11320

20 ºº

MAINTAINING THE LONG-TERM PRODUCTIVITY OF PACIFIC NORTHWEST FOREST ECOSYSTEMS

MAINTAINING THE LONG-TERM PRODUCTIVITY OF PACIFIC NORTHWEST FOREST ECOSYSTEMS

Edited by

D. A. Perry, R. Meurisse, B. Thomas, R. Miller,
J. Boyle, J. Means, C. R. Perry, and R. F. Powers

in cooperation with
College of Forestry, Oregon State University

TIMBER PRESS
Portland, Oregon

ISBN 0-88192-144-0
Printed in The United States of America

TIMBER PRESS, INC.
9999 S.W. Wilshire
Portland, Oregon 97225

Library of Congress Cataloging-in-Publication Data

Maintaining the long-term productivity of Pacific Northwest forest
   ecosystems / edited by D.A. Perry ... [et al.].
        p.   cm.
    "In cooperation with College of Forestry, Oregon State
University."
    "Proceedings of a symposium held at Oregon State University (OSU)
in spring 1987 ... jointly sponsored by the USDA Forest Service, the
UDSI Bureau of Land Management and the OSU College of Forestry."-
-Pref.
    Includes bibliographical references.
    ISBN 0-88192-144-0
    1. Sustainable forestry--Northwest, Pacific--Congresses.
2. Forest productivity--Northwest, Pacific--Congresses. 3. Forest
ecology--Northwest, Pacific--Congresses.   I. Perry, David A.
II. Oregon State University. College of Forestry. III. United
States Forest Service. IV. United States. Bureau of Land
Management.
SD144.A13M35 1989
    634.9'09795--dc20   89-20168
                                                   CIP

Contents

List of Contributors

Albert Abee
Bureau of Land Management
Coos Bay, Oregon

Michael P. Amaranthus
Department of Forest Science
Oregon State University, and
Siskiyou National Forest
Grants Pass, Oregon

Thomas Atzet
Siskiyou National Forest
Grants Pass, Oregon

John H. Beuter
Consulting Forester
Mason, Bruce & Girard, Inc.
Portland, Oregon

Richard E. Bigley
USDA Forest Service
Olympia, Washington

Dan Binkley
Colorado State University

J. G. Borchers
Department of Forest Science
Oregon State University

Bernard T. Bormann
USDA Forest Service
Juneau, Alaska

George Bush
Siuslaw National Forest
Corvallis, Oregon

Bill Carr
Terrasol
Vancouver, British Columbia

R. E. Carter
Faculty of Forestry
University of British Columbia

H. N. Chappell
College of Forest Resources
University of Washington

Stuart W. Childs
Department of Soil Science
Oregon State University

James L. Clayton
USDA Forest Service
Boise, Idaho

Kermit Cromack, Jr.
Department of Forest Science
Oregon State University

Scott Davis
Bureau of Land Management
Eugene, Oregon

Robert E. Denton
(Retired) USDA Forest Service
Moscow, Idaho

Frederick W. Ebel
Boise Cascade Corporation
La Grande, Oregon

Robert L. Edmonds
University of Washington

James A. Entry
Department of Forest Science
Oregon State University

Steve Eubanks
Blue River Ranger District
Blue River, Oregon

Michael C. Feller
University of British Columbia

Jerry F. Franklin
USDA Forest Service, and
College of Forest Resources
University of Washington

H. A. Froehlich
Department of Forest Engineering
Oregon State University

J. M. Geist
USDA Forest Service
LaGrande, Oregon

Donald J. Goheen
USDA Forest Service
Portland, Oregon

Stith Gower
Department of Forestry
University of Wisconsin

R. T. Graham
USDA Forest Service
Moscow, Idaho

Charles Grier
School of Forestry
Northern Arizona University

Edward R. Gross
Siskiyou National Forest
Brookings, Oregon

P. Gum
Okanagan National Forest
Okanagan, Washington

Mark E. Harmon
Department of Forest Science
Oregon State University

A. E. Harvey
USDA Forest Service
Moscow, Idaho

L. S. Heath
College of Forest Resources
University of Washington

Ronald L. Heninger
Weyerhaeuser Company
Springfield, Oregon

Elsie H. Himes
USDA Forest Service
Portland, Oregon

James O. Howard
USDA Forest Service
Portland, Oregon

Jack Hulsey
Washington State Department of
Natural Resources
Olympia, Washington

K. Norman Johnson
College of Forestry
Oregon State University

M. F. Jurgensen
Michigan Technological University

J. P. Kimmins
Department of Forest Sciences
University of British Columbia

K. Klinka
Faculty of Forestry
University of British Columbia, and
B.C. Ministry of Forests and Lands
Burnaby, British Columbia

G. O. Klock
Western Resources Analysis
Wenatchee, Washington

Michael B. Lambert
USDA Forest Service
Portland, Oregon

C. Y. Li
Department of Forest Science
Oregon State University

Susan N. Little
USDA Forest Service
Portland, Oregon

Howard Loewenstein
Department of Forest Resources
University of Idaho

G. I. McDonald
USDA Forest Service
Moscow, Idaho

Arthur McKee
Department of Forest Science
Oregon State University

D. S. McLennan
Faculty of Forestry
University of British Columbia

Angus McLeod
B.C. Ministry of Forests and
Lands
Prince George, British Columbia

David H. McNabb
Forestry Intensified Research
(FIR) Program
Medford, Oregon

J. E. Means
USDA Forest Service
Corvallis, Oregon

Walter F. Megahan
USDA Forest Service
Boise, Idaho

Bob Metzger
Oregon State Office, BLM
Portland, Oregon

R. T. Meurisse
USDA Forest Service
Portland, Oregon

D. W. R. Miles
Department of Forest
Engineering
Oregon State University

Richard E. Miller
USDA Forest Service
Olympia, Washington

Bob Mitchell
B.C. Ministry of Forests and
Lands
Kamloops, British Columbia

R. J. Molina
USDA Forest Service
Corvallis, Oregon

Erin Moore
College of Forest Resources
University of Washington

David D. Myrold
Oregon State University

Chih-Hao Niu
Department of Forest Science
Oregon State University

D. Opalach
College of Forest Resources
University of Washington

David A. Perry
Department of Forest Science
Oregon State University

Robert F. Powers
USDA Forest Service
Redding, California

Roger B. Ryan
USDA Forest Service
La Grande, Oregon

T. D. Schowalter
Department of Entomology
Oregon State University

William Scott
Weyerhaeuser Company
Tacoma, Washington

S. P. Shade
USDI Bureau of Land Management
Medford, Oregon

E. Shepard
USDI Bureau of Land Management
Roseburg, Oregon

Phillip Sollins
College of Forestry
Oregon State University
(currently, School of Forestry
and Environmental Studies,
Yale University)

Thomas A. Spies
USDA Forest Service
Corvallis, Oregon

Douglas Sprugel
College of Forest Resources
University of Washington

N. Stark
School of Forestry
University of Montana

William I. Stein
USDA Forest Service
Corvallis, Oregon

Tim Sullivan
USDA Forest Service
John Day, Oregon

Frederick J. Swanson
USDA Forest Service
Corvallis, Oregon

J. M. Trappe
Departments of Botany and
  Forest Science
Oregon State University

Scott Tunnock
(Retired) USDA Forest Service
Missoula, Montana

Daniel Vogt
School of Forestry and
  Environmental Studies
Yale University

Kristiina Vogt
School of Forestry and
  Environmental Studies
Yale University

Dale R. Waddell
USDA Forest Service
Portland, Oregon

Frank R. Ward
USDA Forest Service
Portland, Oregon

G. F. Weetman
Faculty of Forestry
University of British Columbia

Bruce E. Wilson
Willamette National Forest
McKenzie Bridge, Oregon

H. Zuuring
School of Forestry
University of Montana

This Book is Dedicated to Robert F. Tarrant
Former Director, Pacific Northwest Forest and Range
Experiment Station
Professor Emeritus, Department of Forest Science,
Oregon State University
Pioneer Researcher in the Long-Term Productivity of
Pacific Northwest Forest Ecosystems

Preface

Sustainable Forestry: Managing Ecosystems for the Future

David A. Perry

This book is the proceedings of a symposium held at Oregon State University (OSU) in spring 1987. The symposium, jointly sponsored by the USDA Forest Service, the USDI Bureau of Land Management, and the OSU College of Forestry, was conceived in response to a burgeoning interest among forest managers, forest researchers, and the public in the long-term sustainability of the forest resource in the Pacific Northwest. Symposium organizers had two objectives: first, to produce a state-of-the art summary of knowledge concerning the issue of long-term productivity and how it is affected by various management practices common to the Pacific Northwest; and second, to provide practical guidelines for sustainable forest management. The latter aspect is particularly important—although the chapters herein contain much information of value to researchers and the interested lay public, our primary target audience is forest managers.

Sustainability—or maintenance of long-term productivity (the terms are synonymous)—is a very old concept in forestry: it simply means adopting a level of harvest or management activity that can be perpetuated indefinitely. However, as we discovered during the planning and execution of this symposium, there are many different ideas about exactly what should be sustained in forestry, and how "success" in doing it might be measured.

As used in this book, sustainability refers to a potential only, the productive *capacity* of the land and the ecosystem. Most chapters deal with tree growth, and with good reason. Tree growth is what we have the most information on, and the capacity of forest ecosystems to sustain good tree growth over centuries is probably the simplest and most direct measure of ecosystem health. It does not follow, however, that the volume of wood cut down and delivered to a mill is a good measure of sustainability. Level of harvest is a management decision that has no direct connection with productive potential of the land (although level of harvest can influence productive potential indirectly, for example, through excessive removal of nutrients). Moreover, forests produce numerous values in addition to wood—water, recreation, biological diversity. Though these noncommodity values are difficult to quantify, society nonetheless has an important stake in them, and they must be taken into account as strategies for sustainable forestry are developed.

The current high level of interest in the long-term productivity of managed forests probably has numerous sources, but two in particular are worth mention. First, experience from various areas around the globe has shown that, in at least some instances, the productivity of intensively managed forests declines with time (for more detail, see chapter 1). What has happened elsewhere does not necessarily extrapolate to the Pacific Northwest, but it should raise a clear warning sign and prompt us to carefully evaluate our own practices.

Second, many scientists agree that changes in global climate are a foregone conclusion (see chapter 6). The Earth is probably entering a period of climatic change unique in its history. At no other time have the temperature and precipitation patterns changed at anywhere near the same rates as they are likely to in the next few decades. Add to this, unprecedented global pollution, and the ability of earth's forests to modulate climate and protect soils and water supplies takes on immense significance. The potential for stress and disruption within ecological communities that are no longer well adapted to their environment underscores the need for management systems which foster mechanisms that confer resilience and stability on our forests.

Far more factors influence the stability and productivity of forests than can be dealt with in a single symposium. All chapters except three (chapters 6, 12, and 13) focus primarily on soils. Much work has shown that maintaining healthy soils is a prerequisite to maintaining healthy ecosystems. Soils are directly impacted by harvest and, particularly, site preparation, but in most cases they are also amenable to protection.

The book can be conveniently divided into four sections. The first, chapters 1 through 6, introduces the topic and deals with the general biological and ecological principles underlying forest productivity and stability. Chapters in the second section discuss the issue of long-term productivity as it applies to specific regions or forest types within the Pacific Northwest: the western hemlock/Douglas-fir forest type (chapter 7), upper slope forests (chapter 8), "eastside" forests of the intermountain region and northern Rocky Mountains (chapter 9), and forests of southwest Oregon and northern California (chapter 10). Chapters in the third section deal with modeling the effects of management on long-term productivity (chapter 11), economic aspects (chapter 12), and the approach taken by one District Ranger to develop management strategies that protect ecological diversity (chapter 13). In chapter 14, a forest manager recaps symposium highlights. Finally, the last section aggregates short summaries representing posters displayed and informally discussed by their presenters at a special session of the symposium.

Because ecosystems are highly diverse and the details of their functioning in general poorly understood, researchers do not always agree in their assessments of management effects on long-term productivity. This disagreement is sometimes reflected in this book. Despite the occasionally divergent points of view, however, it is noteworthy that two themes persist throughout. The first is the overriding importance of protecting soil organic matter. Regardless of region or forest type, there is widespread agreement that soil organic matter plays a seminal role in forest productivity and stability. The second is our lack of knowledge concerning many of the key processes that underlie productivity and stability. It is clear that we have much to learn about forest ecosystems in the Pacific Northwest, and this symposium marks a starting point, not the final word.

In closing this preface, I wish to thank the many people, too numerous to name, who contributed their time and ideas. With one exception, the editors of the book are those who played a major role in planning and organizing the symposium. The exception is Carol Rosenblum Perry, who was responsible for technical editing of book chapters, and whose hard work over a period of 18 months turned this from a collection of papers into a coherent product. Early in the planning stages, more than 50 people from all around the region traveled to Corvallis for a workshop which produced the first detailed outline of subject matter to be covered. Many of these appear as authors of one or more chapters. Pam Henderson and Rylee Geboski, OSU College of Forestry, did an outstanding job of managing the logistics of registration and the nuts and bolts of running a 300-person symposium. The Pacific Northwest Forest and Range Experiment Station, USDA Forest Service, contributed several thousand dollars toward the costs of producing this book. Izella Stuivenga and Gretchen Bracher, OSU College of Forestry, graciously provided word processing and drafting, respectively. The interest, cooperation, and patience during preparation of Richard Abel, Timber Press, were instrumental to the publication of this proceedings.

Chapter 1

Maintaining Long-Term Forest Productivity in the Pacific Northwest: Defining the Issues

Robert F. Powers

ABSTRACT

Long-term forest productivity, the inherent capacity or "potential" of the land to sustain vegetation as indexed by tree growth over multiple rotations, is controlled by both fixed and malleable site factors. Although this potential rarely is realized by timber managers, practices impacting fundamental site factors will affect the capacity of the site to grow trees. The factors most easily affected by management pertain to the soil, and they are most apt to be modified during timber harvest and site preparation. Harvest and site-preparation practices have direct impacts on six main ecosystem properties believed to be linked with a site's productive potential—soil volume, soil porosity, soil water availability, soil chemistry, soil biology, and ecological diversity. Soil volume loss has the most dramatic effect on productivity, but other properties can alter productive potential in less obvious ways. Both direct and indirect evidence suggests that long-term productive potential can decline if amounts of site organic matter and total soil porosity are reduced substantially.

INTRODUCTION

Long-term productivity: what is it, and are we maintaining it? Many reasons—legal, financial, and ethical—drew us to Corvallis, Oregon, to tackle this topic head on. Symposium organizers asked authors to meld principles related to long-term productivity with their own experience and judgment to produce state-of-the-art guidelines for forest management in the Pacific Northwest. This was not easy, because much of what we think we know about the subject is based on experience elsewhere and on short-term findings of limited scope. There is a risk in reaching too far afield for information to apply to the Pacific Northwest. Mercifully, this responsibility was not borne solely by the speakers—the chapter authors of this proceedings. The symposium audience shared the load through a vigorous, give-and-take dialogue with the speakers, and much of that has been reproduced here in the "question and answer" sections that follow most chapter texts, as well as in chapter 14.

But the challenge continues beyond the symposium to examine critically what was presented. Does it seem reasonable? How does it compare with practical experience? Are recommendations based on sound assumptions? Are the consequences convincing enough to warrant a change in silvicultural practices? Are there "gray areas" of uncertainty needing further research? This chapter is meant to clarify our understanding of terms, issues, and concepts, and to set the stage for the chapters to come.

DEFINITIONS

Forest Ecosystems

Forest ecosystems are three-dimensional, evolving units of nature containing biotic (living) components—plants, animals, and other associated organisms—and their immediate abiotic environment, of which soil is the most massive component. Conventionally, forest ecosystems are divided into these biotic and abiotic components both above and below ground. Decomposing organic matter—either plant litter, or dead roots and microbes—constitutes a dynamic transition between biotic and abiotic stages. Lateral boundaries of forest ecosystems are broad enough to include all the properties of the smallest unit of management (e.g., the area encompassed by a stand). Vertical boundaries generally extend from the tips of the roots to the tops of the trees.

This symposium focuses on commercial forest ecosystems of the Pacific Northwest.

Productivity

Forest productivity can be defined in several ways. In general, it refers to an ecosystem's output over time. In a plant ecology context, productivity is expressed as total plant mass produced annually per unit area. Depending on the environment, a considerable share of the biomass may be produced belowground (see chapter 8, this volume). Unfortunately, measures of total plant mass are not readily obtained or applied. We lack long historical records of such a measure over a broad range of sites. Nor is total mass production expressed in units familiar—and thereby useful—to practicing foresters. Because of this, forest productivity is defined here to mean the inherent capacity of the land to maintain commercial wood growth. Although a less-than-perfect measure, commercial wood growth is our best documented index of inherent site productivity and is a useful index of ecosystem health. It follows then that "long-term productivity" refers to the ability of the land to sustain such levels of wood growth over several rotations.

The land's ability to sustain wood growth is based on several elements. First, there is an inherent capacity of the land to produce wood—a "potential productivity"—that is fixed by local climatic, topographic, and edaphic conditions, and expressed through the genetically constrained growth of forest trees. Second, there is an "economic productivity," realized by management, which depends on stocking, rotation length, utilization standards, and growth losses caused by forest pests. Economic and potential productivity rarely coincide because of inefficiencies in management operations, or because of constraints levied on management by economic goals, market values, or capital. However, it is the more fundamental question of *potential* long-term productivity that concerns this symposium. Are management practices maintaining the potential of the land to sustain wood production?

The Pacific Northwest

Finally, what is the scope of the "Pacific Northwest" described in this symposium? The region resembles a triangle (Fig. 1.1)—its vertex on the Kenai Peninsula of Alaska (at about lat. 61°N., long. 151°W.), its base spreading south (roughly following lat. 37°N.) and east (between long. 105°W. and 122°W.). More specifically, it extends northwestward from the Sierra Nevada and Coast Ranges of California, through Oregon, Washington, and British Columbia to the narrow extension of western hemlock [*Tsuga heterophylla* (Raf.) Sarg.] in southeastern coastal Alaska. It reaches eastward through British Columbia to the eastern limits of the Douglas-fir [*Pseudotsuga menziesii* (Mirb.) Franco] and lodgepole pine (*Pinus contorta* var. *latifolia* Engelm.) mixture in the Rocky Mountains of western Alberta, and then southward along the eastern boundaries of the same types in Montana, Wyoming, and Colorado. Timber management intensity—and soil impacts—are expected to increase in western portions of this region in the decades ahead (Powers 1987).

THE PRODUCTIVITY OF MANAGED FORESTS

The productive potential, or "site quality," of any land unit emerges from physical, chemical, and climatic factors interacting within a particular biological framework. Disregarding human intervention, biology could be considered a fourth factor in that vegetation fixes (converts to a usable form) carbon (C) and adds organic matter to the system, soil fauna shred and mix fresh organic matter with the soil and improve aeration, soil microbes decompose and further circulate organic matter as well as fix atmospheric nitrogen (N), and forest insects and diseases reduce a site's expression of its potential—for instance, dwarfmistletoe (*Arceuthobium* sp. Bieb.) alone reduces growth of western U.S. forests by over 8 million m^3 annually (Stewart 1985). How much of this potential is converted to products of commercial value depends on management which, almost by definition, makes a site more "productive" if productivity is measured simply by commercial success. For example, stocking control increases economic productivity by focusing more of a site's given resources on particular target trees. Similarly, pest control improves economic productivity by increasing net merchantable growth. Actually, this is a kind of sleight-of-hand in that the site's potential productivity has not been altered, but merely redistributed so that more of it is realized by management.

Can a site's productive potential be changed fundamentally? Yes, because site potential has both fixed and malleable features. "Fixed" features are those constrained by climate and the physical and chemical nature of the

FIG.1.1. The Pacific Northwest forest region as envisioned for the purposes of this Symposium.

soil. These do not seem to change, although over long periods they are dynamic. Climate changes. Atmospheric inputs change. Soil properties change because of the ability of trees to synthesize, accumulate, and cycle organic matter. Because change is a fact of nature, no site factors are static on a larger time scale. But "malleable" features are more dynamic than so-called "fixed" features. Soil may erode. Water tables may change. Soil porosity may decrease. Forest pests may appear or disappear. The "malleability" of a forest ecosystem, or the ease by which site potential is altered by management, depends on its buffering capacity (how well it resists change) and on its resiliency (how well it recovers following disturbance).

How then might management practices affect potential site productivity? In principle, productive potential can be altered at any stage in a rotation, but impacts are most sizable during timber harvest and site preparation—when heavy machinery is present, surface soil is disturbed, organic matter is redistributed, and biological properties are changed. Management impacts during this period affect six main ecosystem properties linked to long-term productivity: soil volume, soil porosity, soil water availability, soil chemistry, soil biology, and ecological diversity. How do changes in these properties relate to long-term productivity?

Soil Volume

Obviously, slope failures triggered by poor road placement reduce potential productivity, and risks are increased in the steep, faulted geological formations of the Pacific Northwest (Swanston and Swanson 1976; see also chapter 5, this volume). Soil movement and even mass failure can occur in undisturbed ecosystems where slopes are steep and rainfall is high, so some change in total soil mass is not unusual. Often, soil slips in mass along a shear plane, leaving behind a surface with reduced productive potential. Five- to 18-year-old Douglas-fir regenerated naturally on landslides in the western Cascade Mountains of Oregon averaged 25% less stocking and 62% less height growth than trees planted on nearby clearcuts (Miles et al. 1984), and one-third of the landslide area was judged unstockable. Less spectacular but much more common than mass movement are losses due to erosion from cut and fill slopes of forest roads (Fredriksen et al. 1975), although the long-term consequences are unknown. A key to reducing erosion is maintaining a surface layer of organic matter to reduce raindrop impact. Another is maintaining soil organic matter because products of humification promote granulation of soil particles into water-stable aggregates that maintain porosity (Youngberg 1979).

Soil volume sometimes is changed deliberately. For instance, surface soil often is bladed—or "scalped"—by a bulldozer into windrows during site preparation. Bladed along with the surface soil is a high proportion of the soil organic matter (Fig. 1.2), which concentrates near the soil surface and decreases with depth. Soil organic matter is the main source of N to sustain plant growth. Thus, displacing a few centimeters of surface soil can have a disproportionate impact on the removal of soil N (see chapter 10, this volume). As seen in Figures 1.2a and 1.2b, mature soils may have substantially more organic matter (and N) stored in their full profiles than do immature soils, but amounts in their surface layers may be similar. Accordingly, the loss of a few centimeters of topsoil could have greater significance for immature than for mature soils.

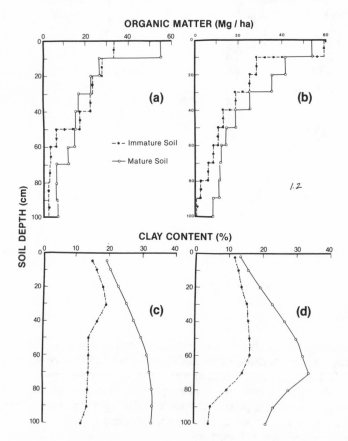

FIG. 1.2. Organic matter and clay contents to 1-m depth for mineral soils typical of northern California and southwest Oregon. Solid lines are for mature soils (Typic Haploxerults and Ultic Haploxeralfs), broken lines for immature soils (Dystric Xerochrepts and Umbric Vitrandepts). Organic matter contents are shown for (a) soft sediments of the Klamath Mountains, (b) volcanic soils of the Cascades. Clay contents are shown for (c) soft sediments of the Klamath Mountains, (d) volcanic soils of the Cascades. Each curve is the average of many profiles. Source: P. J. Zinke and A. G. Stangenberger, unpublished data on file at the University of California, Berkeley.

Research in the Pacific Northwest on impacts of soil displacement on site productivity tends to be short term or circumstantial. Minore (1986), studying early performance of Douglas-fir plantations where logging residues had been tractor piled, concluded that 5-year height growth was much less than would be expected if the slash had been broadcast burned. Not all the effect could be attributed to soil displacement, however, as soil strength was greater where tractors had been used. Powers et al. (1988) compared the performance of ponderosa pine (*Pinus ponderosa* Dougl. ex Laws.) plantations a decade or more after site preparation. Plantations with tractor-piled windrows had lower soil and foliar N than unscalped plantations, and showed N stress (Table 1.1). Unfortunately, "after-the-fact" studies such as these lack the rigor of designed experiments. Consequently, their true significance remains somewhat speculative.

TABLE 1.1. Soil and site characteristics (mean ± 1 standard error) for established plantations of ponderosa pine on 16 scalped and piled sites and 6 unscalped sites (adapted from Powers et al. 1988).

Characteristic	Scalped		Not scalped	
	Mean	*SE*	*Mean*	*SE*
Mineralizable soil N, mg/kg	15.5	2.50	24.9	5.30
Foliar N, %				
Current needles	1.13	0.05	1.24	0.06
1-yr-old needles	1.06	0.06	1.12	0.05
Site index (height, m at 50 yr)	20.1	1.46	26.8	2.17
Relative 5-yr fertilization				
growth response to N, %	37.8	13.2	9.0	4.0

Soil Porosity

The size, abundance, and distribution of soil pores affect the flow of liquids and gases to tree roots and the elongation of roots within the soil. Pore size distribution is changed by compaction—the number and volume of large pores (macropores) decrease, reducing aeration and increasing soil strength (see chapter 4, this volume). In turn, losses in macropore volume can reduce root frequency and growth (Greacen and Sands 1980) and tree growth (Froehlich and McNabb 1984). Forest soils of the Pacific Northwest generally have high porosities and low bulk densities. Consequently, there is a potential for growth loss if soils are compacted (Froehlich and McNabb 1984). Whether such losses occur depends on how closely compaction approaches a growth-limiting bulk density.

Soil organic matter and clay content affect total soil porosity. Generally, the greater the clay content, the lower the macropore volume and the greater the biological impact of compaction. Because clay soils initially have few large pores, a given increase in soil density on clayey soils should have a greater effect on productivity than an equivalent increase on loams or sands.

How does this relate to soil classification? Alfisols and Ultisols have greater clay contents than Inceptisols for a given rock type, and clay content is lower in surface than in subsurface horizons (Fig. 1.2). Soils developed from soft sediments such as siltstone (Fig. 1.2c) weather more readily to clay than do soils from hard, crystalline rocks such as andesite and basalt (Fig. 1.2d), and show comparatively high clay content to a considerable depth. In most cases, subsoils can be compacted more seriously than surface soils because they have lower organic matter and greater clay contents.

Soil organic matter from root and forest-floor decomposition is a key factor in buffering a soil against compaction and in imparting resilience against permanent change (see chapter 3, this volume). In all but a few soils, organic matter content is greatest near the soil surface and declines rapidly with depth. Typically, Alfisols and Ultisols contain more organic matter for a given depth than do Inceptisols, although the contents of the uppermost horizons of immature and mature soils can be surprisingly similar (Figs. 1.2a and 1.2b). Where soil profiles are intact, compaction potential may be relatively low despite high clay contents because intact profiles are relatively high in surface-soil organic matter. However, if the surface horizon is lost, the same soils become much more compactable because organic matter content is lower in subsoil (Figs. 1.2a and 1.2b), whereas clay content is higher (Figs. 1.2c and 1.2d).

What is the evidence that compaction has caused problems? Much of it centers on retrospective comparisons between growth in compacted skid trails and that in adjacent, less disturbed areas. In the Oregon Cascades, Douglas-fir growing in skid trails took 4 years longer to reach breast height (about 1.4 m above the ground) and produced only one-quarter the volume per hectare than adjacent trees in logged but relatively uncompacted areas 32 years after harvest (reflecting both lower stocking and less growth per tree) (Wert and Thomas 1981). In a south-central Washington study, Froehlich et al. (1986) found that volumes of 9–18 year old ponderosa pine growing in compacted skid trails were substantially lower those of pines growing in less dense soils nearby. In a California plantation study, Helms et al. (1986) found that soil bulk density measured around individual ponderosa pine 16 years after planting explained only a small fraction of the variation in periodic height growth. Overall, trees in areas of highest bulk density (1.19 g/cm^3) were 13% shorter at age 15 than those in areas of lowest bulk density (0.83 g/cm^3). Work summarized by Froehlich and McNabb (1984) indicates height growth is reduced in direct proportion to increase in soil density, but this seems simplistic. Growth decline should be increasingly severe as soil macroporosity drops below a critical minimum.

A problem with retrospective studies such as these is that initial soil conditions can only be inferred, and that compaction and other effects often are confounded. For example, clay content increases with depth as soils weather naturally (Figs. 1.2c and 1.2d), producing subsoils with higher bulk densities than surface soils. In Minore's (1986) study, high soil strengths noted in tractor-piled areas probably reflect subsoil exposure as well as compaction. Also in question is how long the effects last, although Wert and Thomas (1981) found that differences in bulk density persisted for over 30 years. Further discussion concerning soil porosity is presented in chapter 4, this volume.

Soil Water Availability

Climate, topographic position, and soil type determine the amount of water potentially available to a forest ecosystem. Either by design or chance, management practices that lower or raise water tables affect productivity. Sometimes water tables are altered deliberately to improve productivity—for example, waterlogged sites may be drained to increase tree survival and growth by improving aeration (Terry and Hughes 1975). However, at other times management practices may have unplanned and unfavorable consequences. For example, species conversion on clayey, lowland hardwood sites in Germany led to reduced soil drainage and progressively poorer yields of Norway spruce [*Picea abies* (L.) Karst.]—the infamous "Saxony spruce sickness" which has been misinterpreted widely as soil degradation caused by pure stands of conifers (Krauss et al. 1939).

Research on droughty sands in southern Australia (Squire et al. 1985) indicates that much of the drop in yields of second-rotation plantations of Monterey pine (*Pinus radiata D.* Don) can be attributed to water stress caused by the removal of a forest-floor mulch during site preparation. Consequently, slash burning and raking are avoided wherever possible. How significant the loss of surface organic matter is on more mesic sites remains to be seen. However, Kittredge (1954) noted that summer evaporation from a bare, clay-loam soil in California was half-again greater than that from the same soil under the litter and shade of pine.

Soil Chemistry

Management impacts on soil chemistry generally are direct and are meant to boost forest productivity. A common, obvious example is fertilization. But how long growth improvement lasts depends on the nutrient, the amount applied, and the initial degree of deficiency. In temperate forests, growth responses to standard rates of N fertilization rarely last beyond 5–8 years. Yet, when southern pines are fertilized with phosphorus (P) at planting, they can grow 2–5 m taller by age 25 than unfertilized trees (Allen 1987). Why is this so?

Annual N requirements in young Northwest stands probably are greater than previously believed. Depending on site quality, species, and stand age, 20–60 kg/ha of N are required to meet yearly aboveground needs (Kimmins et al. 1985), and belowground demand may be twice as great (Meier et al. 1985). However, the mineral soil does not have to satisfy all of the N demand. Some N need is met by internal recycling, or by uptake from decaying roots and mycorrhizae. Thus, although 200–400 kg/ha of N applied operationally *could* meet the annual requirements of a forest, not all will be absorbed. The excess will be immobilized, leached, or possibly lost as gaseous oxides of N (denitrification). In time, fertilizer N disappears in a soil system typically housing between 1,800 and 18,000 kg/ha of N (Zinke et al. 1984). Standard fertilization rates provide little N, compared with that present in most ecosystems (Table 1.2). Unless applied repeatedly, N fertilizer is unlikely to have a lasting effect on potential productivity.

Experiences with phosphorus fertilization have been different from those with N, but the principles are different too. In the Northwest, response to P fertilization has been erratic (Gessel et al. 1981). In contrast, many southern pine stands generally respond well to P (Allen 1987). Two conditions help to explain response differences. First, a genuine P deficiency must exist before trees will respond. Second, P must be applied at a rate that exceeds the P-sorption capacity of the soil. Sandy soils of the southern U.S. have both low sorption capacities and low amounts of mineral P in their upper horizons (Ballard and Pritchett 1974). Thus, typical fertiliza-

TABLE 1.2. Ranges in total nitrogen (N) and phosphorus (P) contents reported for true fir (*Abies* sp. L.), pine, and Douglas-fir ecosystem components in North America (adapted from Kimmins et al. 1985).

Ecosystem component	True fir		Pine		Douglas-fir	
	N	*P*	*N*	*P*	*N*	*P*
	-- kg/ha --					
Trees						
Aboveground	80–686	12–83	180–556	12–31	84–728	18–112
Roots	24–72	4–12	12–117	2–21	30–90	5–18
Understory	2–50	t–14[1]	1–54	t–5	5–66	1–9
Forest floor	666–2,300	55–217	80–1,240	9–103	110–1,249	19–115
Soil to 1-m depth	5,237–14,000	3,212–6,317	1,753–5,554	146–4,457	1,770–15,400	3,878–3,900

[1]t = trace.

tion rates of 50–100 kg/ha of P represent a sizable absolute gain in soil P. That, coupled with relatively low annual uptake needs, leads trees to show a prolonged response to fertilizer P. In contrast, most Northwest forest soils contain relatively large amounts of P (Table 1.2) in primary and secondary minerals in equilibrium with aluminum, iron, and manganese phosphates of varying solubilities, and mycorrhizal roots have long been known to be capable of tapping reserves of soil P not in a readily available form (Mitchell et al. 1937). Further, many Northwest soils have comparatively high P-sorption capacities (Powers et al. 1975), and operational rates of P fertilization are insignificant compared with the levels of P—400–2,000 kg/ha—such soils are capable of sorbing in their surface horizons.

Some management practices applied early in the life of a stand may affect soil chemistry in ways that are not immediately apparent. For example, many site-preparation practices accelerate mineralization (the breakdown of complex organic compounds by soil microbes) which, coupled with low stocking density in very young stands, creates a relative abundance of soil nutrients (Fox et al. 1986). However, this can change as the stand develops. If absolute quantities of site nutrients have been sizably reduced through volatilization, leaching, or displacement, nutrient stress may occur seasonally and then continually as the stand places increasing demands on the capacity of the soil to supply nutrients (McColl and Powers 1984). Thus, activities that seem favorable in the short run may prove deleterious later, as the stand develops. The evidence that this is so, however, tends to be speculative and confounded.

A common example concerns slash burning. Although most evidence—pro or con—tends to be short term (McColl and Powers 1984), one exception is the retrospective study by Kramer and Hermann (1979). In examining 25-year effects in unburned and burned portions of Douglas-fir cutblocks in the Northwest, they detected no appreciable differences in physical or chemical properties of surface soils. However, Miller et al. (see chapter 7, this volume) take a fresh look at this historical study in terms of subsequent tree growth. Generalizations about effects of prescribed burning must be tempered by the specific properties of each site. In Norway, for example, pine and spruce seedlings planted following burning on productive *Oxalis/Myrtillus* sites grew well and had high foliar N concentrations in the first few years after burning, but were inferior to seedlings on unburned sites by age 12 (Skoklefald 1973). On such sites, nutrient leaching probably was increased once fire had consumed the thin humus layers. On poorer *Calluna* sites, however, burning the thick, acid layers of heath humus improved the performance of planted trees.

Soil Biology

Soil organisms work continually, if imperceptibly, in mediating carbon cycling, nutrient transfer, water availability, vegetation vigor, and soil formation itself. Perhaps the significance of soil organisms is shown best by their density and diversity. A square meter of surface soil may encompass a thousand or more species of soil animals and several million individuals (Swift et al. 1979). In comparison, a gram of surface soil may contain over a thousand fungal hyphae and a million bacteria (Swift et al. 1979). Soil from an old-growth Douglas-fir stand in Oregon has been estimated to hold about 4,200 kg/ha of fungal mycelia and 5,400 kg/ha of mycorrhizal root tips (Fogel et al. 1973). Soil organisms play a fundamental role in many site processes by interacting with their environment and with each other, and it is important to recognize that humans can influence their activity—and thus, site processes (see chapters 3 and 9, this volume).

Obviously, human intervention can be favorable. For example, disking during site preparation leads to increased N mineralization (Fox et al. 1986). On sterile coastal sands, lupine (*Lupinus* sp. L.) can be established to fix N and improve site quality for planted pine (Gadgil 1971). In the Pacific Northwest, interplanting red alder (*Alnus rubra* Bong.) into an N-deficient 4-year-old Douglas-fir plantation appeared to increase Douglas-fir productivity by about 7% over a 44-year period. Productivity nearly doubled when alder yields were included (Miller and Murray 1978). But while there clearly is a potential for developing silvicultural systems that benefit from symbiotic N fixation, we must remember that the "success stories" tend to be restricted to sites which are extremely deficient in N and relatively well supplied with water. On drier or more fertile sites, N fixation may be reduced and moisture stress increased through direct competition.

Except for red alder forests, little N is leached from the soil of undisturbed or fully stocked Northwest forest ecosystems. This is because most mineral N is in the form of ammonium—a positively charged ion (cation) held tightly by negatively charged soil colloids, where it can be absorbed by plants. When the rate of ammonium production exceeds that of plant uptake, certain soil microorganisms (nitrifiers) use the ammonium as an energy source and oxidize it to nitrate, a negatively charged ion repulsed by charged soil colloids, causing it to leach from the soil in drainage water. Nitrate production often increases following timber harvest and site preparation, because factors that constrain nitrifier activity (low soil temperature, moisture, and ammonium substrate) are modified. Although this may increase soil N loss through leaching, reports usually have sidestepped direct impacts on tree growth and have focused instead on rates of nitrate leaching and contributing causes. Despite the attention that accelerated nitrification has drawn, its effect on long-term productivity is unknown but probably inconsequential on many sites. "Preventive medicine," therefore, seems a prudent policy (see chapter 2, this volume). One step toward preventive medicine is suggested by Bollen and Lu's (1969) findings that soluble tannins in logging slash inhibit nitrifying bacteria. In fact, Hart et al. (1981) found that soil solutions on a clearcut lodgepole pine site in Wyoming were higher in total phenols and lower in nitrate concentrations where slash had been chipped and left than where slash had been removed. Thus, leachates from such post-logging residues as bark and heartwood probably inhibit nitrifier activity and reduce leaching of nitrates and accompanying cations.

Forests depend on mycorrhizae for survival. Like all fungi, mycorrhizal fungi are aerobes associated with the organic matter components of surface soils. Presumably, management activities that reduce aeration or soil organic matter (tractor piling, slash burning) reduce mycorrhiza activity (Perry and Rose 1983). Certain mycorrhiza types produce their sporocarps below ground and depend on small animals for spore dispersal. Thus, mycorrhizal reinoculation in disturbed sites may be retarded if small-mammal habitat is destroyed (Maser et al. 1978). Greenhouse studies suggest that sites with a harsh, continental climate (Wyoming) may have less fungus diversity than sites with a marine climate (Oregon), and thus may be more poorly buffered against changes in fungus populations caused by disturbance (Perry and Rose 1983). Any practice that retards the development of mycorrhizal fungi can reduce tree growth and the expression of site potential.

Soil fauna play a role central to sustained site productivity that often is overlooked. Macrofauna (rodents, mollusks, and earthworms) stir surface organic matter into the soil and, through their tunneling, create channels for drainage and aeration. Mesofauna (termites, springtails, beetles, and millipedes) reduce organic matter to smaller pieces of greater surface area, making them more readily available for further degradation by microfauna (nematodes, rotifers, mites, and protozoa). For example, intact pine needles decompose slowly, but rates double when needles are cut into small segments (Fyles and McGill 1987), which simulates the action of soil mesofauna. Earthworm casts, fecal material, and organic matter-rich nests of soil macrofauna can produce microsites of high N mineralization because deposited materials have lower C:N ratios than the original organic matter (Gosz 1984). Not all soil fauna necessarily promote growth, however. Animals ranging from gophers to nematodes reduce productivity by feeding on roots. As Hill et al. (1975) point out, it is pertinent to ask what effect silvicultural practices have on soil fauna, and whether the results are beneficial or harmful in the long run.

Ecological Diversity

A popular ecological theory holds that diversity promotes ecosystem stability. Odum (1972) suggests that variety is not merely "the spice of life," but possibly a necessity. Advocates of this principle are concerned that timber management trends toward simplification in the Pacific Northwest work against stability. Yet "ecosystem stability" is not necessarily a goal of timber management. Here and elsewhere, monocultures usually are favored over mixed-species stands because monocultures are easier to manage. Moreover, plantations tend to comprise seral species with high rates of bolewood production. Further, stable, well-buffered systems may reduce management options for raising inherent productivity to higher levels by deliberate practices (Powers 1987).

Granted that stability is not necessarily a management goal in the Pacific Northwest, how important is ecological diversity in long-term productivity? Franklin et al. (1986) suggest that diversity has genetic, structural, landscape, and temporal components that provide a useful framework for discussion (see chapter 6, this volume). Proponents of genetic diversity point out that mixed stands may produce more biomass than monocultures. However, this simply suggests that multiple species probably do not occupy identical niches. And even though mixed stands may better express a site's inherent potential, they do not change it. Stand mixtures containing N-fixing species probably provide the only solid examples of fundamental improvement in site potential (Miller and Murray 1978), but benefits vary with site. For example, DeBell et al. (1987) compared growth performance of separate and mixed plantings of *Eucalyptus saligna* Sm. and N-fixing *Albizia falcataria* (L.) Fosberg at four Hawaiian locations. On one of the wetter sites, eucalyptus was twice as tall when grown in mixture than when grown separately. On the other three sites, differences were negligible.

Understory species sometimes are seen as important in concentrating nutrients in the upper soil. But the understory contains only a small fraction of ecosystem nutrients once stands reach early maturity (Table 1.2), and there is no substantive evidence that tree growth will decline if understory species are eliminated. In fairness, the subject has not been studied rigorously. Recent work by Perry et al. (1987) suggests that the species of plants revegetating clearcuts on coarse-textured soils may influence soil aggregate stability. Following clearcutting, fewer large soil aggregates were found on sites succeeding to grass than on sites stocked with conifers, a finding apparently related to changes in soil microflora and the aggregate-building characteristics of fungal hyphae.

Structural diversity concerns the presence of standing dead trees (snags) and downed woody residues. Snags of particular form become habitat for birds that help control forest pests, and prescriptions can be developed for producing and replacing snags at a desirable rate (see chapter 13, this volume). Downed logs can be habitat for small mammals that carry spores of hypogeous mycorrhizal fungi into disturbed areas (Maser et al. 1978) and for free-living (asymbiotic) N-fixing bacteria (Harmon et al. 1986). Although N-fixation rates are comparatively low in rotting logs, inputs may be important in drier ecosystems lacking symbiotic N-fixing species (see chapter 9, this volume). Thus, large woody residues may play a sizable, previously unrecognized role in maintaining long-term productivity on certain sites.

Landscape diversity refers to stand arrangement and shape on the scale of a watershed or larger, temporal diversity to the array of successional stages. Breaks in forest age classes and species types reduce the risk of catastrophic losses from fire, insects, and disease. Further, the placement and shape of cutting boundaries influence the susceptibility of a stand to windthrow. The link between landscape and temporal diversity and long-term productivity is weak, however, and must be argued more on the basis of abstract principles and other nontimber uses of the forest.

How forest diversity impacts long-term productivity remains open to question. Except in the case of intensive agriculture involving extreme genetic uniformity, convincing examples of simplification leading to ecological disaster are as yet hard to find. See chapter 6, this volume, for further discussion.

EVIDENCE OF PRODUCTIVITY DECLINE

Direct Evidence

Direct evidence of productivity decline requires two conditions. First, there must be a standard reference for comparing the effect of the treatment in question—growth records from either an alternative treatment or a previous stand. Not surprisingly, direct evidence is rare. Timber rotations are long, and historical records seldom survive in sufficient detail to have conclusive value. Most direct evidence comes from experiences with short-rotation silviculture—primarily with successive rotations of Monterey pine in Australia (Keeves 1966). Growth increment in South Australia declined to such a degree on identical sites from first to second rotations that the area was downgraded by more than a site class (Fig. 1.3). The rate of increment decline slows with stand age, stabilizing at about two site-class reductions by crown closure in the seventh or eighth year (Boardman 1979). Although many causes have been proposed for the decline phenomenon, they remain speculative until experiments are conducted to separate cause from coincidence (McColl and Powers 1984).

Recently, results from designed experiments indicate that second-rotation declines in the Australian states of Victoria and South Australia are both explainable and preventable. Working with second-rotation plantations and with first-rotation plantations that were matched with second-rotation sites, Squire et al. (1985) traced growth declines to losses of forest-floor organic matter during site preparation. Slash burning following the first rotation exposes the soil surface to evaporation and promotes weed invasion. Together, these have a major impact in a region characterized by summer drought. Drought further reduces nutrient mineralization and transport to tree roots in the soil solution. The end result is diminishing stand performance until crown closure.

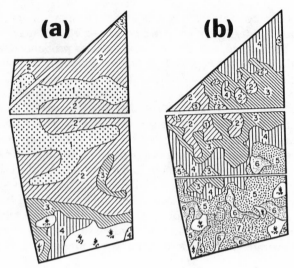

FIG. 1.3. Mappings of site class for first (a) and second (b) rotations of Monterey pine within the Penola Forest Reserve, South Australia. Numbers 1–7 indicate site-quality scales between 1,500 (no. 1) and 400 (no. 7) m³/ha stemwood production over 50 years. Unnumbered sectors indicate unplanted land (adapted from Keeves 1966).

Maintaining surface organic matter not only prevents second-rotation decline, but may improve growth substantially over that noted in the first rotation (Squire et al. 1985).

Most direct evidence does not come from designed experiments, but from retrospective studies lacking adequate control. The advantage of retrospective analyses of long-term productivity is that sites can be found where forest growth has been affected by a condition of interest for a particularly long time. Because the growth record already exists, certain questions can be answered quickly. Unfortunately, only a limited number of questions can be asked. Other drawbacks are that replicated treatments are rare (so there is no way of attaching statistical confidence to retrospective findings), and that initial site conditions often have been blurred by time and can only be inferred. Probably the outstanding examples of retrospective direct evidence of productivity decline are Wiedemann's (1935) growth comparisons of paired plots in pine forests of eastern Germany following decades of litter gathering. Removing litter regularly lowered productivity by more than a full site class (Table 1.3). Even on the best soils, volume increment on litter-free plots was only two-thirds that where litter had been left.

TABLE 1.3. Site-class comparisons between adjacent plots of Scots pine (*Pinus sylvestris* L.) in eastern Germany in relation to cumulative effects of several decades of litter removal (adapted from Wiedemann 1935).

Location	Subsoil condition at each location	Pine site class[1]		
		Litter intact	Litter removed	Apparent change
Neumuhl Cpt. 220/221/91	Moderately fine to coarse gravelly sand. Ground water at 2 m, or with high lime.	1.5	3.4–4.2	2.3
Cpt. 220/91	Moderately fine sand becoming coarse gravel with depth. Ground water at 2.5 m.	2.2	3.7	1.5
Schonthal	Medium-grained sand with lime and loam. Ground water about 3 m.	2.4	4.0	1.6
Neumuhl Cpt. 210/80	Fine to moderately fine sand. Ground water at 3 m.	2.8–3.0	5.0	2.1
Cpt. 208/71	Moderately fine sand. Ground water at 2.5 m.	3.0	5−	>2
Hoyerswerda Cpt. 335	Coarse sand and gravel, growing coarser with depth. Ground water not observed.	4.0	5−	>1
Eichow Cpt. 29	Moderately fine sand with sandy subsoil. Ground water not observed.	4.6	5−	nd[2]
Dobrilugk Cpt. 168	Moderately fine sand with sandy, gravelly subsoil. Ground water not observed.	5	5−	nd

[1]Site class 1 = most productive site. Site class 5− = a site class poorer than 5.
[2]nd = not determined because of unknown site class on litter-removal plots.

Much of our work in the Pacific Northwest also is retrospective. For example, Froehlich et al. (1986) found that ponderosa pine growing in compacted skid trails had poorer growth than pines growing in lower density soils nearby. Powers et al. (1988) found that pine plantations scalped of topsoil during site preparation were nutritionally poorer than unscalped plantations (Table 1.1). However, neither study can guarantee that "impacted" and "nonimpacted" sites were alike initially, or that soil conditions have not changed since impacts occurred. Because sampling was done "after the fact," conclusions from retrospective studies tend to be somewhat speculative.

Indirect Evidence

Because long-term historical records are rare, researchers often develop models of varying complexity to project possible outcomes of alternative management practices. Models basically fall into three categories: empirical, process, and hybrid (see chapter 11, this volume). Although always marred by incomplete information and oversimplification, such models are useful in producing interim guidelines until more conclusive data surface. Work has centered almost entirely on nutritional aspects of long-term productivity, rather than physical or biological interactions. Within this nutritional focus, increased rates of biomass removal (higher utilization, shortened rotations) have drawn most attention.

Most empirical models compare rates of nutrient withdrawal from a site under alternative management strategies. For example, Switzer et al. (1981) developed tables of nutrient contents measured in standing biomass of 20- and 60-year-old stands of loblolly pine (*Pinus taeda* L.). These were used to compare nutrient removal for hypothetical stands managed under short or long rotations and varying degrees of utilization. Assuming stem-only harvesting and no thinning, nutrient removal would be about one-third greater in three 20-year rotations than in one 60-year rotation. If all biomass was removed, nutrient export would be more than 50% greater in three short rotations. The authors admitted that their estimates of nutrient loss were conservative because they ignored losses through accelerated erosion or leaching. Further, on the basis of soil analysis and input/recycling estimates, they warned that although increased nutrient drain probably could be sustained through several rotations, physical impacts of increased utilization on soil properties might be much more serious.

A more flexible and sophisticated model involves process simulation. "Pure" process models—those based on cellular physiology—are sensitive to very short temporal changes and quickly become inaccurate as they expand to whole organisms and communities, decades and rotations. At present, no pure process model with value for long-term projections has been developed (see chapter 11, this volume). Bridging the gap between empirical and process models are "hybrids"—the foremost being the computer model FORCYTE (Kimmins and Scoullar 1984). Hybrid process models have the major advantage of being flexible, thus allowing the user to compare a broad array of management options in a changing environment. Recently, Sachs and Sollins (1986) used FORCYTE to compare management alternatives in hypothetical stands of western hemlock. They concluded that yields and soil organic matter remained stable over multiple rotations if rotations lasted at least 90 years and only boles were harvested. Shorter rotations and higher utilization rates led to depleted soil N and slightly declining yields.

A problem with such ambitious simulators as FORCYTE is that the driving processes and modifying calibrations may reflect the biases of their inventors and users (Rolff and Dyck 1986). Further, input data needed to calibrate process simulators accurately simply do not exist in their entirety for specific sites. An alternative is to use data established for similar locations, such as those compiled by Kimmins et al. (1985), or to array such data along a climatic gradient to derive approximate rate functions mathematically. Although process simulators produce results of unknown validity, they can be immensely helpful in examining relative differences among management alternatives, in pinpointing knowledge gaps involving ecosystem processes, and in setting hypotheses for further testing.

DOES IT REALLY MATTER?

Whether maintaining the long-term productive potential of forest sites is worthwhile in the Pacific Northwest depends on one's point of view. On purely economic grounds, scenarios even worse than those modeled by Sachs and Sollins (1986) may fail to justify the costs of prevention (see chapter 12, this volume). On public lands, however, management must be guided by legal as well as economic principles. By law established by the Multiple Use-Sustained Yield Act of 1960, public forests must be managed to maintain in perpetuity a high level of output "without impairment of the productivity of the land." Essentially every major piece of natural-resource legislation enacted since 1960 has echoed or reinforced that theme (USDA Forest Service 1983).

But beyond economic and legal concerns, there is ethical concern for protecting the long-term capability of the land. We did not create the land, and it will outlast this generation and any that follow. Thus, it is a matter driven more by a sense of stewardship and by a hope for the future that moves us to care for the land and to want to protect it for others. The chapters that follow are meant to show us how.

REFERENCES

Allen, H. L. 1987. Forest fertilizers: nutrient amendment, stand productivity, and environmental impact. *Journal of Forestry* 85(2):37–46.

Ballard, R., and W. L. Pritchett. 1974. Phosphorus retention in Coastal Plain forest soils. II. Significance to forest fertilization. *Soil Science Society of America Proceedings* 38(2):363–366.

Boardman, R. 1979. "Maintenance of productivity in successive rotations of radiata pine in South Australia." In *The ecology of even-aged forest plantations,* edited by E. D. Ford, D.C. Malcolm, and J. Atterson, 543–553. Proceedings, Division I, IUFRO Conference, September 1978, Edinburgh. Cambridge, U. K.: Institute of Terrestrial Ecology.

Bollen, W. B., and K. C. Lu. 1969. *Douglas-fir bark tannin decomposition in two forest soils.* Research Paper No. 85. Portland, Ore.: Pacific Northwest Forest and Range Experiment Station, USDA Forest Service.

DeBell, D., C. D. Whitesell, and T. B. Crabb. 1987. *Benefits of Eucalptus-Albizia mixtures vary by site on Hawaii Island.* Research Paper PSW-187. Berkeley, Calif.: Pacific Southwest Forest and Range Experiment Station, USDA Forest Service.

Fogel, R., M. Ogawa, and J. M. Trappe. 1973. *Terrestrial decomposition: a synopsis.* U.S./International Biological Program, Coniferous Forest Biome Report 135.

Fox, T. R., J. A. Burger, and R. E. Kreh. 1986. Effects of site preparation on nitrogen dynamics in the southern Piedmont. *Forest Ecology and Management* 15:241–256.

Franklin, J. F., T. Spies, D. Perry, M. Harmon, and A. McKee. 1986. "Modifying Douglas-fir management regimes for nontimber objectives." In *Proceedings, symposium on Douglas-fir: stand management for the future,* edited by C. D. Oliver, D. P. Hanley, and J. A. Johnson, 373–379. Contribution No. 55. Seattle, Wash.: College of Forest Resources, University of Washington.

Fredriksen, R. L., D. G. Moore, and L. A. Norris. 1975. "The impact of timber harvest, fertilization, and herbicide treatment on streamwater quality in western Oregon and Washington." In *Forest soils and forest land management,* edited by B. Bernier and C. H. Winget, 283–313. Proceedings, 4th North American Forest Soils Conference, August 1973. Quebec: Les Presses de L'Université Laval.

Froehlich, H. A., and D. H. McNabb. 1984. "Minimizing soil compaction in Northwest forests." In *Forest soils and treatment impacts,* edited by E. L. Stone, 159–192. Proceedings, 6th North American Forest Soils Conference, June 1983. Knoxville, Tenn.: University of Tennessee.

Froehlich, H. A., D. W. R. Miles, and R. W. Robbins. 1986. Growth of young *Pinus ponderosa* and *Pinus contorta* on compacted soils in central Washington. *Forest Ecology and Management* 15:285–294.

Fyles, J. W., and W. B. McGill. 1987. Decomposition of boreal forest litters from central Alberta under laboratory conditions. *Canadian Journal of Forest Research* 17(2):109–114.

Gadgil, R. L. 1971. The nutritional role of *Lupinus arboreus* in coastal sand dune forestry. 3. Nitrogen distribution in the ecosystem before planting. *Plant and Soil* 35(1):113–126.

Gessel, S. P., E. C. Steinbrenner, and R. E. Miller. 1981. "Response of northwestern forests to elements other than nitrogen." In *Proceedings, forest fertilization conference,* edited by S. P. Gessel, R. M. Kenady, and W. A. Atkinson, 140–149. Contribution No. 40. Seattle, Wash.: Institute of Forest Resources, College of Forest Resources, University of Washington.

Gosz, J. R. 1984. "Biological factors influencing nutrient supply in forest soils." In *Nutrition of plantation forests,* edited by G. D. Bowen and E. K. S. Nambiar, 119–146. New York: Academic Press.

Greacen, E. L., and R. Sands. 1980. Compaction of forest soils. A review. *Australian Journal of Soil Research* 18:163–189.

Harmon, M. E., J. F. Franklin, F. J. Swanson, P. Sollins, S. V. Gregory, J. D. Lattin, N. H. Anderson, S. P. Cline, N. G. Aumen, J. R. Sedell, G. W. Lienkaemper, K. Cromack, Jr., and K. W. Cummins. 1986. Ecology of coarse woody debris in temperate ecosystems. *Advances in Ecological Research* 15:133–302.

Hart, G. E., N. V. DeByle, and R. W. Henner. 1981. Slash treatment after clearcutting lodgepole pine affects nutrients in soil water. *Journal of Forestry* 79(7):446–450.

Helms, J. A., C. Hipkin, and E. B. Alexander. 1986. Effects of soil compaction on height growth of a California ponderosa pine plantation. *Western Journal of Applied Forestry* 1(4):104–108.

Hill, S. B., L. J. Metz, and M. H. Farrier. 1975. "Soil mesofauna and silvicultural practices." In *Forest soils and forest land management,* edited by B. Bernier and C. H. Winget, 119–135. Proceedings, 4th North American Forest Soils Conference, August 1973. Quebec: Les Presses de L'Universite Laval.

Keeves, A. 1966. Some evidence of loss of productivity with successive rotations of *Pinus radiata* in the southeast of South Australia. *Australian Forestry* 30(1):51–63.

Kimmins, J. P., D. Binkley, L.Chararpaul, and J. de Catanzaro. 1985. *Biogeochemistry of temperate forest ecosystems: literature on inventories and dynamics of biomass and nutrients.* Information Report PI-X-47E/F. Chalk River, Ontario: Petawawa National Forestry Institute, Canadian Forestry Service.

Kimmins, J. P., and K. A. Scoullar. 1984. "FORCYTE-11: a flexible modelling framework with which to analyse the long-term consequences for yield, economic returns and energy efficiency of alternative forest and agro-forest crop production strategies." In *Proceedings, 5th Canadian bioenergy research and development seminar,* 126–130. National Research Council of Canada.

Kittredge, J. 1954. The influence of shade and litter of pine on evaporation from a clay loam soil at Berkeley, California. *Ecology* 35(3):397–405.

Kramer, J. F., and R. K. Hermann. 1979. Broadcast burning: 25-year effects on forest soils in the western flanks of the Cascade Mountains. *Forest Science* 25(3):427–439.

Krauss, G., K. Muller, G. Gartner, F. Hartel, H. Schanz, and H. Blanckmeister. 1939. Standortsgemasse Durchfuhrung der Abkehr von der Fichtenwirtschaft im nordwestsachsischen Niederland. *Tharandter Forstliches Jahrbuch* 90(7/9):481–715.

Maser, C., J. M. Trappe, and R. A. Nussbaum. 1978. Fungal-small mammal interrelationships with emphasis on Oregon coniferous forests. *Ecology* 59(4):799–809.

Meier, C. E., C. C. Grier, and D. W. Cole. 1985. Below- and aboveground N and P use by *Abies amabilis* stands. *Ecology* 66(6):1928–1942.

McColl, J. G., and R. F. Powers. 1984. "Consequences of forest management on soil-tree relationships." In *Nutrition of plantation forests,* edited by G. D. Bowen and E. K. S. Nambiar, 379–412. New York: Academic Press.

Miles, D. W. R., F. J. Swanson, and C.T. Youngberg. 1984. Effects of landslide erosion on subsequent Douglas-fir growth and stocking levels in the western Cascades. *Soil Science Society of America Journal* 48(3):667–671.

Miller, R. E., and M. D. Murray. 1978. "The effect of red alder on growth of Douglas-fir." In *Utilization and management of alder,* edited by D. G. Briggs, D. S. DeBell, and W. A. Atkinson, 283–306. General Technical Report PNW-70. Portland, Ore.: Pacific Northwest Forest and Range Experiment Station, USDA Forest Service.

Minore, D. 1986. *Effects of site preparation on seedling growth: a preliminary comparison of broadcast burning and pile burning.* Research Note PNW-RN-452. Portland, Ore.: Pacific Northwest Research Station, USDA Forest Service.

Mitchell, H. L., R. F. Finn, and R. O. Rosendahl. 1937. The relation between mycorrhizae and the growth and nutrient absorption of coniferous seedlings in nursery beds. *Black Rock Forest Paper* 10(1):58–73.

Odum, E. P. 1972. "Ecosystem theory in relation to man." In *Ecosystem structure and function,* edited by J. A. Wiens, 11–24. Proceedings, 31st Annual Biology Colloquium. Corvallis, Ore.: Oregon State University Press.

Perry, D. A., R. Molina, and M. P. Amaranthus. 1987. Mycorrhizae, mycorrhizospheres, and reforestation: current knowledge and research needs. Canadian Journal of Forest Research 17(4):929–940.

Perry, D. A., and S. L. Rose. 1983. "Soil biology and forest productivity: opportunities and constraints." In *IUFRO symposium on forest site and continuous productivity,* edited by R. Ballard and S. P. Gessel, 229–238. General Technical Report PNW-163. Portland, Ore.: Pacific Northwest Forest and Range Experiment Station, USDA Forest Service.

Powers, R. F. 1987. "Predicting growth responses to soil management practices: avoiding 'future shock' in research." In *Future developments in soil science,* edited by L. L. Boersma, D. E. Elrick, R. B. Corey, H. H. Cheng, T. C. Tucker, E. M. Rutledge, P. W. Unger, N. W. Foster, S. Kincheloe, and P. H. Hsu, 391–403. Annual meeting, November 30–December 5, 1986, New Orleans, La. Madison, Wis.: Soil Science Society of America, Inc.

Powers, R. F., K. Isik, and P. J. Zinke. 1975. Adding phosphorus to forest soils: storage capacity and possible risks. *Bulletin of Environmental Contamination and Toxicology* 14(3):257–264.

Powers, R. F., S. R. Webster, and P. H. Cochran. 1988. "Estimating the response of ponderosa pine forests to fertilization." In *Proceedings—future forests of the Mountain West: a stand culture symposium,* compiled by W. C. Schmidt, 219–225. General Technical Report INT-243. Ogden, Utah: Intermountain Research Station, USDA Forest Service.

Rolff, C., and B. Dyck. 1986. *An evaluation of FORCYTE-10.* Report No. 4, IEA/FE Project CPC-10. Rotorua, N. Z.: Forest Research Institute.

Sachs, D., and P. Sollins. 1986. Potential effects of management practices on nitrogen nutrition and long-term productivity of western hemlock stands. *Forest Ecology and Management* 17:25–36.

Skoklefald, S. 1973. [Effect of controlled burning on some humus properties and on the establishment and height growth of Norway spruce and Scots pine.] *Meddelelser fra det Norske Skogforsoeksvesen* 30(7):471–504.

Squire, R. O., P. W. Farrell, D. W. Flinn, and B.C. Aeberli. 1985. Productivity of first and second rotation stands of radiata pine on sandy soils. II. Height and volume growth at five years. *Australian Forestry* 48(2):127–137.

Stewart, J. L. 1985. Current use and potential for implementing forest management practices in intensive forest management in the U.S.A. *Forestry Chronicle* 61(3):240–242.

Swanston, D. N., and F. J. Swanson. 1976. "Timber harvesting, mass erosion, and steep land geomorphology in the Pacific Northwest." In *Geomorphology and engineering,* edited by D. R. Coates, 199–221. Stroudsburg, Pa.: Dowden, Hutchinson and Ross, Inc.

Swift, M., O. Heal, and J. Anderson. 1979. *Decomposition in Terrestrial Ecosystems.* Oxford: Blackwell.

Switzer, G. L., L. E. Nelson, and L. E. Hinesley. 1981. "Effects of utilization on nutrient regimes and site productivity." In *Proceedings, forest fertilization conference,* edited by S. P. Gessel, R. M. Kenady, and W. A. Atkinson, 241–259. Contribution No. 40. Seattle, Wash.: Institute of Forest Resources, College of Forest Resources, University of Washington.

Terry, T. A., and J. H. Hughes. 1975. "The effects of intensive management on planted loblolly pine (*Pinus taeda* L.) growth on poorly drained soils of the Atlantic Coastal Plain." In *Forest soils and forest land management,* edited by B. Bernier and C. H. Winget, 351–377. Proceedings, 4th North American Forest Soils Conference, August 1973. Quebec: Les Presses de L'Université Laval.

USDA Forest Service. 1983. *The principal laws relating to Forest Service activities.* Agriculture Handbook No. 243. Washington, D.C.: U.S. Government Printing Office.

Wert, S., and B. R. Thomas. 1981. Effects of skid roads on diameter, height, and volume growth in Douglas-fir. *Soil Science Society of America Journal* 45(3):629–632.

Wiedemann, E. 1935. Über die scháden der streunutzung im Deutschen osten. [Damage due to litter utilization in eastern Germany]. *Forstarchiv* 11(23):386–390.

Youngberg, C.T. 1979 (revised 1981). "Organic matter of forest soils." In *Forest soils of the Douglas-fir Region,* edited by P. E. Heilman, H. W. Anderson, and D. M. Baumgartner, 137–144. Pullman, Wash.: Cooperative Extension Service, Washington State University.

Zinke, P. J., A. G. Stangenberger, W. M. Post, W. R. Emanuel, and J. S. Olson. 1984. *Worldwide organic soil carbon and nitrogen data.* Publication No. 2212. Oak Ridge, Tenn.: Environmental Sciences Division, Oak Ridge National Laboratory.

Chapter 2

Nutrient Cycling: Effects on Productivity of Northwest Forests

Robert L. Edmonds, Dan Binkley, Michael C. Feller, Phillip Sollins, Albert Abee, and David D. Myrold

ABSTRACT

Nutrient availability—the quantity of nutrients available for uptake by trees—limits forest productivity. In the U.S. Pacific Northwest and British Columbia (the Northwest), nitrogen is the major growth-limiting nutrient element, although sulfur potentially may be limiting in southern Oregon, potassium in gravelly outwash soils, phosphorus in coastal Washington, and boron and zinc in southwest British Columbia. This chapter examines, with particular reference to the Northwest: (1) characteristics of nutrient-limited stands, (2) the concept of nutrient availability in relation to nutrient cycling, (3) specific challenges facing forest managers, such as restoring nutrients after harvest, and (4) management options for maintaining long-term productivity. The theory of "optimum nutrition"—providing all necessary elements at a rate determined by tree growth—is discussed. Nutrient-rich sites are generally more robust than nutrient-poor sites, but the nutrient capital even on productive sites should be conserved by using fire carefully and minimizing soil disturbance during site preparation. Weed control generally increases nutrient availability. Maintaining woody debris could be important in managed plantations. Foresters are encouraged to install "low-intensity" nutrient experiments to test ideas on maintaining productivity.

INTRODUCTION

The productivity of many forests is limited by nutrient availability, as seen from plant growth responses to fertilization (Axelsson 1985). But to understand nutrient availability—the quantity of nutrients available for uptake by trees—we must understand nutrient cycling. It is only when we consider how nutrients cycle through an entire ecosystem that we can judge the impact of forest management operations on long-term productivity. Information on nutrient cycling, tree nutrition, and soil chemistry all have some meaning in terms of productivity, but none should be considered in isolation (McColl and Grigal 1979).

The elements commonly limiting tree growth are nitrogen (N), phosphorus (P), potassium (K), magnesium (Mg), sulfur (S), zinc (Zn), and boron (B) (Lavender and Walker 1979, Tamm 1979). Other elements such as iron (Fe), manganese (Mn), copper (Cu), molybdenum (Mo), and chloride (Cl) are required but are rarely limiting. In a classic example of how nutrient availability affects long-term productivity, Ebermayer (1876) as quoted by Tamm (1979) demonstrated that removing litter, and thus nutrients, from middle European forests for use in cow stables adversely affected site quality. Forest growth declined, particularly on infertile sites. In another example, productivity of second-rotation radiata (or Monterey) pine (*Pinus radiata* D. Don) plantations declined in South Australia (Keeves 1966, Woods 1980) and in New Zealand (Stone and Will 1965). In South Australia, the affected plantations were growing in infertile, sandy soils, where slash (harvest residues) from the previous rotation had been burned (Woods 1980). This situation, still of concern in Australia, can be corrected with fertilizers or organic matter management (Farrell et al. 1986). Windrowing also tends to impact long-term productivity (Ballard 1978). Although we have few examples of the effects of management practices on nutrients, and therefore forest productivity in the Northwest, Perry and Rose (1989) suggest that windrowing and broadcast burns are likely to reduce long-term productivity. Skeletal soils in southwest Oregon may be susceptible to harsh site-preparation disturbances (Lewis and Abee 1981).

It is the intent of this chapter to examine—with particular reference to the U.S. Pacific Northwest and British Columbia (the Northwest)—(1) characteristics of nutrient-limited stands, (2) the concept of nutrient availability and its relationship to nutrient cycles in different ecosystems, (3) specific challenges, such as restoring nutrient levels after harvesting, facing forest managers, and (4) management options for maintaining long-term productivity. Productivity may be expressed in two ways—as the total amount of biomass or as merchantable wood volume produced annually. Commercial forest managers are more interested in the latter, most productivity researchers in the former.

NUTRIENTS OF CONCERN IN THE NORTHWEST

Nitrogen is the major growth-limiting nutrient element in the Northwest and is the only one that Douglas-fir [*Pseudotsuga menziesii* (Mirb.) Franco] responds to consistently (Heilman 1979, Peterson and Gessel 1983). Sitka spruce [*Picea sitchensis* (Bong.) Carr.] also appears to benefit from N fertilization (Webster et al. 1976, Farr et al. 1977). Response of western hemlock [*Tsuga heterophylla* (Raf.) Sarg.] has been inconsistent (Webster et al. 1976), but recent work suggests that it will respond better to combined N and P fertilizers (Radwan and Shumway 1983) or to P fertilizer alone on some coastal soils in Washington (Porada 1987). We are just beginning to understand possible effects of nutrient interactions (Radwan and Brix 1986). Lodgepole pine (*Pinus contorta* Dougl. ex Loud.) in interior British Columbia has also been inconsistent in its response to N fertilization (Weetman and Fournier 1982). However, N fixers such as red alder (*Alnus rubra* Bong.) are unlikely to respond to N fertilization.

In the case of Douglas-fir, field experiments with the entire range of essential elements have failed to demonstrate widespread deficiencies of any other element than N (Gessel et al. 1979, Heilman 1979). However, S may be limiting in southern Oregon (Blake 1985, Edmonds and Hsiang 1987), K in gravelly outwash soils (Johnson et al. 1982), and B and Zn in some Douglas-fir, as well as in some western hemlock and Pacific silver fir (*Abies amabilis* Dougl. ex Forbes), plantations in southwestern British Columbia (Carter et al. 1984, 1986).

Concentrations of N, P, K, Calcium (Ca), and Mg as they relate to deficiency in foliage of five western coniferous species are given in Table 2.1; general interpretations (not species specific) are given in Table 2.2 for Mn, Fe, Zn, Cu, B, and Mo. Van den Driessche (1979) determined "adequate" levels of nutrients in current-year needles of Douglas-fir to be 1.8% for N, 0.22% for P, 0.80% for K, 0.20% for Ca, 0.12% for Mg, and 0.18% for S. However, it is difficult to interpret nutrient deficiencies from foliar levels alone because levels in foliage of different ages vary. The New Zealanders have had some success in determining nutrient deficiency levels with radiata pine (Will 1985). The N:S ratio in foliage may also indicate whether N fertilization is likely to induce S deficiency (Turner et al. 1977). Because of the widespread nature and dominance of N deficiency in Pacific Northwest forests, this chapter focuses largely on this element.

CHARACTERISTICS OF NUTRIENT-LIMITED STANDS

Most forest stands are nutrient limited to one degree or another, so trees are well adapted to this type of stress. One way to examine the characteristics of nutrient-limited sites is to contrast the characteristics of a single species in ecosystems which are relatively high and relatively low in nutrients. Douglas-fir is a good test species. Douglas-fir ecosystems with low site quality and relatively moist conditions in northern Oregon, Washington, and British Columbia generally have the following features, compared to those with high site quality (Johnson et al. 1982, Peterson 1982, Vogt and Edmonds 1982, Feller et al. 1983b, Vogt et al. 1983b):

(1)   Lower aboveground production and wood biomass.
(2)   Longer needle retention time.
(3)   Lower photosynthesis rates.
(4)   Lower canopy leaf areas.
(5)   Lower foliar N concentrations.
(6)   Greater translocation of N from old foliage to living tree tissues before litterfall.
(7)   Less litterfall and lower litterfall N concentrations.
(8)   Lower litterfall lignin concentrations.
(9)   Thicker forest floors with well-developed humus layers, perhaps because of more fine-root biomass.
(10) Roughly the same decomposition rates.
(11) Higher forest-floor C:N (carbon:nitrogen) ratios.
(12) More fine-root, but less total live-root, biomass.
(13) More mycorrhizae.
(14) Less total soil N.
(15) Less available soil N (ammonium, NH_4^+, and nitrate, NO_3^- forms).

Values for many of these features are contrasted in Table 2.3. However, some of these may not apply to drier sites in southern Oregon or California. For example, forest floors are thinner in hot, dry areas.

TABLE 2.1. Interpretation of foliar nutrient concentrations for five coniferous species (adapted from Ballard and Carter 1985).

Element[1]	Foliar concentration, % (dry-mass basis)					Interpretation of deficiency
	Douglas-fir	Lodgepole pine	Western hemlock	White spruce[2]	Western redcedar[3]	
N	0.00	0.00	0.00	0.00	0.00	
						Very severe
	1.05	1.05	0.95	1.05	1.15	
						Severe
	1.30	1.20	1.20	1.30	1.50	
						Slight-moderate
	1.45	1.55	1.45	1.55	1.65	
						Adequate
P	0.00	0.00	0.00	0.00	0.00	
						Severe
	0.08	0.09	0.11	0.10	0.10	
						Moderate
	0.10	0.12	0.15	0.14	0.13	
						Slight
	0.15	0.15	0.35[4]	0.16	0.16	
						Adequate
K	0.00	0.00	0.00	0.00	0.00	
						Very severe
	0.35	0.35	0.40	0.25	0.35	
						Moderate-severe
	0.45	0.40	0.45	0.30	0.40	
						Adequate
Ca	0.00	0.00	0.00	0.00	0.00	
						Severe
	0.10	0.05	0.05	0.07	0.07	
						Moderate-severe
	0.15	0.06	0.06	0.10	0.10	
						Slight-moderate possible
	0.20	0.08	0.08	0.15	0.20	
						Little, if any
	0.25	0.10	0.10	0.20	0.25	
						Adequate
Mg	0.00	0.00	0.00	0.00	0.00	
						Severe
	0.06	0.06	0.06	0.05	0.05	
						Moderate-severe
	0.08	0.07	0.07	0.06	0.06	
						Slight-moderate possible
	0.10	0.09	0.09	0.10	0.12	
						Little, if any
	0.12	0.10	0.10	0.12	0.14	
						Adequate

[1] N = nitrogen, P = phosphorus, K = potassium, Ca = calcium, Mg = magnesium.
[2] *Picea glauca* (Moench) Voss.
[3] *Thuja plicata* Donn ex D. Don.
[4] Based on a single sample (Everard 1973) and perhaps not representative.

TABLE 2.2. Interpretation of foliar nutrient concentrations not yet species specific (adapted from Ballard and Carter 1985).

Element[1]	Foliar concentration, ppm (dry-mass basis)	Interpretation of deficiency
Mn	0	
		Severe
	4	
		Probable
	15	
		Possible or near
	25	
		Adequate
Fe	0	
		Likely
	25	
		Possible
	50	
		Unlikely
Active Fe	0	
		Likely
	30	
		Unlikely
Zn	0	
		Probable
	10	
		Possible
	15	
		None
Cu	0	
		Probable
	1	
		Possible
	2	
		Possibly somewhat
	2.6	
		Possible slight
	4	
		None
B	0	
		Deficiency likely
	10	
		Possible; NID[2]
	15	
		Unlikely; N<1.5[3], NID possible; if N>1.5, NID unlikely
	20	
		None
Mo	0	
		Possible
	0.1	
		None

[1]Mn = manganese, Fe = iron, Zn = zinc, Cu = copper, b = boron, Mo = molybdenum.
[2]NID = deficiency inducible by N fertilizer application.
[3]N = percent N concentration.

TABLE 2.3. Features (mean ± standard deviation) of Douglas-fir stands with differing site quality.

Feature	High site quality	Low site quality
Foliar N, %[1]	1.40	1.23
Litterfall N, %[2]	0.63 ± 0.05	0.60 ± 0.07
Litterfall lignin, %[2]	45.6 ± 6.7	43.2 ± 6.6
Forest-floor depth, cm[3]	3.3 ± 1.5	5.2 ± 1.6
Needle weight loss after 2 years' decomposition, %[4]	43.5 ± 5.0	43.0 ± 0.6
N remaining in needles after 2 years' decomposition, %[4]	109 ± 15	133 ± 19
Forest-floor C:N[4]	36 ± 8	51 ± 17
Total live roots, kg/ha[4]	68,000	12,000
Total live fine roots, kg/ha[4]	433 ± 508	1,544 ± 1,295
Mycorrhizal live roots, kg/ha[3]	149 ± 199	426 ± 337
Total fine roots infected by mycorrhizae[3]	69 ± 14	87 ± 11
Total soil N, kg/ha[4]	6,227 ± 3,441	2,895 ± 1,119
Soil NH_4^+, ppm[5]	21.8 ± 2.4	14.0 ± 3.8
Soil NO_3^- ppm[5]	3.1 ± 1.5	1.0 ± 0.2

[1] Edmonds and Bigger (1983); stand age 53 years. N = nitrogen.
[2] R. L. Edmonds, unpublished data, University of Washington, 1987; stand ages range from 11 to 163 years.
[3] Vogt et al. (1983b); stand ages range from 11 to 163 years.
[4] Feller et al. (1983a); stand age 48 years. C = carbon.
[5] Vogt and Edmonds (1982); stand ages range from 45 to 175 years.

Interestingly, total productivity of Douglas-fir stands in Washington with low site quality is not dramatically less than that of stands with high site quality (Keyes and Grier 1981, Grier et al. 1986). The major difference seems to be how carbon is allocated. Lower nutrient availability apparently requires greater investments of photosynthate in fine-root production and mycorrhizae, leaving less photosynthate for wood production. Fine-root production may not always be greater on poor sites, however; for example, Nadelhoffer et al. (1985) found that it was less.

Nutrient-limited Pacific silver fir stands at high elevation tend to have many of the same features as poor Douglas-fir stands, but the features are exaggerated (see chapter 8, this volume). Fine-root and mycorrhizal biomass is much higher, forest floors are thicker (Vogt et al. 1983a), decomposition rates are lower (Edmonds 1980), foliage is retained longer, and N concentrations in litter are lower (Johnson et al. 1982).

Some of the reported differences in site quality can be attributed to different moisture regimes rather than nutrients. To assess the influence of nutrient limitation alone on forest stands, we can examine stands growing on the same site with the same soil moisture, some of which have been fertilized and others not. Several studies have done this. Foliar biomass in Douglas-fir is greater on urea-fertilized sites (Gessel and Turner 1976, Vogt et al. 1986a) as result of (1) increased needle size, (2) more needles per shoot, and (3) greater number of shoots produced (Tamm 1979, Grier et al. 1986). Brix (1971) also found some increase in photosynthetic capacity (milligrams of carbon fixed per unit surface area or biomass of foliage) of Douglas-fir after N fertilization. A much larger response from fertilization can thus be expected in stands in which canopies are not fully closed and there is room for foliage area to increase.

Litterfall may also be influenced by fertilization. Gessel and Turner (1976) indicated that litterfall decreases after fertilization, then increases for at least 5 years. Yet Vogt et al. (1986a) found little difference in litterfall between fertilized and unfertilized stands 14 years later. Berg and Staaf (1980) noted that fertilization only moderately increased decomposition rates of needle litter.

The proportion of photosynthates allocated to shoots relative to roots increases after fertilization (Waring and Schlesinger 1985, Axelsson 1986). Vogt et al. (1986a) found that fine-root biomass decreased after fertilization in Douglas-fir stands in Washington whereas coarse-root and aboveground biomass increased. Fourteen years after fertilization, fine-root biomass was 1,350 kg/ha, while it was 5,620 kg/ha in an unfertilized stand. Fine-root turnover on the fertilized stand was 50% of that on the unfertilized. Axelsson (1986), however, found no decrease in fine-root biomass in fertilized Scots pine (*Pinus sylvestris* L.) stands in Sweden, but an increase in coarse-root and aboveground biomass.

THE CONCEPT OF NUTRIENT AVAILABILITY

The productivity of many forests appears to be controlled by nutrient availability—that is, the quantity of nutrients available for uptake each year. If the current supply is not sufficient, nutrient deficiencies occur. Nutrient availability can be considered similar to dividends earned on financial investments:

$$\text{Dividends} = \text{capital} \times \text{interest rate}$$
$$\text{Nutrient availability} = \text{nutrient capital} \times \text{turnover rate}$$

The availability of nutrients can be changed either by changing the amount of nutrient capital or by changing the turnover rate—the rate at which nutrients are released from the nutrient capital in the soil. Management can do both. Moreover, the total nutrient capital is a conglomerate of various "pools" with various turnover rates. Nutrient capital is fairly easy to measure, but turnover rate is difficult. Detecting changes in turnover rates may be even more difficult.

Many forest-tree species appear to have different nutritional requirements (Tamm 1979) and different nutrient-use efficiencies—that is, net primary production per unit of nutrient accumulated. Wild plants that are restricted to infertile soils generally have lower maximum potential growth rates and are less responsive to added nutrients than related plants from more fertile sites (Chapin et al. 1986) (Fig. 2.1).

Chapin et al. (1986) have contrasted nutrient limitation in individuals with that in the community. Over the range of a dominant species such as Douglas-fir, individuals on infertile sites are more responsive to fertilization than individuals on more fertile sites (Fig. 2.2). Understory vegetation in Douglas-fir stands, however, may respond differently because the understory species on fertile and infertile sites are usually different. The potential productivity of each community depends on the growth potential of each of its component species. Thus, an understanding of both individual- and ecosystem-level processes is necessary if we are to accurately interpret the results of fertilization experiments (see chapter 11, this volume).

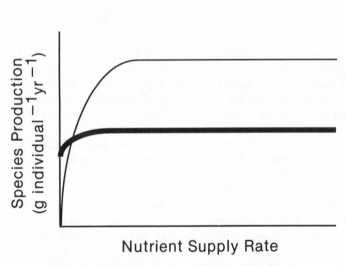

FIG. 2.1. Production by a crop species (light line) and a species adapted to low levels of nutrients (heavy line) in response to variable nutrient supply rate (adapted from Chapin et al. 1986).

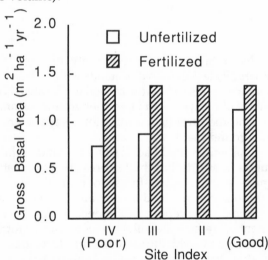

FIG. 2.2. Estimated increase in gross basal area over 10 years for unfertilized and heavily fertilized (450 kg/ha of nitrogen) unthinned Douglas-fir in the Northwest growing on sites of variable quality (adapted from Peterson 1982, Chapin et al. 1986).

Indexes of nutrient availability, including soil incubations (both anaerobic and aerobic in the field and laboratory; Strand 1984) and ion-exchange resins (Binkley and Matson 1983) have been developed. These indexes have been used with mixed success in predicting the response of monospecific (one species) forests to fertilization (Chapin et al. 1986), suggesting that our understanding of this concept in forests is incomplete.

Nutrient availability may be reflected in nutrient concentrations in tree foliage which, in turn, are related to tree growth (Fig. 2.3). Thus, as soil nutrient availability increases, foliar nutrient concentrations and tree growth should increase until some optimum beyond which tree growth levels off and then declines as a result of toxic effects.

Ingestad (1974, 1982), however, challenged the concept of an optimum concentration of nutrients in soil and foliage, suggesting instead that it is the nutrient flux density (amount of nutrients available per unit time) and the total amount of nutrients in the biomass that are important in determining tree growth rates. Ingestad's concept seems to be borne out when relationships between foliar nutrient concentration and stand age are considered. On a site of given productivity, foliar N concentration decreases as trees age (Lavender and Walker 1979). It may be only 0.83% in a 450-year-old Douglas-fir stand with dark green foliage, but 1.2% in a 50-year-old stand with chlorotic foliage. Nutrient availability is adequate to maintain green foliage in the old-growth stand but not in the younger stand despite the presence of higher foliar N concentrations in the latter. Thus, foliar nutrient concentrations alone may not be very useful in characterizing how nutrient limitations affect productivity.

Many conifers, including our western species, have high growth potentials (Axelsson 1985). For example, western hemlock can produce 36 Mg ha^{-1} yr^{-1} aboveground (Fujimori 1971), although this is not often achieved. Most Douglas-fir stands produce less than 20 Mg ha^{-1} yr^{-1} (Long 1982). Net biomass production will increase if maximum leaf area is rapidly achieved. There is a strong relationship between total leaf area and net primary production in Douglas-fir and other Northwest species (Fig. 2.4). Although the leaf areas shown in this figure may be overestimates for old-growth forests (Marshall and Waring 1986), the relationship is still strong. The main factor increasing leaf area of conifers is the nutrient flux density, which can be manipulated to a greater extent than other variables controlling growth (Axelsson 1985). Nutrient availability is thus related to the current requirement of trees. In low-elevation Douglas-fir forests, low nutrient availability may prevent a site from supporting the leaf area possible given that site's water balance (Grier et al. 1986).

Thus, manipulating nutrient availability can increase wood production (Binkley 1986). In Sweden, "optimum nutrition" (adding all necessary elements at a rate determined by tree growth and beginning at an early age) could produce a gain in mean annual volume increment of about 300% for pine and 150% for spruce (Axelsson 1985)—a gain 2–3 times greater than that achieved with conventional fertilization throughout a rotation. The theory behind optimum nutrition and maximum growth is that the whole stand-soil system is saturated with nutrients in 10–20 years (Axelsson 1985). The system then cycles the N necessary for high production throughout the rotation, requiring little or no additional fertilization. The necessary maximum dose thus decreases with time while internal N cycling increases. Extremely high productivity can be expected even in stands carrying moderate amounts of foliage if the nitrogen flux density is high.

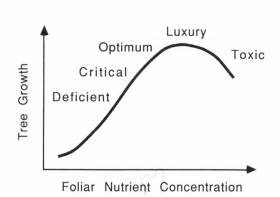

FIG. 2.3. Relationship of tree growth to nutrient concentrations in tree foliage (adapted from Waring and Schlesinger 1985).

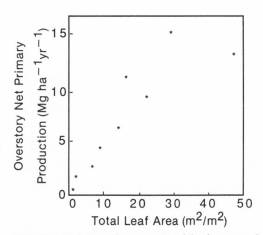

FIG. 2.4. Relations between total leaf area and overstory net primary production in nine Northwest vegetation zones, along a transect from the Pacific coast to the east side of the Cascade Mountains (adapted from Gholz 1982, Grier et al. 1986).

FACTORS INFLUENCING NUTRIENT TURNOVER RATES

Nutrient availability is strongly influenced by nutrient turnover rates, which are generally controlled by the rates of organic matter decomposition. Soil organic matter is extremely complex. The forest floor, for example, contains many different substrates (needles, twigs, cones, bark, branches, and logs), each decomposing and releasing nutrients at different rates. Some substrates (e.g., red alder leaves) decompose quickly and do not immobilize N or any other element (Edmonds 1980). Others (e.g., Pacific silver fir needles and branches) may immobilize N for more than 5 years (Edmonds 1984, 1987). Still others (e.g., very slowly decomposing logs) may immobilize N and other nutrients for more than 25 years (Grier 1978). Most of the N mineralized (i.e., released from decomposing substrates) in conifer stands appears to come from the forest floor rather than the mineral soil. Using buried incubation bags, McClaugherty et al. (1985) determined that up to 18% of the N mineralized in eastern hemlock [*Tsuga canadensis* (L.) Carr.] and white pine (*Pinus strobus* L.) stands was derived from the mineral soil, the rest from the forest floor; in contrast, 53% of the N mineralized in bigtooth aspen (*Populus grandidentata* Michx.) stands came from the mineral soil.

Litter chemistry (mostly C:N and lignin:N ratios and lignin concentrations), site microenvironment (mostly moisture and temperature), and microbial populations (soil microflora and microfauna) are the dominant factors controlling decomposition and mineralization rates (Fogel and Cromack 1977, Edmonds 1980, 1984, 1987).

Today's management practices—clearcutting, shorter rotations, site preparation (including slash burning and yarding unmerchantable material)—strongly influence the type of organic matter on a site, the populations of soil microbes, and the rate of organic matter decomposition and nutrient release (McColl and Powers 1984). Thus, management practices strongly influence nutrient availability. Some research on the effects of harvesting practices in forests has been conducted (Bormann and Likens 1979, Leaf 1979), with a certain amount in western forests (e.g., Jurgensen et al. 1979, Bigger and Cole 1983, Edmonds and Bigger 1983, Entry et al. 1986, Bigger 1988). Harvesting generally is thought to increase decomposition rates by creating warmer, moister conditions. However, conditions immediately after harvesting may be too warm, and the resulting excess drying may actually retard decomposition. Binkley (1984) found that surface litter decomposition may be retarded in clearcuts, but humus decomposition may be increased. Decomposition may also be greater at forest edges adjacent to clearcuts (Edmonds and Bigger 1983); if so, this could have implications with respect to the size, shape, and configuration of clearcuts (see chapter 6, this volume). Although our knowledge of these processes is far from complete, it appears that maintaining organic matter on a site is important to sustaining site productivity.

NUTRIENT AVAILABILITY IN RELATION TO NUTRIENT CYCLING

Nutrient availability is determined by nutrient cycles. Nutrient cycling in forests is well explained in many publications (Cole and Rapp 1981, Johnson et al. 1982, Miller 1984, Waring and Schlesinger 1985, Binkley 1986), so it will only be briefly described here. Forest nutrient cycles involve annual inputs, internal transfers, and annual outputs (Fig. 2.5). This is further elaborated for N in Figure 2.6. Nitrogen cycling is complex and involves the processes of nitrification (microbial transformation of NH_4^+ to NO_2^- and then to NO_3^- under aerobic conditions) and denitrification (microbial transformation of NO_3^- and NO_2^- to the gases N_2O and N_2 under anaerobic conditions). In many cases, episodic events such as fires and harvest are more important than the sum of the annual fluxes through the rotation. Table 2.4 shows some common rates of N transfers for certain processes in several different types of ecosystems.

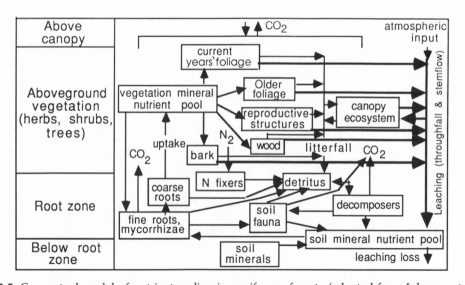

FIG. 2.5. Conceptual model of nutrient cycling in coniferous forests (adapted from Johnson et al. 1982).

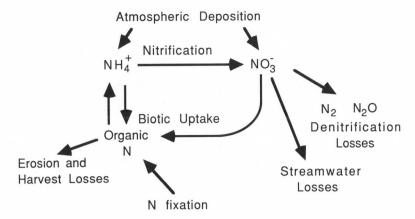

FIG. 2.6. Inputs, internal transfers, and outputs of nitrogen (N) in a forest ecosystem (adapted from Waring and Schlesinger 1985).

TABLE 2.4. Nitrogen transfers (kg ha^{-1} yr^{-1}) among ecosystem components in young, mature, and old-growth coniferous ecosystems (adapted from Johnson et al. 1982).

Process	42-yr-old Douglas-fir	121-yr-old Pacific silver fir	170-yr-old western hemlock/ Sitka spruce	450-yr-old Douglas-fir
Input (precipitation, dry fall)[1]	1.7	5.5	1.3	2.0
Return to forest floor[2]				
Throughfall + stemflow	0.5	—	1.3	3.4
Litterfall	25.4	—	16.3	25.6
Total forest floor	25.9	35.8[3]	17.6	29.0
Within vegetation transfers				
Requirement	45.8	39.9	23.1	33.3
Redistribution	20.7	0.0	12.4	18.5
Uptake	25.1	39.9	10.7	14.8
Soil transfers				
Forest floor to soil	7.3	—	10.3	4.7
Loss from rooting zone	3.4	2.0	2.7	1.5
Input minus loss from rooting zone	−1.7	3.5	−1.4	0.5

[1]Weathering inputs are negligible for nitrogen (N). N fixation is minimal in western conifer stands (Cushon 1985).
[2]Throughfall is rain dripping through the canopy; stemflow is water collected at the base of the stem; litterfall is needles, leaves, twigs and other fine material.
[3]Separate estimates for throughfall, stemflow, and litterfall not available.

Inputs

Atmospheric inputs come dissolved in precipitation, as dry particles deposited on canopies, and, in areas subject to pollution, even as gases (mostly sulfur dioxide and nitrogen oxides). Atmospheric inputs of N in western forests are generally less than 2 kg ha^{-1} yr^{-1} but may be slightly higher (near 5 kg ha^{-1} yr^{-1}) in coastal forests (Table 2.4). Nitrogen fixation, which converts atmospheric N gas into proteins, is an important source of N in forests, particularly those containing large proportions of symbiotic N fixers such as *Ceanothus* spp. and red alder, which can fix up to 100 and 50–200 kg ha^{-1} yr^{-1}, respectively (Bormann and DeBell 1981, Binkley et al. 1982). Once fixed, the N continues to cycle within the forest. Although free-living (asymbiotic) microbes also can fix N, the rates are generally insignificant compared to those of symbiotic N fixers. Cushon (1985) studied gaseous N fluxes in a mature (approximately 100-year-old) Douglas-fir, western hemlock, and western redcedar (*Thuja plicata* Donn ex D. Don) forest in southwestern British Columbia in which no symbiotic N-fixing plants such as alder were present. He found that N fixation added approximately 0.8 kg ha^{-1} yr^{-1} while denitrification losses were less than 0.01 kg ha^{-1} yr^{-1}, for a net gain of approximately 0.8 kg ha^{-1} yr^{-1}. Similar low inputs from free-living N fixers (B. Heath, personal communication, Oregon State University, 1987) and low losses for denitrification (D. Myrold, unpublished data, Oregon State University, 1987) have been found in Oregon. Gaseous inputs and outputs are not included in Table 2.4 because the data are from coniferous forests where such fluxes are very small.

Weathering of soil minerals can release sizable quantities of cation (positively charged) nutrients such as K, Ca, and Mg and sometimes P but usually no N. But such estimates of weathering inputs are difficult to obtain and are not included in Table 2.4. An additional source of nutrients is, of course, fertilization, which has mostly been used to increase productivity. However, future fertilization use might extend to maintaining productivity on sites where natural supplies have been depleted.

Internal Transfers

Organic matter decomposition and subsequent nutrient release are key processes in forest ecosystems, and the rates at which C and nutrients flow through the forest floor can play a large role in regulating ecosystem productivity. Soil microbes are strong competitors for plant nutrients; so when microbes are nutrient limited, trees can become nutrient deficient.

Microbes are also important in nitrogen transformations in forest soils (Fig. 2.5). Highest rates of nitrification are observed in red alder stands. Lower rates are observed in Douglas-fir stands, but rates are higher for sites that are more productive. Little or no nitrification occurs in high-elevation Pacific silver fir stands (Vitousek et al. 1979). The factors controlling nitrification in forest soils are not completely understood, but substrate (ammonium) availability appears to be the most important.

Trees can take up N as ammonium, nitrate, or amino acids. Ammonium is assumed the dominant form taken up, at least by conifers in the Northwest (Johnson et al. 1982). Once absorbed by plants, nutrients move to sites where they are needed. However, some elements are more mobile than others. Potassium, for example, may be leached from needles by rain. Some elements, particularly N and S, and sometimes P, may be translocated back into living tree tissues before needles are lost as litterfall (Johnson et al. 1982). This translocation tends to be greater on more nutrient-limited sites. Other elements, such as Ca, cannot be easily mobilized and are lost with litterfall. Interestingly, a large proportion of the litter (or detritus) is produced belowground through fine-root turnover. In many cases, belowground inputs exceed aboveground (Vogt et al. 1986b). In some ecosystems, woody litter may be an important source of nutrients and could also be an important site for N fixation (Harmon et al. 1986). Of the nutrients taken up annually, on average, roughly 20% are retained and accumulated in tree biomass; the rest are recycled to the soil. Temperate-zone conifers typically take up 47 kg ha^{-1} yr^{-1} of N and return 36 kg ha^{-1} yr^{-1} (Cole 1986). If we assume that uptake regulates productivity, 1 kg ha^{-1} yr^{-1} of N taken up will, on average, produce 194 kg ha^{-1} yr^{-1} of aboveground biomass (Cole 1986).

Outputs

Most forests are very efficient at retaining nutrients. Not only are outputs usually smaller than inputs, but outputs are a small fraction of the amount cycled annually when forests remain undisturbed.

Leaching and erosion are usually the major pathways for loss. Fires can volatilize both N and S and, through fly ash as well, cause significant nutrient losses. Some N can be lost as a gas through denitrification, but this is usually minor for forests growing on well-drained soils. Cushon (1985) found denitrification outputs to be less than 0.01 kg ha^{-1} yr^{-1} in southwestern British Columbia. Many of the significant outputs are episodic in nature, particularly those involving fire and harvest.

Fire. Hot wildfires may remove greater than 500 kg/ha of N annually (Table 2.5), slash fires from 10 to over 1,000 kg/ha of N depending on the severity of the fire (Feller et al. 1983b, Little and Klock 1985, Binkley 1986; M. C. Feller, unpublished data, University of British Columbia, 1987). A typical broadcast slash burn in the coastal Northwest appears to remove more than 200 kg/ha of N (Little and Klock 1985; M. C. Feller, unpublished data, University of British Columbia, 1987).

Harvest. Nutrient loss resulting from harvest depends on the quantity of biomass removed. Long rotations often yield large trees, so more biomass is removed at the time of harvest; however, long rotations remove less biomass than short rotations. This is generally a function of tree species and the amount and type of tissue removed. Whole-tree harvests generally remove about twice as much biomass as bole-only harvests (Leaf

1979). Even the most intensive vegetation removal leaves 87.7% of the total ecosystem N on the site; removing boles typically leaves more than 95% (Table 2.6).

However, determining site N capital depends greatly on the soil depth used in the calculations because different depths contain different amounts. For example, mineral soil usually contains the greatest quantities of N. It is uncertain exactly what depth should be used for calculating soil N capital. Furthermore, much of the soil or total ecosystem N is not readily available to trees because it is bound up in organic matter. Thus, although harvesting may remove only 10% of the site N capital, it may remove a much greater proportion of the N that would be readily available for uptake by plant roots. The significance of harvesting losses cannot always be readily assessed from the type of data given in Table 2.6. What we really need to know is the effect of harvesting on the available N pool, and on the short- and long-term rates of replenishment and depletion of this pool. For instance, amounts of N lost through leaching as a result of harvest appear to be slight in western conifer forests (Johnson et al. 1982, Bigger and Cole 1983, Feller and Kimmins 1984, Bigger 1988).

Whole-tree harvesting in Douglas-fir stands at Pack Forest, Washington, strongly reduced height growth in the first 2 years after treatment on poor sites, but had little influence on highly productive sites (Edmonds and Bigger 1983, Bigger 1988). This effect, however, was not so pronounced after 7 years (Bigger 1988). Thus it appears that poor sites like those at Pack Forest, although susceptible to productivity losses, may be fairly resilient with respect to harvesting.

TABLE 2.5. Total annual nitrogen (N) losses and their mechanisms for Douglas-fir ecosystems (Johnson et al. 1982, Feller et al. 1983b).

Condition	Total N loss $kg\ ha^{-1}\ yr^{-1}$	Loss mechanism
Undisturbed	(Gain of 0–10)	(No loss)
Clearcut only	100–300	Stem removal; leaching
Clearcut and slashburned	300–1,200	Volatilization; leaching; stem removal
Burned by hot wildfire	>500	Volatilization; leaching

TABLE 2.6. Nitrogen (N) capital remaining after harvest in forest ecosystems in Washington (WA) and Oregon (OR) (adapted from Johnson et al. 1982).

Tree species	Age, yr	State	Total ecosystem N, kg/ha	% N remaining after removing		
				Boles only[1]	Whole trees[2]	Vegetation[3]
Douglas-fir	9	WA	3,017	99.6	98.9	97.4
	22	WA	3,281	95.6	93.1	91.0
	30	WA	3,232	95.6	93.2	91.7
	30	WA	3,477	95.1	90.9	90.1
	42	WA	3,366	93.3	89.4	88.3
	49	WA	3,538	95.3	90.6	89.9
	73	WA	3,751	95.4	90.7	90.2
	95	WA	3,686	92.5	87.9	87.7
	95	OR	10,805	97.5	95.2	95.1
	130	OR	8,775	97.9	95.6	95.5
	450	OR	5,725	93.9	90.1	89.9
Western hemlock/Sitka spruce	30	OR	33,781	99.5	98.6	98.6
	121	OR	36,315	98.4	98.0	97.9
Noble fir[4]	130	OR	15,500	97.5	96.0	96.0
Mountain hemlock[4]/Pacific silver fir	130	OR	6,529	97.2	94.0	93.7
Pacific silver fir	23	WA	2,868	99.0	94.1	93.1
Pacific silver fir/mountain and western hemlock	170	WA	4,895	96.9	93.1	92.8

[1] To a minimum top diameter inside bark of 10 cm.
[2] Boles, branches, foliage, and reproductive structures removed from site for all trees greater than 5-cm diameter at breast height (1.4 m above ground).
[3] All living vegetation removed to surface of litter layer.
[4] Noble fir (*Abies procera* Rehd.); mountain hemlock [*Tsuga mertensiana* (Bong.) Carr.].

NUTRIENT CYCLING PATTERNS THROUGHOUT A ROTATION

Natural forest ecosystems usually have balanced nutrient cycles that allow very little nutrient loss (Vitousek and Reiners 1975, Tamm 1979). The balanced cycle, however, is affected by factors such as successional stage of the forest, water regime, mineralogy and rate of soil weathering, external inputs of nutrients and toxic substances, nitrogen fixation, denitrification and nitrification, and natural or human-caused disturbance (Tamm 1979). Trends for net ecosystem production and nutrient losses during primary successional development are shown in Figure 2.7. In a mature forest, nutrient inputs offset outputs. When net ecosystem production is positive, nutrient outputs in streamwater are less than inputs because of plant uptake. Losses for limiting elements such as N may fall to zero while levels of less essential elements such as K show little change during succession (Vitousek and Reiners 1975).

Little is known about N availability, uptake, and limitation in western forest ecosystems. We have, however, hypothesized trends for these three factors in relation to time (Fig. 2.8). We believe that N availability increases dramatically after harvest and then falls back to original levels. If atmospheric inputs are high, N availability may continue to be higher than before harvest; if harvesting was intensive, N availability may decline below original levels. N uptake initially declines after harvest, increases once vegetation is reestablished, and then declines after canopy closure. Nutrients become limiting when availability cannot meet uptake requirements. Broadcast fertilization immediately after clearcutting may actually result in losses of N because uptake is low. However, before canopy closure heavy demands are made on the soil, and fertilizers may increase growth because N availability is declining. Because demands on soil nutrient supplies drop dramatically after canopy closure, Miller (1981) suggested that fertilizers are likely to be of limited value at this stage. However, this is certainly not the view in the Northwest, where fertilizers are applied after canopy closure with good results (Miller et al. 1986). Different management strategies could alter the differences between the two curves shown in Figure 2.8c. Although these hypothesized trends are appealing, data are needed to test them and to apply them on a site-specific basis.

The major problem involved in testing and applying the concept outlined in Figure 2.8 seems to be determining values for N availability, which are difficult to obtain directly. Mineralizable N has been used to index N availability (Shumway and Atkinson 1978, Powers 1980, Shumway 1984) but does not always reflect availability of N to trees.

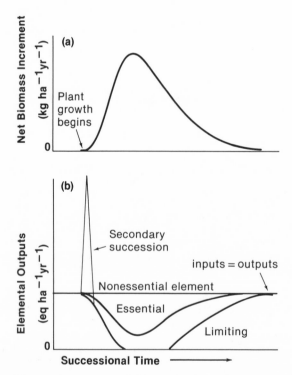

FIG. 2.7. Variation in (a) net biomass increment and (b) nutrient loss of nonessential, essential, and limiting elements (e.g., nitrogen) during plant succession. In (b), the sharply peaked thin line represents a high rate of nutrient loss immediately after disturbance, such as harvesting, during secondary succession; over this period, total ecosystem biomass would decrease (adapted from Vitousek and Reiners 1975).

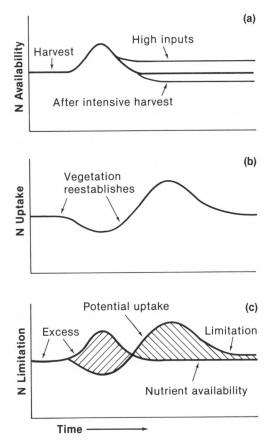

FIG. 2.8. Hypothesized trends for nitrogen (N) (a) availability, (b) uptake, and (c) limitation over time in a Douglas-fir forest.

SPECIFIC CHALLENGES FACING FOREST MANAGERS

The most important of the many challenges facing forest managers with respect to nutrients as they relate to long-term productivity are listed below.

(1) Precisely determining long-term trends in forest productivity.

(2) Determining an "ecological" rotation with natural input rates of nutrients and then decreasing this rotation length through management by, for example, using N-fixing species or less intensive harvesting.

(3) Manipulating nutrient cycling processes by species selection. Stands of mixed tree species would be expected to behave differently from stands of an individual species. The effects of understory species need to be considered, both as nutrient competitors and as producers of readily decomposed litter.

(4) Increasing nutrient availability by increasing the turnover rate of nutrients already on a site by, for example, reconfiguring cutting units.

(5) Understanding the importance of woody debris.

(6) Understanding the relationships between nutrient cycling, water regimes, and soil compaction.

(7) Determining what is required to restore site productivity if management degrades it by removing nutrients.

(8) Determining the nutrient implications of genetically selected trees. Will their nutritional needs be greater? There seems to be some potential for manipulating the efficiency of nutrient uptake by genetic means (Nambiar 1985).

RECOMMENDATIONS AND CONCLUSIONS

Nutrient cycling has been studied in the Northwest for more than 2 decades, and we still have much to learn about the effects of forest management on specific processes and, ultimately, long-term productivity. On the basis of our current knowledge and some "best guesses," we feel we can make the following recommendations to managers:

(1)   Conserve the nutrient capital on a site by using fire carefully and minimizing soil disturbance during site preparation. Fires should be hot enough to meet management objectives but no hotter. Make sure that benefits from fire (e.g., reduced brush competition) are not offset by costs (e.g., reduced nutrient availability). Avoid windrowing if possible, and otherwise minimize disturbance of the forest floor. If a chosen management regime entails substantial nutrient losses, consider writing the cost of replacing nutrients into timber-sale calculations. Organic matter losses, however, cannot be easily or cheaply replaced. Nutrient-rich sites, generally more robust than nutrient-poor sites, have greater nutrient capital and faster turnover rates. However, a 10% reduction in growth on a rich site is more costly in terms of wood production than a 10% reduction on a poor site. On nutrient-poor sites, grow trees over longer rotations, lessen harvest intensity, limb where trees fall, and minimize the use of fire.

   Fertilization can restore lost productivity in Douglas-fir stands on poor sites after intensive harvest, as observed at Washington's Pack Forest (Bigger 1988) and from the South Australian experience (Farrell et al. 1986). Maintenance of woody debris could be important in managed plantations, particularly on poor sites, but we have little evidence for this as yet.

(2)   Aim at "relieving" vegetative competition in young plantations, rather than removing every single noncrop plant. Weed control generally increases nutrient availability. Although too many alders definitely suppress conifers, as few as 50 red alder/ha (20/acre) can substantially increase site N status because the alders fix nitrogen.

(3)   Take the opportunity to install "low-intensity" experiments. Instead of applying one treatment to an entire management unit, be creative—burn only three-quarters of a unit, or put a species mixture on one-tenth of a unit. With some careful recordkeeping, useful information can be collected without big investments in research.

(4)   Tie fertilizer applications to nutrient availability during a rotation—that is, apply the "optimum nutrition" concept. Try adding small amounts of fertilizer to individual trees at planting.

(5)   Communicate with specialists and researchers as much as possible.

QUESTIONS FROM THE SYMPOSIUM FLOOR

Q: Can you critique the use of raw sewage sludge to increase nutrients to soil?

A: Raw sewage is not applied to soils in the U.S.; only treated sewage is applied. It is a source of organic matter, N, P, and many other nutrient elements. Many tree species respond favorably to added sludge, including Douglas-fir, but there are some problems, including nitrate leaching, pathogens, heavy metals, and unwanted organic chemicals (see Cole et al. 1986).

Q: You speculated that it may be possible to increase nutrient availability rather than applying fertilizers. Do you have any suggestions as to how this could be done?

A: Opportunities for increasing wood production through manipulating nutrient availability are possible. What I was referring to was the Swedish "optimum nutrition" idea—adding all necessary elements at a rate determined by tree growth and beginning at an early age. This involves fertilization. Otherwise you would have to use N-fixing plants or increase the rate of decomposition (the latter is difficult to manage).

Q: How significant is large woody debris in long-term nutrient availability? On a good site, would maximum utilization of the stand (removal of all woody debris) have any long-term impact, or would inputs from fine woody debris, foliage, and precipitation be sufficient to maintain long-term productivity?

A: Large woody debris provides organic matter to the soil over a long period and thus is important to consider for maintaining long-term productivity. Woody debris is a site for N fixation but only provides a small fraction of the annual nutrient needs of trees. Needles and fine woody debris provide most of the readily available nutrients. Thus, from a nutrient point of view, maintenance of coarse woody debris may not be all that important for wood production on a good site. However, it may be important for a variety of other reasons, for example, animal habitats.

Q: Is height growth or diameter growth the better measure of tree performance?

A: In the early growth stages, height growth is probably a better measure. However, diameter growth is as good as or perhaps better than height once trees are out of their juvenile phase (e.g., older than 10 years).

Q: On a moist site, where water is not limiting growth, how feasible would it be to accelerate tree height growth beyond that of brush by fertilizing heavily rather than controlling brush to reduce competition?

A: I think it would be feasible as long as you applied the fertilizer so that the trees obtained most of it, e.g., in the planting hole.

Q: Approximately when does nitrogen become deficient in relation to time (see the time axis in Figure 2.8)?

A: Sometime near canopy closure.

Q: How are N-fixation inputs measured? Indirectly, by assessing the presence of symbiotic N-fixing plants (e.g., alder), or directly, by studying actual N-fixation rates of free-living microflora (asymbiotic N fixation in soil and litter)?

A: It has been done both ways in the Pacific Northwest. Nitrogen accretion with time has been determined with red alder and ceanothus. Acetylene reduction techniques have been used for free-living bacteria in litter, logs, and so forth.

Q: Have you considered that some of the "weed" species—such as herbaceous species with rapid turnover of organic matter—may have a long-term benefit?

A: These species are no doubt very important in the early stages of stand development, but their importance probably declines after canopy closure. Some understory species, however, such as Oregon grape (*Berberis aquifolium* Pursh), have sclerophyllous (tough) leaves and probably do not decompose very rapidly.

Q: On sites where nutrients have been reduced by burning and/or whole-tree harvesting, can application of N following harvest return a site to its original level without further treatments?

A: Average N losses by burning can be replaced through operational fertilization at 200 kg/ha of urea N. Thus, provided volatilization and leaching losses are not great, applying N following harvest could bring site N back to original levels. However, not all of the N will be taken up by the trees.

Q: In the Pacific Northwest, is weed competition really a problem? I have planted thousands of trees on my place and they always seem to grow better in the brush. Early in the rotation when nutrients are in excess, weeds capture nutrients for release later in the rotation. Please expand on this.

A: Weed competition is not a problem everywhere in the Pacific Northwest. It is more of a problem on stressed sites, particularly dry sites. It also appears to be a problem in moist areas in British Columbia where weeds establish very rapidly, resulting in inadequate tree stocking. In other areas there is no problem.

Q: You state that "good" sites are more robust than "poor" sites. Don't you think that potential for absolute (not percent) productivity loss is greater on good sites? Similarly, isn't there more opportunity for enhanced productivity (total volume increase) by fertilizing on many good sites?

A: You could realize greater absolute productivity loss on good sites, but in general there is an excess of nutrients on these sites, with a lot of nutrients in the "bank." The treatment has to be pretty drastic to have a lasting effect. This is why good sites are not as responsive to fertilization as poor sites. However, if the value of a log on a good site is increased by a small diameter increase, then it might be worth doing.

Q: Would you comment on the cumulative effect—that is, the effect over several rotations—of losses or gains of nitrogen, phosphorus, and other nutrients without fertilization.

A: Whether or not cumulative effects occur depends on level of utilization, method of site preparation, nutrient replacement rates, and rotation length. Considering only the nutrients removed in logs, there is probably no cumulative effect; sufficient nutrients are added through natural processes over a rotation to balance removals. Whole-tree harvest greatly increases nutrient removals; studies in both western and eastern North America show excessive losses of calcium associated with whole-tree harvest. When clearcuts are broadcast burned, some proportion of the nitrogen and sulfur contained in logging residues and forest floor is volatilized and lost as gas. What proportion depends on the heat of the burn. If N-fixing plants such as alder and ceanothus occupy a site, nitrogen losses even from intense burns are probably replaced within 5–20 years. Without N-fixing plants, annual nitrogen inputs in the Pacific Northwest total 3–5 kg/ha. Over a 60-year rotation, this would amount to 200–300 kg/ha—enough to balance losses from cool burns, but probably not from moderate burns and certainly not from hot ones. Shorter rotations increase the chance of cumulative effects, longer rotations decrease it. Windrowing is a more severe treatment than broadcast burning in that all nutrients in logging residues, forest floor, and frequently topsoil are removed from most of the site and concentrated on a small portion. Much evidence shows that windrowing is bad news.

REFERENCES

Axelsson, B. 1985. "Increasing forest productivity and value by manipulating nutrient availability." In *Forest potentials—productivity and value,* edited by R. Ballard, P. Farnum, G. A. Ritchie, and J. K. Winjum, 5–38. Tacoma, Wash.: Weyerhaeuser Science Symposium 4.

———. 1986. "Difference in yield at different sites: an irrigation-fertilization study of nutrient flux during fast growth." In *Forest site and productivity,* edited by S. P. Gessel, 171–183. Dordrecht/Boston: Martinus Nijhoff Publisher.

Ballard, R. 1978. Effect of slash and soil removal on the productivity of second rotation radiata pine on a pumice soil. *New Zealand Journal of Forest Science* 8:252–260.

Ballard, T. M., and R. E. Carter. 1985. *Evaluating forest stand nutrient status.* Land Management Report No. 20. Victoria, B.C.: British Columbia Ministry of Forests.

Berg, B., and H. Staaf. 1980. Decomposition rate and chemical changes of Scots pine needle litter. II. The influence of chemical composition. *Ecological Bulletin (Stockholm)* 32:373–390.

Bigger, C. M. 1988. *Effects of harvest intensity on nutrient removal, nutrient leaching, and growth of seedlings in individual stands of high and low productivity red alder and Douglas-fir.* Ph.D. Thesis. Seattle, Wash.: College of Forest Resources, University of Washington.

Bigger C. M., and D. W. Cole. 1983. "Effects of harvesting intensity on nutrient losses and future productivity in high and low productivity red alder and Douglas-fir stands." In *Proceedings IUFRO symposium on forest site and continuous productivity,* edited by R. Ballard and S. P. Gessel, 167–178. General Technical Report PNW-163. Portland, Ore.: Pacific Northwest Forest and Range Experiment Station, USDA Forest Service.

Binkley, D. 1984. Does forest removal increase rates of decomposition and nitrogen release? *Forest Ecology and Management* 8:229–233.

———. 1986. *Forest Nutrition Management.* New York: John Wiley.

Binkley, D., K. Cromack, and R. L. Fredricksen. 1982. Nitrogen accretion and availability in some snowbrush ecosystems. *Forest Science* 28:720–724.

Binkley, D., and P. Matson. 1983. Ion exchange resin bag method for assessing forest nitrogen availability. *Soil Science Society of America Journal* 47:1050–1052.

Blake, J. I. 1985. *Characterization of soil nitrogen and sulfur availability in relation to response of Douglas-fir (Pseudotsuga menziesii (Mirb.) Franco) in western Oregon and Washington.* Ph.D. Thesis. Seattle, Wash.: College of Forest Resources, University of Washington.

Bormann, B. T., and D. S. DeBell. 1981. Nitrogen content and other soil properties related to age of red alder stands. *Soil Science Society of America Journal* 45:428–432.

Bormann, F. H., and G. E. Likens. 1979. *Pattern and Process in a forested ecosystem.* New York: Springer Verlag.

Brix, H. 1971. Effects of nitrogen fertilization on photosynthesis and respiration in Douglas-fir. *Forest Science* 17:407–414.

Carter, R. E., J. Otchere-Boateng, and K. Klinka. 1984. Dieback of a 30-year-old Douglas-fir plantation in the Brittain River Valley, British Columbia: symptoms and diagnosis. *Forest Ecology and Management* 7:249–263.

Carter, R. E., A. M. Scagel, and K. Klinka. 1986. Nutritional aspects of distorted growth in immature forest stands in southwestern British Columbia. *Canadian Journal of Forest Research* 16:36–41.

Chapin, F. S., P. M. Vitousek, and K. Van Cleve. 1986. The nature of nutrient limitation in plant communities. *American Naturalist* 127:48–58.

Cole, D. W. 1986. "Nutrient cycling in world forests." In *Forest site and productivity,* edited by S. P. Gessel, 103–115. Dordrecht/Boston: Martinus Nijhoff Publisher.

Cole, D. W., C. L. Henry, and W. L. Nutter (editors). 1986. *The forest alternative for treatment and utliization of municipal and industrial wastes.* Seattle, Wash.: University of Washington Press.

Cole, D. W., and M. Rapp. 1981. "Elemental cycling in forest ecosystems." In *Dynamic properties of forest ecosystems,* edited by D. E. Reichle, 341–409. London: Cambridge University Press.

Cushon, G. H. 1985. *Gaseous nitrogen transformations in a mature forest ecosystem.* M.S. Thesis. Vancouver, B.C.: University of British Columbia.

Ebermayer, E. 1876. *Die gesamte lehre der waldstreu mit rücksicht auf die chemische statik des waldbaues.* Berlin: Julius Springer Publisher.

Edmonds, R. L. 1980. Litter decomposition and nutrient release in Douglas-fir, red alder, western hemlock and Pacific silver fir ecosystems in western Washington. Canadian Journal of Forest Research 10:327–337.

———. 1984. Long-term decomposition and nutrient dynamics in Pacific silver fir needles in western Washington. *Canadian Journal of Forest Research* 14:395–400.

———. 1987. Decomposition rates and nutrient dynamics in small diameter woody litter in four forest ecosystems in Washington, USA. *Canadian Journal of Forest Research* 17:499–509.

Edmonds. R. L., and C. M. Bigger. 1983. "Decomposition and nitrogen mineralization rates in Douglas-fir needles in relation to whole tree harvesting practices." In *Proceedings of the Society of American Foresters national convention,* 187–192. Washington, D.C.: Society of American Foresters.

Edmonds, R. L., and T. Hsiang. 1987. Forest floor and soil influence on response of Douglas-fir to urea. *Soil Science Society of America Journal* 51:1332–1337.

Entry, J. A., N. M. Stark, and H. Loewenstein. 1986. Effect of timber harvesting on microbial biomass fluxes in a northern Rocky Mountain forest soil. *Canadian Journal of Forest Research* 16:1076–1081.

Everard, J. 1973. Foliar analysis sampling methods interpretation and application of results. *Quarterly Journal of Forestry* 67:51–66.

Farr, W. A., A. S. Harris, and S. N. Israilson. 1977. *Effects of an aerial application of urea fertilizer on young Sitka spruce and western hemlock at Thomas Bay, Alaska.* Research Paper PNW-219. Portland, Ore.: Pacific Northwest Forest and Range Experiment Station, USDA Forest Service.

Farrell, P. W., D. W. Flinn, R. O. Squire, and F. G. Craig. 1986. "Maintenance of productivity of radiata pine monocultures on sandy soils in southeastern Australia." In *Forest site and productivity,* edited S. P. Gessel, 127–136. Dordrecht/Boston: Martinus Nijhoff Publisher.

Feller, M. C., and J. P. Kimmins. 1984. Effects of clearcutting and slashburning on streamwater chemistry and watershed nutrient budgets in southwestern British Columbia. *Water Resources Research* 20:29–40.

Feller, M. C., J. P. Kimmins, and K. A. Scoular. 1983a. "FORCYTE 10: calibration data and simulation of potential long-term effects of intensive forest management on site productivity, economic performance, and energy cost/benefit ratio." In *Proceedings IUFRO symposium on forest site and continuous productivity,* edited by R. Ballard and S. P. Gessel, 179–200. General Technical Report PNW-163. Portland, Ore.: Pacific Northwest Forest and Range Experiment Station, USDA Forest Service.

Feller, M. C., J. P. Kimmins, and K. M. Tsze. 1983b. "Nutrient losses to the atmosphere during slashburns in southwestern British Columbia." In *Proceedings of the 7th conference on fire and forest meteorology,* 128–135. Boston, Mass.: American Meteorological Society.

Fogel, R., and K. Cromack, Jr. 1977. Effect of habitat and substrate quality in Douglas-fir needle decomposition in western Oregon. *Canadian Journal of Botany* 55:1632–1640.

Fujimori, T. 1971. *Primary productivity of a young* Tsuga heterophylla *stand and some speculations about biomass of forest communities on the Oregon coast.* Research Paper PNW-123. Portland, Ore.: Pacific Northwest Forest and Range Experiment Station, USDA Forest Service.

Gessel, S. P., E. C. Steinbrenner, and R. E. Miller. 1979. "Response of Northwest forests to elements other than nitrogen." In *Proceedings of forest fertilization conference,* edited by S. P. Gessel, R. M. Kenady, and W. Atkinson, 140–149. Contribution No. 40. Seattle, Wash.: Institute of Forest Resources, College of Forest Resources, University of Washington.

Gessel, S. P., and J. Turner. 1976. Litter production in western Washington Douglas-fir stands. *Forestry* 49:63–72.

Gholz, H. L. 1982. Environmental limits on aboveground net primary production, leaf area and biomass in vegetation zones of the Pacific Northwest. *Ecology* 63:469–487.

Grier, C. C. 1978. A *Tsuga heterophylla—Picea sitchensis* ecosystem of coastal Oregon: decomposition and nutrient balances of fallen logs. *Canadian Journal of Forest Research* 8:198–206.

Grier, C. C., T. M. Hinckley, K. A. Vogt, and S. T. Gower. 1986. "Net primary production in Douglas-fir ecosystems: its relation to moisture and mineral nutrition." In *Douglas-fir: stand management for the future,* edited by C. D. Oliver, D. P. Hanley, and J. A. Johnson, 155–161. Contribution No. 55. Seattle, Wash.: Institute of Forest Resources, College of Forest Resources, University of Washington.

Harmon, M. E., J. F. Franklin, F. J. Swanson, P. Sollins, S. V. Gregory, J. D. Lattin, N. H. Anderson, S. P. Cline, N. G. Aumen, J. R. Sedell, G. W. Lienkaemper, K. Cromack, Jr., and K. W. Cummins. 1986. Ecology of coarse woody debris in temperate ecosystems. *Advances in Ecological Research* 15:133–302.

Heilman, P. E. 1979. "Minerals, chemical properties and fertility of forest soils." In *Forest soils of the Douglas-fir Region,* edited by P. E. Heilman, H. W. Anderson, and D. M. Baumgartner, 121–136. Pullman, Wash.: Cooperative Extension Service, Washington State University.

Ingestad, T. 1974. Towards optimum nutrition. *Ambio* 3:49–54.

———. 1982. Addition rate and concentration. Relative addition rate and external concentration; driving variables used in plant nutrition research. *Plant Cell and Environment* 5:443–453.

Johnson, D. W., D. W. Cole, C. S. Bledsoe, K. Cromack, R. L. Edmonds, S. P. Gessel, C. C. Grier, B. N. Richards, and K. A. Vogt. 1982. "Nutrient cycling in the Pacific Northwest." In *Analysis of coniferous forest ecosystems in the western United States,* edited by R. L. Edmonds, 186–232. Stroudsburg, Pa.: Hutchinson Ross Publishing Company.

Jurgensen, M. F., M. J. Larsen, and A. E. Harvey. 1979. *Forest soil biology—timber harvesting relationships.* General Technical Report INT-69. Ogden, Utah: Intermountain Forest and Range Experiment Station, USDA Forest Service.

Keeves, A. 1966. Some evidence of loss of productivity with successive rotations of *Pinus radiata* in the south-east of South Australia. *Australian Forestry* 30:52–63.

Keyes, M. R., and C. C. Grier. 1981. Above- and below-ground net production in 40 year-old Douglas-fir stands on low and high productivity sites. *Canadian Journal of Forest Research* 11:599–605.

Lavender, D. P., and R. B. Walker. 1979. "Nitrogen and related elements in nutrition of forest trees." In *Proceedings of forest fertilization conference,* edited by S. P. Gessel, R. M. Kenady, and W. A. Atkinson, 15–22. Contribution No. 40. Seattle, Wash.: Institute of Forest Resources, College of Forest Resources, University of Washington.

Leaf, A. L. (editor) 1979. *Proceedings of a conference on the impact of intensive harvesting on forest nutrient cycling.* Syracuse, N.Y.: School of Forestry, State University of New York.

Lewis, R., and A. Abee. 1981. "Site preparation for skeletal soils." In *Reforestation of skeletal soils,* edited by S. D. Hobbs and O. T. Helgerson, 40–49. Corvallis, Ore.: Forest Research Laboratory, Oregon State University.

Little, S. N., and G. O. Klock. 1985. *The influence of residue removal and prescribed fire on distribution of forest nutrients.* Research Paper PNW-338. Portland, Ore.: Pacific Northwest Forest and Range Experiment Station, USDA Forest Service.

Long, J. N. 1982. "Productivity of western coniferous forests." In *Analysis of coniferous forest ecosystems in the western United States,* edited by R. L. Edmonds, 89–125. Stroudsburg, Pa.: Hutchinson Ross Publishing Company.

Marshall, J. D., and R. H. Waring. 1986. Comparison of methods of estimating leaf-area index in old-growth Douglas-fir. *Ecology* 67:975–979.

McClaugherty, C. A., J. Pastor, J. D. Aber, and J. M. Melillo.1985. Forest litter decomposition in relation to soil nitrogen dynamics and litter quality. *Ecology* 66:266–275.

McColl, J. G., and D. F. Grigal. 1979. "Nutrient losses in leaching and erosion by intensive forest harvesting." In *Proceedings of a conference on the impact of intensive harvesting on forest nutrient cycling,* edited by A. L. Leaf, 231–248. Syracuse, N.Y.: School of Forestry, State University of New York.

McColl, J. G., and R. F. Powers. 1984. "Consequences of forest management on soil-tree relationships." In *Nutrition of plantation forests,* edited by G. D. Bowen and E. K. S. Nambiar, 379–412. London: Academic Press.

Miller, H. G. 1981. "Nutrient cycles in forest plantations, their change with age and the consequence for fertilizer practice." In *Proceedings Australian forest nutrition workshop,* edited by N. G. Turvey, 187–199. Canberra: Division of Forest Research, CSIRO.

———. 1984. "Dynamics of nutrient cycling in plantation ecosystems." In *Nutrition of plantation forests,* edited by G. D. Bowen and E. K. S. Nambiar, 53–78. London: Academic Press.

Miller, R. E., P. R. Barker, C. E. Peterson, and S. R. Webster. 1986. "Using nitrogen fertilizers in management of coast Douglas-fir. I. Regional trends of response." In *Douglas-fir stand management for the future,* edited by C. D. Oliver, D. P. Hanley, and J. A. Johnson, 290–303. Contribution No. 55. Seattle, Wash.: Institute of Forest Resources, College of Forest Resources, University of Washington.

Nadelhoffer, K. J., J. D. Aber, and J. M. Melillo. 1985. Fine roots, net primary production, and soil nitrogen availability: a new hypothesis. *Ecology* 66:1377–1390.

Nambiar, E. K. S. 1985. "Increasing forest productivity through genetic improvements of nutritional characteristics." In *Forest potentials—productivity and value,* edited by R. Ballard, P. Farnum, G. A. Ritchie, and J. K. Winjum, 191–215. Tacoma, Wash.: Weyerhaeuser Science Symposium 4.

Perry, D. A., and S. L. Rose. 1989. "Productivity of forest lands as affected by site preparation." In *Proceedings of the California conference on forest tree nutrition and soil fertility,* edited by R. Powers and T. Robson. Berkeley, Calif.: Pacific Southwest Forest and Range Experiment Station, USDA Forest Service. (In press).

Peterson, C. E. 1982. "Regional growth and response analysis for unthinned Douglas-fir." In *Regional forest nutrition project biennial report,* 3–25. Seattle, Wash.: College of Forest Resources, University of Washington.

Peterson, C. E., Jr., and S. P. Gessel. 1983. "Forest fertilization in the Pacific Northwest: results of the regional forest nutrition research project." In *Proceedings IUFRO symposium on forest site and continuous productivity,* edited by R. Ballard and S. P. Gessel, 365–369. General Technical Report PNW-163. Portland, Ore.: Pacific Northwest Forest and Range Experiment Station, USDA Forest Service.

Porada, H. J. 1987. *The effect of aluminum on the growth and mineral composition of Douglas-fir and western hemlock.* Ph.D. Thesis. Seattle, Wash.: College of Forest Resources, University of Washington.

Powers, R. F. 1980. Mineralizable soil nitrogen as an index of nitrogen availability to forest trees. *Soil Science Society of America Journal* 44:1314–1320.

Radwan, M. A., and H. Brix. 1986. "Nutrition of Douglas-fir." In *Douglas-fir stand management for the future,* edited by C. D. Oliver, D. P. Hanley, and J. A. Johnson, 177–188. Contribution No. 55. Seattle, Wash.: Institute of Forest Resources, College of Forest Resources, University of Washington.

Radwan, M. A., and J. S. Shumway. 1983. Soil nitrogen, sulfur, and phosphorus in relation to growth response of western hemlock to nitrogen fertilization. *Forest Science* 29:469–477.

Shumway, J. S. 1984. "Total nitrogen, mineralizable nitrogen and site index as guides to fertilization of Douglas-fir." In *Nitrogen assessment workshop,* compiled by R. F. Strand, 57–59. Report No. 2. Seattle, Wash.: Regional Forest Nutrition Project, College of Forest Resources, University of Washington.

Shumway, J. S., and W. A. Atkinson. 1978. Predicting nitrogen fertilizer response in unthinned stands of Douglas-fir. *Communications in Soil Science and Plant Analysis* 9:529–539.

Stone, E. L., and G. M. Will. 1965. "Nitrogen deficiency of second generation radiata pine in New Zealand." In *Forest soil relationships in North America,* edited by C. T. Youngberg, 118–139. Corvallis, Ore.: Oregon State University Press.

Strand, R. F. (compiler). 1984. *Nitrogen assessment workshop.* Report No. 2. Seattle, Wash.: Regional Forest Nutrition Project, College of Forest Resources, University of Washington.

Tamm, C. O. 1979. "Nutrient cycling and productivity of forest ecosystems." In *Proceedings of a conference on the impact of intensive harvesting on forest nutrient cycling,* edited by A. L. Leaf. Syracuse, 2–21. N.Y.: School of Forestry, State University of New York.

Turner, J., M. J. Lambert, and S. P. Gessel. 1977. Use of foliage sulfate concentrations to predict response to urea application in Douglas-fir. *Canadian Journal of Forest Research* 7:476–480.

van den Driessche, R. 1979. "Estimating potential response to fertilizer based on tree tissue and litter analysis." In *Proceedings of forest fertilization conference,* edited by S. P. Gessel, R. M. Kenady, and W. A. Atkinson, 214–220. Contribution No. 40. Seattle, Wash.: Institute of Forest Resources, College of Forest Resources, University of Washington.

Vitousek, P. M., J. R. Gosz, C. C. Grier, J. M. Melillo, W. A. Reiners, and R. L. Todd. 1979. Nitrate losses from disturbed ecosystems. *Science* 204:469–474.

Vitousek, P. M., and W. A. Reiners. 1975. Ecosystem succession and nutrient retention: a hypothesis. *BioScience* 25:376–381.

Vogt, D. J., and R. L. Edmonds. 1982. Nitrate and ammonium levels in relation to site quality in Douglas-fir soil and litter. *Northwest Science* 56:83–89.

Vogt, D., K. Vogt, S. Gower, and C. Grier. 1986a. *Long-term N fertilization effect on above- and belowground biomass and production for Douglas-fir.* Abstract. Syracuse, N.Y.: 71st Annual Meeting, Ecological Society of America.

Vogt, K. A., C. C. Grier, C. E. Meier, and M. R. Keyes. 1983a. Organic matter and nutrient dynamics in forest floors of young and mature *Abies amabilis* stands in western Washington as affected by fine root input. *Ecological Monographs* 53:139–157.

Vogt, K. A., C. C. Grier, and D. J. Vogt. 1986b. Production, turnover, and nutrient dynamics of above and belowground detritus in world forests. *Advances in Ecological Research* 15:303–377.

Vogt, K. A., E. E. Moore, D. J. Vogt, M. J. Redlin, and R. L. Edmonds. 1983b. Conifer fine root and mycorrhizal biomass within the forest floor of Douglas-fir stands of different ages and site productivities. *Canadian Journal of Forest Research* 13:429–437.

Waring, R. H., and W. H. Schlesinger. 1985. *Forest Ecosystems—Concepts and Management.* New York: Academic Press.

Webster, S. R., D. S. DeBell, K. N. Wiley, and W. A. Atkinson. 1976. "Fertilization of western hemlock." In *Western hemlock management,* edited W. A. Atkinson and R. J. Zasoski, 247–252. Contribution No. 34. Seattle, Wash.: Institute of Forest Products, College of Forest Resources, University of Washington.

Weetman, G. F., and R. Fournier. 1982. Graphical diagnoses of lodgepole pine response to fertilization. *Soil Science Society of America Journal* 46:1280–1289.

Will, G. 1985. *Nutrient deficiencies and fertilizer use in New Zealand exotic forests.* Forest Research Bulletin 97. Rotorua, New Zealand: Forest Research Institute, N. Z. Forest Service.

Woods, R. V. 1980. *An investigation into the relationship between fire and nutrient depletion leading to decline in productivity between rotations of* Pinus radiata *plantations in South Australia.* Miscellaneous Publication 37. Adelaide, South Australia: Woods and Forests Department of South Australia.

36

Chapter 3

Long-Term Forest Productivity and the Living Soil[1]

M. P. Amaranthus, J. M. Trappe, and R. J. Molina

ABSTRACT

A myriad of soil organisms and their interactions profoundly affect forest-site productivity through capture and uptake of nutrients, nitrogen fixation, protection against pathogens, maintenance of soil structure, and buffering against moisture stress. However, some forest practices can reduce or eliminate beneficial soil organisms. To minimize long-term impacts on these beneficial organisms, forest managers should (1) minimize disturbance severity (i.e., intense burns, soil compaction or erosion), (2) emphasize retention of organic matter, (3) emphasize rapid revegetation by indigenous host species and associated beneficial soil organisms, and (4) recognize that sites with harsh environments (i.e., cold, drought) are most susceptible to productivity losses. Although there is no "magic bullet" for maintaining or enhancing forest productivity, there is great opportunity to use soil organisms as "tools." Research is now underway to identify organisms best adapted to specific environmental and biotic conditions and to assess the potential for "managing" these organisms. Incorporating the concept of the "living soil" in evaluation of site productivity is part of a new, expanding view of forest ecosystems. By understanding soil organisms and putting them to wise use, practicing foresters can better achieve short-term management goals while ensuring long-term site productivity.

> No man is an *Island,* intire of it selfe; every
> man is
> a peece of the *Continent,* a part of the *maine;* if a
> Clod bee washed away by the *Sea, Europe* is the lesse,
> as well as if a *Promontorie* were, as well as if a *Mannor*
> of they *friends* or of thine *owne were;* any man's
> death diminishes me, because I am in-
> volved in Mankinde; And therefore
> never send to know for
> whom the bell tolls;
> It tolls for thee.
>
> *John Donne*

INTRODUCTION

Forest researchers and managers are coming to perceive soil resources and site productivity in new ways. Changes in forest-site productivity were once considered as physiological responses to changes in the physical environment. In this view, the impacts of forest-management activities were evaluated as they affected levels of nutrients, light, and water, either increasing or decreasing site potential to generate wood products. By this simple "checkbook balancing" approach, site productivity decreases as "withdrawals" exceed "deposits" until some threshold level is reached and a site is permanently impaired because of "insufficient funds." Maintaining long-term site productivity, therefore, would require that forest-management activities minimize withdrawals of site resources and, when necessary, replenish those depleted resources with deposits. Unfortunately, this conventional approach fails to recognize the diversity and activity of soil organisms that profoundly influence the total "bankroll" of resources determining long-term forest productivity.

---

[1]Paper 2265, Forest Research Laboratory, Oregon State University, Corvallis.

The soil biological community is inevitably impacted by forest-management practices, and much remains to be learned about these impacts. Which organisms are important to site recovery following disturbance? Which are important in the later stages of stand development? How do management activities affect these populations? How much productivity is lost? What are the rates of recovery? Can soil organisms be "managed" to preserve or increase site production? Answers to these important questions have come slowly, deterred by difficulty in identifying organisms, enormous variability within and among sites, and unresolved methodologies (Trappe and Bollen 1979). However, our growing knowledge of the workings of this complex belowground forest system has already enabled us to better predict the consequences of our actions.

In this chapter we (1) briefly review the variety, abundance, and interactions of organisms in forest soils, (2) examine the important functions of these organisms in the context of long-term site productivity, (3) consider the factors that adversely affect populations of beneficial organisms—and thereby site productivity—on managed forest lands, and (4) look at the potential for managing soil organisms to maintain or enhance site productivity.

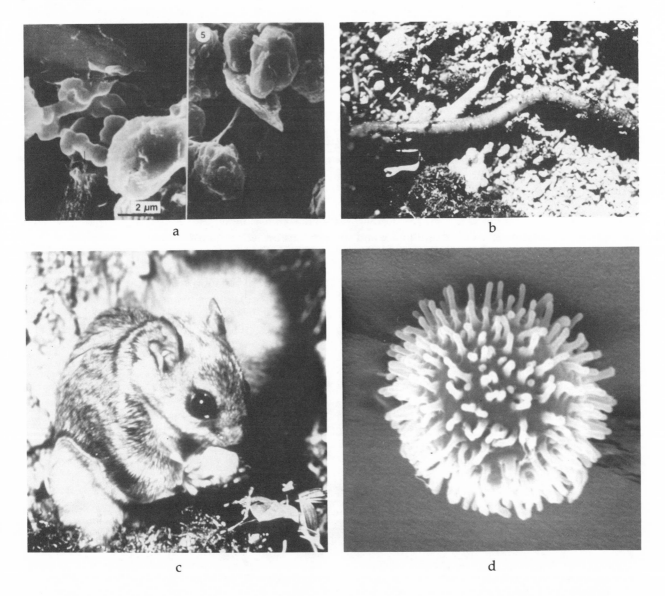

a

b

c

d

FIG. 3.1. A wide variety of life forms reside and interact in the living forest soil: (a) bacteria binding clay particles, enhancing soil aggregation; (b) an earthworm perforating the soil, aerating it and furthering soil weathering and decomposition of organic residues; (c) a northern flying squirrel feeding on a truffle, the belowground fruiting body of a mycorrhizal fungus, and later transmitting spores (d) such as those of *Gymnomyces monosporus* (× 3000) through the forest in its fecal pellets.

VARIETY, ABUNDANCE, AND INTERACTIONS OF SOIL ORGANISMS

The life forms residing and interacting in forest soil range from the smallest, most primitive living organisms all the way up the evolutionary ladder to mammals (Fig. 3.1). Estimates of the types and numbers of these organisms, which vary in function and are strongly interdependent, are staggering. For example, 10–100 million bacteria and actinomycetes, 1,000–100,000 fungal propagules, and several kilometers of fungal hyphae can be present in a single gram of forest soil (Bollen 1974). Mites and nematodes can number from thousands to hundreds of thousands per square meter of surface soil, and larger soil organisms such as worms, insects, and animals from 10 to well over 100 (Dindal 1973). The resulting biomass reflected in these numbers is immense. For example, in the Pacific Northwest, the soil of an old-growth Douglas-fir [*Pseudotsuga menziesii* (Mirb.) Franco] stand can contain some 4,200 kg/ha (3,700 lb/acre) dry weight of fungal mycelium and 5,400 kg/ha (4,800 lb/acre) of mycorrhizal tips alone (Fogel et al. 1973). We can no longer ignore the biological influence of this living mass on site productivity.

The balance of forest-soil organisms can shift dramatically in response to fluctuations of chemical, environmental, and biotic factors caused by natural disturbance or management-related activities such as timber harvest, site preparation, and fertilization (Perry and Rose 1983, Amaranthus and Perry 1989). Although some soil organisms thrive in the aftermath of disturbance (Pilz and Perry 1984), those that cannot compete may decline, lose vigor, or disappear altogether (Perry et al. 1982, Harvey et al. 1986, Amaranthus and Perry 1987). The final equilibrium of soil organisms may or may not facilitate rapid reforestation for sustained conifer growth.

To assess the potential impact of forest-management activities, we must understand where the vast majority of soil organisms live and work. Humus, rotten wood, and the upper mineral soil are the powerhouses of soil biological activity (Harvey et al. 1979, 1986) and thus are essential substrates for maintaining forest productivity. Densities of fine roots in these substrates and populations of organisms near these root surfaces are higher than in surrounding soil (Rambelli 1973). It is in the rhizosphere, the 2–3 mm zone surrounding root surfaces, that biological activity is greatest. Fine roots maneuvering through the soil exude amino acids, carbohydrates, and other compounds that stimulate the growth of microflora such as bacteria, actinomycetes, and fungi, which in turn produce their own compounds that either stimulate or repel other soil organisms. Microflora are also prime food for "grazer" herbivores such as mites, nematodes, and springtails, which themselves fall prey to carnivores such as centipedes and spiders. Saprophytic organisms feed on the dead remains of other microbes and roots accumulating in the rhizosphere and decompose complex organic molecules into basic components. Nutrients released through decomposition, as well as water, are captured and transported to host plants by specialized fungi that colonize root tips in a symbiotic association termed mycorrhizae (Fig. 3.2) (Harley and Smith 1983, Read et al. 1985). The area immediately surrounding mycorrhizae, the "mycorrhizosphere" (Rambelli 1973), supports its own increased levels of microbial activity. Rhizosphere and mycorrhizosphere populations may vary among plant species and are further influenced by season and host maturity (Foster and Marks 1967).

FIG. 3.2. Mycorrhizae, which vary in type and function, colonize the majority of root tips in temperate forest ecosystems. Most of the important timber-producing species in these regions cannot survive in the natural forest environment without mycorrhizae.

Litter and woody debris are also important centers of activity. Plant tissue fallen to the forest floor is attacked by soil organisms called "detritivores." These organisms, including mites, millipedes, snails, and beetles, tear and chew holes in fresh litter, increasing its surface area and utilizing its more soluble components. The remnants are decomposed by other soil flora and fauna. Wood fallen to the forest floor is attacked by beetles and a succession of fungi that "digest" the cellulose and lignin. Insects, earthworms, amphibians, reptiles, and mammals likewise concentrate in and around this woody debris, enhancing site productivity by mixing and aerating the soil and by transporting and excreting nutrients and the spores of mycorrhizal fungi from one microsite to another (Maser et al. 1978).

IMPORTANT FUNCTIONS OF SOIL ORGANISMS

Nutrient Cycling

Most woody host plants require soil organisms to facilitate adequate nutrient uptake. Mycorrhizae enhance such uptake not only by increasing the absorbing surface area of roots but also through active physiological mechanisms. Ectomycorrhizal fungi release enzymes which increase the availability of phosphorus to higher plants (Williamson and Alexander 1975, Ho and Zak 1979, Alexander and Hardy 1981). This "extraction" process also extends to other nutrients and enters them into the forest nutrient cycle. Mycorrhizal fungi, common to members of the Pinaceae, release compounds (chelating agents called siderophores) that are especially important in iron nutrition (Graustein et al. 1977, Powell et al. 1980). Perry et al. (1982) found lower levels of siderophores in soils from both burned and unburned clearcuts than in undisturbed forest soil from 8 of 10 widely scattered sites in southwest, central, and east-central Oregon; the reduction in siderophores was related to poor iron nutrition of Douglas-fir seedlings.

Maintenance of long-term forest productivity requires long-term conservation of nutrient capital. Few nutrients leach out when populations of soil organisms are healthy and active. This is particularly significant for soluble forms of nitrogen (N) such as nitrate, which is mobile and susceptible to leaching. Soil organisms form an intricate web to capture and assimilate N into complex organic compounds and then slowly release them into the ecosystem. This capture, assimilation, and release are critical to the long-term nitrogen capital of forest soils (see chapter 2, this volume).

Nitrogen Fixation

Inadequate nitrogen is the most common limitation to forest productivity in the Douglas-fir Region (Lavender and Walker 1979). Loss of N due to timber harvest, removing harvest residues, and site preparation (especially intense burning) often exceeds natural inputs to the forest over the length of most planned rotations (Perry and Rose 1988). Lost nitrogen must be replaced if long-term site productivity is to be maintained.

FIG. 3.3. Large quantities of nitrogen can be added to the forest ecosystem by bacteria within root nodules of leguminous plants. Bacteria such as *Rhizobium* species help maintain long-term forest productivity by converting ("fixing") atmospheric nitrogen into organic forms that plants can use.

Perhaps the most practical and economical means of replenishing this loss is through biological fixation of nitrogen in the soil (Domingo 1983, Gordon and Avery 1985).

Symbiotic N fixation can add substantial amounts of nitrogen continuously to Pacific Northwest forests (Wollum and Youngberg 1964, Trappe et al. 1968). Common nodulated plants such as lupine, alder, and snow-brush (*Lupinus, Alnus,* and *Ceanothus* species) form a mutually beneficial relationship with certain bacteria (Fig. 3.3) and actinomycetes that convert ("fix") atmospheric N_2 into ammonium N. This fixed nitrogen is released into the roots of host plants, thereby increasing N concentrations in living tissue (Tarrant and Trappe 1971). As N is returned to the soil by litterfall and washing of leaves by rain, other species—including tree species valued for timber—reap benefits.

Through asymbiotic N fixation, "free-living" organisms contribute to the nitrogen pool. N_2-fixing bacteria have been found in association with wood-rotting fungi in coniferous forest residues (Larsen et al. 1980). *Azotobacter* and *Clostridium* species fix nitrogen under conditions characteristic of the rhizosphere, where oxygen levels are low (Giller and Day 1985). Fixation by these and other species, such as the bacterium *Azospirillium,* may be enhanced by or may totally depend on mycorrhizal fungi (Amaranthus et al. 1987a). Silvicultural use of these free-living organisms to improve nitrogen levels is now receiving considerable attention and deserves further research.

Protection against Pathogens

Both symbiotic and free-living soil organisms can protect trees against soil pathogens. Several mycorrhizal fungi protect pine (*Pinus*) species and Douglas-fir from pathogens such as *Phytophthora cinnamomi, Fusarium oxysporum,* and *Rhizoctonia solani* (Wingfield 1968, Marx 1973, Marx and Krupa 1978). The protective mechanisms include physical barriers against root penetration by pathogens, excretions of antibiotics, and stimulation of other pathogen-inhibiting rhizosphere organisms (Zak 1964, Marx 1972). Rose et al. (1980) found that a free-living *Streptomycete* species from the rhizosphere of snowbrush (*Ceanothus velutinus* Dougl.) antagonized three common root pathogens, *Phellinus weirii, Fomes annosus,* and *Phytophthora cinnamomi.* Some nonmycorrhizal fungi also may inhibit pathogens; for example, the fungus species *Trichoderma* can reduce the incidence of root rot in pine seedlings (Kelly 1976).

Soil Structure

Soil structure greatly influences plant growth. Mycorrhizae and other microbes affect soil structure by producing humic compounds (Tan et al. 1978), accelerating the decomposition of primary minerals (Cromack et al. 1979), and secreting organic "glues" (extracellular polysaccharides) that bind soil particles into water-stable aggregates (Sutton and Sheppard 1976, Forster 1979, Tisdall and Oades 1979, 1982). The importance of the first two processes to soil fertility and plant nutrition is well documented. The third—aggregate stability—also is important because the stability of pores, essential for the movement of water and air required by plant roots and soil organisms, is predicated on the stability of aggregates formed when mineral grains and homogeneous clays are linked by organic glues (Lynch and Bragg 1985, Emerson et al. 1986). When the flow of organic materials is interrupted, soil aggregation—and ultimately forest productivity—declines.

Examination of aggregates from granitic soils on a high-elevation site in the Klamath Mountains of south-west Oregon illustrates this decline. This site, logged in 1968, has not become reforested despite several attempts (Amaranthus and Perry 1987). Now dominated by grasses and herbs, it supports different microflora than found associated with conifers. Scanning electron micrographs show that soil structure in the clearcut and adjacent, undisturbed forest differs drastically (Fig. 3.4): an abundance of relatively large (greater than 50 microns) pores and fungal hyphae in the forest soil contrasts with a scarcity of large pores and fungal hyphae in the clearcut soil. Degradation of soil structure in clearcuts is likely to make reforestation difficult, especially on potentially droughty sites. More research is needed on how best to stabilize and maintain soil structure after harvest.

Soil Moisture

Some soil organisms, especially mycorrhizal fungi, seem to benefit associated plants when soil moisture is limited (Mikola 1970). Mycorrhizae are important in water uptake, storage, and transport (Reid 1979). Mycorrhizal fungi substantially increase the surface absorbing area of colonized roots, directly increasing the total soil volume roots can explore for water. They also prevent gaps between roots and soil, preserving "liquid continuity" during drier periods. Differentiated "vessel hyphae" can act as specialized channels for water transport to the host plant (Read et al. 1985).

a

b

FIG. 3.4. Soil aggregates from (a) undisturbed forest and (b) an adjacent, 17-year-old clearcut on a high-elevation site in the Klamath Mountains of southwest Oregon. The clearcut is now dominated by nonectomycorrhizal host species which support different microflora from those associated with the coniferous species that previously dominated the site. Note the abundance of relatively large (greater than 50 microns) pores and fungal hyphae in the undisturbed forest soil—and their absence from the clearcut soil (adapted from Perry et al. 1987).

FACTORS ADVERSELY AFFECTING POPULATIONS OF BENEFICIAL ORGANISMS

What reduces populations of beneficial organisms on disturbed forest land? How do reduced populations affect forest productivity? Under what conditions is forest productivity most likely to be impaired? Final answers are as yet unknown, but recent studies provide sufficient evidence for reasonable speculation.

Much of the research on reductions in populations of beneficial organisms after disturbance has focused on ectomycorrhizae. Although information on other organisms is scanty in the Pacific Northwest, mycorrhizal fungus populations may serve as indicators of the health and vigor of other associated beneficial organisms. Mycorrhizae provide a biological substrate for other microbial processes. For example, in a Douglas-fir system, mycorrhizae provided 50% of the annual biomass returned to the soil and 42% of the annual nitrogen released (Fogel and Hunt 1983). Microbial activity generally is stimulated in soil surrounding ectomycorrhizae (Oswald and Ferchau 1963, Rambelli 1973)—an effect that likely extends along the vast expanse of ectomycorrhizal fungal mycelia in the soil.

Because most forest-tree species in the Douglas-fir Region require ectomycorrhizae for nutrient uptake, the importance of understanding the relationship among disturbance, site conditions, and mycorrhiza impact cannot be overstated. Numerous authors have reported reductions in mycorrhiza populations due to forest disturbance (Harvey et al. 1980, Parke 1982, Perry et al. 1982, Amaranthus et al. 1987b). However, the degree of reduction and its impact on forest productivity vary widely and depend on many factors.

Type and Severity of Disturbance

The most widespread activities which alter both the aboveground and belowground environments and which therefore potentially impact populations of soil organisms are timber harvest and site preparation. In the Pacific Northwest, clearcutting and prescribed burning are the common harvesting and site-preparation practices. Soil nutrient status, moisture, temperature, pH, and organic matter content, litter inputs, and species composition affect the growth and occurrence of soil organisms (Harvey et al. 1980)—and all of these are influenced by harvesting and site preparation. Clearing vegetation and disturbing the forest floor remove nutrients and reallocate them within the ecosystem. Harvesting host trees eliminates the photosynthate source for dependent ectomycorrhizal fungi and associated microbes. Converting a mature forest to a clearcut typically increases soil temperatures once the protective canopy is gone. Prescribed broadcast burning increases soil pH, creates a nutrient flush, and can reduce litter and duff levels (Amaranthus and McNabb 1984). Soil organic matter, humified material, and decaying wood are centers of microbial activity and can substantially diminish as a result of intense fire. Changes in aboveground community composition alter the form of root exudates and litter leachates.

Wright and Tarrant (1958) found fewer ectomycorrhizae on Douglas-fir seedlings growing in burned, compared to unburned, clearcuts (Fig. 3.5). The greatest reductions were associated with the hottest burns. Thus, not only the type of activity, but its severity, is critical. Parke (1982) compared mycorrhiza formation in soils from burned and unburned clearcuts of 36 "difficult to regenerate" sites in northwest California and southwest Oregon. Douglas-fir and ponderosa pine (*Pinus ponderosa* Dougl. ex Laws.) seedlings grown in soils from the burned clearcuts formed 40% fewer ectomycorrhizae, and seedlings grown in soils from the unburned clearcuts 20% fewer ectomycorrhizae, than seedlings grown in undisturbed forest soil. Yet it is difficult to generalize about effects of burning on microbial populations because they are highly dependent on duration and intensity of fire as well as soil and site conditions (Perry and Rose 1983).

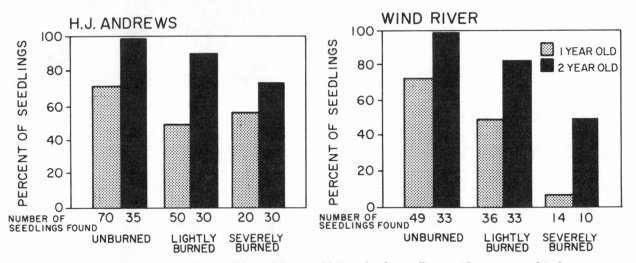

FIG. 3.5. Mean percentages of natural 1- and 2-year-old Douglas-fir seedlings with ectomycorrhizal roots growing in soils on unburned, lightly burned, and severely burned clearcuts on two experimental forests in the Pacific Northwest (adapted from Wright and Tarrant 1958).

Because ectomycorrhizae predominate in the organic layers of the soil (Trappe and Fogel 1977, Harvey et al. 1979), the degree of organic matter lost from a site can influence mycorrhiza populations. Harvey et al. (1979) found more than 87% of the active ectomycorrhizal fungus types in humus and decaying wood in a mature Douglas-fir/larch (*Larix*) forest (Fig. 3.6). Moreover, the physical consumption of humidified material affects not only ectomycorrhizae but an array of other beneficial organisms tied to site productivity. Habitat for small mammals that are important in distributing fungal spores of several belowground mycorrhizal fungi (Maser et al. 1978) also can be lost. Thus, numbers, diversity, and activity of beneficial soil organisms can be reduced by repeated removal of organic matter from a site.

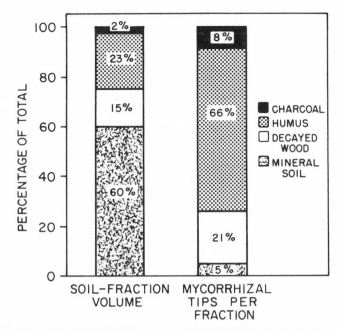

FIG. 3.6. Percentage of soil fraction, by volume, and total active ectomycorrhizal root tips per soil fraction, averaged over 50 10- by 38-cm soil cores taken from a 250-year-old Douglas-fir/larch forest (adapted from Harvey et al. 1979).

Minimizing soil compaction helps maintain healthy populations of soil organisms by preserving soil structure (see also chapter 4, this volume). Pore space is essential for the movement of oxygen and water into soil and the flushing of carbon dioxide out of it; microbial activity is drastically altered when levels of these basic elements become extreme. Undisturbed forest soil is rarely saturated because large pores allow for rapid downward percolation of water. However, when soils are compacted, large pores are destroyed and water movement through soil is reduced. Soil compaction greatly influences the types and activities of soil organisms sensitive to excess soil moisture. Thus, the adverse response of plants to compaction reflects both indirect effects on microbes and direct effects on the plants themselves. Careful selection and skillful implementation of harvest methods to minimize compaction increase the potential for long-term maintenance of beneficial soil organisms.

Topsoil is a reservoir of both nutrients and fungal spores and other propagules important for mycorrhiza formation. Loss of this biological reservoir by erosion will inevitably impair productivity. Reeves et al. (1979) found that the dominant species in a sagebrush (*Artemisia*) community in Colorado all were mycorrhizal. When topsoil was severely disturbed and eroded, numbers of mycorrhizal propagules were greatly decreased (Moorman and Reeves 1979), and nonmycorrhizal weedy species could successfully reestablish. Little is known about the effects of soil erosion from deforested areas, but the density and diversity of mycorrhizal inocula are reduced.

Diversity of Soil Organisms

The diversity of organisms within the soil buffers the impact of disturbance on forest sites. Disturbance did not reduce ectomycorrhiza formation on Douglas-fir seedlings grown in soil from extremely productive sites in the Oregon Cascades, where diversity of ectomycorrhizal fungi is high (Schoenberger and Perry 1982, Pilz and Perry 1984). However, the proportion of each mycorrhizal fungus type shifted significantly with soil disturbance; different soil environments reduced ectomycorrhiza formation by some fungus types and apparently opened niches for others. In contrast, clearcutting significantly lowered ectomycorrhiza formation on Douglas-fir seedlings grown in soil from a harsh, less productive site in southwest Oregon, where soil contained few ectomycorrhiza types (Amaranthus et al. 1987b) (Fig. 3.7). Reduced ectomycorrhiza formation correlated positively with decreased Douglas-fir growth after outplanting (Fig. 3.8). The southwest Oregon soil, with low fungus diversity, was poorly buffered against disturbance, compared to the Cascades soils (see chapter 6, this volume).

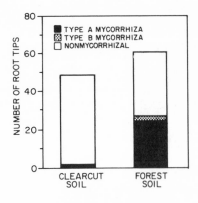

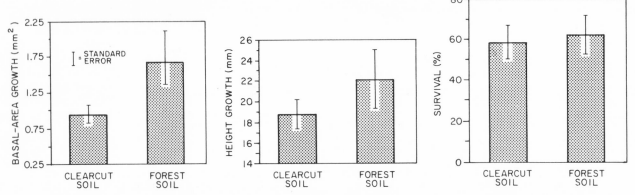

FIG. 3.7. Ectomycorrhiza formation on Douglas-fir seedlings greenhouse-grown in soil from a clearcut and from undisturbed forest in southwest Oregon. Numbers of mycorrhizal root tips in the clearcut and forest soils differed significantly ($p \leq 0.05$) (adapted from Amaranthus et al. 1987b).

FIG. 3.8. Reduced growth and survival of Douglas-fir seedlings greenhouse-grown in soil from a clearcut compared to that from undisturbed forest. Basal-area growth of seedlings grown in the clearcut and forest soils differed significantly ($p \leq 0.05$) (adapted from Amaranthus et al. 1987b).

Climatic Conditions

Climate influences seedling growth and ectomycorrhiza formation (Harvey et al. 1980, Pilz and Perry 1984). The importance of early mycorrhiza formation in dry areas has been emphasized (Parry 1953, Mikola 1970). Dry climates may limit the activity of mycorrhizal fungi by decreasing the length of time for spore production, germination, and optimal mycelial growth, which in turn can decrease the chances for planted seedlings to become colonized. Seedlings in moist climates may be able to survive longer without mycorrhizae than those in dry climates, increasing their chances of becoming colonized. Fungal symbionts differ in their capacity to function in periods of either low or "excessive" soil moisture, and impaired function subsequently affects growth of associated plants (Mexal and Reid 1973, Slankis 1974, Theodorou 1978). Moisture content also affects uptake of certain nutrients by mycorrhizae (Gadgil 1972).

Seedlings growing in cold climates may also require rapid, early mycorrhizal colonization to take advantage of the short growing season and obtain the necessary nutrients and water to survive the long cold season and early frosts. In studies in the Klamath Mountains of northwest California and southwest Oregon, Amaranthus and Perry (1987) found that mycorrhiza formation most strongly influences seedling survival and growth on sites limited by both moisture and temperature.

Biotic Conditions

The importance of aboveground species composition and arrangement to belowground biological functioning is unclear. It is increasingly apparent, however, that an ectomycorrhizal fungus can link some plant species with fungal mycelia (Bjorkman 1970, Read et al. 1985, Finlay and Read 1986). In the natural forest environment, ectomycorrhizal fungi supported by nonconiferous hosts can actively colonize conifer seedlings. Root-chamber analysis of the development of ectomycorrhizal mycelium has shown that expanding hyphal fans not only act as nutrient-absorbing structures but also colonize nonmycorrhizal feeder roots in host-plant combinations within and among species. Using radioactive labeling, Finlay and Read (1986) have demonstrated the free movement of carbon among plants connected by mycorrhizal mycelia. Clearly, the existence of "pipelines" for distributing materials among plant species has important implications for forest regeneration.

Little is known of the persistence and distribution of ectomycorrhizae in the absence of living hosts. It has been suggested (Hacskaylo 1973) that ectomycorrhizal fungi do not persist long in the absence of host-supplied substrates. In the Klamath Mountains of northwest California and southwest Oregon, sites that have been logged and burned are often rapidly invaded by woody shrubs (Gratkowski 1961). Many of these shrubs, members of the Ericaceae and Fagaceae, form mycorrhizae with many of the same fungi as do members of the Pinaceae (Molina and Trappe 1982). This mechanism of natural redundancy preserves mycorrhiza diversity during periods of rapidly changing community structure.

Amaranthus and Perry (1989) transferred small amounts of soil from a Pacific madrone (*Arbutus menziesii* Pursh) stand to planting holes at three locales—a site cleared of whiteleaf manzanita (*Arctostaphylos viscida* Parry), a meadow cleared of annual grasses, and under Oregon white oak (*Quercus garryana* Hook)—on which Douglas-fir seedlings were grown. In the first year, they found more rapid mycorrhizal colonization of Douglas-fir feeder roots, and dramatically improved seedling survival and growth, on the site cleared of manzanita than in the meadow under similar soil, moisture, and temperature conditions. In the second year, Douglas-fir seedling performance continued to increase dramatically on the site cleared of manzanita compared to the other two locales (Fig. 3.9). If mortality and basal-area growth of surviving individuals are taken into account, on an area basis Douglas-fir inoculated with soil from the Pacific madrone stand and growing on the site cleared of manzanita was roughly 10 times that of seedlings growing in the meadow and 100 times that of seedlings growing under oak. The effect of the madrone inoculum on the manzanita site was almost certainly biological: it introduced a new mycorrhiza type and was ineffective when pasteurized. On the other hand, relative ineffectiveness of the madrone inoculum in the meadow and under oak indicates that more is involved in the Douglas-fir response than the simple presence or absence of the "right" organism. Rapid mycorrhiza formation, especially on sites that are difficult to regenerate, increases the chances that succeeding species will become established.

Some woody shrub species may act as reservoirs not only of mycorrhizal fungi but of other microflora as well. Significantly higher rates of nitrogen fixation—and increased seedling survival and growth—were found in association with the roots of Douglas-fir seedlings in a stand cleared of whiteleaf manzanita than in a meadow cleared of annual grass (Amaranthus et al. 1987a). *Azospirillium,* an N_2-fixing bacterium, was isolated within the mycorrhizae of Douglas-fir at the manzanita site. Whiteleaf manzanita occupies particularly hot, dry sites where fire is frequent. Because high N losses can accompany intense fire, natural mechanisms by which N is returned to the soil are important to long-term site productivity. Quite likely, the N fixed and gradually accumulated in association with mycorrhizae is biologically important for individual conifers over their long life.

We suggest that conifers and some woody shrubs form successional guilds, in which the rapidly sprouting pioneer members of the guild maintain the guild's shared soil microflora, forming a biological time bridge between old and new conifer stands. In the long run, maintaining diversity of soil microflora by pioneering shrubs may optimize conifer performance during the varied conditions likely over a rotation.

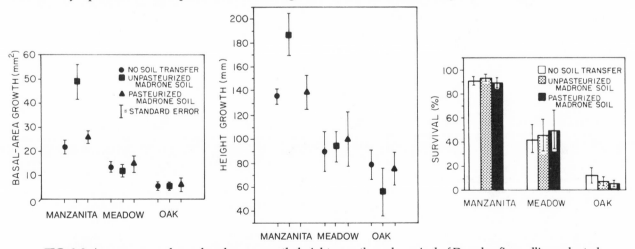

FIG. 3.9. Average second-year basal-area growth, height growth, and survival of Douglas-fir seedlings planted with and without soil transferred from a nearby Pacific madrone stand to a site cleared of whiteleaf manzanita, to a meadow cleared of annual grasses, and under Oregon white oak (adapted from Amaranthus and Perry 1989).

Effect of Nonhosts over Time

Many grass species and shrub species such as ceanothus and *Rubrus* (e.g., blackberry, salmonberry) form vesicular-arbuscular mycorrhizae (VAM) with fungi incompatible with members of the Pinaceae (Rose and Youngberg 1981; J. M. Trappe, unpublished data, Pacific Northwest Research Station, USDA Forest Service). On sites long dominated by VAM species, the ectomycorrhizal fungi needed by members of the Pinaceae may gradually disappear, and the soil microbial complex associated with ectomycorrhizae will shrivel. Invasion of sites by nonectomycorrhizal plants over years can seriously affect reforestation (Amaranthus and Perry 1987) and long-term yield, particularly in the case of ectomycorrhizal tree species growing on difficult sites where seedlings must establish ectomycorrhizae early to survive. Long-term changes in soil microflora associated with nonhost species could affect patterns of decomposition; nutrient and water retention, availability, and uptake; and the balance between pathogens and pathogen-inhibiting organisms.

How long soils retain their mycorrhizal colonization potential in the absence of living hosts is unknown. Ectomycorrhizal spores and hyphal fragments have remained metabolically active after 2 years in Scandinavian forests, though the number of active fragments dropped dramatically over that period (Persson 1982, Ferrier and Alexander 1985). In the Pacific Northwest, mycorrhiza formation generally decreases as the length of time between disturbance and reforestation increases (Pilz and Perry 1984, Perry et al. 1987).

POTENTIAL FOR MANAGING SOIL ORGANISMS

In discussing the practical role of certain beneficial bacteria for stimulating agricultural crop growth, Schroth and Hancock (1982) state: ". . . it has now been demonstrated that the root microflora can be altered qualitatively and quantitatively and that this can lead to substantial increases in yield." For forest crops, similar increases in yield may be achieved through inoculation with soil organisms. Some important advances have already been made.

Survival and growth of tree seedlings inoculated with the ectomycorrhizal fungus *Pisolithus tinctorius* have been enhanced in some areas (Marx 1975, Marx and Krupa 1978). However, the generally disappointing performance of *P. tinctorius* in the Pacific Northwest (Alvarez 1982; M. Castellano and J. M. Trappe, unpublished data, Pacific Northwest Research Station, USDA Forest Service) suggests that there is no "magic bullet." Because of the wide variety of soil, climatic, and biotic conditions characterizing temperate forests, it is improbable that a single fungus could benefit all host species and adapt to all conditions. For example, the types and activities of soil organisms associated with young conifers may be quite different from those associated with mature forests (Mason et al. 1983, Amaranthus and Perry 1987). On an old, high-elevation, nonreforested clearcut, soil inoculum transferred from a plantation significantly increased survival and growth of Douglas-fir seedlings compared to soil inoculum transferred from adjacent, mature forest (Fig. 3.10). Likewise, soil organisms needed to help seedlings establish on difficult sites may differ from those which sustain site productivity over a forest rotation.

In the Pacific Northwest, Douglas-fir seedlings growing in containers in nurseries have been successfully inoculated with the mycorrhizal fungus *Rhizopogon vinicolor* when its spores were added to irrigation water (M. Castellano, unpublished data, USDA Forest Service, 1986). Although not all fungal symbionts can be inoculated in this manner, success was attained with this promising species. *R. vinicolor* is commonly found in

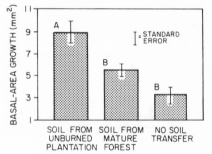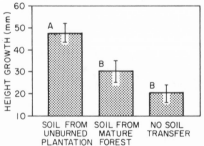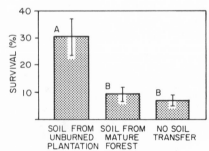

FIG. 3.10. Average second-year basal-area growth, height growth, and survival of Douglas-fir seedlings planted on an old, high-elevation, nonreforested clearcut in southwest Oregon with soil transferred from an unburned plantation or a mature forest and with no soil transferred (M. P. Amaranthus and D. A. Perry, unpublished data, Oregon State University, 1987).

clearcuts on young Douglas-fir seedlings and can improve seedling tolerance to drought (Parke et al. 1983). Preliminary results upon outplanting indicate that seedlings inoculated with *R. vinicolor* also grow better (Castellano et al. 1985).

Inoculating seedlings with beneficial soil organisms in bareroot nurseries has similar potential for improved outplanting performance. However, mycorrhizae adapted to outplanting sites are often lacking in modern bareroot nurseries (Trappe 1977). High fertility levels and routine fumigation, which are common in nurseries, reduce mycorrhizal fungus populations. Methods to increase mycorrhiza formation and diversity on seedlings in the nursery need further attention. Selecting the appropriate organisms is also critical. Seedlings colonized by a diversity of soil organisms adapted to conditions in the outplanting environment may outperform seedlings colonized by less diverse populations adapted to nursery conditions (Trappe 1977).

Forest managers should be aware that the yield-enhancing attributes of soil organisms are the product of diverse, complex interactions within natural systems that have co-evolved over millenia. Thus, the best long-term management approach is to minimize drastic or cumulative impacts to the forest environment so as to retain a balance of beneficial organisms. To do this, forest managers should:

(1)   Minimize disturbance severity—that is, intense burns, extensive soil compaction or erosion.
(2)   Emphasize retention of site organic matter.
(3)   Emphasize rapid revegetation of sites by indigenous host species and associated beneficial soil organisms.
(4)   Recognize that sites with harsh environments such as cold or drought are most susceptible to productivity losses.

A new era is emerging in our understanding of forest ecosystems. Incorporating the concept of the "living soil" in our evaluation of site productivity is part of this new, expanding view. Although much remains to be learned, we are making progress at a rapid rate. By understanding soil organisms, practicing foresters can better achieve short-term management goals while ensuring long-term site productivity. The challenge to forest managers is to assimilate the growing body of information concerning soil organisms in forest ecosystems and put that information to wise use.

QUESTIONS FROM THE SYMPOSIUM FLOOR

Q: Does energy flowing to belowground organisms represent energy lost to trees? How does this energy flow influence a site's ability to resist degradation?

A: An appreciation of the importance of the plant-soil relationship can be acquired from looking at the amount of energy plants divert to soils. In temperate forests, from 50 to 80% of the net carbon fixed in photosynthesis goes to roots and associated organisms such as mycorrhizal fungi (Fogel and Hunt 1983, Perry et al. 1987). Energy flowing into the soil supports a diverse community of soil organisms which in turn influence plant growth through effects on nutrient cycling, water uptake, pathogens, and soil structure.

   Energy flowing to soil organisms may have a specific cost/return for participating host plants. This is likely to vary in time and space and with changes in the physical and biotic environment. Different organisms do different jobs for different hosts in different environments. Some organisms, like mycorrhizal fungi and nitrogen fixers, benefit host plants in clearly definable ways. Others may benefit hosts only during periods of environmental extremes, at certain points in plant development, following disturbance, or indirectly by influencing important ecosystem properties such as soil structure. Maintaining native populations of soil organisms helps minimize site degradation by assuring a diversity of plant responses to unpredictable or varying environments.

Q: Do some hardwoods facilitate the succession of conifers in clearcuts? What other factors may be involved?

A: In southwest Oregon and northwest California, numerous hardwood species in the Ericaceae, Fagaceae, and Pinaceae form ectomycorrhizae, sharing many of the same fungus species as important commercial conifer species (Largent et al. 1980, Molina and Trappe 1982). Ericaceous manzanita and madrone are early pioneers following fire and are often associates of regenerating conifers. In hot, droughty environments, conifer seedlings establishing underneath the cover of brush species likely benefit from the shade. However, they may also be "plugging into" the network of mycorrhizal hyphae supported by ericaceous plants, gaining the advantage of early mycorrhiza formation critical to survival on some "difficult" sites (Amaranthus et al. 1987a, Amaranthus and Perry 1987). The species of hardwoods may affect the degree to which conifers are facilitated early in succession (Amaranthus and Perry 1989). In southwest Oregon, conifers regenerate poorly beneath Oregon white oak, apparently benefiting neither from the shade nor from the microflora associated with this species. The effect of numerous other hardwood species is unknown.

The density of hardwoods may be another important factor. When hardwoods are scattered as clumps, rather than in dense, uniform stands, the net effect may help conifers establish. In the field, Douglas-fir root-tip formation correlated positively with closeness to manzanita (M. P. Amaranthus and D. A. Perry, manuscript in preparation, Oregon State University, 1988). Years after certain high-elevation forests have been clearcut, the only living conifer seedlings are associated with "islands" of manzanita (Amaranthus and Perry 1987). Soils from the feeder root zone of madrone have had a highly stimulatory effect on conifer growth (Amaranthus and Perry 1989). In these experiments, environmental factors could not explain differences in survival and growth. The manzanita and madrone effect was almost certainly biological.

Hardwoods may affect conifer succession in many ways, including improving the microclimate, enhancing nutrient concentrations, and chemically stimulating rooting activity. We believe that at least some hardwoods exert a strong microbiological effect. Mycorrhizal propagules probably concentrate around pioneering hardwoods, and the direct transfer of inocula from hardwood to conifer is likely an effective mode of mycorrhizal colonization (Read et al. 1985). Moreover, a mycorrhizal fungus with an established "food" source (the root of an adjacent hardwood) delivers not only mycorrhizal inocula, but a whole package of rhizosphere organisms which may benefit succeeding conifers.

Q: How do you value large woody debris, especially given Bob Edmond's (chapter 2 author) statement that it may not be critical to nutrient cycling? Does the value of woody debris vary by site?

A: Woody debris is a dynamic component of the forest soil. It provides a storehouse of moisture and is an energy source and refuge for microorganisms critical to forest productivity. Mycorrhiza activity is significantly greater occurs in decaying wood than soils (Harvey et al. 1979). The relative importance of woody debris in supporting feeder roots may be greater on dry sites than on moist sites. During periods of adequate moisture, humus supports the highest level of ectomycorrhiza activity; but during periods of drought, soil wood becomes the most active site (Harvey et al. 1986). Thus, the wood component appears most important on low-productivity sites where moisture is limited or where natural levels of woody debris are low.

Wood on the forest floor forms long-lasting, moist microsites that may aid forest recovery. Following intense wildfire in southwest Oregon, decaying logs retained 25 times more moisture than surrounding soil (M. P. Amaranthus, D. Parrish, and D. A. Perry, manuscript in preparation, Oregon State University, 1988). Such decaying logs may expedite forest recovery by providing important refuge for roots and associated mycorrhizal fungi of pioneering vegetation.

Because most forest stands of the Pacific Northwest appear nitrogen limited, any factor affecting inputs and storage has implications for long-term productivity. Although the amount of nitrogen in sound stemwood may be small compared to that stored on the total site, decaying wood acts as an important locale for asymbiotic nitrogen fixation. Over the long residence time of large wood, inputs and storage of nitrogen are significant for some sites (Larsen et al. 1980, Harvey et al. 1986).

Protecting or enhancing the organic matter in Northwest forest soils is a primary means of maintaining long-term forest growth. Woody debris is a critical component of this organic fraction. The long-term ability of a soil to retain moisture, as well as ectomycorrhizal and nitrogen-fixing organisms, depends upon the continuing input of organic matter. Substantial losses of organic matter, including large wood, from thin, droughty, or infertile soils may result in long-term losses of forest productivity.

Accumulated woody debris, if overly abundant, represents a fuel hazard and increases the potential for wildfire. So there can be too much as well as too little woody debris. A balance must be struck between fuel management guidelines and protection of large woody debris if long-term forest productivity is to be maintained.

Q: Why is rapid mycorrhiza formation more important to conifer seedlings on "difficult" sites?

A: On cold, droughty, nutrient-poor, or otherwise stressful sites, there may be only a brief period favorable for seedling growth. Seedlings that do not become well established within that "window" are unlikely to survive. Mycorrhizae increase the capacity of tree seedlings to capture resources early by enhancing uptake of nutrients and water, lengthening root life, and protecting against pathogens. Rapid mycorrhiza formation assures seedlings a continuing resource supply and the vigor necessary to survive environmental stress. Studies in southwest Oregon indicate that rapid mycorrhiza formation is crucial for survival on "difficult" sites (Amaranthus et al. 1987b, Amaranthus and Perry 1987).

Q: What factors influence a seedling's potential to form mycorrhizae on disturbed forest sites?

A: Numerous factors directly and indirectly influence the potential for mycorrhiza formation, including seedling physiology, environmental conditions, and abundance of soil microorganisms and propagules (Perry et al. 1987). Modification of these conditions may influence a seedling's ability to form mycorrhizae. Mycorrhizal potential following disturbance such as clearcutting and slash burning depends primarily upon (1) the balance between mortality and input of mycorrhiza-forming propagules (such as spores and hyphae of mycorrhizal fungi); (2) the recovery of host plants, which provides the energy to stabilize populations of mycorrhizal fungi and allows them to grow and colonize nonmycorrhizal roots of surrounding plants; and (3) the diversity of fungus species, which buffers the mycorrhizal community against environmental changes following disturbance.

REFERENCES

Alexander, I. J., and K. Hardy. 1981. Surface phosphatase activity of Sitka spruce mycorrhizas from a serpentine site. *Soil Biology and Biochemistry* 13:301–305.

Alvarez, I. 1982. *Nursery, cold storage, and field studies on western conifers inoculated with spores of* Pisolithus tinctorius. Ph.D. Thesis. Corvallis, Ore.: Oregon State University.

Amaranthus, M. P., C. Y. Li, and D. A. Perry. 1987a. "Nitrogen fixation within mycorrhizae of Douglas-fir." In *Proceedings of the North American conference on mycorrhizae,* edited by D. M. Sylvia and J. H. Graham, 80. Gainesville, Fla.: University of Florida.

Amaranthus, M. P., and D. H. McNabb. 1984. "Bare soil exposure following logging and prescribed burning in southwest Oregon." In *New forests for a changing world,* 234–237. Proceedings, 1983 National Convention, Portland, Ore. Washington, D.C.: Society of American Foresters.

Amaranthus, M. P., and D. A. Perry. 1987. Effect of soil transfer on ectomycorrhiza formation and the survival and growth of conifer seedlings on old, nonreforested clear-cuts. *Canadian Journal of Forest Research* 17(8):944–950.

Amaranthus, M. P., and D. A. Perry. 1989. Interacting effects of vegetation type and Pacific madrone soil inocula on survival, growth, and mycorrhiza formation of Douglas-fir. *Canadian Journal of Forest Research* (in press).

Amaranthus, M. P., D. A. Perry, and S. L. Borchers. 1987b. "Reduction of native mycorrhizae reduce growth of Douglas-fir seedlings." In *Proceedings of the North American conference on mycorrhizae,* edited by D. M. Sylvia and J. H. Graham, 79. Gainesville, Fla.: University of Florida.

Bjorkman, E. 1970. Forest tree mycorrhizae—the conditions for formation and the significance for growth and afforestation. *Plant and Soil* 32:589–610.

Bollen, W. B. 1974. "Soil microbes." In *Environmental effects of forest residues management in the Pacific Northwest,* edited by O. Cramer, B1-B41. General Technical Report PNW-24. Portland, Ore.: Pacific Northwest Forest and Range Experiment Station, USDA Forest Service.

Castellano, M. A., J. M. Trappe, and R. Molina. 1985. Inoculation of container-grown Douglas-fir seedlings with basidiospores of *Rhizopogon vinicolor* and *R. colossus:* effects of fertility and spore application rate. *Canadian Journal of Forest Research* 15:10–13.

Cromack, K., P. Sollins, W. C. Graustein, K. Seidel, A. W. Todd, G. Spycher, Y. L. Ching, and R. L. Todd. 1979. Calcium oxalate accumulation and soil weathering in mats of the hypogeous fungus *Hysterangeum crassum. Soil Biology and Biochemistry* 11:463–468.

Dindal, D. L. (editor). 1973. *Proceedings of the first soil micro-communities conference.* A. E. C. Tech. Inf. Ant. CONF-711076.

Domingo, I. L. 1983. "Nitrogen fixation in Southeast Asian forestry: research and practice." In *Biological nitrogen fixation in forest ecosystems: foundations and applications,* edited by J. C. Gordon and C. T. Wheeler, 295–315. The Hague, The Netherlands: Martinus Nijhoff/Dr W. Junk Publishers.

Emerson, W. W., R. C. Foster, and J. M. Oades. 1986. "Organo-mineral complexes in relation to soil aggregation and structure." In *Interactions of soil minerals with natural organics and microbes,* edited by P. M. Huang and M. Schnitzer, 521–548. Special Publication 17. Madison, Wis.: Soil Science Society of America.

Ferrier, R. C., and I. J. Alexander. 1985. "Persistence under field conditions of excised fine roots and mycorrhizas of spruce." In *Ecological interactions in soil,* edited by A. H. Fitter, D. Atkinson, D. J. Read, and M. B. Usher, 175–179. Oxford: Blackwell Scientific Publications.

Finlay, R. D., and D. J. Read. 1986. Translocation of CO_2-labelled carbon between plants interconnected by a common mycelium. *New Phytologist* 103:143–156.

Fogel, R., and G. Hunt. 1983. Contribution of mycorrhizae and soil fungi to nutrient cycling in a Douglas-fir ecosystem. *Canadian Journal of Forest Research* 13:219–232.

Fogel, R., M. Ogawa, and J. M. Trappe. 1973. *Terrestrial decomposition: a synopsis.* U.S./International Biological Program, Coniferous Forest Biome International Report 135.

Forster, S. M. 1979. Microbial aggregation of sand in an embryo dune system. *Soil Biology and Biochemistry* 11:537–541.

Foster, R. C., and G. C. Marks. 1967. Observations of the mycorrhizas of forest trees. II. The rhizosphere of *Pinus radiata* D. Don. *Australian Journal of Biological Sciences* 20:915–926.

Gadgil, P. D. 1972. Effect of waterlogging on mycorrhizas of radiata pine and Douglas-fir. *New Zealand Journal of Forest Science* 2:222–226.

Giller, K. E., and J. M. Day. 1985. "Nitrogen fixation in the rhizosphere: significance in natural and agricultural systems." In *Ecological interactions in soil,* edited by A. H. Fitter, D. Atkinson, D. J. Read, and M. B. Usher, 127–147. Oxford: Blackwell Scientific Publications.

Gordon, J. C., and M. E. Avery. 1985. "Improving tree crops using microorganisms in designed systems." In *Attributes of trees as crop plants,* edited by M. G. R. Cannell and J. E. Jackson, 316–326. Abbots Ripton, Hunts, England: Institute of Terrestrial Ecology.

Gratkowski, H. 1961. *Brush problems in southwestern Oregon.* Portland, Ore.: Pacific Northwest Forest and Range Experiment Station, USDA Forest Service.

Graustein, W., K. Cromack, Jr., and P. Sollins. 1977. Calcium oxalate: occurrence in soils and effect on nutrient and geochemical cycles. *Science* 198:1252–1254.

Hacskaylo, E. 1973. "Carbohydrate physiology of ectomycorrhizae." In *Ectomycorrhizae: their ecology and physiology,* edited by G. C. Marks and T. T. Kozlowski, 207–230. London: Academic Press.

Harley, J. L., and S. E. Smith. 1983. *Mycorrhizal Symbioses.* London: Academic Press.

Harvey, A. E., M. J. Larsen, and M. F. Jurgensen. 1979. Comparative distribution of ectomycorrhizae in soils of three western Montana forest habitat types. *Forest Science* 25:350–360.

Harvey, A. E., M. J. Larsen, and M. F. Jurgensen. 1980. Clearcut harvesting and ectomycorrhizae: survival of activity on residual roots and influence on a bordering forest stand in western Montana. *Canadian Journal of Forest Research* 10:300–303.

Harvey, A. E., M. J. Larsen, M. F. Jurgensen, and J. A. Schlieter. 1986. *Distribution of active ectomycorrhizal short roots in forest soils of the Inland Northwest: effects of site and disturbance.* General Technical Report INT-374. Ogden, Utah: Intermountain Research Station, USDA Forest Service.

Ho, I., and B. Zak. 1979. Acid phosphatase activity of six ectomycorrhizal fungi. *Canadian Journal of Botany* 57:1203–1205.

Kelly, W. D. 1976. Evaluation of *Trichoderma harzianum* integrated clay granules as a biocontrol for *Phytophthora cinnamomi* causing damping off of pine seedlings. *Phytopathology* 66:1023–1027.

Largent, D. L., N. Sugihara, and C. Wishner. 1980. Occurrence of mycorrhizae on ericaceous and pyrolaceous plants in northern California. *Canadian Journal of Botany* 58:2274–2279.

Larsen, M. J., A. E. Harvey, and M. F. Jurgensen. 1980. "Residue decay processes and associated environmental functions in northern Rocky Mountain forests." In *Environmental consequences of timber harvesting,* 157–174. General Technical Report INT-90. Ogden, Utah: Intermountain Research Station, USDA Forest Service.

Lavender, D. P., and R. B. Walker. 1979. "Nitrogen and related elements in nutrition of forest trees." In *Proceedings, forest fertilization conference,* edited by S. P. Gessel, 15–22. Contribution No. 40. Seattle, Wash.: Institute of Forest Resources, University of Washington.

Lynch, J. M., and E. Bragg. 1985. Microorganisms and soil aggregate stability. *Advances in Soil Science* 2:133–171.

Marx, D. H. 1972. Ectomycorrhizae as biological deterrents to pathogenic root infections. *Annual Review of Phytopathology* 10:429–454.

———, D. H. 1973. Growth of ectomycorrhizal and nonmycorrhizal shortleaf pine seedlings in soil with *Phytophthora cinnamomi. Phytopathology* 63:18–23.

———, D. H. 1975. Mycorrhizae and establishment of trees on strip-mined land. *Ohio Journal of Science* 75:288–297.

Marx, D. H., and S. V. Krupa. 1978. "Ectomycorrhizae." In *Interactions between non-pathogenic soil microorganisms and plants,* edited by Y. R. Dommergues and S. V. Krupa, 373–400. Amsterdam: Elsevier Scientific Publishing Company.

Maser, C., J. M. Trappe, and R. Nussbaum. 1978. Fungal-small mammal interrelationships with emphasis on Oregon coniferous forests. *Ecology* 59:799–809.

Mason, P. A., J. Wilson, F. T. Last, and C. Walker. 1983. The concept of succession in relationship to the spread of sheathing mycorrhizal fungi in inoculated tree seedlings growing in unsterile soil. *Plant and Soil* 71:247–256.

Mexal, J., and C. P. P. Reid. 1973. The growth of selected mycorrhizal fungi in response to induced water stress. *Canadian Journal of Botany* 51:1579–1588.

Mikola, P. 1970. Mycorrhizal inoculation in afforestation. *International Review of Forestry Research* 3:123–196.

Molina, R., and J. M. Trappe. 1982. Lack of mycorrhizal specificity by the ericaceous hosts *Arbutus menziesii* and *Arctostaphylos uva-ursi.* New Phytologist 90:495–509.

Moorman, T., and F. B. Reeves. 1979. The role of endomycorrhizae in revegetation practices in the semi-arid West. II. A bioassay to determine the effect of land disturbance on endomycorrhizal populations. *American Journal of Botany* 66:14–18.

Oswald, E. T., and H. A. Ferchau. 1963. Bacterial associations of coniferous mycorrhizae. *Plant and Soil* 28:167.

Parke, J. L. 1982. *Factors affecting the inoculum potential of VA and ectomycorrhizal fungi in forest soils of southwest Oregon and northern California.* Ph.D. Thesis. Corvallis, Ore.: Oregon State University.

Parke, J. L., R. G. Linderman, and C. H. Black. 1983. The role of ectomycorrhizas in drought tolerance of Douglas-fir seedlings. *New Phytologist* 95:83–95.

Parry, M.S. 1953. Tree planting in Tanganyika: methods of planting. *East African Agricultural Journal* 18:102–115.

Perry, D. A., M. M. Meyer, D. Egeland, S. L. Rose, and D. Pilz. 1982. Seedling growth and mycorrhizal formation in clearcut and adjacent undisturbed soils in Montana: a greenhouse bioassay. *Forest Ecology and Management* 4:261–273.

Perry, D. A., R. Molina, and M. P. Amaranthus. 1987. Mycorrhizae, mycorrhizospheres, and reforestation: current knowledge and research needs. *Canadian Journal of Forest Research* 17(8):929–940.

Perry, D. A., and S. L. Rose. 1983. "Soil biology and forest productivity: opportunities and constraints." In *IUFRO symposium on forest site and continuous productivity,* edited by R. Ballard and S. P. Gessel, 229–238. General Technical Report PNW-163. Portland, Ore.: Pacific Northwest Forest and Range Experiment Station, USDA Forest Service.

Perry, D. A., and S. L. Rose. 1989. "The influence of site preparation on forest productivity." In *Proceedings, California conferences on forest nutrition,* edited by R. Powers and T. Robson. Berkeley, Calif.: Pacific Southwest Forest and Range Experiment Station, USDA Forest Service. (In press).

Persson, H. 1982. *Changes in the tree and dwarf shrub fine-roots after clearcutting in a mature Scots pine stand.* Swedish Coniferous Forest Project, Technical Report 31.

Pilz, D. P., and D. A. Perry. 1984. Impact of clearcutting and slashburning on ectomycorrhizal associations of Douglas-fir. *Canadian Journal of Forest Research* 14:94–100.

Powell, P. E., G. R. Cline, C. P. P. Reid, and P. J. Szaniszlo. 1980. Occurrence of hydroxamate siderophore iron chelators in soils. *Nature* 287:833–834.

Rambelli, A. 1973. "The rhizosphere of mycorrhizae." In *Ectomycorrhizae: their ecology and physiology,* edited by G. C. Marks and T. T. Kozlowski, 229–249. London: Academic Press.

Read, D. J., R. Francis, and R. D. Finlay. 1985. "Mycorrhizal mycelia and nutrient cycling in plant communities." In *Ecological interactions in soil,* edited by A. H. Fitter, D. Atkinson, D. J. Read, and M. B. Usher, 193–218. Oxford: Blackwell Scientific Publications.

Reeves, F. B., D. Wagner, T. Moorman, and J. Kiel. 1979. The role of endomycorrhizae in revegetation practices in the semi-arid West. I. A comparison of incidence of mycorrhizae in severely disturbed natural environments. *American Journal of Botany* 66:6–13.

Reid, C. P. P. 1979. "Mycorrhizae and water stress." In *Root physiology and symbiosis,* edited by A. Riedacker and M. J. Gagnaire-Michard, 392–408. Nancy, France: IUFRO Symposium.

Rose, S. L., C. Y. Li, and A. Steibus Hutchins. 1980. A streptomycete antagonist to *Phellinus weirii, Fomes annosus,* and *Phytophthora cinnamomi. Canadian Journal of Microbiology* 26:583–587.

Rose, S. L., and C. Youngberg. 1981. Tripartite associations in snowbrush (*Ceanothus velutinus*): effect of vesicular-arbuscular mycorrhizae on growth, nodulation, and nitrogen fixation. *Canadian Journal of Botany* 59:34–39.

Schoenberger, M. M., and D. A. Perry. 1982. The effect of soil disturbance on growth and ectomycorrhizae of Douglas-fir and western hemlock seedlings: a greenhouse bioassay. *Canadian Journal of Forest Research* 12:343–353.

Schroth, M. N., and J. G. Hancock. 1982. Disease-suppressive soil and root colonizing bacteria. *Science* 26:1376–1381.

Slankis, V. 1974. Soil factors influencing formation of mycorrhizae. *Annual Review of Phytopathology* 12:437–457.

Sutton, J. C., and B. R. Sheppard. 1976. Aggregation of sand dune soil by endomycorrhizal fungi. *Canadian Journal of Botany* 54:326–333.

Tan, K. H., P. Sihanonth, and R. L. Todd. 1978. Formation of humic acid like compounds by the ectomycorrhizal fungus *Pisolithus tinctorius. Soil Science Society of America Journal* 42:906–908.

Tarrant, R. F., and J. M. Trappe. 1971. The role of alder in improving the forest environment. *Plant and Soil, Special Volume:* 335–348.

Theodorou, C. 1978. Soil moisture and the mycorrhizal association of *Pinus radiata* D. Don. *Soil Biology and Biochemistry* 10:33–37.

Tisdall, J. M., and J. M. Oades. 1979. Stabilization of soil aggregates by the root systems of ryegrass. *Australian Journal of Soil Research* 17:429–441.

Tisdall, J. M., and J. M. Oades. 1982. Organic matter and water stable aggregates in soils. *Journal of Soil Science* 33:141–164.

Trappe, J. M. 1977. Selection of fungi for ectomycorrhizal inoculation in nurseries. *Annual Review of Phytopathology* 15:203–222.

Trappe, J. M., and W. B. Bollen. 1979. "Forest soils biology of the Douglas-fir Region." In *Forest soils of the Douglas-fir Region,* edited by P. E. Heilman and H. W. Anderson. Pullman, Wash.: Washington State University.

Trappe, J. M., and R. D. Fogel. 1977. "Ecosystematic functions of mycorrhizae." In *The belowground ecosystem,* 205–214. Fort Collins, Colo.: Colorado State University, Range Science Department Scientific Series.

Trappe, J. M., J. F. Franklin, R. F. Tarrant, and G. M. Hansen (editors). 1968. *Biology of alder. Proceedings of a symposium.* Northwest Science Association. Portland, Ore.: Pacific Northwest Forest and Range Experiment Station, USDA Forest Service.

Williamson, B., and I. J. Alexander. 1975. Acid phosphatase localized in the sheath of beech mycorrhiza. *Soil Biology and Biochemistry* 7:195–198.

Wingfield, E. B. 1968. *Mycotrophy in loblolly pine.* Ph.D. Thesis. Blacksburg, Va.: Virginia Polytechnic Institute and State University.

Wollum, A. G., II, and C. T. Youngberg. 1964. The influence of nitrogen fixation by non-leguminous woody plants on the growth of pine seedlings. *Journal of Forestry* 62:316–321.

Wright, E., and R. F. Tarrant. 1958. *Occurrence of mycorrhizae after logging and slash burning in the Douglas-fir forest type.* Research Note PNW-160. Portland, Ore.: Pacific Northwest Forest and Range Experiment Station, USDA Forest Service.

Zak, B. 1964. Role of mycorrhizae in root disease. *Annual Review of Phytopathology* 2:377–392.

Chapter 4

Soil Physical Properties: Importance to Long-Term Forest Productivity

S. W. Childs, S. P. Shade, D. W. R. Miles,
E. Shepard, and H. A. Froehlich

ABSTRACT

The physical nature of the soil directly affects how a site must be managed to ensure maintenance of site productivity. The most important soil physical properties are porosity, aeration, water storage, infiltration and water flow, heat storage and flow, and strength. Long-term changes in these properties are directly affected by changes in soil density and organic matter content. Because of these direct effects and the fact that soil physical properties are relatively easily measured, the basic relationships between organic matter content, soil density, and each of the important soil physical properties can be examined here. Impacts of four site-disturbance categories—compaction, soil surface disturbance, fire effects, and soil removal—are reviewed. Finally, the effects of specific timber-management practices on soil physical properties are summarized.

INTRODUCTION

The physical nature of the soil directly and indirectly affects how a site must be managed to ensure long-term maintenance of site productivity. Soil physical properties themselves affect plant growth, soil biological activity, nutrient cycling, and transport of heat, water, gases, and solutes at the soil surface and below. In addition, the properties are a subset of the large array of interactive attributes that determine site response to various management practices. The soil is a dynamic system constantly undergoing change and moving towards a seldom attained equilibrium point. For sites where physical improvement of long-term productivity is possible (a classic example is drainage), site equilibrium can be shifted to a new optimum point. In most cases, however, sites are manipulated over a range from which the system can recover to the initial conditions. In this way, the site is managed to maintain productivity.

Long-term effects of soil physical properties on productivity are most easily identified in extreme cases where degradation of these properties limits growth or survival regardless of interactions with other site factors. Examples are excessive soil compaction, removal of all soil organic matter, and topsoil loss from a shallow soil. These conditions can limit overall site productivity, favor growth of undesirable species, or create situations in which short-term conditions required for survival are not met.

The focus of this chapter is the effect that diminished quality of the soil physical environment has on site equilibrium and productivity. Specific issues include decrease in total soil volume (or depth), changes in the properties of the soil surface layer, creation of a short-term harsh environment which delays reforestation after harvest and site preparation, soil resistance to disturbance, and resilience of the soil and site. The soil physical properties affecting site productivity—density, porosity, organic matter content, aeration, water storage and flow, heat storage and flow, and strength—are discussed individually so that their relative importance to long-term productivity can be assessed. They are also treated in disturbance categories—soil compaction, surface mixing and disruption, fire effects, and soil removal. Finally, the impacts of specific timber-management practices are addressed.

SOIL PHYSICAL PROCESSES AND PROPERTIES

The physical properties of a soil are commonly summarized with easily measured quantities: bulk density, porosity, texture, and organic matter content. In the following paragraphs, other soil properties of importance are discussed with particular attention to effects of organic matter and density. These two properties are ones which management practices can alter.

Soil Density and Porosity

These basic properties are common quantitative descriptors of soil structure because they are easily measured and can be used to estimate other properties related to heat, gas, and water flow. Bulk density, the mass of dry soil per unit volume, is related to porosity, the volume of pores per volume of soil. The two quantities characterize the proportions of a soil occupied by solids and fluids (both water and air).

Soil organic matter is important in determining soil density and porosity. Although the direct role of soil organic matter in maintaining site productivity is complex, it is clear that as organic matter percentage increases, soil bulk density decreases and porosity increases (Fig. 4.1). On the basis of the work of Adams (1973) and Rawls (1983), these relationships show that added organic matter would have the greatest effect on a soil initially at a high bulk density. Adding organic matter generally results in: (1) a more favorable growth environment with better drainage of the soil profile and higher infiltration rates (Sands 1983); (2) adequate aeration over a wider range of soil moisture conditions (Bullock et al. 1985); (3) better conditions for microbial activity (Bridge and Rixon 1976); and (4) easier root penetration (Williams and Cooke 1961). Note the effect of organic matter on a sandy soil (bulk density at 0 organic matter = 1.6 Mg/m^3), which is represented by the lowest porosity curve and the highest bulk-density curve (Fig. 4.1). Although total porosity is quite low when no organic matter is present, such a soil will reach 50% porosity and a fine-soil bulk density of 1.2 Mg/m^3 at an organic matter content of 5%. This percentage is commonly met or exceeded in the surface 0.3 m of Pacific Northwest forest soils (Youngberg 1959, Brown 1975, Flint and Childs 1984).

The size distribution of soil pores is also important for maintaining a productive site. Large pores and cracks (macropores) are important for soil drainage, aeration, and root access; smaller pores (micropores) store soil water and are the sites of nutrient retention and microbial activity. Both kinds of pores are required for productive soils. Pore size distribution can be characterized by the soil-water release curve in which water content (water-filled pore space) is plotted against water potential, a measure of the energy required to extract water from the soil. That energy is inversely related to pore size (Fig. 4.2).

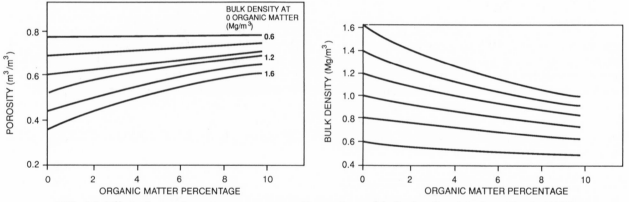

FIG. 4.1. Effect of organic matter content on soil porosity and bulk density; data from Rawls (1983).

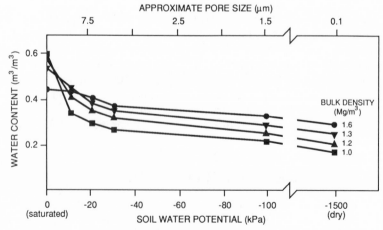

FIG. 4.2. Effect of soil compaction on soil-water release curve; data for Barnes loam at four bulk densities from Reicosky et al. (1981).

Water release curves provide information about the size and number of pores. The data set shown in Figure 4.2 demonstrates the changes in pore structure caused by compaction of a soil initially at 1.0 Mg/m^3 bulk density. The leftmost points indicate the decreases in porosity caused by compaction (because the water content at 0 kPa water potential is equal to total porosity of the soil). In addition, pore size distribution also changes, as evidenced by the shapes of the curves. In fact, several workers have shown that steeply sloping soil-water release curves indicate a favorable pore-size distribution (Cary and Hayden 1973, Reicosky et al. 1981, Lenhard 1986). Flatter curves indicate too few large pores. In Figure 4.2, the soil with the highest density curve has the least total porosity, the fewest macropores (those larger than 14 μm in radius—between 0 and −10 kPa water potential), and the most pores smaller than 1 μm (−1,500 kPa water potential). This point is conveniently shown in a redrawn version of these data (Fig. 4.3). The effect of compaction (increase in bulk density) on total porosity is shown by the total height of the bars. As bulk density increases from 1 to 1.2 Mg/m^3, total porosity decreases slightly and is accompanied by a change in pore size distribution. The volume of macropores, those important for drainage and aeration, decreases. At the same time, the volume of micropores increases. These smaller pores are separated into two categories: those containing water available for extraction by plant roots and those containing water essentially unavailable for root extraction. This distinction is an important measure of the quality of a soil. As bulk density increases from 1.2 to 1.6 Mg/m^3, the number of micropores storing unavailable water increases while that of macropores and of micropores storing available water decreases. At 1.6 Mg/m^3, very few macropores remain, and more than half the soil porosity consists of micropores with unavailable water.

Soil Aeration

Rapid gas exchange in soils is required for optimum microbial activity and growth of plant roots. Adequate supply of oxygen for root growth can be assured if there is a network of continuous, air-filled pores present in a soil. Numerous studies of gas diffusion in soils have demonstrated that supply of oxygen is adequate when less than 90% of the soil pores are filled with water (e.g., Cannell 1977). That is, when there is more than about 10% air-filled pore space, the oxygen concentration in the bulk soil can be maintained at atmospheric levels by gas diffusion. Aeration conditions for a soil can be assessed with a soil-water release curve (see Fig. 4.2) to determine the pore size and water potential at which aeration is adequate. If 10% of the pores are filled with air but those pores are of small size (as is the case for the 1.6 Mg/m^3 bulk density curve in Fig. 4.2), it is likely that a greater percentage of air-filled pores will be required for adequate aeration. This is due to slower air flow in small pores, partly because the flow path created by small pores is more tortuous than that created by large pores. Furthermore, slower drainage rates in small pores prolong poor aeration conditions in a higher density soil.

Oxygen concentration in a specific soil volume may be decreased through consumption by microbes and plant roots. Depletion depends on the amount of biological activity and the percentage of air-filled pores available to replenish the soil atmosphere. Roots generally consume more oxygen than microbes in a given volume of soil and require an oxygen concentration greater than 10% (Glinski and Stepniewski 1985). Microbial populations may be able to grow at lower oxygen concentrations, but the concentration required depends on population size and amount of organic matter present in the soil (Greenwood 1961).

Soil Water Storage

Changes in soil water storage caused by management practices can have important effects on site productivity. The most important changes are decrease in total soil volume when soil is removed, decrease in soil porosity when soil is compacted, and decreased soil organic matter content as a result of harvesting and site preparation. Because total site water use is generally positively correlated with growth (Carmean 1975), factors that decrease soil water storage are detrimental to productivity and those that increase it are beneficial. Decreased soil-water storage is particularly important for sites with little growing-season precipitation, shallow soil profiles, or coarse-textured soils in which water limitations already control productivity. In addition, soil water storage must be evaluated in the context of water needs for plant growth and mechanisms of water loss. Water requirements are larger on well-vegetated sites and sites without surface organic matter or litter layers.

Soil water storage can be changed by altering soil porosity or organic matter content. The data in Figure 4.3 show that available soil water (that water held between −10 and −1,500 kPa) is 0.17 m^3/m^3 for a loam soil at 1 Mg/m^3 bulk density. The amount of available water increases to 0.21 and 0.20 m^3/m^3 when soil is compacted to bulk densities of 1.2 and 1.3 Mg/m^3 but ultimately decreases to 0.13 m^3/m^3 at a bulk density of 1.6 Mg/m^3. That is, an initial increase in density can increase the amount of available water by decreasing the number of pores

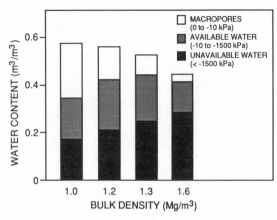

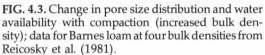

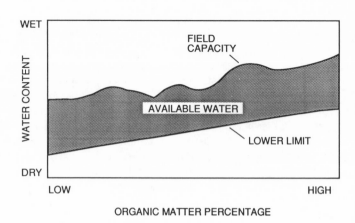

FIG. 4.3. Change in pore size distribution and water availability with compaction (increased bulk density); data for Barnes loam at four bulk densities from Reicosky et al. (1981).

FIG. 4.4. Effect of organic matter percentage on storage of available soil water.

larger than 14 μm and increasing the number of pores between 14 and 0.1 μm. But if density is increased too much, more pores smaller than 0.1 μm are created and available soil water is decreased.

The effect of soil organic matter on water storage is variable. Regression analyses of agricultural soils have demonstrated that increasing amounts of organic matter increase soil water content at a given water potential (Gupta and Larson 1979, De Jong et al. 1983). If the increase in water content at the lower limit of water availability is greater than the increase at the upper limit (called field capacity), soil water storage is decreased (Alexander 1982, De Jong et al. 1983, Sommerfeldt and Chang 1987), as illustrated in Figure 4.4. These studies show that the lower limit of available water (approximately −1,500 kPa) almost always increases as organic matter content increases. However, the effect of organic matter on field capacity is not so predictable, depending on soil particle size, pore size distribution, and soil structure. It is often observed that soils with organic matter amendments develop macropores, are better drained, and have lower water contents at field capacity. This results in a decrease in available water.

Alexander (1982) studied the relationship of organic matter to available water for 400 California forest soil horizons. His data show that organic matter consistently increases water-holding capacity for sandy soils but not for other textural classes. In his study, water storage in soils with high native organic matter contents (greater than 0.6% organic carbon) was never more than 40% greater than that in soils of the same texture but with little organic matter. Sands et al. (1979) showed that water storage of very coarse-textured soils is greatly increased as organic matter content increases from 0 to 3% at constant bulk density.

Infiltration, Permeability, and Soil Water Flow

Water transport properties of forest soils have an effect on long-term productivity at two scales: (1) the hydrologic scale of storm flow and soil movement; and (2) the scale of root water uptake and evapotranspiration. Change in properties is important at the hydrologic scale because it is at this scale that effects such as erosion (Beasley et al. 1986) or change in elevation of a water table (Morris and Pritchett 1983) can occur. Site quality can be seriously degraded when the hydrologic cycle is altered. Notable examples are the decrease in site productivity after mass slope failure (Miles et al. 1984) and changes in nitrogen cycling resulting in stunted tree growth following a rise in water table after logging (Heilman 1966).

Redistribution of water in the soil profile and evapotranspiration both affect plant growth and, therefore, site productivity. Pore size distribution affects water flow and storage, as already illustrated in Figure 4.2. Other factors of importance at a given site are canopy cover and root distribution of competing vegetation (Giles et al. 1985), suppression of soil surface evaporation by the mulching action of surface litter and debris (Ginter et al. 1979), and effects of soil surface cover on infiltration (Henderson and Golding 1983).

Soil water properties are commonly related to soil texture because water flow rate and storage are closely related to pore size. Other factors that influence pore size are bulk density and organic matter percentage. The effects of bulk density and organic matter on the soil-water release curve have already been described as variable. The effects on water flow are illustrated by hydraulic conductivity data shown in Table 4.1. Hydraulic conductivity, the water flow rate per unit hydraulic gradient, can be compared among soils because it repre-

TABLE 4.1. Effect of organic matter (OM) percentage and soil bulk density on hydraulic conductivity of saturated and unsaturated soils. OM effects are demonstrated for three similar soils (Sands 1983); bulk-density effects are shown for the Barnes loam compacted to different bulk densities (Reicosky et al. 1981).

Soil condition or type	Bulk density, Mg/m^3	Hydraulic conductivity, m/day		
		Saturated, 0 kPa	Unsaturated	
			−10 kPa	−1,500 kPa
Sand, 0.01% OM	1.4	38	6×10^{-4}	6×10^{-15}
1.01% OM	1.4	10	5×10^{-4}	2×10^{-11}
2.5% OM	1.4	3.8	2×10^{-3}	2×10^{-8}
Barnes loam	1.0	2.6	1×10^{-3}	1×10^{-7}
	1.2	0.9	9×10^{-3}	5×10^{-7}
	1.3	0.3	5×10^{-2}	1×10^{-6}
	1.6	0.02	1×10^{-2}	5×10^{-8}

sents the flow rate for standardized external conditions. Hydraulic conductivity of saturated soil is largest at low bulk density because water flow is through macropores. Soil compaction decreases macroporosity and lowers the hydraulic conductivity of saturated soil (Eagleman and Jamison 1962, De Kimpe et al. 1982, Incerti et al. 1987). The effect of increased organic matter is commonly observed to be decreased bulk density and increased porosity and hydraulic conductivity of saturated soil (MacRae and Mehuys 1985). The data in Table 4.1 do not show the trend of increasing saturated hydraulic conductivity because bulk density does not show the expected decrease with soil organic matter (see Fig. 4.1).

Effects of organic matter percentage and bulk density on hydraulic conductivity of unsaturated soils are different from those for saturated conditions. As soils lose water, the hydraulic conductivity of unsaturated soil decreases rapidly because macropores drain and flow shifts to the smaller soil pores that are still full of water. For the data shown (Table 4.1), hydraulic conductivity of unsaturated soil increases with small increases in bulk density or organic matter percentage, an effect evident both near field capacity (−10 kPa), where flow occurs in intermediate-sized pores, and for dry soil conditions (−1,500 kPa), where flow occurs in micropores less than 0.1 μm in radius. When compaction is too severe (e.g., 1.6 Mg/m³ in Table 4.1), hydraulic conductivity of unsaturated soil decreases. At this extreme level of compaction, the volume of very small pores is large, and soil conditions for tree growth are poor.

Soil Thermal Properties

The most important manageable soil thermal properties are those associated with the soil surface, the location of large heat and energy exchanges. Maintaining surface litter or slash limits high temperatures in the soil profile (Morris and Pritchett 1983) but causes high temperatures at the surface. Having such a mulch layer is an advantage when surface heat loads can be dissipated to the atmosphere and subsoil temperatures are adequate for root growth and other biological activity. However, the exclusion of heat from the deeper soil by mulch can be a problem on sites where low soil temperatures limit growth and productivity (Dobbs and McMinn 1977). Removing mulch layers may also be advantageous on sites where early season budburst increases opportunities for growth and survival (Sorensen and Campbell 1978), or where sites are managed for natural regeneration and trees must compete for resources (Williamson 1973).

Soil organic matter content and bulk density both affect the soil thermal environment. The net effect of high organic matter content is that it slows the rate of heat transfer in a soil (Childs and Malstaff 1982); this can cause slightly cooler temperatures and delayed soil warming. However, these effects of organic matter are generally small in comparison with heat-transfer effects due to soil water content or increase in soil density. Densification increases the rate of heat transfer in wet soil by increasing mineral particle contact to enhance thermal conductivity. In addition, heat storage is decreased because decreased porosity leads to less soil-water storage. When compacted soils are dry, heat storage is greater because soil particles are more densely packed. This combination of effects results in more rapid spring soil warming (wet soil, rapid heat transfer) and higher late-summer soil temperatures (dry soil, slow heat transfer).

Soil Strength

Shear strength increases with density for a given soil (Froehlich and McNabb 1984) and is well correlated with decrease in root penetration (Sands et al. 1979) and root proliferation (Wronski 1984). The direct effect of organic matter on soil strength is not well documented, but the decrease in soil bulk density with increasing organic matter percentage (see Fig. 4.1) suggests that strength also may decrease.

Surface organic layers have an important effect on soil strength in that they decrease susceptibility to compaction simply by protecting surface horizons (Greacen and Sands 1980, Jakobsen and Moore 1981). Deeper in the soil profile where soil compaction and strength increases are affected by soil water content, any change in water status caused by organic matter indirectly affects soil strength.

MAJOR SOIL DISTURBANCES

Harvest and site-preparation methods can damage the physical soil resource and decrease long-term productivity. The major disturbance categories are soil compaction, surface disturbance, effects associated with fire, and soil removal. Site management practices must be assessed with regard to the potential for damage to soil physical properties in each of these categories. The resistance of a particular soil to change, as well as cumulative effects of damaging events, must be considered in determining whether changes will affect site productivity. Spatial variation of both soil properties and management impacts also influence site damage and response. Localized areas of differing sensitivity to disturbance may be managed differently to minimize impacts on the site as a whole.

Soil Compaction

The effects of soil compaction have been extensively studied, and excellent reviews are available (Greacen and Sands 1980, Froehlich and McNabb 1984). Increase in soil bulk density is correlated with changes in other soil properties (e.g., strength, water storage, aeration), and there is little doubt that compaction affects the physical environment enough to decrease productivity. Reduction in root growth, height, and timber volume have been observed (Froehlich and McNabb 1984) and may result from the compaction produced by as little as one pass of a logging vehicle over a site (Wronski 1984). The percentage decrease in tree height has been linearly correlated to percentage increase in bulk density (Froehlich and McNabb 1984). Productivity loss has been documented for whole sites (Wert and Thomas 1981) as well as for individual trees (Froehlich 1979, Helms and Hipkin 1986). Decreases in microbial populations have been observed in compacted soils for up to 5 years (Smeltzer et al. 1986). In general, however, the effects directly observed in field studies result from environmental degradation due to both compaction and disturbance or removal of surface soil. The specific effects of compaction alone have not been isolated.

A considerable body of literature shows that bulk-density increase due to logging is long lived. Froehlich and McNabb (1984) summarized data that show compaction effects persisting for as long as 40 years. Wert and Thomas (1981) observed decreases in height and volume growth after as long as 32 years.

The mechanism of physical damage responsible for growth loss depends on specific site conditions. A generalized model relating root growth conditions to soil strength, moisture, bulk density, and aeration (Fig. 4.5) shows a root growth "window" bounded by soil conditions of inadequate aeration and excessive soil strength. The range of water contents acceptable for root growth decreases as bulk density increases. When site conditions are such that soil water content is not within the growth window, growth declines. It is clear from Figure 4.5 that, with higher levels of soil compaction, the potential for growth-limiting soil conditions increases and that careful management would be required to maintain optimum growth. The primary forestry practices that can be used to control soil moisture are irrigation and vegetation control.

If soil water content is a site attribute that changes with time and cannot be precisely managed, favorable growth conditions can be maintained in two ways: (1) keeping soil bulk density low, and (2) establishing a large soil volume for water and nutrient extraction. Unfortunately, roots cannot easily explore compacted soil, and a restricted root zone will result in poor growth conditions if the availability of resources is low in the soil volume occupied (Fig. 4.6). If soil-resource availability is high, a small root zone may be adequate to support growth requirements (see chapter 7, this volume). It is tempting to speculate that, if all required resources are available to a tree in sufficient quantities, compaction will not be a problem. However, a well-distributed root system may be required to provide physical support and avoid windthrow even if adequate resources are available in a shallow layer. Because the cumulative effects of changing soil physical processes are unknown, it is prudent to assume that any alteration of the growth environment for plant roots will likely result in increased allocation of

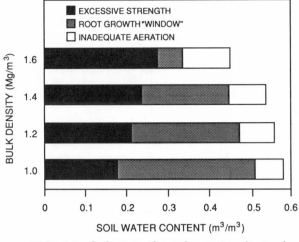

FIG. 4.5. Soil strength and aeration limits for optimizing root growth. Density and total porosity data (right-most extent of each bar) from Reicosky et al. (1981).

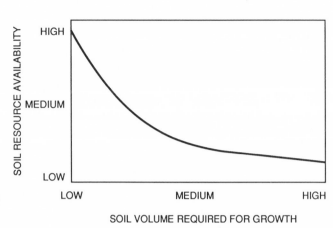

FIG. 4.6. Effect of soil water and nutrient resource status on the soil volume required for adequate tree growth.

resources to root growth and maintenance at the expense of aboveground growth. This may ultimately change productivity equilibrium (Sands 1983, Marshall 1986). A final caution is that, for purposes of maintaining long-term productivity, any alteration of site productivity or the soil physical environment may result in a less resilient ecosystem. Such a weakened system may be more susceptible to future damage (see chapter 6, this volume).

It appears that soil compaction can be partially ameliorated by post-harvest tilling of compacted trails and landings. Improved tree growth after tillage has been widely reported (Froehlich and McNabb 1984). However, the most reasonable approaches to minimizing productivity loss due to compaction are preventive: (1) restrict the area impacted using logging methods such as designated skid trails (Froehlich and McNabb 1984), and (2) protect the soil by keeping surface soil, litter, and slash in place (Greacen and Sands 1980, Jakobsen and Moore 1981).

Soil Surface Disturbance

Mixing and short-distance displacement of topsoil from a site can decrease productivity. Although the areal extent of bare surface exposed by logging is likely to be less than 30% of a given site (Rice et al. 1972, Miller and Sirois 1986), the impact can be severe. Physical effects of surface disturbance include destruction of soil structure and increased erosion potential (see chapter 5, this volume).

Soil structure can be altered in two ways. First, during logging in wet soils, surface structure can be obliterated by the kneading action of machinery and logs (Froehlich and McNabb 1984), producing a damaged surface without deep soil compaction. The surface loses structural features of good pore-size distribution, continuity among soil pores, and aggregation of individual particles into larger groups; the soil is said to be "puddled." Removal of surface slash and litter also decreases the resistance of the soil to puddling or compaction damage caused by tractor logging (Jakobsen and Moore 1981); the resulting surface is sealed to water and gas movement and often dries to a hard, dispersed layer. Second, the disturbed soil surface may cause the common biological agents of structural development (mycorrhizae, fungi, microbes, roots) to be less effective (Morris and Pritchett 1983; see chapter 3, this volume). The exact nature of this effect is unknown but results from changes in soil microclimate as well as interruption of nutrient cycling by removal of or damage to plant roots. Changes in surface soil structure and microbial activity have been documented in harsh, high-elevation environments where reforestation efforts have failed (see poster summary, this volume, J. Borchers and D. Perry).

Once bare soil is exposed, decreased infiltration rates of disturbed surfaces generally result in increased erosion (Johnson and Beschta 1980, Wronski 1984, Beasley et al. 1986) for up to 6 years. It is possible, however, for erosion to be significant during the susceptible period for a given site if infiltration rate or capacity is reduced to less than that required to absorb the water delivered by a storm (Fig. 4.7). The occurrence of a major rainstorm during a susceptible period (e.g., B in Fig. 4.7) could degrade long-term productivity; at other less vulnerable times (e.g., period A), damage might be slight.

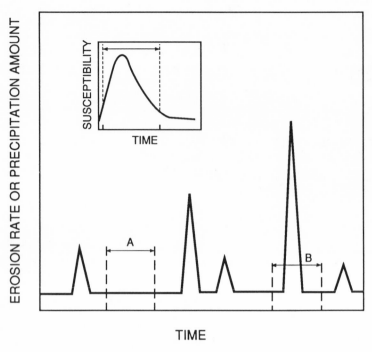

FIG. 4.7. Relation of site susceptibility to erosion damage, depending on frequency and timing of precipitation. Occurrence of a large storm during a particularly susceptible period (see inset) such as B could substantially damage productivity; occurrence at less susceptible times (e.g., A) might have little impact.

Effects of Fire

Fire directly affects the soil physical resource by consuming soil organic matter (Wells et al. 1979), altering soil clay or organic colloids (Tarrant 1956, Ralston and Hatchell 1971), creating hydrophobic (water-repellent) layers (Henderson and Golding 1983), decreasing infiltration rates (Dyrness 1976), and increasing solar energy absorbed by the blackened soil surface (Holbo and Childs 1987). The worst fire effects documented have come from studies of machine piling and burning for site preparation (Tarrant 1956, Wells et al. 1979). However, none of the above-mentioned direct effects is likely to decrease long-term productivity if fire intensities and temperatures are kept low.

Destruction of soil organic matter and alteration of soil colloids are generally observed only after extremely hot fires such as those beneath burning slash piles (Tarrant 1956). Yet severely burned sites generally cover less than 5% of harvested areas following slash burning (Tarrant 1956, Wells et al. 1979). Furthermore, fire almost never consumes the entire forest floor, let alone the organic matter in the mineral soil (Pritchett 1979). Water repellency and increased absorption of solar radiation by the blackened soil surface appear to last only one or two growing seasons. The effects of water repellency are also minimal because the areal extent is commonly patchy.

Prescribed fire has indirect effects on the soil which are more important than the direct effects previously listed. Removal of the forest floor or decrease in forest-floor thickness substantially changes the energy environment at the soil surface. In temperate-zone forests, higher soil-surface temperatures temporarily create a less favorable environment for tree establishment. Increased water loss from surface evaporation may be offset by temporary control of competing vegetation (Haase 1986); however, if the surface litter layer is removed for more than a few years, plants, especially small ones, are likely to be stressed (Ginter et al. 1979). Increase in soil temperature and wetting cycles near the soil surface also accelerates the decomposition of soil organic matter (Morris and Pritchett 1983).

Loss of soil organic matter allows precipitation to strike directly on the exposed surface of the mineral soil. This can result in disaggregation of surface structure (Wells et al. 1979) increasing soil density and decreasing soil aeration and infiltration. Because these effects occur near the surface, they are probably short lived. There is, however, the potential for significant erosion during this period (Tiedemann et al. 1979). If erosion is severe, productivity may decline because enriched topsoil is lost before revegetation and other natural recovery processes stabilize the site.

Although fire generally causes short-term phenomena, the temporarily harsh environment could delay reforestation. Where a soil is quite fragile (e.g., extremely shallow, with very little native fertility or buffering capacity, on steep or exposed areas susceptible to erosion, in a harsh microclimate), even a short initial delay in reforestation may result in conditions which retard reestablishment of a productive stand.

Some evidence suggests that, in many forests, soil organic matter is preserved despite the consumption of the forest floor by fire (Kraemer and Hermann 1979). First, the residence time of organic matter in the forest floor is estimated to be less than 20 years (Waring and Schlesinger 1985). Further, fine-root turnover rates appear to be high enough to maintain soil organic matter (Santantonio 1982). In fact, some studies indicate that soil organic matter levels do not vary significantly with time after logging (Kraemer and Hermann 1979, Durgin 1980). There also is evidence to suggest that soil organic matter levels are increased in fire-prone ecosystems (Wells 1971) and that levels are quite high in western Oregon and Washington where the mesic climate is conducive to rapid decomposition (Boyer and Dell 1980).

Soil Removal

Short-term growth appears to be strongly affected when topsoil is removed. Effects are most severe on shallow soils but can be important on deeper soils as well. The primary effect of soil removal is that it decreases organic matter levels and nutrient supply (Klock 1982). However, the process of removing soil involves use of tractive machines on most of the site, superimposing the added detrimental effects of soil compaction and surface disturbance. Furthermore, where soil is removed during operations such as machine piling and burning, the site may also sustain fire damage.

Soil removal is frequently a by-product of site preparation intended to control competing vegetation. Short-term studies of these practices are, therefore, often inconclusive because the damaging effects of soil removal are mitigated by the short-term benefits of vegetation control (Tuttle et al. 1985). There is little question, however, when studies of long-term growth (e.g., Coile and Schumacher 1953, Glass 1976) or soil nutrient status (Klock 1982, Tuttle et al. 1985) are considered: removing topsoil adversely affects long-term site productivity.

EFFECTS OF SPECIFIC TIMBER-MANAGEMENT PRACTICES

During the harvest-regeneration cycle changes in physical soil properties occur. Effects can take the form of soil surface disturbance, alteration of all or a portion of the soil profile, or soil loss. Specific impacts are:

(1) *Exposure of mineral soil surface:* Loss of organic layers of humus and litter directly reduces nutrient supply. In addition, marked changes in water and energy fluxes may produce a harsh microclimate.

(2) *Changes in soil physical properties:* Properties of the soil profile affected by management practices include (a) soil structure, (b) soil density, (c) organic matter content and distribution, and (d) amount, distribution, and continuity of pore space.

(3) *Soil removal:* Both mass displacement and erosion decrease the effective soil volume for root development and water, heat, and gas storage. Soil removal also decreases nutrient content and microbial activity of the soil profile.

In most situations, the effect of an operation is determined by site-specific factors. Impact of machine piling, for instance, depends on the particular slope, soil type, amount of slash piled, equipment used, operator skill, and soil moisture during the operation. In other cases (e.g., broadcast burning), the effects are quite general. As a result, the information summarized in Table 4.2 serves only as guidelines which should not be used without considering site-specific factors. An understanding of the forest ecosystem must be coupled with field experience or practical guidelines for the effects of forest management on the physical aspects of long-term site productivity to be assessed.

TABLE 4.2. General effects of specific management practices on three categories of impacts on forest soils.

	Exposure of mineral soil surface	Changes in soil physical properties	Soil displacement and erosion
Logging			
Mechanical felling	Little or no change over yarding.	Moderate to high increase in soil density on 40–80% of area. Little loss of OM.[1]	Little or no change over yarding.
Tractive yarding	Soil in 20–40% of area harvested exposed, increases with repeated entries. 7–15% exposed with designated skid trails.	Moderate to high increase in soil density on 20–40% of area. Increases with repeated entries. High increase in density on 7–15% of area with designated skid trails. Low loss of OM.	Little or no change on slopes less than 30% but increases rapidly as skid trails are excavated on steeper slopes.
Skyline or aerial yarding	Soil in 0–10% of area exposed; often dispersed or discontinuous. Varies with tree size and logging layout.	Low to moderate increase in soil density on 0–10% of area. Little or no loss of OM.	Little or no change.
Site preparation by tractive machines			
Machine piling of slash and mechanical control of vegetation (scarification)	Soil in up to 80% of area may be exposed.	Low to high increase in soil density on 60–80% of area not compacted during logging. Moderate to high loss of OM on 30–50% of piled area; some gain in OM in unburned piles and windrows.	20–80% of soil displaced; largest on steep (greater than 35%) slopes.
Site preparation by burning			
Hand piling	5–20% of area burned, with 2–10% exposed soil.	No change in soil density. 5–30% loss of OM.	Little or no change.
Machine piling	10–20% of area burned, with up to 90% exposed soil.	10–60% increase in soil density on 60–80% of area not in skid trails. 5–50% loss of OM.	20–80% of soil displaced; largest on steep slopes.
Broadcast burning of slash or chemical treatment and burning of unwanted vegetation.	40–75% of tractor-logged areas burned between skid trails. Up to 95% of skyline area burned with 10–15% exposed soil.	No increase in soil density or loss of OM except for 2–10% of area, which is severely burned. Effect on soil structure and pore space limited to a few centimeters at severely burned locations.	Little or no change; some surface erosion of soil on steep slopes, especially coarse-textured soils. Streambank erosion accelerated.

[1]Soil organic matter.

QUESTIONS FROM THE SYMPOSIUM FLOOR

Q: Does the development of root systems of seral shrubs and herbs help to ameliorate the impacts of harvest activities on soil structure and other physical properties?

A: Root penetration, other biological activity, organic matter additions, and freeze-thaw cycles are the important natural processes that ameliorate compacted soil conditions. Development of soil structure depends directly on the biological activity in a soil. Therefore, seral shrubs and herbs are important in the process of recovery from damage. Root systems are vital because they ramify through the soil and stimulate biological activity. In addition, shrub canopies may well protect fungi and microbes critical for soil productivity. In situations where other vegetation does not or cannot occupy a site, the presence of brush may be critical for short-term and, therefore, long-term productivity (Amaranthus and Perry 1987, Perry et al. 1987, Borchers and Perry 1989; poster summary, this volume, J. Borchers and D. Perry).

Q: How does one quantitatively define compaction?

A: Compaction is defined as an increase in soil bulk density. The definition is good but very narrow in scope. There are two major inadequacies in the information available about "compaction damage." First, field studies of compaction almost never separate the effects of compaction from the effects of other factors (e.g., soil removal or displacement). The studies provide information about logging damage at a site but do not directly address compaction alone. Second, the areal pattern of compaction has a large impact on the damage caused by the increase in soil density. This dependence on spatial variability makes the study of soil compaction challenging.

Q: Does soil texture affect rate of compaction (e.g., two trips of a logging vehicle over sandy loam vs. two trips over clay loam)?
    AND
    To what degree does soil wetness play a role in the amount of compaction from tractor logging on a site (e.g., if the site is dry, do you have to worry about compaction)?

A: I group these questions together because I feel that the intent is to develop rules to follow based on easily determined soil properties. In my opinion, such rules are too simplistic. Foresters have the knowledge and ability to make more complex decisions about the risks associated with various logging practices; simplifying to averages and rules is inappropriate. I offer these specific views on the two questions:
    (1) The relationship between texture and compaction is drastically affected by soil organic matter content and water content. Furthermore, guidelines to prevent compaction by limiting the number of equipment passes must also account for site slope, water status, and other factors that may influence site productivity.
    (2) The effect of soil wetness is important to soil compaction but is only one of a number of factors that must be considered. It is also worth noting that the original impetus behind developing soil water content guidelines for compaction damage may have had more to do with issues of soil surface disturbance and puddling than with actual compaction.
    (3) The best soil-damage guidelines I know of are those which restrict the total area covered by tractive machines and those which specify that surface damage be kept to a small percentage of total area. Logging practices gentle enough to maintain the soil surface intact will minimize soil compaction as well.

Q: Intense burning has been shown to degrade site. Yet some, but by no means all, of our tractor piles and landing decks that have been burned show significant growth increases over adjacent units. Could you explain?

A: There are a number of reasons why tractor piles or landing decks have good growth over the short term. Tractor piles may well have better nutrient status because of the piled material and less soil compaction because they are the only spots on the landscape without compaction damage. Landings may have good short-term growth if site resources are more available than at other places in the unit. It is commonly observed that less canopy cover and increased rainfall collection along roadsides results in better growth for the adjacent trees. Vegetation control on compacted ground also may improve resource availability (see chapter 7, this volume). (However, it is noteworthy that the trees which may grow well on skid roads during the early years of establishment cease rapid growth after 10–15 years.

Q: Given the following site-preparation techniques, which causes the least soil disturbance: (a) scarification, (b) fire, or (c) herbicides?

A: As a university scientist, I believe that (1) it depends and (2) more research is needed. Now, a more serious answer must treat three facets not specified in the question. First, the intensity of the techniques must be known before a comparison can be made. Second, the resource status of a specific site must be known to determine what the limiting factors on the site are. Third, the long-term effects of these site-preparation techniques may well be different from the short-term effects. After all, herbicides were restricted on federal lands partly because the long-term effects of their application were unknown. Finally, let me note that some comparisons between scarification and burning are given in Table 4.2 of this chapter.

Q: On cold sites, isn't a scattered to broken pattern of organic cover better than total cover or total removal? Too much cover—too cold? Too little cover—too warm and too dry?

A: Your question indicates that you understand both the physics of the situation and spatial variability. An organic cover (mulch) restricts heat and water transport. As a result, covered soils are wet and cold in the spring. Uncovered soils have large fluxes of heat and water that create extremes. Since you want neither of these conditions all the time, the solution is to apply a patchy treatment to get both effects at different places on the landscape. I applaud you for pointing out that the right answer is almost always in the middle; the extremes are seldom proper.

Q: If you could ban one forest-management practice, what would it be?

A: I would ban the adoption of rigid rules governing use of various site-preparation and logging methods. Such rules oversimplify both the effect of a technique on an ecosystem and our knowledge about ecosystem response to forest management. I recognize that there are many things we do not fully understand, but I feel that a thorough analysis should not be replaced by rules in forest management.

Issues of long-term forest productivity will be resolved in political arenas and foresters should be ready to participate effectively. Social politics and communication are the most important skills a land manager can add to technical skills in resource management.

REFERENCES

Adams, W. A. 1973. The effect of organic matter on the bulk and true densities of some cultivated podzolic soils. *Journal of Soil Science* 24:10–17.

Alexander, E. B. 1982. *Available water capacities of California soils in relation to water retention at different matric potentials.* Earth Resources Note 82–133. San Francisco, Calif.: Region 5, USDA Forest Service.

Amaranthus, M. P., and D. A. Perry. 1987. Effect of soil transfer on ectomycorrhiza formation and the survival and growth of conifer seedlings on old nonreforested clear-cuts. *Canadian Journal of Forest Research* 17:944–950.

Beasley, R. S., A. B. Granillo, and V. Zillmer. 1986. Sediment losses from forest management: mechanical versus chemical site preparation after clearcutting. *Journal of Environmental Quality* 15:413–416.

Borchers, S., and D. A. Perry. 1989. Growth and mycorrhiza formation of Douglas-fir seedlings grown in soils collected at different distances from pioneering hardwoods in Southwest Oregon. Submitted to *Canadian Journal of Forest Research.*

Boyer, D. E., and J. D. Bell. 1980. *Fire effects on Pacific Northwest forest soils.* Report R6-WM-040. Portland, Ore.: Region 6, USDA Forest Service.

Bridge, B. J., and A. J. Rixon. 1976. Oxygen uptake and respiratory quotient of field cores in relation to their air-filled pore space. *Journal of Soil Science* 27:279–286.

Brown, R. B. 1975. *Genesis of some soils in the central western Cascades of Oregon.* M.S. Thesis. Corvallis, Ore.: Department of Soil Science, Oregon State University.

Bullock, P., A. C. D. Newman, and A. J. Thomasson. 1985. Porosity aspects of the regeneration of soil structure after compaction. *Soil and Tillage Research* 5:325–341.

Cannell, R. Q. 1977. Soil aeration and compaction in relation to root growth and soil management. *Applied Biology* 2:1–86.

Carmean, W. H. 1975. Forest site quality evaluation in the United States. *Advances in Agronomy* 27:209–269.

Cary, J. W., and C. W. Hayden. 1973. An index for soil pore size distribution. *Geoderma* 9:249–256.

Childs, S. W., and G. Malstaff. 1982. *Final report: heat and mass transfer in unsaturated porous media.* PNL-4036. Richland, Wash.: Battelle Pacific Northwest Laboratory.

Coile, T. S., and F. X. Schumacher. 1953. Relation of soil properties to site index of loblolly and shortleaf pines in the Piedmont region of the Carolinas, Georgia and Alabama. *Journal of Forestry* 51:739–744.

De Jong, R., C. A. Campbell, and W. Nicholaichuk. 1983. Water retention equations and their relationship to soil organic matter and particle size distribution for disturbed samples. *Canadian Journal of Soil Science* 63:291–302.

De Kimpe, C. R., M. Bernier-Cardou, and P. Jolicoeur. 1982. Compaction and settling of Quebec soils in relation to their soil water properties. *Canadian Journal of Soil Science* 62:165–175.

Dobbs, R. C., and R. G. McMinn. 1977. "Effects of scalping on soil temperature and growth of white spruce seedlings." In *Proceedings, 6th British Columbia soil science workshop.* Richmond, B.C., Canada. Victoria, B.C.: British Columbia Ministry of Agriculture.

Durgin, P. B. 1980. *Organic matter content of soil after logging of fir and redwood forests.* Research Note PSW-346. Berkeley, Calif.: Pacific Southwest Forest and Range Experiment Station, USDA Forest Service.

Dyrness, C. T. 1976. *Effect of wildfire on soil wettability in the high Cascades of Oregon.* Research Paper PNW-202. Portland, Ore.: Pacific Northwest Forest and Range Experiment Station, USDA Forest Service.

Eagleman, J. R., and V. C. Jamison. 1962. Soil layering and compaction effects on unsaturated moisture movement. *Soil Science Society of America Proceedings* 26:519–522.

Flint, A. L., and S. W. Childs. 1984. "Physical properties of rock fragments and their effect on available water in skeletal soils." In *Erosion and productivity of soils containing rock fragments*, edited by J. D. Nichols, P. L. Brown, and W. J. Grant, 91–103. Special Publication 13. Madison, Wis.: Soil Science Society of America.

Froehlich, H. A. 1979. Soil compaction from logging equipment: effects on growth of young ponderosa pine. *Journal of Soil and Water Conservation* 34:276–278.

Froehlich, H. A., and D. H. McNabb. 1984. "Minimizing soil compaction in Pacific Northwest forests." In *Forest soils and treatment impacts*, edited by E. L. Stone, 159–192. Proceedings of the 6th American Forest Soils Conference, Knoxville, Tenn.

Giles, D. G., T. A. Black, and D. L. Spittlehouse. 1985. Determination of growing season soil water deficits on a forested slope using water balance analysis. *Canadian Journal of Forest Research* 15:107–114.

Ginter, D. L., K. W. MacLeod, and C. Sherrod. 1979. Water stress in longleaf pine induced by litter removal. *Forest Ecology and Management* 2:13–20.

Glass, G. G., Jr. 1976. *The effects from rootraking on an upland Piedmont loblolly pine* (Pinus taeda L.) *site*. Technical Report No. 56. Raleigh, N.C.: School of Forest Resources, North Carolina State University.

Glinski, J., and W. Stepniewski. 1985. *Soil Aeration and Its Role in Plants*. Boca Raton, Fla.: CRC Press.

Greacen, E. L., and R. Sands. 1980. Compaction of forest soils. A review. *Australian Journal of Soil Research* 18:163–189.

Greenwood, D. J. 1961. The effect of oxygen concentration on the decomposition of organic materials in soil. *Plant and Soil* 14:360–376.

Gupta, S.C., and W. E. Larson. 1979. Estimating soil water retention characteristics from particle size distribution, organic matter percent, and bulk density. *Water Resources Research* 15:1633–1635.

Haase, S. M. 1986. *Effect of prescribed burning on soil moisture and germination of southwestern ponderosa pine seed on basaltic soil*. Research Note RM-462. Fort Collins, Colo.: Rocky Mountain Forest and Range Experiment Station, USDA Forest Service.

Heilman, P. E. 1966. Changes in distribution and availability of nitrogen with forest succession on north slopes in interior Alaska. *Ecology* 47:825–831.

Helms, J. A., and C. Hipkin. 1986. Effects of soil compaction on tree volume in a California ponderosa pine plantation. *Western Journal of Applied Forestry* 1:121–124.

Henderson, G. S., and D. L. Golding. 1983. The effect of slash burning on the water repellency of forest soils at Vancouver, British Columbia. *Canadian Journal of Forest Research* 13:353–355.

Holbo, H. R., and S. W. Childs. 1987. Summertime radiation balances of clearcut and shelterwood slopes in southwest Oregon. *Forest Science* 33:504–516.

Incerti, M., P. F. Clinnick, and S. T. Willatt. 1987. Changes in the physical properties of a forest soil following logging. *Australian Forest Research* 17:91–98.

Jakobsen, B. F., and G. A. Moore. 1981. Effects of two types of skidders and of a slash cover on soil compaction by logging of mountain ash. *Australian Forest Research* 11:247–255.

Johnson, M. G., and R. L. Beschta. 1980. Logging, infiltration capacity, and surface erodibility in western Oregon. *Journal of Forestry* 6:334–337.

Klock, G. O. 1982. "Some soil erosion effects on forest soil productivity." In *Determinants of soil loss tolerance: proceedings of a symposium*, 53–66. Special Publication 45. Madison, Wis.: Soil Science Society of America.

Kraemer, J. F., and R. K. Hermann. 1979. Broadcast burning: 25-year effects on forest soils in the western flanks of the Cascade Mountains. *Forest Science* 25:427–439.

Lenhard, R. J. 1986. Changes in void distribution and volume during compaction of a forest soil. *Soil Science Society of America Journal* 50:462–464.

MacRae, R. J., and G. R. Mehuys. 1985. The effect of green manuring on the physical properties of temperate-area soils. *Advances in Soil Science* 3:71–94.

Marshall, J. D. 1986. Drought and shade interact to cause fine root mortality in Douglas-fir seedlings. *Plant and Soil* 91:51–60.

Miles, D. W. R., F. J. Swanson, and C. T. Youngberg. 1984. Effects of landslide erosion on subsequent Douglas-fir growth and stocking levels in the western Cascades, Oregon. *Soil Science Society of America Journal* 48:667–671.

Miller, J. H., and D. L. Sirois. 1986. Soil disturbance by skyline yarding vs. skidding in a loamy hill forest. *Soil Science Society of America Journal* 50:1579–1583.

Morris, L. A., and W. L. Pritchett. 1983. "Effects of site preparation on *Pinus elliottii-P. palustris* flatwoods forest soil properties." In *IUFRO symposium on forest site and continuous productivity*, edited by R. Ballard and S. P. Gessel, 243–251. General Technical Report PNW-163. Portland, Ore.: Pacific Northwest Forest and Range Experiment Station, USDA Forest Service.

Perry, D. A., R. Molina, and M. P. Amaranthus, 1987. Mychorrhizae, mycorrhizospheres, and reforestation: current knowledge and research needs. *Canadian Journal of Forest Research* 17:929–940.

Pritchett, W. L. 1979. *Properties and Management of Forest Soils*. New York: John Wiley & Sons.

Ralston, C. W., and G. E. Hatchell. 1971. "Effects of prescribed burning on physical properties of soil." In *Prescribed burning symposium proceedings*, 68–85. Asheville, N.C.: Southeastern Forest Experiment Station, USDA Forest Service.

Rawls, W. J. 1983. Estimating soil bulk density from particle size analysis and organic matter content. *Soil Science* 135:123–125.

Reicosky, D.C., W. B. Voorhees, and J. K. Radke. 1981. Unsaturated water flow through a simulated wheel track. *Soil Science Society of America Journal* 45:3–8.

Rice, R. M., J. S. Rothacher, and W. F. Megahan. 1972. "Erosional consequences of timber harvesting: an appraisal." In *Watersheds in transition*, 321–329. Urbana, Ill.: American Water Resources Association Proceedings Series 14.

Sands, R. 1983. "Physical changes to sandy soils planted to radiata pine." In *IUFRO symposium on forest site and continuous productivity*, edited by R. Ballard and S. P. Gessel, 146–152. Portland, Ore.: General Technical Report PNW-163. Pacific Northwest Forest and Range Experiment Station, USDA Forest Service.

Sands, R., E. L. Greacen, and C. J. Gerard. 1979. Compaction of sandy soils in radiata pine forests. I. A penetrometer study. *Australian Journal of Soil Research* 17:101–113.

Santantonio, D. 1982. *Production and turnover of fine roots of mature Douglas-fir in relation to site*. Ph.D. Dissertation. Corvallis, Ore.: College of Forestry, Oregon State University.

Smeltzer, D. L. K., D. R. Bergdahl, and J. R. Donnelly. 1986. Forest ecosystem responses to artificially induced soil compaction. II. Selected soil microorganism populations. *Canadian Journal of Forest Research* 16:870–872.

Sommerfeldt, T. G., and C. Chang. 1987. Soil-water properties as affected by twelve annual applications of cattle feedlot manure. *Soil Science Society of America Journal* 51:7–9.

Sorensen, F. C., and R. K. Campbell. 1978. Comparative roles of soil and air temperatures in the timing of spring bud flush in seedling Douglas-fir. *Canadian Journal of Botany* 56:2307–2308.

Tarrant, R. F. 1956. Effects of slash burning on some soils of the Douglas-fir Region. *Soil Science Society of America Proceedings* 20:408–411.

Tiedemann, A. R., C. E. Conrad, J. H. Dietrich, J. W. Hornbeck, W. F. Megahan, L. A. Viereck, and D. D. Wade. 1979. *Effects of fire on water*. General Technical Report WO-10. Washington, D.C.: USDA Forest Service.

Tuttle, C. L., M.S. Golden, and R. S. Meldahl. 1985. Surface soil removal and herbicide treatment: effects on soil properties and loblolly pine early growth. *Soil Science Society of America Journal* 49:1558–1562.

Waring, R. H., and W. H. Schlesinger. 1985. *Forest Ecosystems: Concepts and Management*. New York: Academic Press.

Wells, C. G. 1971. "Effects of prescribed burning on soil chemical properties and nutrient availability." In *Prescribed burning symposium proceedings*, 86–99. Asheville, N.C.: Southeastern Forest Experiment Station, USDA Forest Service.

Wells, C. G., R. E. Campbell, L. F. DeBano, C. E. Lewis, R. L. Fredrickson, E. C. Franklin, R. C. Froelich, and P. H. Dunn. 1979. *Effects of fire on soil*. General Technical Report WO-7. Washington, D.C.: USDA Forest Service.

Wert, S., and B. R. Thomas. 1981. Effects of skid roads on diameter, height, and volume growth in Douglas-fir. *Soil Science Society of America Journal* 45:629–632.

Williams, J. B., and G. W. Cooke. 1961. Some effects of barnyard manure and of grass residues on soil structure. *Soil Science* 92:30–39.

Williamson, R. L. 1973. *Results of shelterwood harvesting of Douglas-fir in the Cascades of western Oregon*. Research Paper PNW-242. Portland, Ore.: Pacific Northwest Forest and Range Experiment Station, USDA Forest Service.

Wronski, E. B. 1984. Impact of tractor thinning operations on soils and tree roots in a Karri forest, western Australia. *Australian Forest Research* 14:319–332.

Youngberg, C. T. 1959. The influence of soil conditions following tractor logging on the growth of planted Douglas-fir seedlings. *Soil Science Society of America Proceedings* 23:76–78.

Chapter 5

Erosional Processes and Long-Term Site Productivity

Frederick J. Swanson, James L. Clayton, Walter F. Megahan, and George Bush

ABSTRACT

Both natural and management-imposed disturbances of forest ecosystems lead to accelerated soil erosion. However, the areal extent, degree, and duration of management-accelerated erosion vary among erosion processes. Some studies report dramatic increases in surface and debris-slide erosion for periods of a year to a decade or more following clearcutting and slash burning. However, the long-term (multirotational) consequences of these periods of accelerated erosion are unknown at present. In a few situations in the Pacific Northwest, erosion alone appears to have been the primary cause of pronounced, extensive (10+ ha), and prolonged (rotation time scale) reduction of site productivity. More commonly, where severe disturbance has diminished site productivity, erosion acts in combination with other factors, such as loss of nutrients, soil biota such as mycorrhizae, and soil organic matter. Loss of biological integrity of a site leads to loss of physical stability, and the resulting erosion may prolong the period of recovery.

INTRODUCTION

Soil erosion affects long-term site productivity in several ways in the steep, unstable forest land of the Pacific Northwest. Here, we discuss soil erosion—the detachment, transport, and deposition of particles—and distinguish it from soil disturbance (treated in chapter 4)—the modification of soil properties, by processes such as compaction, while soil is in place. Various soil-erosion processes (defined in Table 5.1) can influence site productivity by removing soil and propagules and by disrupting tree growth chronically (frequently, relative to the age of the vegetation) or episodically. Where erosion removes soil from potential tree-growing sites, nutrients and growing medium are lost. This loss can be very serious in mountainous areas because the entire soil mantle may be stripped away, exposing bedrock or infertile subsoil. Where surface erosion and freeze-thaw processes remove propagules such as seedlings or seeds, reestablishment of desired species may be delayed or even prevented. Where chronic soil movement such as large, slow-moving landslides disrupts tree growth by tipping and splitting boles and shearing roots, quantity and quality of forest products are degraded. Unfortunately, few of the effects of any of these processes on site productivity have been assessed. In response to public pressure through legislation and litigation, erosion research in Pacific Northwest forest lands has centered mainly on effects on water quality and fish habitat.

In this chapter, we summarize the relations between erosion processes and site productivity by considering general perspectives on soil loss, the character of forest soils from an erosion viewpoint, the erosion regime in the natural system and in managed forests, and some possible long-term impacts. Time scales of interest range from the short term—for instance, the response time of a forest-soil system to a single disturbance such as wildfire or timber harvest—to the much longer term—for instance, a set of responses, over a thousand years or more, to multiple disturbances such as wildfire or timber harvest. The multiple-disturbance framework is relevant because this is the time scale over which the soil has formed.

DETERMINING SOIL-LOSS TOLERANCE

Many of our perspectives on soil loss come from nonforested agricultural lands. Since 1950, world food output has more than doubled, but this gain has often been achieved by adopting agricultural practices that lead to excessive erosion. Brown (1981) estimates that at least one-fifth, and perhaps as much as one-third, of the world's cropland is eroding at rates sufficiently high to result in long-term declines in productivity. Concern

TABLE 5.1. Definitions of soil erosion processes.

Term	Definition
Creep	Very slow (mm/yr) downslope movement of the soil mantle resulting from deformation of soil under the influence of gravity.
Debris flow	Very fast (m/sec) movement of water-charged soil, alluvium, and vegetation down stream channels.
Debris slide	Very fast movement down hillslopes of soil under the influence of gravity. Commonly containing high concentration of water. Initial sliding surface generally 1–4 m below ground surface.
Earthflow	Slow (cm to m/yr) downslope movement of earth material under the influence of gravity. Moving mass generally 3–20 m thick. Sliding surface is much thinner, and may be planar to irregular in form.
Gully erosion	Removal of soil by running water and development of channels greater than about 0.1 m^2 in cross-sectional area.
Mass movement	Downslope movement of a mass of earth under the influence of gravity. Includes creep, debris flow, debris slide, slump, and earthflow.
Overland flow erosion	Soil movement resulting from unchannelized flow of water in a thin film over the ground surface.
Raindrop splash erosion	Detachment and transport of soil particles resulting from the impact of rain or throughfall drops.
Ravel	Downslope particle-by-particle movement of soil on steep slopes resulting from soil detachment by wetting-drying, freezing-thawing, animal activity, or other processes not involving precipitation and overflow.
Rill erosion	Soil movement by channelized flow of surface water as it erodes rills (small channels less than about 0.1 m^2 in cross-sectional area).
Slump	Slow to fast (m/hr to cm/yr) rotational mass movement along concave sliding surface.
Surface erosion	Particle-by-particle movement of soil over the ground surface as a result of gravity or flowing water. Includes ravel, raindrop splash, and overland flow erosion.

about erosion of croplands has led to the concept of soil-loss tolerance (T values), defined as the maximum rate of annual soil erosion that will permit high crop productivity to be sustained economically and indefinitely (Wischmeier and Smith 1978).

Soils vary in their ability to withstand losses from erosion. T values on croplands commonly range from 1 to 10 Mg/ha, depending on soil depth and thickness of the A horizon (uppermost zone of the soil profile where organic matter has accumulated and soluble salts have been leached). T values on forested lands have not been established, principally because of the difficulty in isolating the magnitude of productivity declines accompanying soil loss. Establishing this link in forest stands is greatly complicated by large variation in erosion rates over small areas, variability in annual precipitation (no irrigation), length of growth cycle from planting to harvest and the changing dynamics of crop growth over this cycle, variable effects of diseases, pests, and fertility levels, and differences in dominant erosion processes between steep forest terrain and relatively flat agricultural fields.

Determining soil-loss tolerance also requires estimating the rate of soil formation (pedogenesis) to offset erosion losses. Most cropland soils are formed on relatively deep, unconsolidated alluvium (deposits of stream-transported sediment) or colluvium (deposits of material transported by gravitational processes), and soil-formation rates are dictated by pedogenic processes such as accretion of organic matter, transport of dissolved bases, and redistribution of free silica, sesquioxides, and clays. Large areas of Northwest forest land are located on montane sites (Coast Range, Cascade Range, Northern Rocky Mountains) marked by poorly developed soils formed over consolidated bedrock. Although the same pedogenic processes are at work, rates of soil formation are more often limited by the rates of advance of the bedrock weathering front, soil mixing, and erosion processes characteristic of steep forested slopes. McCormack et al. (1982) suggest that soil-forming processes are much slower on mountain slopes than in unconsolidated alluvium. To arrive at estimates of soil-formation rates on upland slopes, we rely on watershed studies of chemical and erosional denudation, by measuring the amount of weathered material removed in solution and sediment transport. This approach assumes that soil depth averaged over an undisturbed watershed is in a state of quasi-equilibrium, so the weathering front advances at a rate equal to that of the denudation loss (Clayton and Megahan 1986). This is probably a reasonable assumption on the time scales of centuries to a few millennia for mountain areas of the Pacific Northwest.

Calculating T values for forest land is further complicated because the land-use systems and physical environment of forestry in the western United States differ from those of agricultural lands in several important respects. First, the forest crop is harvested much less frequently than agricultural crops. Second, forestry disturbs the land in different ways and to differing degrees than agriculture, generally involving less intensive individual site treatment, but requiring road construction. Finally, erosion in steep landscapes is unlikely to be uniform in space, concentrated on localized sites and commonly involving considerable deposition downslope, or in time, dominated by landslides which occur infrequently.

THE FOREST SOIL RESOURCE

As the rooting medium for higher plants, soils provide four essentials: water, most nutrients, structural support, and soil biota. First, according to the National Soil Erosion-Soil Productivity Research Planning Committee (1981), erosion reduces crop productivity mainly by decreasing the amount of soil water available to plants; this is a result of changing the water-holding characteristics and thickness of the rooting zone. Even for deep-rooted trees, this is a likely consequence of erosion except in deep depositional soils in swales or on terraces. Second, erosion removes nutrients available to plants. Fertilizer applications can partly offset these losses in intensively managed stands, but at greatly increased cost. Third, erosion may reduce productivity by degrading soil structure. Removal of loose, organic surface soils promotes surface sealing and crusting, decreasing infiltration capacity and increasing erosion (see chapter 4, this volume). Fourth, erosion results in loss of important soil biota, such as mycorrhizal fungi, which facilitate nutrient uptake by plants (see chapter 3, this volume).

Surface erosion proceeds downward, removing first the surface layers of organic matter (O horizon), then A horizon material, and so forth. Soil horizons have differing capacities for supplying nutrients and holding water, so loss of productivity is not directly proportional to depth of erosion. Because the highest concentrations of nutrients and biota and the maximum water-holding capacity are in the uppermost soil horizons (Table 5.2, Fig. 5.1), incremental removals of soil nearer the surface are more damaging than those of subsoils.

TABLE 5.2. Distribution of available nutrients and water-holding capacity (WHC), by soil horizon, for a granitic soil in central Idaho. Nutrient extraction procedures are described by Clayton and Kennedy (1985); available water is 0.033 minus 1.5 MPa extractable percentage by volume.

Soil parameter	Soil horizon		
	O	A	C
	----------------------%----------------------		
Potassium	0.11	0.015	0.007
Calcium	1.08	0.052	0.033
Magnesium	0.12	0.006	0.004
Nitrogen	0.57	0.071	0.025
Phosphorus	0.06	0.005	0.002
Sulfur	0.044	0.006	0.004
WHC	—	11.3	4.1

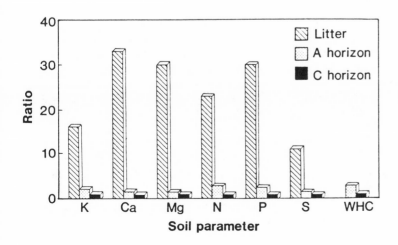

FIG. 5.1. Vertical distribution of nutrient elements potassium (K), calcium (Ca), magnesium (Mg), nitrogen (N), phosphorus (P), and sulfur (S) and available water-holding capacity (WHC) for a granitic soil in central Idaho, expressed as ratios of concentration in the C horizon (soil material relatively little affected by organisms and chemical and physical weathering).

EROSION IN THE NATURAL SYSTEM

In the natural system, soil and sediment move downslope and into streams by a variety of surface erosion processes (Table 5.1), interrupted by periods of temporary storage. Soil is stored on hillslopes behind downed logs, in upturned root wads, and in the soil mantle itself. Bedrock hollows (also termed swales, headwalls, and zero-order basins) are important temporary storage sites that fill slowly over decades to millennia and empty abruptly by small-scale sliding (Dietrich et al. 1982).

These processes of soil transfer and temporary storage are commonly referred to as the sediment-routing system and are quantified in terms of a sediment budget (Dietrich and Dunne 1978, Swanson et al. 1982, Megahan et al. 1986). Comparing sediment budgets of several basins reveals both similarities and differences (Swanson et al. 1987). In the published sediment budgets for the Pacific Northwest, landsliding is a major source of sediment, and surface erosion is of minor importance. However, cohesionless soils formed from granitic rocks (e.g., in the Idaho Batholith) and skeletal soils in general are prone to erosion by raindrop splash and dry ravel, especially when soil strength imparted by roots, mycorrhizae, and other organic matter is reduced (Megahan 1981). Areas with clay-rich soils, such as parts of north coastal California and southwest Oregon, and areas where soil compaction is widespread experience high surface erosion by overland flow and gullying (Kelsey 1980, Kelsey et al. 1981).

Sediment production rates by individual erosion processes, however, are not closely related to site productivity. More relevant measures of erosion impact include the extent of the area affected by erosion; the extent of the affected area that had the potential to grow trees; the water-holding capacity and nutrient and biotic content of the material moved; and the availability of the eroded material to support tree growth elsewhere. Soil creep and deep-seated, slow-moving slumps and earthflows mobilize large volumes of soil, but only a very small fraction of it is removed from potential tree-growing sites. Shallow, rapid debris slides, on the other hand, mobilize smaller volumes of soil, but commonly a large percentage of the moved soil is transported to stream channels. All of these processes of mass soil movement typically involve the entire rooting zone and even sub-soil. The average nutrient content of material transported by mass movement processes is lower than that of the nutrient-rich materials transported by surface erosion processes.

Surface erosion processes are also widespread, but scars of debris slides generally cover less than 1 or 2% of slide-prone landscapes (Ice 1985). Soil creep, though widespread, produces little soil disruption, and movement rates are very slow, measured in millimeters per year. Slump and earthflow terrain may cover more than 20% of the landscape, and movement rates may be high enough (greater than 1–2 m/year) to cause severe disruption of forest vegetation, although areas of such rapid movement are rather rare.

In many steep basins, debris slides may be the dominant mechanism of sediment production and downstream damage to fish habitat, but may have only a minor impact on long-term site productivity because they involve small areas. To assess the effects of slide scars on long-term site productivity, we must consider establishment (stocking) and growth of desired species, loss of canopy and rooting space, and percentage of total landscape area occupied by slide scars young enough to have an effect. In a study of 5–18 year old Douglas-fir [*Pseudotsuga menziesii* (Mirb.) Franco] slide scars in the Oregon Cascade Range, Miles et al. (1984) observed 38% less height growth and 25% lower stocking than in restocked clearcuts of the same age. One-third of the area of slide scars (mean area/scar 460 m^2, range 36–1,287 m^2) was estimated to be nonstockable because of unstable or impenetrable substrate. However, Douglas-fir had the highest percentage of cover on slide scars of the more than 140 species identified (Miles and Swanson 1986).

Conditions at this site in the central western Oregon Cascades appear to be more favorable for recovery of commercial forest on slide scars than elsewhere in the Pacific Northwest. In other areas, for example, competition from noncommercial species [e.g., where alder (*Alnus* spp.) establishes dense stands (Smith et al. 1986)], persistent physical instability from surface erosion (e.g., in raveling soils in southwest Oregon), large areas of scars (e.g., common in glaciated terrain), and other factors may considerably slow recovery of commercial productivity on slide scars. This difference has not been quantified to any significant extent, however. Not all areas with high susceptibility to sliding ever had complete cover of commercial species; consequently, assessing productivity losses by comparing slide scars with adjacent, unaffected sites well stocked with conifers may be misleading. Furthermore, establishment of alder, ceanothus (*Ceanothus* spp.), or other nitrogen-fixing, noncrop plants may be an important step in the recovery process.

Active earthflows can significantly affect site productivity as a result of chronic disruption—measurable in terms of the mean angle of lean of trees and percentage of tree stems with curved ("pistol") butts. In the Douglas-fir forests of the central Oregon Cascades, tree disruption increases with increased earthflow velocity (Vest 1988) (Fig. 5.2). If the land moves more than several meters per year, the conifer overstory breaks up and hardwoods are more prevalent. The tilt and deformation of stems increase progressively with increased earthflow-movement rate (Fig. 5.2).

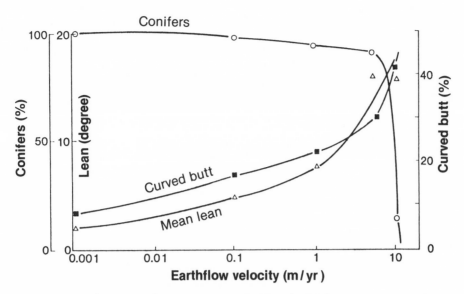

FIG. 5.2. Characteristics of trees in relation to movement rate of earthflow on which they grow (Vest 1988). Mean lean is mean angle between vertical and the axis of stem at breast height (about 1.37 m above the ground). At these sites, the major failure plane of the earthflow occurs well below the root zone.

EROSION IN THE MANAGED FOREST

We have emphasized that erosion is a part of the natural landscape. Forest-management activities alter the natural erosion regime by suppressing some processes, accelerating the rates of others, and introducing some new processes and conditions. This array of effects makes assessing the consequences for long-term site productivity difficult. We review here some of the limited information available on impacts of management on erosion.

Sediment Yield from Small Basins

Paired basin studies have been widely used to assess soil loss as a result of forestry practices. In this approach, two or more basins with similar vegetation, topography, and hydrology are monitored for several years before treatment. After this calibration period, one or more basins are "managed" (treated by logging, road construction, or both), and one basin is left undisturbed as a control. A summary of such data (e.g., Table 5.3, Fig. 5.3) reveals substantial variation in suspended-sediment yield, both in the rates for forested control basins and in the magnitudes of increase resulting from management activities. Increased sediment production following logging and road construction can result from increased availability of material for transport and magnitude of peak flows.

Some of the effects of forest management on suspended-sediment yield can be seen in a comparative analysis of results from experimental basins in western Oregon with at least 5 years of record (Fig. 5.3). This sample, selected to minimize climatic and geologic sources of variation, comprises three groups: basins with gentle (less than 35%) slopes, which yield very low levels of suspended sediment, even after road construction, clearcutting, and broadcast burning; basins with steep (greater than 35%) slopes, which yield higher sediment levels, especially where managed; and basins with steep slopes and debris slides, which yield the highest sediment levels and have among the highest increases relative to their control basins. Generally, suspended-sediment yields increase several-fold after logging and road construction. To put these estimates of sediment yield in perspective, all but the highest values are less than 200 Mg km^{-2} yr^{-1} (about the annual yield of the Siuslaw River at Mapleton, Oregon) but less than one-tenth the annual yield of several rivers in northern California, notorious for their extremely high sediment production due to both highly erodible soils and past forestry practices.

However, observations in the experimental basin studies may not accurately reflect accelerated soil loss from logging and road construction. In several basins, much of the soil delivered to channels by debris slides remained stored there through the period of the published record and was not sampled at the gauging station. Furthermore, sediment that entered the channel and was stored there before basin treatment may have been

TABLE 5.3. Site characteristics and mean annual suspended-sediment yield for six sets of experimental basins in western Oregon for which at least 5 years of data exist for each site condition (Larson and Sidle 1980, Swanson et al. 1987).

Basin name and location	Basin area, ha	Mean basin slope, %	Site condition[1]	Suspended-sediment yield, Mg km^{-2} yr^{-1}	Period of record, water yr
Fox Creek, Bull Run, N. Western Cascade Mountains					
Fox 1	59	8	R, 25CC, BB	2.9	1972–79
Fox 2	254	8	R	2.0	70–79
Fox 3	71	8	R, 25CC	2.7	73–79
Coyote Creek, South Umpqua River, S. Western Cascade Mountains					
Coyote 1	69	40	R, 50PC	22	72–79
Coyote 2	68	40	R, 30CC	16	72–79
Coyote 3	50	40	R, 90CC, BB	181	72–79
Coyote 4	50	40	F	47	70–79
H. J. Andrews Experimental Forest, Central Western Cascade Mountains					
HJA 1	96	63	F	8	57–61
HJA 1	96	63	100CC, BB	183	67–76
HJA 2	60	61	F	11	57–76
HJA 3	101	53	R, 25CC, BB	456	65–76
HJA 6	13	28	R, 100CC, BB	13	76–79
HJA 7	15	31	50PC	2.5	72–79
HJA 8	21	30	F	11	72–79
HJA 9	9	60	F	3.4	69–79
HJA 10	10	60	F	9.5	76–79
HJA 10	10	60	100CC	57	76–79
Alsea River, Coast Range					
Deer	303	50	F	97	59–65
Deer	303	50	R, 25CC, BB	136	66–73
Needle	71	37	F	53	59–65
Needle	71	37	90CC, BB	146	66–73
Flynn	202	50	F	98	59–73

[1]F = forested, R = roaded, 50CC = 50% of area clearcut, BB = broadcast burned, 50PC = 50% of stand removed in partial cut.

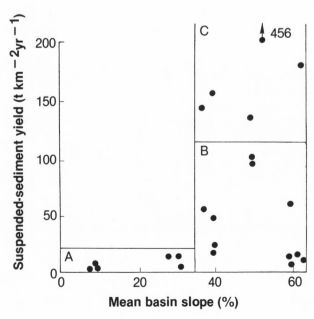

FIG. 5.3. Summary of annual suspended-sediment yield for small experimental basins in western Oregon with at least 5 years of record for forest or treated conditions. (Data are from Table 5.3.). Group A: gentle slopes; 0–100% logged, burned, roaded. Group B: steep slopes; 0–100% logged, roaded. Group C: steep slopes and debris slides; 25–100% logged, burned, roaded.

released when large woody debris was manipulated during logging and road construction. Increased sediment yield resulting from release of this material does not represent soil erosion accelerated by management practices.

In summary, although studies of small experimental watersheds reveal substantial increases in sediment yield after timber harvest and road construction, interpretation is complicated by the importance of localized sediment sources and sites of deposition. The basins with the greatest increases in sediment yield experienced soil and sediment movement by debris slides and debris flows. Slides mobilize material in localized parts of a drainage basin; so soil and sediment volume, even if large, may not represent widespread loss of site productivity. Debris flows may also mobilize large volumes, but most of it may be material that entered the channel previously and had already been removed from the soil mantle used by the growing forest crop. None of the published sediment-budget studies has been designed to consider site-productivity issues specifically.

Debris Slides

Clearcutting and road construction generally increase the frequency and areal extent of debris slides (Ice 1985). However, the proportion of Pacific Northwest landscape in slide scars less than 10–30 years old is generally less than a few percent, even after a major storm that triggers many debris slides (Ice 1985). Moreover, slide scars in this region have little tendency to expand, although some undocumented cases of expansion have been reported. Elsewhere in the world, slide scars have been known to expand progressively to cover 20% or more of the landscape and reduce site productivity over substantial areas. In New Zealand, for example, where volcanic ash mantles steep, hilly country, heavy grazing combined with periodic intense rain storms have progressively stripped the soil developed in the ash from the slopes (Crozier et al. 1980). The initially small slide scars have grown by lateral and headward expansion over a series of large storms. The new soil-vegetation-erosion regime established as a result of management practices (conversion of forest to pasture and subsequent intensive sheep grazing) has resulted in a 21% decrease in site productivity on old slide scars as long as 75 years after sliding (Trustrum et al. 1983). In the area as a whole, total productivity has dropped 16%.

Are current forestry practices in the Pacific Northwest likely to produce similar changes in system function and productivity? Probably not of the type observed in New Zealand, where vegetation type was completely converted on slide-prone soils. But our management practices may change the frequency and size distribution of slides—which may have a greater effect on stream and riparian (streamside) resources than on timber production. This view is based in part on the hypothesis that debris slides in many areas of the Pacific Northwest originate in bedrock-defined depressions (hollows) on hillslopes, which fill slowly and fail periodically, triggering debris slides and flows. In this view, sliding is restricted to those hollows; and because hollows occupy a small percentage of the total landscape area, loss of site productivity is not expected to be widespread.

Debris slides related to roads can occur on landforms that would have little chance of sliding otherwise. By contributing to occurrence of slides, roads further increase the amount of land removed from timber production. Furthermore, slide scars from failed road fills may be slower to recover site productivity than slide scars elsewhere on the landscape because they are less likely to receive material sloughed from adjacent, intact soil and are subject to repeated surface erosion from road runoff. The road surface at the head of a road-fill slide scar may be a source of infertile material that disturbs vegetation recovery on the slide scar rather than enhancing it, as would be true for slide scars with natural soil in the headscarp.

Surface Erosion

Sediment-budget studies suggest that surface erosion, although not a major source of sediment in many forested watersheds, may have disproportionately large significance in terms of site productivity because it is widespread and affects the nutrient-rich surface of the soil. Overland flow and rill erosion produced by overland flow are rare under forest cover in the Pacific Northwest, but are common where soils are compacted or where they are hydrophobic (water repellent) as a result of wildfire or slash burning.

Effects of timber harvest and site preparation on surface erosion have been examined in a few studies of limited scope in the region. A summary of some research at the H. J. Andrews Experimental Forest, near Blue River, Oregon, and neighboring areas of the Willamette National Forest provides examples of the type, duration, and magnitude of effects of forest practices on surface erosion (Tables 5.4, 5.5) (Swanson and Grant 1982). Conducted by different workers using different methods and with different objectives, these studies are not strictly comparable, but do reveal important trends. All studies used erosion collector boxes open on the upslope side; overland flow, if it existed, was usually not sampled. Erosion rates are expressed per unit area,

TABLE 5.4. Description of surface erosion studies in Oregon's Willamette National Forest (Swanson and Grant 1982). Surface erosion data are summarized in Table 5.5. Entries without citations are unpublished data on file at the Forestry Sciences Laboratory, Pacific Northwest Research Station, USDA Forest Service, Corvallis, Oregon, which is the affiliation of all the investigators who furnished unpublished data.

Investigators	Site location[1]	Slope range, %	Length of record, yr	Number of erosion boxes	Width of box opening, m	Contributing catchment area, m²	Frequency of collection, no./yr
Mersereau and Dyrness[2] (1972)	HJA 1	60–80	1.18	10	2.45	62–262 (range)	6
G. W. Lienkaemper and F. J. Swanson[3]	HJA 1	60–80	1.00	8	2.10	63–262	8
Stream Team[4]	HJA 9	26–55	5.50	34	0.5	—[8]	8
	HJA 10	26–55	2.15	34	0.5	—[8]	8
F. J. Swanson[5]	HJA 10	26–55	0.87	34	0.5	—[8]	12
F. M. McCorison[6]							
Site VI	HJA 10	80	3.00	1	16.5	776	4
Sites I, II	HJA 9	95–100	3.25	2	15.7–20.2	214–458	4
Sites III-V	HJA 10	80–88	3.00	3	8.9–9.6	124–171	4
George[7] (1984)	SFM	19–61	1.00	24	1.5	2.3	4

[1]HJA 1–10 = H. J. Andrews Experimental Forest watershed number; SFM = Ryder Creek, South Fork McKenzie River.
[2]Results given by aspect, slope, and duff cover conditions.
[3]Follow-up study to Mersereau and Dyrness (1972) 12 years after burning; erosion boxes in about the same location as before.
[4]Research group at Oregon State University, Corvallis. Erosion boxes placed in clusters along 1400-m stream perimeter.
[5]Erosion boxes placed at 20-m intervals along stream perimeter.
[6]All sites selected to represent maximum surface-erosion rates for forested conditions.
[7]Results given by slope and duff cover; duff removed by burning; site artificially cleaned of slash.
[8]Unbounded erosion boxes; contributing area not determined.

TABLE 5.5. Surface-erosion data, by slope class and treatment, for studies in Oregon's Willamette National Forest (Swanson and Grant 1982). Study descriptions and affiliations of those furnishing unpublished data are summarized in Table 5.4.

Slope class, %	Annual surface-erosion rate, m³ ha⁻¹ yr⁻¹				
	Undisturbed forest	Clearcut, unburned (2 yr after treatment)	Clearcut, unburned (1st decade)	Clearcut, burned (2 yr after treatment)	Clearcut, burned (1st decade)
0–30[1]	6.9×10^{-7}	0.0018	0.00088	0.10	0.050
31–60	0.014[2]	0.18[3]	0.11	0.57[4]	0.32[5]
60+	0.19[6]	—	—	2.9[7]	1.6[8]

[1]All values for this slope class, except that for clearcut, unburned sites (first decade), are averages from George (1984); the value 0.050 is the average of 6.9×10^{-7} and 0.10.
[2]Average of streamside erosion boxes, watersheds 9 and 10, and upslope boxes.
[3]Average of Stream Team (unpublished data; see footnote 4, Table 5.4) and George (1984; first year after cutting).
[4]Average of George (1984; clearcut, burned sites) and Mersereau and Dyrness (1972; sites 5–8).
[5]Average of Mersereau and Dyrness (1972) and G.W. Lienkaemper and F.J. Swanson (unpublished data; sites 5–8).
[6]Average of F.M. McCorison (unpublished data; sites I-IV).
[7]Average of Mersereau and Dyrness (1972; sites 1–4).
[8]Average of Mersereau and Dyrness (1972) and G.W. Lienkaemper and F.J. Swanson (unpublished data; sites 1–4).

based on estimates of contributing area above the collector, except on watersheds 9 and 10 (H. J. Andrews Experimental Forest); in these two watersheds, erosion boxes were located along the stream edge, and soil delivery to the channel was estimated by multiplying the average rate of soil collection per meter of channel perimeter by the total stream perimeter. Surface erosion per unit of hillslope area was then estimated by dividing by total watershed area (9 ha for watershed 9, 10 ha for watershed 10).

Summarized mean surface-erosion rates for various sites and treatments exhibit expected trends (Table 5.5), despite great variability in surface erosion rate among erosion boxes at individual sites. For example, in forested watershed 9, 30 of 47 sample periods had 40% or more of the total soil collected in only one of the 33 erosion boxes. Surface erosion rate greatly increased with increasing slope gradient and was much higher in burned than in unburned clearcuts (Table 5.5). Within 5 years of clearcutting without burning, surface erosion rate (organic + inorganic material) measured at watershed 10 (Fig. 5.4), a steep (average slope gradient = 65%) drainage with hillslopes extending directly to the stream banks along much of their length, appears to have stabilized at about 0.07 m^3 ha^{-1} yr^{-1}, which is about 3 times the rate observed in the forested control, watershed 9. At such sites with moderate disturbance (skyline yarding, no broadcast burning), the period of accelerated surface erosion appears to be brief, relative to the rotation length of 80–100 years.

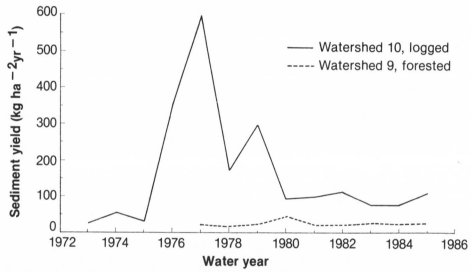

FIG. 5.4. Surface erosion rates 1973–85 for watersheds 9 (forested control) and 10 (clearcut June 1975 without broadcast burning), H. J. Andrews Experimental Forest, Oregon Cascades.

Elsewhere in the region, other types and magnitudes of surface erosion have been observed. Rates of soil ravel are very high in the Oregon Coast Range during and following slash burning on loamy soils developed on the Yachats Basalt Formation and on clay loam to gravel loam soils in sedimentary rocks of the Tyee/Flournoy Formation. Sampling over the first year after burning, Bennett (1982) measured surface erosion at 176 m^3 ha^{-1} yr^{-1} on burned clearcuts with slopes over 60%, 22 m^3 ha^{-1} yr^{-1} on gentler slopes. Unburned clearcut slopes steeper than 60% lost 13 m^3 ha^{-1} yr^{-1}. On the steep, burned sites, 65% of the first year's erosion occurred in the 24-hour period including the fire; the high rates of the immediate post-burn period declined after 8 months to 6.2 m^3 ha^{-1} yr^{-1} and returned to preharvest levels after 2 years. No surface erosion was detected in four erosion boxes placed in the forest.

Surface erosion by ravel is also locally severe in the Klamath Mountains and Idaho Batholith where skeletal soils are widespread. Where roads, streams, and small slide scars cut a steep slope, soil removal to a depth of 1+ m by raveling can progress upslope for distances of 50 m and more over several decades. The rate and extent of soil raveling appear to be greatest where vegetation has been severely disturbed by clearcutting and hot slash burning. Studies of pervasive surface ravel are underway by D. McNabb (McNabb 1985) and by H. Froehlich and M. Pyles (Oregon State University) as part of the Forestry Intensified Research (FIR) program in southwest Oregon. McNabb (1985) observed a 42-fold increase in ravel rate during the harvest period relative to preharvest and control rates, but the ravel rate for 5 post-harvest summer months differed little from that before harvest. Ravel over the following winter declined to half the preharvest rate, a pattern McNabb interprets to be a result of the unburned slash stabilizing the soil surface. The percentage of organic debris in the transported material doubled from before to after harvest (from 10 to 22%), but the relative abundance of coarse and fine fractions changed little.

Several of these studies can be compared on the basis of movement rate of soil into erosion boxes, expressed as soil mass per length of collector opening per unit of time (Table 5.6). The clearcut and burn treatments on steep (greater than 60%) Coast Range slopes produced by far the greatest rate of surface erosion. Unfortunately, no other sites are available with full measurements for the first year after clearcut and burn treatments on slopes greater than 60%. Cutting without burning substantially increased surface movement rate in two of the three cases.

TABLE 5.6. Surface erosion for forested areas in Oregon and Idaho for 1 year after treatment, expressed as grams of organic and inorganic soil collected per meter of contour line per day[1].

Erosion study sites, by treatment and slope gradient	Number of erosion boxes	Surface-erosion rate, $g \ m^{-1} \ day^{-1}$
>60% Slope		
Undisturbed forest		
Coast Range	4	0
Klamath Mountains	6	9
Cascade Range	30–34	0.4
Clearcut, burned		
Coast Range	24	230
Clearcut, unburned		
Coast Range	4	33
Klamath Mountains	19	7
Cascade Range	34	8
<60% Slope		
Clearcut, burned		
Coast Range	8	8
Idaho Batholith	11	0.5

[1]Assuming bulk density = 1.0 g/cm³, except for Idaho Batholith, where bulk density = 1.3 g/cm³. Coast Range from Bennett (1982), Klamath Mountains from McNabb (1985), Cascade Range from the H. J. Andrews Experimental Forest (G. W. Lienkaemper and F. J. Swanson, unpublished data, Pacific Northwest Research Station, USDA Forest Service), and Idaho Batholith from Clayton (1981).

The data summarized in Table 5.6 are for the first year after treatment only. Studies covering longer periods typically have found higher surface-movement rates in the second year after treatment (Clayton 1981; George 1984; D. McNabb, personal communication, Oregon State University, 1987) (Fig. 5.4). Several workers have speculated that decomposition of slash may be a factor. If so, surface erosion rates for sites that lose fine litter when burned probably peak earlier than those for unburned sites.

Even modest rates of downslope movement of slash and soil, perhaps with the help of the downhill creep of a snowpack, can damage seedlings, resulting in substantial loss of management investment and perhaps delayed regeneration. The title of an early paper on the subject—"Are your seedlings being buried?" (Franklin and Rothacher 1962)—raises the issue. In the only recent study, McNabb (1986) observed minor ravel-related mortality of seedlings on a steep, clearcut, but unburned site. In this case, use of ravel guards to protect seedlings was unnecessary.

In summary, surface erosion is important to site productivity because it can be widespread and may retard reforestation. As pointed out by Rice et al. (1971), burning is the major factor in accelerating surface erosion where cable yarding has been used. Results of studies indicate that the period of accelerated surface erosion is generally short relative to the rotation length. Unfortunately, we have few samples of surface erosion rates in areas experiencing wildfire and its erosional aftermath as a point of reference for judging effects of forestry practices [the work of Megahan and Molitor (1975) is a notable exception].

Forest Roads

Forest roads can have significant effects on site productivity through mechanisms of both site disturbance and erosion. In a recent review paper, Megahan (1988) summarizes results of published and unpublished studies on effects of roads on the area removed from timber production and on road-related impacts on hydrology and soil properties that influence tree establishment and growth. He finds that road construction can initially affect 1–30% of the landscape—much of which may be available for tree growth after construction. Site conditions are poorest on the cut portion of the road bed and backslope, but tree height growth is typically no different for fills and adjacent areas. Growth may be greater on fill slopes than on undisturbed slopes in some locales. Cutslopes and road drainage to downslope areas can increase or decrease productivity, depending on local site conditions and the importance of water as a limiting factor in tree growth.

Generally, Megahan (1988) concludes that productivity loss is less than that reflected in the area directly affected by initial road construction. At some sites, however, debris slides and substantial modification of the ground-water system translate road impacts up and down the slope.

LONG-TERM CONSIDERATIONS

Stability or change in site productivity must be evaluated on the scale of thousands of years, because this is the scale of soil development. The residence time of soil on steep slopes in a small Cascade Range drainage basin, for example, is about 10,000 years, assuming average soil thickness of 1 m in a 10-ha basin divided by average annual export of 1 m^3/ha for soil and sediment with bulk density of 1,000 kg/m^3 (Swanson et al. 1982). Important considerations at this time scale include the effects of management practices on the rate of soil formation by processes such as weathering and the rate of soil loss, including that induced by vegetation disturbance. Unfortunately, very little is known about the effects of forestry on soil formation in Northwest forest soils. A bit more is known about the effects of disturbance on soil erosion rates, so we will discuss this subject briefly.

Ultimately, analysis of long-term site conditions must consider the natural disturbance regime of the landscape. By disturbance regime, we refer to the characteristic types, frequencies, intensities, and durations of events that alter vegetation and soil properties. Forestry replaces the natural disturbance regime (wildfire, "blowdown," landslides) with a management disturbance regime (harvest, roads, prescribed fire, vegetation control).

In many steep areas, an important part of the long-term soil loss occurs in pulses of erosion after vegetation has been disturbed. Swanson (1981) suggested a simple approach to evaluating the effect of a disturbance regime on soil erosion by assessing the frequency, magnitude, and duration of an erosion peak resulting from a disturbance such as wildfire. The amount of erosion produced by a series of disturbances is compared to the baseline erosion in the period between peaks, yielding a measure of the contribution of major vegetation disturbances to the long-term erosion rate. On the basis of some simple assumptions, Swanson (1981) estimated that wildfire-accelerated erosion accounted for about 23% of long-term erosion in the central western Cascade Range. In a chaparral system with more frequent, intense fire and greater erosional response to fire, about 75% of the long-term erosion rate was apparently fire related. Depending on the frequency and intensity of vegetation disturbance, as well as the sensitivity of a landscape to erosion, a particular area may have greater or lesser erosional response to disturbance.

Consideration of the frequency and magnitude of episodes of accelerated erosion is a useful frame of reference for discussing the effects of forestry on erosion and site productivity. Soil erosion and site productivity in ecosystems where the management disturbance regime differs negligibly from the natural disturbance regime are likely to remain basically unchanged. We know little about natural disturbance regimes, however, and even less about their effects on soil for many ecosystems where intensive forestry is being practiced. In the Douglas-fir forests of the western Oregon Cascades, for example, the perception of the natural fire regime is now changing substantially. These forests were thought to have experienced very infrequent (return period of several centuries), widespread, stand-replacement fires as the dominant element of the disturbance regime. Recent field studies (Morrison 1984, Stewart 1986, Teensma 1987) suggest that more frequent (return period of about 100 years) fires of moderate and low severity are an important part of the disturbance story.

In summary, an important, neglected ingredient in analyzing effects of forestry on site productivity is management of changes in the disturbance regime on the scale of centuries before and after first entry. From a management perspective, we should be concerned about changing the natural disturbance regime on sites sensitive to erosion. For instance, steep areas in which vegetation and soils have developed in a regime of frequent, low-intensity, short-duration fire may experience severe erosion problems as a result of slash burning; if unusually prolonged, high soil-surface temperature kills sprouting brush species, destroys soil structure stabilized by organic matter, and disturbs other soil-stabilizing mechanisms. In central Idaho, Steele et al. (1986) observed that, before 1895, the fire regime was dominated by low-severity fire at 10–20 year intervals. Suppression efforts since then have lengthened the interval, but increased the potential for severe, stand-replacement fires which can substantially reduce long-term site productivity.

CONCLUSIONS

Although forestry practices in the Pacific Northwest can accelerate soil loss, erosion alone is seldom the cause of greatly reduced site productivity, except on slide scars and sites of persistent ravel, which are generally local in extent. On severely disturbed sites, however, erosion acts in combination with other factors to reduce productivity on the scale of decades to centuries. Extreme disturbance by intense wildfire or tractor yarding, for example, may cause loss of nutrients, mycorrhizae, and organic matter. These losses not only reduce long-term site productivity, but may also lead to sustained periods of accelerated erosion because the soil-stabilizing effects of live and dead organic matter are reduced or even eliminated. The two major influences of erosion processes in such cases are to remove soil and chronically disturb sites, thus delaying establishment. By these mechanisms, severe disruption can exceed thresholds of ecosystem resistance both physically and biologically. Under these conditions recovery will likely be slow, initiated perhaps in localized patches (relatively "safe sites"), stabilized by structures such as stumps, clumps of residual vegetation, large woody debris, and rock outcrops. Furthermore, a significant amount of soil development will be required to replace lost soil and recover degraded soil properties.

The short-term (year to decade) effects of erosion on site productivity are generally not dramatic in this region of low-intensity precipitation and rather rapid revegetation. Longer term effects of erosion are poorly understood and difficult to interpret from studies of erosion after harvest of natural stands, which leaves much greater amounts of residual vegetation and woody litter than would be likely from future harvest of managed stands. To evaluate long-term effects of erosion on productivity of managed sites, we need further field studies coordinated with modeling to simulate long-term aspects of system behavior (see chapter 11, this volume). Thus far, study of long-term development of forest soils in the region has been sketchy, and little effort has been made to incorporate erosion into the analysis of long-term site productivity.

The best recommendation for managing the soil resource is to be judicious with the disturbance regime, especially with fire and physical disruption of the soil. Poor forestry practices can trigger long-term degradation of site productivity. We believe that in most areas where sound, modern forestry is practiced, accelerated erosion alone is unlikely to cause widespread, major loss of long-term productivity.

ACKNOWLEDGMENTS

We thank L. Finnegan (Bureau of Land Management, Coos Bay, Oregon), D. McNabb (Oregon State University, Corvallis), and W. Power (Bureau of Land Management, Salem) for helpful discussion in early stages of manuscript preparation, and D. Perry and J. Means for reviews. This work was supported in part by National Science Foundation Grants BSR-8514325 and BSR-8508356.

QUESTIONS FROM THE SYMPOSIUM FLOOR

Q: If Coast Range headwalls have no trees to leave, should trees be left upslope from the headwall and, if so, how many?

A: The major argument for establishing headwall "leave areas" (patches of forest or shrub vegetation) has been to preserve root strength in order to reduce occurrence of landslide associated with clearcutting. From this point of view, cutting trees at the upper edge of an unstable headwall basin may not directly impact the slide-prone area. There also may be hydrologic and other stabilizing influences of vegetation left in headwall basins, but these have not been studied. Felling and bucking of trees above headwalls may reduce stability of slide-prone parts of headwalls by direct physical damage caused by sliding logs, and through slash accumulation which suppresses revegetation and increases the possibility of slash fires burning into the headwall area.

Q: How does removing large woody debris (commonly referred to as YUM yarding or gross yarding) from steep harvested sites (to lessen broadcast burning intensity) affect erosion rates? Is it a good trade-off?

A: I would favor leaving large woody debris and timing the burning (e.g., spring rather than fall burning) to keep the fire intensity down so that nutrients and sediment-trapping structures are retained.

Q: If you have an active slide within a proposed timber-sale boundary, what preventive measures do you suggest prior to harvest, particularly if the slide area cannot be deleted from the harvest area?

A: If it is a shallow slide (failure plane 1–2 m deep), consider managing the root systems, such as leaving brush and hardwoods around the slide perimeter. If it is a deeper slide (earthflow or slump), consider managing the hydrology of the site by, for instance, road drainage systems to divert water from upslope areas or from the slide surface itself.

Q: Considering the Coast Range headwalls are often geologically weak areas that naturally tend to seed to alder—a deep-rooting species that probably tends to further chemically and physically weaken the site—would it not be better to do something like plant Douglas-fir just outside the area and species like hemlock (*Tsuga*), Sitka spruce [*Picea sitchensis* (Bong.) Carr.], and western redcedar (*Thuja plicata* Donn ex D. Don) on the area? Thus the root mat over the headwall would be anchored to the Douglas-fir on the edge.

A: The jury is still out on whether headwall leave areas prevent management-accelerated sliding (Swanson and Roach 1987). Such suggestions are interesting to discuss, but we are a long way from knowing if they would be worth the investment. Ziemer (1981) has examined the relative root strength of a number of species and found that many brush species have relatively high strength.

Q: On steep coastal slopes, do you advocate gross yarding of draws to reduce occurrence of debris flows and probable debris dams?

A: Some very large, stable pieces of woody debris in draws may help to stabilize them by preventing release of accumulated finer slash that could trigger debris flows downstream. The best practice is to keep slash out of highly sensitive sites in the first place.

Q: Regarding erosion and landsliding, have you studied the effects (increased erosion and slides) of the second year following clearcutting and broadcast burning on steep slopes? Studies on the Entiat Experimental Forest (east slope of the Washington Cascades) show increased slump and slide activity the second year following wildfire.

A: The actual year of sliding after a fire or clearcutting is probably determined more by storm history than anything else. However, the timing of sliding appears to vary in a broadly systematic fashion after disturbance, presumably as a result of declining strength of decaying roots of killed vegetation and the lag before roots of invading vegetation fully reestablish a root network. A study in Mapleton in the Oregon Coast Range, for example, found 63% of slides occurring 0–3 years after logging and burning, 29% 4–10 years, and 6% 11+ years. In the Oregon Cascades (Swanson and Dyrness 1975), the values were 46, 42, and 12%. In the Idaho Batholith (Megahan et al. 1978), they were 24, 41, and 35%. The apparent delay in sliding in the more interior areas may reflect slower revegetation and decomposition resulting from colder winters and drier summers.

Q: Logging roads are frequently built on the lower slopes of steep-sided valleys. Has there been any research to examine how these roads may affect the flow of water and nutrients to the lower slope sites and, ultimately, the long-term productivity of these productive ecosystems?

A: The paper by Megahan (1988) summarizes the scanty and anecdotal information on this subject. There has been too little research to make a general statement.

Q: On slopes with a history of debris slides, have you noted differences in soil profile characteristics or degree of development within bedrock hollows vs. more stable positions on the same slope? If so, does this indicate any degree of hazard?

A: To my knowledge this has not been studied systematically. Some textural properties and radiocarbon dates of soils filling hollows have been examined (Dietrich et al. 1982, Reneau et al. 1986), but with little comparison to "nonhollow" soils. I believe that landform (steepness of axis and sideslope of hollow) and soil thickness are key criteria for judging debris-slide potential of a site.

Q: When quantifying soil loss due to surface erosion, how much loss is significant and how much can be replaced through natural soil building within an 80-year rotation?

A: As discussed in the chapter, we have no information on the soil-loss tolerance of forest ecosystems.

Q: You mentioned that the Drift Creek slide in the Coast Range was an example of a natural mass movement. Is there any disagreement among researchers as to whether road construction had any effect on the timing or magnitude of the slide?

A: I have heard no discussion of this question, but personally consider it possible, though not probable, that the road and logging contributed to catastrophic failure at Drift Creek.

Q: What do you think of grass seeding as a measure to prevent surface erosion or mass movement?

A: Establishing grass can locally reduce surface erosion; however, its potential effectiveness depends on timing of seeding relative to heavy rains, nutrient status of treated soils, and other factors. I believe that grass seeding has no significant effect on sliding in the Pacific Northwest landscape.

Q: Have the multirotational European forests seen an increase or decrease of erosion landslides over time? Does this relate to a decrease in organic matter?

A: I know of no data on the subject. The issue of the effects of Waldsterben (forest decline) on erosion and runoff is now being confronted by the Europeans, and results of a small workshop and brief field exercise on this subject were recently published by the Swiss government.

REFERENCES

Bennett, K. A. 1982. *Effects of slash burning on surface soil erosion rates in the Oregon Coast Range.* M.S. Thesis. Corvallis, Ore.: Oregon State University.

Brown, L. R. 1981. World population growth, soil erosion, and food security. *Science* 214:995–1002.

Clayton, J. L. 1981. *Soil disturbance caused by clearcutting and helicopter yarding in the Idaho Batholith.* Research Note INT-305. Ogden, Utah: Intermountain Research Station, USDA Forest Service.

Clayton, J. L., and D. A. Kennedy. 1985. Nutrient losses from timber harvest in the Idaho Batholith. *Soil Science Society of America Journal* 49:1041–1049.

Clayton, J. L., and W. F. Megahan. 1986. Erosional and chemical denudation rates in the southwestern Idaho Batholith. *Earth Surface Processes and Landforms* 11:389–400.

Crozier, M. J., R. J. Eyles, S. L. Marx, J. A. McConchie, and R. C. Owen. 1980. Distribution of landslides in the Wairarapa hill country, New Zealand. *Journal of Geology and Geophysics* 23:579–586.

Dietrich, W. E., and T. Dunne. 1978. Sediment budget for a small catchment in mountainous terrain. *Zeitschrift fuer Geomorphologie* 29:191–206.

Dietrich, W. E., T. Dunne, N. Humphrey, and L. M. Reid. 1982. "Construction of sediment budgets for drainage basins." In *Sediment budgets and routing in forested drainage basins,* edited by F. J. Swanson, R. J. Janda, T. Dunne, and D. N. Swanston, 5–23. General Technical Report PNW-141. Portland, Ore.: Pacific Northwest Forest and Range Experiment Station, USDA Forest Service.

Franklin, J. F., and J. S. Rothacher. 1962. Are your seedlings being buried? *Tree Planters' Notes* 51:7–9.

George, D. 1984. *Surface erosion on a clearcut in the Willamette National Forest.* M.S. Thesis. Corvallis, Ore.: Oregon State University.

Ice, G. G. 1985. *Catalog of landslide inventories for the Northwest.* Technical Bulletin 456. New York, N.Y.: National Council of the Paper Industry for Air and Stream Improvement.

Kelsey, H. M. 1980. A sediment budget and an analysis of geomorphic process in the Van Duzen River Basin, north coastal California, 1941–1975. *Geological Society of America Bulletin* 91(4):1119–1216.

Kelsey, H., M. A. Madej, J. Pitlick, M. Coghlan, D. Best, R. Belding, and P. Stroud. 1981. *Sediment source and sediment transport in the Redwood Creek Basin: a progress report.* Technical Report 3. Arcata, Calif.: Redwood National Park.

Larson, K. R., and R. C. Sidle. 1980. *Erosion and sedimentation data catalog of the Pacific Northwest, September 1980.* Report R6-WM-050-1981. Portland, Ore.: Pacific Northwest Region, USDA Forest Service.

McCormack, D. E., K. K. Young, and L. W. Kimberlin. 1982. *Current criteria for determining soil loss tolerance.* Special Publication 45. Madison, Wis.: Soil Science Society of America.

McNabb, D. 1985. Ravel before, during, and after harvesting. *FIR Report* 7(3):4–5.

———. 1986. Impact of ravel on newly planted seedlings. *FIR Report* 7(4):3–4.

Megahan, W. F. 1981. "Effects of silviculture practices on erosion and sedimentation in the Interior West—a case for sediment budgeting." In *Proceedings, symposium on Interior West watershed management,* edited by D. M. Baumgartner, 169–181. Pullman, Wash.: Cooperative Extension, Washington State University.

———. 1988. "Roads and forest site productivity." In *Degradation of forested land—forest soils at risk,* edited by J. D. Lousier and G. W. Still. Proceedings, 10th British Columbia Soil Science Workshop, February 20–21, 1986. Land Management Report. Victoria, B.C.: Research Branch, British Columbia Ministry of Forests and Lands. (In press).

Megahan, W. F., N. F. Day, and T. M. Bliss. 1978. "Landslide occurrence in the western and central Northern Rocky Mountain physiographic province in Idaho." In *Forest soils and land use,* edited by C. T. Youngberg, 116–139. Proceedings of the 5th Northern American Forest Soils Conference. Fort Collins, Colo.: Colorado State University.

Megahan, W. F., and D.C. Molitor. 1975. Erosional effects of wildlife and logging in Idaho. *Journal of Irrigation and Drainage Division, American Society of Civil Engineers:* 423–444.

Megahan, W. F., K. A. Seyedbagheri, and T. L. Mosko. 1986. "Construction phase sediment budget for forest roads on granitic slopes in Idaho." In *Proceedings, symposium on drainage basin sediment delivery,* edited by R. F. Hadley. Albuquerque, N. Mex.: International Association of Scientific Hydrology.

Mersereau, R., and C. T. Dyrness. 1972. Accelerated mass wasting after logging and slash burning in western Oregon. *Journal of Soil and Water Conservation* 27(3):112–114.

Miles, D. W. R., and F. J. Swanson. 1986. Vegetation composition on recent landslides in the Cascade Mountains of western Oregon. *Canadian Journal of Forest Research* 16:739–744.

Miles, D. W. R., F. J. Swanson, and C. T. Youngberg. 1984. Effects of landslide erosion on subsequent Douglas-fir growth and stocking levels in the western Cascades, Oregon. *Soil Science Society of America Journal* 48:667–671.

Morrison, P. H. 1984. *The history and roles of fire in forest ecosystems of the central western Cascades of Oregon determined by forest stand analysis.* M.S. Paper. Seattle, Wash.: University of Washington.

National Soil Erosion-Soil Productivity Research Planning Committee. 1981. Soil erosion effects on soil productivity: a research perspective. *Journal of Soil and Water Conservation* 36:82–90.

Reneau, S. L., W. E. Dietrich, R. I. Dorn, C. R. Berger, and M. Rubin. 1986. Geomorphic and paleoclimatic implications of latest Pleistocene radiocarbon dates from colluvium-mantled hollows, California. *Geology* 14:655–658.

Rice, R. M., J. S. Rothacher, and W. F. Megahan. 1971. "Erosional consequences of timber harvesting: an appraisal." In *National symposium on watersheds in transition,* 321–329. Fort Collins, Colo.: American Water Resources Association.

Smith, R. B., P. R. Commandeur, and M. W. Ryan. 1986. *Soils, vegetation, and forest growth on landslides and surrounding logged and old-growth areas on the Queen Charlotte Islands.* Land Management Report 41. Victoria, B.C.: British Columbia Ministry of Forests, Canadian Forestry Service.

Steele, R., S. F. Arno, and K. Geier-Hayes. 1986. Wildfire patterns change in central Idaho's ponderosa pine–Douglas-fir forest. *Western Journal of Applied Forestry* 1:16–18.

Stewart, G. H. 1986. Population dynamics of a montane conifer forest, western Cascade Range, Oregon, USA. *Ecology* 67:534–544.

Swanson, F. J. 1981. "Fire and geomorphic processes." In *Proceedings of the conference on fire regimes and ecosystem properties,* edited by H. A. Mooney, T. M. Bonnicksen, N. L. Christensen, J. E. Lotan, and W. A. Reiners 159–170. General Technical Report WO-26. Washington, D.C.: USDA Forest Service.

Swanson, F. J., L. E. Benda, S. H. Duncan, G. E. Grant, W. F. Megahan, L. M. Reid, and R. R. Ziemer. 1987. "Mass failures and other processes of sediment production in Pacific Northwest forest landscapes." In *Proceedings, streamside management: forestry and fishery interactions symposium,* edited by E. O. Salo and T. W. Cundy, 9–38. Seattle, Wash.: Institute of Forest Resources, University of Washington.

Swanson, F. J., and C. T. Dyrness. 1975. Impact of clear-cutting and road construction on soil erosion by landslides in the western Cascade Range, Oregon. *Geology* 3:393–396.

Swanson, F. J., R. L. Fredriksen, and F. M. McCorison. 1982. "Material transfer in western Oregon forested watershed." In *Analysis of coniferous forest ecosystems in the western United States,* edited by R. L. Edmonds, 233–266. Stroudsburg, Pa.: Hutchinson Ross Publishing Company.

Swanson, F. J., and G. E. Grant. 1982. *Rates of soil erosion by surface and mass erosion processes in the Willamette National Forest.* Report on file. Corvallis, Ore.: Forestry Sciences Laboratory, Pacific Northwest Research Station, USDA Forest Service.

Swanson, F. J., and C. J. Roach. 1987. *Mapleton leave area study.* Administrative Report on file at Siuslaw National Forest. Corvallis, Ore.: Pacific Northwest Research Station, USDA Forest Service.

Teensma, P. D. A. 1987. *Fire history and fire regimes of the central western Cascades of Oregon.* Ph.D. Dissertation. Eugene, Ore.: University of Oregon.

Trustrum, N. A., M. G. Lambert, and V. J. Thomas. 1983. "The impact of soil slip erosion on hill country pasture production in New Zealand." In *Second international conference on soil erosion and conservation,* edited by C. L. O'Loughlin and A. J. Pearce. Honolulu, Hawaii: East-West Center, University of Hawaii.

Vest, S. B. 1988. *Effects of earthflows on stream channel and valley floor morphology, western Cascade Range, Oregon.* M.S. Thesis. Corvallis, Ore.: Oregon State University.

Wischmeier, W. H., and D. D. Smith. 1978. *Predicting rainfall erosion losses—a guide to conservation planning.* Agriculture Handbook 537. Washington, D.C.: U.S. Department of Agriculture.

Ziemer, R. R. 1981. "Roots and the stability of forested slopes." In *Erosion and sediment transport in Pacific Rim steeplands,* edited by T. R. H. Davies and A. J. Pearce, 343–361. Science Publication 132. International Association of Hydrology.

Chapter 6

Importance of Ecological Diversity in Maintaining Long-Term Site Productivity

Jerry F. Franklin, David A. Perry, Timothy D. Schowalter,
Mark E. Harmon, Arthur McKee, and Thomas A. Spies

ABSTRACT

Long-term site productivity is ultimately dependent upon ecosystem resilience—an ability to absorb stress or change without significant loss of function—and not simply soil properties. Forest ecosystems are faced with dramatic changes in climate, pollutants, and pests and pathogens. These uncertainties, coupled with our demonstrably inadequate knowledge of ecosystem function, strongly indicate management approaches which retain the genetic, structural, landscape, and temporal diversity critical to resilience. Current management emphases simplify forests. Alternative management programs that retain diversity, including schemes which accommodate early successional species, provide for coarse, woody debris, create mixed stands, protect streamside habitats, and provide for diverse and functional landscapes, are suggested. Foresters must manage to retain greater ecological margins in order to sustain long-term productivity and buffer against uncertainties.

INTRODUCTION

Scientists and land managers tend to focus primarily on soil nutrients when considering the issue of long-term site productivity. But long-term site productivity extends beyond plant nutrition to soil physical properties and the biotic contribution to both chemical and physical properties. The importance of woody organic matter incorporated into the soil (Harvey et al. 1979) and of roots as pumps and points of energy ("white holes") in the soil matrix are good examples (Perry et al. 1987).

Long-term site productivity goes far beyond soil considerations, however, to the larger issue of maintaining resilience in forest ecosystems and landscapes. By "resilience" we mean an ecosystem's ability to absorb stress or change without significant loss of function. It is this ability which must be the concern of resource managers.

In this chapter, we address the changes and stresses to which forest ecosystems currently are subjected; reexamine simplification of forest ecosystems, which has been our traditional management approach; and propose altering practices to assure ecosystem resilience, in the face of stresses and the uncertainty they bring, through maintaining diversity and complexity in our forests to keep all future options open. Our concern extends to a forest's ability to sustain production of a complete array of goods and services, from wood fiber to wildlife habitat. We focus primarily upon forest growth or production, however, in the belief that by maintaining a site's capacity for photosynthetically converting the sun's energy to the complex organic structures known as trees, we retain the potential to create any specific set of forest goods and services. If we reduce a sites's potential to convert energy to trees then we have limited society's options.

CHANGE AND STRESS IN OUR FOREST ENVIRONMENTS

We relatively short-lived humans tend to view forests and soils as essentially eternal in their current form. Indeed, it is difficult for us to imagine these ecosystems in other conditions or to sense gradual or subtle changes in their character. But forests and forest environments are not immutable. There are many profound examples of current, ongoing changes.

Global Climatic Change

Increased levels of carbon dioxide, methane, and other trace gases are producing global climatic changes through the "greenhouse effect," whereby more of the sun's radiant energy is trapped in the atmosphere. A 4–5°C increase in mean temperature is predicted for the Pacific Northwest during the next 30–40 years, along with perhaps a slight decrease in summer precipitation (Schneider 1989). This change in climate is equivalent to an upward 1,000-m change in elevation—that is, the climate currently found at 1,000 m elevation on a mountain slope would occur at 2,000 m elevation (Franklin et al. 1989). The net effect, on site, will be increased droughtiness as the effective moisture declines.

Certain major impacts on northwestern forests due to climatic change seem likely (Franklin et al. 1989), although some (e.g., Woodman 1987) suggest that it will have little consequence. For example, environmental changes could profoundly alter the present match of species and their genetic strains with site. Leverenz and Lev (1987) have discussed effects on species ranges based upon physiological factors. If major shifts in species dominance seem far-fetched, we need only note that Douglas-fir [*Pseudotsuga menziesii* (Mirb.) Franco] has been a major species in this region only during this interglacial period and a dominant for only about 7,000 years (Brubaker 1988); other currently dominant species, such as ponderosa pine (*Pinus ponderosa* Dougl. ex Laws.), have similar histories. Profound changes have taken place in northwestern vegetation in response to past fluctuations in climate which were much smaller than those projected for the next 40 years; for example, the maximum temperatures experienced during this interglacial period were only 2° warmer than those at present (Brubaker 1986), yet lowland areas of the Pacific Northwest were apparently more sparsely forested than at present.

Perhaps the most profound effects of global climatic change will be on disturbance regimes—frequency, intensity, scale, and locale of wildfire, wind and rain storms, and outbreaks of pests and pathogens. In some cases, altered disturbance regimes will create a "double whammy," as the existing forests are destroyed and hotter, drier conditions make tree regeneration even more difficult (Franklin et al. 1989).

Pollutants

Pollutant loadings of all types, including photooxidants, ozone, acid precipitation, and heavy metals, are increasing dramatically. Moreover, such pollutants typically behave in concert (synergistically), further accentuating their impact on productivity. Although pollution problems in forested areas are more acute in the eastern United States, central and southern California, and Europe, levels of various chemical pollutants are also increasing in parts of the Pacific Northwest, and the potential for serious problems exists (e.g., Sun 1985).

Air pollutants stress forests in various ways depending upon their intensity and type (Kozlowski and Constantinidou 1986). Reduced growth, reduced reproduction, and increased mortality due either to increased susceptibility to pests or pathogens or to direct induction of disease are typical at intermediate pollutant dosages. Highly elevated levels of mortality and complete elimination of species may result from high dosages. Tree species do vary substantially in their susceptibility to air pollutants—with conifers generally more susceptible than hardwoods.

Pests and Pathogens

Human society is dramatically altering the pest and pathogen loads on forests by introducing new pests, making forest communities more vulnerable by altering their structure and composition, and increasing physiological stresses (e.g., through global climatic change). Conversion of old-growth to younger stands was once thought to be a key in reducing losses to pests and pathogens; this conversion has instead brought other problems, such as the necessity to deal with infection centers of *Phellinus weirii* root rot (Childs 1970).

Shigo (1985) has commented that disease problems appear to be much more serious in managed than in natural stands. For example, monocultures (stands of single species) of southern pines, especially planted monocultures of the most susceptible species, create conditions for immense and unimpeded outbreaks of the southern pine bark beetle (*Dendroctonus frontalis*) (Schowalter 1986). Frequent management entries may be detrimental in themselves by, for instance, facilitating spread of damaging root rots. We find that silvicultural practices as common as thinning can create major problems. Thinning can increase the occurrence of root rots such as *Fomes annosus* (Ross 1973). As another example, precommercial thinning of Douglas-fir can dramatically increase levels of the Douglas-fir root bark beetle (*Hylastes nigrinus*) (Fig. 6.1), which is the vector for black stain fungus (*Ceratocystis wageneri*) (Witcosky et al. 1986). Young Douglas-fir plantations are also more seriously affected by foliage diseases. Moreover, damage by herbivorous insects may increase in importance as the old-growth component of forests is lost. Old-growth stands are a net source of insect predators (Table 6.1) and also hamper the progress of herbivorous host-seeking insects which must pass through areas of unfavorable vegetation in search of desirable young trees (Schowalter 1989).

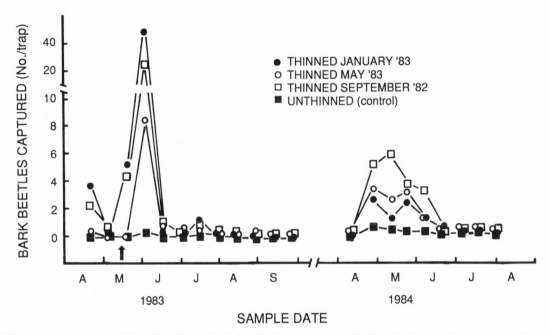

FIG. 6.1. Occurrence of Douglas-fir root bark beetle, the vector for black stain fungus, for 2 years following precommercial thinning in a 20-year-old Douglas-fir stand; thinning greatly elevated levels of beetles over those encountered in the unthinned control (adapted from Witcosky et al. 1986).

TABLE 6.1. Mean arthropod densities in a young (10-year-old) Douglas-fir and old-growth (450-year-old) Douglas fir-western hemlock stand. Numbers of species are in parentheses. One interpretation of these data is that greater plant and arthropod diversity of old-growth forests limits pest populations; old-growth forest have over 100 times as many predators as young forests (adapted from Schowalter 1989).

Arthropod type	Young Douglas-fir	Old-growth Douglas-fir	Old-growth hemlock
	---------- No. of individuals/kg ----------		
Folivores			
Gall aphids	29,000 (1)	48 (1)	28 (1)
Aphids	100 (1)	0	0
Scale insects	2 (1)	49 (2)	110 (3)
Budmoths	0	1 (7)	0
Other folivores	2 (2)	1 (7)	2 (5)
Pollen and seed feeders			
Seed bugs	0	1 (1)	12 (3)
Thrips	0	3 (2)	1 (2)
Detritivores			
Oribatid mites	0	17 (5)	50 (5)
Insects	0	1 (4)	12 (4)
Predators			
Ants	2 (1)	1 (2)	0
Aphid predators	9 (1)	3 (5)	1 (4)
Parasitic wasps	8 (4)	2 (5)	1 (4)
Other insects	3 (2)	2 (3)	0
Spiders	19 (3)	14 (15)	15 (15)
Other arachnids	0	5 (2)	7 (2)
	---------- Predators: folivore ----------		
	0.0014	0.26	0.18

INADEQUATE INFORMATION AND HUMILITY

Along with change and the uncertainty that it brings, our woefully inadequate knowledge of forest ecosystems should humble us. The last 2 decades have brought important discoveries with many surprises, including the following basic findings:

(1) The importance of photosynthesis outside the growing season in northwestern forests (Waring and Franklin 1979). We previously believed that photosynthesis was primarily confined to spring and summer, but we now know that is not the case. This knowledge has allowed us to understand how mild winter climates give conifers an advantage over deciduous hardwood species;

(2) The high rate of turnover of roots and mycorrhizae in forest ecosystems and the high energy requirements for their maintenance—requirements often far out of proportion to the 20% of biomass typically found belowground. In one subalpine (high-elevation) forest, 73% of the net primary productivity went to belowground dry-matter production, 66% to fine roots and mycorrhizae (Grier et al. 1981). One implication of this finding is that fertilization and irrigation may simply shift production from below the ground to above it without altering total forest productivity; and

(3) The numerous pathways for fixation (conversion to usable form) and loss of biologically available nitrogen, including microbial fixation in woody debris (Cornaby and Waide 1973, Sharpe and Milbank 1973) and fixation by canopy lichens (Denison 1979, Carroll 1980). Previously, all sources of biologically available nitrogen had been largely unknown in forests. These findings have provided us with opportunities to increase nitrogen fixation, and thus fertility, in forests.

Recognizing the importance of coarse, woody debris has been a particularly conspicuous reversal in resource managers' thinking. We have matured from viewing such materials as fire hazards, physical impediments, and waste (Cramer 1974) to understanding them as essential structures in forests, streams, and rivers (Maser and Trappe 1984, Harmon et al. 1986, Maser et al. 1988).

We have just now entered a period of rapid expansion in our knowledge of forest ecosystems. Already we are learning that parts of forests that we have never considered seriously are proving significant, even essential, to ecosystem functioning. And through this new information, we are finally recognizing the many fallacies and weaknesses in our traditional forestry dogma. In pursuit of high, short-term returns we have attempted to mimick intensive agriculture, which moves us toward a homogenized, simplified forest, one requiring large energy subsidies. Simultaneously, we have been wondering how far the system can be pushed and rationalizing with "don't worry too much—we can fix it later." But can we? Considering the uncertainties of the future and our still inadequate knowledge base, we must ask ourselves: have we been proceeding prudently? The answer, inescapably, is no.

SIMPLIFICATION—THE TRADITIONAL EMPHASIS

Forest ecosystems may be homogenized or simplified at several levels: genetic, structural (the stand: small spatial scale), landscape (larger spatial scale), and temporal (successional).

Genetic simplification takes many forms, including elimination or exclusion of some species and reduction of genetic variability in others. Elimination and exclusion usually occur by accident rather than by design, as when certain animal species associated with old-growth forests are lost because the old-growth component is eliminated from a landscape. Reduced genetic variability within species is often by design, through programs of genetic improvement or, even more drastically, programs for cloning commercial tree species. Other forestry activities, such as artificial regeneration of trees from wild seed, can result in substantial, unplanned modification of their natural genetic variability even when the seed is from the same area because the seedlings undergo very different selection processes in a nursery than in the wild. Creating uniform stands with a narrowed genetic base increases the vulnerability of forests to changes in climate, pollutants, and pests and pathogens.

More generally, excessive promotion of dense populations of any host-tree species, even without a narrowed genetic base, can be expected to lead to outbreaks and other pest-management problems. Most pests and pathogens have narrow host ranges including one or a few congeneric plant species; even polyphagous insects such as the gypsy moth (*Lymantria dispar* L.) accept as hosts plants from only a few temperate families (Daterman et al. 1986, Schowalter 1986). Many pests focus on specific genotypes (e.g., Alstad and Edmonds 1983, Perry and Pitman 1983, Whitham 1983). Most hosts also have specific ages during which they are vulnerable (Schowalter et al. 1986). Hence, reducing the distance, in time or space, between suitable host trees increases the likelihood that the pest will "discover" and propagate rapidly through the host. Simplifying stand composition or forest age structures creates high host density in space and time, reducing natural barriers. Conversely, potential pests are limited naturally in diverse ecosystems by the high cost (in terms of time and energy) of locating suitable resources in a structurally complex matrix of hosts and nonhosts (Kareiva 1983, Schultz 1983, Courtney 1986, Schowalter et al. 1986).

Structural simplification within forests includes eliminating dead trees and downed logs, reducing the range of tree sizes and growth forms, and using geometrical tree spacings. Long before intensive forest management was initiated, foresters removed dead wood because of concerns over wildfire. Practices such as YUM (yarding unmerchantable material) and PUM (piling unmerchantable material) are the ultimate result of such efforts (Cramer 1974). Fortunately, major changes in these practices are underway because the structural diversity afforded by this "unmerchantable material" (i.e., woody debris) can yield numerous ecological benefits. For example, retention or re-creation of structural diversity can significantly enhance biological diversity by providing a greater array of habitat (and, often, higher quality habitat) for plant and vertebrate and invertebrate animal species. As another example, coarse woody debris contributes to long-term site productivity by providing organic matter.

Landscape modifications have been mixed in their effects. Management practices have most often increased the number of discrete patches of forest (Fig. 6.2) but have reduced the range of patch sizes, homogenized conditions within the patches, and increased, sharpened, and straightened boundaries between patches. Such activities can have some benefits, such as creating large amounts of habitat for wildlife species that live at the forest edge. On the other hand, landscape manipulations have sometimes produced patches which are too small to provide suitable conditions for species requiring interior habitat, and extensive areas of forest edge can contribute significantly to accelerated tree mortality in residual stands (Franklin and Forman 1987).

Temporal simplification results when the length of early successional stages is shortened and late successional stages are eliminated (Fig. 6.3). An intensive forestry goal is usually rapid reestablishment of a fully stocked, closed-canopy forest. However, tree planting and control of competing vegetation—practices intended to achieve this goal—in turn can drastically shorten the period of herb and shrub dominance which precedes closure of the tree canopy. Federal forest lands generally are harvested at "culmination of mean annual increment," or the time when cumulative tree productivity is maximized: this is the transition from young (up to 80–100 year old) to mature (100–200 year old) forest. Hence, both the mature and old-growth (greater than 200-year-old) forest stages are eliminated under intensive forest management.

In general, we have tended to forget that what is good for wood production is not necessarily good for other organisms or processes in a forest ecosystem. Fully stocked young forests, the forester's ideal, are the most simplified stage of forest development in terms of structure and function, and the most impoverished in terms of biological diversity. Essentially all of the site resources are co-opted by the rapidly growing young trees.

Although some simplification is essential, much of it is not. Indeed, simplification—genetic, structural, landscape, and temporal—reduces ecosystem resilience, eliminating redundancies that could be important in saving the ecosystem, and us. Because the ability of an ecosystem to tolerate or absorb new kinds of stresses or changes is clearly of increasing consequence, the key to retaining resilience must be in maintaining ecological complexity or diversity. Thus we see that a sustainable forestry is in fact supported by three legs: ecological diversity, genetic diversity, and soils (Fig. 6.4).

It may be useful to think about forest ecosystems in the same way that we think about our personal health or finances. If we utilize such resources to their limits (or, perhaps, even borrow a little on our future), we have no reserves to draw on when subjected to an unexpected stress. Similarly, if we push our forest ecosystems (or most other natural resources) to their limits—maximum sustainable yield—little reserve will be available for the unforeseen contingencies that are the inevitable by-products of change.

FIG. 6.2. Dispersed patch clearcutting on National Forest lands in the Douglas-fir Region has typically increased the number of discrete patches of forest but reduced the range of patch sizes and drastically increased, straightened, and sharpened boundaries between patches.

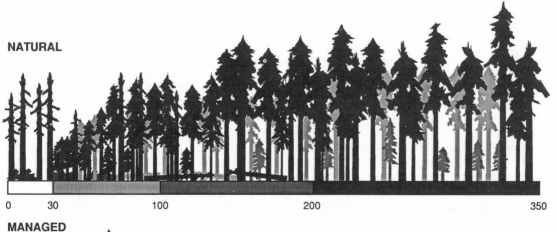

FIG. 6.3. Contrast between the natural and typical, managed forest rotation in northwestern Oregon and western Washington; mature and old-growth stages are eliminated under management and the period before the canopy closes is drastically shortened (adapted from Franklin et al. 1986).

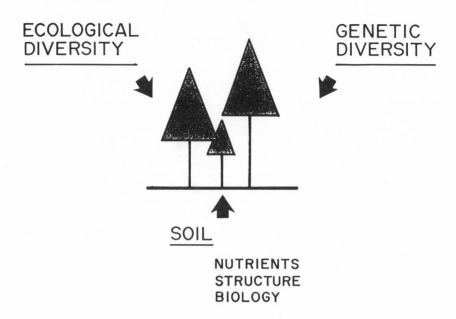

FIG. 6.4. The three legs of sustainable forestry (adapted from Perry 1988).

DIVERSIFICATION—THE NEW IMPERATIVE

How can we retain the natural resilience, assure the potential long-term site productivity of our forest ecosystems? We need to develop strategies which maintain or enhance ecological complexity whenever possible. Such management practices must accommodate early successional species; provide coarse, woody debris; create multistructured and multispecies stands; protect riparian (streamside) habitats; and provide for diverse and functional landscapes.

Accommodating Early Successional Species

We can achieve several ecological objectives when accommodating early successional species. Much of the diversity before the forest canopy closes is associated with weedy generalist plant species but also includes many game birds and mammals. This is also the successional stage during which symbiotic nitrogen-fixing plants, such as alder, ceanothus, and lupine (*Alnus, Ceanothus,* and *Lupinus* spp.), carry on most of their activity. Some relationships may be very complex. For example, mixed stands of ceanothus and Douglas-fir create an environment less favorable for the herbivorous insects feeding on Douglas-fir and for root pathogens (Schowalter 1989).

Silvicultural prescriptions that delay full canopy closure and maintain open forest conditions for long periods include wide spacings in plantings and in early precommercial thinnings. Wide spacings can also reduce planting and thinning costs (Oliver et al. 1986). Furthermore, spacing trials in the region suggest that the economics of growing such stands might suffer very little; although total yields are less, such stands produce trees with larger than average diameters (Reukema 1979, Hoyer, and Suanzy 1986).

One such strategy is followed in growing Monterey pine (*Pinus radiata* D. Don) in New Zealand. Stands are precommercially thinned to crop-tree spacing early in stand development (e.g., 9 years). Although of usable size, the thinned material is left as slash because of its marginal economic value. Crop trees are pruned in three stages to produce clear logs. The thinned stands are very open in structure for most of their history and can generate a variety of other products, including forage for domestic animals. Monterey pine is not native to New Zealand; a silvicultural system of this type (i.e., extreme monoculture) would have to be carefully considered when applied to a native species to insure that risks of outbreaks of pests, such as bark and root beetles, were not excessive.

Providing Coarse, Woody Debris

Standing dead trees (snags) and downed logs play a large variety of ecological roles in forests and associated streams and rivers. Ecologically, a dead tree is as important to the forest ecosystem as a live one (Maser and Trappe 1984, Harmon et al. 1986, Franklin et al. 1987, Maser et al. 1988). At the time a tree dies, it has probably fulfilled only about half of its "life" in the ecosystem. The importance of dead wood, especially snags, for wildlife has long been recognized (e.g., Brown 1985). As noted by Elton (1966), ". . . dying and dead wood provides one of the two or three greatest resources for animal species in a natural forest . . . if fallen timber and slightly decayed trees are removed the whole system is gravely impoverished of perhaps more than a fifth of its fauna." Coarse, woody debris is also an important component in nutrient and energy flows, as a source of soil organic matter, as a site for asymbiotic nitrogen fixation, and in erosion control. In waterways, logjams dissipate energy to reduce channel erosion. Logs also provide major structures for retaining food and sediments in stream reaches serving as habitat for an array of organisms, including fish. Additional functions for woody debris exist in large rivers and estuaries, where debris influences channel formation, and even in open ocean and deep marine regions, where it provides a food or energy base for marine organisms; some of these functions are described in Maser et al. (1988).

Nature provides for substantial amounts of coarse, woody debris at all successional stages in unmanaged forests (Spies et al. 1988). However, assuring a continuous flow of such material in managed stands, spatially and temporally, is a major challenge to silviculturists. Woody structures are transient and require constant replacement. For example, Douglas-fir snags in the Pacific Northwest rarely persist in forms useful to animals that create and utilize cavities beyond 60 or 70 years (Cline et al. 1980, Graham 1982).

Therefore, managers must plan to preserve existing coarse, woody debris and to assure future sources (essentially to create new material). Preservation can be greatly aided by modifying or eliminating YUM and PUM practices. Existing snags may be retained in many situations (Fig. 6.5). Creation of new material is probably a more effective strategy than preservation, however, because of the transient nature of wood structures. Green trees of various ages can be retained as sources of future snags and downed woody debris on cutover areas; by spacing mortality of these trees over the rotation, silviculturists can assure a continuing supply of woody debris in varying stages of decay.

FIG. 6.5. Silviculturists can provide for snags in managed stands by retaining existing snags as well as green trees that will become snags, as has been done on this clearcut on the Willamette National Forest, Oregon.

Creating Mixed Stands

Stands of mixed composition, structure, or both promote ecological diversity, but foresters often avoid planning for such stands because it is simpler not to do so and because timber production objectives have not required it. However, benefits such as improved soil fertility and reduced susceptibility to pests can accrue from mixed stands. Indeed, mixed stands may sometimes produce greater total yields.

Incorporating hardwood species into mixed stands is one major way to retain ecological diversity. Hardwoods can contribute substantially to improved soil fertility: both chemical and physical properties are generally enhanced. Most deciduous hardwoods produce a base-rich litter and mull-type humus. Nitrogen-fixing alders make an additional contribution, although increased soil acidity and lower base saturation may be an undesired consequence (Franklin et al. 1968). Deciduous hardwoods also produce an open canopy for part of the year, creating diversity in environmental conditions in and on the forest floor; shifts in animal populations as well as more rapid carbon and nutrient cycling are probable responses to the increased insolation (Seastedt and Crossley 1981). The hardwood trees themselves offer a very different habitat for epiphytes such as mosses and lichens and for animals large and small. Bigleaf maple (*Acer macrophyllum* Pursh) is, for example, an outstanding substrate for development of epiphytic plants (Coleman et al. 1956).

Use of a greater variety of coniferous species could also enhance soil conditions and increase diversity of live and dead tree structures. For example, cedars and related species (Cupressaceae and Taxodiaceae) are calcium accumulators (Zinke and Crocker 1962, Kilsgaard et al. 1987). Their litter contributes to development of soils richer in bases, lower in acids, and generally more favorable to biological productivity (see, e.g., Alban 1969, Turner and Franz 1985). Because they also produce high-quality wood products, it is somewhat surprising that these species have not been incorporated into more managed stands.

Stands of mixed structure could take many forms and might have many objectives. Classical uneven-aged stands would fall into this category. A simple and broadly relevant example of such a mixed stand would be a two-layered forest comprising two distinct age classes, perhaps created by a shelterwood-type cutting in which the "leave" trees were allowed to remain through the entire next rotation. This approach might be taken to create greater canopy diversity (perhaps for wildlife or moisture condensation purposes), to provide a source of coarse, woody debris, or to produce high-quality wood. Experimental stands of this type have already been created in the Douglas-fir Region (Fig. 6.6).

FIG. 6.6. Cutover area on which dominant trees have been left for the next rotation to provide a stand of mixed structure; Douglas-fir on the Willamette National Forest, Oregon.

Protecting Riparian Habitats

Managers of riparian habitats should conserve as much as possible of the rich structural and compositional diversity found in streamside areas (Fig. 6.7). The number and complexity of forest and stream linkages are great. The forest controls the environment (light, temperature, nutrient regimes), provides the food or energy base, and creates the physical structure for small- to medium-sized streams (Gregory et al. 1989).

In forests, the most obvious linkage between a riparian stand and the stream is shading. In-stream photosynthesis and stream temperature are directly regulated by the amount of sunlight received (Minshall et al. 1983, Beschta et al. 1987); therefore, the height, density, and character of the foliage (evergreen or deciduous) determine the light regime. This linkage is tightest along small streams and decreases in proportion to the ratio of vegetation height to width of stream channel.

Riparian stands also function as a nutrient filter between terrestrial and aquatic systems, capturing some of the nutrients moving in the soil solution from the uplands to the stream and adding nutrients through litterfall. Our understanding of the processes of nutrient capture by riparian vegetation is currently rudimentary (Correll 1986), but we do know that riparian plant species differ considerably among themselves in rooting habits and phenology. Consequently, it is probable that a riparian zone consisting of a mixture of species and communities will be more effective than a monotypic stand in capturing and retaining nutrients.

Litterfall, from leaves to logs, is a major transfer of nutrients and carbon (energy) from the terrestrial to the aquatic system. These "allochthonous" inputs (materials from outside the aquatic ecosystem) are the primary energy source for small, heavily shaded streams. Plant species differ considerably in the quality of their leaves and the rate at which the leaves are processed by aquatic organisms (Webster and Benfield 1986), as well as in the timing of leaf fall to the stream (Campbell and Franklin 1979). In addition, plant communities can differ greatly in the total amounts of leaf material delivered to the stream. Land managers can make decisions to create or maintain specific conditions in riparian communities on the basis of the amount and quality of leaf material, and timing of leaf fall (Gregory et al. 1989). For example, if a manager opts for as rich a mix of riparian vegetation as possible to maximize diversity and maintain options, then the simplest management decision might be to stay out of late mature and old-growth areas immediately adjacent to streams; such areas have been found to have a rich diversity of allochthonous inputs relative to recent clearcuts and (especially) young coniferous stands.

The large litterfall component—coarse, woody debris—performs many functions in the stream ecosystem (Harmon et al. 1986), including improvement of fish habitat (Bisson et al. 1987). But amounts of coarse, woody debris have been drastically reduced in most managed areas (Sedell and Swanson 1984). It seems clear that in order to maintain the productivity of the streams flowing through forested landscapes, the land manager must ensure a continuing source of large dead wood; small pieces of wood simply do not have the necessary stability during high flows. This means that large trees must be left in riparian stands being harvested for the first time and that special consideration must be given to rapid regrowth of large trees on already logged lands. The area required to assure appropriate supplies of coarse, woody debris need not be terribly large; for example, McDade et al. (1989) found that 90% of all such material originated within 30 m of the stream.

FIG. 6.7. Streamside (riparian) zones such as that at Cherry Creek Research Natural Area, Oregon, are rich in structural, compositional, and functional diversity; management strategies should aim at retaining this complexity to maintain the productivity of aquatic environments.

Providing for Diverse and Functional Landscapes

Land managers must become much more aware of landscape-level needs and effects. We have tended to focus on individual stands and stream reaches without fully appreciating the ways in which all the pieces fit together. The increased concerns with cumulative effects and related issues indicate an increased recognition of landscape-level concerns.

Retaining patches of old-growth forest in managed landscapes is one way to promote diversity. Such patches provide habitat not only for dependent wildlife species, but also for insect predators. A recent survey has shown a much greater diversity and higher numbers of insect predators and parasites in old-growth forests than in adjacent Douglas-fir plantations (see Table 6.1); conversely, numbers of herbivorous insects, especially aphids, were much higher in the plantations, in part because of the abundance and proximity of young succulent shoots (Schowalter 1989). Old-growth forests retain snow in amounts and patterns that are dramatically different from those in clearcut areas; smaller snowpacks and a protected environment in old-growth forests reduce the potential contribution to winter floods, especially where a warm, intense rainstorm melts much of an existing snowpack (Harr 1986). Old-growth forests are also especially effective at scavenging atmospheric moisture and converting it to fog drip because of their high leaf areas (Harr 1982).

The pattern of cutting also affects the way the landscape functions as a whole. Clearcutting in dispersed patches fragments the forest landscape early in a cutting cycle, increases the potential for catastrophic events such as windthrow and wildfire, and rapidly reduces habitat suitable for interior forest species (Fig. 6.8) (Franklin and Forman 1987). Pattern and size of cut areas should be evaluated from the standpoint of multiple resource values and potential risks. Prescriptions should be flexible enough to fit the features and phenomena of the landscape, the nature of the resource, and management objectives. Aggregating, rather than dispersing, cutting activities may also prove desirable economically. It is essential that managers retain greater structural diversity (e.g., green trees and coarse, woody debris) if larger areas are cut over.

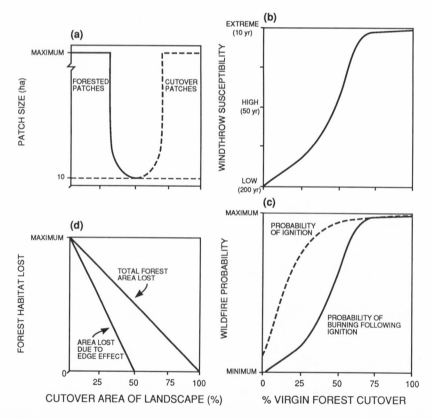

FIG. 6.8. Dispersed patch clearcutting leads to (clockwise): (a) rapid fragmentation of forests, increased susceptibility to catastrophic events such as (b) windthrow and (c) wildfire, and (d) rapid loss of habitat for interior forest species (adapted from Franklin and Forman 1987). Note in (d) that the patches of forest created when about 50% of the area is cut over lose all interior habitat because the patches are so small as to be all edge ("edge effect").

CONCLUSIONS

Forestry in the Pacific Northwest is at a unique stage in development—a stage that calls for the lessons only recently learned to be applied through practices that conserve and even enhance ecological diversity. We in forestry have tended to follow a technical heritage that emphasizes symmetry, order, cleanliness, and efficiency. Evidence is rapidly mounting that we must now foster something of a new tradition which accepts a little disorder or chaos as part of the natural order of things.

Achieving long-term site productivity is a much broader matter than simply maintaining fertile soils. It requires that resilience be maintained throughout forest ecosystems so they can absorb stresses. Ecological complexity is the key to such resilience, just as it is one of the keys to maintaining soil fertility. Thus, foresters should avoid simplifying ecosystems whenever possible—that is, they should "save all the parts to keep future options open."

Forest landscapes are under constant assault by management practices and other human impacts, local to global, planned to unforeseen. To combat uncertainty, we must retain as much ecological margin as possible.

QUESTIONS FROM THE SYMPOSIUM FLOOR

Q: What harvest system would you replace dispersed patch cutting with? Would you, for instance, advocate fewer, but larger cutting units?

A: One alternative to dispersed patch cutting is aggregating cutting areas, i.e., cutting new areas next to existing units, rather than skipping over areas of green forest. Aggregating cuttings in this way can reduce the amount of edge and maximize the size of residual forest islands.

Q: Do you feel the maintenance of ecological diversity is a technical, social/political, or forestry decision? How can we assure this diversity 200 years from now?

A: Basically, the decision to maintain ecological diversity is a societal decision. Resource managers, including foresters, are the technical personnel who will implement society's decision. To assure diversity in the future, society must develop both a national and an international commitment, in conjunction with generating the knowledge base and financial resources needed to support that commitment.

Q: Would you give us a few examples of where simplification has led to management disasters?

A: The recent bark beetle epidemics in the extensive young forests of southern pines probably fall into the category of a management disaster. That is, foresters contributed significantly to the problem through their decisions. The problem with spruce budworm in spruce-fir forests in Maine and southeastern Canada may be another example.

Q: My reading of the scientific evidence is that both simple and complex forest ecosystems can be equally stable. Can you give any proof, other than opinion, to support your argument that ecological diversity improves ecological stability in forest ecosystems?

A: Much of the debate about the relation between diversity and stability has been based upon simple mathematical models and not on experimentation or empirical study. The relationship has been neither proved nor disproved by theoretical ecologists. Back in the real world, however, common sense and empirical evidence clearly show that forest ecosystems which have redundancy in structure and function are more likely to be able to absorb stresses, including species losses, without catastrophic damage to the forest. For example, a stand composed of several tree species is less likely to experience 100% loss of the overstory to a pest or pathogen than one composed of a single species. Engineers recognize the value of redundancy in their work (e.g., as in aircraft), and it is an even more appropriate strategy in the art of ecological engineering known as forestry.

Q: Others have suggested using low-elevation, less productive farm land for intensive, short forest rotations and using upper elevation, steeper slopes for minimally managed and much longer rotations. What is your view on this?

A: Converting marginal agricultural lands to the structurally more complex ecosystems known as forests seems like a sound idea—such could provide wood fiber, wildlife habitat, and a variety of other "products." Moreover, including these marginal farm lands into the forest land base could reduce the pressures for intensive management of more fragile upper slope stands (see chapter 8, this volume).

Q: Would uneven-aged management be better for the Douglas-fir Region than clearcutting? Would it allow more management options for ecological diversity and resilience?

A: Some alternative to the current even-aged emphasis would probably allow for many more management options, but I am reluctant to refer to it as uneven-aged management. That suggests selective cutting systems, which I believe have a limited role in the Region. Unfortunately, the broad spectrum of possible cutting methods is not described in textbooks or taught in most silviculture courses. In this chapter, we mention one type of alternative scheme, in which a stand of various age classes is created by allowing selected green trees to remain at the time of harvest for one or more subsequent rotations. I believe the future of silviculture, at least on public lands, lies in this middle ground between clearcutting, on the one hand, and selection systems, on the other.

Q: What is your opinion of forest management policies recommending leaving 2 or more wildlife trees per acre in clearcuts?

A: I favor it. It is a start on developing practices which retain more structural (and, thereby, ecological) diversity on cutover lands.

Q: Are YUM and PUM totally negative when they replace burning, which often reduces genetic and species diversity and also removes dead wood?

A: Of course there are trade-offs between YUM and slash burning. However, light and medium, rather than heavy, fuels are typically the primary objective of broadcast slash burning, so one practice generally does not replace the other. If I had to choose one practice over the other, I would probably prefer burning because tends to leave much more of the large woody debris than YUM. Overall, YUM and PUM remove, at substantial cost, structures which should remain on site to enhance long-term productivity and provide animal habitat.

ACKNOWLEDGMENTS

We acknowledge the contribution of several associates, including W. K. Ferrell, S. V. Gregory, J. Lattin, and J. E. Means, to the development of the concepts presented here. R. F. Tarrant, J. Boyle, and K. Cromack, Jr., provided us with extensive and helpful review of earlier drafts. Students in a graduate ecology seminar in the College of Forest Resources, University of Washington, also provided many helpful comments. C. Perry greatly improved the readability of the manuscipt with her extensive and sound editing. Financial support was provided from a wide variety of sources including the home institutions of the authors and the National Science Foundation via Grants BSR-8315174 and BSR-8514325.

REFERENCES

Alban, David H. 1969. The influence of western hemlock and western redcedar on soil properties. *Soil Science Society of America Proceedings* 33:453–457.

Alstad, D. G., and G. F. Edmonds, Jr. 1983. "Adaptation, host specificity, and geneflow in the black pineleaf scale." In *Variable plants and herbivores in natural and managed systems,* edited by R. F. Denno and M.S. McClure, 413–426. New York: Academic Press.

Beschta, R. L., R. E. Bilby, G. W. Brown, L. B. Holtby, and T. D. Hofstra. 1987. "Stream temperature and aquatic habitat: fisheries and forestry interaction." In *Streamside management: forestry and fisheries interaction,* edited by E. O. Salo and T. W. Cundy, 191–232. Contribution No. 57. Seattle, Wash.: Institute of Forest Resources, University of Washington.

Bisson, P. A., R. E. Bilby, M. D. Bryant, C. A. Dolloff, G. B. Grette, R. H. House, M. L. Murphy, K. V. Koski, and J. R. Sedell. 1987. "Large woody debris in forested streams in the Pacific Northwest: past, present and future." In *Streamside management: forestry and fisheries interaction,* edited by E. O. Salo and T. W. Cundy, 143–190. Contribution No. 57. Seattle, Wash.: Institute of Forest Resources, University of Washington.

Brown, F. Reade. 1985. *Management of wildlife and fish habitats in forests of western Oregon and Washington. Part 1— chapter narratives.* Publication No. R6-F&WL-192-1985. Portland, Ore.: USDA Forest Service.

Brubaker, Linda B. 1986. Responses of tree populations to climatic change. *Vegetatio* 67:119–130.

———. 1988. "Vegetation history and anticipating future vegetation change." In *Ecosystem management for parks and wilderness,* edited by J. Agee. Seattle, Wash.: College of Forest Resources, University of Washington. (In press).

Campbell, A. G., and J. F. Franklin. 1979. *Riparian vegetation in Oregon's Western Cascade Mountains: composition, biomass, and autumn phenology.* U.S. International Biological Program, Coniferous Forest Biome Bulletin 14. Seattle, Wash.: College of Forest Resources, University of Washington.

Carroll, George C. 1980. "Forest canopies: complex and independent subsystems." In *Forests: fresh perspectives from ecosystem analysis,* edited by Richard H. Waring, 87–107. Corvallis, Ore.: Oregon State University Press.

Childs, T. W. 1970. *Laminated root rot of Douglas-fir in western Oregon and Washington.* Research Paper PNW-102. Portland, Ore.: Pacific Northwest Forest and Range Experiment Station, USDA Forest Service.

Cline, S. P., A. B. Berg, and H. M. Wright. 1980. Snag characteristics and dynamics in Douglas-fir forests, western Oregon. *Journal of Wildlife Management* 44:773–786.

Coleman, Babette Brown, Walter C. Muenscher, and Donald R. Charles. 1956. A distributional study of the epiphytic plants of the Olympic Peninsula, Washington. *American Midland Naturalist* 56:54–87.

Cornaby, B. W., and J. B. Waide. 1973. Nitrogen fixation in decaying chestnut logs. *Plant and Soil* 39:445–448.

Correll, D. L. 1986. *Watershed Research Perspectives.* Washington, D.C.: Smithsonian Institution Press.

Courtney, S. P. 1986. The ecology of pierid butterflies: dynamics and interactions. *Advances in Ecological Research* 15:51–131.

Cramer, Owen P. (editor). 1974. *Environmental effects of forest residues management in the Pacific Northwest.* General Technical Report PNW-24. Portland, Ore.: Pacific Northwest Forest and Range Experiment Station, USDA Forest Service.

Daterman, G. E., J. C. Miller, and P. E. Hanson. 1986. "Potential for gypsy moth problems in southwest Oregon." In *Forest pest management in southwest Oregon,* edited by O. T. Helgerson, 37–40. Corvallis, Ore.: Forest Research Laboratory, Oregon State University.

Denison, William C. 1979. "*Lobaria oregana,* a nitrogen-fixing lichen in old-growth Douglas-fir forests." In *Symbiotic nitrogen fixation in the management of temperate forests,* edited by J. C. Gordon, C. T. Wheeler, and D. A. Perry, 266–275. Corvallis, Ore.: Forest Research Laboratory, Oregon State University.

Elton, Charles S. 1966. *The Pattern of Animal Communities.* New York: John Wiley & Sons.

Franklin, Jerry F., Virginia H. Dale, David A. Perry, Frederick J. Swanson, Mark E. Harmon, Thomas A. Spies, Arthur McKee, David Larsen, and William K. Ferrell. 1989. "Effects of global climatic change on forests in northwestern North America." In *Consequences of the greenhouse effect for biological diversity.* New Haven, Conn.: Yale University Press. (In press).

Franklin, Jerry F., C. T. Dyrness, Duane G. Moore, and Robert F. Tarrant. 1968. "Chemical soil properties under coastal Oregon stands of alder and conifers." In *Biology of alder,* edited by J. M. Trappe, J. F. Franklin, R. F. Tarrant, and G. M. Hansen, 157–172. Portland, Ore.: Pacific Northwest Forest and Range Experiment Station, USDA Forest Service.

Franklin, Jerry F., and Richard T. Forman. 1987. Creating landscape patterns by forest cutting: ecological consequences and principles. *Landscape Ecology* 1:5–18.

Franklin, Jerry F., H. H. Shugart, and Mark E. Harmon. 1987. Tree death as an ecological process. *BioScience* 37:550–556.

Franklin, J. F., T. Spies, D. A. Perry, M. Harmon, and A. McKee. 1986. "Modifying Douglas-fir management regimes for nontimber objectives." In *Douglas-fir: stand management for the future,* edited by C. D. Oliver, D. P. Hanley, and J. A. Johnson, 373–379. Seattle, Wash.: College of Forest Resources, University of Washington.

Graham, Robin Lambert. 1982. *Biomass dynamics of dead Douglas-fir and western hemlock boles in mid-elevation forests of the Cascade Range.* Ph.D. Thesis. Corvallis, Ore.: Oregon State University.

Gregory, S. V., F. J. Swanson, and W. A. McKee. 1989. An ecosystem perspective of riparian zones; submitted to *BioScience.*

Grier, C. C., K. A. Vogt, M. R. Keyes, and R. L. Edmonds. 1981. Biomass distribution and above- and below-ground production in young and mature *Abies amabilis* zone ecosystems of the Washington Cascades. *Canadian Journal of Forest Research* 11:155–167.

Harmon, M. E., J. F. Franklin, F. J. Swanson, P. Sollins, S. V. Gregory, J. D. Lattin, N. H. Anderson, S. P. Cline, N. G. Aumen, J. R. Sedell, G. W. Lienkaemper, K. Cromack, Jr., and K. W. Cummins. 1986. Ecology of coarse woody debris in temperate ecosystems. *Advances in Ecological Research* 15:133–302.

Harr, R. Dennis. 1982. Fog drip in the Bull Run Municipal Watershed, Oregon. *Water Resources Bulletin* 18:785–789.

_____. 1986. Effects of clearcutting on rain-on-snow runoff in western Oregon: a new look at old studies. *Water Resources Research* 22:1095–1100.

Harvey, A. E., M. J. Larsen, and M. F. Jurgensen. 1979. Comparative distribution of ectomycorrhizae in soils of three western Montana habitat types. *Forest Science* 25:350–358.

Hoyer, G. E., and J. D. Suanzy. 1986. *Growth and yield of western hemlock in the Pacific Northwest following thinning near the time of initial crown closing.* Research Paper PNW-365. Portland, Ore.: Pacific Northwest Forest and Range Experiment Station, USDA Forest Service.

Karieva, P. 1983. "Influence of vegetation texture on herbivore populations: resource concentration and herbivore movement." In *Variable plants and herbivores in natural and managed systems,* edited by R. F. Denno and M. S. McClure, 259–289. New York: Academic Press.

Kilsgaard, C. W., S. E. Greene, and S. G. Stafford. 1987. Nutrient concentrations in litterfall from some western conifers with special reference to calcium. *Plant and Soil* 102:223–227.

Kozlowksi, T. T., and Helen A. Constantinidou. 1986. Environmental pollution and forest growth. Part II. Factors affecting responses to pollution and alleviation of pollution effects. *Forestry Abstracts* 47:105–132.

Leverenz, Jerry W., and Deborah J. Lev. 1987. "Effects of carbon dioxide-induced climate changes on the natural ranges of six major commercial trees species in the western United States." In *The greenhouse effect, climate change, and U.S. forests,* edited by William E. Shands and John S. Hoffman, 123–155. Washington, D.C.: The Conservation Foundation.

Maser, Chris, Robert F. Tarrant, James M. Trappe, and J. F. Franklin (editors). 1988. *From the forest to the sea: a story of fallen trees.* General Technical Report. Portland, Ore.: Pacific Northwest Forest and Range Experiment Station, USDA Forest Service. (In press).

Maser, Chris, and James M. Trappe (editors). 1984. *The seen and unseen world of the fallen tree.* General Technical Report PNW-164. Portland, Ore.: Pacific Northwest Forest and Range Experiment Station, USDA Forest Service.

McDade, M. H., F. J. Swanson, W. A. McKee, and J. F. Franklin. 1989. The source area for coarse woody debris in small streams in western Oregon and Washington. *Canadian Journal of Forest Research* (in press).

Minshall, G. W., R. C. Peterson, K. W. Cummins, T. L. Bott, J. R. Sedell, C. R. Cushing, and R. L. Vannote. 1983. Interbiome comparison of stream ecosystem dynamics. *Ecological Monographs* 53:1–25.

Oliver, Chadwick Dearing, Kevin L. O'Hara, George McFadden, and Ichiro Nagame. 1986. "Concepts of thinning regimes." In *Douglas-fir: stand management for the future,* edited by C. D. Oliver, D. P. Hanley, and J. A. Johnson, 246–257. Contribution No. 55. Seattle, Wash.: Institute of Forest Resources, University of Washington.

Perry, D. A. 1988. An overview of sustainable forestry. *Journal of Pesticide Reform* 8:8–12.

Perry, D. A., R. Molina, and M. P. Amaranthus. 1987. Mycorrhizae, mycorrhizospheres, and reforestation: current knowledge and research needs. *Canadian Journal of Forest Research* 17:929–940.

Perry, D. A., and G. B. Pitman. 1983. Genetic and environmental influences on host resistance to herbivory: Douglas-fir and the western spruce budworm. *Zeitschrift fuer Angewandte Entomologie* 96:217–228.

Reukema, D. L. 1979. *Fifty-year development of Douglas-fir stands planted at various spacings.* Research Paper PNW-253. Portland, Ore.: Pacific Northwest Forest and Range Experiment Station, USDA Forest Service.

Ross, E. W. 1973. *Fomes annosus in the southeastern United States: relation of environmental and biotic factors to stump colonization and losses in the residual stand.* Technical Bulletin 1459. Washington, D.C.: U.S. Department of Agriculture.

Schneider, Stephen H. 1989. "Climate-change scenarios for impact assessment." In *Consequences of the greenhouse effect for biological diversity.* New Haven, Conn.: Yale University Press. (In press).

Schowalter, T. D. 1986. Ecological strategies of forest insects: the need for a community-level approach to reforestation. *New Forests* 1:57–66.

———. 1989. Canopy arthropod community structure and herbivory in old-growth and regenerating forests in western Oregon. *Canadian Journal of Forest Research* (in press).

Schowalter, T. D., W. W. Hargrove, and D. A. Crossley, Jr. 1986. Herbivory in forested eocsystems. *Annual Review of Entomology* 31:177–196.

Schultz, J. C. 1983. "Habitat selection and foraging tactics of caterpillars in heterogenous trees." In *Variable plants and herbivores in natural and managed systems,* edited by R. F. Denno and M.S. McClure, 61–90. New York: Academic Press.

Seastedt, T. R., and D. A. Crossley, Jr. 1981. Microarthropod response following cable logging and clear-cutting in the southern Appalachians. *Ecology* 62:126–135.

Sedell, J. R., and F. J. Swanson. 1984. "Ecological characteristics of streams in old-growth forests of the Pacific Northwest." In *Fish and wildlife relationships in old-growth forests: proceedings of a symposium,* edited by W. R. Meehan, T. R. Merrill, Jr., and T. A. Hanley, 9–16. Washington, D.C.: American Institute of Fishery Research Biologists.

Sharpe, R. F., and J. W. Milbank. 1973. Nitrogen fixation in deteriorating wood. *Experimentia* 29:895–896.

Shigo, A. L. 1985. Wounded forests, starving trees. *Journal of Forestry* 83:668–673.

Spies, Thomas A., Jerry F. Franklin, and Ted B. Thomas 1988. Coarse woody debris in Douglas-fir forests of western Oregon and Washington. *Ecology* 69:1689–1702.

Sun, Marjorie. 1985. Possible acid rain woes in the West. *Science* 228:34–35.

Turner, D. P., and E. H. Franz. 1985. The influence of western hemlock and western redcedar on microbial numbers, nitrogen mineralization, and nitrification. *Plant and Soil* 88:259–267.

Waring, R. H., and J. F. Franklin. 1979. Evergreen coniferous forests of the Pacific Northwest. *Science* 204:1380–1386.

Webster, J. R., and E. F. Benfield. 1986. Vascular plant breakdown in freshwater ecosystems. *Annual Review of Ecology and Systematics* 17:567–594.

Whitham, T. G. 1983. "Host manipulation of parasites: within plant variation as a defense against rapidly evolving pests." In *Variable plants and herbivores in natural and managed systems,* edited by R. F. Denno and M.S. McClure, 15–41. New York: Academic Press.

Witcosky, J. J., T. D. Schowalter, and E. M. Hansen. 1986. The influence of time of precommercial thinning on the colonization of Douglas-fir by three species of root-colonizing insects. *Canadian Journal of Forest Research* 16:745–749.

Woodman, James N. 1987. "Potential impact of carbon dioxide-induced climate changes on management of Douglas-fir and western hemlock." In *The greenhouse effect, climate change, and U.S. forests,* edited by William E. Shands and John S. Hoffman, 277–283. Washington, D.C.: The Conservation Foundation.

Zinke, P. J., and R. L. Crocker. 1962. The influence of giant sequoia on soil properties. *Forest Science* 8:2–11.

Chapter 7

Maintaining and Improving Site Productivity in the Douglas-Fir Region

Richard E. Miller, William I. Stein, Ronald L. Heninger, William Scott, Susan N. Little, and Donald J. Goheen

ABSTRACT

Land managers need to know which forest practices may be used on a given site without impairing productivity, as well as where and when intensive practices may best improve current and long-term stand growth. Concerns and knowledge about long-term productivity in the Douglas-fir Region are summarized in this chapter. The focus is on direct evidence (measured effects on tree growth); indirect evidence (measured effects on site factors or processes likely to affect tree growth and from which impacts may be inferred) is also considered but requires more substantiation to be of greater value. Direct evidence about tree response to practices is short term and uncomfortably scarce; longer term effects are unknown. Moreover, impacts vary depending on site, practice, and operator. This shortage of quantitative information makes managers uncertain and skeptical about the consequences of their operations and raises specific concerns. Some concerns, such as nutrient loss, are common to two or more practices, suggesting that the successive combination of individual practices will have cumulative effects on site productivity. Timber harvest, site preparation, and vegetation control can alter factors that influence short-term and, potentially, long-term site productivity. Harvesting and site preparation (1) seldom increase inherent productivity and (2) always disturb soil and cause nutrient loss. Substituting intensive silvicultural practices may offset some long-term losses. In the final analysis, however, the comparative biological and economic costs of soil conservation vs. soil substitution or replenishment must be evaluated. To cope with uncertainty and reduce skepticism, managers should, for example, avoid unnecessary soil disturbance and loss of organic matter through the common-sense approach of conservation, and monitor some sites to document responses of trees and site factors to specific forest practices. Simultaneously, technical staff and researchers face the formidable task of quantifying potential trade-offs between short-term production and efficiency and long-term site productivity in complex ecosystems.

INTRODUCTION

The Douglas-fir Region, typically rich in soil resources, water, and species diversity, comprises part of northwestern California and most of western Oregon, Washington, and British Columbia located between the coast and the higher elevation true fir (*Abies* spp.) and mountain hemlock [*Tsuga mertensiana* (Bong.) Carr.] forests. Southeast Alaska is included as a natural extension of the coastal forest.

In distribution and commercial importance, Douglas-fir [*Pseudotsuga menziesii* (Mirb.) Franco] dominates in the Region. Ecologists in the United States generally describe the area as the Sitka spruce/western hemlock [*Picea sitchensis* (Bong.) Carr.]/[*Tsuga heterophylla* (Raf.) Sarg.] zone, or western hemlock zone, because of the assumed eventual climax dominance of these shade-tolerant species if left undisturbed by wildfire and humans (Franklin and Dryness 1969). Ecologists in British Columbia, however, regard Sitka spruce as a successional species and Douglas-fir as a climax species on many mesic or drier sites in their coastal Douglas-fir biogeoclimatic zone and under similar conditions in coastal Washington (Klinka et al. 1984). Regardless of classification, these evergreen forests are adapted to a winter-wet, summer-dry environment. Trees continue to photosynthesize, store food, and take up nutrients during the relatively mild winters (Waring and Franklin 1979). Subregional variations in geology, soils, climate, and vegetation are amply described by Franklin and Dyrness (1969) and Heilman et al. (1979).

Major natural factors which limit production of some commercial forests in the Region include available water, available nitrogen, pathogens, and wildfire. In addition, effects of management activities on soil physical and chemical properties and on species composition, stand density, and vegetation can be of concern. In this chapter, we focus on direct evidence—as measured by response in tree growth—of the positive and negative effects of management activities on productivity. Direct evidence is not abundant for any practice, and is poor or lacking for some. Moreover, the cumulative effects of management activities, either individually (successive harvests) or in combination, have not been scientifically documented. Where direct evidence is weak, we draw on indirect evidence—measured effects on site factors or processes such as soil properties, microclimate, or biology, from which consequences on tree growth may be inferred. We discuss individual management practices (timber harvesting, site preparation, vegetation control, and site improvement and protection) and then suggest ways to conserve and monitor site productivity and thereby improve our understanding of complex ecosystems.

CONCEPTS AND DEFINITIONS

The sustained production of timber relies on a series of activities to harvest and renew forest stands. Some activities, such as construction of road systems and landings or burning of old-growth slash (harvest residue), are primarily one-time events associated with the conversion of virgin old-growth to managed forests. Other activities, such as road maintenance, biomass removal, site preparation, reforestation, and vegetation control are integral components in the production and harvest of successive forest crops, although their uses and applications are likely to differ; even the percentage of biomass removed, the objective of production, may differ in successive crops.

Every forest practice is undertaken for immediate or long-term benefits, but it may also have negative impacts. Predicting the net impact on timber production is difficult, given the change in practices over time, the mix of practices that may be used, the interactions among practices, the variability of sites, and the difference in expertise by which practices are carried out. Such uncertainty provides ample room for divergent opinions about the effects of forest practices on site productivity, as illustrated in Figure 7.1. Optimists assume that harvest of old-growth stands has no effect on future productivity and that individual silvicultural practices increase timber production. In contrast, pessimists assume that harvest reduces inherent site productivity and that most silvicultural practices have negative or no effect on timber production. For illustrative purposes, the percentage gains in Douglas-fir timber production assumed by the USDA Forest Service for silvicultural practices in a typical forest on the west side of the Cascade Mountains are also shown (Timber Management Staff, personal communications, Region 6, USDA Forest Service, Portland, 1984, 1988). The estimated gains from genetics, precommercial thinning, vegetation control, and fertilization are assumed to be additive for specified periods after treatment. Potentially, the effects could be additive, less than additive, or more than additive (synergistic).

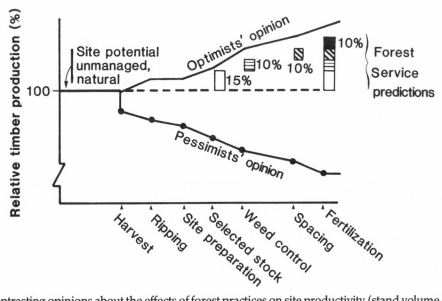

FIG. 7.1. Contrasting opinions about the effects of forest practices on site productivity (stand volume growth) of coast Douglas-fir; the validity of these opinions and predictions for specific site conditions remains uncertain.

Site Productivity

Maintenance and enhancement of site productivity are easily understood objectives and concepts. But translating that objective from concept to quantitative practice is not easy. What is site productivity and how should it be measured? In the National Forest Management Act of 1976 (PL 94-588, 90 Stat. 2949 as amended; 16 USC 472a), "long-term productivity" is defined as the potential of the land to produce wood at consistent levels of quality and volume over hundreds of years without significant reduction in the quality of soil or water resources. If site productivity is defined in terms of wood production, volume growth per unit area would be a useful measure. But volume growth of wood is influenced strongly by site (climate and soil) and other factors. In equation form, forest site productivity may be partly defined as:

Site productivity = (f) soil, climate, tree species, stand density,
silvicultural practices, time, and their interactions.

It is important to recognize, first, that the effect of a change in one factor may be enhanced or counterbalanced by changes in other factors. For example, reductions in soil volume or quality might be compensated for by silvicultural practices that alter tree species, stand density, competing vegetation, or nutrient availability. Thus, to isolate the effects of forest practices on the soil resource, one must specify, hold constant, or separate the effects of silviculture and climate. Second, although critically important, soil is not a fully independent variable in the site-productivity equation; it is affected by other site factors and especially by management practices.

Judging whether any practice has a positive or negative effect on wood production per unit area requires comparison to a baseline level for specified duration. But what is an appropriate baseline? As a first approximation, growth in natural stands has been broadly grouped into site quality classes which indicate what nature produced in about a century encompassing changes in climate and with usually unknown stand densities and site histories. But do these quality classes adequately define baseline levels against which to detect trends in site productivity and the effects of forest practices? If not, what baseline should be used? The first problem is to measure a change in stand growth, the second to determine how much of that measured change is explained by a specified management activity rather than by change in climate or other factors.

Forecasts of timber yields often assume that inherent site productivity will be maintained or enhanced by intensive forest management (Beuter et al. 1976). Is this assumption realistic and for how long? Timber harvest levels may, in fact, be sustained or increased by substituting intensive silvicultural practices such as fertilization and thinning. In the final analysis, however, the comparative costs of soil conservation and substitutions must be evaluated.

Long-Term Site Productivity

In the Douglas-fir Region and elsewhere, long-term effects (e.g., those over several rotations or centuries) on site productivity are not well identified. Most reports contain predictions based on short-term observations of soil properties or seedling growth. Such effects may be of only short duration and might be favorable, adverse, or synergistic. Geppart et al. (1984) posed the following questions for judging whether a forest practice can have long-term effects on site productivity:

(1)   What properties or processes are changed by the practice?
(2)   What are the relative magnitude and direction of change?
(3)   What is the duration of the effect?
(4)   What interactions with other changes are likely?
(5)   Over what time and space are forest practices occurring on the site?

These questions may help both the authors and readers of this chapter place different components of long-term site productivity in perspective.

TIMBER HARVESTING: EFFECTS ON PRODUCTIVITY

Clearcutting is the most common final harvest system in the Douglas-fir Region—about 100,000 acres (40,500 ha) are clearcut annually in Washington and Oregon. The effect this harvesting has on site productivity depends on several factors, including:

(1)   Standards of utilization and yarding methods.
(2)   Frequency of cutting cycles and length of rotation.
(3)   Initial site conditions (e.g., nutrient quantities and distribution, soil moisture, and snow cover).
(4)   Changes in microclimate and soil physical properties which affect rates of organic matter decom-

position and vegetation succession.

(5)   Additive, subtractive, or synergistic interactions among these and other factors.

Some effects of timber harvesting in the Douglas-fir Region have been reviewed by Bell et al. (1975), Cromack et al. (1978), Kimmins (1974, 1977), and Perry and Norgren (1983). For additional information on North American conditions in general, see Leaf (1979) and Harvey et al. (1980).

Timber harvest involves the use of heavy equipment to construct roads and yard logs. Major concerns about harvesting and long-term site productivity include:

(1)   Initial displacement of soil and subsequent displacement or loss through accelerated erosion or landslides (mass failure); this is a strong concern on steep slopes where road construction and harvesting can reduce soil stability (see chapter 5, this volume).

(2)   Compaction of mineral soil; this reduces infiltration rate, changes drainage patterns, and increases resistance of soil to root penetration. Compaction is a major concern on landings and skid trails (see chapter 4, this volume).

(3)   Initial nutrient loss from harvest and subsequent loss by leaching; nutrient loss is a particular concern in infertile soils and where vegetation is slow to develop after disturbance (see chapter 3, this volume).

Area Dedicated to Roads

Commercial forests in the Douglas-fir Region are commonly harvested by clearcuts staggered in time and place; about 2–15% of the gross land area is dedicated to the permanent transportation system (Sidle 1980). Long-span cable yarding generally requires less area for haul roads than tractor yarding. Regardless of yarding system, steep slopes require more area for roads. In addition, land is allocated to spur roads and to landings either permanently or temporarily (if rehabilitated and planted).

Growth of roadside trees, however, may benefit from the increased light, increased moisture, and reduced competition afforded by their location. Indeed, Pfister (1969) reported for an Idaho location that diameter and height growth of western white pine (*Pinus monticola* Dougl. ex D. Don) within 24 ft. (8 m) of single-lane roads averaged about 30% greater than growth of trees located farther from the road. Similar data are not available for the Douglas-fir Region, but we may assume that not all of the area cleared for permanent roads is removed from timber production.

Megahan's (1986) summary is pertinent:

> "On balance, the percentage of area devoted to construction of forest roads is a poor index of changes in site productivity. Actual productivity losses will tend to be considerably less than the percentage of area devoted to roads except possibly in areas where off-road groundwater or landslide problems exist. Adverse effects tend to increase with exceptional road width and vary by biogeoclimatic regions. A lack of change in site productivity does not mean that forest roads are environmentally benign. Downstream effects of forest roads, especially with respect to sedimentation, can be an important consideration in many areas."

Initial Soil Disturbance

Sources of disturbance. Initial soil disturbances from harvesting include compaction, kneading, churning, and removal of surface soil and subsoil. After harvesting, erosion and mass movement of soil can cause additional disturbance. Differing amounts and combinations of disturbance occur depending on the logging system used, skill of operator, time of year harvested (wet or dry soil conditions), number of trips, amount of slash and forest floor on the soil, depth and extent of the root mat, and soil texture. Investigators seldom separate the various types of disturbance, often compositing them as "compaction." Because ground-based logging systems usually cause more disturbance than cable systems, most research has examined the former.

Soil disturbance from ground-based systems is caused by both machine and logs. Logs may be transported with the leading ends raised in an arch or on a bunk behind the skidder or may be dragged full length on the ground. Soil compaction and churning begin when the skidder and its load first move over the ground. With repeated trips, soil compaction becomes severe and occurs at greater depths; surface soil churning also increases. Many trips can be made with no direct soil contact, however, thereby avoiding churning, in areas where slash is deep and continuous and if logs are carried with the leading ends raised. Hence, soil compaction is the only disturbance. Where slash is light or discontinuous and the leading ends of logs are not lifted, the "plowing action" of the logs exposes mineral soil in relatively few trips. Under wet conditions with repeated "plowing" by the trailing logs and compaction by the tractor, the surface soil is churned, puddled, and mixed with the forest floor and slash. In this way, heavily used trails can be disturbed to a depth of 12+ in. (30+ cm).

Soil can be disturbed more directly. On steeper slopes or in deep slash, an operator may blade a skid trail, especially where tractors traverse on contour. Blading immediately exposes soil to churning, puddling, and compacting. More significantly, blading removes (displaces) surface soil and exposes subsoil generally of much poorer quality for plant growth.

Having observed the above sequences and resulting soil disturbances from a number of ground-based systems (rubber-tired skidders, crawler or rigid-tracked tractors, and FMC bombadiers), Scott et al. (1979) suggested four classes of soil disturbance based on the type and degree of disturbance (Fig. 7.2). This qualitative classification system is easy to use and to communicate to loggers, foresters, and researchers because the four disturbance classes are readily recognized. This system is used subsequently in this chapter.

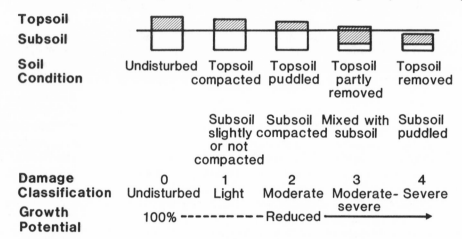

FIG. 7.2. Site-disturbance classification system used by Weyerhaeuser Company (Scott et al. 1979).

TABLE 7.1. Areal extent of soil disturbance in the Douglas-fir Region caused by tractor logging after clearcutting.

Location, by source	Results (% of gross area affected)
Western Washington	
Steinbrenner and Gessel (1955a)	Skid trails (17–34)
Scott et al. (1979)	Skid trails (33)
	Primary trails (14)
	Secondary trails (14)
	Tertiary trails (6)
Western Oregon	
Dyrness (1965)	Area compacted (27)
	Deeply disturbed (9)
	Slightly disturbed (26)
Froehlich (1973)	Heavy disturbance (20–30)
	Some disturbance (40–60)
Aulerich et al. (1974)	Skid trails (16–27)
	Major trails (10)
	Secondary trails (8)
	Lightly used trails (2)
Froehlich (1978)	Skid trails (12–15)
Sidle and Drlica (1981)	Skid trails (14)
	Low-use trails (4)
Wert and Thomas (1981)	Area compacted (25)
Western British Columbia	
Bockheim et al. (1975)	Total area disturbed (87)
	Mineral soil exposed (69)
	Deep disturbance (58)

Area in skid trails. In clearcuts harvested by tractors in the Douglas-fir Region, skid trails cover 12–87% of the area (Table 7.1). Least disturbance results when low volumes per unit area are removed and when yarding systems that primarily lift rather than drag logs (e.g., skyline, balloon, or helicopter) are used. Area disturbed by cable systems in one investigation ranged from 35–45%; moreover, 7–11% of the logged area was compacted and 6–14% deeply disturbed to the subsoil (Dyrness 1965). Balloon logging caused the least amount of disturbance, with only 4% of the logged area compacted or deeply disturbed (Dyrness 1972). Because these yarding methods are more costly, skidding logs with tractors, especially rubber-tired tractors, is more common where slopes are less than about 30% and skidding distances less than about 800 ft. (240 m).

Early tree growth on skid trails. Survival of seedlings planted on skid trails is seldom lower than that on other areas in clearcuts (Youngberg 1959, Miller et al. 1988), possibly because vegetation competition is less on skid trails compared to the remaining area. In naturally seeded stands, however, Steinbrenner and Gessel (1955a) reported 20% less stocking on skid trails than in adjacent logged-only portions of nine clearcuts in western Washington.

Total height of Douglas-fir on skid trails 2–8 years after seeding or planting has ranged from 8% more to 21% less than that on adjacent cutover areas (Fig. 7.3). Steinbrenner and Gessel (1955a) reported that skid trails with a 35% increase in soil bulk density resulted in a 20% reduction in average height of 2–4 year old, artificially seeded Douglas-fir seedlings (average sample size/age group = 17 for skid trail, 99 for control). However, portions of these skid trails either were also deeply churned or had significant amounts of surface soil displaced. Froehlich (1979b) reported that height of 5-year-old planted seedlings on Dunn Forest in western Oregon was 8 and 12% less on skid trails where soil bulk densities were increased 10% after 6 and 10 trips, respectively, compared to controls (average sample size = 48 trees/treatment). On the Molalla Forest in Oregon, a 9–14% increase in soil bulk density for 6 and 10 trips, respectively, resulted in an 11–21% decrease in total height of 6-year-old seedlings (average sample size = 50 trees/treatment); no information was provided about vegetative competition and other soil disturbance which may have occurred (Froehlich 1979b).

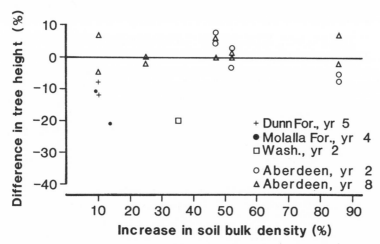

FIG. 7.3. Relationship between the increase in soil bulk density and Douglas-fir seedling height at sites in Oregon and Washington.

In contrast, Miller et al. (1988) detected little difference in height of 2-0 and 2+1 Douglas-fir seedlings in the second and seventh year after planting at three sites (960 seedlings/site) in coastal Washington. These study areas were on productive, silt loam soils where large volumes were harvested in midwinter. At two of the sites, soil disturbance on skid trails was mostly Class 2 (moderate), with approximately 25% Class 3 (moderate-severe) interspersed in small portions. Soil bulk densities immediately after logging increased an average of 55% on these two sites, yet average heights of seedlings growing on skid trails and on logged, slash-burned areas in the second year after planting did not differ. Height differences for the two stock types and locations ranged from +7 to −3%, with an average difference of 2.3% in favor of the skid-trail planting.

At the third site, soil disturbance from logging on the major skid trails was more severe and ranged from Class 2 through Class 4 (severe). Increases in soil bulk density averaged 86% on the Class 4 portions and 36–41% on the Class 2 and 3 portions. Two years after planting, both stock types on skid trails averaged 3–4% taller (over all disturbance classes) than those on logged, scarified areas and 0–3% shorter than those on nonscarified controls.

By the seventh and eighth years after planting at all three sites, however, height of both Douglas-fir stock types growing on skid trails and on scarified and nonscarified control areas did not differ significantly (differences ranged from +12 to −2%); results for average stem volumes were similar. Soil bulk density 8 years after logging was still 6–31% greater in the surface 12 in. (30 cm) on skid trails (Miller et al. 1988).

Equal numbers of western hemlock and Sitka spruce were also planted at these three sites. By the second year after planting, height of 2+1 hemlock seedlings on skid trails averaged 15% less and that of 2-0 spruce 11% less than height of seedlings growing off skid trails. In the seventh and eighth years after planting, hemlock trees growing on skid trails averaged 4% shorter than those off skid trails. Sitka spruce, however, had recovered from early height reductions and were equal to or slightly taller (+7%) than those growing off skid trails.

Four explanations may be offered for these results. First, the maximum soil bulk density recorded at the three sites was only 1.1 g/cc for the Class 4 disturbance level; thus, a growth-limiting density was probably not attained. Forristall and Gessel (1955) estimated that the upper limit of soil bulk density for Douglas-fir root growth is 1.25 g/cc. Heilman (1981) estimated the limiting bulk density for root penetration to be 1.7–1.8 g/cc for Douglas-fir seedlings in artificially compacted cores of sandy loam to loam-textured soils; height growth, however, was not affected at these soil densities. Singer (1981) reported a laboratory study in which bulk densities ranging from 0.9 to 1.1 g/cc for clay loam and from 1.06 to 1.35 g/cc for sandy loam had no significant effect on shoot growth of 2-year-old Douglas-fir seedlings. Minore et al. (1969) also found that bulk densities as high as 1.59 g/cc had no significant effect on shoot dry weight of 2-year-old Douglas-fir. Thus, increases in bulk density expressed as a percentage may be less meaningful than absolute values (see also chapter 4, this volume).

Second, seedlings may not have been stressed by soil damage at these sites because environmental conditions were favorable enough to compensate for the unfavorable soil condition. Third, soil bulk density may have returned to near normal levels; however, this speculation is not supported by measurements made 8 years after planting, although some recovery did occur. Last, and most plausibly, root growth may have been inhibited for a few years until roots began to exploit the adjacent, relatively undisturbed soil. These four possible explanations need not be mutually exclusive. The low soil bulk density and favorable climate at all three sites are probably strong contributors to all explanations.

To better understand or assess the impact of soil disturbance caused by harvesting, we need to observe height and volume growth through time coupled with more detailed evaluations of changes in soil properties. So far, few studies have measured and reported trends in height growth over time on skid trails or attempted to relate changes in height or volume growth to changes in soil physical properties caused by logging.

Midrotation yields and skid trails. Growth of trees beyond the seedling stage should be an improved predictor of growth over a rotation, but its significance to long-term productivity remains unknown. To evaluate fully the effects of skid trails on site productivity of established stands, we must quantify (1) tree growth on specified strata or conditions, and (2) extent of these strata or conditions within the total logged area.

Wert and Thomas (1981) estimated yield losses associated with major skid trails in an older clearcut by comparing tree size and numbers; both components were reduced on skid trails. They measured all trees on 11 acres (4.45 ha) of a 32-year-old, unmanaged Douglas-fir stand in western Oregon which had 10% of its total area in skid trails. Total standing volume, estimated for skid trails, a buffer zone (10 ft., or 3.0 m, on either side of the trail), and the logged-only remainder, was 486, 1,386, and 1,843 ft.^{3}/acre (34, 97, and 129 m^3/ha) for the three zones, respectively. The estimated volume loss was 12% for the entire 11 acres at age 32. Trees in the skid trails took 4 more years to reach breast height (4.5 ft., or 1.4 m above ground) than did trees in the cutover areas. Once the skid-trail trees reached breast height, however, subsequent height growth was at the same rate as on the logged-only areas. The fact that early differences in height growth were not maintained over the entire period is consistent with the observations made by Miller et al. (1988).

More recently, Scott and others (Bill Scott, personal communication, Weyerhaeuser Co., 1987) investigated seven 28–39 year old, natural or planted Douglas-fir stands on tractor-logged clearcuts in western Washington and Oregon. In each stand, two plots ranging from 0.5 to 5.0 acres (0.20 to 2.01 ha) were installed in well-stocked portions of the stand, but the percentage of plot area in skid trails differed. Three site conditions were recognized in each plot: distinct skid trails, a 16-ft. (5-m) buffer on either side of the skid trail, and a logged-only control with no visible evidence of skid trails. Area and standing volume for each condition were determined. Yield changes were estimated as the difference between the volume per unit area on the logged-only control and that of the total plot.

Distinct skid trails averaged 16% of total plot area and ranged from 7 to 30% among the 14 plots (7 locations each with 2 plots). Soil disturbance level was Class 3 and 4; the small amounts of Class 2 were seldom identifiable and showed no measurable losses in tree growth. Yield changes on the 14 plots ranged from −17 to +18% (Fig. 7.4). For four stands where competing vegetation was not severe or was overtopped by Douglas-fir, plot yield averaged 10% lower because of the skid trails. For three of the seven stands, however, brush competi-

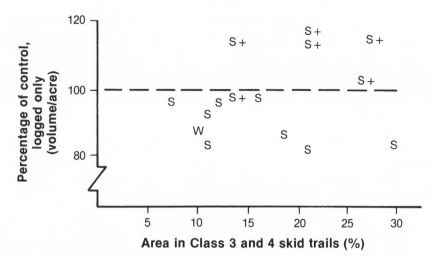

FIG. 7.4. Volume per unit area on an entire plot (comprising skid trails, buffer, and remaining logged-only control) as a percentage of volume on the control area for 28–39 year old Douglas-fir stands on tractor-logged clearcuts in western Washington and Oregon. Data sources: S, S+ = B. Scott (personal communication, Weyerhaeuser Co., 1987), W = Wert and Thomas (1981); Scott's locations with severe vegetation competition have + symbol.

tion was strong on the logged-only areas but nearly absent on the skid trails; brush reduced production on the logged-only areas to less than that on the skid trails and buffers. Consequently, volume production for entire plots was reduced by 11%. We believe that on these sites, where water is probably the most limiting growth factor, reduced vegetation competition on skid trails proved more beneficial than the potentially poorer soil conditions that also resulted from soil disturbance.

Commercial thinning. Skidding logs in commercial thinning can reduce short-term growth of trees near skid trails; longer term effects on growth and productivity are unknown. Froehlich and Berglund (1976) compared basal-area growth of 93 trees before and after thinning in five Douglas-fir stands in Oregon. Cores were extracted from 10 to 28 trees in each stand; no trees with bole damage were sampled. Disturbance was classified at each tree according to the percentage of the root zone affected, measured increase in soil bulk density, and distance from stem to the major disturbance. For lightly, moderately, and heavily disturbed trees, respectively, 4, 14, and 60% showed reduced growth in the 5–15 years after thinning. Moderately disturbed trees averaged 14% less basal-area growth. Growth loss was related to distance of soil disturbance from the tree and severity of disturbance; growth loss also appeared proportional to the affected percentage of the root zone. No undisturbed trees were measured, so the effects of disturbance cannot be separated from the effects of thinning. If thinning had increased growth, then the 14% reduction in basal-area growth after trees were moderately disturbed underestimates the impact of skidding on growth.

In a 22-year-old western hemlock stand near Seaside, Oregon, commercial thinning resulted in 15% reduction in 5-year basal-area growth of individual trees whose root zones had been moderately disturbed (Froehlich 1979a).

In neither thinning study, however, can one translate results to a total stand basis; this is critical for properly evaluating the effect of ground skidding on yield. Any tree root system transected by a skid rut is either wounded or completely severed. Although reduced growth of damaged trees is likely, poorer tree growth near skid trails may improve the growth of adjacent trees. Root damage by logging equipment may also reduce tree vigor and therefore resistance to insects and disease. For example, black stain disease in Douglas-fir plantations in western Oregon is believed to be related to soil disturbance (Hansen et al. 1986).

Summarized below are some of the difficulties confounding interpretation of results for most studies of soil disturbance:

(1) Tree growth on skid trails is influenced by soil compaction and other disturbance, but simultaneously by shrubs, grasses, and trees on the trails and in adjoining areas.

(2) Height growth is often used as a measure of early tree growth, but it is only one component. Diameter and volume growth may be better measures but have seldom been used.

(3) When effects on large trees (poles or larger) are investigated, trees measured on both compacted and noncompacted areas should have about the same growth potential. They should, for example, have similar crown class and surrounding density.

(4)   Effects on stand growth are more important than effects on tree growth, but more difficult to quantify.

Indirect evidence. Activities associated with harvesting can compact soil (Froehlich 1978, Froehlich et al. 1980, Sidle and Drlica 1981, Smith and Wass 1985). The most commonly reported changes in soil physical conditions are summarized in Table 7.2. Soil compaction is associated with decreased macropore (large soil pore) space, reduced soil aeration, reduced infiltration rates, increased volumetric water storage capacity with light to moderate compaction but reduced capacity with severe compaction (see chapter 4, this volume), increased or reduced nutrient availability, breakdown of soil structure, increased shear strength, and increased potential for runoff and erosion (see chapter 5). Changes in these factors could ultimately affect tree growth (see reviews by Greacen and Sands 1980, Froehlich and McNabb 1984, Alexander 1985).

TABLE 7.2. Changes in soil properties caused by ground-based skidding in the Douglas-fir Region.[1]

Location, by source	Results
Western Washington Steinbrenner and Gessel (1955b)	Tractor roads vs. undisturbed 93% loss in permeability 53% loss in macropore space 35% increase in BD
Western Oregon Youngberg (1959)	Cutover (control): 0.87–0.98 BD, 0% change Berm: 1.01–1.05 BD, 11% increase in BD Road: 1.58–1.73 BD, 78% increase in BD
Dyrness (1965)	Undisturbed: 0.60 BD Slightly disturbed: 0.58 BD, 3% decrease in BD Deeply disturbed: 0.77 BD, 28% increase in BD Compacted: 0.98 BD, 63% increase in BD
Aulerich et al. (1974)	Major trails: +21% (0–15 cm), +17% (15–30 cm) in BD Secondary trails: +16% (0–15 cm), +12% (15–30 cm) in BD Lightly used: +13% (0–15 cm), +6% (15–30 cm) in BD
Power (1974)	Area 2, skid trails: 34–45% increase in BD Area 3, skid trails: 26–52% increase in BD
Froehlich (1976)	Skid trails: 13–21% increase in BD

Froehlich (1978)	Mt. Hood NF (sandy loam)
	    Undisturbed: 0.65 BD (at 5 cm), 0.87 BD (at 15 cm)
	    1–3 trips: 1.03 BD (at 5 cm), 0.89 BD (at 15 cm)
	    6–10 trips: 1.06 BD (at 5 cm), 1.01 BD (at 15 cm)
	Umpqua NF (sandy clay loam)
	    Undisturbed: 1.06 BD (at 5 cm), 1.06 BD (at 15 cm)
	    1–3 trips: 1.09 BD (at 5 cm), 1.17 BD (at 15 cm)
	    6–10 trips: 1.08 BD (at 5 cm), 1.07 BD (at 15 cm)

Sidle and Drlica (1981)	Skid trails: average exceeded 40% increase in BD
Wert and Thomas (1981)	Skid trails: after 32 years 8–16% increase in BD

[1]BD = bulk density (g/cc); NF = National Forest.

In addition to compaction, surface soils, subsoils, and organic debris in skid trails may be churned and mixed together in various proportions. Varying depths of soil can also be displaced to expose subsoils which are generally less fertile than surface soils. Subsoils also tend to have greater bulk density and poorer structure with fewer macropores than surface soils. Exposed subsoils usually become compacted further during logging. These soil changes may reduce tree growth and yield, a result generally attributed to reduced root growth.

Soils vary in their susceptibility to compaction; soil texture and moisture content are key variables. Clay soils are more vulnerable to serious compaction and puddling than are sandy or gravelly soils and are particularly vulnerable when near field-moisture capacity. On fine-textured soils under the wet soil conditions typical for the Northwest, Froehlich et al. (1980) reported that six trips with track-laying or rubber-tired skidder, or a crawler tractor, produced 60% of the change in soil bulk density that 20 trips produced. Steinbrenner (1955) reported that logging when soils were wet caused significantly greater decreases in macropore space and infiltration rate and increases in soil bulk density than did logging when soils were dry. For a given soil texture, forest soils with low organic matter content are more susceptible to compaction than those with high organic matter content (Howard et al. 1981).

In most literature about soil disturbance, a change in bulk density is treated as an index of change in soil productive capacity. Yet plotting reported percentage differences in total height of 4- to 11-year-old (from seed) Douglas-fir stands against percentage increases in soil bulk density immediately after logging does not appear to produce a significant relationship (Fig. 7.3). The average of 21 data points shows a 2.7% reduction in total height for young Douglas-fir stands established on skid trails compared to the same-aged stands growing off skid trails. Childs et al. (in chapter 4, this volume) suggest additional reasons why the relationship between decreased height and percent increase in bulk density needs reanalysis. Moreover, height growth is but one component of volume growth; diameter growth and stand density should also be measured. The critical issue is this: Do measured changes in soil properties provide reliable indicators of change in short- or long-term site productivity?

Some methods of yarding or residue treatment cause more soil disturbance than others. The amount and types of disturbance also vary from site to site and from operator to operator, and the effects on tree growth can be negative, neutral, or positive. Critical variables include size and amount of residue, equipment used, irregularity of terrain, moisture content at time of traffic, and inherent soil fragility. For quality land management, treatment and equipment should be specially prescribed for each site and situation. On most soils, deep compaction and displacement probably will have some undesirable effects on tree growth and soil organisms (see chapter 3, this volume). Without designed and long-term studies to separate the potentially positive and negative effects of skid trails on stand growth, skepticism about net effects will remain.

Subsequent Soil Loss

Road construction and maintenance in steep terrain are major and recurring causes of landslides and surface soil erosion in the Douglas-fir Region (Swanston and Dyrness 1973, Swanson et al. 1982). Although occupying 2–15% of the total management area, roads account for a much higher percentage of landslide and erosion problems. Erosion potential is also increased both by harvesting, which can expose mineral soil on as much as 70% of the clearcut area (Bockheim et al. 1975), and by site preparation.

Tree growth after landslides. Land management activities, especially road building, can accelerate landslide occurrence on steep mountainous terrain of the Coast Range and western Cascades (Gresswell et al. 1979). The effects of landslides on short-term forest productivity were estimated at 16 locations in the upper Blue River drainage in Oregon. Stocking levels and recent height growth of Douglas-fir on naturally regenerated 11–28 year old landslides were compared with those of nearby plantations of similar topography and age (Miles et al. 1984). For 16 paired areas, most recent 5-year height growth averaged 62% less on landslides. More sample plots were stocked in clearcuts than in the slide area (82 vs. 62%), and this was attributed to the greater amount of unstable or impenetrable substrata. Note, however, that the difference in stand origin help explain the differences in stocking and growth. The authors reaffirmed the need to determine the areal extent of landsliding and growth reductions over at least one rotation.

Smith et al. (1986) investigated landslides from 1 to 155 years old on the Queen Charlotte Islands in British Columbia. The slides were not caused by logging; practically all were debris slides, avalanches, and flows, and a few were rotational slumps. Over about 60 years, productivity on these naturally regenerated slides was about 70% less than that of equal-aged, natural stands on adjacent logged areas. Differences were due largely to poorer growth rates and stocking of the upper portions of slide areas and to severe competition from red alder (*Alnus rubra* Bong.) in middle and lower slide areas. Logged stands over 55 years old were not sampled, so it was not possible to determine directly whether this 70% volume reduction would continue. Yield-table projections indicated that the reduction at 85 years would be about 45% for all species and 65% for conifers. We speculate, however, that (1) future growth of conifers may be increased by the nitrogen added by the nitrogen-fixing alder, and (2) yield reductions would be lower if slide areas were planted and brush competition was controlled. Our point is that silvicultural expenditures can offset at least some losses from soil disturbance. Moreover, a long-term perspective must be used when projecting effects of soil disturbance and competition. Bormann's observations (Bernard Bormann, personal communication, USDA Forest Service, Juneau, Alaska, 1988) about landslides on Queen Charlottes Island and in southeastern Alaska are cogent. Older (perhaps 80–200 years) landslide depositional areas are readily apparent from the air or ground. The pure spruce stands have dark blue-green foliage, in stark contrast to the adjacent chlorotic spruce-hemlock stands. Alder may initially reduce conifer growth on depositional areas, but may improve site productivity in later stages and, perhaps, future rotations.

Soil erosion. Soil erosion and site productivity are closely linked (see chapter 5, this volume). Erosion affects productivity and, through its support of protective vegetative growth, site productivity affects future erosion (Stocking 1984). Erosion causes productivity loss through a variety of responses. Because erosion selectively removes the finer, more fertile soil particles, overall soil fertility is reduced. Erosion also causes crusting, compaction, and increased soil strength, all of which can suppress plant growth. Reduced moisture-holding capacity and soil rooting depth are major reasons why erosion degrades site productivity (Stocking 1984). The National Soil Erosion-Soil Productivity Research Planning Committee (1981) also concluded that "erosion reduces productivity first and foremost through loss of plant-available soil moisture capacity." Productivity inevitably declines as erosion causes root-restricting layers to be nearer the surface and as the water-holding constituents of the soil (organic matter and fine particles) are washed away. Consequently, the decline is most likely in marginal, particularly drier, environments.

Assessing the effects of erosion on site productivity is difficult. Erosion rates are poor indicators of loss in productivity because most soil is redistributed within a catchment and is not necessarily lost to crop production (Stocking 1984). Moreover, the effects of erosion on site productivity vary; some soils or locations show considerable erosion but site productivity remains unaffected (Larson et al. 1983). Soils differ in their tolerance to erosion losses. For example, andosols (e.g., volcanic ash) have relatively high water-holding capacity and natural fertility. Erosion may be severe on sites with such soils, but productivity may decline little. In contrast, sites with eroded spodosols (podsols) frequently lose productivity because those soils are commonly highly leached and naturally infertile, retain fertilizers poorly, and have low water-holding capacity.

The effects of erosion on site productivity have been simulated in agriculture, but not forestry, by removing soil to various depths and measuring subsequent plant growth. Klock (1982), however, described a greenhouse bioassay to simulate the effect of erosion on growth of grass and conifer seedlings on four forest soils of northeast Washington. This bioassay showed that (1) the top few inches (centimeters) of soil were most critical to plant growth, (2) the four soils varied greatly in their productivity after topsoil losses, and (3) plant species differed in their response to soil removal. How to interpret yield reductions found in simulated erosion studies, however, remains unclear. Greenhouse bioassays, for example, probably underestimate reductions in the field because greenhouse-grown plants are well watered. Observed differences in greenhouse tests are mostly due to nutrient losses. Stocking (1984) concluded that (1) in every field comparison, natural erosion reduced yields more than the experimental "erosion" of an equivalent depth of surface soil, and (2) simulated removal underestimates yield reductions because erosion due to water selectively removes the finer, more fertile particles.

In summary, we agree with McColl and Grigal (1979) that evaluating net, long-term loss in site productivity from measured erosional loss or mass movement is uncertain. In some places, soil is only displaced downslope, and, overall, the slope may remain just as productive. On complex slopes, eroded material deposited downslope may even increase growth locally, offsetting upslope losses.

Initial Nutrient Loss

Tree growth after intensive utilization. Bigger and Cole (1983) provide the only published quantification of growth of coast Douglas-fir after varying degrees of biomass removal. In their study area at Pack Forest, Washington, an average-quality (site III) and a poorer quality (site IV) Douglas-fir stand were harvested at three intensities of utilization: bole only, whole tree (bole + crown), and complete aboveground biomass including subordinate vegetation. There was no additional site preparation or vegetation management. Douglas-fir seedlings (2-0) were planted on the two clearcuts shortly after harvest and measured each year. Harvesting intensity had no statistically significant impact on 2-year survival, which averaged 73% at the site IV location and 92% at the site III (Bigger and Cole 1983). Equating height growth for the conventional bole-only level to 100%, whole-tree and complete harvest decreased 6-year height growth by 22 and 23%, respectively, at the site IV location, but increased height growth by 11 and 3%, respectively, at the site III location (Table 7.3). Diameter growth showed greater percentage decreases (site IV) and increases (site III). The significance of the initial differences in growth will be determined in future measurements.

Nutrient export. Inferences about long-term site productivity can be based on nutrient balance sheets. Loss of nitrogen (N) is of particular concern in Douglas-fir forests. Johnson (1983) estimated that conventional bole-only harvest removed only 2–8% (194–304 lb./acre, or 218–349 kg/ha) of the total nitrogen capital of Douglas-fir ecosystems, but whole-tree harvest generally removed about twice as much. Increased removal of nutrients by whole-tree harvesting in Douglas-fir stands has also been projected by Kimmins (1977) and Miller et al. (1976).

Further investigations of N losses at Pack Forest, Washington, after various harvest intensities indicate greater absolute and percentage losses than those cited previously for these site III and IV locations (Table 7.4). The preharvest nitrogen supply (vegetation, forest floor, and mineral soil) at the site III location was about 3-fold greater than that of the site IV location. Conventional bole-only harvest removed about 3-fold more nitrogen from the site III than from the site IV location. Increasing harvest intensity from bole only through whole tree and complete aboveground biomass doubled nitrogen loss at the site III location, but more than tripled loss at the site IV location. Leaching losses were also greater on the poorer site, so that the combined losses (leaching + complete biomass removal) exceeded 50% of the initial nitrogen supply at the site IV location (Table 7.4). These major losses in N supply relate to reduced seedling growth at site IV, but not at site III (Table 7.3).

Researchers generally agree that harvesting most of the bole will not greatly deplete nutrients, but that short rotations and whole-tree harvests remove more nutrients and accelerate other losses at a rate that will diminish reserves and availability of N, phosphorus, potassium, calcium, and possibly other elements. Harvesting crowns is particularly undesirable because they contain a large proportion of stand nutrient content. Yet whole-tree harvesting of 50- to 100-year-old Douglas-fir can leave many of the branches on site because they are broken during felling and yarding (Bill Webb, personal communication, consulting forester, 1987).

TABLE 7.3. Six-year diameter and height growth of 2-0 Douglas-fir seedlings planted after three harvest treatments of varying intensities on two sites of differing quality, Pack Forest, Washington (Dale Cole, personal communication, University of Washington, Seattle, 1987).[1]

Harvest treatment	Height growth			Diameter growth		
	Ft.	(m)	Relative	In.	(cm)	Relative
	Site III (average)					
Bole only	5.7	(1.74)a	100	1.13	(2.87)a	100
Whole tree	6.4	(1.94)b	111	1.27	(3.22)b	112
Complete[2]	5.9	(1.81)ab	104	1.40	(3.55)c	124
	Site IV (poor)					
Bole only	4.5	(1.37)a	100	0.85	(2.16)a	100
Whole tree	3.5	(1.07)b	78	0.64	(1.62)b	75
Complete[2]	3.4	(1.05)b	77	0.57	(1.45)b	67

[1]Among treatments within each site type, values with different letters are significantly different (p = 0.05).
[2]Complete removal of all aboveground biomass.

TABLE 7.4. Losses from the total nitrogen (N) pool (to 20-in., or 50-cm, depth) after harvest of Douglas-fir on two sites (same as in Table 7.3) of differing quality, Pack Forest, Washington.

Treatment	Total N[1]	Harvest loss[1]	3-yr leaching loss[2]	% lost
	lb./acre (kg/ha)			
	Site III (average)			
Uncut	—	0 (0)	0.3 (0.3)	—
Bole only	2,621 (2,935)	419 (470)	4.0 (4.4)	16
Whole tree	2,525 (2,827)	606 (678)	0.5 (0.5)	24
Complete	2,428 (2,719)	777 (870)	0.6 (0.7)	32
	Site IV (poor)			
Uncut	—	0 (0)	0.9 (1.0)	—
Bole only	879 (984)	141 (157)	1.8 (2.1)	16
Whole tree	806 (903)	258 (289)	4.2 (4.7)	32
Complete	834 (934)	434 (486)	4.9 (5.5)	53

[1]Total nitrogen above and in soil to specified depth; derived from Bigger and Cole (1983) except where noted in footnote 2.
[2]Dale Cole, personal communication, University of Washington, Seattle, 1987.

Subsequent Nutrient Loss

Nutrient losses can also be accelerated after harvesting by three other processes: (1) gaseous losses of N to the atmosphere, (2) leaching of ions beyond the root zone, and (3) soil erosion (Stone 1975; see also earlier in this chapter).

Clearcutting increases soil temperature, available moisture, and amounts of residues on the forest floor. The rate of organic matter decomposition and the amounts of nutrients released to the soil and plants are usually accelerated (Cole and Grier 1965), as shown by analysis of soil leachates (Table 7.4). By removing vegetation, clearcutting temporarily reduces the ability of a site to retain nutrients. Reestablishment of nutrient cycling and reduced leaching losses accompany the luxuriant development of shrubs and herbs that survive logging or rapidly invade clearcuts; this vegetation provides soil protection, organic matter, and a nutrient "sink."

Increased nutrient concentrations have been measured in streams draining conventionally harvested and site-prepared watersheds (Fredriksen 1972, Brown et al. 1973, Scrivener 1982, Feller and Kimmins 1984); these increases are due to the combined contribution of increased leaching, erosion, mass soil movement, and deposition of slash in streams. Sampling soil solutions below the rooting zone provides more reliable evidence about leaching losses and forest productivity. Such measurements taken from a coarse-textured, N-poor soil in western Washington showed that leaching losses after clearcut harvest and slash burning are temporal and small (Cole and Grier 1965). In more nutrient-rich ecosystems with a high component of red alder, however, more intensified harvesting released much greater quantities of nutrients in the soil solution (Miller 1974; written communication with Dale Cole, University of Washington, Seattle, 1987).

In summary, forest sites in the Pacific Northwest generally have a high capacity to retain nutrients and to limit losses to ground water (Cole 1981) or surface streams (Fredriksen 1972). Ordinary leaching losses of N in the Douglas-fir Region are commonly less than amounts of N added by precipitation. McColl and Grigal (1979) opined that under well-managed harvest and post-harvest conditions, temporarily increased leaching losses may degrade quality of surface water, but generally are not great enough to reduce site quality.

SITE PREPARATION: EFFECTS ON PRODUCTIVITY

Timber harvest in the Douglas-fir Region is usually followed by slash disposal or other site preparation to reduce fire hazard, facilitate planting, and provide initial control of competing vegetation. Treatment methods most commonly used, singly or in combination, are (1) mechanical removal of boles during or after harvest, (2) burning logging residue, and (3) chemical or manual techniques to control competing vegetation. Concerns about effects of mechanical site preparation on productivity are similar to those about harvesting—displacement, compaction, and loss of mineral soil and rearrangement or loss of nutrients and organic matter. Site preparation by controlling competing vegetation raises additional concerns addressed in the next section in this chapter. In this section, we concentrate on effects of site preparation by burning.

Slash is most commonly disposed of by broadcast burning. Residues are sometimes piled by machine on slopes less than 30% if the risk of soil disturbance appears minimal. Piled residues can be burned on a more controlled basis than scattered debris; fire intensity is increased but the effects are concentrated on a limited area. The further soil disturbance from machine piling, however, is an added concern. Closer utilization and improved markets for firewood, hogged fuel, and nontraditional wood products can reduce the amounts of logging residues remaining on sites and therefore the need for further site treatment. For these reasons, as well as to reduce costs and attain environmental objectives, fewer harvested units are being burned in the Northwest states, and more seedlings are being planted in unburned slash; where units are being burned, timing has been shifted to reduce emissions and consumption of forest floor. In British Columbia, however, use of broadcast burning is increasing (Mike Feller, personal communication, University of British Columbia, Vancouver, 1987).

Site-preparation methods have been summarized by Stewart (1978), different aspects of fire effects by Zivnuska (1972), Wells et al. (1979), Boyer and Dell (1980), Feller (1982), and Loucks et al. (1986). A compendium (Cramer 1974) covers environmental effects of residue management and specifics for major forest types (Miller et al. 1974, Ruth and Harris 1974) in the Douglas-fir Region.

Broadcast Burning

When fire is prescribed for site preparation, the most common method is broadcast burning. However, the multiple effects of broadcast burning in the Douglas-fir Region have been debated and studied for over half a century. Substantial information has been accumulated, yet the evidence is so fragmentary and sufficiently contradictory that an adequate balance sheet on the effects of burning on forest productivity is still not possible. Among its important effects, broadcast burning reduces advance regeneration (the numbers of tree seedlings established before clearcutting); increases the mineral soil surface available for establishment of naturally regenerating seedlings; increases the potential for soil erosion and nutrient leaching; makes areas more accessible for planting and big game; may temporarily reduce rodent populations; eliminates residual competing vegetation but may also trigger germination of other species; changes the status of organic matter, nutrients, and surface soils; reduces the amount of fuel available for wildfire; and contributes to air pollution and risk of escaped fire.

These effects are not uniformly distributed but are influenced by the kind, amount, moisture content, and distribution of slash and residual vegetation; the topographic features—slope, aspect, and drainage pattern; and the atmospheric conditions when the burn occurs. Consequently, even on a single clearcut, broadcast burning creates a mosaic of effects. Previously bare areas and those where slash was sparse or its moisture content high may hardly be affected. Additional soil exposure may range from as little as 8% to more than 40% (Miller et al. 1974, Smith and Wass 1983, Little et al. 1986). Soil impacts are severe where heavy accumulations of fuels are concentrated—landings, crossed logs, and piles of large slash. Typically, less than 10% of the area is severely affected when old-growth Douglas-fir slash is burned in early fall (Tarrant 1956, Dyrness 1966, Morris 1970). Given the multiplicity of possible consequences and the mosaic of conditions created on burned areas, the net influence on timber yield is not yet predictable.

Survival and early tree growth. In general, broadcast burning tends to directly or indirectly facilitate establishment and growth of Douglas-fir seedlings, one of the prime objectives of burning. Burning bares more mineral soil, a prerequisite for the natural establishment and early growth of Douglas-fir and other pioneering species but not necessarily of true firs and hemlocks (Isaac 1938, 1963). Broadcast burning also reduces physical obstacles for planting crews; these effects are generally recognized and investigations to quantify them are underway (John Zasada, personal communication, Forestry Sciences Laboratory, USDA Forest Service, Corvallis, 1988). Several studies have shown that survival or early growth of Douglas-fir was less on severely burned spots than on lightly or moderately burned spots (Isaac and Hopkins 1937, Austin and Baisinger 1955, Lavender et al. 1956, Knight 1965, Baker 1968), but no significant difference was reported in another study (Tarrant and Wright 1955). Because severity of burn classes was retrospectively and subjectively rated, it is not certain whether these outcomes are truly contradictory; nor is it possible to judge to what minor percentage of a burned clearcut they apply.

Published results of two regeneration surveys provide evidence that burning sometimes has mixed or negative effects on conifer regeneration. Surveys on 4,130 acres (1,700 ha) of clearcuts regenerated between 1958 and 1963 in coastal forests of northwest Washington showed that (1) survival of planted Douglas-fir was equal, and distribution of 1- to 4-year-old planted trees better, on burned than unburned areas, but (2) early growth was less and animal damage (primarily by elk and deer) greater (Gockerell 1966). Including naturally established seedlings, total stocking on 4-milacre (0.0016-ha) plots averaged only 4% greater on unburned areas (77 vs. 73%); seedlings of western hemlock, Sitka spruce, and western redcedar (*Thuja plicata* Donn. ex D. Don) were taller, but those of Pacific silver fir (*Abies amabilis* Dougl. ex Forbes) shorter, on unburned than burned areas. In northern California, where regeneration was compared on one unburned and two burned clearcuts located on soil derived from granite, the percentage of stocked quadrats after 6 years was much higher (36 vs. 10%), dominant trees were nearly twice as tall, and brush cover was less (46 vs. 55%) on the unburned than on the two burned areas (Heavilin 1977). Stocking of conifer seedlings, however, was highest in adjacent uncut stands (62%); thus burning apparently eliminated much more advance regeneration than was lost during harvest. Although regeneration surveys provide valuable insights, they are not pure comparisons; such retrospective studies leave in doubt the comparableness of the planting efforts and the initial conditions that prompted clearcuts to be designated to be burned or left unburned.

Such reservations are greatly reduced in direct, side-by-side comparisons. On 10 Coast Range clearcuts in Oregon, survival and total height of planted Douglas-fir were greater after 5 years on burned than unburned sites (Stein 1984, 1986). The differences in survival, however, were not as large when trees were protected by plastic mesh that prevented mountain beaver from clipping stems (Table 7.5). Height differences of trees growing in burned and unburned areas were about the same for protected and unprotected trees. Amount and composition of competing vegetation also differed on burned and unburned areas. Continued monitoring of tree and vegetation development will provide a longer term comparison.

Effects at midrotation. Morris (1958, 1970) conducted an extensive long-term study on effects of burning old-growth slash on fire hazard and conifer regeneration in the Pacific Northwest. The study design originally included pairs of burned and unburned plots at 62 locations in western Washington and Oregon. At each location, Morris (1958) attempted to match the paired plots in slope, aspect, soil, and logging disturbance. Plots were established within 1 year after burning, but no specific data on burning conditions before or during treatment were available for most plots. All burns were conducted in fall, although under a variety of fuel and moisture conditions. Transects of post-burn conditions, supplemented with photographs taken when plots were established, allow comparison of burned and unburned plots (Fig. 7.5); at a few locations, more large woody debris on the burned than the unburned plot indicates that the unburned was not a perfect match.

TABLE 7.5. Survival and average total height of unprotected Douglas-fir and those protected by plastic mesh 5 years after planting on broadcast-burned and unburned sites in the Oregon Coast Range.

Site treatment	Survival, %		Total height, ft. (m)	
	Unprotected	Protected	Unprotected	Protected
Systems study, 6 sites (Stein 1984)				
Broadcast burned	59	88	4.6 (1.4)	5.6 (1.7)
Unburned control	46	83	3.8 (1.2)	5.0 (1.5)
Difference	13	5	0.8 (0.2)	0.6 (0.2)
Site-preparation study, 4 sites (Stein 1986)				
Broadcast burned	79	85	7.3 (2.2)	8.2 (2.5)
Unburned control	54	72	5.3 (1.6)	6.1 (1.9)
Difference	25	13	2.0 (0.6)	2.1 (0.6)

A   B

FIG. 7.5. Burning logging slash after clearcut harvest can remove large quantities of aboveground organic matter. Burned (A) and unburned (B) plots established by Morris (1958) in 1950 near Enumclaw, Washington.

In 1986 and 1987, 44 of the original 62 pairs were reestablished by Miller et al. (1986). Measurement of these stands in the Cascade Range of western Washington and Oregon 35–42 years after first harvest provides the longest yield comparisons available for quantifying the net effects of slash burning in the Douglas-fir Region. Preliminary analysis of these recent data (paired t-tests) indicates that, Cascade-wide, the average difference in site index between paired burned and unburned plots was not statistically significant. For some locations (e.g., nos. 30, 40, 49), site index of the two plots seemed considerably different (Fig. 7.6), but the lack of treatment replication at any location precludes a statistical test at individual locations. No consistent pattern related to burning is evident. Despite the mosaic of burn intensities in burned plots, variation in site index within burned and unburned plots did not differ.

Twenty-eight of these stands regenerated naturally; 14 were planted to Douglas-fir and two to ponderosa pine (*Pinus ponderosa* Dougl. ex Laws.). Results were similar for both planted and naturally regenerated locations. Species composition varied among the locations and between the burned and unburned plots at most locations. Number and volume of Douglas-fir were greater on burned plots, but those of other conifers were greater on unburned plots. Advance regeneration of hemlock and true fir species was more likely to survive on unburned areas, whereas the greater extent of exposed mineral soil on burned areas initially favored Douglas-fir (Morris 1970). The stem volume of current live and past cut and dead trees was estimated for each species. For all species combined, the average difference in cumulative gross volume growth for the 44 reestablished burned and unburned plot pairs was not statistically significant even though volume was obviously much greater on burned plots at some locations and on unburned at others (Fig. 7.7):

Stand component	Treatment	Cumulative gross volume, ft.³/acre (m³/ha)
Trees 1.6 in. (4.1 cm) and larger diameter at breast height (DBH)	Burned	2,628 (184.0)
	Unburned	2,543 (178.0)
	Difference	85 (6.0) [3%]
Trees 7.6 in. (19.3 cm) and larger DBH	Burned	1,996 (139.7)
	Unburned	1,958 (137.1)
	Difference	38 (2.7) [2%]

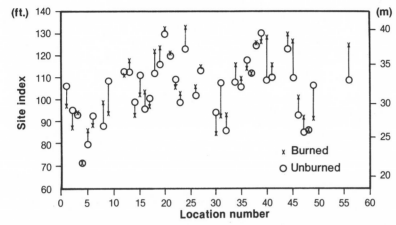

FIG. 7.6. Douglas-fir site index (tree height at 50 years; age determined at breast height) on 42 paired burned and unburned plots 35–42 years after harvest. Locations are numbered in ascending order from the most northerly (no. 1) near Enumclaw, Washington, to the most southerly (no. 49) near Roseburg, Oregon. No. 56 is west of Corvallis, Oregon. (Unpublished data on file at the Forestry Sciences Laboratory, USDA Forest Service, Olympia, Washington.)

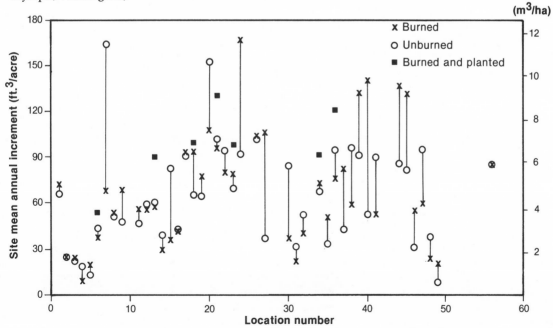

Fig. 7.7. Mean annual gross volume growth in 35–42 years since old-growth harvest or slash burning for trees 1.6 in. (4.1 cm) DBH and larger of all species on 44 paired burned and unburned plots. The 44 locations are numbered in ascending order from the most northerly (no. 1) near Enumclaw, Washington, to the most southerly (no. 49) near Roseburg, Oregon. No. 56 is west of Corvallis, Oregon. At seven locations, a third plot (burned and planted) was recently (1986) established in the plantation surrounding the original burned plot that was naturally regenerated. (Unpublished data on file at the Forestry Sciences Laboratory, USDA Forest Service, Olympia, Washington.)

The current data indicate that the net effect of s lash burning on site index and stand productivity in the western Cascades can range from positive to negative depending on location. Although some of the difference in tree growth between burned and unburned plots could be due to site differences that existed before logging and burning, Morris (1958, 1970) minimized this source of error by matching the plots. Delayed seedling establishment clearly reduced volume growth, but the delay was not consistently related to the treatment. Future analyses will attempt to define the characteristics of locations showing the greatest and least effects of burning on productivity.

At seven locations, cumulative gross volume growth on a burned and planted plot was compared to that on an adjacent burned and naturally regenerated plot. Planted plots averaged 903 ft.^{3}/acre (63.2 m^3/ha)—or 33% more volume growth in trees 1.6 in. (4.1 cm) and larger—and this difference was statistically significant. This result indicates the benefits of planting to avoid vagaries of advance and subsequent natural regeneration.

Indirect evidence. Burning rapidly oxidizes organic matter and releases nutrients. When organic matter is consumed by burning, most of its nitrogen (Knight 1966, DeBell and Ralston 1970, Grier 1972) and sulfur (Allen 1964), and much phosphorus (Grier 1972), are lost as gases or in particulates to the atmosphere. Most ash from consumed organic matter remains on site, where precipitation leaches it into the soil, temporarily increasing pH which may favor nitrate production and nutrient availability; this is termed the "ash effect." The amount of nutrients lost depends on intensity and duration of the burn (Little and Klock 1985, Little and Ohman 1988). Feller et al. (1983) reported the following nutrient losses to the atmosphere during an intermediate- and a low-intensity burn in coastal British Columbia:

Element	Amount lost, lb./acre (kg/ha) at	
	Intermediate intensity	Low intensity
Nitrogen	876 (981.9)	431 (483.1)
Phosphorus	14 (15.7)	7 (7.8)
Potassium	33 (37.0)	15 (16.8)
Calcium	136 (152.4)	78 (87.4)
Magnesium	26 (29.1)	6 (6.7)

Broadcast burning increases the amount of mineral soil exposed by a varying amount, depending on the depth and consumption of forest floor. Additional soil exposure, beyond that due to logging, can be as little as 8% or over 40% (Miller et al. 1974, Little et al. 1986). Thus, slash burning can increase the number of microsites favorable for Douglas-fir seed or make planting of all species easier; however, exposing additional soil on sloping terrain is likely to increase erosion. The effects of burn severity on erosion have been summarized by Dyrness (1966, p. 605):

"Although severe burning may alter surface soil characteristics sufficiently to bring about some increase in erodability, moderate and light burning often have very little direct effect on soil properties. Therefore, the most important changes caused by fire are often not in the mineral soil itself, but rather in the vegetation and litter which protect the soil surface. If essentially all surface fuel is consumed by an intense fire, exposure of mineral soil will often result in decreased infiltration rates largely due to destruction of surface structure by rain drop impact. A light surface fire, on the other hand, will generally only char the litter, leaving most of the mineral soil at least partially covered. In many instances, this remaining litter may afford sufficient protection to maintain soil porosity, and, therefore, to avoid a large-scale increase in accelerated erosion."

However, the significance of erosion to tree growth has not been measured. Erosional and leaching losses are reduced by vegetation that survives slash burning or invades soon afterward (Fredriksen and Harr 1979). Most soil movement occurs during the first season after slash is burned (Bennett 1982), and rapid establishment of vegetative cover can halt soil movement (Mersereau and Dyrness 1972). Areas with delayed vegetative cover, however, are more likely to experience soil movement. For example, vegetation recovery is generally slower on southerly than northerly aspects (Mersereau and Dyrness 1972) and on skid trails.

Physical, chemical, and biological properties of soil are affected on severely burned portions (Isaac and Hopkins 1937, Youngberg 1953, Tarrant 1956, Dyrness and Youngberg 1957, Wright and Tarrant 1958, Neal et al. 1965, Kraemer and Hermann 1979, Schoenberger and Perry 1982, Pilz and Perry 1984). Where burning is severe (generally, less than 10% of the total area), most aboveground organic matter, nitrogen, sulfur, and some phosphorus are lost, but available nitrogen, ash, and pH are likely to increase. Organic matter content and moisture-holding capacity of mineral soil are reduced (Neal et al. 1965). Water-stable soil aggregates are reduced in number and size (Dyrness and Youngberg 1957). Clay and silt fractions decrease with corresponding increase in coarse fractions because water in the clay lattice structure is evaporated; expanding clay types (montmorillonitic) permanently lose their capacity to expand and contract. The net effect on severely burned areas is for clay aggregates near the surface to assume the moisture characteristics of sand and gravel (Ralston and Hatchell 1971). This altering of surface soil characteristics on severely burned patches on steep slopes increases the potential for soil erosion (Dyrness 1966).

Gases released during burning contain hydrophobic substances which condense on cooler surfaces within the soil to cause water repellency that lasts at least 5–10 years (Dyrness 1976). Water repellency is most likely to occur with high-temperature fires. Coarse-textured soils become more water repellent than finer textured soils, possibly because there is less surface area to be coated with hydrophobic substances (DeBano 1981). Water repellency can increase erosion and reduce plant-available water.

Finally, slash burning changes species composition and abundance. Burning eliminates some species found in the original forest and delays expansion of others. On many sites in the Cascades, however, heat from slash burning may stimulate germination of long-dormant seeds of several brush species not present in the stand at harvest (Morris 1958, 1970). These include several species of ceanothus (*Ceanothus*) which host N_2-fixing organisms and which can subsequently increase soil nitrogen status (Zavitkowski and Newton 1968, McNabb et al. 1979, Youngberg et al. 1979). Generally, seedbeds created by light to moderate burning are quickly populated by herbaceous species from windblown seed, soon curtailing soil erosion and nutrient leaching (Dyrness 1965). In the western Cascade and Coast Ranges, total herbaceous growth 3–5 years after burning is not significantly different on burned and unburned areas (Morris 1970). On severely burned spots, however, equivalent cover is delayed by several years.

Piling and Burning

Residue to be burned may be machine piled on areas with mild (less than 30%) slopes where the risk of soil disturbance from machines is thought to be minimal. These piles are subsequently burned in most situations. The long-term effects of such piling and burning on stand productivity are unknown; information about short-term effects is scanty.

Seedling growth. Seedling growth after tractor piling, with or without subsequent burning, was recently documented by Minore (1986) for numerous sites in southwest Oregon. Using his data, we estimate that 5-year height of Douglas-fir seedlings in this area of the Douglas-fir Region was reduced an average of 26% by tractor-piling slash instead of broadcast burning. These current data, however, do not permit estimating effects of broadcast burning on seedling growth.

Indirect evidence. Use of tractors increases disturbance to mineral soil. For example, tractor yarding and slash piling in 11 small clearcuts on 0–15% slopes left an average of 5% undisturbed soil, compared with 44% after high-lead yarding on a 35% slope (Dyrness 1965). Piling of slash also involves redistribution and additional loss of organic matter in affected portions of the site. Soil and much fine logging slash will also be mixed with large debris unless brush blades are used carefully to minimize soil disturbance.

Piled slash burns hotter than broadcast slash, increasing consumption of organic matter and nutrient losses. High soil temperatures generated under burning piles (typically, about 5–10% of the harvested area) severely and negatively affect soil properties by physically changing soil texture and structure and reducing nutrient content. Herbaceous plants invade larger patches of severely burned soil much more slowly than they do adjacent moderately or lightly burned areas (Morris 1970).

Positive and negative effects of slash burning on timber production have been cited; no conclusive evidence on long-term effects is available. Lack of adequate controls and of accurate descriptions of sites and treatments has weakened existing evidence. In general, the consequences of prescribed fire depend on fire severity. Immediate effects can be minimal to substantial; most are controllable through fire management. Loss of soil cover and subsequent erosion by water, wind, or gravity on steep slopes may be of more concern to long-term productivity than initial loss of nutrients.

VEGETATION MANAGEMENT: EFFECTS ON PRODUCTIVITY

As discussed previously, harvesting and site preparation contribute to vegetation management. In this section, we consider known effects on current stand growth and potential impacts on inherent site productivity from weeding, release, and precommercial thinning, the post-stand establishment phases of vegetation management. Various aspects of vegetation management in the Douglas-fir Region have been summarized by Kimmins (1975), Eckhouse et al. (1981), Knapp et al. (1984), Stewart et al. (1984), Perry et al. (1985), and Perry and Tappeiner (1986).

Reducing competition between trees and associated vegetation (weeding and release) and among trees (thinning) has been shown to maintain and enhance volume growth of wood per unit area, increasing yield or actual productivity (see chapter 1, this volume). Even so, we still have much to learn about their wise application—where and when to weed, release, or thin. Weeding, release, and precommercial thinning have little physical impact on the soil because little mechanical rearrangement of the landscape can be tolerated without endangering the developing conifer stand. Biological changes triggered by these treatments are of some concern, for example, in the amount and composition of competing vegetation and, most particularly, in the environmental consequences of herbicide application.

Potential Benefits

Weeding and release. The principle that reducing competing vegetation enhances conifer growth is generally supported by studies in the Douglas-fir Region (e.g., Hawkes 1953, Ruth 1956, 1957, Fritz and Rydelius 1966, Zavitkowski et al. 1969, Gratkowski and Lauterbach 1974, Radosevich et al. 1976, Preest 1977, Peterson and Newton 1982, Howard and Newton 1984, Cole and Newton 1986, McDonald 1986, Walstad et al. 1986). Weeding or release (from overtopping vegetation) often forestalls two kinds of negative impacts on productivity of existing stands: (1) lower stocking levels because potential crop trees died as the result of over-topping, and (2) slowed volume growth due to the competitive effects of associated vegetation. Only short-term gains in tree growth (in most studies, for a decade or less) have been clearly proven. Rotation-length benefits from forestalling mortality can be projected from some short-term results. Longer studies are needed, however, to confirm that short-term gains in volume growth do, in fact, shorten the rotation or result in greater yield over a given period.

Potential gains from release are burdened with another source of uncertainty—identifying the appropriate conditions under which a release treatment will improve growth enough to warrant its cost and side effects. To prevent a substantial setback in growth or even mortality, weeding or release treatments must be applied before tree growth is materially affected. In both operational practice and research studies, it is not uncommon to misjudge the imminence of overtopping and growth slowdown. If this happens, the cost of weeding or release treatment may provide little gain in stand growth. Efforts are underway to develop objective measures of competition which could lead to more selective and effective use of weeding and release.

The need for weeding or release may develop at distinctly different phases of plantation development. The first phase occurs during and immediately after establishment when trees are likely to be affected by pioneering vegetation. Weeding or release may be helpful or even critical in this phase if the site preparation and nursery stock used have not produced trees that dominate competing vegetation. Use of site preparation and large stock can minimize the need for release to overcome short competitors. Tall competitors such as alder (*Alnus* spp.), cherry (*Prunus* spp.), bigleaf maple (*Acer macrophyllum* Pursh), and tanoak [*Lithocarpus densiflorus* (Hook. & Arn.) Rehd.] may overtop crop trees when a plantation is somewhat older; an adequate release treatment is the chief option for maintaining stand productivity in the presence of such competition.

Precommercial thinning. Providing adequate space for crop trees is a proven way to develop usable wood volume more quickly. Therefore, in practice, overstocked young stands are often precommercially thinned. Although thinning temporarily lowers the total amount of biomass produced, it enhances production of usable material. If cut stems are not removed, the impacts of precommercial thinning on soil and other inherent productivity factors should be negligible because dead organic matter is added; moreover, the reduced tree canopy lets in more light, prolonging the life of other vegetation. If thinning slash is burned to reduce fire hazard, however, potential productivity could be lowered (see preceding section of this chapter).

Potential Adverse Effects

In contrast to the clearly demonstrated short-term gains in stand productivity from weeding and release, the potential long-term effects are much more uncertain because vegetation management may:
(1) Remove protective soil cover.
(2) Remove or diminish the amount of vegetation as a nutrient sink.
(3) Remove or reduce the number of nitrogen-fixing plants.
(4) Change species composition or diversity.
Management practices that release crop trees usually result in rearrangement, rather than total elimination, of vegetative cover; their effects are obviously less drastic than those of harvesting and site preparation on competing vegetation.

Protective soil cover. Live vegetation and accumulated organic debris protect the soil surface from the direct impact of rainfall and reduce surface erosion. Vegetation also moderates soil temperature in both hot and cold weather. Consequently, vegetation-control treatments that keep the surface soil bare for extended periods might increase erosion and would increase surface soil temperatures, with attendant positive or negative effects on soil microorganisms and rate of organic matter decomposition. In those parts of the Douglas-fir Region where vegetation competition is most severe, a single weeding or release treatment rarely bares the mineral soil. Most often, the dominant competitors are knocked back but quickly recover or, if eliminated, are replaced by a secondary layer or by a new crop of vegetation. Reductions in competing vegetation are also partially offset by accelerated expansion of tree crowns. Animal use and attendant soil disturbance, however, may be greater in released than unreleased areas. In summary, the potential exists for reduced infiltration capacity and physical loss of soil following vegetation control, but this is unlikely to have lasting consequences on long-term site productivity, particularly compared to the certainty of reduced stand productivity without release where needed.

Vegetation as a nutrient sink. Vegetation that rapidly develops on cleared areas holds nutrients that might otherwise be leached from the site. This living biomass serves as a sink that later yields nutrients as vegetation is gradually suppressed by the developing conifer stand. Whether done manually or with chemicals, weeding, release, and precommercial thinning accelerate decomposition and nutrient release. Limited evidence indicates that nitrogen levels in the soil solution are increased (Sollins et al. 1981, Bigley and Kimmins 1983), but the actual losses of N and other elements from the site are unknown. Undoubtedly, the potential for losses following release is less than that during harvest and site preparation and varies depending on the degree and duration of vegetation reduction.

Nitrogen-fixing plants. Several strongly competitive species, red alder and ceanothus in particular, host nitrogen-fixing bacteria and thus may enhance soil quality and site productivity. If development of these species is curtailed by treatment, a portion of their nitrogen production is forgone. Their N contribution can be important—after crown closure, about 70% of the Douglas-fir stands in the Region benefit from added nitrogen (Miller et al. 1986). Greatest growth increases from added N can be expected on lower quality sites; measurable benefits are fewer where the natural nitrogen supply is high (Miller and Murray 1978, Binkley and Greene 1983, Miller et al. 1986). As expressed by Perry and Tappeiner (1986), "Since far more N is removed in harvest and in site preparation than is input through natural sources other than alder, continued site productivity will require either fertilization at high dosages or incorporation of alder into the conifer rotation in some way."

Nitrogen fixation appears highest during the early years of site occupancy (Youngberg and Wollum 1976), when conifers are most likely to need release. In an age-sequence study over a wide range of western Oregon sites, dense stands of red alder apparently fixed approximately 300 lb./acre (336 kg/ha) of N annually during the first 15 years; little nitrogen was added after 20 years (Newton et al. 1968). In a second age-sequence study, restricted to one soil in western Washington, however, annual N accretion to the ecosystem was estimated at 89 lb./acre (100 kg/ha), and this rate was considered to be maintained for at least 40 years (Bormann and DeBell 1981).

Fortunately, most release treatments do not totally remove competitive species, but generally reduce their density and retard height development. On N-deficient soils, suppression of nitrogen-fixing species like red alder should be minimized to ensure release and, therefore, a conifer stand that can benefit from the nitrogen fixation. Mixed conifer-alder stands or a short rotation of nitrogen-fixing plants can be promoted through silvicultural practices; however, these strategies need additional testing and study.

Species diversity. The term "species diversity" refers to the richness and variety of plants, animals, fungi, and bacteria that naturally inhabit a defined area—an ecological community, a watershed, a region, and even the entire world. A current concern is that some forest practices may increase populations of widespread species at the expense of rarer or more sensitive species (Wilcove 1988).

It is unclear whether vegetation management, as practiced in the Douglas-fir Region to foster forest growth and other objectives, reduces or actually increases species diversity relative to what would occur if stands were left unmanaged. At the inception of managed stands, early successional vegetation is probably as diverse as that which follows natural disturbance. The regeneration period is usually shorter, however, because site preparation and release treatments speed tree growth (see chapter 6, this volume). Release treatments are usually applied when a competitive undesired species has naturally assumed dominance, often as a solid stand of a single species such as salmonberry (*Rubus spectabilis* Pursh), ceanothus, or red alder. Release fosters diversity because the canopy generally is opened enough to allow another wave of annuals and the survival and recovery of trees and understory species overtopped by the previously dominant competitor. Thinnings also foster diversity by reducing tree density, which invigorates the understory. Clearly, the diversity found in overmature old-growth stands cannot develop to the same extent in managed stands because rotations are shorter. Yet considering one aspect of diversity, managed forests in the Douglas-fir Region present a mixture of age classes and species representing greater diversity over the broad landscape than did many mature, natural stands that covered thousands of acres.

In summary, unmanaged stands of Douglas-fir have great diversity at establishment and after a lengthy progression to old growth; but the mix of managed stands can provide substantial species diversity at any point in time. Much study will be required to determine if and to quantify how much vegetation management and other forestry practices affect species diversity and long-term productivity.

MANAGEMENT OPTIONS TO CONSERVE PRODUCTIVITY

"A fundamental long-term question of forest management must be: what are the most efficient strategies to insure a sustained supply of water and nutrients to the growing crop? The answer will require an understanding and quantification of various options of management." (Raison and Crane 1981)

In this context, we have reviewed existing information about the effects of several individual forestry practices on tree growth (our measure of site productivity) and on specific site-productivity factors, especially soil properties. We conclude that limited data are available to quantify the effects of conventional harvesting, site preparation, and vegetation management on even short-term site productivity. This lack of information raises specific concerns which we enumerated and discussed. Some concerns, such as nutrient loss, are common to two or more practices (Table 7.6), suggesting that the successive combination of these individual practices will have a cumulative effect on site productivity.

On the basis of current knowledge, it is prudent to assume that impact of heavy machinery and logs on soil and large losses of N can reduce inherent site productivity at many locations. Conversely, it seems less likely that these actions could improve site productivity at many locations. Managers can minimize negative impacts through good planning and control of operations. Assuming that every action has a reaction, managers should try to control what actions are taken and where, when, and how they will be executed. We agree with Bengtson's (1978) basic thesis that actions taken in anticipation are more effective in the long run than attempts at restoration.

In the remainder of this chapter, we suggest ways to protect, restore, and improve long-term site productivity. Lacking solid evidence, we must speculate, basing many of our suggestions on "best guesses."

TABLE 7.6. Level of concern about how forest practices affect long-term site productivity.

	Forest practice				
		Site preparation		Vegetation management	
Current concern	Timber harvest	Fire	Mechanical	Herbicide	Other
Nutrient and organic matter losses	**	**	**	*	*
Soil displacement and erosion	**	*	**	*	*
Soil compaction	**	—	**	—	*
Leaching losses	**	**	*	*	*
Species diversity	*	*	*	*	*

* = minor concern, ** = major concern.

Conserving Nutrient Capital

Considerations in planning. Setting rotation length, which clearly influences frequency of harvesting, site preparation, and other silvicultural practices, is a major planning decision which can affect long-term productivity. Most soil erosion and leaching losses, for example, occur in the first 3–5 years after harvest and diminish thereafter as sites become fully revegetated (Fredriksen and Harr 1979, McColl and Grigal 1979). Short rotations are especially undesirable on unstable sites. Fredriksen and Harr (1979) determined from watershed sampling that annual outflow after timber harvest may exceed 10 lb./acre (11 kg/ha) of N and speculated that rotations of up to 200 years may be necessary to maintain adequate nitrogen capital on steep, unstable sites subject to mass wasting. For most sites, less frequent entries mean less risk of soil damage and less loss of nutrients.

Intensity of harvest and site preparation can affect long-term productivity; retaining branches and foliage on site can be especially important where nutrient reserves are limited. Natural nutrient inputs to forests are likely insufficient to balance losses associated with intense, short-rotation harvesting (Kimmins 1977, Wells and Jorgensen 1979). A sustained supply of organic matter to the soil is critical for maintaining soil tilth and nutrients. Farrell et al. (1981) concluded that conservation of organic matter and nutrients is the main factor in maintaining site productivity on sandy soils after multiple rotations of pine in Australia. Logging slash can be a nutrient sink. Vitousek and Matson (1985) estimated that the temporary immobilization of N by microbes in logging residues was the most important process for reducing nitrogen losses after clearcut harvesting of loblolly pine (*Pinus taeda* L.); uptake by plants accounted for only 13% of the nitrogen conservation.

Wells and Jorgensen (1979) suggested midcourse corrections after one or more rotations. Asserting that soil moisture supply and site productivity in forests change relatively slowly, they reasoned that intensity of harvest can be reduced, if necessary, after one or two rotations without permanent impairment of long-term productivity. This strategy, however, implies that foresters can monitor and detect changes in stand growth before irreversible levels are reached.

Leaching losses, though relatively small in the Douglas-fir Region after conventional harvesting and site preparation, are greatest where: (1) organic matter mineralization releases large amounts of ammonium that can be converted to leachable nitrate-N by nitrifying bacteria; (2) soils have low cation exchange capacity because organic matter and clay contents are low; (3) precipitation is high; and (4) root and microbial uptake provide insufficient nutrient sinks (McColl and Powers 1984).

Some sites are more robust or resilient to practices than others (Klock 1983). Higher quality sites are generally more robust because they have the following characteristics: (1) relatively large amounts of nitrogen and organic matter in the mineral soil; (2) deep, well-drained soils with high infiltration and moisture-holding capacity—such soils are more stable and have minimal potential for surface erosion and mass movement, or are relatively less affected if these occur; (3) favorable climatic conditions that compensate for degradation of chemical or physical soil properties; and (4) rapid secondary succession by a wide variety of plants that reestablish the nutrient and organic matter cycles. In contrast, lower quality sites generally have (1) less total nutrient and organic matter capital, a higher proportion of which is in the forest floor and stand where it is vulnerable to losses by burning; (2) shallower soils or soils with higher gravel or rock content, which further reduces storage capacity for nutrients and moisture; and (3) steep slopes, which are more vulnerable to mechanical damage and slash burning, especially on southerly aspects—fires are hotter, potential for erosion is greater, and soils are usually shallower than those on level or gentle slopes.

It is important to recognize vulnerable areas and adjust methods and scheduling to reduce impact. Soil maps and supporting interpretations can help managers recognize fragile or robust soils. For example, Klinka et al. (1984) suggested this approach to making slash-burning decisions: (1) identify and diagnose the sensitivity of sites to proposed slash burning, (2) determine the site-preparation needs, and (3) assess the potential effects of slash burning on the site.

To conserve nutrients, land managers can minimize the amounts removed from or relocated within a site by keeping tree foliage and branches in place. Thus, felling, lopping, and scattering are more desirable than whole-tree yarding, piling, or burning unmerchantable material. Further, they can use site-preparation methods that minimize soil disturbance and loss of nutrients and organic matter from wood, forest floor, and surface soil (Raison and Crane 1981, Little and Ohman 1988). Regarding choice of site-preparation method, Bengtson (1978) concluded that any method that effectively controls unwanted vegetation, leaves topsoil in place, and incorporates organic matter with topsoil will leave a far more productive site than methods that remove topsoil and existing vegetation; this advice suggests that herbicides should be preferred to both fire and tractor scarification for site preparation.

Control during operations. Field supervisors can influence when and how well forest practices are executed. The supervisor must inform the crew of objectives and actions that are potentially harmful or beneficial. In particular, machine operators can minimize or maximize disturbance as needed to influence surface drainage and distribution of organic matter and soil. Informed operators can also reduce physical damage to residual trees.

Preventing Soil Displacement, Compaction, and Loss

Considerations in planning. McColl and Grigal (1979) recommend (1) good engineering in road placement and harvesting; (2) minimal disturbance of vegetation, forest floor, and soil; and (3) rapid regeneration and revegetation. Klock's (1979) additional suggestions include (1) identifying unstable slopes with thorough soils and geotechnical examination, (2) avoiding trouble spots or redesigning to accommodate them, and (3) planning to control surface and ground water during and after road construction and logging. Paeth et al. (1971)

describe how soil color and rock type in an extensive area of western Oregon can be used to predict slope stability.

Methods to limit compaction and other soil disturbance include use of designated skid trails, use of arches on tractors, replacement of ground skidding with aerial yarding systems, use of small skidders and low ground-pressure skidders, stricter adherence to soil management guidelines, improved equipment design and operator training, and, when possible, scheduling harvest on sensitive soils when they are dry, frozen, or snow covered (Froehlich and McNabb 1984, Poff 1985).

If harvests during wet weather are necessary, they should be restricted to sandy or gravelly soils whenever possible; conversely, harvests during dry weather should be reserved for clayey soils (McNabb and Campbell 1988). McNabb and Campbell (1988) also suggest coordinating felling and yarding operations on fragile soils. Evapotranspiration is much less after trees are felled. Consequently, soil retains more water and is more susceptible to compaction and puddling. Yarding shortly after felling can reduce this risk. Combining harvesting and site preparation into one contract can facilitate scheduling during drier seasons of the year.

Hatchell et al. (1970) concluded that on moist, medium-to-heavy-textured soils, one yarding trip may do as much damage as several trips; therefore, yarding should be confined to a few primary skid trails which can be retained for future use or restored to some degree by tillage or other treatment (Froehlich and McNabb 1984). On dry or sandy soil, however, little damage is done by one or two trips, so yarding could be dispersed over many different trails. Figure 7.8 provides some useful information about equipment choice and the tolerance of different soil textures to rutting. Note that the ground pressure exerted with cable-logging systems is unlikely to result in soil rutting even when soils are saturated to the soil surface (0 depth to wet-season water table). As the saturated zone moves deeper into the soil, more pressure can be exerted by logging equipment without rutting. Rubber-tired skidders could be used on sandy soils when the saturated zone is at about 6 in. (13 cm) without causing rutting; on clayey soils, however, drainage to about 12 in. (25 cm) would be necessary.

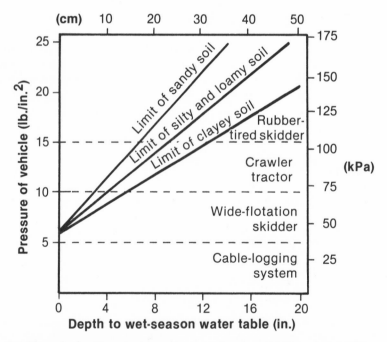

FIG. 7.8. Hazard of rutting during wet-season logging (McKee et al. 1985).

Control during operations. Gouging and compaction of mineral soil should be avoided. Loss of vegetation or forest floor increases the physical impact of precipitation on mineral soil and may channel water to cause surface and rill erosion; potential for dry raveling also increases (Mersereau and Dyrness 1972).

Soils near field capacity are most likely to compact or puddle; puddling occurs when soil aggregates are sheared. Yet direct evidence presented earlier showed that compaction does not always result in reduced tree growth. Nonetheless, it is prudent to (1) avoid machine operations when soils are near field capacity, (2) use organic debris as a cushion, and (3) match equipment size to material being removed. Other ways to reduce compaction and soil disturbance include felling trees to lead, winching logs to skid trails, using equipment with wide tires or tracks or with different suspension systems, and using skilled and informed equipment operators.

Piling slash and vegetation in rows with one pass of the machine decreases soil compaction (McNabb and Campbell 1988), but the piles may not be compact enough to burn well.

Temporary roads and skid trails abandoned between entries should be water-barred to divert water from the road, then reforested or revegetated. Unacceptably high soil bulk densities may be decreased by tilling skid trails after thinning or clearcut harvesting. The procedures for alleviating compaction in forest soils have been reviewed by Andrus and Froehlich (1983) and Froehlich and McNabb (1984); however, neither short- nor long-term growth gains have been evaluated.

Managing Vegetative Cover

Managing nitrogen-fixing plants such as red alder and ceanothus presents an obvious dilemma. These species commonly are strong competitors of conifer crop trees, yet are also potential alternatives to commercial fertilizer in some areas. The value of non-N_2-fixing plants to site productivity is not documented. Generally, some species show (1) an unusually large capacity to accumulate readily leached nitrate-N after clearcutting and fire (e.g., *Epilobium* spp. and *Rubus* spp.), or (2) intense rooting patterns that can reduce surface soil erosion (e.g., grasses).

Both retention and control of vegetation have costs and benefits to be considered during planning and controlling forest practices. The short-term effects to the current crop or rotation are more easily projected from existing information than are those for several rotations. The clearest example is the probable consequence of eliminating nitrogen-fixing red alder in successive rotations of conifers without substituting other sources of nitrogen. We recommend that silviculturists (1) control vegetation where a competition problem exists, but not at all sites, (2) control problem species, but not all species, and (3) promote nitrogen-fixing species on N-deficient sites.

OPPORTUNITIES TO ENHANCE SITE PRODUCTIVITY

Despite good planning and field supervision, one or more factors that influence long-term site productivity may be damaged. If the area and severity of damage exceed the manager's standards, then restorative measures may be justified. Some restoration toward preharvest conditions will occur through natural processes, so we discuss both natural and imposed amelioration.

Productivity in natural Douglas-fir stands is determined largely by soil and climatic factors and can be changed for better or worse by timber harvest and other forest practices. In theory, inherent productivity can be increased on all sites. In practice, however, costs and attendant benefits determine economic feasibility. A general investigative procedure for assessing economic feasibility is to: (1) determine which site productivity factor(s) limit growth, (2) change the factor(s) experimentally, (3) measure resulting changes in tree growth until no further response is detectable, and (4) evaluate the changes in stand value from this treatment relative to its cost. This general procedure was followed to justify operational programs for fertilizing Douglas-fir forests with nitrogen.

Fertilization to remove nutrient limitations and drainage to remove excess moisture are examples of major practices which may improve long-term productivity. Remedial actions to combat root rots also invigorate sites and foster productivity.

Increasing Available Nutrients

Accelerating nutrient cycling. Forest residues must be decomposed before nutrients can be recycled and residues converted to the soil humus important for both soil fertility and moisture relations. A rapid rate of organic matter decomposition is desirable as long as vegetation is present to capture the released nutrients. Conversely, excessive accumulations of forest litter above the soil are undesirable because this usually indicates that nutrients and organic matter are cycling slowly.

Soil fertility, a major factor in determining site productivity, depends strongly on soil microbial activity associated with decomposition of organic matter and mineralization of nutrients (see chapter 3, this volume). Rates for microbial processes, like rates of tree growth, are controlled by environmental conditions and available food supply (Table 7.7). To the extent that silvicultural practices change soil environment or quantity and quality of organic matter returned to the soil, we can shift conditions toward or away from optimum levels of microbial activity. For example, N fertilization invariably increases nitrogen content of foliage and amount of litterfall, especially on poor-quality sites. These changes can increase rates of organic matter decomposition and amounts of available nitrogen and soil organic matter. Thus, reducing a nutrient deficiency for either plants or

TABLE 7.7. Environmental factors and their approximate values controlling microbial activity in soil (adapted from Bollen 1974).

| Factor | Rate of microbial activity | | |
	Minimum	Optimum	Maximum
Moisture, %[1]	5	50	80
Temperature, °C	2	28	40
Aeration, %	Variable	At 50[1]	Variable
pH	4	7	10
Food supply	Variable	Balanced[2]	Variable

[1]Percent of field capacity.
[2]Carbon:nitrogen = 25/1.

microorganisms can accelerate organic matter decomposition rate (Miller et al. 1976, Turner 1977, Heilman et al. 1982, Powers 1983) and improve at least short-term productivity on some sites.

Physical and chemical characteristics of residues affect decomposition rates. In general, the higher the nitrogen concentration and the lower the lignin content of organic matter, the greater the potential for microbial activity and reproduction (Fogel and Cromack 1977, Youngberg 1978, Edmonds 1987). Thus, wood decomposes more slowly than foliage because it has less N and more resistant lignin-cellulose complexes. For optimum rates of decomposition, the ratio of readily available carbon to nitrogen (C/N ratio) in residues should be about 25:1 (Table 7.7).

Moisture-temperature relations are also critical for microbial activity. During winter and spring, moisture content of forest residues in most of the Douglas-fir Region is favorable for microbial activity, but temperatures are below optimum. During summer and autumn, temperatures may be optimum but moisture limiting. The characteristic, rain-free periods in the growing season probably limit moisture supplies for both trees and soil microorganisms that mineralize organic nitrogen. Thus, narrow tree growth rings associated with droughty years reflect N and water deficiency.

Silvicultural practices in the Douglas-fir Region affect nutrient cycling in several ways (see chapter 2, this volume). First, some of the total nutrient capital of the site is removed or changed qualitatively by timber harvest or site preparation; weeding and release that reduce the supply of nitrogen-fixing plants reduce the potential for added N. Second, nutrients can be added by fertilization or by promoting N_2-fixing plants. Third, silvicultural practices may substantially alter the rate of organic matter decomposition and hence nutrient cycling.

Replacing lost nutrients. The supply of available nutrients in the soil largely depends on rates of organic matter decomposition and weathering of soil parent material. Small contributions to the pool of available nutrients also come from nutrients dissolved in precipitation and from nitrogen fixation. Except for nitrogen, the major source of new nutrients is weathering of soil parent material.

Rates of natural additions of new nutrients—other than N—to Northwest forests are not yet quantified. Rainfall annually adds about 1 lb./acre (1 kg/ha) of N, an amount which exceeds normal leaching losses to streams in undisturbed watersheds (Fredriksen 1972, Gessel et al. 1972). According to current estimates, fixation by free-living microorganisms may add annually up to 1 lb./acre (1 kg/ha) of N (Cushon 1985); annual fixation rates are much higher for microorganisms hosted by plants than free-living organisms. For example, red alder stands have contributed annually 50–300 lb./acre (56–336 kg/ha) of N; the estimated period of these rates of fixation after logging and soil disturbance ranges from 15 years (Newton et al. 1968) through 40 years (Bormann and DeBell 1981).

Fertilization, particularly with nitrogen, has been suggested for replacing nutrients and organic matter lost in harvesting. The practicality of replacement fertilization, however, has been questioned. On the basis of N recovery by conifers from fertilizers, Bengtson (1978) concluded that we would have to apply at least twice as much nitrogen as lost by harvesting, topsoil removal, or prescribed burning to "stay even." Wells and Jorgensen (1979) and Ballard (1979) also doubt that productivity can be easily maintained by fertilizers to balance the natural input-output cycle because fertilizers are not 100% utilized. They stated that considerably more research is required to develop efficient fertilizer practices to compensate for increases in nutrient removal.

Crop rotations alternating between conifers and N_2-fixing species have been proposed (e.g., Atkinson et al. 1979, DeBell 1979, Tarrant et al. 1983). In some areas, crop rotations mimic the normal successional pattern following harvest or natural disturbance. In other areas, however, nitrogen-fixing species like red alder and deerbrush (*Ceanothus integerrimus* H. & A.) are not normally succeeded by Douglas-fir (John Tappeiner, personal communication, Oregon State University, Corvallis, 1988). Therefore, costs of converting forest types must be evaluated. Although theoretically feasible, purposeful crop rotation has only been attempted to restore productivity on some Douglas-fir sites infected with the laminated root rot *Phellinus weirii* (Murr.) Gilbertson. Thus, red alder, which is not affected by *Phellinus*, has been planted to provide some timber production during the many decades necessary for *Phellinus*-infected organic matter to decay.

Long-term effects of forest fertilization. Fertilization has short-and long-term implications for site productivity in the Douglas-fir Region. In western Washington and Oregon, more than 1.4 million acres (566,580 ha) have been fertilized in the last 2 decades (Chappell and Opalach 1984). To what extent has this nitrogen fertilization been a long-term, *site*-improving measure rather than a short-term, *stand*-improving measure? If we assume that some of the added N will recycle in future forests, then this fertilization will improve long-term productivity.

Fertilizer trials in Douglas-fir stands have shown that nitrogen increased growth in about 70% of the locations studied (Miller et al. 1986). The extent to which this regional inadequacy of available N is related to the common fire history of the Region and paucity of N-fixing plants at some locations is unknown. Because gains in total volume from nitrogen fertilization are inversely related to site quality, site index is a good predictor of need for fertilization.

Decreasing Excessive Soil Moisture

There have been few attempts to reduce seasonal, saturated soil conditions in some forests of the Douglas-fir Region; the potential for improving growth by soil drainage is unknown. Small, localized areas with poor drainage occur when natural drainages are rearranged or blocked by road construction or harvesting activities. In aggregate, production could be improved over considerable areas. Forest productivity may be also limited by excessive moisture on level topography associated with windblown or lake sediments. More than 200,000 acres (83,500 ha) of forests in western Washington and Oregon could be involved (Table 7.8). Although drainage may prove economically feasible on only a fraction of this area, we will not know until this treatment is experimentally applied and tree response measured.

TABLE 7.8. Area of forest soils in western Washington and Oregon with seasonal water table within 24 in. (60 cm) of the soil surface (Lynn Townsend, personal communication, Soil Conservation Service, Portland, Oregon, 1987).

Soil series	Slope, %	Acres (ha)
Washington		
Bellingham		
Silty clay loam	0–3	17,300 (7,000)
Other	0–1	10,600 (4,290)
Lacamas, silt loam	0–3	40,600 (16,440)
Norma		
Loam	0–3	2,650 (1,070)
Fine sandy loam	—	13,300 (5,380)
Subtotal		84,450 (34,150)
Oregon		
Coquille-Brenner, silt loam	—	13,000 (5,260)
Coquille-Clatsop	0–1	15,800 (6,400)
Dayton		
Silt loam	—	84,200 (34,090)
Silt loam, clay subsoil	—	4,300 (1,740)
Hebo, silty clay loam	0–3	4,700 (1,900)
Subtotal		122,000 (49,390)
Grand total		206,450 (83,580)

Douglas-fir seedlings have low tolerance to flooding and poor aeration associated with compaction or temporary water saturation (Minore and Smith 1971). Western hemlock tolerated a winter water table within 6 in. (15 cm) of the soil surface, but Douglas-fir required 14 in. (36 cm) (Minore and Smith 1971). Power (William E. Power, personal communication, Bureau of Land Management, Salem District, Oregon, 1987) observed 95% mortality in two 1-year-old Douglas-fir plantations where the water table was at the surface for at least 30 days. He also observed increased survival of Douglas-fir seedlings at two locations after artificial drainage. In the South Fork Alsea River locale, this drainage was provided by a ditch to intercept water from an upslope area. In a second locale, installation of a subsurface drain improved survival of Douglas-fir in a swale where the seasonal water table was within 14 in. (36 cm) of the surface. These observations show that localized opportunities exist to enhance growth of some species by drainage or perhaps by the bedding technique (ridge and furrow construction) practiced in the southern U.S.

Technical and economic feasibility of improving drainage is unknown. Although some gains in timber productivity could be achieved, potential negative effects on water and wildlife resources also must be investigated.

Combatting Root Rot

Current situation. Several root diseases of forest trees can persist on an infected area from one tree generation to another; these are considered "diseases of the site." Laminated root rot, caused by *Phellinus weirii*, can significantly reduce long-term site productivity in the Pacific Northwest. *P. weirii*, clearly the most damaging root disease in the Douglas-fir Region, has been estimated to cause annual losses of 32 million ft.^{3} (0.9 million m^3) of wood in Oregon and Washington (Childs and Shea 1967) and 37 million ft.^{3} (1.05 million m^3) in British Columbia (Wallis 1967).

P. weirii spreads little, if at all, by wind-borne spores; virtually all spread is by mycelia on or within roots. The fungus survives in root systems of infected dead or harvested trees for up to 50 years (Buckland and Wallis 1956, Hansen 1979). Disease-induced resin impregnation of infected wood and the ability of *P. weirii* to form a protective hyphal sheath around itself are responsible for the pathogen's long-term survival. When roots of susceptible hosts contact infected residues, their root systems are colonized (Tkacz and Hansen 1982).

P. weirii extensively decays roots of susceptible hosts and thus causes growth loss, butt rot, windthrow, and tree mortality. Any conifer species can be infected, but some conifers tolerate the pathogen better than others (Filip and Schmitt 1979, Hadfield et al. 1986). Among tree species of the Douglas-fir Region, Douglas-fir and grand fir [*Abies grandis* (Dougl. ex D. Don) Lindl.] are considered highly susceptible (readily infected and killed), western hemlock and Sitka spruce moderately susceptible (frequently infected but rarely killed), and cedars and pines tolerant or resistant (rarely infected and almost never killed). Hardwoods including red alder are immune to *P. weirii*.

When a site with *P. weirii*-infected stumps or snags is regenerated with susceptible tree species, root contacts develop within 15 years between new trees and old stumps and snags. Mortality in the new stand first involves scattered individuals close to the old stumps. Unfortunately, by the time this is noticeable, stands often have been precommercially thinned and have received other expensive cultural treatments. After stand age exceeds about 15 years, *P. weirii* begins to spread from tree to tree and thus expand disease centers. The average annual rate of radial enlargement is about 1 ft. (30 cm) (Nelson and Hartman 1975, McCauley and Cook 1980). Ultimately, laminated root rot centers appear as variable-sized, understocked openings that containing standing dead trees, stubs, windthrown trees, and some unaffected trees. Unhealthy conifers occur around the margins of these openings, which frequently fill with shrubs, hardwood trees, resistant conifers, and, sometimes, regenerating seedlings of susceptible conifer species.

No published evidence indicates that laminated root rot is influenced by soil or site factors. The disease is damaging on a variety of site types and appears well adapted to the same environmental conditions that favor its hosts (Hadfield et al. 1986).

Remedial actions. Managing laminated root rot offers an opportunity to increase productivity on a substantial area in the Pacific Northwest. Control on infected sites, best attained at final harvest, requires accurate knowledge of the distribution of the disease. Recommended is that all susceptible hosts in infection centers and within a 50-ft. (15-m) wide buffer be cut, then that either (1) the remaining stumps and roots be removed or treated, or (2) the site be regenerated with less susceptible tree species (Hadfield 1985, Hadfield et al. 1986)

The first option, inoculum treatment, involves either removing infected stumps and roots from the soil or leaving them in place but killing the fungus within them. Physical removal of stumps with heavy equipment or stump injection with such chemical fumigants as allyl alcohol or possibly chloropicrin, Vapam®, or Vorlex® appears to effectively control *P. weirii* (Thies 1984). Use of biological agents like *Trichoderma* spp. that are antagonistic to *P. weirii* also shows promise for stump treatment (Nelson and Thies 1981). Drawbacks to inoculum treatments include high costs and, in the case of stump removal, much soil disturbance (Smith and Wass 1984) and limited applicability on steep terrain. An advantage to inoculum treatment is that sites can be regenerated immediately with a highly susceptible tree species such as Douglas-fir. The estimated costs and benefits of these alternatives become factors in any economic analysis to indicate financial return.

The second option, tree species manipulation, involves regenerating diseased areas with tree species that are adapted to the site but also immune, resistant, tolerant, or only moderately susceptible to *P. weirii*. If immune, resistant, or tolerant tree species can be planted, and ingrowth of susceptible species prevented for at least 50 years, the pathogen should die out in most, if not all, of the area. Subsequent rotations of susceptible species can then be grown with little probability of significant reinfection. If moderately susceptible tree species are regenerated on a diseased site, there should be limited loss due to mortality. However, because many trees will be infected and inoculum retained on the site, highly susceptible species should not be grown in the following rotation.

SUMMARY AND RECOMMENDATIONS

Biologically sound forest management requires that factors controlling tree growth be maintained in suitable quantities and balance for sustained high levels of forest productivity. In the Pacific Northwest—as in most forest regions—reliable and long-term quantitative data about long-term stand productivity are not available to support or reject most current practices. Absence of reliable information requires that interim decisions be made. Such decisions remain generally unsatisfactory to most participants and observers; thus, the same or related controversies continually resurface. Current forest managers are generally more aware than their predecessors of the costs and benefits of conserving and increasing inherent site productivity. Their awareness creates a demand for new quantitative information about maintaining and improving long-term site productivity.

Current Knowledge

Our conclusions from this review of site productivity in the Douglas-fir Region of the Pacific Northwest follow:
(1)   Scientific evidence about the effects of forest practices on site productivity is inferred mostly from effects on soil or other site factors. Direct evidence about tree response to practices is short term and uncomfortably scarce. Duration of short-term impacts is unknown because long-term data are nonexistent. Therefore, managers may be justifiably uncertain or skeptical about the consequences of their forest operations on long-term growth and yield.
(2)   Timber harvest, site preparation, and vegetation control can alter several factors influencing short-term and, potentially, long-term site productivity. Harvesting and site preparation seldom increase inherent long-term productivity and always result in soil disturbance and some loss of nutrient capital. The location and frequency of occurrence of forest practices contribute to their cumulative effects.
(3)   Effects of forest practices on productivity factors are likely to vary among sites, practices, and operators. Measured negative effects on soil properties, however, do not always reduce growth of trees and stands. Such variation means that (a) predicting consequences is uncertain, (b) techniques or prescriptions must fit the local situation, and (c) information on tree response is needed to improve predictions.
(4)   Maintaining or even increasing timber production over one or more rotations may be possible by substituting intensive silvicultural practices for some losses of inherent site productivity. In the final analysis, however, the comparative biological and economic costs of soil conservation vs. soil substitution or replenishment must be evaluated.

Recommendations

Prudent-manager concept. We suggest two basic strategies for coping with uncertainty or reducing skepticism about the real effects of forest practices on long-term site productivity:
(1)   In general, avoid unnecessary soil disturbance and loss of organic matter. Conservation is a common-sense approach to soil management. Conserve premanagement conditions or status of the soil—when in doubt, minimize change.
(2)   Use existing information and keep abreast of new developments. If information is inadequate, then base decisions on biological principles, common sense, and past experience.
Long-term monitoring. To reduce current uncertainty and skepticism, we must establish long-term plots to monitor and compare the cumulative effects of our forest practices on tree growth. These long-term plots should be relatively large (about 1 acre, or 0.4 ha), be located, for example, at several typical locations per 100,000 acres (40,000 ha) of ownership, and compare two or more management options. Stand growth in these plots should be measured precisely at intervals during successive rotations. A data retrieval and evaluation system should be maintained to insure systematic summaries and objective interpretation of monitoring data.

Forest research. Our critical review uncovered many gaps and conflicts in current knowledge about the effects of harvesting and forestry practices on long-term site productivity in the Douglas-fir Region. Paramount is the fact that we have no long-term evidence. Thus, current forest-management decisions are often made without potentially critical information. Current uncertainty provides ample room for divergent viewpoints about the effects of commercial forestry on sustained timber growth and yield.

Forest researchers have much to do. To know the effects of timber harvest and forest practices on long-term stand growth and inherent factors of site productivity, we must measure volume growth on permanent plots in an adequate sampling of stands. The current data base is inadequate and short term. Means to predict tree and stand response to forest practices are also inadequate. Measuring changes in soil characteristics or other substitutes can provide indirect evidence—when these substitutes are proven to be reliable predictors of tree growth.

Research should determine additional means to accelerate the natural rate of nutrient turnover in some stands. Through stand density control, soil temperature and moisture relations may be improved. Further, fertilizing with nutrients other than N—which may enhance microbial activity and forest growth—should be investigated. Use of nitrogen-fixing plants to replace or complement use of commercial fertilizers on N-deficient sites needs additional investigation.

ACKNOWLEDGMENTS

Additional members of the working group who contributed information or comments for this chapter are: Dale Cole, College of Forest Resources, University of Washington, Seattle, Wash.; Mike Feller, University of British Columbia, Vancouver, B.C.; Norm Gartley, Bureau of Land Management, Eugene, Ore.; Jack Hulsey, Washington State Department of Natural Resources, Olympia, Wash.; Miles Hemstrom, Willamette National Forest, Eugene, Ore.; Joe Means, Forestry Sciences Laboratory, Corvallis, Ore.; Bill Power, Bureau of Land Management, Salem, Ore.; Robert F. Tarrant, retired, USDA Forest Service, Corvallis, Ore.; and Tom Turpin, Siuslaw National Forest, Corvallis, Ore.

Technical reviews by the following persons were helpful and appreciated: James K. Agee, Bernard Bormann, Dean DeBell, Robert F. Powers, Ken Russel, Richard B. Smith, and John C. Tappeiner II.

QUESTIONS FROM THE SYMPOSIUM FLOOR

Q: About the effects of harvesting and site preparation on site productivity, does the weight of the evidence support the optimist or the pessimist (see Figure 7.1)?

A   (R. E. Miller): Either viewpoint can be supported for some practices and some locations. We attempt to provide more detail in specific sections of the text to indicate situations where either viewpoint could be reasonable. The current scarcity of reliable and long-term data about tree growth convinces us to urge caution and conservation of inherent soil properties.

Q: Would you prescribe compaction to increase tree growth on sites of "abundant resources"?

A   (Miller): No.

A   (R. L. Heninger): Compacting soil would not be prescribed to increase tree growth. Until recently, however, it has been assumed that compaction (i.e., increase in bulk density) is always bad for tree growth. Data presented in this chapter show that this is not always the case. Some compaction may be beneficial in that it may allow some soils to hold more available water longer into the growing season, which would benefit tree growth (Froehlich et al. 1980). We do not know if an optimum bulk density exists for a given species on a given soil. For example, if we knew that Douglas-fir growth was optimized at a specific bulk density on a given soil, then we could determine how much the soil could be compacted before effects would be deleterious and develop guidelines on acceptable levels of compaction in logging operations. These could vary by soil type, structure, and texture as well by climate, elevation, and precipitation.

Q: How long does it take soils to recover from the various compaction classes?

A   (Miller): Few data are available. Wert and Thomas (1981) reported that compaction in subsoil was still measurable after 30 years. Bill Power (Bureau of Land Management, Salem District) reported that the soil on landings was still compacted 60 years after railroad logging in his area. "Recovery" can be that to the original bulk density or to a bulk density that no longer is restrictive to tree growth.

Q: What types of mitigations for soil disturbance and damage does Weyerhaeuser Company favor and why?

A   (Heninger): Since Bill Scott developed the soil disturbance class system, it has been discussed and reviewed with logging foremen and their logging crews as well as contract logging crews. The emphasis has been to avoid, or at least to minimize, any Class 3 or 4 damage in ground-based logging units. The technology transfer has been well received by loggers, and overall damage reduced. However, there are still incidents of Class 3 and 4 damage. In these cases, the amelioration technique usually depends on the forestry manager and the amount and extent of the damage. For example, it is routine to rip most skid trails with Class 3 and 4 damage and thereby till the soil and create more favorable planting spots. Traditionally, this has been done with a "cat"-type tractor pulling either a two- or three-tooth road construction rock ripper in late summer or early fall when soils are dry. In 1986, we tried the winged ripper on a couple of units with very satisfactory results. At the same time we are continuing our research efforts in this area.

Q: I think I am hearing some speakers say that impacts to potential productivity really aren't all that important as long as overall we increase total production through brush control, slash removal, and so forth. To me, this sounds like a lazy way out of developing new practices capable of avoiding negative impacts to potential productivity. It assumes that we have only two choices: (1) compacted soil (12% volume loss) or (2) brushfields with poor stocking! Please comment.

A: (Miller): I hope I didn't say that. I think we should conserve inherent factors of site productivity and try to improve them through soil management. Silvicultural practices may offset our shortcomings in site management and provide additional gains in wood production.

Q: With all the negative impacts to a forest site from site preparation (burning, piling, etc.), are Weyerhaeuser and other private timber companies reducing these activities?

A: (Heninger): I can't speak for other companies' policies relating to this question. However, at Weyerhaeuser, it is well understood that soil is one of the most important resources the company has because their long-term success will depend on the soil's productive capacity to grow trees. As has come out in this symposium, the question should be restated to acknowledge a general lack of long-term scientific evidence to support the practices you have asked about. Decisions about these practices are based on short-term scientific data, fundamental biological principles, common sense, past experience, and economics. There will probably always be some reasonable risk to successfully establishing plantations and providing an efficient supply of timber despite a relatively negative climate for vegetative management, animal control, and political decisions.

Q: Can you elaborate on the impacts caused by disturbing and mixing the duff layer with the soil, specifically, on a site where soil temperature is not severe. Wouldn't the nutrients be retained?

A: (Miller): Disturbing and mixing should increase the rate of organic matter decomposition, providing that concomitant compaction does not lead to anaerobic conditions. Yes, nutrients should be retained unless some unusual circumstances favoring leaching were to occur, e.g., lack of vegetation, or low cation-exchange capacity in the soil.

Q: Hot burns have been shown to reduce site productivity. Yet some burned piles and decks show the best regeneration growth within a unit. Why might this be?

A: (Miller): Hot burns undoubtedly lead to losses of organic matter and some nutrients. Offsetting these losses somewhat are increases in pH and available nutrients. Severely burned areas are slower to revegetate through natural succession, so the greater initial growth of regeneration in severely burned areas may be due to the potentially favorable effects of increased nutrient availability and reduced vegetative competition; moreover, mechanically piled areas receive topsoil and nutrients at the loss of nearby "nonpile" areas. Ballard (1978) is a good reference.

Q: So far, the scientific jury at this symposium is in with a verdict on site preparation: *guilty*, as charged, of organic matter and nutrient losses, mycorrhiza destruction, soil erosion, loss of productivity, and air-quality degradation. Comments?

A: (Miller): The verdict is true in some locations and to some degree; we should look for less damaging alternatives. Elsewhere, burning may be the preferred option. We have attempted in the chapter text to indicate where the concern is greatest. Certainly, we have destruction of organic matter, nutrient losses, and increased soil erosion; at issue, however, is the question: to what extent is long-term productivity affected by these?

A: (Heninger): Let's remember that fire has played an essential and continued role in forest history, contributing to the vast Pacific Northwest forests that exist today and to their species makeup. There may be short-term (1–10 year) negative impacts of prescribed fire, but the verdict is not yet in about long-term effects.

Q: The Washington Department of Natural Resources apparently has backed off its burning program. What led to this decision? Do you feel there will be difficulty in obtaining stocking standards as a result of this decision?

A: (Jack Hulsey): The decision is not to "back off" from burning. The Department believes that prescribed fire is a viable and vital tool. However, issues both external and internal to the agency have caused the Department to reanalyze the entire site-preparation scenario. Changes in the legal climate in Washington have transferred increased liability to the landowner. That, coupled with the high cost of burning, led to a reassessment of options. The need and the willingness to accept both biological and economic risk have served to identify new options.

Simultaneously, our analyses have shown that fewer trees per unit area are needed for maximum present net worth, our decision criterion. The poor economic return from large-scale, operational commercial thinning has left the Department with numerous overstocked stands and the intent to limit further additions to the commercial thinning acreage. Reduced slash burning has not resulted in restocking problems; however, restocking standards have been reduced because of the economic interpretations of our recent analyses.

Q: You mentioned vegetation management but did not discuss herbicides. Please discuss the obvious benefits of herbicides (as well as problems, if any) in maintaining productivity without disturbance.

A: (W. I. Stein): Vegetation management may be necessary to optimize volume production on some sites. Prescribed fire, herbicides, mechanical site preparation, and control with hand tools are options for doing this job. Of these options, aerially applied herbicides have the least impact on soil physical properties and organic matter losses. The key issue of concern is the fate of herbicides once applied and unknown effects on human and other populations.

Q: Are industry or any public agencies on the west side of the Cascades interplanting alder with conifers on a regular operational basis?

A: (Miller): Unknown. Several organizations are retaining some volunteer red alder at precommercial thinning. This is a relatively cheap option, but only appropriate where red alder naturally regenerates.

A: (Heninger): Weyerhaeuser is not interplanting at this time. However, as more information becomes available—and some is encouraging—the option will be continuously reviewed and considered. We are retaining some alder at precommercial thinning where appropriate.

A: (Hulsey): The Washington Department of Natural Resources is not operationally planting any red alder. However, we are tolerating higher levels of naturally regenerating red alder in our plantations.

Q: Losses to root diseases seem to be increasing dramatically with intensive management in Northwest forests. Will root diseases become *the* major limiting factor in maintaining long-term productivity?

A: (D. J. Goheen): Root diseases will be a major factor in decreasing long-term site productivity (measured in terms of wood volume) in many Pacific Northwest forests if not properly managed. We estimate that, if susceptible tree species are managed on sites affected by laminated root rot, yields will be only 50% as great as those on similar undiseased sites. Furthermore, *Phellinus weirii* will be retained on such sites and cause similar or greater losses in subsequent rotations. Impacts of other root diseases (black stain, *Armillaria*, and *Annosus*) could also be substantial if not addressed in silvicultural prescriptions. These diseases are favored in managed stands (especially single-species plantations) and have greater capabilities for long distance or rapid spread than does laminated root rot. Recognition of root diseases and of their control through tree species manipulation offers silviculturists an excellent opportunity to maintain or increase site productivity in the long run.

Q: I am sensitive to Jerry Franklin's presentation (see chapter 6, this volume) on maintaining natural diversity. However, where we have done this, losses to root rots have become significant. Can someone comment on working with root diseases and maintaining diversity?

A: (Goheen): The most widely used prescription for managing laminated root rot is to regenerate diseased areas with tree species which are adapted to the site and which are intermediately susceptible, tolerant, resistant, or immune to the disease. This usually involves establishing hardwoods, pines, cedars, larch, hemlocks, spruce, or mixtures of these species on sites that would, if not diseased, be regenerated to Douglas-fir or true firs. Successful disease management can contribute substantially to species diversity, especially in stands on the west side of the Cascades where Douglas-fir is normally preferred over other species in the absence of disease.

Q: Is there any evidence that nitrogen fertilization can reduce tree growth losses from *Phellinus weirii*?

A: (Goheen): Nitrogen fertilization could offset losses from *Phellinus* by increasing growth rates of surviving trees. Alternatively, fertilization could affect *Phellinus* directly or indirectly by benefiting competitive pathogens. However, there is no conclusive evidence that nitrogen fertilization influences infection or rate of growth of infected trees in diseased stands of susceptible species.

Q: What is the current status of silvicultural activity monitoring?

A: (Miller): Most organizations monitor planting activities by regeneration surveys. A few attempt to measure the effects of operational precommercial thinning or fertilization; doing this requires careful measurement of tree growth on treated and *untreated* areas whose initial conditions are similar. Region 6 (USDA Forest Service) is monitoring the extent and severity of soil disturbance on a sampling of harvested areas.

Q: Do you believe we should develop strong monitoring programs for "operational" practices or projects by managers as well as for research projects?

A   (Miller): If it is important to know how operationally treated stands are growing, then it is necessary to monitor or measure growth. Monitoring information can be checked against estimates or predictions made for planning purposes. If we want to determine gains in growth after expenditures for fertilization, thinning, or other practices, then we must measure trees on treated and untreated areas; this will require procedures similar to those used in monitoring research trials.

REFERENCES

Alexander, E. B. 1985. *Soil disturbance and compaction in wildland management.* Earth Resources Monograph 8. Berkeley, Calif.: Pacific Southwest Region Watershed Management Staff, USDA Forest Service.

Allen, S. E. 1964. Chemical aspects of heather burning. *Journal of Applied Ecology* 1:347–367.

Andrus, C. W., and H. A. Froehlich. 1983. *An evaluation of four implements used to till compacted forest soils in the Pacific Northwest.* Research Bulletin 45. Corvallis, Ore.: Forest Research Laboratory, Oregon State University.

Atkinson, W. A., B. T. Bormann, and D. S. DeBell. 1979. Crop rotation of Douglas-fir and red alder: a preliminary biological and economic assessment. *Botanical Gazette* 140 (suppl.): S102-S107.

Aulerich, D. E., K. N. Johnson, and H. A. Froehlich. 1974. Tractors or skylines: what's best for thinning young-growth Douglas-fir. *Forest Industries* 101:42–45.

Austin, R. C., and D. H. Baisinger. 1955. Some effects of burning on forest of western Oregon and Washington. *Journal of Forestry* 53:275–280.

Baker, J. 1968. *Growth response and chemical composition of Douglas-fir seedlings on burned and unburned soil samples.* Information Report BC-X-28. Victoria, B.C.: Forest Research Laboratory, Canadian Department of Fisheries and Forestry.

Ballard, R. 1978. The effect of slash and soil removal on the productivity of second rotation radiata pine on a pumice soil. *New Zealand Journal of Forestry Research* 8:248–258.

_____. 1979. "Use of fertilizers to maintain productivity of intensively managed forest plantations." In *Impact of intensive harvesting on forest nutrient cycling,* edited A. L. Leaf, 321–342. Syracuse, N.Y.: College of Environmental Science and Forestry, State University of New York.

Bell, M. A. M., J. M. Beckett, and W. F. Hubbard. 1975. *Impact of harvesting on forest environments and resources: a review of the literature and evaluation of research needs.* Victoria, B.C.: Pacific Forestry Research Centre, Canadian Forestry Service.

Bengtson, G. W. 1978. "Strategies for maintaining forest productivity: a researcher's perspective." In *Principles of maintaining productivity on prepared sites,* edited by T. Tippin, 123–159. State College, Miss.: Mississippi State University.

Bennett, K. A. 1982. *Effects of slash burning on surface soil erosion rate in the Oregon Coast Range.* Masters Thesis. Corvallis, Ore.: Oregon State University.

Beuter, J. H., K. N. Johnson, and H. L. Scheurman. 1976. *Timber for Oregon's tomorrow; an analysis of reasonably possible occurrences.* Corvallis, Ore.: Forest Research Laboratory, Oregon State University.

Bigger, C. M., and D. W. Cole. 1983. "Effects of harvesting intensity on nutrient losses and future productivity in high and low productivity red alder and Douglas-fir stands." In *IUFRO symposium on forest site and continuous productivity,* edited by R. Ballard and S. P. Gessel, 167–178. General Technical Report PNW-163. Portland, Ore.: Pacific Northwest Forest and Range Experiment Station, USDA Forest Service.

Bigley, R. E., and J. P. Kimmins. 1983. "Herbicide effects on ecosystem nitrogen loss." In *New forests for a changing world,* 199–203. Portland, Ore.: Society of American Foresters.

Binkley, D., and S. Greene. 1983. "Production in mixtures of conifers and red alder: the importance of site fertility and stand age." In *IUFRO symposium on forest site and continuous productivity,* edited by R. Ballard and S. P. Gessel, 112–117. General Technical Report PNW-163. Portland, Ore.: Pacific Northwest Forest and Range Experiment Station, USDA Forest Service.

Bockheim, J. G., T. M. Ballard, and R. Willington. 1975. Soil disturbance associated with timber harvesting in southwestern British Columbia. *Canadian Journal of Forest Research* 5:285–290.

Bollen, Walter B. 1974. "Soil microbes." In *Environmental effects of forest residues management in the Pacific Northwest, a state-of-knowledge compendium,* edited by O. P. Cramer, B-2 to B-41. General Technical Report PNW-24. Portland, Ore.: Pacific Northwest Forest and Range Experiment Station, USDA Forest Service.

Bormann, B. T., and D. S. DeBell. 1981. Nitrogen content and other soil properties related to age of red alder stands. *Soil Science Society of America Journal* 45:428–432.

Boyer, Donald E., and John D. Dell. 1980. *Fire effects on Pacific Northwest soils.* R6-WM-040-1980. Portland, Ore.: Pacific Northwest Region, USDA Forest Service.

Brown, G. W., A. R. Gahler, and R. B. Marston. 1973. Nutrient losses after clearcut logging and slash burning in the Oregon Coast Range. *Water Resources Journal* 9:1450–1453.

Buckland, D.C., and G. W. Wallis. 1956. The control of yellow laminated root rot of Douglas-fir. *Forestry Chronicle* 32:14–16.

Chappell, H. N., and D. Opalach. 1984. *Forest fertilization and stand management in western Oregon and Washington: status and prospect.* RFNRP Report No. 1 (unpublished). Seattle, Wash.: College of Forest Resources, University of Washington.

Childs, T. W., and K. R. Shea. 1967. *Annual losses from disease in Pacific Northwest forest.* Research Bulletin PNW-20. Portland, Ore.: Pacific Northwest Forest and Range Experiment Station, USDA Forest Service.

Cole, Dale W. 1981. "Mineral cycling in forest ecosystems of the Pacific Northwest." In *Forest fertilization conference,* 29–36. Contribution No. 40. Seattle, Wash.: Institute of Forest Resources, College of Forest Resources, University of Washington.

Cole, Dale W., and Charles C. Grier. 1965. *Influence of slash burning on ion transport in a forest soil.* Seattle, Wash.: College of Forest Resources, University of Washington.

Cole, Elizabeth C., and Michael Newton. 1986. Fifth-year responses of Douglas-fir to crowding and nonconiferous competition. *Canadian Journal of Forest Research* 17:181–186.

Cramer, Owen P. (editor). 1974. *Environmental effects of forest residues management in the Pacific Northwest.* General Technical Report PNW-24. Portland, Ore.: Pacific Northwest Forest and Range Experiment Station, USDA Forest Service.

Cromack, K., Jr., F. J. Swanson, and C. C. Grier. 1978. "A comparison of harvesting methods and their impact on soils and environment in the Pacific Northwest." In *Forest soils and land use,* edited by C. T. Youngberg, 449–476. Fort Collins, Colo.: Colorado State University.

Cushon, G. 1985. *Gaseous nitrogen transformations in a mature ecosystem.* M.S. Thesis. Vancouver, B.C.: University of British Columbia.

DeBano, L. F. 1981. Water repellent soils: a state-of-the-art. General Technical Report PSW-46. Berkeley, Calif.: Pacific Southwest Forest and Range Experiment Station, USDA Forest Service.

DeBell, Dean S. 1979. "Future potential for use of symbiotic nitrogen in forest management." In *Symbiotic nitrogen fixation in the management of temperate forests,* edited by J. C. Gordon, C. T. Wheeler, and D. A. Perry, 451–466. Corvallis, Ore.: Forest Research Laboratory, Oregon State University.

DeBell, D. S., and C. W. Ralston. 1970. Release of nitrogen by burning light forest fuels. *Soil Science Society of America Proceedings* 34:936–938.

Dyrness, C. T. 1965. Soil surface condition following tractor and high-lead logging in the Oregon Cascades. *Journal of Forestry* 63:272–275.

————. 1966. Erodability and erosion potential of forest watershed. *National Science Foundation, Advanced Seminar Proceedings* 1965:599–611.

————. 1972. *Soil surface conditions following balloon logging.* Research Note PNW-182. Portland, Ore.: Pacific Northwest Forest and Range Experiment Station, USDA Forest Service.

————. 1976. *Effect of wildfire on soil wettability in the high Cascades of Oregon.* Research Paper PNW-202. Portland, Ore.: Pacific Northwest Forest and Range Experiment Station, USDA Forest Service.

Dyrness, C. T., and C. T. Youngberg. 1957. *Some effects of logging and slash burning on physical soil properties in the Corvallis watershed.* Research Paper No. 19. Portland, Ore.: Pacific Northwest Forest and Range Experiment Station, USDA Forest Service.

Eckhouse, Katherine L., Daniel L. Galt, and Robert N. Stavins. 1981. *An economic analysis of alternative vegetation management practices in commercial forests of the Pacific Coast region.* Berkeley, Calif.: Cooperative Extension and Giannini Foundation of Agricultural Economics, University of California.

Edmonds, Robert L. 1987. Decomposition rates and nutrient dynamics in small-diameter woody litter in four forest ecosystems in Washington, USA. *Canadian Journal of Forest Research* 17:499–509.

Farrell, P. W., D. W. Flinn, R. O. Squire, and F. G. Craig. 1981. "On the maintenance of productivity of radiata pine monocultures on sandy soils in southeast Australia." In *Proceedings, XVII IUFRO World Congress,* 117–128. Congress Group S1.02, Division 1. Japan.

Feller, M. C. 1982. *The ecological effects of slashburning with particular reference to British Columbia: a literature review.* Land Management Report No. 13. Victoria, B.C.: Province of British Columbia Ministry of Forests.

Feller, M. C., and J. P. Kimmins. 1984. Effects of clearcutting and slash burning in streamwater chemistry and watershed nutrient budgets in southwestern British Columbia. *Water Resources Research* 20:29–40.

Feller, M. C., J. P. Kimmins, and K. M. Tsze. 1983. "Nutrient losses to the atmosphere during slashburns in southwestern British Columbia." In *Proceedings, 7th conference on fire and forest meteorology,* 123–135. Boston, Mass.: American Meteorological Society.

Filip, G. M., and C. L. Schmitt. 1979. Susceptibility of native conifers to laminated root rot east of the Cascade Range in Oregon and Washington. *Forest Science* 25:261–265.

Fogel, R., and K. Cromack, Jr. 1977. Effect of habitat and substrate quality on Douglas-fir litter decomposition in western Oregon. *Canadian Journal of Botany* 55:1632–1640.

Forristall, F. F., and S. P. Gessel. 1955. Soil properties related to forest cover type and productivity on the Lee Forest, Snohomish County, Washington. *Soil Science Society of America Proceedings* 19:384–389.

Franklin, Jerry F., and C. T. Dyrness. 1969. *Vegetation of Oregon and Washington.* Research Paper PNW-80. Portland, Ore.: Pacific Northwest Forest and Range Experiment Station, USDA Forest Service.

Fredriksen, R. L. 1972. "Nutrient budget of a Douglas-fir forest on an experimental watershed in western Oregon." In *Proceedings, research on coniferous forest ecosystems, a symposium,* edited by Jerry F. Franklin, L. J. Demster, and R. H. Waring, 115–131. Portland, Ore.: Pacific Northwest Forest and Range Experiment Station, USDA Forest Service.

Fredriksen, Richard L., and R. Dennis Harr. 1979. "Soil, vegetation, and watershed management." In *Forest soils of the Douglas-fir Region,* 231–259. Pullman, Wash.: Cooperative Extension Service, Washington State University.

Fritz, Emanual, and James A. Rydelius. 1966. "Response of suppressed redwood and Douglas-fir seedlings after release from over-topping brush." In *Redwood reforestation problems, an experimental approach to their solution,* 97–104. Buena Park, Calif.: Foundation for American Resource Management.

Froehlich, H. A. 1973. "The impact of even-age forest management on physical properties of soils." In *Even-age management,* edited by R. K. Hermann and D. P. Lavender, 199–220. Corvallis, Ore.: Oregon State University.

_____ . 1976. "The influence of different thinning systems on damage to soil and trees." In *Proceedings, XV IUFRO World Congress IV,* 333–374. Norway.

_____ . 1978. *Soil compaction from low ground pressure, torsion-suspension logging vehicles on three forest soils.* Research Paper 36. Corvallis, Ore.: Forest Research Laboratory, Oregon State University.

_____ . 1979a. *Skid trails and competition reduced growth rate of residual western hemlock.* Unpublished Report (mimeo). Corvallis, Ore.: School of Forestry, Oregon State University.

_____ . 1979b. *The effect of compaction by logging on forest productivity.* Final Report (mimeo). Contract No. 53500-CT4-5(N). Portland, Ore.: Bureau of Land Management, USDI.

Froehlich, H. A., J. Azevedo, R. Cafferata, and D. Lysne. 1980. *Predicting soil compaction on forested land.* Final Project Report (mimeo) to USDA Forest Service, Cooperative Agreement 228. Corvallis, Ore.: Oregon State University.

Froehlich, H. A., and E. R. Berglund. 1976. *Soil compaction during thinning affects growth rate of residual trees.* Unpublished Report (mimeo). Corvallis, Ore.: School of Forestry, Oregon State University.

Froehlich, H. A., and D. H. McNabb. 1984. "Minimizing soil compaction in Pacific Northwest forests." In *Forest soils and treatment impacts,* edited by Earl L. Stone, 159–192. Knoxville, Tenn.: University of Tennessee.

Geppart, Rollin, Charles W. Lorenz, and Arthur G. Larson. 1984. *Cumulative effects of forest practices on the environment, a state of the knowledge.* Unpublished Report prepared for the Washington Forest Practices Board. Olympia, Wash.: Ecosystems, Inc.

Gessel, S. P., D. W. Cole, and E. C. Steinbrenner. 1972. Nitrogen balances in forest ecosystems of the Pacific Northwest, *Soil Biology and Biochemistry* 5:19–34.

Gockerell, E. C. 1966. Plantations on burned versus unburned areas. *Journal of Forestry* 64:392–393.

Gratkowski, H., and P. Lauterbach. 1974. Releasing Douglas-firs from varnishleaf ceanothus. *Journal of Forestry* 72:150–152.

Greacen, E. L., and R. Sands. 1980. Compaction of forest soils: a review. *Australian Journal of Soils Research* 18:163–189.

Gresswell, S., D. Heller, and D. N. Swanston. 1979. *Mass movement response to forest management in the central Oregon Coast Ranges.* Research Bulletin PNW-84. Portland, Ore.: Pacific Northwest Forest and Range Experiment Station, USDA Forest Service.

Grier, C. C. 1972. *Effects of fire on the movement and distribution of elements within a forest ecosystem.* Ph.D. Dissertation. Seattle, Wash.: University of Washington.

Hadfield, J. S. 1985. *Laminated root rot, a guide for reducing and preventing losses in Oregon and Washington forests.* Portland, Ore.: Pacific Northwest Region, USDA Forest Service.

Hadfield, J. S., D. J. Goheen, G. M. Filip, C. L. Schmitt, and R. D. Harvey. 1986. *Root diseases in Oregon and Washington conifers.* R6-FPM-250-86. Portland, Ore.: Pacific Northwest Region, USDA Forest Service.

Hansen, E. M. 1979. Survival of *Phellinus weirii* in Douglas-fir stumps after logging. *Canadian Journal of Forest Research* 9:484–488.

Hansen, E. M., D. J. Goheen, P. F. H essburg, J. J. Witcosky, and T. D. Schowalter. 1986. "Biology and management of black-stain root disease in Douglas-fir." In *Forest pest management in southwest Oregon,* edited by O. T. Helgerson, 13–19. Corvallis, Ore.: College of Forestry, Oregon State University.

Harvey, A. E., M. F. Jurgensen, and M. J. Larsen. 1980. "Biological implication of increasing harvest intensity on the maintenance and productivity of forest soils." In *Environmental consequences of timber harvesting in Rocky Mountain coniferous forests,* 211–220. General Technical Report INT-90. Ogden, Utah: Intermountain Forest and Range Experiment Station, USDA Forest Service.

Hatchell, G. E., C. W. Ralston, and R. R. Foil. 1970. Soil disturbance in logging: effects on soil characteristics and growth of loblolly pine in the Atlantic Coastal Plain. *Journal of Forestry* 68:772–775.

Hawkes, Carl. 1953. Planes release tree plantation. *Journal of Forestry* 51:345–348.

Heavilin, Danny. 1977. *Conifer regeneration on burned and unburned clearcuts on granitic soils of the Klamath National Forest.* Research Note PSW-321. Berkeley, Calif.: Pacific Southwest Forest and Range Experiment Station, USDA Forest Service.

Heilman, P. 1981. Root penetration of Douglas-fir seedlings into compacted soils. *Forest Science* 27:660–666.

Heilman, P. E., H. W. Anderson, and D. M. Baumgartner (editors). 1979. *Forest soils of the Douglas-fir Region.* Pullman, Wash.: Cooperative Extension Service, Washington State University.

Heilman, P. E., T. H. Dae, H. H. Cheng, S. R. Webster, and L. Christensen. 1982. Comparison of fall and spring applications of 15N-labeled urea to Douglas-fir. Part 2: fertilizer nitrogen recovery in trees and soil after two years. *Soil Science Society of America Journal* 46:1300–1304.

Howard, Kerry M., and Michael Newton. 1984. Overtopping by successional Coast-Range vegetation slows Douglas-fir seedlings. *Journal of Forestry* 82:178–180.

Howard, R. F., M. M. Singer, and G. A. Frantz. 1981. Effects of soil properties, water content, and compactive effort on the compaction of selected California forest and range soils. *Soil Science Society of America Journal* 45:231–236.

Isaac, Leo A. 1938. *Factors affecting establishment of Douglas-fir seedlings.* Circular No. 486. Washington, D.C.: U.S. Department of Agriculture.

———. 1963. "Fire—a tool not a blanket rule in Douglas-fir ecology." In *Proceedings 2nd annual Tall Timbers fire ecology conference,* 1-17. Tallahassee, Fla.: Tall Timbers Research Station.

Isaac, L. A., and H. G. Hopkins. 1937. The forest soils of the Douglas-fir Region and the changes wrought upon it by logging and slash burning. *Ecology* 18:264–279.

Johnson, D. W. 1983. "The effects of harvesting schedules on nutrient depletion from forests." In *IUFRO symposium on forest site and continuous productivity,* edited by R. Ballard and S. P. Gessel. General Technical Report PNW-163. Portland, Ore.: Pacific Northwest Forest and Range Experiment Station, USDA Forest Service.

Kimmins, J. P. 1974. Sustained yield, timber mining, and the concept of ecological rotation, a British Columbian view. *Forestry Chronicle* 50:27–31.

———. 1975. *Review of the ecological effects of herbicide usage in forestry.* Information Report No. BC-X-139. Victoria, British Columbia: Pacific Forest Research Centre, Canadian Forestry Service.

———. 1977. Evaluation of the consequences for future tree productivity of the loss of nutrients in whole-tree harvesting. *Forest Ecology and Management* 1:169–183.

Klinka, K., R. N. Green, P. J. Courtin, and F. C. Nuszdorfer. 1984. *Site diagnosis, tree species selection, and slash-burning guidelines for the Vancouver forest region.* Land Management Report No. 25. Vancouver, B.C.: British Columbia Ministry of Forests.

Klock, G. O. 1979. "Some engineering aspects of forest soils of the Douglas-fir Region." In *Forest soils of the Douglas-fir Region,* 269–277. Pullman, Wash.: Cooperative Extension Service, Washington State University.

———. 1982. "Some soil erosion effects on forest soil productivity." In *Determinants of soil loss tolerance,* 53–66. Madison, Wis.: American Society of Agronomy.

———. 1983. "The productivity resilience of forest soils." In *IUFRO symposium on forest site and continuous productivity,* edited by R. Ballard and S. P. Gessel, 81–85. General Technical Report PNW-163. Portland, Ore.: Pacific Northwest Forest and Range Experiment Station, USDA Forest Service.

Knapp, W. H., T. C. Turpin, and J. H. Beuter. 1984. Vegetation control for Douglas-fir regeneration on the Siuslaw National Forest: a decision analysis. *Journal of Forestry* 82:168–173.

Knight, H. 1965. *Some effects of slash-burning and clear-cut logging on soil properties and initial tree growth.* Ph.D. Dissertation. Seattle, Wash.: University of Washington.

_____.1966. Loss of nitrogen from the forest floor by burning. *Forestry Chronicle* 42:149–152.

Kraemer, James F., and Richard K. Hermann. 1979. Broadcast burning: 25-year effects on forest soils in the western flanks of the Cascade Mountains. *Forest Science* 25:427–439.

Larson, W. E., F. J. Pierce, and R. H. Dowdy. 1983. The threat of soil erosion to long term crop production. *Science* 219:458–465.

Lavender, D. P., M. H. Bergman, and L. D. Calvin. 1956. *Natural regeneration on staggered settings.* Research Bulletin No. 10. Salem, Ore.: Oregon Board of Forestry.

Leaf, A. L. (editor). 1979. *Proceedings, impact of intensive harvesting on forest nutrient cycling.* Syracuse, N.Y.: College of Environmental Science and Forestry, State University of New York.

Little, S. M., and G. O. Klock. 1985. *The influence of residue removal and prescribed fire on distributions of forest nutrients.* Research Paper PNW-338. Portland, Ore.: Pacific Northwest Forest and Range Experiment Station, USDA Forest Service.

Little, Susan N., and Janet L. Ohmann. 1988. Estimating nitrogen lost from forest floor during prescribed fires in Douglas-fir/western hemlock clearcuts. *Forest Science* 34:152–164.

Little, Susan N., Roger D. Ottmar, and Janet L. Ohman. 1986. *Predicting duff consumption from prescribed burns on conifer clearcuts in western Oregon and western Washington.* Research Paper PNW-362. Portland, Ore.: Pacific Northwest Research Station, USDA Forest Service.

Loucks, Donna M., Steven Radosevich, Timothy B. Harrington, and Robert G. Wagner. 1986. *Prescribed burning in Pacific Northwest forests: an annotated bibliography.* CRAFTS Report. Corvallis, Ore.: College of Forestry, Oregon State University.

McCauley, K. J., and S. A. Cook. 1980. *Phellinus weirii* infestation of two mountain hemlock forests in the Oregon Cascades. *Forest Science* 26:23–29.

McColl, John G., and David F. Grigal. 1979. "Nutrient losses in leaching and erosion by intensive forest harvesting." In *Impact of intensive harvesting on forest nutrient cycling,* edited by A. L. Leaf, 231–248. Syracuse, N.Y.: College of Environmental Science and Forestry, State University of New York.

McColl, J. G., and R. F. Powers. 1984. "Impacts of forestry practices on soil-tree relationships." In *Nutrition of plantation forests,* edited by G. D. Bowen and E. K. Nambiar, 379–412. New York: Academic Press.

McDonald, Philip M. 1986. Grasses in young conifer plantations—hindrance and help? *Northwest Science* 60:271–278.

McKee, W. H., Jr., G. E. Hatchell, and A. E. Tiarks. 1985. *Managing site damage from logging.* General Technical Report. Asheville, N.C.: Southeastern Forest Experiment Station, USDA Forest Service.

McNabb, D. H., and R. G. Campbell. 1988. Managing the soil physical environment to maintain and enhance forest productivity. Submitted to *Journal of Forestry.*

McNabb, D. H., J. M. Geist, and C. T. Youngberg. 1979. "Nitrogen fixation by *Ceanothus velutinus* in northern Oregon." In *Symbiotic nitrogen fixation in the management of temperate forests,* edited by J. C. Gordon, C. T. Wheeler, and D. A. Perry, 481–482. Corvallis, Ore.: Forest Research Laboratory, Oregon State University.

Megahan, Walter F. 1986. "Roads and forest site productivity." In *10th British Columbia soil science workshop.* Unpublished Report. Vancouver, B.C.: University of British Columbia.

Mersereau, R. C., and C. T. Dyrness. 1972. Accelerated mass wasting after logging and slash burning in western Oregon. *Journal of Soil and Water Conservation* 27:112–114.

Miles, D. W. R., F. J. Swanson, and C. T. Youngberg. 1984. Effects of landslide erosion on subsequent Douglas-fir growth and stocking levels in the western Cascades, Oregon. *Soil Science Society of America Journal* 48:667–671.

Miller, J. H. 1974. *Nutrient losses and nitrogen mineralization on forested watersheds in Oregon's Coast Range.* Ph.D. Dissertation. Corvallis, Ore.: Oregon State University.

Miller, R. E., P. R. Barker, C. E. Peterson, and S. R. Webster. 1986. Using nitrogen fertilizers in management of coast Douglas-fir: regional trends of response. In *Douglas-fir: stand management for the future,* 290–303. Seattle, Wash.: College of Forest Resources, University of Washington.

Miller, R. E., R. E. Bigley, and S. N. Little. 1986. *The effects of burning Douglas-fir logging slash on subsequent stand development and site productivity.* Unpublished Report on file. Olympia, Wash.: Forestry Sciences Laboratory, USDA Forest Service.

Miller, R. E., D. P. Lavender, and C. C. Grier. 1976. Nutrient cycling in the Douglas-fir type—silvicultural implications. *Proceedings Society of American Foresters* 1975:359–399.

Miller, R. E., and M. D. Murray. 1978. "The effects of red alder on growth of Douglas-fir." In *Utilization and management of alder,* compiled by D. G. Briggs, D. S. DeBell, and W. A. Atkinson, 283–306. General Technical Report PNW-70. Portland, Ore.: Pacific Northwest Forest and Range Experiment Station, USDA Forest Service.

Miller, R. E., W. Scott, and J. Hazard. 1988. *Soil disturbance and conifer growth after tractor yarding at three coastal Washington locations.* Unpublished Report. Olympia, Wash.: Forestry Sciences Laboratory, USDA Forest Service.

Miller, Richard E., Richard L. Williamson, and Roy Silen. 1974. "Regeneration and growth of coastal Douglas-fir." In *Environmental effects of forest residues management in the Pacific Northwest,* edited by O. P. Cramer, J-1 to J-41. General Technical Report PNW-24. Portland, Ore.: Pacific Northwest Forest and Range Experiment Station, USDA Forest Service.

Minore, D. 1986. *Effects of site preparation on seedling growth: a preliminary comparison of broadcast burning and pile burning.* Research Note PNW-RN-452. Portland, Ore.: Pacific Northwest Research Station, USDA Forest Service.

Minore, D., and C. E. Smith. 1971. *Occurrence and growth of four northwestern tree species over shallow water tables.* Research Note PNW-160. Portland, Ore.: Pacific Northwest Forest and Range Experiment Station, USDA Forest Service.

Minore, Don, Clark E. Smith, and Robert F. Wollard. 1969. *Effects of high soil density on seedling root growth of seven northwestern tree species.* Research Note PNW-112. Portland, Ore.: Pacific Northwest Forest and Range Experiment Station, USDA Forest Service.

Morris, William G. 1958. *Influence of slash burning on regeneration, other plant cover, and fire hazard in the Douglas-fir Region.* Research Paper 29. Portland, Ore.: Pacific Northwest Forest and Range Experiment Station, USDA Forest Service.

_____ . 1970. Effects of slash burning in overmature stands of the Douglas-fir Region. *Forest Science* 16:258–270.

National Soil Erosion-Soil Productivity Research Planning Committee. 1981. Soil erosion effects on soil productivity: a research perspective. *Journal of Soil and Water Conservation* 36:82–90.

Neal, J. L., E. Wright, and W. B. Bollen. 1965. *Burning Douglas-fir slash: physical, chemical and microbial effects in the soil.* Research Paper No. 1. Corvallis, Ore.: Forest Research Laboratory, Oregon State University.

Nelson, E. E., and T. Hartman. 1975. Estimating spread of *Poria weirii* in a high elevation mixed conifer stand. *Journal of Forestry* 73:141–142.

Nelson, E. E., and W. G. Thies. 1981. "Chemical and biological means of reducing laminated root rot inoculum." In *Proceedings, 20th annual western international disease work conference,* 71–73. Vernon, B.C.

Newton, M., B. A. El Hassan, and J. Zavitkovski. 1968. "Role of red alder in western Oregon forest succession." In *Biology of alder,* edited by J. M. Trappe, J. F. Franklin, R. F. Tarrant, and G. M. Hansen, 73–84. Portland, Ore.: Pacific Northwest Forest and Range Experiment Station, USDA Forest Service.

Paeth, R. C., M. E. Jarward, E. G. Knox, and C. T. Dyrness. 1971. Factors affecting mass movement of four soils in the western Cascades of Oregon. *Soil Science Society of America Proceedings* 35:943–947.

Perry, D. A., and J. Norgren. 1983. "Impact of biomass harvest on soil and nutrient loss." In *Generating electricity with wood and solid wastes in southern Oregon,* edited by D. A. Perry, 6–68. Corvallis, Ore.: Forest Research Laboratory, Oregon State University.

Perry, D. A., and J. Tappeiner. 1986. *A review of literature pertaining to vegetation management on the Siuslaw National Forest: phase II—environmental impacts.* Unpublished Report. Corvallis, Ore.: College of Forestry, Oregon State University.

Perry, D. A., J. Tappeiner, and B. McGinley. 1985. *A review of literature pertaining to vegetation management on the Siuslaw National Forest: phase I—early successional patterns, competition between trees and associated vegetation, and efficacy of vegetation control techniques.* Unpublished Report. Corvallis, Ore.: College of Forestry, Oregon State University.

Petersen, Terry D., and Michael Newton. 1982. Growth of Douglas-fir following control of snowbrush and herbaceous vegetation in Oregon. *Down to Earth* 41:21–25.

Pfister, R. D. 1969. *Effect of roads on growth of western white pine plantations in northern Idaho.* Research Paper INT-65. Ogden, Utah: Intermountain Forest and Range Experiment Station, USDA Forest Service.

Pilz, D. P., and D. A. Perry. 1984. Impact of clearcutting and slashburning on ectomycorrhizal associations of Douglas-fir seedlings. *Canadian Journal of Forest Research* 14:94–100.

Poff, R. 1985. *Soil disturbance and compaction in wildland management.* Earth Resources Monograph 8. Berkeley, Calif.: Pacific Southwest Region Watershed Management Staff, USDA Forest Service.

Power, W. E. 1974. *Effects and observations of soil compaction in the Salem District.* Technical Note 256. Portland, Ore.: Bureau of Land Management, USDI.

Powers, R. F. 1983. "Forest fertilization research in California." In *IUFRO symposium on forest site and continuous productivity,* edited by R. Ballard and S. P. Gessel, 388–396. General Technical Report PNW-163. Portland, Ore.: Pacific Northwest Forest and Range Experiment Station, USDA Forest Service.

Preest, D. S. 1977. Long-term growth response of Douglas-fir to weed control. *New Zealand Journal of Forestry*

Science 7:329–332.

Radosevich, S. R., P. C. Passof, and O. A. L eonard. 1976. Douglas-fir release from tanoak and Pacific madrone competition. *Weed Science* 24:144–145.

Raison, R. J., and W. J. B. Crane. 1981. "Nutritional costs of shortened rotations in plantation forestry." In *Proceedings, IUFRO World Congress XVII, Division 1,* 63–72. Japan.

Ralston, G. W., and G. E. Hatchell. 1971. "Effects of prescribed burning on physical properties of soil." In *Prescribed burning symposium,* 68–84. Asheville, N.C.: Southeastern Forest Experiment Station, USDA Forest Service.

Ruth, Robert H. 1956. *Plantation survival and growth in two brush-threat areas in coastal Oregon.* Research Paper 17. Portland, Ore.: Pacific Northwest Forest and Range Experiment Station, USDA Forest Service.

_____ . 1957. *Ten-year history of an Oregon coastal plantation.* Research Paper 21. Portland, Ore.: Pacific Northwest Forest and Range Experiment Station, USDA Forest Service.

Ruth, R. H., and A. S. Harris. 1974. *Forest residues in hemlock-spruce forests of the Pacific Northwest and Alaska—a state-of-knowledge review with recommendations for residue management.* General Technical Report PNW-39. Portland, Ore.: Pacific Northwest Forest and Range Experiment Station, USDA Forest Service.

Schoenberger, M. M., and D. A. Perry. 1982. The effect of soil disturbance on growth and ectomycorrhizae of Douglas-fir and western hemlock seedlings: a greenhouse bioassay. *Canadian Journal of Forest Research* 12:343–353.

Scott, W., G. C. Gillis, and D. Thronson. 1979. *Ground skidding soil management guidelines.* Weyerhaeuser Internal Report. Federal Way, Wash.: Weyerhaeuser Technical Center.

Scrivener, J. C. 1982. "Logging impacts on the concentration patterns of dissolved ions in Carnation Creek, British Columbia." In *Proceedings, Carnation Creek workshop, a 10-year review,* edited by G. Hartman, 64–80. Nanaimo, B.C.: Pacific Biological States, British Columbia Fisheries Research Branch.

Sidle, R. C. 1980. *Impacts of forest practices on surface erosion.* Extension Publication PNW-195. Corvallis, Ore.: Cooperative Extension Service, Oregon State University.

Sidle, R. C., and D. M. Drlica. 1981. Soil compaction from logging with a low-ground pressure skidder in the Oregon Coast Ranges. *Soil Science Society of America Journal* 45:1219–1224.

Singer, M. J. 1981. *Soil compaction-seedling growth study.* Final Technical Report to USDA Forest Service, Region 5, for Cooperative Agreement USDA-7USC-2202, Supplement 43. Berkeley, Calif.

Smith, R. B., P. R. Commandeur, and M. W. Ryan. 1986. *Soils, vegetation, and forest growth on landslides and surrounding logged and old-growth areas on the Queen Charlotte Islands.* Land Management Report No. 41. Victoria, B.C.: British Columbia Ministry of Forests.

Smith, R. B., and E. F. Wass. 1983. "Changes in ground-surface characteristics and vegetative cover associated with logging and prescribed broadcast burning." In *Proceedings, Carnation Creek workshop, a 10-year review,* edited by G. Hartman, 100–109. Nanaimo, B.C.: Pacific Biological States, British Columbia Fisheries Research Branch.

Smith, R. B., and E. F. Wass. 1984. "Preliminary assessment of impacts of two stumping operations on site productivity, interior British Columbia." In *Proceedings of the 1983 Society of American Foresters national convention,* 247–251. Portland, Ore.

Smith, R. B., and E. F. Wass. 1985. *Some chemical and physical characteristics of skidroads and adjacent undisturbed soils.* Report BC-X-261. Victoria, B.C.: Pacific Forest Research Centre, Canadian Forestry Service.

Sollins, P., K. Cromack, Jr., F. M. McCorison, R. H. Waring, and R. D. Harr. 1981. Changes in nitrogen cycling at an old-growth Douglas-fir site after disturbance. *Journal of Environmental Quality* 10:37–42.

Stein, William I. 1984. *The coastal reforestation systems study—five year results.* Unpublished Research Progress Report. Corvallis, Ore.: Forestry Sciences Laboratory, USDA Forest Service.

_____ . 1986. *Comparison of site preparation methods on Coast Range sites.* Unpublished Research Progress Report. Corvallis, Ore.: Forestry Sciences Laboratory, USDA Forest Service.

Steinbrenner, E. C. 1955. The effects of repeated tractor trips on the physical properties of forest soils. *Northwest Science* 41:155–159.

Steinbrenner, E. C., and S. P. Gessel. 1955a. "Effect of tractor logging on soils and regeneration in the Douglas-fir Region of southwestern Washington." In *1955 Proceedings, Society of American Foresters,* 77–80. Washington, D.C.

Steinbrenner, E. C., and S. P. Gessel. 1955b. The effect of tractor logging on physical properties of some soils in southwestern Washington. *Soil Science Society of America Proceedings* 19:372–376.

Stewart, R. E. 1978. "Site preparation." In *Regenerating Oregon's forests,* edited by B. D. Cleary, R. D. Greaves, and R. K. Hermann, 100–129. Corvallis, Ore.: Oregon State University.

Stewart, Ronald E., Larry L. Gross, and Barbara H. Honkala. 1984. *Effects of competing vegetation on forest trees: a bibliography with abstracts.* General Technical Report WO-43. Washington, D.C.: USDA Forest Service.

Stocking, Michael. 1984. *Erosion and soil productivity: a review.* Consultants' Working Paper No. 1. Rome: Soil Conservation Programme, Food and Agriculture Organization of the United Nations.

Stone, E. L. 1975. "Soil and man's use of forest land." In *Forest soils and forest management,* edited by B. Bernier and C. H. Winget, 1–9. Quebec: Laval University Press.

Swanson, Frederick J., Richard J. Janda, Thomas Dunne, and Douglas N. Swanston. 1982. *Sediment budgets and routing in forested drainage basins.* General Technical Report PNW-141. Portland, Ore.: Pacific Northwest Forest and Range Experiment Station, USDA Forest Service.

Swanston, D. N., and C. T. Dyrness. 1973. Stability of steep land. *Journal of Forestry* 71:264–269.

Tarrant, R. F. 1956. Effect of slash burning on some physical soil properties. *Forest Science* 2:18–22.

Tarrant, R. F., Bernard T. Bormann, Dean S. DeBell, and William A. Atkinson. 1983. Managing red alder in the Douglas-fir Region: some possibilities. *Journal of Forestry* 81:787–792.

Tarrant, R. F., and E. Wright. 1955. *Growth of Douglas-fir seedlings after slash burning.* Research Note No. 115. Portland, Ore.: Pacific Northwest Forest and Range Experiment Station, USDA Forest Service.

Thies, W. G. 1984. Laminated root rot, the quest for control. *Journal of Forestry* 82:345–346.

Tkacz, B. M., and E. M. Hansen. 1982. Damage by laminated root rot in two succeeding stands of Douglas-fir. *Journal of Forestry* 80:788–791.

Turner, J. 1977. Effect of nitrogen availability on nitrogen cycling in a Douglas-fir stand. *Forest Science* 23:307–316.

Vitousek, Peter M., and Pamela A. Matson. 1985. Disturbance, nitrogen availability, and nitrogen losses in an intensively managed loblolly pine plantation. *Ecology* 66:1360–1376.

Wallis, G. W. 1967. "Poria weirii root rot." In *Important forest insects and diseases of mutual concern to Canada, the United States, and Mexico.* Publication 1180. Ottawa, Canada: Department of Forestry and Rural Development.

Walstad, J. D., J. D. Brodie, B.C. McGinley, and C. A. Roberts. 1986. Silvicultural value of chemical brush control in the management of Douglas-fir. *Western Journal of Applied Forestry* 1:69–73.

Waring, R. H., and J. F. Franklin. 1979. Evergreen coniferous forests of the Pacific Northwest. *Science* 204:1380–1386.

Wells, Carol G., Ralph E. Campbell, Leonard F. Debano, Clifford E. Lewis, Richard L. Fredriksen, E. Carlyle Franklin, Ronald E. Froelich, and Paul H. Dunn. 1979. *Effects of fire on soil.* General Technical Report WO-7. Washington, D.C.: USDA Forest Service.

Wells, C. G., and J. R. Jorgensen. 1979. "Effects of intensive harvesting on nutrient supply and sustained productivity." In *Impact of intensive harvesting on forest nutrient cycling,* edited by A. Leaf, 212–230. Syracuse, N.Y.: College of Environmental Science and Forestry, State University of New York.

Wert, Steve, and Byron R. Thomas. 1981. Effects of skid roads on diameter, height, and volume growth in Douglas-fir. *Soil Science Society of America Journal* 45:629–632.

Wilcove, David S. 1988. *National Forests, policies for the future; vol. 2, Protecting biological diversity.* Washington, D.C.: The Wilderness Society.

Wright, E., and R. F. Tarrant. 1958. *Occurrence of mycorrhizae after logging and slash burning in the Douglas-fir forest type.* Research Note No. 160. Portland, Ore.: Pacific Northwest Forest and Range Experiment Station, USDA Forest Service.

Youngberg, C. T. 1953. Slashburning and soil organic matter maintenance. *Journal of Forestry* 51:202–203.

―――――. 1959. The influence of soil conditions following tractor logging on the growth of planted Douglas-fir seedlings. *Soil Science Society of America Proceedings* 23:76–78.

―――――. 1978. Nitrogen mineralization and uptake from Douglas-fir forest floors. *Soil Science Society of America Journal* 42:499–502.

Youngberg, C. T., and A. G. Wollum II. 1976. Nitrogen accretion in developing *Ceanothus velutinus* stands. *Soil Science Society of America Journal* 40:109–112.

Youngberg, C. T., A. G. Wollum, and W. Scott. 1979. "Ceanothus in Douglas-fir clearcuts: nitrogen accretion and impact on regeneration." In *Symbiotic nitrogen fixation in the management of temperate forests,* edited by J. C. Gordon, C. T. Wheeler, and D. A. Perry, 224–233. Corvallis, Ore.: Forest Research Laboratory, Oregon State University.

Zavitkovski, J., and M. Newton. 1968. Ecological importance of snowbrush (*Ceanothus velutinus*) in the Oregon Cascades. *Ecology* 49:1134–1145.

Zavitkovski, J., Michael Newton, and Babiker El-Hassan. 1969. Effects of snowbrush on growth of some conifers. *Journal of Forestry* 67:242–246.

Zivnuska, J. A. 1972. "Economic tradeoffs in fire management." In *Fire in the environment,* 69–74. Washington, D.C.: USDA Forest Service.

Chapter 8

Productivity of Upper Slope Forests in the Pacific Northwest

Kristiina Vogt, Erin Moore, Stith Gower, Daniel Vogt, Douglas Sprugel, and Charles Grier

ABSTRACT

Sustaining long-term productivity and managing upper slope forests necessitate understanding the climatic, biological, and edaphic factors controlling tree growth. Upper slope (high-elevation, or subalpine) forests are generally characterized by colder annual temperatures, heavy winter snowpacks, forest floors as important "sinks" of total ecosystem nitrogen, greater importance of mycorrhizae in nutrient uptake, slower growth rates of trees, greater carbon allocation to root biomass, long retention of foliage, and long life span of trees. These characteristics may reduce management options because of our inability to modify climate or require management criteria different from those developed for lower slope stands. Much more information on the diverse forest zones composing the upper slope forests is needed before management options for maintaining productivity can be stated. Too little research has been conducted on upper slope forests. On the basis of current information, managers of these stands must consider that (1) long rotations are needed to reestablish current biomass levels, (2) any practice that destroys the surface organic layers (e.g., fire) must be minimized to insure nitrogen conservation, (3) erosion must be minimized because upper slopes are susceptible to nutrient losses through this mechanism, and (4) uneven-aged management may be required for successful regeneration.

CONCEPTUAL FRAMEWORK FOR EXAMINING LONG-TERM PRODUCTIVITY

To begin to understand how to maintain long-term productivity of upper slope (high-elevation, or subalpine) forests in the Pacific Northwest, we must examine the question in a broad conceptual framework that looks at ecosystem change and development over time. It is not enough to confine ourselves to an approach which only considers a specific time interval. Upper slope forests take longer to establish and mature than lower slope (low-elevation) forests. Existing under arduous environmental conditions, they are sensitive to changes in that environment.

Tree growth within stands follows certain developmental stages. Within each stage, trees may respond differentially to the same environmental or biological modification. Sometimes, only individual components of an ecosystem will respond, at other times an entire stand. Time scale is critical for predicting long-term forest productivity—especially for long-lived or slow growing species such as those found in upper slope forests.

Ultimately, the ability to predict long-term productivity will arise from forecasting models that identify the most sensitive ecosystem components (e.g., environmental conditions, nutrient availability) and how these components vary with time (see Graham et al. 1984; see also chapter 11, this volume). Current attempts to predict forest growth have focused on yield functions obtained from correlations with site index and soil characteristics (Herman et al. 1978). These predictive relationships are indirect in that the dominant characteristics considered—tree height and age (i.e., site-index curves)—are only end products resulting from the interaction of environmental and physiological characteristics of specific tree species.

But site-index curves cannot predict how a specific site might accumulate tree biomass after a major disturbance such as clearcutting or whether a site could sustain current productivity in the future. Yield functions reflect past productivity and do not incorporate changes caused by management practices. To understand and model long-term productivity within the scope of a planned management regime require measuring the key variables that directly control volume growth.

But what does managing long-term productivity in these upper slope forests entail? If we are managing for wood production, time scale becomes extremely important. One or two rotations for upper slope forests may require a minimum of 120–250 years—scales 2–4 times those of lower slope forests. However, certain factors controlling productivity cannot be manipulated by humans or are not economically feasible, which limits management options. Some current forest programs reflect these limitations. The Swedes, for instance, have determined that it is only economically or biologically feasible to fertilize 20% of their forest lands to maintain or improve site productivity; the remaining lands either do not respond to treatment or are impractical to treat (Axelsson 1984). Moreover, present management practices are geared to maintaining productivity of existing species on a site, even though we know little about how they became established hundreds of years ago. This raises provocative questions about how long-lived species should be managed.

Few studies have been conducted on upper slope forests. Because the discussion in this chapter is based on limited data from a few sites, and because subalpine forests are very diverse, it is impossible to form broad generalizations. Working within these limitations, we try to identify dominant factors regulating productivity in the different forest zones of the upper slopes and to determine whether it is even feasible to manage upper slope forests. If management is feasible, then the following questions must be asked:

(1) What uses—wood production, recreation, wildlife—should these upper slope forests be managed for on the basis of our current knowledge?
(2) Do we have the technology to manage these forests to maintain wood production into the future in light of their long life spans?
(3) Do we have sufficient knowledge to predict long-term consequences of management practices?
(4) Should management practices be geared to maintaining existing tree species, or should productivity be maintained regardless of species?

DESCRIPTIONS OF UPPER SLOPE FOREST ZONES

We define upper slope forests generally as those 900 m and above in elevation, even though the dominant tree species in a zone may be found growing at lower elevations. The significant upper slope forest zones in the Pacific Northwest are the *Abies amabilis* (Pacific silver fir), the *Tsuga mertensiana* (mountain hemlock), the *Abies lasiocarpa* (subalpine fir), and east slope of Cascades mixed conifer. Specific descriptions largely follow Franklin and Dyrness (1973).

Above the closed subalpine forests is meadow-forest mosaic of subalpine parklands considered a sub-zone of the upper reaches of the *T. mertensiana/A. lasiocarpa* zones (Franklin and Dyrness 1973). Although widespread in the Pacific Northwest, these parklands have significantly less value for timber production than for watershed protection, landscape rehabilitation, and recreation and are largely excluded from this discussion.

Abies amabilis Zone

The *Abies amabilis* zone is considered the most commercially valuable timber region of the upper slope forests. Lying between the *Tsuga heterophylla* (western hemlock) and *T. mertensiana* zones, it ranges from the northern extension of the Cascade Mountains in British Columbia, Canada, including areas in the Olympic Mountains, south to 44° latitude in Oregon. Elevations vary with latitude, in northern Washington from 600 to 1,300 m, in southern Washington from 900 to 1,300 m, and in Oregon from 1,000 to 1,500 m. Pacific silver fir (*A. amabilis* Dougl. ex Forbes), the species for which the zone is named, also occurs in locally limited stands on wetter, cooler sites on the east side of the Cascades and within the *T. mertensiana* zone on the west side. Some Pacific silver fir forests have been characterized as cool temperate or montane rather than subalpine because they support vegetation similar to that of lower slope forests. (Breaking the zone into two has been suggested, one to include a lower *A. amabilis* zone, where western hemlock dominates all except the very oldest stands [Long 1976]).

Species composition within the *A. amabilis* zone depends on site, stand history, and age (Franklin and Dyrness 1973). Codominant tree species are noble fir (*A. procera* Rehd.), western hemlock [*Tsuga heterophylla* (Raf.) Sarg.], Douglas-fir [*Pseudotsuga menziesii* (Mirb.) Franco], western redcedar (*Thuja plicata* Donn ex D. Don), and western white pine (*Pinus monticola* Dougl. ex D. Don). At the uppermost elevations, mountain hemlock [*Tsuga mertensiana* (Bong.) Carr.] and Alaska yellow-cedar [*Chamaecyparis nootkatensis* (D. Don) Spach] also occur. Grand fir [*Abies grandis* (Dougl. ex D. Don) Lindl.]., subalpine fir [*Abies lasiocarpa* (Hook.) Nutt.], Engelmann spruce (*Picea engelmannii* Parry ex Engelm.), and lodgepole pine (*Pinus contorta* Dougl. ex Loud.) are associates on the east side of the Cascades. Understory, largely members of the Ericaceae, also includes members of Vaccinium, Gaultheria, Menziesia, and Rhododendron.

The first tree species to establish on upper slope sites are shade-intolerant Douglas-fir, western white pine, and noble fir. For the latter two, the inability to regenerate under canopy shade and the typically heavy mortality after 250–300 years (J. F. Franklin, personal communication, University of Washington, 1987) means they are not present on sites over the long term. In contrast, shade-intolerant Douglas-fir can live 750 years or more (Table 8.1). The more shade-tolerant western hemlock and Pacific silver fir can establish initially or later, in larger numbers, under the forest canopy. Pacific silver fir can survive decades as suppressed, older trees ("advance regeneration") in the understory before a gap opens in the overstory, releasing them.

TABLE 8.1. Average life span and shade tolerance of some upper and lower slope tree species (Waring and Franklin 1979, Packee et al. 1982).

Tree species	Minimum age, yr	Shade tolerance
Upper Slope		
Pacific silver fir	400	Very tolerant
Mountain hemlock	400	Tolerant
Subalpine fir	250	Tolerant
Lodgepole pine	250	Intolerant
Western larch[1]	700	Intolerant
Lower Slope		
Sitka spruce[1]	800	Tolerant
Douglas-fir	750	Intolerant
Western hemlock	400	Very tolerant

[1]Western larch (*Larix occidentalis* Nutt.); Sitka spruce [*Picea sitchensis* (Bong.) Carr.].

Tsuga mertensiana Zone

Occurring above the *A. amabilis* zone, the *T. mertensiana* zone is the highest forest zone on the west side of the Cascades. Elevations range from 1,300 to 1,700 m in northern Washington, from 1,250 to 1,850 m in central Washington, and from 1,700 to 2,000 m in Oregon. It is replaced by spruce-fir associates on the east side. The *T. mertensiana* zone consists of closed-canopy forests at lower elevations, and a mosaic of bald spots and clumped forest—transitional to "timberline" and alpine vegetation—at higher elevations.

Mountain hemlock has fewer common tree associates than Pacific silver fir; the major ones are Pacific silver fir and Alaska yellow-cedar on wetter sites and subalpine fir and lodgepole pine on drier sites. Minor associates are Douglas-fir, subalpine fir, and western white pine. Understory species are members of Ericaceae, Rosaceae, and Asteraceae.

Abies lasiocarpa Zone

The *A. lasiocarpa* zone, occurring at the highest elevations on the east side of the Cascades, is the "continental" analog of the *T. mertensiana* zone. Subalpine fir forests range in elevation from a minimum of 1,500 m eastward into the Cascades, and from 1,300 to 1,700 m in the other mountain ranges of Oregon and Washington (Franklin and Dyrness 1973). Subalpine fir is also found in the Okanogan highlands of northeastern Washington, and in the Blue and Wallowa Mountains of northeastern Oregon and southeastern Washington. At higher elevations, subalpine fir forests intergrade into subalpine parklands.

Discussion of long-term productivity in this zone is limited by lack of data.

East Slope of Cascades Mixed Conifer Zone

Franklin and Dyrness (1973) classified the mixed conifer forests into three distinct zones based on dominant tree species: lodgepole pine, Douglas-fir, and grand fir. Because of the paucity of data on the stand structure and function of these three forest zones and the common occurrence of all three species in all three zones, we discuss the three zones collectively and, for brevity, refer to them as the "mixed conifer zone."

The mixed conifer zone typically is bound by the *Abies lasiocarpa* and *Pinus ponderosa* (ponderosa pine) zones at its upper and lower limits, respectively (Franklin and Dyrness 1973). Stands in this zone may consist of Engelmann spruce, mountain hemlock, Douglas-fir, western larch (*Larix occidentalis* Nutt.), ponderosa pine (*Pinus ponderosa* Dougl. ex Laws.), and grand fir. Lodgepole pine is considered a minor (or dominant seral) species on upper slopes dominated by subalpine fir and Engelmann spruce. Extensive stands of pure lodgepole pine are found on very poor sites such as those in eastern Oregon where the rooting medium consists of deep tephra deposits (Mazama pumice). One of the most widespread conifers in the western United States and Canada, lodgepole pine ranges in elevation from 1,200 to 1,525 m in the Pacific Northwest (up to 3,500 m in Colorado) and represents 5% of Northwest commercial forest lands (Schmidt and Alexander 1985).

FACTORS REGULATING PRODUCTIVITY

Climatic

Moisture and temperature. For west-side conifers, moisture stress is not a consideration during the growing season (Zobel et al. 1976). Some species, such as Pacific silver fir, do not seem physiologically adapted to dry conditions and are restricted to relatively narrow ecological ranges where moisture stress does not occur (Schmidt 1957, Kotar 1972, Keyes 1982). Pacific silver fir also appears to be located where soils are not frozen under winter snowpacks. However, for east-side conifers, moisture stress is a factor during summer months (Zobel et al. 1976, Teskey et al. 1984) and therefore strongly influences productivity because the period for tree growth is restricted. Growth conditions for species such as lodgepole pine are ideal only for a short time preceding snowmelt.

In these upper slope forests, 80% or more of the precipitation occurs as rain or snow between autumn and spring. Average annual precipitation may vary from 160 to 270 cm for the *A. amabilis* zone, from 160 to 280 cm for the *T. mertensiana* zone, and from 35 to 70 cm for the mixed conifer zone. In the *A. amabilis* zone, winter snowpacks commonly average 3 m deep but may exceed 6 m in some years. Snowpacks are smaller in the mixed conifer zone.

All upper slope forests have cold temperatures that strongly limit productivity. On the west side of the Cascades, January soil temperatures ranged from −2.6 to 3.3°C for sites occupied by Pacific silver fir and from −3 to −4°C for sites occupied by mountain hemlock; July temperatures ranged from 9.4 to 15°C (Vogt et al. 1981a, Brockway et al. 1983, Greene and Klopsch 1985). On the east side, summer temperatures are higher (July average = 14.3–18.4°C) than on the west side, but January temperatures (−1.3 to −4.6°C) are similar to those of the *T. mertensiana* zone (Franklin and Dyrness 1973). The important effect of temperature on productivity was shown by Gholz (1982), who reported an inverse relationship between mean minimum January air temperatures and maximum leaf area index, biomass, and net primary production.

Length of growing season. The growing season for upper slope forests is short, determined by the number of frost-free days in which photosynthesis is possible (Emmingham and Waring 1977). For Pacific silver fir growing on the west side of the Cascades, the number of growing days between conifer bud swell and the first hard fall frost was 130 days for a stand located at Findley Lake (Grier et al. 1981) and 64–136 days in Mount Rainier National Park (Greene and Klopsch 1985). For a mixed lodgepole pine/western larch stand on the east side of the Cascades, the number of growing days was 137 (S. T. Gower, unpublished data, University of Wisconsin, 1987). Subalpine fir had the shortest growing season, 30–60 days (Alexander et al. 1984).

Biological

Stand developmental stages. Natural, undisturbed conifer forests pass through several defined developmental stages: (1) tree initiation—trees becoming established on site, (2) competitive tree-stem exclusion—the canopy has closed, resulting in the period of greatest competition between trees and selective mortality of suppressed individuals, (3) redevelopment of angiosperms in the understory due to gaps formed in the canopy when individual trees die, (4) cessation of tree height growth, and (5) old growth—trees are usually older than 250 years, and tree growth rate drastically slows, relative to that in stages 1–3 (Oliver 1981, Vogt et al. 1987c). In general, foliage and fine-root biomass, litterfall, net primary production (NPP; the amount of carbon annually fixed, or converted to usable form, by a plant), and nutrient accumulation reach a plateau at stage 2, which occurs 5–60 years after stage 1 at low elevations (Vogt et al. 1987c).

In west-side, upper slope forests, trees reach stage 2 at about age 70 years on productive sites but at greater than age 100–150 years on the poorest sites (J. F. Franklin, personal communication, University of Washington, 1987). Slow early growth lengthens each developmental stage. Revegetation after disturbance can take 10–20 years, seedling growth 20–50 years because of heavy winter snowpack and reduced winter photosynthesis. In contrast, an east-side species such as lodgepole pine may be overtopped by other species 30–80 years after initiation (Eis et al. 1982); this growth pattern probably reflects the shorter life span (250+ years, Table 8.1) of lodgepole pine compared to its associates.

Foliage biomass and life span. To achieve high productivities, trees need sufficient foliage biomass to adequately utilize solar radiation (Ford 1984). The positive correlations between foliage biomass and annual branch and bole (tree stem) production in some ecosystems (Ford 1984) further underline the importance of foliage biomass to productivity. The slow accumulation of foliage biomass in upper slope forests helps to explain the low productivities reached there. In the Pacific silver fir stands on the west side of the Washington Cascades, foliage biomass was optimized when stands were about 50 years old (Table 8.2). In lodgepole pine stands on the east side, foliage biomass was not optimized until stands were 70–100 years old (Table 8.2). These contrast low-elevation species whose foliage biomass was optimized in less than 30 years (Ford 1984).

TABLE 8.2. Foliage biomass and estimated life span of upper and lower slope forest ecosystems.

Tree species[1]	Stand age, yr	Foliage biomass, Mg/ha	Foliage life span, yr[2]	Reference
			Upper Slope	
PSF	3	0.3	—	Keyes (1982)
PSF	9	0.9	—	Keyes (1982)
PSF	23	13.6	13.1	Grier et al. (1981)
PSF	50	23.2	—	Keyes (1982)
PSF	180	21.7	21.0	Grier et al. (1981), Vogt et al. (1987a)
MH	120–200	15	5	Gholz (1982)
PSF/MH	260	19.3	18.7	Grier et al. (1985)
PSF/MH	280	18.5	17.9	Grier et al. (1985)
PSF/MH	130	19.7	19.1	Grier et al. (1985)
NF	100–130	17.5	18–203	Fujimori et al. 1976
LP	3	0.2	—	S. T. Gower, A. Friend, and C. C. Grier (unpublished)
LP	10	2.9	—	S. T. Gower and A. Friend (unpublished)
LP	50	10.0	—	S. T. Gower and A. Friend (unpublished)
LP/WL	70	8.4	6	S. T. Gower, A. Friend, and C. C. Grier (unpublished)
LP	110	18.5	—	A. Friend, S. T. Gower, and C. C. Grier (unpublished)
LP	>180	15.3	—	Tiedemann and Klock (1977)
			Lower Slope	
DF	22	5.0	2.4	Long and Turner (1975)
DF	30	6.2	2.0	Long and Turner (1975)
DF	32	5.3	5.3	Cannell (1982)
DF	38	9.0	5.0	Cannell (1982)
DF	42	8.3	3.7	Long and Turner (1975)
DF	52	12	8	Cannell (1982)
DF	73	10.8	4.7	Long and Turner (1975)
DF/WH	90–110	11.1	4.3	Fujimori et al. (1976)
DF	up to 450	12.4	5.6	Grier and Logan (1977)
WH	26	21.1	3.5	Grier (1976)
WH	130	23	3.8	Cannell (1982)
WH	130	32	4	Cannell (1982)
WH/SS	120	7.9	2.6	Fujimori et al. (1976)

[1]PSF = Pacific silver fir
MH = Mountain hemlock
NF = Noble fir
LP = Lodgepole pine
WL = Western larch
DF = Douglas-fir
WH = Western hemlock
SS = Sitka spruce
[2]Estimated foliage life span (years) = foliage biomass/foliage litterfall.

Foliage life span has a strong relationship to foliage biomass supported (Kira and Shidei 1967). For instance, Kira and Shidei (1967) recorded that temperate-zone deciduous hardwood forests had the least leaf biomass as well as an average leaf life span of less than 1 year. They noted that subalpine fir and spruce forests had greater foliage biomass and could retain foliage for 3–5 years.

This relationship between foliage biomass and life span is very apparent for cold, wet, high-elevation sites (Table 8.2). Foliage biomass was greater (15–22 Mg/ha) as foliage was retained longer (18–21 years) in mature forests. These high foliage-biomass values suggest that wood production also should be high in these forests; however, other limitations, such as low temperatures and short frost-free periods, reduce the time in which photosynthesis is possible, limiting actual growth. Teskey et al. (1984) suggested that the longer life span of Pacific silver fir foliage may be a survival mechanism that decreases dependence on any one year of foliage for fixing carbon for growth. The estimated short life span (see Table 8.2) of noble fir and mountain hemlock foliage in Oregon is attributed to the substantial winter pruning of green foliage by wind, suggesting a short foliage life span; however, Fujimori et al. (1976) noted that foliage was retained 18–20 years in this noble fir stand.

The lower foliage biomass accumulation and shorter life span of east-side lodgepole pine probably reflect moisture limitations (Table 8.2). Grier and Running (1977) demonstrated that site water balance governs the leaf area a site can support; and leaf area, in turn, has been highly correlated with aboveground NPP in Pacific Northwest forests (Gholz 1982).

High levels of foliage biomass similar to those of cold, wet, upper slope forests were also maintained by low-elevation western hemlock; however, foliage life span was only 3–4 years for western hemlock, in contrast to 18–21 years for stands dominated by Pacific silver fir (Table 8.2). It is not unusual for foliage life span of low-elevation species to be only 2–8 years (Table 8.2). Even though needle life span for Douglas-fir growing in the lowland Puget Sound area in Washington was 3–6 years, Douglas-fir growing at high elevations in New Mexico had a foliage life span greater than 21 years (S. T. Gower, unpublished data, University of Wisconsin, 1987).

Belowground carbon allocation. Except for stands dominated by Pacific silver fir in Washington, data on carbon (C) allocation to belowground tissues do not exist for upper slope forests. Pacific silver fir characteristically invests a significant portion of NPP in maintaining a root system that is larger than that of most other tree species (Vogt et al. 1982, 1986). For example, 30 and 54% of NPP were in fine roots and mycorrhizal root tips in a young and mature Pacific silver fir stand, respectively (Vogt et al. 1982). If coarse roots are included in these estimates, NPP in total belowground tissues rises to 45 and 67% for these same two stands. These values for Pacific silver fir contrast those of the low-elevation Douglas-fir, which had 15–50% of NPP in fine and coarse roots (Keyes and Grier 1981, Vogt et al. 1985).

Large C allocations to belowground tissues are probably restricted to cold, wet, upper slope forests where soils are not frozen during winter (Vogt et al. 1986). East-side high-elevation forests probably cannot maintain a large root biomass similar to that of Pacific silver fir because the site water balance would limit leaf area and, thus, achievable production.

When moisture is not the primary factor limiting root growth, nutrients—especially nitrogen (N)—appear to regulate C allocation patterns. For a variety of sites supporting conifers in the Pacific Northwest, there was a significant inverse relationship between the amount of N cycled in aboveground litterfall and root biomass: that is, the more N cycled aboveground (and the greater its availability on site), the less root biomass supported (Vogt et al. 1986). This same relationship between N availability and root biomass has been shown experimentally by manipulating the N status of low-elevation sites (Axelsson 1981, Linder and Rook 1984, Vogt et al. 1985). The large allocations of carbon to roots seen for Pacific silver fir are probably due to the high accumulations of total ecosystem N in the surface organic layers above the soil, removing this N from the plant-available pools.

Mycorrhizae. Upper slope forests appear to have structurally well-developed mycorrhizae on root tips, compared to lower slope stands (Vogt and Grier 1982; K. A. Vogt, unpublished, Yale University, 1987). Most conifers depend on these mycorrhizal associations for increasing nutrient uptake where availability is naturally low (Harley and Smith 1983). Because there is a strong, direct relationship between increasing accumulations of surface organic matter and decreasing availability of nutrients in forest ecosystems (Vogt et al. 1986), it follows that the greatest density of mycorrhizal root tips will be found in organic "pockets" in the soil, decaying wood, or surface organic layers (Mikola and Laiho 1962, Mikola 1973, Harvey et al. 1978, 1979, Kimmins and Hawkes 1978, Vogt et al. 1981a). The thick surface organic matter accumulations that have been recorded in west-side, upper slope forests in Washington (Williams and Dyrness 1967, Vogt et al. 1986; see "Forest floor," this chapter) suggest that biomass of mycorrhizal root tips is greater in these forests. In fact, Vogt et al. (1981b) found many mycorrhizal root tips within the thick surface organic layer in a mature Pacific silver fir forest. Comparable data on both mycorrhizal root biomass and forest-floor biomass are not available for east-side, upper slope forests in the Pacific Northwest.

Because the relationship between tree roots and mycorrhizal fungi is symbiotic, the increased uptake of nutrients by trees via mycorrhizae is offset by the carbon requirements of the fungal associate; that is, mycorrhizal fungi "cost" the tree carbon because they obtain their C from tree photosynthate (Harley and Smith 1983). In two Pacific silver fir stands in Washington, an estimated 14–15% of C annually fixed by the trees was translocated to mycorrhizae alone for their growth and maintenance (Vogt et al. 1982). If the mycorrhizal component increases, more C must be allocated to it—leaving less C available to aboveground tissues. This is especially important at high elevations because the length of the growing season is restricted by the number of frost-free days (see "Snowpack, frost, and winter desiccation").

Edaphic

Rooting depth and wind. Trees on naturally steeper, less stable slopes, trees at the edges of stands, and trees growing on ridges and mesic (moist) sites where root systems tend to be shallower all are susceptible to loss from wind ("windthrow," or "blowdown"). If windthrown trees are not immediately salvaged, stand volume is lost. Trees in upper slope forests in Washington commonly root in shallow soils that limit rooting depth. For example, the rooting depth for Pacific silver fir in Washington is typically restricted to the upper 30–50 cm of soil (Vogt et al. 1983). The effective rooting depth will be greater in soils where tephra (airborne volcanic material) is thick. In Oregon, Williams and Dyrness (1967) found that effective rooting depths were twice as deep where soils consisted of pumice sands and gravels. The much greater effective rooting depth—as deep as 120 cm—observed by Fujimori et al. (1976) for one noble fir stand in Oregon may prevent trees from being windthrown and help explain the high productivities measured in that stand.

In the long term, windthrow may be a mechanism for rejuvenating a site: roots of windthrown trees break up the impervious layers created when the soil was formed (Ugolini and Mann 1979). In the ecosystems studied by Ugolini and co-workers in southeast Alaska, such impermeable soil layers limit rooting to the upper soil and inhibit decomposition of surface organic matter. Ugolini has hypothesized that windthrow is the most important mechanism for reversing bog formation and allowing forests to grow on these sites. Mounds created by the root systems of uprooted, windthrown trees have younger, better drained soils directly beneath them (Ugolini and Mann 1979).

Soils. Podzolization is a common soil-forming process in the Cascades and Olympic Peninsula of Washington and in the high Oregon Cascades (Ugolini 1982). Podzolized soils are characterized by the presence of incompletely decomposed organic surface layers, and soil horizons that have a bleached surface layer followed by a deeper layer in which iron (Fe) and aluminum (Al) precipitate. Podzolization may be the dominant soil-forming process on upper slopes in Oregon and southern Washington; however, these areas do not have the distinct profile characteristic of this process (J. F. Franklin, personal communication, University of Washington, 1987). Further information on the diverse soil types existing in the west-side, upper slope forests of Oregon and Washington is presented in Franklin and Dyrness (1973). Tree species typically growing in podzolized soils are Pacific silver fir, western hemlock, mountain hemlock, and subalpine fir; the presence of noble fir seems to prevent podzolization (Ugolini 1982).

Many of the soils in Washington and Oregon are developed in tephra, which has been repeatedly deposited in these upper slope forests. Some of the properties associated with ash-derived soils are low bulk density, high moisture contents, and high phosphorus (P) retention due to high levels of extractable Al and Fe oxides (Ugolini and Zasoski 1979).

Soils of the mixed conifer zone exhibit minimal horizon development, although they are generally deep because of their volcanic origin (Franklin and Dyrness 1973). The forest floor is relatively shallow, and podzolization, if present, is not well developed. A wide range of soil types exists on the east side of the Cascades (Franklin and Dyrness 1973). Some tree species (e.g., lodgepole pine) grow both in poorly drained soils and in coarsely textured, droughty soils. Although lodgepole pine is found on a wide range of soils, it seems to thrive on granite, shale, and coarse-grained lavas and is often the only tree species to grow on very infertile soils (Franklin and Dyrness 1973).

Forest floor. The depth and mass of the forest floor seem to vary considerably on upper slopes, with west-side sites in central and northern Washington having deeper accumulations (Williams and Dyrness 1967).

Many upper slope forests accumulate litter layers that can be as much as twice as deep as those of lower slope forests (Williams and Dyrness 1967, Vogt et al. 1986). These accumulations are deep because of (1) slow litter-decomposition rates resulting from cooler temperatures and the lack of nutrients available to the microorganisms decomposing the litter, and (2) the large amounts of litter added to the forest floor to be decomposed (Vogt et al. 1980, 1983). In mature, west-side Pacific silver fir forests in Washington, surface accumulations of organic matter are commonly 100 Mg/ha or greater (Vogt et al. 1986). In a series of true fir-hemlock plots in Washington, Williams and Dyrness (1967) measured surface organic matter accumulations varying from 19 to 106 Mg/ha at Mount Adams, from 28 to 171 Mg/ha at Mount Rainier, and from 58 to 146 Mg/ha at Mount Baker. In Oregon, these values ranged from 22 to 43 Mg/ha at Mount Hood, from 33 to 49 Mg/ha at Willamette, from 44 to 85 Mg/ha at Crater Lake, and from 26 to 88 Mg/ha at Three Sisters (Williams and Dyrness 1967).

On east-side, upper slope sites in Washington, forest-floor accumulations were comparable to those reported by Williams and Dyrness (1967) for west-side, upper slope forests: 47, 58, and 42 Mg/ha for a 50-, 110-, and greater than 180-year-old mixed lodgepole pine/western larch stand, respectively (S. T. Gower, A. Friend, and C. C. Grier, unpublished, 1987). These mixed-stand values are at the upper extreme of the 20–50 Mg/ha range measured in low-elevation forests of the Pacific Northwest (Vogt et al. 1986). Forest-floor accumulation in an old-growth Douglas-fir forest studied by Grier and Logan (1977) was 51 Mg/ha.

Significant amounts of nutrients are stored in thick organic layers. Mature west-side, upper slope forests averaged 0.3–2 Mg/ha N in the forest floor, lower slope forests 0.1-0.4 Mg/ha (Williams and Dyrness 1967, Vogt et al. 1986). Upper slope sites in central and northern Washington have greater amounts of N immobilized in the forest floor than do sites in Oregon; Williams and Dyrness (1967) found that total N content of forest floors varied from 330 to 487 kg/ha in Oregon and from 577 to 690 kg/ha in Washington (these values did not always include the humus layers and therefore are probably lower than others reported). East-side, upper slope forests accumulate N at rates similar to those at the lower end of the range for west-side forests; 0.6 Mg/ha was reported for a 110-year-old lodgepole pine stand (A. Friend, S. T. Gower, and C. C. Grier, unpublished, 1987).

Nutrient cycling. There is a strong positive linear relationship between plant uptake of N and P and a plant's aboveground NPP—that is, as a plant takes up more N or P, aboveground productivities are higher (Miller 1981). At each stand developmental stage, availability of nutrients to trees and requirement for nutrients by trees also vary. Most newly regenerating stands have sufficient N available to support seedling growth, much of it from decomposing forest floor and any slash (harvest residue) left on site after logging. At stand developmental stage 2 (competitive tree-stem exclusion), foliage and root biomass reach an optimum (Vogt et al. 1987c) when demand for nutrients is greatest. As trees age, a greater proportion of tree nutrient requirement is satisfied by cycling of nutrients within the tree itself (resorption) than by nutrients released during the decomposition of litter in the forest floor (Turner 1975). This can culminate in a situation in which insufficient N is available annually on a site to support new growth on older trees because so much of the N is immobilized either in tree biomass (Matson and Boone 1985) or the forest floor (Krause et al. 1979). Stand growth may naturally slow when N deficiencies limit growth in cold, temperate, high-elevation forests.

Because nutrient data are lacking for upper slope forests, most of this discussion centers on west-side, upper slope Pacific silver fir stands and one east-side lodgepole pine/western larch stand in Washington. On Pacific silver fir sites, most N is stored in the forest floor, whereas most P, calcium (Ca), potassium (K), and magnesium (Mg) are stored in the soil (Table 8.3). N is mineralized (converted by microorganisms) more quickly from the forest floor than from the soil (Pritchett 1979). In a mature Pacific silver fir stand, only 10% of the stand's N was distributed in aboveground tree components, in contrast to 40% in the forest floor and 47% in the soil (Table 8.3). That more N is stored in the forest floor of a cold, wet, upper slope forest than warm, temperate, or tropical, moist forests has been previously reported (Pritchett 1979). Because site N availability is so closely tied to productivity, this large accumulation of forest floor N on west-side, upper slope sites identifies the forest floor as an important management focus.

The smaller amounts of surface organic matter in east-side forests (see "Forest floor") are reflected in the smaller amounts of N in the forest floor. In a lodgepole pine/western larch stand, only 6% of ecosystem N was in the forest floor, but 91% in the soil (A. Friend, S. T. Gower, and C. C. Grier, unpublished, 1987). Nitrogen accumulation in surface organic layers seems less significant in east- than west-side, upper slope forests. The pattern of N distribution in east-side forests is similar to that of low-elevation Douglas-fir forests, which held 5–11% of site N in the forest floor and 76–83% in the soil (Turner 1975, Miller et al. 1976).

TABLE 8.3. Distribution of biomass and nutrient contents in a 185-year-old Pacific silver fir stand in Washington (Grier et al. 1981, Meier 1981, Vogt et al. 1987a). The sum of the components may not equal 100% because of rounding.

Forest component	Biomass or nutrient content, kg/ha or % of total					
	Biomass		Nitrogen		Phosphorus	
	kg/ha	%	kg/ha	%	kg/ha	%
Stemwood and stem bark	356,200	38	285	6	37	1
Foliage and branches	89,450	10	177	4	64	2
Understory	170	t[1]	t	t	t	t
Roots (fine and coarse)	141,410	15	228	5	61	2
Forest floor	149,500	16	1,971	40	83	3
Soil	194,800	21	2,320	47	2,894	92
	Calcium		Potassium		Magnesium	
	kg/ha	%	kg/ha	%	kg/ha	%
Stemwood and stem bark	369	<1	332	<1	45.5	<1
Foliage and branches	300	<1	289	<1	53.3	<1
Understory	t[1]	t	t	t	t	t
Roots (fine and coarse)	183	<1	206	<1	46.6	<1
Forest floor	246	<1	123	<1	61.0	<1
Soil	180,960	99	85,780	99	136,840	100

[1]t = trace.

Because podzolization is the dominant soil-forming process in west-side, upper slope forests, Al and Fe are present in mobile forms, creating the potential for plant toxicity (Ugolini et al. 1977a,b, Vogt et al. 1987a,b). But where pollution is not a consideration, upper slope forests appear to be adapted to these higher Al levels (Vogt et al. 1987a). Existing tree species either avoid taking up Al or can accumulate it in their tissues without effect; for example, Pacific silver fir avoids taking up Al, whereas mountain hemlock accumulates and tolerates it (Vogt et al. 1987b). Thus, Al toxicity may not be an issue unless tree species composition changes, Al levels in soil increase significantly, or acid deposition becomes a problem in the Pacific Northwest. Acidification facilitates the release of elements such as Al into soil solution (Khanna and Ulrich 1984). Plants may be tolerant of existing levels but incapable of adjusting to higher ones. We do not currently know what Al concentrations are naturally toxic.

In some west-side forests, vegetation appears to play an important role in cycling Al. In a Pacific silver fir stand in Washington, 82% of total ecosystem Al was cycled annually as part of detritus production by trees (Vogt et al. 1987a), most (97%) resulting from root turnover. Belowground Al cycling dominates because a large proportion of the Al taken up by plants precipitates in root tissues.

We have hypothesized that the large root biomass of west-side, upper slope forests may allow existing species to avoid Al toxicity. When Al accumulates in roots at levels in which nutrient uptake mechanisms are impaired, roots can be selectively senesced by soil layer or microsite, removing Al from metabolically active tissues. That this mechanism is plausible and functioning on these sites is seen in the rapid turnover rate of roots containing high Al levels in the deeper soil layers where soil Al levels are greatest (Vogt et al. 1981a, 1987a).

PRODUCTIVITY OF UPPER SLOPE FORESTS

In evaluating potential upper slope productivity, it is important to recognize that high-elevation stands develop more slowly than low-elevation stands; many may not even reach maximal productivity until they are well over 100 years old. To estimate future biomass or volume, we must examine total productivity and how the components used to determine productivity vary by stand developmental stage. Because production peaks earlier at low than high elevations, lower slope forests cannot be compared with upper slope forests on the basis of age.

Aboveground NPP for upper slope forests (Table 8.4) is generally lower than the world average of 7.9 Mg ha^{-1} yr^{-1} reported for temperate-zone forests (Olson 1975, Rodin et al. 1975). For west-side, upper slope forests in Washington, aboveground NPP ranged from 4 to 6 Mg ha^{-1} yr^{-1}; by contrast, values for low-elevation Douglas-fir are 7–14 Mg ha^{-1} yr^{-1}, for western hemlock 13–32 Mg ha^{-1} yr^{-1} (Table 8.4).

One exception to this pattern is the west-side, upper slope noble fir forest in Oregon studied by Fujimori et al. (1976), which had an aboveground NPP almost 3 times higher than NPPs reported for west-side, upper slope forests in Washington (Table 8.4). This high value may be characteristic of stands in which rooting volume is not restricted (Fujimori et al. 1976); such stands are common to west-side, upper slope forests in the central and northern Washington Cascades (Vogt and Grier 1982). Currently, lack of information prevents us from generalizing about biomass accumulation or productivity levels in upper slope forests.

The percentage of aboveground NPP lost to detritus production (litterfall and grazing) (Table 8.5) shows that as stands age, trees allocate more resources to producing deciduous tissues such as leaves and branches and fewer resources to producing wood. Wood production actually becomes negative as stands approach old age

TABLE 8.4. Aboveground tree productivity (net primary production, NPP) for upper and lower slope forest ecosystems.

Tree species[1]	Stand age, yr	Aboveground NPP, Mg ha^{-1} yr^{-1}	Reference
		Upper Slope	
PSF	3	0.4	Keyes (1982)
PSF	9	1.6	Keyes (1982)
PSF	23	6.1	Grier et al. (1981)
PSF/MH	130	4.9	Grier et al. (1981, 1985)
PSF	185	4.5	Grier et al. (1981)
PSF/MH	260	5.9	Grier et al. (1981, 1985)
PSF/MH	280	4.6	Grier et al. (1981, 1985)
MH	120–200	4.2	Gholz (1982)
NF/DF	100–130	16.5	Fujimori et al. (1976)
LP/WL	70	8.6	S. T. Gower, A. Friend, and C. C. Grier (unpublished)
		Lower Slope	
DF	22	8.8	Cannell (1982)
DF	30	8.4	Cannell (1982)
DF	40	9.3	Cannell (1982)
DF	40	7.3	Keyes and Grier (1981)
DF	40	13.7	Keyes and Grier (1981)
DF	73	5.1	Cannell (1982)
DF	450	7.0	Grier and Logan (1977)
WH	30	28.0	Grier et al. (1985)
WH	130	15.0	Cannell (1982)
WH	130	13.0	Cannell (1982)
WH/SS	26	32.2	Grier (1976)
WH/SS	100–120	19.5	Grier (1976)
DF/WH	90–110	12.6	Fujimori et al. (1976)

[1]PSF = Pacific silver fir
MH = Mountain hemlock
NF = Noble fir
DF = Douglas-fir
LP = Lodgepole pine
WL = Western larch
WH = Western hemlock
SS = Sitka spruce

TABLE 8.5. Percent of aboveground net primary production (NPP) lost to litterfall and grazing for upper and lower slope forest ecosystems.

Tree species[1]	Stand age, yr	Aboveground NPP, %[2]	Reference
		Upper Slope	
PSF	23	33	Grier et al. (1981)
PSF	180	49	Grier et al. (1981)
LP/WL	70	59	S. T. Gower, A. Friend, and C. C. Grier (unpublished)
		Lower Slope	
DF	22	30	Cannell (1982)
WH/SS	26	23	Grier (1976), Fujimori et al. (1976)
DF	30	42	Cannell (1982)
DF	40	30	Keyes and Grier (1981)
DF	40	28	Keyes and Grier (1981)
DF	73	73	Cannell (1982)
WH/SS	100–120	62	Grier (1976), Fujimori et al. (1976)
DF	450	59	Grier and Logan (1977)

[1]PSF = Pacific silver fir
LP = Lodgepole pine
WL = Western larch
DF = Douglas-fir
WH = Western hemlock
SS = Sitka spruce
[2]Calculated as [(litterfall + grazing)/aboveground NPP]100.

and die (cf. Grier and Logan 1977). Interestingly, about half of the aboveground NPP in west-side, upper slope Pacific silver fir forests in Washington occurred as wood even when stands were 180 years old. This finding is consistent with the pattern of slow initial growth, followed by maintenance growth for a longer period, at high- compared to low-elevation sites. An east-side, upper slope forest already had a large proportion of aboveground NPP in deciduous tissues by 70 years with 59% lost as part of detritus production. The pattern here is similar to the patterns exhibited by lower slope forests. For example, detritus production was 73 and 62% of aboveground NPP in a 70-year-old Douglas-fir forest and a 100–120 year old western hemlock/Sitka spruce [*Picea sitchensis* (Bong.) Carr.] forest, respectively. Slower growing upper slope forests in western Washington allocated more annually fixed carbon to wood production over a longer time.

For upper slope forests, the amount of total aboveground tree biomass reflects the lower productivity of these sites and their slow early growth (Table 8.6). According to available data, biomass accumulates in west-side, upper slope forests in Washington until stand age averages 200 years; maximum accumulations are 450–550 Mg/ha. In east-side, upper slope forests in Washington, aboveground biomass accumulates more rapidly, peaking by 110 years for lodgepole pine/western larch stands (Table 8.6). In addition, east-side forests had lower maximums (350 Mg/ha) than west-side forests. The slower accumulation of aboveground biomass in the mixed conifer zone is largely attributed to the slower replacement of optimal foliage biomass and the smaller amounts of foliage supported by these forests. Patterns of biomass accumulation for low-elevation stands of Douglas-fir, a long-lived species, are similar to those of west-side, upper slope forests (up to 200 years). For shorter lived western hemlock, rates of biomass accumulation for a single stand (which may have been atypical) apparently decreased by age 150. Even though the time span for accumulating biomass may be similar for high- and low-elevation species, maximum accumulations are greater at low elevations—about 700–800 Mg/ha for Douglas-fir and 1,000–1,100 Mg/ha for western hemlock.

Height growth also reflects the slow growth rate of upper slope forests and continued growth later into stand development. West-side, upper slope forests continue to grow taller to very advanced ages (Herman and Franklin 1976, Herman et al. 1978). Herman and Franklin (1976) measured almost constant height growth for mountain hemlock until trees were felled at age 263. Trees grew taller at a slower rate and continued to grow over a longer time at high- than low-elevation sites. Similarly, Curtis et al. (1974) found slower height growth rates for Douglas-fir at high than low elevations. This does not imply, however, that high-elevation tree species are not capable of achieving heights of low-elevation species. For instance, Grant (1980) found greater total heights on Pacific silver fir than Douglas-fir or western hemlock 80 years after establishment. But this observation may be uncommon because the distribution of Pacific silver fir is limited by its inability to compete with faster growing trees found at lower elevations (Kotar 1972).

TABLE 8.6. Total aboveground tree biomass for upper and lower slope forest ecosystems.

Tree species[1]	Stand age, yr	Aboveground tree biomass, Mg/ha	Reference
		Upper Slope	
PSF	3	1.1	Keyes (1982)
PSF	9	3.1	Keyes (1982)
PSF	23	49.1	Grier et al. (1981)
PSF	50	282.0	Keyes (1982)
PSF/MH	130	453.1	Grier et al. (1981)
PSF	180	445.5	Grier et al. (1981)
PSF/MH	417	467.3	Krumlik and Kimmins (1976), Grier et al. (1985)
PSF/MH	300–350	542.2	Cannell (1982)
MH	120–200	278	Gholz (1982)
NF/DF	100–130	880.4	Fujimori et al. (1976)
LP/WL	3	0.3	A. Friend, and S. T. Gower, and C. C. Grier (unpublished)
LP/WL	10	14.1	S. T. Gower and A. Friend (unpublished)
LP/WL	50	183.2	S. T. Gower and A. Friend (unpublished)
LP/WL	70	199.1	S. T. Gower, A. Friend, and C. C. Grier (unpublished)
LP	110	361.6	A. Friend, S. T. Gower, and C. C. Grier (unpublished)
LP/WL	>180	338.7	C. C. Grier and A. R. Tiedemann (unpublished), Tiedemann and Klock (1977)
		Lower Slope	
DF	22	131.5	Long and Turner (1975)
DF	30	159.2	Long and Turner (1975)
DF	40	239.6	Keyes and Grier (1981)
DF	40	453.3	Keyes and Grier (1981)
DF	42	204.8	Long and Turner (1975)
DF	70	233	Vogt (1987)
DF	70	411	Vogt (1987)
DF	70	357	Vogt (1987)
DF	70	288	Vogt (1987)
DF	73	303.6	Long and Turner (1975)
DF	125	449	Cannell (1982)
DF/GF	150	865	Gholz (1982), Cannell (1982)
DF	150–200	536	Vogt (1987)
DF	150–200	765	Vogt (1987)
DF	150–200	772	Vogt (1987)
DF	450	711.1	Grier and Logan (1977)
DF	up to 500	632	Cannell (1982)
DF/WH	up to 450	1,064	Waring and Franklin 1979
WH/SS	26	192.7	Fujimori (1971)
WH/SS	120	915.6	Fujimori et al. (1976)
WH/SS	100–120	871.3	Fujimori et al. (1976)
WH	130	1,080	Cannell (1982)
WH	130	1,492	Cannell (1982)
WH/SS	up to 250	558.1	Cannell (1982)
PP	120–200	136	Gholz (1982)

[1]PSF = Pacific silver fir
MH = Mountain hemlock
NF = Noble fir
DF = Douglas-fir
LP = Lodgepole pine
WL = Western larch
GF = Grand fir
WH = Western hemlock
SS = Sitka spruce
PP = Ponderosa pine

MANAGING UPPER SLOPE PRODUCTIVITY

Considerations

Management considerations for upper slope forests should include the environmental impacts of any rotation schedule. These forests are adapted to the extreme stresses of their environments through mechanisms such as strict growth timing and conservative nutrient use and retention. Disrupting nutrient cycling through poor management practices may cause irreparable damage. The system is resilient to a certain point but finely tuned to its environment and sensitive to any change (see chapter 6, this volume).

Snowpack, frost, and winter desiccation. Two important limitations to growth of subalpine areas are the extensive duration of winter snowpacks and short, cool, growing seasons. Snowpack duration directly affects the length of the growing season and therefore the period of aboveground production. At these elevations, patches of snow may persist until July, allowing ideal growth conditions for only 2–3 months. Despite species adaptation to these cold sites, snow depth and duration influence the amount of annual growth increment achievable. Graumlich (1985) found a strong negative relationship between length of snowpack and width of annual growth rings for mountain hemlock. Despite the deleterious effects of snowpacks on tree growth, melt-water from snowpacks recharges the soil and represents a major annual source of water.

Tree species on upper slopes are well adapted to their sites. For instance, Pacific silver fir is frost hardy and relatively resistant to snow breakage, which allows it to grow where snowpacks are deep (Thornburgh 1969). Mountain hemlock commonly regenerates and survives on these cold sites. Subalpine fir is conspicuous in cold-air drainages and frost pockets (small depressions where cold air settles) and is an important pioneer species on many severe sites (Franklin 1966). Lodgepole pine seedlings are quite cold resistant and tend to establish in lower lying areas that are potential frost pockets (Cochran 1969).

Brockway et al. (1983) considered frost to be the most important variable determining revegetation success of upper slope forests. Frost is common late in the season; there may be a 2–3 month period of frequent frosts until continuous snowpacks are formed. Frost is especially prevalent at high elevations on slopes less than 15%, ridgetops and benches, and small depressions (Brockway et al. 1983). Those areas commonly vegetated by lodgepole pine are especially subject to frost. Seeds that do germinate often encounter frost heaving in autumn if soils become wet without first being covered by snow (Cochran 1985) and may have problems germinating in spring because of dry, cold soils.

Winter desiccation can dramatically decrease site productivity and may be responsible for the formation of the timberline in upper slope forests where soils are frozen during the winter (easily recognizable by the resulting "Red Belt Zone") (Tranquillini 1979). The red color arises from foliage desiccation—when warm air temperatures cause stomates to open even though the plant cannot take up water from the frozen soil.

Soil erosion and compaction. High-elevation forests grow on slopes of varying steepness. Slopes tend to be gentler in the High Cascades of Oregon and the plateau-like region around Mount Adams in Washington (J. F. Franklin, personal communication, University of Washington, 1987). Where slopes are steep, managers must critically examine how management practices affect soil erosion because of its impact on water quality and streamflow.

Dominant causes of serious erosion are the construction of logging roads and wildfires (Klock 1982). Presence of forest vegetation and a high infiltration capacity of forest soils protect slopes from surface erosion; volcanic soils have particularly high infiltration rates (R. T. Meurisse, personal communication, 1987). Road building disturbs already marginally stable slopes, thus changing surface-subsurface water movement (Swanston and Swanson 1976). "Cut and fill" roads increased erosion from debris avalanches 25–350 times for east-side, compared to west-side, forests (Swanston 1976). In the H. J. Andrews Experimental Forest and at Alder Creek in Oregon, clearcutting appeared to increase the occurrence of debris torrents 4.5–8.8 times that in the forested system; road building increased this occurrence 42.5–133 times (Swanston 1976). Several studies have shown road building to be a significant cause of increased sedimentation in streamwater (Megahan 1976).

In the *A. amabilis* and *T. mertensiana* zones, Brockway et al. (1983) identified soil compaction as one of the more serious soil-related management problems. Soil compaction problems are especially prevalent in areas with high water tables, where soils are moist throughout most of the year and easily compressed. According to Brockway et al. (1983), conventional equipment with wheels used to harvest trees can cause 90% of the potential compaction damage during the first pass over a skid trail. Cochran (1985) suggested that lodgepole pine is very susceptible to growth reductions due to soil compaction because of its shallow rooting characteristics. He warned managers to be careful operating equipment when soils are wet and thus more susceptible to compaction. Soil compaction also affects site fertility status since it influences root penetration, and therefore the ability of roots to take up nutrients (see chapters 2, 4, and 5, this volume).

The needs of silviculture and watershed management may conflict. For example, the exposure of mineral soil is favored for the successful regeneration of some species (Alvarez et al. 1979, Vogt and Grier 1982). However, the process of exposing mineral soil also compacts it and may subsequently inhibit regeneration. Assessing slash removal with various logging methods, Swanston and Swanson (1976) showed that only 12% of the soil was bared after skyline logging, but 55% after broadcast slash burning.

Because soil disturbance and compaction contribute the most to soil erosion, management practices must be designed to minimize erosion (Sidle 1980). Reducing the number of miles of road and using skyline and balloon logging have been suggested as the most direct means of minimizing erosion from road building (Dyrness 1967). Klock (1982) has shown how using advanced logging techniques (helicopter and skyline), and harvesting when winter snowpacks are present, significantly reduce compaction and erosion. However, in many cases, it is not economically feasible to use advanced techniques because of their excessive cost, especially for typically less productive upper slope forests.

Regeneration potential. Regeneration on upper slopes is generally slower than on lower slopes. Even so, restocking may be adequate if given sufficient time. For example, Minore and Dubrasich (1981) noted that even though regeneration of mountain hemlock near Windigo Pass, Oregon, was initially poor after clearcutting, it was adequate 9–12 years later. This regeneration occurred on gentle slopes with deep deposits of Mazama pumice.

Most upper slope species produce medium to heavy cone crops every 2–3 years; thus shelterwood trees or seedtrees must be left on site. Franklin et al. (1974) noted a rapid decline in seedfall of Pacific silver fir and noble fir as distance from the edge of stands increased. In lodgepole pine stands, they observed seeds to disperse 114 m in bumper years, suggesting adequate seed supplies for natural restocking of 4–8 ha clearcuts.

Once seeds are distributed, regenerating species depend on a suitable microsite for germination. Some species are more dependent on specific microsites for germination than others. For example, mountain hemlock is a prolific seeder but prefers germination beds of well-decomposed, large woody debris (Christy and Mack 1984). However, if whole trees are harvested, this type of bedding may not be available. Likewise, leaving less large, woody debris after harvesting could influence the regeneration of western hemlock, an important Pacific silver fir associate on lower slopes, because hemlock seedlings prefer to establish on rotting logs.

The presence of mycorrhizae may be very important for regenerating dry upper slopes (Amaranthus and Perry 1987). Amaranthus and Perry (1987) observed a 50% increase in first-year seedling survival at high elevations in Oregon when nonmycorrhizal Douglas-fir seedlings were planted in soil containing mycorrhizal inoculum. (See also chapter 3, this volume.)

Brush species that reestablish after logging can create problems for regenerating conifer seedlings. On more productive sites, intense shrub competition can inhibit conifer establishment (Franklin 1966, Sullivan 1978) because forest regeneration is slow after disturbance of upper slopes; frequently, huckleberry (*Vaccinium*) species first dominate the site, competing with regenerating seedlings. Mountain hemlock and Pacific silver fir can pioneer on wetter sites, lodgepole pine and subalpine fir on drier sites. Pacific silver fir often prevails because it regenerates at regular intervals, whereas mountain hemlock remains small until the canopy opens up.

Because of the extreme site variability in the *A. amabilis* zone and the "erratic" results of tree planting (artificial regeneration) (Franklin 1966, Sullivan 1978), natural regeneration has been a primary focus in reforestation of upper slopes (Brockway et al. 1983). A major feature of the *A. amabilis* zone is the ubiquitous presence of old, "regenerating" trees (advance regeneration). Pacific silver fir can survive decades in a suppressed state in the understory before a gap or patch in the dominant overstory opens, releasing it. The number of old, regenerating trees in old-growth stands varies depending on the association (Franklin 1966); Herring and Etheridge (1976) found the age and size of such trees highly variable even within the same stand.

Susceptibility to disturbance. *Disease.* Little is known about the impact of disease on upper slope productivity, although disease seems to play a part in the natural cycle of tree mortality for old, west-side forests.

In mature mountain hemlock stands on the west side of the Cascades, tree life span appears to be related to availability of site N and incidence of disease, which themselves are related (Matson and Boone 1985). Matson and Boone (1985) hypothesized that trees in a 300-year-old mountain hemlock stand died as a result of an increasing deficiency in soil N. As trees age, increasing amounts of N are sequestered in long-lived tissues, limiting the soil available N for uptake by plants and disabling the trees from producing defensive chemicals to protect against disease. In such cases, infection by the root fungus *Phellinus weirii* can ultimately kill weakened or susceptible trees (McCauley and Cook 1980).

Insects. Productivity losses due to insects in upper slope forests of the Pacific Northwest have not been determined. On the east side of the Cascades, numerous studies have been conducted to produce control programs to reduce lodgepole pine mortality due to the mountain pine beetle (*Scolytidae* species) (Amman and Safranyik 1985, Waring and Pitman 1985, Waring and Schlesinger 1985). Apparently, thinning can reduce tree losses to this insect and increase the growth of the remaining trees (Waring and Pitman 1985). A similar increase in growth of the remaining trees following an insect outbreak has been observed in other forest ecosystems (Mattson and Addy 1975, Klein et al. 1978, Wickman 1978). Even if the impact of the mountain pine beetle can be reduced, the beetle's preference for larger diameter trees may limit the ability to manage lodgepole pine stands for timber production in many areas (Wellner 1978). However, if tree growth can be maintained at a high growth efficiency (e.g., by fertilizing trees with N), trees appear capable of surviving beetle attack (Waring and Pitman 1985).

Gara et al. (1985) hypothesized a strong relationship between fire, white rot fungi, pine beetles, and the perpetuation and maintenance of lodgepole pine in the Pacific Northwest. They suggested that fires create fungal infection courts in damaged roots. Advanced decay develops with time in butts and stems of trees which are then selectively attacked by mountain pine beetles. The death of some trees allows for the regeneration of lodgepole pine after another major fire and a rejuvenation of the site.

There is some evidence for the Rocky Mountain region that long-term productivity may not be drastically affected by the mountain pine beetle, and that beetle outbreaks may actually sustain lodgepole pine productivity. Even though site productivity initially decreases because large trees die, it recovers rapidly (Romme et al. 1986): stand productivity first decreased by about 25%, but wood production returned to or exceeded pre-attack levels within 10–15 years.

Balsam woolly aphids (*Adelges piceae* [Ratz.]) have heavily damaged Pacific silver fir in herb-rich habitats (Franklin 1966) and subalpine fir at the lower end of its range. Actual loss of productivity due to aphids is not known.

Forest decline and pollution. Productivity of upper slope spruce and fir forests on the eastern coast of the U.S. is thought to be declining—the decline linked to air pollution from ozone, "acid rain," or both (Hornbeck et al. 1986, Linzon 1986). Productivity of higher elevation forests in heavily polluted areas of Europe definitely is declining, though no single pollution factor can explain regional patterns (Hauhs and Wright 1986).

Effects of such pollution on upper slope forests in the Pacific Northwest are not currently a consideration because these forests are not being impacted. But if this situation changes in the near future, maintaining long-term productivity of upper slope forests may be seriously hampered. In Europe, subalpine regions were the first to show the characteristic symptoms of forest decline (Krause et al. 1986); the first tree species to be affected were silver fir (*Abies alba* Mill.) and then Norway spruce [*Picea abies* (L.) Karst.] (Krause et al. 1986). The significance of upper slope forests for use in environmental monitoring of long-term environmental changes may be an important consideration. Upper slope forests, if left intact, are more sensitive to environmental changes and can be used as an indicator of the health of the environment.

Potential Practices

Regeneration. Successful regeneration will require a longer time between clearcutting and new stand establishment for upper than lower slopes. Areas dominated by mountain hemlock and Pacific silver fir may not regenerate within 5 years of clearcutting at stocking levels desired by managers because of the extreme environmental stresses, especially frost hazard (Sullivan 1978, Minore and Dubrasich 1981, Brockway et al. 1983). To maximize regeneration, managers can reduce frost hazard by, for instance, protecting advance regeneration, assuring sufficient thermal cover (e.g., snowpack), and allowing cold air to drain away from recent clearcuts (Brockway et al. 1983). In frost-prone areas, Cochran (1969) suggested that lodgepole pine should be harvested by creating openings not exceeding twice the height of standing trees to retain effective thermal cover.

Pacific silver fir regenerates quite successfully from large seeds that germinate rapidly after snowmelt (Thornburgh 1969, Edwards 1973). However, regeneration may be hampered because the seedtrees required are largely absent, because seeds have a limited dispersal range, or because seeds sprout slowly. Carkin et al. (1978) found that Pacific silver fir seed supply fell beyond 38 m from the forest edge and that the percentage of unsound seed increased. Franklin (1966) observed a 15–30 m dissemination distance for Pacific silver fir seed.

After seed has germinated, Pacific silver fir seedlings experience less moisture stress than western hemlock seedlings because they quickly develop an extensive root system. However, even though germination and initial establishment are rapid, growth is suppressed for many years because trees are buried in winter by snow.

This advance regeneration seems to be an important reproduction mechanism for Pacific silver fir. However, mortality rates of these old trees are high not only because their leaders, extending above the snowpack, may be desiccated by heat or wind, but also because logging abruptly alters microclimate (Keyes 1982) and logging equipment and operations can mechanically damage trees. In one study (Herring and Etheridge 1976), 30% of advance regeneration sampled had logging injuries, most of which were stem wounds; further, they suggest that the 20% reduction in advance regeneration they noted from edge to open environments was due to logging damage.

Once released from overhead shade, old, regenerating trees are subject to extreme environmental stress. If unable to reestablish a new root:shoot ratio appropriate to open growing conditions (Kotar 1972), they succumb. Pacific silver fir grows better in the partially shaded areas near the stand edges. Wagner (1980), looking at natural regeneration at the edge of an *A. amabilis* zone clearcut on the western slopes of the Cascades, found that Pacific silver fir grew best near the forest edge, whereas western hemlock increased its growth rate and abundance with increasing distance from the edge. In these stands, old, regenerating trees represented 33% of total regeneration after clearcutting. More of these old trees have been found in older, than younger, stands (Long 1976). Chadwick Oliver (personal communication, University of Washington, 1987) has suggested that creating stands with a variety of age classes (uneven-aged management) should be practiced for Pacific silver fir to allow advance regeneration to develop and insure continued stand replacement.

Clearcutting. Before initiating large-scale harvesting operations of upper slope forests, managers must understand the long-term consequences of logging and site preparation practices on site productivity. Unfortunately, only recently have these forests been extensively harvested, so little information exists regarding the long-term effects of harvesting on their productivity. At present, clearcutting is the preferred harvesting method for Pacific silver fir, largely because it facilitates regeneration, but also because difficult slopes, close tree spacing, and available equipment dictate its use. However, loss of nutrients can be substantial when a site is clearcut.

N losses are of greatest concern for west-side, upper slope forests. Because much of the site N may be in the forest floor (40%) and tree biomass (15%) (Table 8.3), type and intensity of harvesting technique strongly influence site N capital. Bolewood harvesting alone would reduce N losses to 6% of total in the Pacific silver fir stand; if branches and foliage are also harvested, N losses would increase to 10% (Table 8.3). Almost the same percentage of ecosystem N was removed when boles only were harvested in lower slope Douglas-fir stands as when boles, branches, and foliage were harvested in upper slope forests (Miller et al. 1976, Table 8.3). In contrast, when whole trees were harvested, less than 1% of K was lost from high-elevation Douglas-fir sites, but 20–39% of K from lower elevation sites (Miller et al. 1976). Because many upper slope forests naturally cycle nutrients, especially N and P, annually to detritus at levels not much lower than those reached when bolewood is harvested—for example, Pacific silver fir contributed almost half of the N and a third of the P removed with bole harvesting to detritus (Table 8.3)—actual aboveground loss of nutrients to harvesting may be low.

That so little P, Ca, Mg, and K were found in tree biomass of the Pacific silver fir stand in Table 8.3 suggests that loss of these nutrients to harvesting may be minor. Decreasing the harvesting intensity can decrease these low-level losses even further. For example, leaving branches and foliage on a site prevents 38% more N, 63% more P, 45% more Ca, 47% more K, and 54% more Mg from being removed (Table 8.3).

Harvesting woody biomass of lodgepole pine can result in N losses similar to those for Pacific silver fir. Removing 80% of stemwood and bark biomass of a 110-year-old lodgepole pine stand resulted in losses of 13% N, 1% P, 9% sulfur (S), 8% K, 6% Ca, and 2% Mg (A. Friend, S. T. Gower, and C. C. Grier, unpublished, 1987).

In many ecosystems, the nutrients removed by tree harvesting may be replenished from soil weathering, N fixation, or atmospheric inputs to sustain future productivity (Curlin 1970). However, in some upper slope forests, N lost to tree harvesting may have to be replaced if site N availability is low, atmospheric inputs are minimal, and N-fixing plants are not present. Atmospheric nitrogen inputs varying from 20 to 25 and exceeding 50 kg ha^{-1} yr^{-1} have been reported from industrial sources in the eastern United States and Europe (Bormann et al. 1977, Van Breemen et al. 1982, Van Praag and Weissen 1986). However, such inputs are only about 1 kg ha^{-1} yr^{-1} in Washington (Gessel et al. 1972) and 1–5 kg ha^{-1} yr^{-1} in Oregon (Fredriksen 1975); these levels are low enough that considerable time would be required to replenish N losses naturally. Other atmospheric nutrient inputs need to be determined across a range of sites in the Pacific Northwest. However, loss of nutrients other than N to harvesting does not appear to be a concern for upper slope forests because these nutrients are replenished through soil weathering (Russell 1973).

Residue management. On steep upper slopes, broadcast burning of slash is common (Miller et al. 1976). Slash burning reduces wildfire hazard and competition to tree seedlings from brushy understory, increases the ease of planting seedlings, minimizes forest insect and disease outbreaks, and creates desirable habitats for wild-life, especially ungulates such as deer and elk (Fellin 1979). It may be especially important in creating a mineral seedbed for regenerating seedlings by consuming the thick humus layers present in mature stands (Bakshi et al. 1972, Alvarez et al. 1979). Alvarez et al. (1979) found that white fir [*Abies concolor* (Gord. & Glend.) Lindl. ex Hildebr.] seedlings survived best when grown just in mineral soil than in mineral soil interspersed with organic horizons. However, in west-side, upper slope forests, loss of the forest floor to burning could rob sites of as much as 40% of ecosystem N (Table 8.3). And with forest floor gone, new vegetation would have to depend on the nutrient-poor soil for nutrient uptake. This situation raises the questions: Is sufficient N available in the soil to satisfy plant growth requirements? How much of the N requirement is satisfied by the forest floor alone?

The forest floor appears to be an important reservoir of N and P in Pacific silver fir stands in Washington. The amount of N and P annually released from the forest floor of a mature Pacific silver fir stand would satisfy the annual requirement of a young stand. Meier (1981) estimated that a young Pacific silver fir stand annually needs 79.1 kg/ha of N and 11.26 kg/ha of P; these estimates are similar to those of annual N and P mineralization (74.9 and 12.03 kg/ha, respectively) from the forest floor in a mature stand (Table 8.7). Such values suggest that managers should try to maintain a relatively intact forest floor during harvesting, restrict the use of burning as a management tool, and, to reduce leaching losses, limit management practices that accelerate forest-floor decomposition rates after clearcutting.

TABLE 8.7. Annual mineralization rates of forest-floor nutrients, based on decay of aboveground and belowground litter (Vogt et al. 1983), and annual aboveground and belowground contributions to detritus production (Vogt et al. 1987a) in a mature, 180-year-old Pacific silver fir stand.

Activity	Organic matter	Nutrients[1]				
		N	P	Ca	Mg	K
		$kg\ ha^{-1}yr^{-1}$				
Forest-floor mineralization	—	74.9	12.03	23.0	3.2	5.1
Annual contribution to detritus						
Aboveground	4,360	20	3.4	12.0	2.3	15.0
Belowground	20,085	110	6.7	23.9	4.0	7.5

[1]N = nitrogen; P = phosphorus; Ca = calcium; Mg = magnesium; K = potassium.

Conserving nitrogen in the surface organic layers does not seem to render it deficient in mature Pacific silver fir in Washington; similar total NPPs were maintained in a 23- and a 180-year-old stand (Vogt et al. 1982), although a larger proportion of NPP is allocated to belowground than aboveground components. If these forests are managed only for timber, a greater allocation to belowground components would be undesirable. However, if these forests are managed to sustain total productivity, the mature stand would be considered healthy since its productivity is similar to that of the young stand.

In west-side, upper slope forests, reduced ecosystem N due to the destruction of the forest floor may result in long-term decreases in tree productivity as trees expend more energy to support the belowground structures needed to acquire nutrients. Under such conditions, trees would have to invest too large a portion of annual photosynthate to obtain nitrogen for growth; these trees already invest more than 50% of annual photosynthate in supporting fine roots and mycorrhizae (Vogt et al. 1982). There arises a point at which it is impossible to support the belowground biomass needed to maintain growth at the expense of the rest of the plant. Productivity could not be sustained under these conditions and existing stands would degrade.

For Pacific silver fir, little site P, Ca, Mg, and K are held in the forest floor. Thus, mineralization from this fraction contributes less to annual plant requirement; an undisturbed forest floor annually mineralizes P, Ca, Mg, and K equivalent to 33, 7, 6, and 2%, respectively, of that which would be lost through bole wood harvesting (Tables 8.3, 8.7). Because P, Ca, Mg, and K are replenished on sites through rock weathering, loss of an intact forest floor may not be as detrimental for insuring their continued availability. Weathering data are not available for these high-elevation forests, but a significant portion of plant requirement for these nutrients may be satisfied through weathering processes in other ecosystems (Fredrikson 1972, as cited in Clayton 1979). Recent data for the H. J. Andrews Experimental Forest in Oregon suggest that the forest floor may be an important source of Ca for tree growth (D. Perry, personal communication, Oregon State University, 1987).

In east-side, upper slope forests, slash should not be burned so that the low soil organic matter content is not further reduced (Carter 1978). Instead, slash left after logging should be lopped and scattered on the site to provide additional organic matter. In the mixed conifer zone, both organic matter and nutrients are affected by residue management. A. Friend, S. T. Gower, and C. C. Grier (unpublished, 1987) estimated that 24% of the total N pool was lost because of factors associated with burning and disturbance in a lodgepole pine stand, and that 9 and 6% of the total S pool were lost because of wood removal and volatilization, respectively. This S loss may be significant in light of the fact that forests in the mixed conifer zone may be S deficient (Klock et al. 1971).

Wildfire is a major natural disturbance vector in east-side, upper slope forests. Wildfires, like prescribed fires, can result in high nutrient losses if hot enough. Tiedemann et al. (1978) monitored stream chemistry and nutrient economy in several watersheds in the Entiat Experimental Forest (eastern Washington) following the dramatic wildfire of 1972. Nitrate N concentrations in streams in burned watersheds increased up to 50 times those in streams in unburned watersheds; however, concentrations in the former did not exceed U.S. Environmental Protection Agency standards for water quality (Tiedemann et al. 1978).

The deleterious effect of soil erosion following wildfire is an additional concern. Surface erosion increases direct export of nutrients from a site (Fredrikson 1971) and adversely affects soil physical properties (Ahlgren and Ahlgren 1960). If soils are of volcanic origin, surface erosion may be minor, but avalanche or debris flows may displace soils (Helvey et al. 1985).

In sum, managers should restrict the use of fire to control residues in upper slope forests because nutrient-rich forest floors would be destroyed. Depending on the heat of burn, N and S are volatilized and lost from the system, and Ca, Mg, K, and P are oxidized and rapidly leached (Grier 1975). Destruction of the organic layers removes a site's ability to buffer against nutrient losses; Vitousek (1985) found that in lower slope forests N availability initially increased after disturbance (increased mineralization) but declined as the forest recovered.

Fertilization. Many forests become deficient in specific major nutrients (especially N and P) or trace elements (Porada 1987) because of intensive management practices. The magnitude of these losses varies by tree species, inherent site fertility, and nutrient. Nitrogen frequently is of greatest concern because it is the nutrient which is most often deficient and which can be replenished only through atmospheric inputs or N fixation, not soil weathering.

One of the most common ways to manipulate or ameliorate a site's nutrient capital is by adding fertilizers. If a nutrient is deficient, fertilizers are used to achieve maximal productivities and reduce rotation lengths. Growth increases due to N fertilization can last from 5 to 10 years depending on site and tree species; however, repeated applications are needed to maintain long-term effects on aboveground productivity (Miller 1981). For example, Waring and Pitman (1985) reported that N concentrations in the soil, litter, and plants returned to prefertilization levels 3–4 years after N was added to a lodgepole pine stand.

Nitrogen fertilizers affect both aboveground and belowground components. For example, when fertilized with N, low-elevation conifers allocate carbon to shoots, rather than roots (Axelsson 1981, Alexander and Fairley 1983, Linder and Rook 1984, Vogt et al. 1985, Waring and Schlesinger 1985). Although aboveground productivity increases, belowground productivity decreases. For low-elevation Douglas-fir, long-term experimental manipulation of site N decreased total NPP from 30 to 15% in fine roots (Vogt et al. 1986). Additional evidence for a strong relationship between site N cycling and C allocation to roots is seen in the strong negative correlation between root production and aboveground N turnover (Vogt et al. 1986). However, although fertilization programs for low-elevation Douglas-fir have been in operation for several decades, once again little information exists for high-elevation forests, and no one knows whether east- or west-side stands will respond similarly or differently.

Lack of data for east-side conifers is due to the generally low productivity of these forests. Forests growing on soils derived from volcanic material are often N deficient (Cochran 1975, 1979). Cochran (1975) fertilized a pole-size lodgepole pine stand with 673, 336, and 101 kg/ha of N, P, and S, respectively, and observed increases in volume and basal-area growth as a result. For example, volume increments (1971–74 and 1975–78 growth periods) for the unfertilized and fertilized stands were 2.6 and 3.4 m^3 ha^{-1} yr^{-1} and 5.2 and 5.5 m^3 ha^{-1} yr^{-1}, respectively (Cochran 1979). A positive growth response also was observed for a predominantly western larch stand in the Colville National Forest treated with urea N. Based on biannual growth measurements and regression equations developed for western larch (Gower et al. 1987), aboveground NPP values of 5.7, 8.0, and 7.9 Mg ha^{-1} yr^{-1} were calculated for unfertilized plots, plots fertilized with 200 kg/ha of urea N, and plots fertilized with 400 kg/ha of urea N, respectively. The insignificant difference in growth response between the two fertilizer treatments may be due to the low nutrient-absorbing capacity of forests in the mixed conifer zone.

Despite the above studies, all demonstrating a positive growth response to N fertilization, absolute increases in wood production were small (see Cochran 1979). Given this low increase in wood production and the uncertainty of stand response, fertilization of east-side, upper slope conifers may not be an economical management practice, especially in light of the restrictive moisture and temperature conditions of these environments.

We do not now know if west-side, upper slope forests would respond to N fertilization—tree growth in these environments is regulated by winter stress. Moreover, we may have to be especially cautious about adding N fertilizers to these sites if the "ammonium hypothesis" for forest dieback in Europe is proven valid (Nihlgard 1985). According to this hypothesis, conifers in Europe are being exposed to increased levels of available N through atmospheric inputs. Because conifers are adapted to low N levels, this saturation of N could produce faster growing trees that are more susceptible to wind damage, drought, and parasites.

According to what we do know about west-side, upper slope ecosystems, we hypothesize the following possible scenarios as a result of fertilizing these sites: (1) decreased frost hardiness of trees because their aboveground growth period has been extended into fall when temperatures are lower, (2) increased foliage surface areas and life spans, and (3) decreased root biomass (supported by lower slope studies; see Vogt et al. 1986). Decreased carbon allocation to roots may be positive if C previously sent to roots is instead sent to boles. However, any decreases in mycorrhizal and fine-root biomass due to N fertilization may hamper the ability of trees to avoid taking up Al (Vogt et al. 1987a). If sites are very N deficient, fertilization may increase foliage life span (Waring and Pitman 1985). At lower elevations, Cochran et al. (1986) observed increased diameter growth and increased needle surface areas for fertilized Pacific silver fir. However, they also observed a significantly greater number of broken tree tops; this was attributed to longer needles which accumulated larger amounts of ice and snow and were more susceptible to wind damage.

If inadequate nutrition were the only factor limiting tree growth at upper elevations, fertilization would be a good management option. However, the environmental limitations of these forests temper the effective use of fertilizers.

CONCLUSIONS

Most highly manageable lands will continue to be those which are readily accessible and which have favorable climate and soil nutrient conditions to promote rapid plant growth. Lacking these factors, upper slope forests are not as conducive to management. Heavy snowpacks and cool temperatures restrict the period during which management is possible and limit management options. For instance, rotations cannot be shortened at these elevations because biomass accumulates slowly as a result of temperature limitations.

Considerably more research needs to be conducted on these upper slopes. Much of the process-level discussion in this chapter was developed from a few stands which, though thoroughly studied, may not be "typical" for their respective vegetation zones. Moreover, the species now present may not, in fact, exist under optimal conditions. For example, the ectomycorrhizal fungus *Cenoccocum graniforme* was found to colonize 70% of the tips of Pacific silver fir roots under natural conditions, but competed poorly against other mycorrhizal fungi and grew poorly at temperatures common at high elevations under laboratory conditions (Vogt et al. 1981b).

Regional climates have shifted over time, and with them, the mosaic of species in a forest. However, we cannot predict how climate may change or how climatic change would influence forest composition (see chapter 6, this volume). Paleoecological interpretations of fossil and pollen records indicate that species associations are different today than they were thousands of years ago (Wright 1983); interactions among the biological factors controlling composition can prompt many possible population responses to climatic change (Brubaker 1986). Dunwiddie (1986) suggested that vegetation at higher elevations is potentially more sensitive to climatic change than is lowland vegetation and that forest composition may respond to climatic changes most dramatically after stand disturbance—such a response influencing which seedlings survive to reestablish a site. Oliver (1981) proposed that most tree species in a forest are what first establish after the last stand-leveling disturbance. Specific climatic conditions existing at time of establishment could dictate forest composition for decades to come.

People often assume that the current forest composition is the "normal" one. Yet most field studies on the topic have been conducted over short periods and under specific conditions. It is difficult to predict long-term productivity or future success of a species if dominance patterns or other factors change after a disturbance resulting from management practice.

Impact of harvesting on sites can be examined at the stand or watershed level. At the stand level, changes in site organic matter content, future productivity, and wildlife habitat are concerns. At the watershed level, changes in snowmelt, surface runoff, and soil movement, as they relate to quality of water and stream habitat as well as soil erosion, are concerns. Tree harvesting on sites with long rotations will have less influence on soil nutrient reserves because the amounts removed are small and the system has time to recover.

In areas vegetated by lodgepole pine in the Rocky Mountains where watershed sizes are limited, forests are often selectively clearcut to maximize the amount of water outflow to ranchers and farmers (Hibbert 1979). Selective clearcutting is the only way that snow accumulation can be manipulated to increase water outflow. In these systems, maintaining tree productivity for lumber is secondary to enhancing water flow from stands. A by-product of such clearcutting is increased big-game activity (Crouch 1985); however, managers must bear in mind that grazing of large ungulates can also influence species composition on these sites (Edgerton 1987).

Generally, sites will be most heavily affected by management practices such as harvesting (and road building), site preparation for planting, and fertilization. These practices often require use of heavy machinery, which displaces, compacts, or erodes soil. This is especially a problem in high-elevation forests, which are cold and wet much of the year and have a large proportion of fine rooting in the surface organic layers which act to structurally hold the soil.

Of all the nutrients, N will be the most affected by management practices because large quantities accumulate in surface organic horizons and in vegetative biomass, which are either disturbed or removed by harvesting and site preparation. Most critical is disturbance of the forest floor; if the forest floor is burned, the N lost cannot be readily replenished. N uptake might be increased by allocating more carbon to nutrient-acquiring organs such as roots. However, because trees already allocate a large portion of photosynthate to root systems, it might be impossible to increase their C allocation without detrimentally affecting the trees' ability to support foliage.

If N fertilization were feasible at high elevations, then replenishing N lost because of harvesting or residue management would be possible. Some growth increases have been reported after fertilizing upper slope forests. Fertilization of east-side, upper slope forests is influenced by site moisture and temperature; limited water and low temperatures (short growing season) may be more constraining to growth than insufficient N. Fertilization may also increase the decomposition rate of surface organic layers; yet more rapid decomposition may not be desirable at these elevations if the nutrients immobilized in organic layers form a critical reservoir. How N fertilization affects such nutrient conservation mechanisms as well as tree growth mechanisms, such as frost hardiness or carbon allocation to roots, needs to be examined at these elevations.

Some management practices may have to be implemented without concern for impact because total lack of management would almost certainly result in greater loss of productivity. For instance, it may be necessary to thin lodgepole pine stands to decrease their susceptibility to bark beetle mortality (Waring and Pitman 1985). However, questions about the real effect of insects on site productivity remain. Romme et al. (1986) suggested that despite initial losses, ecosystem productivity recovers from insect attack and may exceed pre-attack levels; long-term productivity therefore has not been jeopardized. The possibility also exists that some of the need for present management stems from prior practices, such as strict fire control.

QUESTIONS FROM THE SYMPOSIUM FLOOR

Q: Because high-elevation trees retain foliage for 18–21 years, (a) what is the role of understory vegetation in maintaining the forest floor, and (b) how does long-term foliage retention influence fine-root production and abundance of mycorrhizae?

A: In mature high-elevation stands, the understory has a very small role in maintaining the forest floor. Most litter inputs to the forest floor are from roots. Since tree foliage tissues are retained for a long time and the understory is such a small proportion of ecosystem biomass, aboveground components contribute little to the developing surface organic layer. In contrast, the belowground component, which is large, turns over once annually and contributes about 80% of total ecosystem detritus.

Long foliage retention reduces the "carbon cost" of replacing aboveground tissues and may be responsible for the large annual allocation of carbon to producing and maintaining fine roots and mycorrhizal fungi. These high-elevation stands have one of the highest annual allocations of carbon (14–15%) to fine roots and mycorrhizae, compared to other forest ecosystems.

Q: On precommercially thinned, east-side, mixed Pacific silver fir sites, we have had good response to N-S fertilization, except in an overly dense stand. Why?

A: Because east-side, upper slope forests are moisture limited. Any management practice reducing the number of trees competing for belowground resources (i.e., water) will increase the capability of the remaining trees to respond to fertilizer with increased growth. Furthermore, if a stand is very dense, light can become limiting to growth. In that case, trees are incapable of responding to fertilizer because increased growth rates are not possible. Thinning a stand will minimize light as a limiting factor for growth.

Q: It has been suggested that intensively harvesting upper slope forests is a way to ease the pressure of harvest on lower slopes and to bridge the timber supply gap while we wait for second growth. Comments?

A: Intensive harvesting of upper slope forests should be approached with caution and should not occur until we know more about our abilities to manage these forests. The management options currently available for low-elevation stands may not be feasible at high elevations (see chapter text). High-elevation forests have environmental limitations and edaphic characteristics which we cannot manage. We do not now know whether we can regenerate these areas; some results do not look very promising. In addition, the long life span and slow growth of upper slope species make it difficult for us to know the implications of managing at one stand developmental stage for maintaining future site productivity at present levels.

Q: You focus on tying rotation length to biomass levels. If biomass levels are managed for timber production, why should we instead focus on some other measure of production, such as changes in the mean annual increment?

A: We should never use biomass alone to determine rotation length, but only to compare the ability of different tree species to accumulate biomass over time. Rotation length should be determined from estimates of annual productivity such as mean annual increment. Even a better way of estimating rotation length would be to determine how much of annual production is in bolewood and how much in deciduous tissues such as foliage and fine roots; when a significantly greater proportion of production is in deciduous tissues than in bolewood, trees should be clearcut (see chapter text).

Q: Because the rate of mineralization is partially a function of temperature, why was there such a high N input ($75 \text{ kg ha}^{-1} \text{ yr}^{-1}$) from the forest floor in cold Pacific silver fir forests? How general are these high mineralization rates?

A: These high N mineralization rates occurred in a Pacific silver fir stand which had 2–3 times greater accumulation of forest-floor biomass than average for such stands and one of the highest annual inputs of fine-root and mycorrhizal tissue to detritus compared to inputs from other ecosystems (see chapter text). The thick forest floor suggests that mineralization rates would be low, but in fact rates were high because of large amounts of highly decomposable tissue. In addition, temperature does not seem to limit activity of decomposer organisms in this ecosystem—more than 80% of litter decomposed during the winter under snow.

   Results from this silver fir stand cannot be generalized for all high-elevation forests because most have frozen soils during winter, whereas this stand does not.

Q: You mentioned that in one study the trees responded to the addition of carbon. In what form was it applied? Could adding carbon be a management tool?

A: Carbon, as starch + sucrose, has been applied to high-elevation Douglas-fir stands in New Mexico. On these sites, trees grew better with starch additions but not with N fertilization. Similar results have been obtained in Alaska and Scotland. These sites all had cold environmental conditions where decomposition is incomplete, and incomplete decomposition may limit the carbon available to decomposer organisms. The addition of a more readily available carbon source probably stimulated microbial activity and increased the amount of mineralizable N available to trees. Sufficient N appears to be present on these sites for microbial activity, so adding N does not increase the level of mineral N. These changes at the microbial level are evident at the tree level because trees obtain little from nitrogen fertilization itself where, when decomposition is slow, carbon-limited microbes immobilize the added N. Adding carbon therefore may be a very good management tool for increasing tree growth on specific sites, many at high elevation, where decomposition is incomplete and microbes are carbon limited.

REFERENCES

Ahlgren, I. F., and C. E. Ahlgren. 1960. Ecological effects of forest fire. *Botanical Review* 26:483–533.

Alexander, I. J., and R. I. Fairley. 1983. Effects of N fertilisation on populations of fine roots and mycorrhizas in spruce humus. *Plant and Soil* 71:49–53.

Alexander, R. R., R. C. Shearer, and W. D. Shepperd. 1984. *Silvical characteristics of subalpine fir.* General Technical Report RM-115. Fort Collins, Colo.: Rocky Mountain Forest and Range Experiment Station, USDA Forest Service.

Alvarez, I. F., D. L. Rowney, and F. W. Cobb, Jr. 1979. Mycorrhizae and growth of white fir seedlings in mineral soil with and without organic layers in a California forest. *Canadian Journal of Forest Research* 9:311–315.

Amaranthus, M. P., and D. A. Perry. 1987. Effect of soil transfer on ectomycorrhiza formation and the survival and growth of conifer seedlings on old, nonreforested clear-cuts. *Canadian Journal of Forest Research* 17:944–950.

Amman, G. D., and L. Safranyik. 1985. "Insects of lodgepole pine: impacts and control." In *Proceedings of the symposium on lodgepole pine species and its management,* edited by D. W. Baumgartner, R. G. Krebill, J. T. Arnott, and G. F. Weetman, 107–124. Pullman, Wash.: Cooperative Extension Service, Washington State University.

Axelsson, B. 1981. *Site differences in yield-differences in biological production or in redistribution of carbon within trees.* Report 9. Uppsala, Sweden: Department of Ecology and Environment, Swedish University of Agricultural Science.

———. 1984. "Increasing forest productivity and value by manipulating nutrient availability." In *Forest potentials, productivity and value,* Weyerhaeuser Science Symposium 4, 5–37. Tacoma, Wash.: Weyerhaeuser Corporation.

Bakshi, B. K., M. A. Ram Reddy, H. S. Thapar, and S. N. Khan. 1972. Studies on silver fir regeneration. *Indian Forestry* 98:135–144.

Bormann, F. H., G. E. Likens, and J. M. Melillo. 1977. Nitrogen budget for an aggrading northern hardwood forest ecosystem. *Science* 196:981–983.

Brockway, D. G., C. Topik, M. A. Hemstrom, and W. H. Emmingham. 1983. *Plant associations and management guide for the Pacific silver fir zone.* R6-Ecol-130a-1983. Portland, Ore.: Gifford Pinchot National Forest, Pacific Northwest Region, USDA Forest Service.

Brubaker, L. B. 1986. Response of tree populations to climatic change. *Vegetatio* 67:119–130.

Cannell, M. G. R. 1982. *World Forest Biomass and Primary Production Data.* New York: Academic Press.

Carkin, R. E., J. F. Franklin, J. Booth, and C. E. Smith. 1978. *Seeding habits of upper-slope tree species. IV. Seed flight of noble fir and Pacific silver fir.* Research Note PNW-312. Portland, Ore.: Pacific Northwest Forest and Range Experiment Station, USDA Forest Service.

Carter, S. W., Jr. 1978. "Potential impacts of mountain pine beetle and their mitigation in lodgepole pine forests." In *Theory and practice of mountain pine forests,* 27–36. Moscow, Idaho: Forest, Wildlife, and Range Experiment Station, University of Idaho.

Christy, E. J., and R. N. Mack. 1984. Variation of juvenile *Tsuga heterophylla* across the substratum mosaic. *Journal of Ecology* 72:75–91.

Clayton, J. L. 1979. "Nutrient supply to soil by rock weathering." In *Proceedings, impact of intensive harvesting on forest nutrient cycling,* 75–96. Syracuse, N.Y.: State University of New York.

Cochran, P. H. 1969. *Lodgepole pine clearcut size affects minimum temperatures near the soil surface.* Research Paper PNW-86. Portland, Ore.: Pacific Northwest Forest and Range Experiment Station, USDA Forest Service.

———. 1975. *Response of pole-sized lodgepole pine to fertilization.* Research Note PNW-247. Portland, Ore.: Pacific Northwest Forest and Range Experiment Station, USDA Forest Service.

———. 1979. *Response of thinned lodgepole pine after fertilization.* Research Note PNW-335. Portland, Ore.: Pacific Northwest Forest and Range Experiment Station, USDA Forest Service.

———. 1985. "Soils and productivity of lodgepole pine." In *Proceedings of the symposium on lodgepole pine species and its management,* edited by D. W. Baumgartner, R. G. Krebill, J. T. Arnott, and G. F. Weetman, 89–93. Pullman, Wash.: Cooperative Extension Service, Washington State University.

Cochran, P. H., W. Lopushinsky, and P. D. McColley. 1986. *Effects of operational fertilization on foliar nutrient content and growth of young Douglas-fir and Pacific silver fir.* Research Note PNW-445. Portland, Ore.: Pacific Northwest Forest and Range Experiment Station, USDA Forest Service.

Crouch, G. L. 1985. *Effects of clearcutting a subalpine forest in central Colorado on wildlife habitat.* Research Paper RM-285. Fort Collins, Colo.: Rocky Mountain Forest and Range Experiment Station, USDA Forest Service.

Curlin, J. W. 1970. "Nutrient cycling as a factor in site productivity and forest fertilization." In *Tree growth and forest soils,* edited by C. T. Youngberg and C. B. Davey, 313–325. Corvallis, Ore.: Oregon State University Press.

Curtis, R. O., R. F. Herman, and D. J. DeMars. 1974. Height growth and site index for Douglas-fir in high-elevation forests of the Oregon-Washington Cascades. *Forest Science* 20:307–316.

Dunwiddie, P. W. 1986. A 6000-year record of forest history on Mount Rainier, Washington. *Ecology* 67:58–68.

Dyrness, C. T. 1967. *Mass soil movement in the H. J. Andrews Experimental Forest.* Research Paper PNW-42. Portland, Ore.: Pacific Northwest Forest and Range Experiment Station, USDA Forest Service.

Edgerton, P. J. 1987. "Influence of ungulates on the development of the shrub understory of an upper slope mixed conifer forest." In *Proceedings of the symposium on plant-herbivore interactions,* 162–167. General Technical Report INT-222. Ogden, Utah: Intermountain Forest and Range Research Station, USDA Forest Service.

Edwards, D. G. W. 1973. Effects of stratification on western hemlock germination. *Canadian Journal of Forest Research* 3:522–527.

Eis, S., D. Craigdallie, and C. Simmons. 1982. Growth of lodgepole pine and white spruce in the central interior of British Columbia. *Canadian Journal of Forest Research* 12:567–575.

Emmingham, W. H., and R. H. Waring. 1977. An index of photosynthesis for comparing forest sites in western Oregon. *Canadian Journal of Forest Research* 7:165–174.

Fellin, D. G. 1979. "Effects of silvicultural practices, residue utilization and prescribed fire on some forest floor arthropods." In *Environmental consequences of timber harvesting in Rocky Mountain coniferous forests*, 287–316. General Technical Report INT-90. Ogden, Utah: Intermountain Research Station, USDA Forest Service.

Ford, E. D. 1984. "The dynamics of plantation growth." In *Nutrition of plantation forests*, edited by G. D. Bowen and E. K. S. Nambiar, 17–52. New York: Academic Press.

Franklin, J. F. 1966. *Vegetation and soils in the subalpine forests of southern Washington Cascade Range.* Ph.D. Dissertation. Pullman, Wash.: Washington State University.

Franklin, J. F., R. E. Carkin, and J. Booth. 1974. *Seeding habits of upper-slope tree species. 1. A 12-year record of cone production.* Research Note PNW-213. Portland, Ore.: Pacific Northwest Forest and Range Experiment Station, USDA Forest Service.

Franklin, J. F., and C. T. Dyrness. 1973. *Natural vegetation of Oregon and Washington.* General Technical Report PNW-8. Portland, Ore.: Pacific Northwest Forest and Range Experiment Station, USDA Forest Service.

Fredrikson, R. L. 1971. "Comparative chemical water quality in natural and disturbed streams following logging and slash burning." In *Proceedings of the symposium on forest land uses and stream environments*, 125–137. Corvallis, Ore.: Oregon State University.

———. 1972. "Nutrient budget of a Douglas-fir forest on an experimental watershed in Oregon." In *Proceedings of the symposium on research on coniferous forest ecosystems*, 115–131. Bellingham, Wash.

———. 1975. *Nitrogen, phosphorus, and particulate matter budgets of five coniferous forest ecosystems in the western Cascade Range, Oregon.* Ph.D. Dissertation. Corvallis, Ore.: Oregon State University.

Fujimori, T. 1971. Analysis of forest canopy on the basis of a *Tsuga heterophylla* forest. *Japanese Journal of Ecology* 21:134–140.

Fujimori, T., S. Kawanabe, H. Saito, C. C. Grier, and T. Shidei. 1976. Biomass and primary production in forests of three major vegetation zones of the northwestern United States. *Journal of Japanese Forest Society* 58:360–373.

Gara, R. I., W. R. Littke, J. K. Agee, D. R. Geiszler, J. D. Stuart, and C. H. Driver. 1985. "Influence of fires, fungi and mountain pine beetles on development of a lodgepole pine forest in south-central Oregon." In *Proceedings of the symposium on lodgepole pine species and its management*, edited by D. W. Baumgartner, R. G. Krebill, J. T. Arnott, and G. F. Weetman, 153–162. Pullman, Wash.: Cooperative Extension Service, Washington State University.

Gessel, S. P., D. W. Cole, and E. C. Steinbrenner. 1972. Nitrogen balances in forest ecosystems of the Pacific Northwest. *Soil Biology and Biochemistry* 5:19–34.

Gholz, H. L. 1982. Environmental limits on aboveground net primary production, leaf area, and biomass in vegetation zones of the Pacific Northwest. *Ecology* 63:469–481.

Gower, S. T., C. C. Grier, D. J. Vogt, and K. A. Vogt. 1987. Allometric relations of deciduous (*Larix occidentalis*) and evergreen (*Pinus contorta* and *Pseudotsuga menziesii*) of the Cascade Mountains in central Washington. *Canadian Journal of Forest Research* 17:630–634.

Graham, R. L., P. Farnum, R. Timmis, and G. A. Ritchie. 1984. "Using modeling as a tool to increase forest productivity and value." In *Forest potentials, productivity and value*, Weyerhaeuser Science Symposium 4, 101–130. Tacoma, Wash.: Weyerhaeuser Corporation.

Grant, J. C. 1980. *Growth comparisons between Pacific silver fir and western hemlock on the western slopes of the northern Washington Cascades.* Master's Thesis. Seattle, Wash.: University of Washington.

Graumlich, L. 1985. *Long-term records of temperature and precipitation in the Pacific Northwest derived from tree rings.* Ph.D. Dissertation. Seattle, Wash.: University of Washington.

Greene, S. E., and M. Klopsch. 1985. *Soil and air temperatures for different habitats in Mount Rainier National Park.* Research Paper PNW-342. Portland, Ore.: Pacific Northwest Forest and Range Experiment Station, USDA Forest Service.

Grier, C. C. 1975. Wildfire effects on nutrient distribution and leaching in a coniferous ecosystem. *Canadian Journal of Forest Research* 5:599–607.

———. 1976. "Biomass, productivity, and nitrogen-phosphorus cycles in hemlock-spruce stands of the central Oregon coast." In *Proceedings of western hemlock management*, edited by W. A. Atkinson and R. J. Zasoski, 71–81. Institute of Forest Products Contribution No. 34. Seattle, Wash.: College of Forest Resources, University of Washington.

Grier, C. C., and R. S. Logan. 1977. Old-growth *Pseudotsuga menziesii* communities of a western Oregon watershed: biomass distribution and production budgets. *Ecological Monographs* 47:373–400.

Grier, C. C., and S. W. Running. 1977. Leaf area of mature northwestern coniferous forests: relation to site water balance. *Ecology* 58:893–899.

Grier, C. C., K. A. Vogt, M. R. Keyes, and R. L. Edmonds. 1981. Biomass distribution and above- and belowground production in young and mature Abies amabilis zone ecosystems of the Washington Cascades. *Canadian Journal of Forest Research* 11:155–167.

Grier, C. C., K. A. Vogt, K. M. Lee, and R. O. Teskey. 1985. "Factors affecting root production in subalpine forests of the northwestern United States." In *Establishment and tending of subalpine forests: research and management*, edited by H. Turner and W. Tranquillini, 143–149. Berichte 270, Switzerland: Eidgenossische Anstalt fur das forstliche Versuchswesen.

Harley, J., and S. Smith. 1983. *Mycorrhizal Symbiosis.* New York: Academic Press.

Harvey, A. E., M. J. Larsen, and M. F. Jurgensen. 1979. Comparative distribution of ectomycorrhizae in soils of three western Montana forest habitat types. *Forest Science* 25:350–358.

Harvey, A. E., M. F. Jurgensen, and M. J. Larsen. 1978. Seasonal distribution of ectomycorrhizae in a mature Douglas-fir/larch forest soil in western Montana. *Forest Science* 24:203–208.

Hauhs, M., and R. F. Wright. 1986. Regional pattern of acid deposition and forest decline along a cross section through Europe. *Water, Air and Soil Pollution* 31:463–474.

Helvey, J. D., A. R. Tiedemann, and T. D. Anderson. 1985. Plant nutrient losses by soil erosion and mass movement after wildfire. *Journal of Soil and Water Conservation* 40:168–173.

Herman, F. R., R. O. Curtis, and D. J. Demars. 1978. *Height growth and site index estimates for noble fir in high-elevation forests of the Oregon-Washington Cascades.* Research Paper PNW-243. Portland, Ore.: Pacific Northwest Forest and Range Experiment Station, USDA Forest Service.

Herman, F. R., and J. F. Franklin. 1976. *Errors from application of western hemlock site curves to mountain hemlock.* Research Paper PNW-276. Portland, Ore.: Pacific Northwest Forest and Range Experiment Station, USDA Forest Service.

Herring, L. J., and D. E. Etheridge. 1976. *Advance amabilis-fir regeneration.* Joint Report No. 5. Victoria, B.C.: British Columbia Forest Service, Canadian Forestry Service.

Hibbert, A. R. 1979. *Managing vegetation to increase flow in the Colorado River Basin.* General Technical Report RM-66. Fort Collins, Colo.: Rocky Mountain Forest and Range Experiment Station, USDA Forest Service.

Hornbeck, J. W., R. B. Smith, and C. A. Federer. 1986. Growth decline in red spruce and balsam fir relative to natural processes. *Water, Air and Soil Pollution* 31:425–430.

Keyes, M. R. 1982. *Ecosystem development in* Abies amabilis *stands of the Washington Cascades: root growth and its role in net primary production.* Ph.D. Dissertation. Seattle, Wash.: University of Washington.

Keyes, M. R., and C. C. Grier. 1981. Above-ground and below-ground net production in 40-year-old Douglas-fir stands on low and high productivity sites. *Canadian Journal of Forest Research* 11:599–605.

Khanna, P. H., and B. Ulrich. 1984. "Soil characteristics influencing nutrient supply in forest soils." In *Nutrition of plantation forests*, edited by G. D. Bowen and E. K. S. Nambiar, 79–117. London: Academic Press.

Kimmins, J. P., and B. C. Hawkes. 1978. Distribution and chemistry of fine roots in a white spruce-subalpine fir stand in British Columbia: implications for management. *Canadian Journal of Forest Research* 8:265–279.

Kira, T., and T. Shidei. 1967. Primary production and turnover of organic matter in different forest ecosystems of the western Pacific. *Japanese Journal of Ecology* 17:70–87.

Klein, W. H., D. L. Parker, and C. E. Jensen. 1978. Attack, emergence, and stand depletion trends of the mountain pine beetle in a lodgepole pine stand during an outbreak. *Environmental Entomology* 7:732–737.

Klock, G. O. 1982. "Chapter 5. Some soil erosion effects on forest soil productivity." In *Determinants of soil loss tolerance,* 53–66. Madison, Wis.: American Society of Agronomy.

Klock, G. O., J. M. Geist, and A. R. Tiedemann. 1971. Erosion control fertilization: from pot study to field testing. *Sulfur Institute Journal* 7:7–10.

Kotar, J. 1972. *Ecology of* Abies amabilis *in relation to its altitudinal distribution and in contrast to the common associate* Tsuga heterophylla. Ph.D. Dissertation. Seattle, Wash.: University of Washington.

Krause, G. H. M., U. Arndt, C. J. Brandt, J. Bucher, G. Kenk, and E. Matzner. 1986. Forest decline in Europe: development and possible causes. *Water, Air and Soil Pollution* 31:647–668.

Krause, H. H., G. F. Weetman, and P. A. Arp. 1979. "Nutrient cycling in boreal forest ecosystems of North America." In *5th North American forest soils conference,* edited by C. T. Youngberg. Corvallis, Ore.: Oregon State University Press.

Krumlik, G. J., and J. P. Kimmins. 1976. "Studies of biomass distribution and tree form in old virgin forests in the mountains of south coastal British Columbia." In *Forest biomass studies,* edited by H. E. Young, 361–373. Orono, Maine: University of Maine.

Linder, S., and D. A. Rook. 1984. "Effects of mineral nutrition on carbon dioxide exchange and partitioning of carbon in trees." In *Nutrition of forest trees in plantations,* edited by G. D. Bowen and E. K. S. Nambiar. New

York: Academic Press.

Linzon, S. N. 1986. Effects of gaseous pollutants on forests in eastern North America. *Water, Air and Soil Pollution* 31:537–550.

Long, J. N. 1976. *Forest vegetation dynamics within the* Abies amabilis *zone of a western Cascade watershed.* Ph.D. Dissertation. Seattle, Wash.: University of Washington.

Long, J. N., and J. Turner. 1975. Aboveground biomass of understory and overstory in an age sequence of four Douglas-fir stands. *Journal of Applied Ecology* 12:178–188.

Matson, P. A., and R. D. Boone. 1985. Natural disturbance and nitrogen mineralization: wave-form dieback of mountain hemlock in the Oregon Cascades. *Ecology* 65:1511–1516.

Mattson, W. H., and N. D. Addy. 1975. Phytophagous insects as regulators of forest primary production. *Science* 190:515–522.

McCauley, K. J., and S. A. Cook. 1980. *Phellinus weirii* infestation of two mountain hemlock forests in the Oregon Cascades. *Forest Science* 26:23–29.

Megahan, W. F. 1976. "Effects of forest cultural treatments upon streamflow." In *Proceeding of the symposium on the forest acts dilemma,* 14–34. Missoula, Mont.: Montana Forest and Conservation Experiment Station, University of Montana.

Meier, C. E. 1981. *The role of fine roots in nitrogen and phosphorus budgets of young and mature* Abies amabilis *ecosystems.* Ph.D. Dissertation. Seattle, Wash.: University of Washington.

Mikola, P. 1973. "Mycorrhizal symbiosis in forestry practice." In *Ectomycorrhizae, their ecology and physiology,* edited by G. C. Marks and T. T. Kozlowski, 383–411. New York: Academic Press.

Mikola, P., and O. Laiho. 1962. Mycorrhizal relations in the raw humus layers of northern spruce forests. *Commicationes Instituti Forestalis Fenniae* 58(18):1–13.

Miller, H. G. 1981. Forest fertilization: some guiding concepts. *Forestry* 54:157–167.

Miller, R. E., D. P. Lavender, and C. C. Grier. 1976. "Nutrient cycling in the Douglas-fir type—silvicultural implications." In *Proceedings of the 1975 annual convention,* 359–390. Bethesda, Md.: Society of American Foresters.

Minore, D., and M. E. Dubrasich. 1981. Regeneration after clearcutting in subalpine stands near Windigo Pass, Oregon. *Journal of Forestry* 79:619–621.

Nihlgard, B. 1985. The ammonium hypothesis—an additional explanation to the forest dieback in Europe. *Ambio* 14:2–8.

Oliver, C. D. 1981. Forest development in North America following major disturbances. *Forest Ecology and Management* 3:153–168.

Olson, J. S. 1975. "Productivity of forest ecosystems." In *Productivity of world ecosystems,* edited by D. E. Reichle, J. F. Franklin, and D. W. Goodall, 33–43. Washington, D.C.: National Academy of Sciences.

Packee, E. C., C. D. Oliver, and P. D. Crawford. 1982. "Ecology of Pacific silver fir." In *Proceedings of the symposium on the biology and management of true fir in the Pacific Northwest,* edited by C. D. Oliver and R. M. Kenady, 19–34. Contribution No. 45. Seattle, Wash.: College of Forest Resources, University of Washington.

Porada, H. 1987. *The effect of aluminum on the growth and mineral composition of Douglas-fir and western hemlock.* Ph.D. Dissertation. Seattle, Wash.: University of Washington.

Pritchett, W. L. 1979. "Soil as a reservoir: soil nutrient supplies and mobilization rates." In *Proceedings of the symposium on the impact of intensive harvesting on forest nutrient cycling,* 49–61. Broomall, Pa.: Northeastern Forest Experiment Station, USDA Forest Service.

Rodin, L. E., N. E. Bazilevich, and N. N. Rozov. 1975. "Productivity of the world's main ecosystems." In *Productivity of world ecosystems,* edited by D. E. Reichle, J. F. Franklin, and D. W. Goodall, 13–26. Washington, D.C.: National Academy of Sciences.

Romme, W. H., D. H. Knight, and J. B. Yavitt. 1986. Mountain pine beetle outbreaks in the Rocky Mountains: regulators of primary production. *The American Naturalist* 127:484–494.

Russell, E. W. 1973. *Soil Conditions and Plant Growth.* 10th ed. London: Longman.

Schmidt, R. L. 1957. *The silvics and plant geography of the genus* Abies *in the coastal forest of British Columbia.* Forest Service Technical Publication T. 46. British Columbia.

Schmidt, W. D., and R. R. Alexander. 1985. "Strategies for managing lodgepole pine." In *Proceedings of the symposium on lodgepole pine species and its management,* edited by D. W. Baumgartner, R. G. Krebill, J. T. Arnott, and G. F. Weetman. Pullman, Wash.: Cooperative Extension Service, Washington State University.

Sidle, R. C. 1980. *Impacts of forest practices on surface erosion.* Extension Publication PNW-195. Portland, Ore.: Pacific Northwest Forest and Range Experiment Station, USDA Forest Service.

Sullivan, M. J. 1978. *Regeneration of tree seedlings after clearcutting on some upper slope habitat types in the Oregon Cascade Range.* Research Paper PNW-245. Portland, Ore.: Pacific Northwest Forest and Range Experiment

Station, USDA Forest Service.

Swanston, D. N. 1976. "Erosion processes and control methods in North America." In *Proceedings of XVI IUFRO World Congress, Division 1,* 251–275.

Swanston, D. N., and F. J. Swanson. 1976. "Timber harvesting, mass erosion, and steepland forest geomorphology in the Pacific Northwest." In *Geomorphology and engineering,* edited by D. R. Coats, 199–221. Stroudsburg, Pa.: Dowden, Hutchinson, and Ross.

Teskey, R. O., C. C. Grier, and T. M. Hinckley. 1984. Change in photosynthesis and water relations with age and season in *Abies amabilis. Canadian Journal of Forest Research* 14:77–84.

Thornburgh, D. A. 1969. *Dynamics of the true fir-hemlock forests of the west slope of the Washington Cascade Range.* Ph.D. Dissertation. Seattle, Wash.: University of Washington.

Tiedemann, A. R., J. D. Helvey, and T. D. Anderson. 1978. Stream chemistry and watershed nutrient economy following wildfire and fertilization in eastern Washington. *Journal of Environmental Quality* 7:580–588.

Tiedemann, A. R., and G. O. Klock. 1977. "Development of vegetation after fire, seeding and fertilization on the Entiat Experimental Forest." In *Annual proceedings of the Tall Timbers fire ecology conference,* no. 15. Tallahassee, Fla.: Tall Timbers Research Station, USDA Forest Service.

Tranquillini, W. 1979. *Physiological ecology of alpine timberline.* Ecological Studies 31. Berlin: Springer-Verlag.

Turner, J. 1975. *Nutrient cycling in a Douglas-fir ecosystem with respect to age and nutrient status.* Ph.D. Dissertation. Seattle, Wash.: University of Washington.

Ugolini, F. C. 1982. "Soil development in the *Abies amabilis* zone of the central Cascades, Washington." In *Proceedings of the symposium on the biology and management of true fir in the Pacific Northwest,* edited by C. D. Oliver and R. M. Kenady, 165–176. Contribution No. 45. Seattle, Wash.: College of Forest Resources, University of Washington.

Ugolini, F. C., H. Dawson, and J. Zachara. 1977a. Direct evidence of particle migration in the soil solution of a podzol. *Science* 198:603–605.

Ugolini, F. C., and D. H. Mann. 1979. Biopedological origin of peatlands in the south east Alaska. *Nature* 281:366–368.

Ugolini, F. C., R. Minden, H. Dawson, and J. Zachara. 1977b. An example of soil processes in the *Abies amabilis* zone of the central Cascades, Washington. *Soil Science* 124:291–302.

Ugolini, F. C., and R. J. Zasoski. 1979. "Chapter 4. Soils derived from tephra." In *Volcanic activity and human ecology,* 83–124. New York: Academic Press.

Van Breemen, N., P. A. Burrough, E. J. Velthorst, H. F. Van Dobben, T. de Wit, T. B. Ridder, and H. F. R. Reijnders. 1982. Soil acidification from atmospheric ammonium sulphate in forest canopy throughfall. *Nature* 299:548–550.

Van Praag, H. J., and F. Weissen. 1986. Foliar mineral deposition and dieback of Norway spruce. *Tree Physiology* 1:169–176.

Vitousek, P. M. 1985. "Community turnover and ecosystem nutrient dynamics." In *The ecology of natural disturbance and patch dynamics,* edited by S. T. A. Pickett and P. S. White, 325–333. New York: Academic Press.

Vogt, D. J. 1987. *Douglas-fir ecosystems in western Washington: biomass and production as related to site quality and stand age.* Ph.D. Dissertation. Seattle, Wash.: University of Washington.

Vogt, K. A., R. A. Dahlgren, F. Ugolini, D. Zabowski, E. E. Moore, and R. J. Zasoski. 1987a. Aluminum, Fe, Ca, Mg, K, Mn, Cu, Zn and P in above- and belowground biomass. II. Pools and circulation in a subalpine *Abies amabilis* stand. *Biogeochemistry* 4:295–311.

Vogt, K. A., R. A. Dahlgren, F. Ugolini, D. Zabowski, E. E. Moore, and R. J. Zasoski. 1987b. Aluminum, Fe, Ca, Mg, K, Mn, Cu, Zn and P in above- and belowground biomass. I. Concentrations in subalpine *Abies amabilis* and *Tsuga mertensiana. Biogeochemistry* 4:277–294.

Vogt, K. A., R. L. Edmonds, G. C. Antos, and D. J. Vogt. 1980. Comparisons between carbon dioxide evolution, ATP concentrations and decomposition in red alder, Douglas-fir, western hemlock and Pacific silver fir ecosystems in western Washington. *Oikos* 35:72–79.

Vogt, K. A., R. L. Edmonds, and C. C. Grier. 1981a. Seasonal changes in biomass and vertical distribution of mycorrhizal and fibrous-textured conifer fine roots in 23- and 180-year-old subalpine *Abies amabilis* stands. *Canadian Journal of Forest Research* 11:223–229.

Vogt, K. A., R. L. Edmonds, and C. C. Grier. 1981b. Dynamics of ectomycorrhizae in *Abies amabilis* stands: the role of *Cenococcum graniforme. Holarctic Ecology* 4:167–173.

Vogt, K. A., and C. C. Grier. 1982. "Root growth and mycorrhizae in true firs." In Proceedings of the symposium on the biology and management of true fir in the Pacific Northwest, edited by C. D. Oliver and R. M. Kenady, 97–101. Contribution No. 45. Seattle, Wash.: College of Forest Resources, University of Washington.

Vogt, K. A., C. C. Grier, R. L. Edmonds, and C. E. Meier. 1982. Mycorrhizal role in net primary production and nutrient cycling in Abies amabilis [Dougl.] Forbes ecosystems in western Washington. Ecology 63:370–380.

Vogt, K. A., C. C. Grier, C. E. Meier, M. R. Keyes, and R. L. Edmonds. 1983. Organic matter and nutrient dynamics in forest floors of young and mature Abies amabilis stands in western Washington, as affected by fine root input. Ecological Monographs 53:139–157.

Vogt, K. A., C. C. Grier, and D. J. Vogt. 1986. Production, turnover, and nutrient dynamics of above- and belowground detritus of world forests. *Advances in Ecological Research* 15:303–377.

Vogt, K. A., D. J. Vogt, E. E. Moore, B. A. Fatuga, M. R. Redlin, and R. L. Edmonds. 1987c. Conifer and angiosperm fine root biomass in relation to stand age and site productivity in Douglas-fir forests. *Journal of Ecology* 75:857–870.

Vogt, K. A., D. J. Vogt, E. E. Moore, W. Littke, C. C. Grier, and L. Leney. 1985. Estimating Douglas-fir fine root biomass and production from living bark and starch. *Canadian Journal of Forest Research* 15:177–179.

Wagner, R. 1980. *Natural regeneration at the edge of an* Abies amabilis *zone clearcut on the west slope of central Washington Cascades.* M.S. Thesis. Seattle, Wash.: University of Washington.

Waring, R. H., and J. F. Franklin. 1979. Evergreen coniferous forests of the Pacific Northwest. *Science* 204:1380–1386.

Waring, R. H., and G. B. Pitman. 1985. Modifying lodgepole pine stands to change susceptibility to mountain pine beetle attack. *Ecology* 66:889–897.

Waring, R. H., and W. H. Schlesinger. 1985. *Forest Ecosystems: Concepts and Management.* New York: Academic Press.

Wellner, C. A. 1978. "Management problems resulting from mountain pine beetles in lodgepole pine forests." In *Theory and practice of mountain pine beetle management in lodgepole pine forests,* 9–15. Moscow, Idaho: Forest, Wildlife, and Range Experiment Station, University of Idaho.

Wickman, B. E. 1978. *A case study of Douglas-fir tussock moth budbreak and stand conditions 10 years later.* Research Paper PNW-244. Portland, Ore.: Pacific Northwest Forest and Range Experiment Station, USDA Forest Service.

Williams, C. B., Jr., and C. T. Dyrness. 1967. *Some characteristics of forest floors and soils under true fir-hemlock stands in the Cascade Range.* Research Paper PNW-37. Portland, Ore.: Pacific Northwest Forest and Range Experiment Station, USDA Forest Service.

Wright, H. E. (editor). 1983. *Late Quaternary Environments of the United States. Vol. 2. The Holocene.* Minneapolis, Minn.: University of Minnesota Press.

Zobel, D. B., A. McKee, G. M. Hawk, and C. T. Dyrness. 1976. Relationships of environment to composition, structure, and diversity of forest communities of the central western Cascades of Oregon. *Ecological Monographs* 46:135–156.

Chapter 9

Managing Productivity Processes in the Inland Northwest—Mixed Conifers and Pines

A. E. Harvey, R. T. Meurisse, J. M. Geist, M. F. Jurgensen,
G. I. McDonald, R. T. Graham, and N. Stark

ABSTRACT

A myriad of interacting factors govern long-term productivity in forest ecosystems, and each site—species combination is likely to be unique. However, many common threads weave through these "unique" forest systems. For example, in the Inland Northwest, maintaining soil organic matter levels in all forest soils is important, but the relatively moist, fertile soils characteristic of mixed conifer forests, or sites with substantial deposits of volcanic ash, are usually less vulnerable to organic matter-based productivity losses than are dry, infertile soils characteristic of pine forests. Similarly, the effects of competing vegetation may differ in these forest types. Losses to root pathogens likely depend on ability of the host species to deal with harvest-caused increases in fungal inoculum and host stress. Compaction, displacement, and burning of soil surface horizons are particularly relevant to all these processes. Most Inland conifer species grow best, over the long term, when soil surface disturbances are minimal. Prescribed burns and mechanical site preparation should be practiced with great care (while accomplishing the important silvicultural objectives of reducing fuel loads, preparing seedbeds, and controlling brush only where necessary). Adequate attention should be directed to species and seed source, particularly in complex topography. In short, managers need to apply well-informed common sense within the framework of a commitment to long-term tree, site, and soil productivity.

INTRODUCTION

Many likely changes to Inland Northwestern forest ecosystems (i.e., those from the Cascade to Rocky Mountain crests) brought about by either natural or human disturbances could constitute a threat to long-term productivity. Obviously, the most drastic disturbances, or combinations of disturbances—such as those associated with wildfires or harvesting, particularly floristic (including genetic) alterations, mechanical site preparation, and prescribed burning—have the greatest potential to initiate substantial productivity losses. Here we discuss the relevant Inland ecosystems (pine and mixed conifer), selected problem conifers, and management actions that should prevent or minimize losses.

THE NATURE OF POTENTIAL PRODUCTIVITY PROBLEMS

Microclimate Changes

Harvesting and site preparation usually result in substantial microclimatic changes that strongly influence subsequent biological processes. The most important of these changes include increased light, temperature, and moisture (Gates 1980). Although most significant at the soil surface, these changes also occur well below in mineral horizons (see chapter 4, this volume). Thus, not only is a regenerating stand exposed directly to changes in proximal environment, which can be either beneficial or lethal (Levitt 1980), but soil chemical and microbial processes in the forest floor and shallow mineral horizons also can be affected (Hungerford and Babbitt 1987). This includes nutrient cycling or establishment of symbiotic and pathogenic associations, which can also be either beneficial or detrimental to long-term productivity processes (see chapters 2 and 3, this volume; Harvey et al. 1987b).

In most cases, appropriate mitigation of extreme changes in microclimate above or below the soil surface involves leaving sufficient overstory, low shrub and herb layers, or surface debris to provide shade, soil organic matter (OM), or both, to act as an environmental buffer (Harvey 1982, Harvey et al. 1987b, Hungerford and Babbitt 1987).

Nutrient Availability

The relationships between nutrients and plant growth processes are highly complex. In general, forest ecosystems have nutrient cycling processes that tend to store nutrients, even at the expense of short-term productivity (Chapin et al. 1986). Conifers, particularly the pines, are mostly well adapted for growth in infertile ecosystems subject to periodic nutrient (and moisture) shortages because they tend to store nutrients, presumably as a means of surviving periodic shortage (Chapin 1980). Such a conservative system protects long-term nutrient resources and is especially important to the more infertile sites where nutrient replacement is slow (Tiedemann 1981, Harvey et al. 1987b, Perry and Rose 1989). Increasing efforts are being made to better assess nutrient dynamics of forest soils as an aid to diagnosing nutrient-deficient sites (Geist 1977). It is, however, frequently difficult to predict how conifers on any given site will react to nutrient limitations, losses, and additions. Evidence is accumulating that most sites and soils in the Inland Northwest will experience reduced productivity if nutrient losses and associated soil degradation occur. Nutrient additions alone, in the absence of restoration of good soil physical conditions (structure and organic content), may or may not restore productivity.

One of the problems in dealing with nutrients for management of long-term productivity is that they tend to accumulate and cycle at the soil surface in organic horizons and feeder roots (Vogt et al. 1983, Harvey et al. 1987b). Thus located, nutrients are particularly vulnerable to disturbance and dislocation processes that can result in outright loss or reduced capacity for replacement (Harvey et al. 1987b, 1988a, Perry and Rose 1989).

Erosion

Although the direct effects of erosion seem obvious enough, few studies from the Inland Northwest demonstrate losses of forest productivity resulting from erosion. However, the close tie between soil surface horizons and tree growth leaves little doubt that removing surface soil could significantly reduce stand productivity (Harvey et al. 1987b, Perry and Rose 1989). In particular, loss of organic horizons (Flinn et al. 1980, Terry and Campbell 1981, Weber et al. 1985, Harvey et al. 1987b) or volcanic ash deposits (Geist and Strickler 1970, 1978, Geist 1977, Breuer 1988, Miller and Breuer 1988) is likely to decrease site fertility and productivity. Even loss of the parent surface mineral horizon (Ballard 1978, Terry and Campbell 1981, Miller 1984, Clayton and Kennedy 1985) is likely to cause productivity problems. Thus, as we will see, all due caution to prevent physical losses of surface soil horizons by erosive or any other means will pay large dividends in retaining forest productivity (see chapter 5, this volume).

Mechanical Compaction and Displacement

Donnelly and Shane (1986) reviewed physical soil changes resulting from induced soil compaction, Greacen and Sands (1980) the various problems related to soil compaction in forestry practice. Froehlich and McNabb (1984) discussed the effects of soil compaction on tree growth and soil conditions in Pacific Northwest forests. However, few data that assess the effects of soil compaction and displacement on tree growth are available specifically for interior forests. Froehlich (1979) has reported a 6–12% reduction in growth of individual ponderosa pine (*Pinus ponderosa* Dougl. ex Laws.) trees from heavily compacted soil in eastern Oregon. Cochran and Brock (1985) concluded that compaction reduced height growth of young ponderosa pine during the first 5 years after planting in central Oregon. Clayton et al. (1987) concluded that soil displacement and compaction resulted in significant declines in one or more growth attributes of lodgepole (*Pinus contorta* Dougl. ex Loud.) and ponderosa pines in central Idaho. These soils generally have a surface layer of volcanic ash about 1 ft. (0.3 m) thick.

In many areas of the Inland Northwest, ash and pumice layers deposited by Cascade Range volcanoes supply important horizons that significantly influence the physical structure and the moisture- and nutrient-holding capacity of regional forest soils and thus their productivity (Dyrness and Youngberg 1966, Geist and Strickler 1970, 1978, Geist 1977). Ash layers also provide rooting horizons with low bulk densities, and, in the case of pumice, the layers can both buffer against and complicate certain types of compaction problems (Cochran 1971).

In California, Helms et al. (1986) showed reduced growth of ponderosa pine in plantations, a result of compacted soils. Nielsen-Gerhardt (1986) has shown large displacement-related losses to the volcanic ash layers of northern Idaho soils brought about by mechanical site preparation. Miller (1984) demonstrated a reduction of Douglas-fir [*Pseudotsuga menziesii* (Mirb.) Franco] seedling growth in northern Idaho as a result of mechanical site preparation, presumably brought about by a combined loss of volcanic ash deposits and increases in bulk density. Perry and Rose (1989) review many effects of site preparation on potential productivity problems of western forest soils. Possible indirect effects of soil compaction include increases in feeder root pathogens (*Fusarium*) (Smeltzer et al. 1986) or increases in host stress, predisposing trees to insect and disease attack (Wargo and Shaw 1985, McDonald et al. 1987a,b).

The extent of damage from compaction and displacement is highly variable, depending on timber type and volume, soil type, equipment type and use, and moisture conditions. Table 9.1 summarizes soil monitoring results from four National Forests in eastern Oregon and Washington for a variety of conifers, including cedars (*Thuja* spp.), white fir [*Abies concolor* (Gord. & Glend.) Lindl. ex Hildebr.], lodgepole pine, Douglas-fir, and western larch (*Larix occidentalis* Nutt.). These data were collected using procedures for sampling surface soil conditions as described by Howes et al. (1983). The total damage, which was largely soil compaction and displacement, ranged from 11 to more than 40% of the surface area of disturbed units. All but two of the monitored sites were on soils derived largely from volcanic ash. Natural recovery from compaction may take longer than 40 years on many Inland Northwestern soils (Froehlich et al. 1985, Vora 1988).

Several techniques are available for minimizing the extent of area compacted and displaced during harvest and site preparation. One of the common approaches is to designate skid trails and confine equipment to those trails. This often requires pulling line to reach downed logs. Another approach is to limit the number of passes of equipment over a site (Froehlich and McNabb 1984). However, this is difficult to manage in many stands, and unfortunately, most of the compaction occurs in the first few passes anyway. Site preparation by broadcast burning, compared to tractor piling and burning, can be an effective means of reducing the potential for damage by compaction or displacement.

Tillage is becoming a common technique for ameliorating compacted soils. Use of winged subsoilers and forest cultivators seems to be effective (Froehlich and Miles 1984). Costs range from about $50–70/acre ($125–175/ha), which should encourage efforts to limit impacts in new or subsequent entries, whether precommercial or commercial. However, if soil compaction is not the only problem, productivity may only be partially restored.

TABLE 9.1. Soil damage associated with various harvesting practices in the Inland Northwest. Note that damage levels are relatively high when heavy machinery is used (damage = primarily compaction and displacement). Adapted from USDA Forest Service (1983, 1985), Geist et al. (1988).[1]

Harvest type	Yarding method	Site preparation	Conifer species	Damage, %[2]
Clearcut	FB RTS	Whole tree	Cedar	42
Clearcut	CT	B-burn	White fir	31
Clearcut	CT	B-burn	White fir	14
Clearcut	CT	B-burn	White fir	12
Clearcut	CT	B-burn	White fir	19
Clearcut	CT	B-burn	White fir	17
Clearcut	CT	B-burn	White fir	22
CC-salvage	CT	Unknown	Lodgepole pine	36
CC-salvage	CT	Unknown	Lodgepole	11
CC (non-ash soil)	FB RTS	Tractor pile	Lodgepole or Douglas-fir	30
Commercial thin (non-ash soil)	RTS	Tractor pile	Unknown	13
CC-RTP	N45-RTS	SCAR RTS	White fir, Douglas-fir, western larch	18
CC-RTP	D6-RTS	D6-RTS pile	Lodgepole	41
CC-RTP	D6-RTS	D6-RTS pile	Lodgepole	30
Seedtree	Unknown	Windrow	Lodgepole	17
Seedtree	Unknown	Windrow	Lodgepole	19
Clearcut	Unknown	Pile	Mixed conifer	33

[1]CC = clearcut, FB = feller buncher, RTS = rubber-tired skidder, CT = crawler tractor, RTP = reserve trees protected, B-burn = broadcast burn, SCAR = scarified.
[2]Damage is defined by standards published in R-6, FSM 2520, Supp. 50 (Region 6, USDA Forest Service, Portland, Oregon).

Utilization Intensity

Several recent reports discuss the probable effects of intensive harvesting on subsequent forest development (Cramer 1974, Leaf 1979, Barger 1980, Perry et al. 1982). To summarize, these reports and several others point out that removal of soil OM or its parent materials must be kept within reasonable limits to maintain soil structure (see chapter 3, this volume; Perry et al. 1982), nitrogen (N) storage, and asymbiotic N-fixation capacity (Geist and Strickler 1978, Jurgensen et al. 1979a, Harvey et al. 1987b), general nutrient storage and cycling (Leaf 1979), temperature moderation (Fowler and Helvey 1981, Hungerford and Babbit 1987), water storage capacity (see chapter 4, this volume; Geist and Strickler 1978, Perry et al. 1982, Graham et al. 1988), and small mammal and seedling microsites (Harvey 1982, Maser and Trappe 1984). Overuse of parent materials for forest organic reserves may be a particular problem on harsh sites or on sites with thin, skeletal, or otherwise infertile soils (Harvey et al. 1979a, 1987b, Perry and Norgren 1983).

Growth losses have been directly attributed to intentional physical removal of organic horizons from infertile forest soils in various regions of the world (Ballard 1978, Flinn et al. 1980, Weber et al. 1985). Substantial areas of the Inland Northwest are representative of sites potentially sensitive to such losses.

When appropriately applied, intensive utilization should maintain adequate organic reserves and allow at least moderate site sanitation where insect and disease problems emanate from accumulated residues (Fellin 1980). With moderate treatment of productive sites, more intensive use than currently practiced should be possible with minimal or no adverse impacts on new forests (Jurgensen et al. 1979b, Debyle 1980, Perry and Norgren 1983).

Slash Disposal

In the absence of intensive use associated with harvesting, western ecosystems tend to accumulate slash (carbon/fuel) more rapidly than it decays under the relatively cold or dry conditions that characterize western mountain terrain (Olsen 1963). Thus, natural wildfire plays a major role in cycling slow-to-decay woody debris in the interior West (Hayes 1970, Wellner 1970). Enter humans with their usual economic limitations for harvest removal, and even greater amounts of woody residue accumulate. Such accumulations frequently represent fuel buildups that create a hazard not only for fire that is unwanted but also for fire that is likely to be extremely hot and therefore damaging to soil. Obviously, then, if woody debris cannot be used economically and represents a danger to future or adjacent crops, the danger must be either destroyed in place or removed and destroyed elsewhere.

Safe, effective, and economical methods for removing unwanted slash are limited, commonly involving use of heavy equipment to concentrate slash before burning. In recent years, broadcast burns have been used more frequently, but extremely demanding burn prescriptions can have severe constraints, such as narrow (sometimes nonexistent) time windows when weather and other conditions are suitable plus relatively high personnel costs. However, from a soils (productivity) point of view, broadcast burns or no treatment at all are, in most instances, clearly the methods of choice (Harvey et al. 1979b, 1987b, 1988a, Perry and Rose 1989). The underlying factors behind these choices involve the intent to reduce potential for severe disturbance (including compaction) of surface soil horizons and the need to improve predictability of fire effects at or slightly below the soil surface (Ryan and Noste 1985). Roots, nutrients, and beneficial microbes almost always concentrate at the soil surface (see chapter 3, this volume; Harvey et al. 1987b)—where machines must manipulate fuels. So minimizing the affected area is a must. Managers should keep piles and windrows small and well scattered to break up large-fuel continuity but leave plenty of large slash between the rows (Harvey et al. 1987b).

Interactions among fire, soils, flora, and nutrients have been extensively reported, particularly over the last 10 years (Harvey et al. 1979b, 1988a, Raison 1979, Wells et al. 1979, Lotan et al. 1981, Tiedemann 1981, Boerner 1982). A common theme in these reports is concern for interruption of nutrient cycles or significant loss of nutrients subject to volatilization (Harvey et al. 1988a). Loss of N, a nutrient commonly found to limit growth in western ecosystems, has been a primary focus. The potential for N losses to be translated into losses of long-term productivity has been noted (Jurgensen et al. 1979b, Klock and Grier 1981, Tiedemann 1981, Harvey et al. 1987b, 1988a). Because large percentages of total soil N are stored in easily disrupted surface soil layers and because the microbial activities associated with N input and turnover are frequently concentrated in those layers, the concern is warranted. Tables 9.2 and 9.3 show how extensively N can be displaced or lost with burning or mechanical site preparation (Niehoff 1985, Nielsen-Gerhardt 1986). There seems little doubt that severe soil disturbance caused by either force can bring about catastrophic reductions of soil N supplies. There is also little doubt that, modestly and properly applied, either fire or machines can be compatible with long-term N conservation (Debyle 1980, Jurgensen et al. 1981, Stark 1982, Landsberg et al. 1984, Harvey et al. 1987b, Perry and Rose 1989).

TABLE 9.2. Effect of various levels of burn intensity on mineralizable nitrogen (N that can be converted to "available" forms by microbial action, determined by the anaerobic method) stored in an Idaho Panhandle forest soil in two organic (OM) horizons of differing depths. Note the high losses associated with "hot" fire and modest losses or gains associated with "light" fire. Calculated from Niehoff (1985) and Nielson-Gerhardt (1986).

| Treatment[1] | N level, ppm, at | | N change, % |
	0–2.5 cm OM	2.5–7.5 cm OM	
Undisturbed	68	9	0
Clearcut, no burn	97	10	+28
Clearcut, slight burn	75	9	+8
Clearcut, severe burn	5	9	−92
Clearcut, extreme burn	0	1	−99

[1]Slight burn = less than 200°C at mineral surface; severe burn = complete loss of organic horizon; extreme burn = severe, plus discoloration of mineral soil.

TABLE 9.3. Effect of various levels of mechanical site preparation on mineralizable N (as in Table 9.2) stored in an Idaho Panhandle forest soil. Note the high losses associated with heavy treatment and modest losses or gains associated with moderate treatment. Calculated from Nielson-Gerhardt (1986).

Treatment[1]	Horizon	N level, ppm	N change, %
Undisturbed	Mineral	12	0
	Organic	66	0
Clearcut, no scarification	Mineral	15	+20
	Organic	97	+32
Clearcut, moderate scarification	Mineral	13	+8
	Organic	50	−24
Clearcut, heavy scarification	Mineral	10	−17
	Organic	14	−79

[1]Moderate scarification = 50% organic horizon removed; heavy scarification = 100% organic horizon removed or mixed with mineral horizons.

TABLE 9.4. Distribution of nitrogen (N) storage and asymbiotic N fixation in forest soils from a dry (PSME/PHMA)[1] and a wet (TSHE/CLUN) habitat type of western Montana. Note that both storage and fixation are concentrated in surface organic (OM) horizons. Adapted from Harvey et al. (1987b).

| Soil horizon[1] | OM, mg/ha | N storage | | N-fixation rate | |
		kg/ha	%	g/yr	%
Douglas-fir/ninebark (PSME/PHMA)					
Residue	45	68	3	160	21
Soil wood	37	419	16	94	12
Humus	26	438	17	93	12
Top mineral[2]	29	543	21	106	14
Deep mineral[3]	73	1,162	44	32	41
Western hemlock/clintonia (TSHE/CLUN)					
Residue	83	125	5	230	26
Soil wood	50	341	14	120	14
Humus	49	787	33	125	14
Top mineral	29	264	11	117	13
Deep mineral	693	867	36	290	33

[1]Habitat-type designations from Pfister et al. (1977); western hemlock [*Tsuga heterophylla* (Raf.) Sarg.].
[2]Sampling to 5-cm depth
[3]Sampling to 30-cm depth.

The primary tie between slash removal, N, and productivity is, of course, soil OM or the parent materials for soil organic horizons (Flinn et al. 1980, Perry and Norgren 1983, Harvey et al. 1987b). Not only is N stored in organic horizons (as are many other nutrients), but on sites without symbiotic N-fixing plants, the primary source for N input (fixation) may be related to microbial populations that derive energy from OM decay (Table 9.4) (see chapter 3, this volume; Harvey et al. 1987b). Decomposing woody residue, primarily in the form of old decaying logs, may be a particularly good source of N (Larsen et al. 1978, Jurgensen et al. 1979a). Decaying logs also form important microsites for a variety of beneficial plants, microbes, and other organisms (Fellin 1980, Harvey 1982, Maser and Trappe 1984, Harmon et al. 1986). However, where woody residues represent sources of disease inoculum or pest refugia—that is, where pests may be more limiting, at least in the short term, than lower levels of N—sanitation through physical removal or burning can be highly beneficial (Hardison 1976, Harvey et al. 1976, 1987a, Fellin 1980).

In recent years, the tie between soil OM and productivity has been strengthened through direct observation of cause-effect experiments in field situations. For example, lowering OM content in sandy soils of New Zealand reduced tree growth as well as N content (Ballard 1978). Similarly, in Canada, reducing slash by methods that removed surface soil horizons or simply removing forest-floor organic horizons had substantial impacts on growth of trees from affected areas (Weber et al. 1985). More locally, Cole and Schmidt (1986) found that removing slash with heavy machinery can reduce growth rates of 25-year-old western larch and Douglas-fir in western Montana. Breuer (1989), Miller (1984), and Miller and Breuer (1989) reported that site preparation and slash disposal measures displacing soil surface horizons, including ash cap layers, can substantially hinder the performance of seedling crops and forests in northern Idaho. Similarly, both Bosworth (1989) and Eramian and Neuenschwander (1989) reported decreased tree growth associated with pile and burn treatments, compared to broadcast burning, in stands up to 40 years old in northern Idaho. Clayton et al. (1987) reported decreased growth following mechanical site preparation in central Idaho. Minore (1986) noted similar results in southwestern Oregon. Growth reductions reported for these studies varied from 10 to 25%. Removing slash with heavy machinery in the southeastern United States has resulted in productivity losses well over 50% (Haines et al. 1975).

Slash manipulation also affects microsite temperatures. Slash substantially moderates temperatures at or near the soil surface, particularly when blackened by fire (Fowler and Helvey 1981, Hungerford and Babbitt 1987). Thus, because seedlings can either be damaged by temperature extremes or their growth improved by temperature control (Cochran 1972), slash management would seem to provide an opportunity to regulate temperatures to benefit trees, particularly in harsh environments (Hungerford and Babbitt 1987).

As might be expected from the previous discussion, slash management methods that avoid excessive use of heavy machinery (resulting in compaction or displacement of surface soil) or high temperatures can be consistent with maintaining site productivity. However, many times slash disposal may be unwarranted as long as danger from wildfire is reasonably low. Thus, slash should be removed only where there is a specific need, particularly where site-preparation requirements are modest. Obviously, there are strong interactions between slash control and site-preparation needs.

Site Preparation

Because site preparation is an extension or a result of slash disposal, effects are similar though frequently far more pronounced than with the former. Usually, soil disturbance and at least partial removal of organic horizons are major objectives of site preparation, along with control of competing vegetation. Though at times extensive disturbance (mechanical or fire) is required to achieve adequate seedling survival in southwestern Oregon (Ross et al. 1986), the same costs, in terms of potential losses to long-term productivity, as those associated with slash control likely apply (Harvey 1982, Ross and Walstad 1986, Ross et al. 1986, Graham et al. 1989, Perry and Rose 1989). By the same token, the "light touch" can also be used on many Inland sites to achieve adequate seedling survival (Kracht 1985) and appears imperative to maintain long-term productivity (Harvey et al. 1987b, Graham et al. 1989, Perry and Rose 1989).

It bears reemphasizing that, in most cases, past literature has projected decreased growth from reduced soil OM, N, or compaction, primarily based on poorly understood principles of soil and biological science related to nutrient cycling, physical properties, or microbial activities. But recent experience is building an ever stronger argument, based on measured losses, that high levels of disturbance or removal of organic horizons are linked to substantial reductions in conifer performance in both seedling and intermediate-aged stands (Brendemuehl 1967, Ballard 1978, Burger and Pritchett 1979, Perry et al. 1982, Miller 1984, Weber et al. 1985, Cole and Schmidt 1986, Minore 1986, Clayton et al. 1987, Bosworth 1989, Eramian and Neuenschwander 1989, Miller and Breuer 1989). J. M. Geist, K. W. Seidel, and J. W. Hazard (unpublished data, USDA Forest Service,

LaGrande, Oregon, 1988) assessed growth differences in juvenile lodgepole and ponderosa pine after soils were severely or minimally disturbed by clearcut harvesting of mixed conifer stands. Their study was conducted on volcanic ash soils with silt loam textures in eastern Oregon and Washington. Growth was lower when disturbance was severe. Differences, expressed as a percentage of tree parameters measured under minimal disturbance, ranged from 21 to 29% for total height, recent height growth, and recent radial growth.

In at least one instance in the Inland Northwest, a greenhouse experiment showed that reduced growth brought about by harvesting was largely restored by the simple addition of N (Perry et al. 1982). In the absence of natural N replacement, however, recovery times may be long (Tables 9.5, 9.6). Assuming total loss of N from shallow soil horizons, recovery would take roughly 108 years (1468/13.6 = 107.8) with N-fixing ceanothus (*Ceanothus* spp.) on the site, roughly 506 years (1468/2.9 = 506.2) without it (Table 9.6). In addition, where growth reduction may have many causes, including loss of soil structure and compaction (Froehlich 1979), fertilization can be expected to have little effect. We do not know how long recovery of soil structure and related moisture-holding capacity may take—possibly as long as it takes to replace lost OM. Where displacement of mineral soil horizons has been significant (e.g., volcanic ash), in a practical sense, recovery may never occur. With compaction, an estimate of over 40 years has been made for central Idaho and northeastern California (Froehlich et al. 1985, Vora 1988).

TABLE 9.5. Distribution of nitrogen (N) input (asymbiotic and symbiotic) potential in a hypothetical mountain western soil. Note high rates of N fixation associated with symbiotic plants, relative to those for asymbiotic organisms.

Source	N, kg ha^{-1} yr^{-1}	Reference	Assumptions
Asymbiotic			
Humus	0.02	Jurgensen et al.	180-day activity
Soil wood	0.22	(1979a)	
Shallow mineral soil (5 cm)	0.52		
Deep mineral soil (5–30 cm)	0.92		
Residue decay	0.63		
Total	2.3		
Symbiotic			
Ceanothus	10.7	McNabb et al. (1979)	21% crown cover
Alder (*Alnus*)	100	Zavitkovski and Newton (1968)	100% crown cover
Atmospheric			
Rain (1978)	2	Tiedemann et al.	Eastern Washington

TABLE 9.6. A nitrogen (N) balance sheet, based on the assumption that all N associated with surface soil horizons was lost from severe disturbance (see Niehoff 1985 or Nielson-Gerhardt 1986). Input rates based on Table 9.5.

Source	N input, kg ha^{-1} yr^{-1}	N storage, kg/ha
Humus	0.02	438
Soil wood	0.22	419
Residue	0.63	68
Shallow mineral soil (5 cm)	0.52	543
		1,468[1]
Deep mineral soil (5–30 cm)	0.92	1,162
Ceanothus	10.7	—
Rain	2.0	0
	13.6	

[1]Subtotal of nitrogen in shallow soil horizons.

The increased use of machinery and associated high levels of disturbance, frequently part of intensive management in the Inland Northwest (Ross et al. 1986), obviously increase the risk of long-term productivity losses, particularly with piling and windrowing (Froehlich 1979, Harvey et al. 1979b, Cochran and Brock 1985, Helms et al. 1986, Clayton et al. 1987). Pumice-sized ash layers in many Inland soils help buffer against compaction. However, particle bridging in some pumice layers can increase resistance to root penetration (Cochran 1971). We previously mentioned the important contribution of fine ash and pumice deposition to productivity. Unfortunately, these layers are easily displaced by mechanical activities associated with forest management (Cochran 1971, Geist and Strickler 1978, Geist et al. 1988).

Thus, productivity can be lost by combinations of many factors, depending on site and soil. Some facets of this problem, however, are abundantly clear. Lost ash-cap horizons cannot be replaced, lost organic layers or N stores (in absence of fertilization) can require long periods to replace (Harvey et al. 1987b), and relief from compaction can require long periods on many sites (Froehlich et al. 1985, Vora 1988). Because repair is difficult, frequently unreliable, expensive, and time-consuming, the bottom line is to avoid the problem.

Spot use of herbicides (Boyd 1986) and broadcast burning at moderate or mild intensities (Graham et al. 1989) are good examples of "minimal impact" alternatives that can work on many sites. Other examples involve setting operating guidelines to achieve minimal damage but adequate disturbance for regeneration needs (Froehlich and McNabb 1984, Harvey et al. 1987b). Where impacts are already excessive, compaction damage may be repaired with winged subsoilers or similar equipment (Froehlich and Miles 1984). However, results can be inconsistent. An approach currently being tried in northern Idaho is avoiding site preparation where competition levels are modest and planting is the regeneration method of choice (Graham et al. 1989); in much of the Idaho Panhandle region, this approach can be used if planting is prompt. So far, results on the Fernan Ranger District appear as good as when traditional site-preparation guidelines were followed (unpublished data, on file at USDA Forest Service at Fernan Ranger District, Coeur d'Alene, Idaho, 1987–88).

Activity of Microorganisms

The significant roles of beneficial microbes in long-term productivity have been extensively reviewed in this volume in chapter 3 and elsewhere by Harvey et al. (1976, 1987b) and Maser and Trappe (1984). Therefore, the discussion of microbes here concentrates on pathogens of Inland Northwestern conifers. We emphasize those most likely to be affected by management actions that disturb the soil, i.e., endemic, soil-borne root pathogens. Of these, shoestring root rot (*Armillaria* spp. complex), laminated root rot [*Phellinus weirii* (Murr.) Gilberts. (=*Poria weirii*)], annosus root rot [*Heterobasidion annosus* (Fr.) Bref. (=*Fomes annosus*)], black stain root disease [*Ceratocystis Ophiostoma wageneri* Goheen et Cobb], and brown cubical root rot [*Phaeolus (Polyporus) schweinitzii* (Fr.) Pat.] individually or in combination probably cause the greatest damage to forests of the Inland Northwest (J. W. Byler, personal communication, USDA Forest Service, Missoula, Montana, 1987; Filip 1977, Hobbs and Partridge 1979, Filip and Goheen 1982, James et al. 1982, 1984, USDA Forest Service 1984, McDonald et al. 1987a).

Discussion of this important group of pathogens is particularly relevant to the subject of long-term productivity. There is an emerging view that host stress may have a predisposing influence on susceptibility, at least for *Armillaria* and *Phellinus*, the most damaging organisms of this group (Waring 1985, 1987, Entry et al. 1986, McDonald et al. 1987a). Other root-rot organisms may act similarly, with perhaps more restrictive habitat ranges. Thus, even if our management actions only slightly reduce soil productivity but increase tree stress, there is likely to be a postharvest "epidemic explosion" of root-rot problems where previously the organisms were only endemic, causing little damage. Harvest-related increases in root-rot damage (Filip 1977, Filip and Goheen 1982, McDonald et al. 1987a) and increased damage associated with low nutrient status or light levels have been reported with western root rots (Sheilds and Hobbs 1979, Entry et al. 1986); this impact could be greatly increased if site preparation is highly inappropriate.

Our experience in the Coeur d'Alene area of northern Idaho indicates that sites experiencing multiple harvest-related disturbances since the late 1800s are now losing as much as 50% of their potential productivity to root rots, with as much as 50% of the land area affected. These observations indicate that past management actions—including fire control with resulting increases of susceptible hosts, "offsite" planting, inappropriate seed sources, soil degradation, and increased inoculum from infected roots and residue—produced a major root-rot epidemic, at least locally and perhaps more extensively in the Inland Northwest. These epidemics will significantly affect future productivity by reducing product flow to forest industries, employment, and both regional and National Forest revenues.

Past efforts to control root rot have not been very effective. The only completely effective method is total control of inoculum by removing infected wood. However, this results in removal of virtually all the soil organic base and forest floor. The extensive disturbance required will almost surely bring on other productivity problems. Other partially effective methods are based primarily on silvicultural manipulation of stand composition to favor conifers (pines or larch) that tolerate root rots. But these species are usually difficult to retain in adequate quantities to be effective, and shade-tolerant species highly susceptible to root rots are quick to regenerate. Methods used to accomplish species conversions include: (1) destroying damaged stands and planting; (2) accelerating harvesting to capture volume in infected trees before it is lost, while favoring tree species tolerant of root rots; or (3) avoiding preharvest entries if disease-tolerant species are already well represented in the stand—particularly if damage to the more susceptible species is low to moderate. The first two of these methods require aggressive and continuing species control so that species tolerant to root rots remain the major component of treated stands (Thies 1984, Thies and Russell 1984, Hadfield 1985, Wargo and Shaw 1985).

Recent perceptions of root-rot epidemiology suggest that anything that can be done to improve or protect site productivity (reduce stress) is likely to improve prospects of containing root-rot damage (McDonald et al. 1987a; Waring 1987). Futhermore, McDonald et al. (1987a) reported that there are definitive interactions among habitat type, disturbance, and *Armillaria* infection which suggest that risk rating Inland sites will help, at least in a broad sense, to concentrate control efforts on those habitat type-species combinations most likely to experience damage (Tables 9.7, 9.8). Unfortunately, current high-risk habitat types include many of the more productive forest types in the Inland Northwest (Williams and Marsden 1982, McDonald et al. 1987a). Considerable refinement of the habitat risk rating system is required to make it reliable in differentiating among high-risk types.

Under sufficient stress, even *Armillaria*-resistant species such as pines and larch can experience considerable damage. Other pests, through debilitating effects on the host, may increase root rot or other damage (Kulhavy et al. 1984, Tkacz and Schmitz 1986). In the case of black stain root disease, an insect vector is a major source of spread, and control strategy must consider limiting the vector as well as the pathogen (Witcosky and Hansen 1985). White pine blister rust (*Cronartium ribicola* J. C. Fisch. ex Rab.) had a major effect on root-rot epidemiology by decimating one of the major root-rot tolerant species that otherwise would have been well represented in stands now heavily damaged by root disease. A Westwide root-rot model is available that considers most of the concepts previously described. It can help managers evaluate control options for many areas (Shaw et al. 1985).

One arena for possible root-rot control not currently well understood is that of using inherent resistance of certain tree species. Past harvesting which removed the more resistant trees from many Inland sites may have contributed to the high level of damage we are now experiencing. Increasing resistance of more heavily damaged species, particularly Douglas-fir and grand fir [*Abies grandis* (Dougl. ex D. Don) Lindl.], could negate the expensive sanitation requirement for soil-damaging destruction of infected residues and root systems in heavily impacted areas. It may be the only practical means of control where alternative species more tolerant of the pathogens are difficult to manage.

The potential for this method of control with an endemic disease is only now receiving some research attention. However, it is complicated by lack of good methods to assess stress-susceptibility interactions and the genetic nature of several of the pathogens; so widespread use of such an option remains well in the future. In any case, interactions between the beneficial soil microbes supporting soil productivity processes and endemic root pathogens should be major considerations in silvicultural prescriptions for most Inland forests, particularly (though not exclusively) for the mixed conifer forest types.

THE NATURE OF THE ECOSYSTEMS

Lodgepole Pine

Lodgepole pine forests of the Inland Northwest usually occupy relatively moist, cool to cold sites where mean annual precipitation ranges from 20 to 50 in. (50 to 127 cm) and mean annual air temperature from 40 to 60°F (4 to 16°C). Mean summer soil temperatures range from 44–60°F (7 to 16°C). Lodgepole pine forests in much of Oregon, Washington, and Idaho grow predominantly on soils derived from silt loam volcanic ash and loamy sands from pumice and ash (medial and cindery Typic Vitrandepts and Cryandepts). In the pumice plateau of central Oregon, these forests are usually in nearly flat basins that may have water tables at depths of 1 ft. (30 cm) or more. These soils generally have high levels of readily available water storage, low bulk densities, and moderate to low fertility. Most nutrients are concentrated within 6 in. (15 cm) of the surface (Youngberg and Dyrness 1959, Cochran 1971, 1985, Geist and Strickler 1978). In the northern Rockies, lodgepole pine commonly grows on granites and rhyolites, with some stands on shales. In Canada, extensive stands occur on calcareous glacial tills (Lotan and Perry 1983).

TABLE 9.7. Presence of *Armillaria* and *Armillaria* damage across random plots located throughout northern Idaho, western Montana, eastern Oregon, and eastern Washington. Note high presence and damage in productive, relative to less productive (harsh), habitat types. Adapted from McDonald et al. (1987a).

		Plots, %	
Habitat type	Climate/no. plots	With pathogen	With pathogen plus damage
PSME/VAGL[1]	Cool-dry/2	0	—
PSME/PHMA	Warm-dry/6	67	75
PSME/CARU	Hot-dry/6	0	—
ABLA/VASC	Cold-dry/8	0	—
ABLA/MEFE	Cold-moderate/6	83	60
ABLA/CLUN	Cool-moderate/5	80	100
ABGR/VAGL	Cool-dry/5	100	40
ABGR/CLUN	Cool-moderate/12	92	45
ABGR/PHMA	Warm-dry/6	100	17
TSHE/CLUN	Warm-moderate/11	91	20

[1]Habitat-type designations from Pfister et al. (1977). PSME = Douglas-fir; ABLA = subalpine fir [*Abies lasiocarpa* (Hook.) Nutt.]; ABGR = grand fir [*Abies grandis* (Dougl. ex D. Don) Lindl.]; TSHE = western hemlock.

TABLE 9.8. Distribution of *Armillaria* damage on various conifer species across habitat series throughout northern Idaho, western Montana, eastern Oregon, and eastern Washington. For all plots with *Armillaria* present, see Table 9.7. Note that damage (as indicated by infection) to some species is conditioned by habitat series. Adapted from McDonald et al. (1987b).

	Habitat series, %[1]			
Host species	Douglas-fir	Subalpine fir	Grand fir	Western hemlock
Ponderosa pine	33	—[2]	0	—
Lodgepole pine	0	13	14	13
Douglas-fir	50	25	21	25
Western larch	0	0	0	0
Western white pine[3]	—	—	0	0
Western hemlock	—	—	—	0
Grand fir	—	—	23	0
Engelmann spruce[3]	0	21	24	20
Subalpine fir	—	40	0	33

[1]Percent of infected trees of that species on plot.
[2]Species not found on plots from this habitat series.
[3]Western white pine (*Pinus monticola* Dougl. ex D. Don); Engelmann spruce (*Picea engelmannii* Parry ex Engelm.).

Minimizing soil displacement and conserving OM are keys to maintaining long-term productivity of lodgepole pine (Harvey et al. 1987a). Soil compaction is a significant hazard on the fine ash soils (Geist and Strickler 1978). Particle bridging in pumice from vibrating equipment may restrict root penetration and seedling growth on the pumiceous soils (Cochran 1971).

Ponderosa Pine

Ponderosa pine forests occupy the warmest, driest sites of the Inland Northwest. Available soil moisture is closely related to pine distribution and productivity. However, in the central Oregon pumice plateau, distribution is also limited by frost pockets, where ponderosa pine is often replaced by lodgepole pine (Cochran 1973, 1975). Sugar pine (*Pinus lambertiana* Dougl.) commonly occurs on volcanic cones and buttes. Mean annual precipitation, ranging from 16 to 35 in. (41 to 89 cm), generally falls during the autumn and winter months when evapotranspiration is low. Mean annual temperatures range from 42 to 65°F (6 to 19°C). Mean summer soil temperatures range from 45 to 65°F (7 to 18°C). The soils are usually dry at depths of 4–24 in. (10–61 cm) for 60 or more consecutive days during summer and autumn (Daubenmire and Daubenmire 1968, Hall 1973, Donaldson and DeFrancesco 1982).

Ponderosa pine forests generally grow on three broad but distinct groups of soils (Dyrness and Young-berg 1966). Probably the most prominent and contiguous of these soils in Oregon are those from air-laid pumice and ash. These cindery and pumiceous soils often overlie older, loamy, buried soils at depths of about 12 to more than 60 in. (30–150 cm). These soils are coarse textured but store relatively high amounts of readily available soil moisture (Dyrness and Youngberg 1966, Larson 1976, Carlson 1979). Soil OM is concentrated within 6–10 in. (15–25 cm) of the surface, and nutrient content declines rapidly with depth. Although these soils are relatively resilient, assurance of site productivity potential requires that the nutrient regime be maintained by conserving OM and minimizing soil displacement.

The second most prominent group of ponderosa pine soils are those that are moderately deep and dark colored, fine, and fine-loamy, derived from basalts, andesites, and clayey sediments. These soils are easily puddled and compacted when wet but have relatively high strength when dry. On slopes greater than 30%, surface erosion is especially significant when vegetation is removed (Carlson 1974, Paulson 1977, Wenzel 1979).

The third group of ponderosa pine soils are those that are coarse, loamy, and shallow to deep, derived from rhyolite, andesite, granitics, glacial till, and outwash. They usually have low OM content and low plant-available water-holding capacity (less than 3–4 in., or 8–10 cm). Soil displacement and erosion represent potential hazards to long-term productivity, particularly on slopes greater than 30%. Organic matter, surface soil nutrients, and moisture conservation are likely critical on all these soils for maintaining long-term productivity of ponderosa pine (Harvey et al. 1989b, Powers et al. 1989).

Mixed Conifers

Mixed conifer forests occupy a wide range of conditions. At their lowest elevations, they are relatively warm and dry, grading to the low, even warmer and drier ponderosa pine sites; at their highest elevations, they are cold and wet. Species composition is diverse. Both species composition and stand productivity are mainly governed by available soil moisture, nutrient supply, and temperature (Daubenmire and Daubenmire 1968, Hall 1973).

One of the most dominant and essentially universal features of interior mixed-conifer sites is the presence of varying amounts of surface-deposited pumice and volcanic ash. Deposition thickness ranges from about 6 to more than 30 in. (15 to 76 cm). This layer is generally underlain by older, buried soils of varied origin with textures from sandy loams to clays. Some buried portions are gravelly and stony. Total soil depth varies from about 1 to more than 5 ft. (0.3 to 1.5 m) (Donaldson and DeFrancesco 1982).

Because temperature is a major factor affecting productivity and species composition in this forest type, two distinct temperature-related soil groups can be described. The larger and more productive—the frigid regime—has mean annual air temperatures of about 42–46°F (6–8°C) and mean summer soil temperatures of 60–62°F (16–17°C). Elevation ranges from 2,000 to 5,500 ft. (600 to 1,672 m). Mean annual precipitation ranges from 18 to 50 in. (46 to 127 cm). The soils are dry at depths of 8–24 in. (20–61 cm) for 60 consecutive days or more on most sites. A few localized areas, dry for less than 45 consecutive days, usually have western red-cedar/clintonia or western hemlock/clintonia habitat types. Vegetation, from lowest elevation to highest, and driest to wettest, is Douglas-fir, western larch, lodgepole pine, grand fir, white fir, western white pine (*Pinus monticola* Dougl. ex D. Don), western redcedar (*Thuja plicata* Donn ex D. Don), and western hemlock [*Tsuga heterophylla* (Raf.) Sarg.]. Douglas-fir is the major climax species on the driest sites, grand fir and white fir on the coldest sites, and western redcedar on the wettest sites. This soil temperature group supports the most productive forests within the ecosystem. Productivity commonly ranges from 85 to 115 ft.^{3} acre^{-1} yr^{-1} (5.9 to 8.0 m^3 ha^{-1} yr^{-1}) (Hall 1973, Donaldson and DeFrancesco 1982, Volland 1985, Johnson and Simon 1987). Root disease problems are particularly common in these types (McDonald et al. 1987a).

The other major temperature-related soil group—the cryic regime—has mean annual air temperatures of about 37–45°F (3–7°C) and mean summer soil temperatures of less than 60°F (16°C). Elevation ranges from 3,500 to 7,000 ft. (1064 to 2128 m). Mean annual precipitation ranges from 20 to 50 in. (51 to 127 cm). Although most of the soils are dry for 45–60 consecutive days during the summer, some localized areas are dry for less than 45 days. Vegetation is dominantly white fir, grand fir, Douglas-fir, lodgepole pine, Engelmann spruce (*Picea engelmannii* Parry ex Engelm.), and subalpine fir [*Abies lasiocarpa* (Hook.) Nutt.]. Western redcedar, western hemlock, western larch, and western white pine are minor components. Site productivity potentials generally range from 50 to 85 ft.^{3} acre^{-1} yr^{-1} (3.5 to 5.9 m^3 ha^{-1} yr^{-1}), except on the driest, coldest sites, where they can be less (Hall 1973, Donaldson and DeFrancesco 1982, Volland 1985, Johnson and Simon 1987).

Because so many of the soils within the mixed conifer forests are derived from volcanic ash or are strongly influenced by ash, they generally have relatively high water-holding capacities. Plant available water capacities of 10–12 in. (25–30 cm) are common. Natural soil bulk densities average about 0.6 g/cc but can vary, depending on location and management impacts. These low densities provide for rapid infiltration, high water-storage capacity, and good aeration (Donaldson and DeFrancesco 1982, Volland 1985). Maintenance of long-term productivity requires protection from excessive compaction and displacement of the surface soil (ash and OM components). The soils in both the frigid and cryic regimes are among the most fertile of the Inland forests, but management of nutrient reserves and organic matter is critical to maintain productivity levels (Geist and Strickler 1978, Sachs and Sollins 1986, Harvey et al. 1987b).

The Nature of Selected Species

Although we will not describe autecological characteristics of conifer species appropriate for the Inland Northwest here (see Minore 1979), some selective mention is appropriate. For example, when considering interactions between tree species and OM, it seems likely that climax species will be more dependent on well-developed OM horizons than will most seral species. Species such as Douglas-fir and lodgepole pine are likely to be more sensitive to being "off site" than species such as western white pine, ponderosa pine, or western larch (Rehfeldt 1979, 1982, 1983, 1986, Rehfeldt et al. 1981). All species probably will experience less stress during stand development if they are managed well within their ecological ranges. Stands with a history of severe disturbance, natural or human caused, are likely to be under more stress than those without such disturbance, a result of altered soil development. In some instances and particularly with sensitive species, even minor soil degradation may cause substantial impacts on the expected present net worth of future harvests (Routledge 1987).

CONCLUSIONS

For the land manager there seems no alternative but to consider management of each site as a separate entity. Success requires considering history, soils, soil microbes (beneficial and pathogenic), fire effects (past and probable future), and suitable tree species. This may be truer for the Inland Northwest than for most other areas of the country. Although Inland forests can be productive, they have diverse climates, soils, tree species, and microbes. They are subjected to frequent natural perturbations. Many if not all species experience at least episodic stress, perhaps on some sites constant stress.

Methods for assessing ecosystem and individual tree health are currently receiving considerable research attention (in addition to this volume, Hazard and Geist 1984, Stark et al. 1985, Stark and Spitzner 1985, USDA Forest Service 1985, Van Cleve et al. 1985). However, the utility of these methods as an aid to land management is yet to be determined.

QUESTIONS FROM THE SYMPOSIUM FLOOR

Q: You defined a "light burn" as one achieving a temperature in the mineral soil of not over 200°C. Over what percentage of the area do temperatures over 200°C occur? For how long?

A: Definition of the burn was based on procedures described in Ryan and Noste (1985). Generally speaking, it depends more on temperature than time. Interactions between temperature and time also are described by Ryan and Noste.

Q: Is it possible to group soil series or types into susceptibility classes (i.e., high, moderate, low) relative to burning effects?

A: Yes, a system for doing this is included as an addendum to Niehoff's M.S. thesis (1985) at the University of Idaho.

Q: How do you quantitatively define detrimental soil displacement? Compaction? (i.e., percent increases in density, depths, etc.?)

A: There have been some systems developed to do this; one is reported in Nielsen-Gerhardt's M.S. thesis (1986) at the University of Idaho. Another is being developed by Geist et al. (1988).

Q: You showed a slide in which tree growth through age 25 on a scarified site was greater than on a cut site with no slash treatment. Stands younger than 25–30 years have lower nutrient needs than older stands with more leaf area and biomass. Could this response be reduced by age 60–80 years?

A: Yes. If nutrients held in the undisturbed organic material are released through decay action rapidly enough, the situation may well be reversed in 60–80 years.

Q: What do you suggest for site preparation in the Douglas-fir/pinegrass habitat type?

A: Pinegrass (*Calamagrostis rubescens* Buckl.) is an aggressive competitor in many instances. If it is not controlled, regenerating conifers may not survive. Soil productivity at the planting spot is not a limiting consideration. In such instances, spot herbicide applications or minimal scalping may be the only effective site preparation. We are *not* recommending no site preparation. We are advocating using site preparation only to address a problem such as the one described and using the "light touch" if possible. Do not use methods such as scalping organic layers unless the alternatives are even less desirable. In other words, do not employ them automatically, over large areas, where problems may well not exist.

Q: When you talk about wood as a major contributor to long-term N input—how much wood should there be and how big, and how long does it take for N to become available from the large pieces?

A: Recommendations thus far suggest that 15 tons/acre, greater than 6-in. (15-cm) diameter, preferably with heartwood or Douglas-fir, will suffice (Harvey et al. 1987a). However, as long as fuel loading and fire danger specifications are acceptable and the slash does not create other problems, leave it on the site.

Q: Have specific soil-site-management practice combinations given poor regeneration success in the systems you have studied?

A: Our work indicates that high disturbance levels hamper good growth. Many reports in the literature equate good regeneration success only with high early survival percentages, a common occurrence with mineral seedbeds. However, our observations suggest later performance will suffer in such circumstances. Most current literature agrees (see References).

Q: You showed the comparative differences in seedling survival for different site-preparation methods (mounds, scalping, etc.), and the optimum results were to mound and spray release. Would you care to predict the anticipated survival *without* site preparation after logging, but with competition controlled through spray release?

A: Our observations suggest your treatment would be a good option. For example, see Boyd (1986). However, mounding provides a benefit that most natural soils do not have: a loose rooting medium and, thus, greater capacity for root extension. So odds may still favor the mound if other aspects of the prescription are satisfied.

Q: What effect does repeated light underburning have on long-term productivity in immature ponderosa pine stands?

A: It should have little effect. There is some available literature on the general subject, e.g., Harvey et al. (1988a; see References).

Q: If I understood Kristiina Vogt (chapter 8 author) correctly, she implied that high utilization or whole-tree harvest may be beneficial at high elevations because it leaves the small, more nutrient-rich debris while alleviating the need for site preparation. Would you comment on this idea with respect to mixed conifer forests?

A: Within reason, there is considerable opportunity for "high utilization" in the Inland Northwest on the more productive conifer sites without undue negative impacts. However, whole-tree harvesting is another matter. It removes nutrient-rich small material and is not generally recommended for this ecosystem.

Q: *Armillaria*—are there data on success of a short rotation of nonhost tree species to eliminate this root rot?

A: I'm not familiar with any.

Q: Fire—isn't duration more important than maximum temperature in assessing fire effects?

A: Because there is a relatively predictable interaction between the two, either can be used to assess fire to some extent. However, with biological systems, either could be critical.

Q: Are mycorrhizae and dead wood like spotted owls and old growth? In other words, do we really know what is preferred habitat and what is required habitat?

A: Not yet, except in general terms. Importance of rotten wood in soils relative to mycorrhizae is conditioned by soil type and moisture at least. However, prudence demands we assume both are especially important on infertile, thin, skeletal soils characteristic of most of the Inland Northwest.

Q: In the Blue Mountains where ceanothus happens to be the most common N fixer found in our commercial forest base, in what plant community types would ceanothus tend not to colonize after a prescribed fire?

A: Where ceanothus seed was not in the soil before the burn, dependent on site history.

Q: Given a harsh, ponderosa pine/Douglas-fir site, if natural regeneration were the objective, would a light underburn cause much more of a nitrogen depletion than lopping and scattering?

A: Light underburning should be a viable option with minimal N loss. Can it be kept light and still achieve prescription for seedbed? That remains the question. The use of heavy machinery for lopping and scattering suggests potential for compaction.

Q: When we have selectively harvested timber or managed for advance regeneration in the past, root pathogens have become a major concern. Do you feel that it is possible to manage on fir sites in this manner, as Vogt (chapter 8) and Franklin (chapter 6) have encouraged, without significant losses to root pathogens?

A: Perhaps, if specifications can be met. However, it probably is more difficult in Inland ecosystems, and there are good alternative species Inland. In heavily damaged systems in the northern Rocky Mountains, success would be unlikely.

Q: A couple of observations in the literature have correlated presence of *Armillaria* with presence of 2,4-D killed roots of species that have been controlled serving as substrate. Can you comment?

A: Because *Armillaria* is quick to capitalize on available substrate (such as killed root systems) and has an extremely wide host range, this is not surprising. There is at least one instance in the northern Rocky Mountains where birch control by herbicides in a cedar plantation may have increased *Armillaria* populations, with no damage to cedar yet. Herbicides probably have no direct link, but it's not impossible.

Q: On dry pumice soils in central Oregon where decomposition of residue and soil wood is slow, is the presence of small and large woody debris important for N fixation?

A: Likely not as much as on more moderate sites. Although pines seem better adapted to low OM environments, our observations indicate they will respond favorably to OM. So, why not manage for building up organic reserves? Productivity of these limited sites should be enhanced.

Q: Often said: "When planting, scarification should be limited." What kind of scarification are you talking about? How deep? Are you including disking to a depth of 5–10 in.?

A: What do you need for success? Apply no more scarification than required. Accelerated decay will increase exposure of mineral soil the first season. Let silviculture determine need, and do no more than the minimum required for the job.

Q: Legumes as N fixers—review briefly the rates of fixation for some of the endemic legumes relative to the more popular shrubs such as ceanothus.

A: Rates of fixation are highly variable, from substantial inputs to depletion. Variation is significant within species, among sites, and at different times of year. There is a relatively rich literature, including several books.

Q: Have there been any studies of the effect of chemical vegetation control on the mycorrhiza activity on or near soil surface in the early spring?

A: Not directly. However, there have been studies on the effect of herbicidal weed control in nursery management. These studies suggest that detrimental effects of herbicide application to conifers are rare.

Q: Both Kristiina Vogt (chapter 8) and you recommend avoiding entry when stand conditions are such that regeneration may be difficult to achieve. What do you recommend as viable arguments to justify no entry, given land base and allowable cut pressures on managers? And do data exist that support removal of particular site types from the land base?

A: Because regeneration is required in 5 years, regeneration probability seems a strong argument. So is maintaining productivity, until more predictable methods of dealing with problems characterizing sensitive areas are developed. In most cases there is not a good enough data base to make strong arguments. We hope better management records and an improving research base will alleviate the problem in the future. Meanwhile, the power of persuasion is our best, if largely ineffective, ally.

Q: Are there shrub species that can be used to stock a site infected with root-rot diseases to help rid that site of those pathogens?

A: There has been some hope that alder or perhaps other N fixers might be of some value. At this time, reported results are not encouraging. In the future, we believe that effects of certain plants or microbes may be of value.

Q: How long does it take for a site to cleanse itself of root diseases (after harvest)?

A: In the case of *Phellinus,* probably a rotation. But *Armillaria,* with its wide host range, is probably a natural component of many ecosystems with a recycling function. This may be true of some other root-rot organisms as well. It is not so important to "cleanse" a site of such organisms as to work within their limitations so they are not "recycling" what we are trying to produce.

Q: How did northern Idaho reduce planting costs 40% by not doing any site preparation?

A: Harvest action does some site preparation. The point is that nothing extra was done if seedlings were planted, if planting was prompt, and if there were no obvious problems (competition, etc.). So all costs associated with postharvest site preparation designed specifically to establish new seedlings were not incurred. District silviculture staff estimated the saving at about 40%.

Q: Are site-preparation costs *included* as part of planting costs? Are you carrying these as part of the new stand?

A: Yes.

Q: How does large-animal grazing affect the N capital, and amount and distribution of mycorrhizae?

A: I'm not familiar with any studies on this subject. I would estimate that effects would be minimal, if intensity is not otherwise damaging to vegetation and soils (trampling, compaction, etc.). However, insect grazing does have major effects on the cycling of N and other nutrients.

Q: What do you mean by the term "mound" as a site-preparation method?

A: Creating spots with high OM and low bulk density for planting seedlings, generally shaped as a low mound. This technique has been used in the Southeast for cold-air and water drainage. We used it to selectively alter planting sites to optimize soil conditions for early seedling growth. It should be noted that this method has not been widely used in the West and is not without risk on at least some soils.

Q: The Idaho Batholith contains some of the harshest sites in the interior forests. Would you alter management recommendations (i.e., burning, site preparation) on these types of sites?

A: Because of their instability, these soils are being handled with more care than most. Presumably as a result of downslope movement, they also seem less developed from the standpoint of horizonation. In any case, as would be true of any harsh site, the "light touch" seems the most prudent approach.

Q: What is your estimation of percent OM lost because of oxidation after clearcutting?

A: A few percent, depending on utilization intensity and other factors. Actual soil OM can increase after harvest: see Nielsen-Gerhardt (1986).

Q: Reducing fuel hazard is often coupled with site preparation and slash treatment. Fire management is concerned with large buildup of fuels that pose high potential for wildfire. Would you recommend treating or leaving the slash fuels?

A: Because extremely hot fires can virtually eliminate OM reserves and N stores (see Niehoff 1985), risk of hot wildfires is a legitimate concern with regard to long-term productivity. As always, the situation contains trade-offs. Organic reserves represent both fertility and, as fuels, danger to fertility.

Do not create a wildfire hazard in the name of increasing fertility. If you lose the bet, the cost can be high. Again, look at results in Niehoff (1985).

REFERENCES

Ballard, R. 1978. Effect of slash and soil removal on the productivity of second rotation radiata pine on a pumice soil. *New Zealand Journal of Forest Science* 8:248–258.

Barger, R. L. (technical coordinator). 1980. *Environmental consequences of timber harvesting in Rocky Mountain coniferous forests.* Symposium proceedings, September 11–14, 1979, Missoula. General Technical Report INT-90. Ogden, Utah: Intermountain Forest and Range Experiment Station, USDA Forest Service.

Boerner, R. E. 1982. Fire and nutrient cycling in temperate ecosystems. *BioScience* 32:187–192.

Bosworth, B. 1988. "Height growth and height analysis of selected trees in regenerating clearcuts." In *Prescribed fire in the Intermountain region: forest site preparation and range improvement,* coordinated by L. F. Neuenschwander and D. W. Breuer. Silviculture Symposium Proceedings, March 3–5, 1986, Spokane. Pullman, Wash.: Washington State University. (In press).

Boyd, R. J. 1986. "'Spot' herbicide treatments for site preparation and conifer release—a viable alternative to aerial broadcast application on many sites." In *Weed control for forest productivity,* edited by D. M. Baumgartner, R. J. Boyd, D. W. Breuer, and D. L. Miller, 105–106. Pullman, Wash.: Cooperative Extension Service, Washington State University.

Brendemuehl, R. H. 1967. *Loss of topsoil slows slash pine seedling growth in Florida sandhills.* Research Note S0-53. New Orleans, La. Southern Forest Experiment Station, USDA Forest Service.

Breuer, D. W. 1989. "Harvest impacts on the productivity of ponderosa pine forests." In *Ponderosa pine: the species and its management,* coordinated by J. E. Lotan and D. A. Baumgartner. Symposium, September 29-October 2, 1987. Pullman, Wash.: Washington State University. (In press).

Burger, J. A., and W. L. Pritchett. 1979. "Clearcut harvesting and site preparation can dramatically decrease nutrient reserves of a forest site." In *Impact of intensive harvesting on forest nutrient cycling: symposium proceedings,* edited by A. L. Leaf, 393. Syracuse, N.Y.: State University of New York.

Carlson, G. W. 1974. *Malheur National Forest soil resource inventory.* Portland, Ore.: Pacific Northwest Region, USDA Forest Service. (Atlas of maps, separate document).

_____ . 1979. *Winema National Forest soil resource inventory.* Portland, Ore.: Pacific Northwest Region, USDA Forest Service. (Maps included).

Chapin, F. S., III. 1980. The mineral nutrition of wild plants. *Annual Review of Ecological Systems* 11:233–260.

Chapin, F. S., III, P. M. Vitousek, and K. Van Cleve. 1986. The nature of nutrient limitation in plant communities. *American Naturalist* 127:48–58.

Clayton, J. L., G. Kellogg, and N. Forrester. 1987. *Soil disturbance-tree growth relations in central Idaho clearcuts.* Research Note INT-372. Ogden, Utah: Intermountain Forest and Range Experiment Station, USDA Forest Service.

Clayton, J. L., and D. A. Kennedy. 1985. Nutrient losses from timber harvest in the Idaho Batholith. *Soil Science Society of America Journal* 49:1041–1049.

Cochran, P. H. 1971. *Pumice particle bridging and nutrient levels affect lodgepole and ponderosa pine seedling development.* Research Note PNW-150. Portland, Ore.: Pacific Northwest Forest and Range Experiment Station, USDA Forest Service.

_____ . 1972. Temperature and soil fertility affect lodgepole and ponderosa pine seedling growth. *Forest Science* 18:132–134.

_____ . 1973. *Natural regeneration of lodgepole pine in south-central Oregon.* Research Note PNW-204. Portland, Ore.: Pacific Northwest Forest and Range Experiment Station, USDA Forest Service.

_____ . 1975. "Soil temperatures and natural forest regeneration in south-central Oregon." In *Proceedings, 4th North American forest soils Conference,* edited by B. Bernier and C. H. Winget, 37–52. Quebec, Canada: Les Presses de l'Université Laval.

_____ . 1985. "Soils and productivity of lodgepole pine." In *Lodgepole pine, the species and its management,* edited by D. M. Baumgartner, R. G. Krebill, J. T. Arnott, and G. F. Weetman, 89–93. Pullman, Wash.: Washington State University.

Cochran, P. H., and T. Brock. 1985. *Soil compaction and initial height growth of planted ponderosa pine.* Research Note PNW-434. Portland, Ore.: Pacific Northwest Forest and Range Experiment Station, USDA Forest Service.

Cole, D. M., and W. C. Schmidt. 1986. *Site treatments influence first 25 years' development of mixed conifers in Montana.* Research Paper INT-364. Ogden, Utah: Intermountain Forest and Range Experiment Station, USDA Forest Service.

Cramer, O. P. (technical editor). 1974. *Environmental effects of forest residues management in the Pacific Northwest, a state-of-knowledge compendium.* Portland, Ore.: Pacific Northwest Forest and Range Experiment Station, USDA Forest Service.

Daubenmire, R., and J. B. Daubenmire. 1968. *Forest vegetation of eastern Washington and northern Idaho.* Technical Bulletin 60. Pullman, Wash.: Washington Agricultural Experiment Station.

Debyle, N. V. 1980. "Harvesting and site treatment influences on the nutrient status of lodgepole pine forests in western Wyoming." In *Environmental consequences of timber harvesting in Rocky Mountain coniferous forests,* 137–156. General Technical Report INT-90. Ogden, Utah: Intermountain Forest and Range Experiment Station, USDA Forest Service.

Donaldson, N., and J. T. DeFrancesco. 1982. *Soil survey of Stevens County, Washington.* Spokane, Wash.: Soil Conservation Service, USDA Forest Service. (Maps included).

Donnelly, J. R., and J. B. Shane. 1986. Forest ecosystem responses to artificially induced soil compaction. 1. Soil physical properties and vegetation. *Canadian Journal of Forest Research* 16:750–754.

Dyrness, C. T., and C. T. Youngberg. 1966. Soil-vegetation relationships within the ponderosa pine type in the central Oregon pumice region. *Ecology* 47:122–138.

Entry, J. A., N. E. Martin, K. Cromack, Jr., and S. G. Stafford. 1986. Light and nutrient limitation in *Pinus monticola:* seedling susceptibility to *Armillaria* infection. *Forest Ecology and Management* 17:189–198.

Eramian, A., and L. Neuenschwander. 1989. "Comparison of broadcast burn vs. dozer site preparation methods on the growth of bareroot Douglas-fir seedlings." In *Prescribed fire in the Intermountain region: forest site preparation and range improvement.* Silviculture Symposium Proceedings, March 3–5, 1986, Spokane. Pullman, Wash.: Washington State University. (In press).

Fellin, D. G. 1980. "A review of some relationships of harvesting, residue management and fire to forest insects and disease." In *Environmental consequences of timber harvesting in Rocky Mountain coniferous forests,* coordinated by R. L. Barger, 287–316. Symposium Proceedings, September 11–14, 1979, Missoula. General Technical Report INT-90. Ogden, Utah: Intermountain Forest and Range Experiment Station, USDA Forest Service.

Filip, G. W. 1977. An *Armillaria* epiphytotic on the Winema National Forest, Oregon. *Plant Disease Reporter* 61:708–711.

Filip, G. W., and D. J. Goheen. 1982. Tree mortality caused by root pathogen complex in Deschutes National

Forest, Oregon. *Plant Disease* 66:240–243.

Flinn, D. W., R. O. Squire, and P. W. Farrell. 1980. The role of organic matter in the maintenance of site productivity in sand soils. *New Zealand Journal of Forestry* 25:229–236.

Fowler, W. B., and J. D. Helvey. 1981. *Soil and air temperature and biomass after residue treatment.* Research Note PNW-383. Portland, Ore.: Pacific Northwest Forest and Range Experiment Station, USDA Forest Service.

Froehlich, H. A. 1979. Soil compaction from logging equipment: effects on growth of young ponderosa pine. *Journal of Soil and Water Conservation* 34:276–278.

Froehlich, H. A., and D. H. McNabb. 1984. "Minimizing soil compaction in Pacific Northwest forests." In *Forest soil treatment impacts,* edited by E. L. Stone, 159–192. Knoxville, Tenn.: Department of Forestry, Wildlife, and Fisheries, University of Tennessee.

Froehlich, H. A., and D. W. R. Miles. 1984. Winged subsoiler tills compacted forest soil. *Forest Industries,* February.

Froehlich, H. A., D. W. R. Miles, and R. W. Robbins. 1985. Soil bulk density recovery in compacted skid trails in central Idaho. *Soil Science Society of America Journal* 49:1015–1017.

Gates, D. M. 1980. *Biophysical Ecology.* New York: Springer-Verlag.

Geist, J. M. 1977. Nitrogen response relationships of some volcanic ash soils. *Soil Science Society of America Journal* 41:996–1000.

Geist, J. M., J. W. Hazard, and K. W. Seidel. 1988. *Assessing physical conditions of some Pacific Northwest volcanic ash soils after forest harvest.* Unpublished Report. J. B. Geist, LaGrande, Ore.

Geist, J. M., and G. S. Strickler. 1970. *Chemical characteristics of some forest and grassland soils of northeastern Oregon. I. Results from reference profile sampling on the Starky Experimental Forest and Range.* Research Note PNW-137. Portland, Ore.: Pacific Northwest Forest and Range Experiment Station, USDA Forest Service.

Geist, J. M., and G. S. Strickler. 1978. *Physical and chemical properties of some Blue Mountain soils in northeastern Oregon.* Research Paper PNW-236. Portland, Ore.: Pacific Northwest Forest and Range Experiment Station, USDA Forest Service.

Greacen, E. L., and R. Sands. 1980. Compaction of forest soils: a review. *Australian Journal of Soil Research* 18:163–189.

Graham, R. T., A. E. Harvey, and M. F. Jurgensen. 1989. "Site preparation strategies for artificial regeneration: can prescribed burning fill the bill?" In *Prescribed fire in the Intermountain region: forest site preparation and range improvement.* Symposium Proceedings, March 3–5, 1986, Spokane. Pullman, Wash.: Cooperative Extension Service, Washington State University. (In press).

Hadfield, J. S. 1985. *Laminated root rot: a guide for reducing and preventing losses in Oregon and Washington forests.* Portland, Ore.: Forest Pest Management, Pacific Northwest Region, USDA Forest Service.

Haines, L. W., R. E. Maki, and S. G. Sanderford. 1975. "The effect of mechanical site preparation treatments on soil productivity and tree growth." In *Proceedings, 4th North American forest soils conference,* edited by B. Bernier and C. H. Winget, 379–395. Quebec, Canada: Les Presses de l' Université Laval.

Hall, F. C. 1973. *Plant communities of the Blue Mountains in eastern Oregon and southwestern Washington.* Portland, Ore.: Pacific Northwest Region, USDA Forest Service.

Hardison, J. R. 1976. Fire and flame for plant disease control. *Annual Review of Phytopathology* 14:355–379.

Harmon, M. E., J. F. Franklin, F. J. Swanson, P. Sollins, S. V. Gregory, J. D. Lattin, N. H. Anderson, S. P. Cline, N. G. Aumen, J. R. Sedell, G. W. Lienkaemper, K. Cromack, Jr., and K. W. Cummins. 1986. The ecology of coarse woody debris in temperate ecosystems. *Advances in Ecological Research* 15:133–202.

Harvey, A. E. 1982. "The importance of residual organic debris in site preparation and amelioration for reforestation." In *Site preparation and fuels management on steep terrain,* 75–85. Symposium Proceedings, February 15–17, 1982, Spokane. Pullman, Wash.: Cooperative Extension Service, Washington State University.

Harvey, A. E., M. F. Jurgensen, and R. T. Graham. 1989a. "Fire-soil interactions governing site productivity in the northern Rocky Mountains." In *Prescribed fire in the Intermountain region: Forest site preparation and range improvement.* Symposium Proceedings, March 3–5, 1986, Spokane. Pullman, Wash.: Cooperative Extension Service, Washington State University. (In press).

Harvey, A. E., M. F. Jurgensen, and R. T. Graham. 1988b. "Role of woody residues in the soil of ponderosa pine forests." In *Ponderosa pine: the species and its management.* Symposium Proceedings, September 29-October 2, 1987. Pullman, Wash.: Washington State University. (In press).

Harvey, A. E., M. F. Jurgensen, and M. J. Larsen. 1976. *Intensive fiber utilization and prescribed fire: effects on the microbial ecology of forests.* General Technical Report INT-28. Ogden, Utah: Intermountain Forest and Range Experiment Station, USDA Forest Service.

Harvey, A. E., M. F. Jurgensen, and M. J. Larsen. 1987a. "Residues, beneficial microbes, diseases, and soil management in cool, east slope, Rocky Mountain lodgepole pine ecosystems." In *Management of small-stem stands of lodgepole pine—workshop proceedings,* 137–149. General Technical Report INT-237. Ogden, Utah: Intermountain Forest and Range Experiment Station, USDA Forest Service.

Harvey, A. E., M. F. Jurgensen, M. J. Larsen, and R. T. Graham. 1987b. *Decaying organic materials and soil quality in the Inland Northwest: a management opportunity.* General Technical Report INT-225. Ogden, Utah: Intermountain Forest and Range Experiment Station, USDA Forest Service.

Harvey, A. E., M. J. Larsen, and M. F. Jurgensen. 1979a. Comparative distribution of ectomycorrhizae in soils of three western Montana forest habitat types. *Forest Science* 25:350–360.

Harvey, A. E., M. J. Larsen, and M. F. Jurgensen. 1979b. *Fire-decay: interactive roles regulating wood accumulation and soil development in the northern Rocky Mountains.* Research Note INT-263. Ogden, Utah: Intermountain Forest and Range Experiment Station, USDA Forest Service.

Hayes, G. I. 1970. "Impacts of fire on forested ecosystems." In *The role of fire in the Intermountain West,* 99–118. Missoula, Mont.: Intermountain Fire Research Council.

Hazard, J. W., and J. M. Geist. 1984. "Sampling forest soil conditions to assess impacts of management activities." In *Forest soils and treatment impacts,* edited by E. Stone, 421–430. Proceedings of the 6th North American Forest Soils Conference, June 1983. Knoxville, Tenn.: University of Tennessee.

Helms, J. A., C. Hipkin, and E. B. Alexander. 1986. Effects of soil compaction on height growth of a California ponderosa pine plantation. *Western Journal of Applied Forestry* 1:104–108.

Hobbs, S. D., and A. D. Partridge. 1979. Wood decays, root rots and stand composition along an elevation gradient. *Forest Science* 25:31–42.

Howes, S. W., J. Hazard, and J. M. Geist. 1983. *Guidelines for sampling some physical conditions of surface soils.* R6-RWM-146. Portland, Ore.: Pacific Northwest Region, USDA Forest Service.

Hungerford, R. D., and R. E. Babbitt. 1987. *Overstory removal and residue treatments affect soil surface, air, and soil temperature: implications for seedling survival.* Research Paper INT-377. Ogden, Utah: Intermountain Research Station, USDA Forest Service.

James, R. L., C. A. Stewart, and R. E. Williams. 1984. Estimating root disease losses in northern Rocky Mountain National Forests. *Canadian Journal of Forest Research* 14:652–655.

James, R. L., C. A. Stewart, R. E. Williams, and J. W. Byler. 1982. Root disease mortality of northern Rocky Mountain conifers. *Phytopathology* 72:966 (abstract).

Johnson, C. G., and S. Simon. 1987. *Plant associations of the Wallowa-Snake Province, Wallowa-Whitman National Forest.* R6-ECOL-TP-255B-86. Portland, Ore.: Pacific Northwest Region, USDA Forest Service.

Jurgensen, M. F., S. F. Arno, A. E. Harvey, M. J. Larsen, and R. D. Pfister. 1979a. "Symbiotic and nonsymbiotic nitrogen fixation in northern Rocky Mountain forest ecosystems." In *Symbiotic nitrogen fixation in the management of temperate forests,* edited by J. C. Gordon, C. T. Wheeler, and D. A. Perry, 294–308. Corvallis, Ore.: Forest Research Laboratory, Oregon State University.

Jurgensen, M. F., A. E. Harvey, and M. J. Larsen. 1981. *Effects of prescribed fire on soil nitrogen levels in a cut-over Douglas-fir/western larch forest.* Research Paper INT-275. Ogden, Utah: Intermountain Forest and Range Experiment Station, USDA Forest Service.

Jurgensen, M. F., M. J. Larsen, and A. E. Harvey. 1979b. *Forest soil biology-timber harvesting relationships: a perspective.* General Technical Report INT-69. Ogden, Utah: Intermountain Forest and Range Experiment Station, USDA Forest Service.

Klock, G. O., and C. C. Grier. 1981. "Effects of fire on the long-term maintenance of forest productivity." In *Proceedings of a forest fertilization conference,* 247–250. September 27, 1979. Seattle, Wash.: University of Washington.

Kracht, R. L. 1985. "Site preparation—the light touch." In *Proceedings of the national silvicultural workshop,* 109–124. May 13–16, 1985, Rapid City, S. Dak. Washington, D.C.: USDA Forest Service.

Kulhavy, D. L., A. D. Partridge, and R. W. Stark. 1984. Root diseases and blister rust associated with bark beetles (Coleoptera: Scolytidae) in western white pine in Idaho. *Environmental Entomology* 13:813–817.

Landsberg, J. D., P. H. Cochran, M. M. Finck, and R. E. Martin. 1984. *Foliar nitrogen content and tree growth after prescribed fire in ponderosa pine.* Research Note PNW-412. Portland, Ore.: Pacific Northwest Forest and Range Experiment Station, USDA Forest Service.

Larsen, M. J., M. F. Jurgensen, and A. E. Harvey. 1978. Nitrogen fixation associated with wood decayed by some common fungi in western Montana. *Canadian Journal of Forest Research* 8:341–345.

Larson, D. M. 1976. *Deschutes National Forest soil resource inventory.* Portland, Ore.: Pacific Northwest Region, USDA Forest Service. (Atlas of maps, separate document).

Leaf, A. L. (technical coordinator). 1979. *Impact of intensive harvesting on forest nutrient cycling.* Symposium Proceedings, August 13–16, 1979, Syracuse. Syracuse, N.Y.: College of Environmental Science and

Forestry, State University of New York.

Levitt, J. 1980. *Responses of Plants to Environmental Stresses.* 2nd ed. New York: Academic Press.

Lotan, J. E., M. E. Alexander, S. F. Arno, R. E. French, O. G. Langdon, R. M. Loomis, R. A. Norum, R. C. Rothermel, W. C. Schmidt, and J. V. Wagtendonk. 1981. *Effects of fire on flora.* General Technical Report WO-16. Washington, D.C.: USDA Forest Service.

Lotan, J. E., and D. A. Perry. 1983. *Ecology and regeneration of lodgepole pine.* Agriculture Handbook No. 606. Washington, D.C.: USDA Forest Service.

Maser, C., and J. M. Trappe. 1984. *The seen and unseen world of the fallen tree.* General Technical Report PNW-164. Portland, Ore.: Pacific Northwest Forest and Range Experiment Station, USDA Forest Service.

McDonald, G. E., N. E. Martin, and A. E. Harvey 1987a. *Occurrence of* Armillaria *in the northern Rocky Mountains.* Research Paper INT-381. Ogden, Utah: Intermountain Research Station, USDA Forest Service.

McDonald, G. E., N. E. Martin, and A. E. Harvey. 1987b. Armillaria *in the northern Rockies: pathogenicity and host susceptibility on pristine and disturbed sites.* Research Paper INT-371. Ogden, Utah: Intermountain Research Station, USDA Forest Service.

McNabb, D. H., J. M. Geist, and C. T. Youngberg. 1979. "Nitrogen fixation by *Ceanothus velutinus* in northern Oregon." In *Symbiotic nitrogen fixation in the management of temperate forests,* edited by J. C. Gordon, C. T. Wheeler, and D. A. Perry, 481–482. Corvallis, Ore.: Forest Research Laboratory, Oregon State University.

Miller, D. L. 1984. *Effects of site preparation by burning and dozer scarification on seedling performance.* Forestry Technical Paper TP-84–1. Lewiston, Idaho: Wood Products, Western Division, Potlatch Corp.

Miller, D. L., and D. Breuer. 1988. "Site preparation method affects white pine and Douglas-fir seedling growth." In *Prescribed fire in the Intermountain region: forest site preparation and range improvement.* Silviculture Symposium Proceedings, March 3–5, 1986, Spokane. Pullman, Wash.: Washington State University. (In press).

Minore D. 1979. *Comparative autecological characteristics of northwestern tree species—a literature review.* General Technical Report PNW-87. Portland, Ore.: Pacific Northwest Forest and Range Experiment Station, USDA Forest Service.

———. 1986. *Effects of site preparation on seedling growth: a preliminary comparison of broadcast burning and pile burning.* Research Note PNW-452. Portland, Ore.: Pacific Northwest Forest and Range Experiment Station, USDA Forest Service.

Niehoff, G. J. 1985. *Effects of clearcutting and varying severity of prescribed burning on levels of organic matter and the mineralization of ammonium nitrogen in the surface layer of forest soils.* M.S. Thesis. Moscow, Idaho: University of Idaho.

Nielsen-Gerhardt, M. 1986. *Effects of logging and mechanical site preparation on levels of mineralizable nitrogen and organic matter in forest soils.* M.S. Thesis. Moscow, Idaho: University of Idaho.

Olsen, J. S. 1963. Energy storage and the balance of producers and decomposers in ecological systems. *Ecology* 44:322–331.

Paulson, D. J. 1977. *Ochoco National Forest resource inventory.* Portland, Ore.: Pacific Northwest Region, USDA Forest Service. (Maps included).

Perry, D. A., M. M. Meyer, D. Egeland, S. L. Rose, and D. Pilz. 1982. Seedling growth and mycorrhizal formation in clearcut and adjacent, undisturbed soils in Montana: a greenhouse bioassay. *Forest Ecology and Management* 4:261–273.

Perry, D. A., and J. Norgren. 1983. "Impact of biomass harvest on soil nutrient loss." In *Generating electricity with wood and solid wastes in southern Oregon,* edited by D. A. Perry, 56–68. Research Bulletin 40. Corvallis, Ore.: Forest Research Laboratory, Oregon State University.

Perry, D. A., and S. L. Rose. 1989. "Productivity of forest lands as affected by site preparation." In *Proceedings, California conference on forest nutrition,* edited by R. Powers and T. Robson. General Technical Report. Berkeley, Calif.: Pacific Southwest Forest and Range Experiment Station, USDA Forest Service. (In press).

Pfister, R. D., B. L. Kovalchik, S. F. Arno, and R. C. Presby. 1977. *Forest habitat types of Montana.* General Technical Report INT-34. Ogden, Utah: Intermountain Forest and Range Experiment Station, USDA Forest Service.

Powers, R. F., J. Klemmedson, and S. Webster. 1989. "Nutrition and fertilization of ponderosa pine." In *Ponderosa pine: the species and its management.* Symposium, September 29–October 2, 1987. Pullman, Wash.: Washington State University. (In press).

Raison, R. J. 1979. Modifications of the soil environment by vegetation fires, with particular reference to nitrogen transformations: a review. *Plant and Soil* 51:73–108.

Rehfeldt, G. E. 1979. Ecological adaptations in Douglas-fir (*Pseudotsuga menziesii* var. *glauca*) populations. I. North Idaho and northeastern Washington. *Heredity* 43:383–397.

———. 1982. Differentiation of *Larix occidentalis* populations from the northern Rocky Mountains. *Silvae*

Genetica 31:13–19.

———. 1983. Adaptation of *Pinus contorta* populations in heterogeneous environments in north Idaho. *Canadian Journal of Forest Research* 13:405–411.

———. 1986. Adaptive variation in *Pinus ponderosa* from Intermountain regions. I. Snake and Salmon River basins. *Forest Science* 32:79–92.

Rehfeldt, G. E., R. J. Hoff, and R. J. Steinhoff. 1981. Geographic patterns of genetic variation in *Pinus monticola. Botanical Gazette* 145:229–239.

Ross, D. W., W. Scott, R. L. Heninger, and J. D. Walstad. 1986. Effects of site preparation on ponderosa pine (*Pinus ponderosa*), associated vegetation, and soil properties in south central Oregon. *Canadian Journal of Forest Research* 16:612–618.

Ross, D. W., and J. D. Walstad. 1986. *Vegetative competition, site preparation, and pine performance: a literature review with reference to south-central Oregon.* Research Bulletin 58. Corvallis, Ore.: Forest Research Laboratory, Oregon State University.

Routledge, R. D. 1987. The impact of soil degradation on the expected present net worth of future timber harvests. *Forest Science* 33:823–834.

Ryan, K. C., and N. V. Noste. 1985. "Evaluating prescribed fires." In *Symposium and workshop on wilderness fire*, coordinated by J. E. Lotan, B. M. Kilgore, W. C. Fischer, and R. W. Mutch, 230–238. Symposium Proceedings, November 15–18, 1983, Missoula. General Technical Report INT-182. Ogden, Utah: Intermountain Forest and Range Experiment Station, USDA Forest Service.

Sachs, D., and P. Sollins. 1986. Potential effects of management practices on nitrogen nutrition and long-term productivity of western hemlock stands. *Forest Ecology and Management* 17:25–36.

Shaw, C. G., III, A. R. Stage, and T. M. Webb. 1985. Development of a root disease subroutine for use with stand growth models of western forests. In *Proceedings, 33rd annual western international forest disease work conference*, 48–54. September 24–27, Olympia, Wash. Corvallis, Ore.: Oregon State University.

Sheilds, W. J., and S. D. Hobbs. 1979. Soil nutrient levels and pH associated with *Armillariella mellea* on conifers in northern Idaho. *Canadian Journal of Forest Research* 9:45–48.

Smeltzer, D. L. K., D. R. Bergdahl, and J. R. Donnelly. 1986. Forest ecosystem responses to artificially induced soil compaction. II. Selected soil microorganism populations. *Canadian Journal of Forest Research* 16:870–872.

Stark, N. 1982. The impacts of logging and burning on soil fertility. *Canadian Journal of Forest Research* 12:679–686.

Stark, N., and C. Spitzner. 1985. Xylem sap analysis for determining the nutrient status and growth of *Pinus ponderosa. Canadian Journal of Forest Research* 15:783–790.

Stark, H., C. Spitzner, and D. Essing. 1985. Xylem sap analysis for determining the nutritional status of *Pseudotsuga menziesii. Canadian Journal of Forest Research* 15:429–437.

Terry, T. A., and R. G. Campbell. 1981. "Soil management considerations in intensive forest management." In *Proceedings of the symposium on engineering systems for forest regeneration*, 98–106. March, 2–6, 1981, Raleigh, N.C. ASAE Publication 10–81. St. Joseph, Mich.: American Society of Agricultural Engineers.

Thies, W. G. 1984. Laminated root rot: the quest for control. *Journal of Forestry* 82:345–356.

Thies, W. G., and K. W. Russell. 1984. "Controlling root rots in coniferous forests of northwestern North America." In *Proceedings of the 6th international conference on root rots and butt rots of forest trees*, edited by G. A. Kile, 379–386. Queensland, Australia.

Tiedemann, A. R. 1981. "Stream chemistry, nutrient economy, and site productivity consequences of wildland management and wildfire." In *Symposium, Interior West watershed management*, edited by D. M. Baumgartner, 182–201. April 8–9, Spokane. Pullman, Wash.: Cooperative Extension Service, Washington State University.

Tiedemann, A. R., J. D. Helvey, and T. D. Anderson. 1978. Stream chemistry and watershed nutrient economy following wildfire and fertilization in eastern Washington. *Journal of Environmental Quality* 7:580–588.

Tkacz, B. M., and R. F. Schmitz. 1986. *Association of an endemic mountain pine beetle population with lodgepole pine infected by* Armillaria *root disease in Utah.* Research Note INT-353. Ogden, Utah: Intermountain Research Station, USDA Forest Service.

USDA Forest Service. 1983. *Soil monitoring report, best shot timber sale.* Administrative Report. Colville, Wash.: Colville National Forest.

———. 1984. *Root disease-caused losses in the commercial coniferous forests of the western United States.* Report 84–5. Fort Collins, Colo.: Forest Pest Management, Methods Applications Group.

———. 1985. *Management guidelines for ash soils in the Blue Mountains.* Technical Report. Portland, Ore.: Pacific Northwest Region.

Van Cleve, K., O. W. Heal, and D. Roberts. 1985. Bioassay of forest floor nitrogen supply for plant growth.

Canadian Journal of Forest Research 16:1320–1326.

Vogt, K. A., C. Grier, E. Meir, and M. R. Keyes. 1983. Organic matter and nutrient dynamics in forest floors of young and mature *Abies amabalis* stands in western Washington as affected by fine root input. *Ecological Monographs* 53:139–157.

Volland, L. 1985. *Plant associations of the central Oregon pumice zone.* R6-ECOL-104-1985. Portland, Ore.: Pacific Northwest Region, USDA Forest Service.

Vora, R. S. 1988. Potential soil compaction forty years after logging in northern California. *Great Basin Naturalist* 48:117–120.

Wargo, P. M., and C. G. Shaw III. 1985. *Armillaria* root rot: the puzzle is being solved. *Plant Disease* 69:826–832.

Waring, R. H. 1985. Imbalanced forest ecosystems: assessments and consequences. *Forest Ecology and Management* 12:93–112.

————. 1987. Characteristics of trees predisposed to die. *BioScience* 37:569–574.

Weber, M. G., I. R. Methven, and C. E. Van Wagner. 1985. The effect of forest floor manipulation on nitrogen status and tree growth in an eastern Ontario jack pine stand. *Canadian Journal of Forest Research* 15:313–318.

Wellner, C. A. 1970. "Fire history in the northern Rocky Mountains." In *The role of fire in the Intermountain West,* 42–64. Symposium Proceedings, October 27–29, 1970, Missoula. Missoula, Mont.: University of Montana.

Wells, C. G., R. E. Campbell, L. F. Debano, C. E. Lewis, R. L. Fredriksen, E. C. Franklin, R. C. Froelich, and P. H. Dunn. 1979. *Effects of fire on soil.* General Technical Report WO-1. Washington, D.C.: USDA Forest Service.

Wenzel, D. L. 1979. *Fremont National Forest soil resource inventory.* Portland, Ore.: Pacific Northwest Region, USDA Forest Service. (Maps included).

Williams, R. E., and M. A. Marsden. 1982. Modeling probability of root disease center occurrence in northern Idaho forests. *Canadian Journal of Forest Research* 12:876–882.

Witcosky, J. J., and E. M. Hansen. 1985. Root-colonizing insects recovered from Douglas-fir in various stages of decline due to black-stain root disease. *Phytopathology* 75:399–402.

Youngberg, C. T., and C. T. Dyrness. 1959. The influence of soils and topography on the occurrence of lodgepole pine in central Oregon. *Northwest Science* 33:111–120.

Zavitkovski, J., and M. Newton. 1968. Ecological importance of snowbrush *Ceanothus velutinus* in the Oregon Cascades. *Ecology* 49:1134–1135.

Chapter 10

Maintaining Long-Term Forest Productivity in Southwest Oregon and Northern California

Thomas Atzet, Robert F. Powers, David H. McNabb,
Michael P. Amaranthus, and Edward R. Gross

ABSTRACT

The Southwest Oregon/Northern California Area differs from the rest of the Pacific Northwest in the age, composition, and variety of its rock types, its terrain, and its Mediterranean climate, which is hot and dry with a mix of oceanic and continental influences. This geology and climate combine to support endemic species not found elsewhere, a fire regime that limits stand age and organic capital, and some of the most, and least, productive forests in the world. Yet the effects of forest practices on long-term productivity do not differ in principle from those in any other area. Management of organic matter is paramount to maintaining productivity. However, quantifications from other areas do not apply. Rates of production, decomposition, and incorporation of organic matter differ, as do patterns of storage, input, and cycling. Opportunities for a variety of forest-management strategies are provided by site and species diversity. Maintaining long-term productivity in this area is a challenge to the creative resource manager.

INTRODUCTION

The Southwest Oregon/Northern California (SWO/NC) Area roughly forms a square between Coos Bay and Crater Lake to the north and Eureka and Redding to the south (Fig. 10.1). The Area comprises the Klamath Geological Province (about 60% of SWO/NC) and the southern Cascade Range, and the Cascade Geological Province, which lies to the east. The inland border of the Klamath Province abuts the Cascade Province at Redding, Medford, and Tiller. The Cascade Province ranges from Mt. Lassen to Mt. Thielsen but does not include the Sierra Nevada. These two Provinces are environmentally, geologically, and ecologically different from each other and generally are steeper, drier, and climatically more extreme than most of the rest of the Pacific Northwest.

The Area includes six National Forests (Rogue River, Umpqua, Siskiyou, Six Rivers, Klamath, and Shasta Trinity); the Medford, Roseburg, Coos Bay, and Ukiah Districts of the Bureau of Land Management; and state, county, and private forest lands, managed for a full range of forest products.

Although the SWO/NC Area has unproductive sites (dry, ultrabasic soils), biomass production is unsurpassed in coastal areas where temperatures are moderate and even. The climate is similar to that of coast redwood (*Sequoia* spp.) forests. Moreover, inland sites with deep soils and frequent summer fog or thundershowers have produced some of the highest volumes of Douglas-fir [*Pseudotsuga menziesii* (Mirb.) Franco] in the Pacific Northwest (Williamson and Staebler 1971). However, shrubs and hardwoods, considered serious competitors for resources (Gratkowski 1961) on productive sites, may in the long term reduce timber output. Thus, site preparation and vegetation management are often prescribed to prevent volume loss.

The complex geology and climate, which make prescribing management activities difficult, also support a rich variety of species, which provide a number of potential solutions to resource problems. In this chapter, we detail the varied environmental setting of SWO/NC and examine how management practices influence the long-term forest productivity of this unique area.

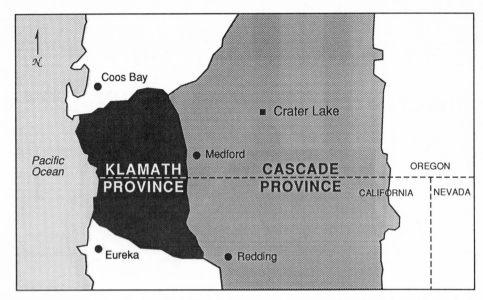

FIG. 10.1. The Southwest Oregon/Northern California Area, comprising the Klamath and Cascade Geological Provinces.

ENVIRONMENTAL SETTING

The Klamath Province

Geology. The Klamath Province is known for its variety of rock types and ages. Igneous and sedimentary rocks have been folded and faulted so intensively that the original nature of the rock often is masked. Formations decrease in age from east to west; the Condrey Mountain schists straddling the California-Oregon border southwest of Ashland are at least 200 million years old, whereas the Hunters Cove Formation, near coastal Gold Beach, is approximately 65 million years old.

Other metamorphic rocks are more common, but less distinct. Their composition relates to site productivity. For example, the Dothan Formation is largely sandstone, but varies from conglomerate to mudstone and, near the coast, includes volcanic rocks. Sites with mudstones and siltstones are generally more productive than those with conglomerates and volcanics. Composition is similar in the Applegate Formation. The differences in fertility and degree of fracturing affect root penetration, rates of soil weathering, stability, coarse-fragment content, and plantability.

Fertility, productivity, and stability often are linked to variations in mineralogy and geology. Granodiorites and ultrabasic peridotites and serpentinites represent mineralogic extremes. Sites with these rock types are the most difficult in the Area to manage. However, these rock types are easily recognized, and serpentinitic sites are not often classified as commercial forest. On the other hand, a significant percentage of silvicultural problems in SWO/NC are found on granodioritic sites, although this rock type occurs in just a small percentage of the Area.

Terrain. Although the Klamath Mountains are geologically old, their dendritic dissection pattern is characteristic of youthful terrain. Uplift periodically resets the base level of the drainages, and downcutting continues. Most surfaces are erosional rather than depositional, the natural rates of erosion varying with parent rock, slope steepness, and precipitation.

Landslides are the dominant erosional mechanism in the Klamath Mountains. Because much of the productive forest land is marginally stable, particularly where rainfall is high, management activities can accelerate landslide frequency (natural rates). Coastal granitics and sandstones, the most highly dissected materials, are easily eroded and prone to slippage during heavy rains. Finer grained metamorphosed sediments can also be a problem where the beds are tilted and faulting has weakened their structure. The implications for long-term productivity are significant (see the section on landslides later in this chapter).

The highest peaks are over 2,133 m, and the slopes are steep. Slopes of the Siskiyou Mountains, in the northern part of the Klamaths, average 39%, those of the north coastal area 50% (Atzet and Wheeler 1984).

Climate. Unlike the rest of the Pacific Northwest, SWO/NC has a Mediterranean climate, combining marine and continental weather. Marine influence extends about 80 km inland, to the coastal crest and up major drainages where cloud cover or fog lowers temperatures and evapotranspiration. Inland areas, on the other hand, generally are clear both day and night during the growing season. The clear nights allow long-wave radiation to escape into the upper atmosphere. Thus, early fall and late spring frosts shorten the growing season. Radiation loads make water the most limiting resource for survival and growth of trees except at higher elevations, where low temperatures are limiting.

Precipitation in the Klamath Province varies from 406 cm near the Coast Range crest to less than 76 cm near Grants Pass (Froehlich et al. 1982). In the central Klamath Province, about 17% of precipitation occurs between April and July as thundershowers (USDA Forest Service fire weather data, on file with the Siskiyou National Forest).

Summer temperatures in the interior valleys often reach 38°C where marine influence is lacking. However, extremes are significantly dampened inland where fog is frequent and persistent. Average August temperatures for Brookings and Grants Pass are about 15 and 21°C respectively.

Soils. The variety of soils reflects the diversity of climate, topography, and parent rock types (Table 10.1). Parent rock, depth, texture, and coarse-fragment content influence soil water-holding capacity and compactability, and therefore site productivity.

TABLE 10.1. Common soil series of the Klamath and Cascade Geological Provinces.

Soil series	Parent rock	Depth, cm	Texture class	Coarse-fragment content
		Klamath Province		
Althouse	Mixed metamorphic	50–100	Loam	Moderate
Beekman	Metavolcanic	50–100	Loam	Moderate
Deadwood	Mixed metamorphic	<50	Sandy loam	High
Josephine	Metasediment	50–150	Loam	High
Neuns	Mixed metamorphic	50–100	Loam	Moderate
Pearsoll	Ultrabasic	25–50	Clay loam	High
Siskiyou	Quartz diorite	50–100	Sandy loam	Low
		Cascade Province		
Freezener	Andesite/tuffs	150+	Loam	High
Rustler Pk.	Andesite	50–100	Sandy loam	Moderate
Alcot	Pumice/ash	150+	Sandy loam	High
Windy	Ash	100–150	Sandy loam	Moderate
McCarthy	Andesite/mudflow	50–100	Sandy loam	Moderate/high
Cohasset	Andesite/basalt	100–150	Loam	Low
Shasta	Ash	150+	Loamy sand	Low

The Pearsoll and Siskiyou series present some special problems. Pearsoll soils, derived from ultrabasic parent rock, often are unstable. Road and landing construction can cause mass soil movement. High coarse-fragment content and nutrient imbalances normally create severe tree-growth problems, making Pearsoll soils unsuitable for commercial forest production. Siskiyou soils, developed from acid-igneous rock, often are coarse textured and subject to erosion. As with pumice, fertility is inherently low, and surface soil disturbance could affect long-term productivity.

Vegetation. Species diversity is high and spatial pattern complex. Whittaker (1960) found the diversity to be comparable to that of the Smokey Mountains in the eastern U.S. The area supports 20 commercial conifer species and several commercial hardwood species as well as endemic trees with ranges limited to SWO/NC (Sawyer and Thornburgh 1977). Plant associations—identifiable portions of the environment with a unique management response—can be grouped into series, based on a common dominant climax species; these associations can be used to simplify an otherwise complex pattern. Figure 10.2 illustrates the elevational and geographical distribution of plant series within the Province. Productivity is highest, and sites are most diverse, in the mid-elevation series; high-elevation series are limited by temperature, low-elevation series by moisture.

Efforts are now underway to classify public and private lands into plant associations to help managers understand the productive potential and response to management activities (Sawyer et al. 1977, Atzet and Wheeler 1984, Atzet et al. 1986, Jimerson 1986).

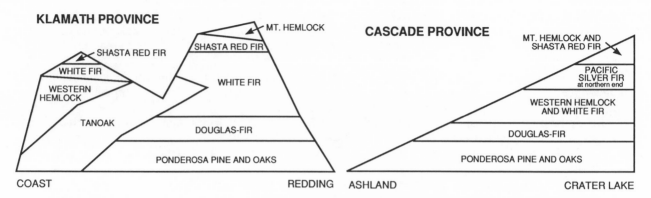

FIG. 10.2. Cross section of the relative distribution of major plant series of the Klamath and Cascade Geological Provinces along elevational and longitudinal gradients. Red fir (*Abies magnifica* A. Murr.), western hemlock [*Tsuga heterophylla* (Raf.) Sarg.], tanoak [*Lithocarpus densiflorus* (Hook. & Arn.) Rehd.], mountain hemlock [*Tsuga mertensiana* (Bong.) Carr.], Douglas-fir, ponderosa pine (*Pinus ponderosa* Dougl. ex Laws.), oaks (*Quercus* spp.), Pacific silver fir (*Abies amabilis* Dougl. ex Forbes), and white fir [*Abies concolor* (Gord. & Glend.) Lindl. ex Hildebr.]. In the Cascade Province, the pine/oak and Douglas-fir series are larger in the Southwest Oregon, Northern California Area than in the rest of the Province.

Fire history. Generally, the frequency of wildfire increases from west to east, away from the marine influence. On the coastal side of the Province, the fire-free period varies between 100 and 200 years. On the Klamath crest, fire scars occur, on the average, every 50 years. In the Ashland watershed, areas with a 20-year fire frequency are common. Overall, the variation in periodicity is high.

Wildfire intensity is related to frequency: the longer the fire-free period, the greater the accumulation of fuels and the greater the risk of high-intensity fires. However, even frequent, low-intensity fires can reduce levels of site nitrogen (N) and carbon (C), lowering potential productivity. Thus, fire history and nutrient status are related.

The Cascade Province

Geology. The Cascade Province is often divided into the Western Cascades and the High Cascades because of their differences in age and composition. The Western Cascades—volcanic flows of andesite and basalt—are approximately 60 million years old. The High Cascades—mostly pyroclastic (pumice and ash) are 1,400–2 million years old. Young (1,400–1,700 year old) pumice, such as that in the Medicine Lake Highlands near Mt. Shasta, and the 7,000-year-old pyroclastics from the Mazama eruption are common. Breccia and tuffs are less common. Ash and pumice have been redeposited by streams in some areas. Metamorphosed rock is essentially absent from the Cascades.

Terrain. Because steepness significantly affects site productivity, managers should be acutely aware of differences in terrain when planning any activity. The most outstanding features of the Province are the volcanic peaks and the Rogue, Smith, and Klamath River drainages. However, they do not typify the Province. Slopes are gentler throughout, and steepness and degree of dissection vary. The Western Cascades generally are steeper (slopes average 40%) and more dissected than the High Cascades (slopes average 26%).

Although the Western Cascades generally are composed of less erodible basalts and andesites, they are more dissected because they are older and at lower elevation than the High Cascades. Deep, incised drainages are common in the headwaters of the High Cascades, particularly where water accumulates on the more erodible ash and pumice.

Climate. The Cascade climate is slightly influenced by marine air during the summer, particularly where such major drainages as the Rogue, Smith, and Klamath Rivers facilitate inland penetration. More generally, the climate is continental, with clear nights and days leading to temperature extremes. Spring frosts can damage or kill regenerating seedlings. And soil surface temperatures can be lethal at midday.

Annual precipitation varies from 80 to 127 cm along the western edge of the Cascades and increases with elevation eastward toward the crest. Summer thunderstorms are common and provide about one-fifth of the total annual precipitation (USDA Forest Service fire weather data, on file with the Siskiyou National Forest). Yet prolonged drought is common during the growing season.

Soil. Cascade Province soils vary in age and degree of development, from the youthful soils of the recent Mazama and Medicine Lake tephras to the relatively old soils of the western Cascades, which have developed from andesite and basalt (Table 10.1).

The Freezener and Rustler Peak series are typical of the Oregon Cascade soils derived from andesites and basalts. The Freezener series is deep, loamy, and moderately productive although coarse-fragment content can be high. The Rustler Peak series tends to be shallow, sandy, and moderately productive, similar to the McCarthy and Cohasset series in the California Cascades. The Alcot, Windy, and Shasta series typify soils developed on pumice and ash. They may be deep but sandy, and have a high coarse-fragment content, low specific heat, and low water-holding capacity. At high elevations or in frost pockets, these soils present regeneration difficulties and are easily damaged once the soil surface is disturbed.

Soil fertility in the Cascades is affected by the Mediterranean climate. Powers (1988) found that N mineralization per unit of soil organic matter was reduced by soil drought at low elevations and by low soil temperatures at higher elevations.

Vegetation. Plant series in the Cascades follow an elevational gradient (Fig. 10.2). The series roughly indicate temperature-moisture regimes relating to the speed and limitations of ecosystem processes such as decomposition and nutrient cycling and availability. Series at high elevations generally are the least productive and slowest to recover from disturbance.

Fire history. Fire is less frequent in the Cascade than in the Klamath Province. Frequency decreases toward the Cascade crest, as elevation and amounts of summer precipitation increase. The higher the elevation and the greater the precipitation, the longer the fire-free period. However, east of the Cascade crest, fires are more frequent (McNeil and Zobel 1980). Fire has been most frequent in the foothills, although some areas show no sign of fire for the last 150–200 years; for example, the Dead Indian Plateau east of Ashland has many stands over 400 years old with an uneven-aged stand structure (many age classes) and no evidence of fire. Individual trees with fire scars can be found, but in most cases, adjacent trees were not burned. The lack of fire in the Cascade Province has left many stands with a bank of organic matter and relatively fertile.

MANAGEMENT PRACTICES AFFECTING LONG-TERM PRODUCTIVITY

Little is known about long-term effects of management practices on site productivity. Most studies in the SWO/NC Area, spanning a few decades or less, reveal only short-term trends. However, longer term studies in temperate-zone ecosystems, although not specifically applicable to the SWO/NC Area, show similar trends. Soil compaction, for example, generally results in slower initial plant growth rates, and severe burning depletes soil N and organic matter regardless of climate. In view of the consistent trends and wide correspondence among studies, some extrapolation is warranted.

Road Building and Harvest

Landslides. The frequency of landslides has increased following road building and clearcutting in the Pacific Northwest (Dyrness 1967, Swanson and Dryness 1975, Swanson et al. 1977; see also chapter 5, this volume). A similar pattern is evident in the Klamath Province of the SWO/NC Area. In roadless areas of the Siskiyou National Forest, landslide frequency over a 20-year period (1955–75) was about 1 slide/2,471 ha every 4.3 years (Amaranthus et al. 1985), with an annual rate of approximately 0.9 m³/ha. In forests that were roaded and harvested, rates were 7 times the natural rate for the same period.

Landslide occurrence is related to rock type. On the Siskiyou National Forest, the Umpqua Formation (bedded sandstone and mudstone) has the greatest landslide risk (Fig. 10.3). Highly faulted and sheared areas which provide zones of weakness, water seeps, bedding planes, jointing, or fracturing of a parent rock parallel to a slope indicate increased landslide potential within a geologic type.

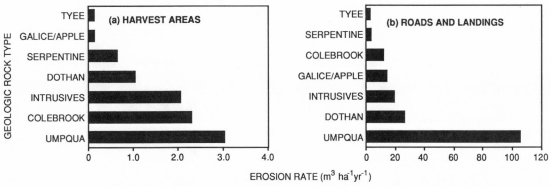

FIG. 10.3. Erosion due to debris slides, by major geologic rock type, from (a) harvest areas and (b) roads and landings, on the Siskiyou National Forest, 1956–76 (adapted from Amaranthus et al. 1985).

The immediate effects of landslides include damage to roads, water quality, and aquatic habitat, and loss in tree stocking and growth. In the Western Cascades, Miles et al. (1984) found that the average height growth of 5–18 year old Douglas-fir regenerating naturally on landslides was reduced 25% compared to that of planted trees in clearcuts. Furthermore, one-third of the landslide area was judged nonstockable because it lacked soil or was unstable. Accelerated soil loss with associated loss of nutrients, organic matter, and microbial populations reduces long-term productivity. Methods of calculating losses vary, but should include a term for changes in the rate of the soil-building processes.

Similar decreases in forest productivity can be seen on slide scars in the Klamath Province. The amount of growth loss depends on soil depth and bedrock characteristics. Losses are greatest in the scarp zone and least in the depositional area, unless slide debris is directly deposited into the stream channel. The impact on productivity can be estimated by summing the extent and rates of landslides over the area of concern.

Landslide frequency and erosion rate are associated strongly with slope steepness (Amaranthus et al. 1985). On the Siskiyou National Forest, slopes steeper than 70% are 20 times more likely to fail than slopes between 50 and 70%, and 200 times more likely to fail than slopes less than 50% (Fig. 10.4). Therefore, managers should avoid locating roads on slopes steeper than 70%, particularly where geologic and hydrologic conditions (faults, seeps, and areas with tilted trees) indicate questionable slope stability. Steep headwalls or the heads of small drainages beneath convex breaks in slope also should be avoided.

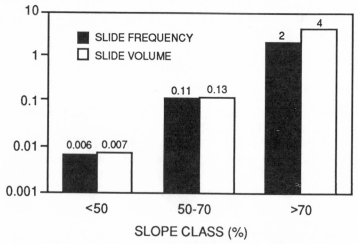

FIG. 10.4. Frequency of debris slides (per 1,000 acres/yr) and erosion rates (yd.^{3} acre^{-1} yr^{-1}) on the Siskiyou National Forest (adapted from Amaranthus et al. 1985). Conversion factors: frequency/1,000 acres × 2.47 = frequency/1,000 ha; yd.^{3}/acre × 1.89 = m^3/ha.

Because 60% of slides occur on lower slopes but only about 15% on ridgetops, ridgetops are preferred road locations. Managers should avoid swales near streams or just above slope breaks; water should not be concentrated in drainages unadjusted for increased flows. Drainage should be routed away from potential slide areas. The sidecasting method of road construction should not be used, and road-construction debris should be deposited on stable slopes.

Steep areas supporting water-loving plants should be avoided. Tilted, jackstrawed, or pistol-butted trees usually indicate shifts in the soil mantle. Where landslides appear imminent, managers should consider leaving the vegetation to stabilize soil. Root systems increase shear strength in unstable soils; roots can anchor the soil mass to bedrock and provide support along locally weak zones. Large downed logs trap sediment, promote infiltration, and decrease the potential for overland flow and water concentration, helping to lower the risk of slides.

Soil compaction. The SWO/NC Area contains the greatest diversity of soils in the Pacific Northwest. Nevertheless, this diversity does not apparently create large differences in susceptibility of the soils to compaction during harvest operations.

Bulk densities range from higher than 1.3 Mg/m^3 for residual soils in the interior valleys to less than 0.7 Mg/m^3 in pumice and volcanic ash in the Cascades. Regardless of initial bulk density, however, all soils are susceptible to compaction, which decreases soil volume and pore space and modifies soil structure (see chapter 4, this volume). The reduction in pore space decreases gas, water, and nutrient exchange, slows root penetration, and usually decreases growth and stocking (Wert and Thomas 1981, Froehlich and McNabb 1984). Moreover, compaction aggravates soil drought, a common summer phenomenon and production limitation in

Mediterranean climates such as that of the SWO/NC Area.

Ground-based skidders are likely to compact soil because they are used on relatively flat ground over which they travel repeatedly to remove logs. Cable yarding systems also can compact soils, but can be designed to minimize compaction and displacement where suspending one or both ends of the logs is possible. Site preparation and slash piling also can increase compaction. The potential for compaction increases with the number of entries during the rotation because natural recovery is slow (Wert and Thomas 1981, Froehlich and McNabb 1984).

The number of passes a machine makes over a soil is a major factor affecting compaction (Froehlich et al. 1980). The greatest increases in bulk density occur in the first few passes. Thus, dispersed skidding may cause widespread compaction. Confining operations to a few, well-spaced skid trails substantially reduces the area compacted without greatly increasing the bulk density of soil in the compacted area. Therefore, designating skid trails before felling is recommended (Froehlich et al. 1981).

Soil moisture content, soil characteristics, and force also affect compaction. The effects of soil moisture content depend on soil characteristics. Soil most likely to compact when moist are fine-textured soils, dominated by expandable clay minerals such as montmorillonite, and well-graded, coarser textured soils, although most of these are found on sites considered too steep for machine operation. The compaction of finer textured soils, dominated by nonexpandable clay minerals such as kaolinite, and of poorly graded, coarser textured soils, such as most pumice and coarse ash soils, is far less affected by soil moisture. And even where soil moisture may be a factor, it is still a minor one relative to the compactive force applied (Froehlich et al. 1980).

Puddling and rutting are affected by soil moisture and can destroy soil structure. However, soils may be puddled or rutted without large changes in bulk density (Froehlich and McNabb 1984). Such conditions are most likely to result from machine site preparation. Thus, managers can most effectively reduce soil damage by limiting the number and area of skid trails.

Growth losses due to compaction have been reported throughout the Area, although the effect has yet to be measured for an entire rotation. Froehlich (1979) reported a 14% reduction in growth of a 17-year-old stand of ponderosa pine (*Pinus ponderosa* Dougl. ex Laws.), Wert and Thomas (1981) a 12% reduction in growth of Douglas-fir after 31 years, on compacted soils in southwest Oregon.

Recovery from compaction is universally slow. In the SWO/NC Area, Wert and Thomas (1981) measured significantly higher bulk densities in skid trails 31 years after use. Other studies in the Pacific Northwest give comparable results (Froehlich and McNabb 1984). Natural soil loosening from freezing and thawing, wetting and drying, and animal activity is inadequate to reverse the effects of compaction except over long periods of time. Because amelioration, even through tilling (see later in this chapter), is difficult, managers should seek every opportunity to avoid or at least minimize compaction.

Site Preparation

Scalping (removing the vegetation including the roots near the surface), piling (pushing logging slash into rows), slash burning, and tilling are the most common methods of site preparation. Regardless of method, the primary objectives of site preparation are to increase survival and growth of crop trees by increasing the number of spots for planting and by controlling vegetative competition. Reducing fuel loads and wildfire risk often are secondary objectives. Site-preparation practices are effective but can have long-term adverse effects on site productivity if improperly applied.

Site preparation has a direct impact on surface-soil organic matter, which in turn is an important link in maintaining desirable physical, chemical, and biological soil properties (see chapter 3, this volume). Organic matter and associated microbes concentrate near the soil surface, and giving soil resilience against deformation. Clayey soils with few large soil pores (macropores) can withstand less compaction than soils of other textures (see chapter 4, this volume), and soils weathered from soft sediments of the Klamath Mountains tend to have greater clay contents than soils weathered from the basalts and andesites of the Cascades (see chapter 1, this volume). Consequently, loss of surface soil in site preparation has a double impact on soil biological and physical properties: it removes resilient organic matter and disrupts the functions of microorganisms, and it exposes subsoil with greater clay content, increasing the risk of productivity decline from soil compaction and erosion.

Beyond physical changes, site-preparation practices that remove a small amount of surface soil may have a disproportionately greater impact on soil fertility (see chapter 2, this volume). Regardless of the material from which soil is formed, nutrients concentrate near the soil surface; their concentrations decline rapidly with depth. For example, between one-third and one-half of the N contained in a soil profile 1 m deep is stored in the top 20 cm (Figs. 10.5a,b). The effect is greatest on immature soils, where between one-third and one-quarter of total soil

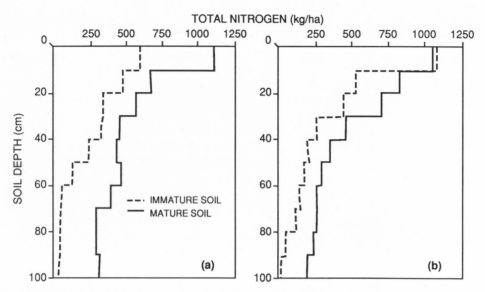

FIG. 10.5. Total nitrogen content of the mineral soil to a depth of 1 m for soils derived from (a) soft sediments of the Klamath Mountains and (b) volcanic soils of the Cascades. Each curve is the average of many profiles. Source: P. J. Zinke and A. G. Stangenberger, unpublished data, University of California, Berkeley.

N is found in the surface 10 cm. Because of their shallowness and high coarse-fragment content, immature soils formed from metasedimentary rocks of the Klamaths contain little N, storing less than 2,300 kg/ha of N on average (Fig. 10.5a). In the Cascades, both mature and immature volcanic soils have similar N storage near the surface (Fig. 10.5b). This similarity may reflect N fixation in previous plant communities, because ceanothus (*Ceanothus*) species are much more common in the Cascades than in the Klamaths. Despite nearly equivalent N contents near the surface, however, immature Cascades soils contain less N deeper in their profiles than do mature soils.

Scalping and piling. Although scalping and other site-preparation methods usually increase survival (Stewart 1978), they may decrease subsequent growth. Minore (1986) found that the combination of piling and burning reduced seedling height more than burning alone. Seedlings were taller on sites with higher humus content. However, short-term results show that loss of forest floor or surface soil may increase early growth by reducing weed competition (D. McNabb, unpublished data, FIR Program, Medford, Oregon, 1986). In the long term, removal of surface layers is likely to decrease site productivity, particularly where soil is thin (Ballard 1978, Steinbrenner 1979).

Powers et al. (1988) compared nutritional characteristics of larger ponderosa pine planted on 16 sites where topsoil had been scalped and piled by tractors into windrows during site preparation and on 6 unscalped sites. Where topsoil had been scalped, mineralizable soil N appeared to be lower by about one-third, and foliar N by one-tenth, than on sites with topsoil left intact (see chapter 1, Table 1.1, this volume). Scalping seemed to induce a sizable N deficiency. However, whereas N fertilization increased 5-year volume growth only slightly in unscalped plantations, response in scalped plantations was more than 4 times greater.

The longer term effect of topsoil scalping on tree growth is illustrated by a 26-year-old ponderosa pine plantation growing on a droughty volcanic ash soil in the southern Cascades (Fig. 10.6). Stem volumes were measured on 66 trees along 9 transects extending at right angles from the toes of windrows to the center of 30-m-wide scalped bays. Trees planted within 3 m of the windrows averaged twice the volume of trees at any greater distance—presumably because they were able to tap the windrowed topsoil. The gradient in tree volumes (Fig. 10.6) suggests that large trees bordering the windrows may be reducing tree growth for a considerable distance outward, or that less topsoil was scalped near the center of bays than near the edges, affecting nutrient availability. A similar study in New Zealand (Ballard 1978) indicates that superior growth near windrows will not offset growth losses over the remainder of the plantation. In general, scalping topsoil into windrows probably reduces site productivity in the long and short term.

Slash burning. Burning, like other site-preparation methods, is applied to improve planting access or seedbed conditions and to reduce competition, fuel loads, and wildfire risk. Long-term effects include the reduction of organic matter (logs, duff, and litter), exposure of mineral soil and the potential for erosion, the volatilization of N and sulfur (S), and changes in soil biology.

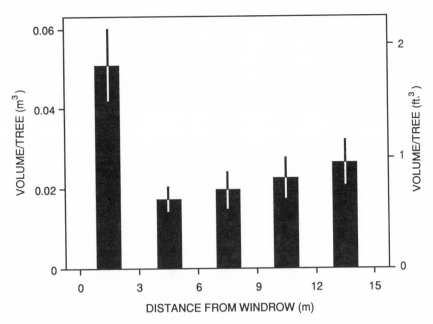

FIG. 10.6. Average volume of 26-year-old ponderosa pine at Edson Creek, southern Cascades, growing on a droughty volcanic ash soil, in relation to distance from edge of windrows. Means and standard error bars are for about 13 trees in each distance class. Source: R. F. Powers, unpublished data, Pacific Southwest Research Station, Redding, California, 1988.

Research on the effects of burning in SWO/NC shows essentially the same pattern of results as elsewhere in the Pacific Northwest. Duff consumption is one of the most obvious impacts. Sandberg (1980) found that the amount of duff consumed was related to the amount and fuel moisture content of duff before burning. His results were not separated by province, but it is highly likely that fuels are drier in the SWO/NC Area with its low rainfall and high evaporative demand. Sandberg also noted that burning after logging increased mineral soil exposure an average of 22%, the percentage of soil exposed related to the amount of duff, its moisture content, and the duration of the burn. Although results for SWO/NC were not specifically reported, the average difference between a spring and fall burn can mean another 47 metric tons of organic matter consumed per hectare, another 28% of soil exposed, and increased risk of erosion. Amaranthus and McNabb (1985) reported similar but more variable results in areas clearcut with skyline logging. Postharvest burning increased the amount of exposed soil from 18 to 75% depending on initial duff depth, duff moisture content, and slope.

Duff and woody debris represent a storehouse of minerals and protection for the soil surface. Since N losses are roughly proportional to the amount of duff consumed, burn prescriptions that allow greater retention of woody debris benefit long-term site productivity. Burning volatilizes organic N or changes it into a readily available form. Large proportions of the total N budget can be lost through volatilization (White et al. 1973). Total foliar N content also is reduced (14% in moderate burns, 33% in intense burns), and the effects last at least 4 years (Landsberg et al. 1984). Reported losses in total site N can be as high as 713 kg/ha after a wildfire (Grier 1975).

At Swain Mountain Experimental Forest, near the southern limit of the Cascades, soil N deficiency seems to be tied to slash burning in a 1,750-m elevation clearcut. A particularly heavy load of logging slash was broadcast burned 5 years after clearcutting an old-growth, true fir (*Abies* spp.) forest. Burning consumed all surface organic matter except the largest cull logs. Despite subsequent planting efforts and abundant natural seedfall, true fir regeneration was sparse. However, lodgepole pine (*Pinus contorta* Dougl. ex Loud.) had regenerated naturally over portions of the site. Ten years after burning, soil samples were taken from the 18–22 cm depth on burned and unburned portions of the clearcut and from the adjacent, old-growth forest. Ten samples from each condition were analyzed for mineralizable N (Powers 1980). Nitrogen concentrations also were measured in current-year needles of the 26 largest lodgepole pine in the clearcut, and lodgepole height growth for the previous 5-year period was noted. Results (Table 10.2) show that a decade after burning, mineralizable soil-N concentrations were about one-third less in the burned clearcut than in either unburned portions of the clearcut or adjacent, undisturbed forest. Foliar N concentrations were about one-quarter lower in lodgepole pine, and recent height growth was 28% less, where slash had been burned.

TABLE 10.2. Conditions (mean ± standard error) in and adjacent to a 1,750-m elevation clearcut at Swain Mountain Experimental Forest, southern Cascades, 10 years after slash burning.

| Characteristic | Clearcut | | Adjacent old-growth forest |
	Burned	Unburned	
Mineralizable nitrogen (N), %	18.1±2.2	26.8±5.4	28.4±3.1
Total foliar N,[1] %	1.40±0.03	1.80±0.13	—
Soluble foliar N, %	0.16±0.01	0.22±0.02	—
Annual height growth,[2] cm	23.0±11.9	31.8±9.4	—

[1]Measured in current-year foliage of naturally regenerated lodgepole pine.
[2]Averaged over most recent 5 years of growth in lodgepole pine.

Soil N and site index (tree height at a specified base age) are related. Nitrogen fertilization seldom fails to increase volume production (Powers 1984a). But such an increase would be expected because lack of N commonly limits growth in the Pacific Northwest. The reverse also should hold true. Where N is lost, growth would be expected to decline. However, the form and distribution of N are important factors influencing N availability, and the interaction is complex. Miller (see chapter 7, this volume) found no difference in volume production or site index between burned and unburned stands after 39 years for three sites in southwest Oregon.

A recent study in the Klamath Mountains (Powers and Weatherspoon 1984) examined long-term impacts of clearcutting on soil properties and site productivity. Three 20-year-old cutblocks 14–41 ha on the Fox Planning Unit, Six Rivers National Forest, were paired with an adjacent old-growth stand of Douglas-fir of the same aspect, slope, and soil type. Soils were of the Galice Formation and typical of a broad geographic region. Logging slash had been broadcast burned before planting with Douglas-fir on two of the clearcuts, and had been tractor piled on the third.

Results (Table 10.3) reveal no long-term differences in site index or most soil properties. However, concentration of mineralizable N in surface soil was consistently lower in clearcuts, and that of exchangeable calcium (Ca) in the full profile was consistently higher (p < 0.10, Fig. 10.7). Lower mineralizable N concentrations probably reflect N losses during site preparation 2 decades earlier, when surface organic matter was burned or pushed into windrows, and a slow rebuilding and turnover of N in the forest floor beneath young, aggrading stands. On the basis of Shumway and Atkinson's (1978) index for Douglas-fir, all forest soils in uncut stands ranked low in N availability, and management operations seem to have aggravated this condition slightly. Higher Ca concentrations in clearcuts probably reflect an effect of residual ash from broadcast burning and accelerated decomposition of Ca-rich hardwood leaves tilled into the soil during tractor operations.

Research is needed on the rates of losses related to management practices and the natural rate of replenishment on a site-specific basis. To avoid site degradation, a balance must be achieved. Yet attention to fuel moisture, amount of duff, soil type and texture, and terrain when using fire will help managers conserve organic matter and N, and maintain or enhance long-term site productivity (McNabb 1988).

TABLE 10.3. Site and soil findings from analysis of 20-year-old clearcuts and adjacent, uncut, old-growth Douglas-fir stands on the Fox Planning Unit, Klamath Mountains (adapted from Powers and Weatherspoon 1984).

| Characteristic[1] | Treatment mean | | Clearcut: uncut | Probability that treatments do not differ |
	Clearcut	Uncut		
Site index (height, m, at 100 yr)	38.7	36.6	1.06	0.45
Soil depth, cm	90.7	91.4	0.99	0.80
Organic matter, g/kg	84.2	83.3	1.01	0.78
Mineralizable N, mg/kg	30.9	33.9	0.91	0.09
Total soil N, g/kg	2.6	2.4	1.08	0.23
Extractable P, mg/kg	39.1	30.4	1.29	0.42
Exchangeable K, mol +/kg[2]	13.0	13.7	0.95	0.80
Exchangeable Ca, mol +/kg	106.5	84.7	1.26	0.07
Exchangeable Mg, mol +/kg	14.3	16.2	0.88	0.43

[1]Organic matter and mineralizable N are for the surface 15 cm of soil. Remaining chemical analyses are averaged over the full soil profile. N = nitrogen, P = phosphorus, K = potassium, Ca = calcium, Mg = magnesium.
[2]mol+/kg = mole of charge per kilogram of soil.

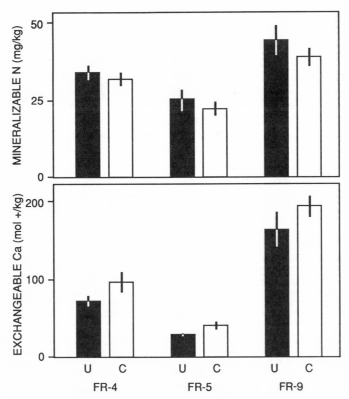

FIG. 10.7. Average concentrations of mineralizable nitrogen (N) in the surface 15 cm and exchangeable calcium (Ca) in the full soil profile in uncut, old-growth, Douglas-fir stands (U) and adjacent clearcuts (C) in the Klamath Mountains. mol+/kg = mole of charge per kilogram of soil. Means and standard error bars are for 25 samples for each U-C plot pair on three Fox Ridge Planning Unit sites (FR-4, -5, and -9). Adapted from Powers and Weatherspoon (1984).

Tilling. Tilling compacted soil is a common practice in SWO/NC following harvesting and machine site preparation, particularly on skid trails and landings. Rock rippers typically are used, although the use of winged subsoilers is increasing (Andrus and Froehlich 1983).

Ameliorating compacted soils has improved seedling survival and growth throughout the Northwest. Seedlings planted in tilled soil in greenhouse experiments have shown increased root and shoot growth (Froehlich and McNabb 1984). However, tilling skid trails in southwest Oregon did not increase volume growth of ponderosa pine seedlings after 5 years (D. McNabb and S. Hobbs, unpublished data, FIR Program, Medford, Oregon, 1985). Soils were poorly tilled in this experiment; rock rippers penetrated only about 1 ft. (0.3 m), and a very small volume of soil was loosened. Ripping, particularly when shallow, does not guarantee improved survival or growth, although occasionally it has been successful.

Successful tilling to increase the number of planting spots, survival, or growth depends partly on the volume of soil tilled and on its original density. Moisture content, texture, rock content, and soil strength are important site considerations (see chapter 4, this volume). Winged subsoilers are extremely effective under most conditions at ripping through the compacted zone to improve internal drainage and reestablish aeration. Because natural recovery by freezing and thawing, root penetration, and animal activities may take 40–70 years, tilling could shorten the recovery period and reduce productivity losses (McNabb and Froehlich 1983), although gains may not be immediately apparent.

Fertilization

Nitrogen and other nutrients sometimes are applied to young stands to increase early volume growth. Amelioration of nutrient losses caused by harvesting, burning, or site preparation is becoming more common. Nitrogen is the most commonly applied fertilizer because it generally limits growth throughout the Pacific Northwest. In SWO/NC, response usually exceeds that predicted by the DFSIM model (Curtis et al. 1981) for stands younger than 40 years, and the increased growth, compared with that of unfertilized stands, lasts longer on low-quality sites. Volume growth of ponderosa pine increases linearly with fertilization rate through 356 kg/ha of N (Powers et al. 1988); average increase in 5-year volume growth is 30%.

Nitrogen deficiencies in true fir stands are common on disturbed soils, and applying 178 kg/ha of N can increase height growth from 30 to 80% in young stands. However, little is known about long-term effects in true fir stands where low soil temperatures restrict mineralization and nitrogen availability (Powers 1981, 1988).

Summer soil drought is common on most SWO/NC sites. Thus, competing vegetation usually must be controlled to realize appreciable fertilizer response in crop trees. Table 10.4 shows 5-year responses of adjacent, scalped plantations of ponderosa pine to combinations of N fertilization and weeding. Treatments were applied when trees were 9 years old. On the drier site (schist soil), volume growth was not appreciably affected by N fertilization at 224 kg/ha on unweeded plots, but increased 8-fold when fertilization was combined with weeding. On the wetter site (basalt soil), fertilization improved volume growth by 3 m³/ha even without weeding. However, fertilization effects will not last as long on the poorer pine sites on schist as on the better Douglas-fir sites on basalt. On the schist site, foliar N concentrations for all treatments were near or below critical level by tree age 14 (Powers 1983). By age 17, foliar biomass N on the basalt site was at least 7 times greater than on the schist site (Powers 1984b). Apparently, the poorer site is unable to retain fertilizer N for very long.

TABLE 10.4. Five-year effects of fertilization and weeding on volume growth and nitrogen (N) status in 9-year-old northern California plantations of ponderosa pine growing on soils derived from schist and basalt (adapted from Powers 1983).

	Schist soil			Basalt soil		
Treatment	Min. N,[1] mg/kg	Foliar N,[2] %	5-yr volume growth, m³/ha	Min. N,[1] mg/kg	Foliar N,[2] %	5-yr volume growth, m³/ha
Control (No N or weeding)	2.6	0.87	0.4	7.1	0.98	5.1
N alone	3.5	0.83	0.5	9.4	1.05	8.0
Weeding alone	4.4	0.92	1.4	9.4	1.14	10.8
N + weeding	4.6	0.98	3.6	11.6	1.26	15.7

[1]Mineralizable soil N 18–22 cm deep.
[2]Total N concentration in current-year needles.

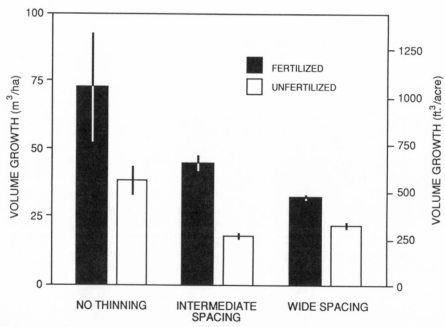

FIG. 10.8. Five-year volume growth for a 60-year-old natural stand of red fir in the Medicine Lake Highlands pumice region, fertilized at two levels (none and 300 kg/ha of nitrogen) and thinned at three levels (none, 16,680 stems/ha; intermediate spacing, 4,444 stems/ha; and wide spacing, 1,111 stems/ha). Means and standard error bars are for three plots in each treatment. Source: R. F. Powers and W. W. Oliver, unpublished data, Pacific Southwest Research Station, Redding, California, 1988.

In older stands, fertilization and thinning are effective silvicultural combinations. In the Medicine Lake Highland region of the Cascades, a very dense 60-year-old natural stand of Shasta red fir (*Abies magnifica* A. Murr.) saplings and poles, growing on pumice overlying a cobbly loam subsoil and testing low in soil and foliar N, received six treatments: two levels of fertilization (none and 300 kg/ha) in combination with three levels of thinning (none, 16,680 stems/ha; intermediate spacing, 4,444 stems/ha—trees 1.5 m apart; and wide spacing, 1,111 stems/ha—trees 3.0 m apart). Three years later, fertilization had increased volume growth in all treatments by an annual average of 1.6 m³/ha (Powers 1981). Results after 5 years indicate that the fertilizer effect is continuing at all spacings (Fig. 10.8). Fertilization response in unthinned plots probably is exaggerated because unthinned, unfertilized plots suffered exceptionally heavy snow damage. However, in plots with intermediate and wide spacings, which received negligible damage, volume growth averaged 1.7 m³ ha⁻¹ yr⁻¹ over the first 3 years and 3.6 m³ ha⁻¹ yr⁻¹ over the first 5 years. How long this will last is uncertain. Five years after treatment, foliar N concentrations in fertilized trees had dropped nearly to pretreatment levels (R. F. Powers, unpublished data on file, Pacific Southwest Research Station, Redding, California).

SUMMARY

In the SWO/NC Area as in the rest of the Pacific Northwest, management practices can significantly affect long-term productivity. Research shows that trends are similar regardless of the climatic regime. Most practices that manipulate the top layer of soil, and particularly those that remove it, degrade productivity as measured by any standard. Nitrogen fertilization, on the other hand, consistently improves productivity. Perhaps these overall results indicate the need to assess the balance of inputs and outputs associated with current management practices.

Although trends are similar among climatic regimes, the details presented show that rates of change differ. The higher temperatures and drier climate of the Mediterranean regime affect rates of soil development. But generalization is difficult because the SWO/NC Area is so variable. The warm, wet climate of coastal sites accelerates decomposition and incorporation of organic matter into the soil system, but the cold, dry climate of high-elevation inland sites allows organic matter to accumulate on the soil surface. Local research is our best source of information. Site-specific dynamics must be considered when planning management strategy.

The fate of organic matter is loosely related to site N and productivity. It plays an important role in the C and N cycles, stores nutrients and energy, and hosts plants and animals that build soil. Organic matter is visible, easily measured, and sensitive to management activities and could be used to indicate trends in long-term productivity.

QUESTIONS FROM THE SYMPOSIUM FLOOR

Q: I agree with the general thrust of your comments about conserving organic matter. However, different types of organic matter have different temporal dynamics, and different implications for long- and short-term productivity. Can you comment on this?

A: As you point out, soil organic matter is a heterogenous potpourri that plays numerous different roles in soil structure and processes. Excluding soil organisms, three types of soil organic matter might be distinguished: transient compounds (mostly polysaccharides), stable humified compounds, and logs. Transient compounds, which disappear rapidly in the absence of plants, are thought to stabilize large soil aggregates. Humified compounds, stable for periods ranging from a few years to several decades, also play a role in soil structure and in addition are nutrient reservoirs. Partially decayed logs are water reservoirs and centers of root, mycorrhizal, and other biological activity (including asymbiotic nitrogen fixation) during dry periods (see chapter 9, this volume). Reduction of any of these components is likely to influence both long- and short-term productivity. In the long term, however, the proportion of logs will decline more than the two other types of soil organic matter because they are a unique product of old-growth forests and are not being replenished in current silvicultural systems. At this point, it is impossible to say how the loss of logs from Pacific Northwest forest soils might affect productivity.

Q: Southwest Oregon is known for its skeletal soils which are sometimes very gravelly. How can we keep these soils in place on the steep slopes?

A: In 1981, Oregon State's Forestry Intensified Research (FIR) program sponsored a workshop on the reforestation of skeletal soils. The proceedings from this workshop (Hobbs and Helgerson 1981) offers some good site-specific information.

Regardless of soil classification, it is important to keep the soil in place, particularly the first few inches or centimeters, to maintain site productivity. With skeletal soils on steep slopes, the risk of reducing site productivity is high with some harvest and site-preparation methods. The solution begins with analyzing the economic viability of harvest and reforestation methods. Some sites with skeletal soils may not support the logging systems needed to prevent soil loss.

Q: Do you think it helpful and/or possible to include mycorrhizal associations with plant associations or habitat types?

A: We need to learn all we can about mycorrhizal associations, which are as important as aboveground systems. As we learn, we should incorporate that knowledge into our classification. In the future, mycorrhiza species may be used as indicators just as vascular species are. However, keys will continue to feature easily recognized plants.

   It may be possible to identify mycorrhiza types important to early establishment of some plant associations or habitat types. For example, significant increases in Douglas-fir seedling performance have been demonstrated following inoculation with the mycorrhizal fungus *Rhizopogon vinicolor*. However, we are far from developing a mycorrhiza classification system based on plant association or habitat type. Thousands of fungus species form ectomycorrhizae, and host-symbiont specificity is generally low. Some ecosystems contain diverse populations of mycorrhizae whose presence can shift dramatically following disturbance and in response to environmental factors.

Q: You stated that fertilization is a good technique for restoring growth lost to other management practices. Would it not be better to avoid the losses and use fertilization to increase growth over the base level?

A: Absolutely! The whole purpose of this symposium is to identify the kinds of management practices that may degrade a site, and then avoid them in the future. Unfortunately, preventive medicine does not do much for problems carried over from the past. Where sites have already been degraded, fertilization may be helpful in restoring some of the lost productivity, but it will not replace organic matter, or improve soil structure, or increase soil water-holding capacity. Intelligent forest managers will avoid creating such problems in the future. And if they do fertilize, they will tailor their treatment only to those sites capable of responding well.

Q: You mentioned that trees continue to respond to fertilization after initial application. How many years beyond the time of application can we expect continued benefits?

A: Nitrogen is not retained forever. Some of it leaches away in drainage water, and more of it is immobilized in microbially resistant humus. Generally, stands treated with 200–400 kg/ha of N should retain higher foliar N concentrations for 5–10 years before dropping back to control (that is, prefertilization) levels. Thus, the "direct" effect of better nutrition on growth should last 5–10 years.

Q: Is the long-term response of N fertilization a result of residual N in the soil or of increased tree vigor from the initial boost?

A: That's hard to determine—although it can be approximated by some sophisticated regression techniques.

   In the strictest sense, fertilization must actually improve the fundamental capacity of the site for carrying foliage to have any long-lasting value. However, two things are working against this for N. One is that conventional rates of N fertilization are such a small fraction of total ecosystem N (generally less than 10%) that they hardly make a ripple in the overall N cycle once the N is incorporated into organic matter. The other is that moisture is such an important limiting factor from the middle of the growing season on in much of the SWO/NC Area that large increases in foliar biomass could not be sustained anyway. Thus, N fertilization tends to push stands along to the point where they've tapped the site's carrying capacity for foliage. This is one of the main reasons why it is better to fertilize thinned than unthinned stands—the crowns grow more, and so do the stems. But once the foliar carrying capacity is reached, growth rates follow those expected for closed-canopy stands of that site quality.

Q: Because fire is as an important component in southwest Oregon ecosystems, doesn't site productivity largely depend on fire frequency and intensity, and can't prescribed burning practices actually be easier on the site than wildfires?

A: Yes, fuel management and prescribed fire can be easier on a site, in the sense that they consume less organic debris than natural fire. However, we don't know if such an artificial regime performs all the same functions as natural fire.

Q: Assuming that you agree with Jerry Franklin (chapter 6 author) about the need to enhance diversity in the forest, what can be done in the Klamath-Siskiyou Province to preserve natural diversity? How do brush-field conversions accomplish this?

A: Diversity in the ecosystem is like diversity in investment; it provides some protection against catastrophes. However, it cannot be "preserved." Diversity is largely a result of dynamic events we often think of as catastrophes, such as fires, floods, epidemics, or storms. We must either accept these as natural ecosystem functions or learn enough about them to reasonably imitate their effects. Currently we should maintain as much structural and compositional richness as possible when managing. Although the objective of brush-field conversion is to increase conifer stocking, much could be done to maintain diversity in composition. The scale and juxtaposition of structural changes (from forest to early seral grass and brush) should be evaluated on a landscape basis.

Q: You mentioned that fire frequency in the Klamath Province, approximately 20 years, limits amounts of large woody debris on sites. Does this have an effect on site productivity?

A: The fire frequency has a profound effect on site productivity. Intensity, frequency, duration, and extent are the variables that determine the overall impacts. I feel that frequent (10–20 years), low-intensity fires generally are more damaging to site productivity than infrequent (200+ years), more intense fires, although others might disagree with this.

Q: Most of the speakers (chapter authors) have alluded to the difficulty of generalizing about long-term productivity in our forests, which reflects, I believe, the great amount of ecological variation among our sites. In Region 6 (Forest Service) we use plant associations to understand this variation. Do you think plant associations could be used to "unconfound" some of the research that has been presented? Can you comment on the relationships between long-term productivity and plant associations?

A: Stratification (classification) has been a standard strategy to reduce variation in research. I have found that plant associations used as a basis for statistical stratification can significantly improve prediction of regeneration success and vegetation-management needs. Such use is increasing. Plot locations are being identified by plant association for stratification and extrapolation of research results.

Because classifying plant associations is a crude method of estimating the primary environment, it follows that rates of decomposition, incorporation, fixation, and production of biomass vary by plant association.

Q: Management accountability in your agency for percent survival of planted trees appears to be in conflict with maintaining long-term productivity in that practices to maximize survival are not always the best ones for maintaining productivity. Is a change in your accountability system warranted?

A: Yes. While we should expect success in reforestation, we should also expect our managers to maintain long-term site productivity. Perhaps accountability for maintaining site productivity should be added to the manager's report card. We have a few indicators that could be used, but they are not easy to evaluate because they are not as strongly related to long-term productivity as percent survival of planted trees is to reforestation success.

Q: How do you define forest productivity, and how should we manage it within the known ecological zones today (1987)?

A: Productivity is the site's potential to produce biomass (organic matter). It is not easily measured, but is an indicator of how we should manage for the long term. We should focus on maintaining organic matter in the soil and on the forest floor. We need to know the quantity and location of the organic matter stored, the processing rates for releasing nutrients, and the rates of input and output for each "zone." We should know how management practices and natural events affect these processes over several rotations to manage effectively for long-term productivity.

REFERENCES

Amaranthus, M. P., and D. H. McNabb. 1985. "Bare soil exposure following logging and prescribed burning in southwest Oregon." In *New forests for a changing world,* 235–237. Proceedings of the National Convention, Portland, Ore. Washington, D.C.: Society of American Foresters.

Amaranthus, M. P., R. M. Rice, N. R. Barr, and R. R. Ziemer. 1985. Logging and forest roads related to increased debris slides in southwestern Oregon. *Journal of Forestry* 83(4):229–233.

Andrus, C. W., and H. A. Froehlich. 1983. *An evaluation of four implements used to till compacted forest soils in the Pacific Northwest.* Research Bulletin 45. Corvallis, Ore.: Forest Research Laboratory, Oregon State University.

Atzet, T., and D. L. Wheeler. 1984. *Preliminary plant associations of the Siskiyou Mountain Province.* Unpublished Report on file. Grants Pass, Ore.: USDA Forest Service.

Atzet, T., D. L. Wheeler, J. F. Franklin, and B. Smith. 1986. Vegetation classification in southwestern Oregon—preliminary report. *FIR Report* 4(4):6–8.

Ballard, R. 1978. Effect of slash and soil removal on the productivity of second rotation radiata pine on a pumice soil. *New Zealand Journal of Forest Science* 8:248–258.

Curtis, R. O., G. W. Clendenen, and D. J. DeMars. 1981. *A new stand simulator for coast Douglas-fir: DFSIM user's guide.* General Technical Report PNW-128. Portland, Ore.: Pacific Northwest Forest and Range Experiment Station, USDA Forest Service.

Dyrness, C. T. 1967. *Soil surface conditions following skyline logging.* Research Note PNW-55. Portland, Ore.: Pacific Northwest Forest and Range Experiment Station, USDA Forest Service.

Froehlich, H. A. 1979. Soil compaction from logging equipment: effects on growth of young ponderosa pine. *Journal of Soil and Water Conservation* 34:276–278.

Froehlich, H. A., D. E. Aulerich, and R. Curtis. 1981. *Designing skidtrail systems to reduce soil impacts from tractive logging machines.* Research Paper 44. Corvallis, Ore.: Forest Research Laboratory, Oregon State University.

Froehlich, H. A., J. Azevedo, P. Cafferata, and D. Lysne. 1980. *Predicting soil compaction on forested land.* Final Project Report, Cooperative Agreement No. 228. Missoula, Mont.: Equipment Development Center, USDA Forest Service.

Froehlich, H. A., and D. H. McNabb. 1984. "Minimizing soil compaction in Pacific Northwest forests." In *Forest soils and treatment impacts,* edited by E. L. Stone, 159–192. Proceedings of the 6th North American Forest Soils Conference, June 1983. Knoxville, Tenn.: Department of Forestry, Wildlife and Fisheries, University of Tennessee.

Froehlich, H. A., D. H. McNabb, and F. Gaweda. 1982. *Average annual precipitation, 1960–1980, in southwest Oregon.* Corvallis, Ore.: Cooperative Extension Service, Oregon State University.

Gratkowski, H. 1961. *Brush problems in southwestern Oregon.* Portland, Ore.: Pacific Northwest Forest and Range Experiment Station, USDA Forest Service.

Grier, C. C. 1975. Wildfire effects on nutrient distribution and leaching in a coniferous ecosystem. *Canadian Journal of Forest Research* 5:599–607.

Hobbs, S. D., and O. T. Helgerson (editors). 1981. *Reforestation of skeletal soils.* Proceedings of a workshop, November 17–19, 1981. Medford, Ore.: FIR Program.

Jimerson, T. M. 1986. *Ecological types of the red fir zone, Six Rivers National Forest.* Unpublished Draft. Eureka, Calif.: USDA Forest Service.

Landsberg, J. D., P. H. Cochran, M. M. Finck, and R. E. Martin. 1984. *Foliar nitrogen content and tree growth after prescribed fire in ponderosa pine.* Research Note PNW-412. Portland, Ore.: Pacific Northwest Forest and Range Experiment Station, USDA Forest Service.

McNabb, D. H. 1988. "Interpreting the effects of broadcast burning on forest productivity." In *Degradation of forested lands—forest soils at risk,* edited by J. D. Lousier and G. W. Stills. Proceedings, 10th Soils Science Workshop. Victoria, B.C.: British Columbia Ministry of Forests and Lands.

McNabb, D. H., and H. A. Froehlich. 1983. "Conceptual model for predicting forest productivity losses from soil compaction." In *New forests for a changing world,* 261–265. Proceedings of the National Convention, Portland, Ore. Washington, D.C.: Society of American Foresters.

McNeil, R. C., and D. B. Zobel. 1980. Vegetation and fire history of a ponderosa pine-white fir forest in Crater Lake National Park. *Northwest Science* 54:30–46.

Miles, D. W. R., F. J. Swanson, and C. T. Youngberg. 1984. Effects of landslide erosion on subsequent Douglas-fir growth and stocking levels in the western Cascades, Oregon. *Soil Science Society of America Journal* 48:667–671.

Minore, D. 1986. *Effects of site preparation on seedling growth: a preliminary comparison of broadcast burning and pile burning.* Research Note PNW-RN-452. Portland, Ore.: Pacific Northwest Forest and Range Experiment Station, USDA Forest Service.

Powers, R. F. 1980. Mineralizable soil nitrogen as an index of nitrogen availability to forest trees. *Soil Science Society of America Journal* 44:1314–1320.

———. 1981. "Response of California true fir to fertilization." In *Proceedings, forest fertilization conference,* edited by S. P. Gessel, R. M. Kenady, and W. A. Atkinson, 95–101. Contribution No. 40. Seattle, Wash.: Institute of Forest Resources, College of Forest Resources, University of Washington.

———. 1983. "Forest fertilization research in California." In *IUFRO symposium on forest site and continuous productivity,* edited by R. Ballard and S. P. Gessel, 388–398. Portland, Ore.: Pacific Northwest Forest and Range Experiment Station, USDA Forest Service.

———. 1984a. "Site productivity and soil nitrogen status." In *Nitrogen assessment workshop,* compiled by R. F. Strand, 60–68. Regional Forest Nutrition Research Project Report No. 2. Seattle, Wash.: College of Forest Resources, University of Washington.

———. 1984b. "Estimating soil nitrogen availability through soil and foliar analysis." In *Forest soils and treatment impacts,* edited by E. L. Stone, 353–379. Proceedings, 6th North American Forest Soils Conference, June 1983. Knoxville, Tenn.: Department of Forestry, Wildlife and Fisheries, University of Tennessee.

———. 1988. Nitrogen mineralization along an altitudinal gradient: interactions of soil temperature, moisture, and substrate quality. *Forest Ecology and Management* (in press).

Powers, R. F., and C. P. Weatherspoon. 1984. *Analysis of soil and site properties in paired clearcut and uncut Douglas-fir stands on the Galice Formation, Fox Planning Unit, Six Rivers National Forest.* Final Report. Berkeley, Calif.: Pacific Southwest Region, USDA Forest Service.

Powers, R. F., S. R. Webster, and P. H. Cochran. 1988. "Estimating the response of ponderosa pine forests to fertilization." In *Proceedings—future forests of the Mountain West: a stand culture symposium,* compiled by W. C. Schmidt, 219–225. General Technical Report INT-243. Ogden, Utah: Intermountain Research Station, USDA Forest Service.

Sandberg, D. V. 1980. *Duff reduction by prescribed underburning in Douglas-fir.* Research Paper PNW-272. Portland, Ore.: Pacific Northwest Forest and Range Experiment Station, USDA Forest Service.

Sawyer, J. O., and D. A. Thornburgh. 1977. "Montane and subalpine vegetation of the Klamath Mountains." In *Terrestrial vegetation of California,* edited by M. Barbour and J. Major, 699–732. New York: John Wiley & Sons.

Sawyer, J. O., D. A. Thornburgh, and J. R. Griffen. 1977. "Mixed evergreen forest." In *Terrestrial vegetation of California,* edited by M. Barbour and J. Major, 359–381. New York: John Wiley & Sons.

Shumway, J., and W. A. Atkinson. 1978. Predicting nitrogen fertilizer response in unthinned stands of Douglas-fir. *Committee on Soil Science and Plant Analysis* 9:529–539.

Steinbrenner, E. C. 1979. "Forest soil productivity relationships." In *Forest soils of the Douglas-fir Region,* edited by P. E. Heilman, H. W. Anderson, and D. M. Baumgartner, 199–229. Pullman, Wash.: Cooperative Extension Service, Washington State University.

Stewart, R. E. 1978. "Site preparation." In *Regenerating Oregon's forests: a guide for the regeneration forester,* edited by B. D. Cleary, R. D. Greaves, and R. K. Hermann, 100–129. Corvallis, Ore.: Cooperative Extension Service, Oregon State University.

Swanson, F. J., and C. T. Dyrness. 1975. Impact of clearcutting and road construction on soil erosion by landslides in the western Cascade Range. *Oregon Geology* 1:393–396.

Swanson, F. J., N. M. Swanston, and C. Woods. 1977. *Inventory of mass erosion in the Mapleton Ranger District, Siuslaw National Forest.* Unpublished Report on file. Corvallis, Ore.: Forestry Sciences Laboratory, Pacific Northwest Forest and Range Experiment Station, USDA Forest Service.

Wert, S., and B. R. Thomas. 1981. Effects of skid roads on diameter, height, and volume growth in Douglas-fir. *Soil Science Society of America Journal* 45:629–632.

White, E. M., W. W. Thompson, and F. R. Gartner. 1973. Heat effects on nutrient release from soils under ponderosa pine. *Journal of Range Management* 26(1):22–24.

Whittaker, R. H. 1960. Vegetation of the Siskiyou Mountains, Oregon and California. *Ecological Monographs* 30:279–338.

Williamson, R. L., and G. R. Staebler. 1971. *Cooperative levels-of-growing stock study in Douglas-fir. Report no. 1, description of study and existing study areas.* Research Paper PNW-111. Portland, Ore.: Pacific Northwest Forest and Range Experiment Station, USDA Forest Service.

Chapter 11
Modelling Long-Term Forest Productivity

J. P. Kimmins and P. Sollins

ABSTRACT

In spite of short-term variations in the global timber supply:demand ratio, pre-AIDS projections of world population growth suggest that demand will exceed supply sometime in the first half of the 21st century unless forest productivity is increased. As global demand more closely approaches global supply, forest management is expected to intensify in an attempt to increase stand-level forest growth. Because many forests grow on inherently poor soils, management intensification will be accompanied by an increased risk of damage to long-term productivity through soil degradation. Productivity may also change as a result of climatic change accompanying alteration of atmospheric chemistry. These and other changes will affect the way in which we predict (model) future forest productivity at the stand level. Traditionally, yield prediction in forestry, and therefore most forest yield models (yield tables and equations, mensurational models), has been based on a "historical bioassay"—the record of tree growth over the past crop rotation. Unfortunately, such model predictions are only valid if growth conditions of the future (soils, climate, biotic factors) are similar to those of the past. But growth conditions are unlikely to remain the same for more than 1 or 2 decades beyond the rotation on which a bioassay is based. Because tree growth under these changed conditions may either increase or decrease, a new flexible approach to yield prediction in forestry is needed. This chapter briefly examines the nature of models, compares various approaches to modelling long-term forest productivity ("first-" and "second-generation" models), and examines one hybrid, "third-generation" model, FORCYTE-11.

INTRODUCTION

Foresters and farmers have traditionally been concerned about yield: the economic productivity of the land. For foresters, this productivity has normally been expressed as mean annual increment of stemwood volume, down to some minimum diameter. In a predictable and relatively unchanging market, the ability to predict stemwood volume may satisfy the planning needs of forest managers. However, in a world with uncertain and changing markets, and with a wide and varying spectrum of tree biomass components that may be marketable (e.g., stemwood, bark, branches, foliage, stumps, and roots), prediction of stemwood volume is not enough. The forester must be able to predict the total net biomass production (net primary production, or NPP) of a site to be able to predict the yield of any particular assortment of biomass products at any time in the future. The ability to predict NPP permits the effects of social, economic, and political factors on yield to be separated from the effects of human-induced alterations of inherent ecosystem productivity.

This chapter examines the nature of models used to predict the productivity and yield of forest ecosystems. At the start, common misunderstandings about models are discussed. The strengths and weaknesses of the traditional approach to predicting forest yield—the historical bioassay—are addressed ("first-generation" models), and the conventional "scientific" solution to the shortcomings of the historical bioassay—process simulation—is evaluated ("second-generation" models). The design criteria and desired capabilities of an improved approach to predicting stand-level productivity (through hybrid, "third-generation" models, specifically FORCYTE-11) are examined. The chapter concludes with a brief presentation of the concepts of "resource renewability" and "ecological rotation," both important in any consideration of long-term productivity.

MODELS AND MODELLING

Many people have negative attitudes towards "models" and "modelling" (i.e., computer simulation models and simulation modelling). These individuals apparently feel that there is something unusual about models and modellers, and they frequently reject "models" in favor of "empirical data." This section of the chapter is addressed to such individuals, not in the hope of reducing their skepticism about models, but of clarifying the nature of models and modelling—to point out that computer simulation models are merely a way of representing what we know about the natural phenomena of the ecosystems we are managing.

A model is simply some human-made abstract or physical representation of some real object or phenomenon ("reality") perceived in the environment. All models have their origins in our ability to perceive "reality," to understand our perceptions, and to formulate them into clear, accurate thoughts and memories. Such thoughts and memories constitute *conceptual models* that exist (are stored) in the minds of the individuals who have perceived the "reality" (Fig. 11.1) or who have had the perceptions communicated to them.

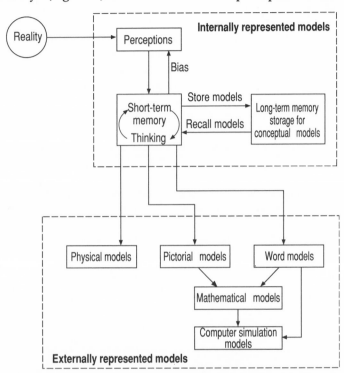

FIG. 11.1. Relationship between some perceived "reality" (e.g., forest biomass and its growth) and various models (abstract representations) of that reality. The first model developed of the perceived reality is always a mental model (internal conceptual model). From this, external models can be developed (Kimmins and Scoullar 1984; used with permission of Academic Press).

Most humans seem to have a strong desire to share their internally stored conceptual models (their perceptions) of the world, which typically are externalized as spoken and written word models. This is why we talk and write so much. However, most of our *word models*—whether a young person's casual verbal model of Saturday night exploits, or a scientist's erudite written model of experimental research—are descriptive, and lack sufficient quantitative definition to provide the basis for accurately predicting future events and conditions.

Where word models are quantitative, scientists may translate them into mathematical language to produce *mathematical models*. Biomass regression equations, equations describing stem taper, and volume/age equations are all mathematical models derived from word models based on conceptual models, which were based in turn on our understanding of natural phenomena. If one or more of these equations is "solved" or "run" on a computer, it is called a *computer model*, although this term does not refer exclusively to equations implemented on a computer. Any set of computer-language instructions that causes a computer to mimic some real system in some way can be called a computer model of that system. Word models can be translated directly into computer language to produce so-called mechanistic computer models. But because computer models can handle much more complexity than can a mathematical model used in conjunction with a slide rule or simple hand calculator, the former generally are more complex. This difference in complexity is really the only fundamental difference between these two types of model.

It should be apparent from Figure 11.1 that our perception of some reality and a computer model thereof are simply different points along a continuum of models, *all* of which have their origins in, and depend for their accuracy on, human perception and understanding of some phenomenon.

Different types of models vary in the accuracy with which they represent reality. For example, some models of airplanes look externally like real airplanes but do not fly; some mimic the flight of a particular real airplane rather accurately, but not its visual appearance; and others mimic both the appearance and performance of real airplanes so accurately that they *are* real airplanes and not models. In contrast, modern technologists can build a model bird that looks, sings, and even flies remarkably like the real bird it mimics, but cannot yet build a model bird that can lay an egg which will hatch into another self-perpetuating bird of the same type.

There is a continuity between models of human-made systems and the systems themselves, because both the models and the reality they represent involve the same materials and construction techniques. The models can be made so much like the reality that they become it. However, no such continuity exists between models of biological or ecological systems and the systems they represent: we can never make such models exact, error-free duplicates of reality. All models of biological or ecological systems—whether textbook or scientific journal descriptions of natural phenomena, the simple mathematical models that describe them, or the more complex computer models derived therefrom—are to some degree wrong. And it is on this basis that many foresters have rejected modelling, and especially computer modelling, of biological phenomena such as tree growth, forest yield, or the response of forest ecosystems to management. We would like to remind readers that *everything* done and said about tree growth and forest yield is based on some type of model, and that *all* these models are imperfect representations of reality. There is no "right" model of yield, and evaluation of a yield model should be based on whether it represents forest productivity accurately enough for its intended purpose and is the best available representation.

Many people have criticized computer models on the basis that "they do not tell us anything that we did not already know." Because computer models are merely alternative representations of conceptual models, it should not be surprising that conclusions reached by that most remarkable "biological computer," the human brain, can be similar to the predictions of human-made computer models. However, the enormous computational speed and memory of electronic computers permit the quantitative evaluation and prediction of complex phenomena that can only be dealt with qualitatively by brains. With "20-20" hindsight, we might reach the same conclusion as a computer model, but would find it far more difficult to think through the enormous complexities of ecosystem-level phenomena and predict future values of ecosystem parameters such as productivity and yield.

DETERMINANTS OF LONG-TERM FOREST PRODUCTIVITY

What exactly is meant by long-term forest productivity, and what determines it?

Long-term *regional* productivity (regional timber supply) is greatly influenced by international, national, and regional market forces, forest policy, tax structures, and government funding of and incentives for forestry. These economic, political, and management factors affect the productive land base and the economic accessibility of existing forest biomass. Current and future regional productivity also depend upon historical factors that have influenced the age-class distribution and species composition of the forest.

Long-term *stand* and *individual-tree* productivity are determined by the availability of growth-determining resources (light, moisture, nutrients), by climatic and physical soil conditions, and by a variety of biotic interactions (e.g., competition for resources; diseases and defoliators). Animals, diseases, and fire can affect productivity at either the regional or stand level.

The long-term productivity referred to in this chapter is stand-level productivity, which can be considered in either ecological or economic terms. Ecological productivity is the NPP per unit area of land per unit of time. NPP is a function of leaf area, and of the photosynthetic efficiency and spatial arrangement of this leaf area. Leaf area and photosynthetic efficiency are determined by many factors, including availability of water and nutrients, shade tolerance of foliage, and loss of foliage to pests, diseases, and leaf fall. Economic productivity (yield) is a function of NPP and "harvest index," the proportion of NPP allocated to and stored in permanent structures which have economic value and which can be harvested and marketed by the available technology.

MODELLING LONG-TERM PRODUCTIVITY: WHAT TYPE OF MODEL IS NEEDED?

As previously noted, long-term productivity can be considered at several levels representing different temporal and spatial scales related to research, stand or whole-forest management, and state (provincial) or national forest policy (Fig. 11.2). Models of forest productivity are needed at each of these levels. Different questions need to be answered at the different levels, and different types of models are needed to answer them:

(1) Process models are well suited to many types of research on mechanisms of productivity at the soil, leaf, or individual-plant level, and can also sometimes apply at the stand level. However, although such models are useful for developing an understanding of individual growth-determining processes, they have not yet proven useful for predicting rotation-length, stand-level productivity and yield.

(2) Stand models at a higher (ecosystem) level of aggregation are needed to predict the productivity and yield of different stand-management strategies.

(3) Whole-forest and large-scale economic models are needed so managers can examine the policy questions related to regional, national, and international timber supply. However, the accuracy of long-term predictions at this level is influenced considerably by the accuracy of stand-level predictions—which means that stand-level models play a powerful pivotal role in predicting productivity. They can facilitate application at the stand and higher levels of the results of research conducted below the stand level, and can have an important influence on the accuracy of higher level productivity predictions. Stand-level models are the focus of the rest of this chapter, which presents the argument that such models should be of the "hybrid simulation" type.

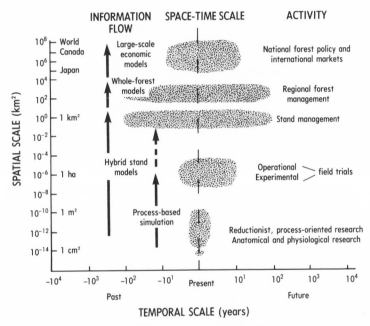

FIG. 11.2. Temporal and spatial scales generally associated with different levels of forestry activity, and the role of models in bridging the space-time gaps. Note that some process-oriented research may have a longer temporal scale than suggested here (see Kimmins 1986). "Past" refers to the importance of historical events to current research or management decisions at any level. "Future" refers to how far into the future research results may be extrapolated, or how far the consequences of management decisions or policy implications may extend. Recent developments in process-based simulation models extend their range up to the stand level (see also Baskerville 1986).

TRADITIONAL AND "SCIENTIFIC" APPROACHES TO MODELLING LONG-TERM FOREST PRODUCTIVITY AT THE STAND LEVEL

Traditional Approaches

The traditional stand-level productivity model used by foresters is a yield table derived from volume/age curves or equations. These "first-generation" models are based on the correlation between accumulated stemwood volume and stand age for a particular species on a particular site. This correlation may be obtained by periodically remeasuring the accumulated volume in a stand over an entire rotation, by remeasuring a series of permanent sample plots of different ages (to construct a synthetic age sequence that mimics the growth of a single stand over time), or simply by making single measurements on stands of different ages (a chronosequence). Alternatively, yield tables may be based on a site-index approach using stem analysis measurements (to give height/age and diameter/age curves) in combination with volume equations and stand-table data.

Yield tables, or the mensurational computer models derived from them, have both advantages and disadvantages. The major advantage is that they are developed from a "historical bioassay" (HB) of the growth potential of trees on a site: the pattern of biomass accumulation in a tree crop on the site over the past rotation. What better basis could there be from which to predict the integrated consequences for growth and yield of the complex of interacting, site-specific, growth-determining factors operating over an entire rotation? The method is not limited by research budgets or by scientists' still inadequate understanding of the complex of factors which determine productivity and harvest index. The predictive power of such empirical correlations is well recognized and widely applied through yield models that use regression equations.

The major disadvantage of the yield table (HB approach) is that it is inflexible. It cannot predict productivity and yield for future growth conditions that are significantly different from those that existed when the trees forming the historical bioassay were growing. Just as regression equations with a single independent variable are of little value for prediction if one or more important independent variables not represented in the model are significantly altered, continued reliance on the HB approach is very questionable if past and future growth conditions differ substantially.

It would be hard to imagine a better way of predicting future forest productivity than the traditional HB approach if growth conditions did not change. But because they do, new yield predictors are needed. Ideally, researchers would establish empirical field experiments to quantify over time how forests grow under the changed conditions. However, obtaining such new HBs (e.g., managed stand yield tables for various future management regimes and environments) takes decades or even centuries, and by the time the new predictors were available, conditions probably would have changed again. This has been referred to as "future shock in forest yield forecasting" (Kimmins 1985): by the time we get the answers, the questions may no longer be relevant. Besides, what do we do while waiting for the new HBs? Apparently, some other type of yield predictor must be developed.

Mechanistic Models

Even the German forest scientists who developed the yield-table approach commented as early as the mid-19th century on its inflexibility. They suggested that yield and productivity should be predicted on the basis of an *understanding* of growth determinants, not on a simple correlation between volume and age. This suggestion became the foundation of the subsequent 130 years of yield science, production ecology and ecophysiology, and the "process simulation" approach to yield prediction. Process models, which can be considered "second-generation" yield models, consist of empirically established relationships (correlations) between a series of independent variables and the dependent variable, tree growth. These relationships are programmed into a computer simulation model and used to predict future growth under defined future conditions.

Although there appears to be no theoretical reason why process simulation should not produce satisfactory yield predictions, there are many practical reasons why it has failed to do so. Process models of forest ecosystem productivity have generally been both too complex and too simple at the same time. They have been too complex in that most have attempted to predict events that occur over decades or even centuries by simulating processes that vary weekly, daily, or even hourly; they have tended to predict events at the landscape level by simulating processes at an individual organism or organ level. Process models have been too simple in that most have tended to focus on only a subset of the full range of growth determinants. Many process models are limited to the individual-tree or population level because of the overwhelming complexity required at the ecosystem level in this type of model. However, yields must be predicted at the ecosystem level because only at that level are all the major determinants (climatic, edaphic, biotic) of productivity identified, and only in such models do we achieve the flexibility in prediction that we need (Fig. 11.3). Process models at levels below the ecosystem contribute more to our understanding of productivity than to accurate prediction of productivity when future conditions change.

Conceptually and scientifically elegant, and extremely valuable in education and research, process models by themselves have not yet provided a satisfactory replacement for the traditional HB yield model in production forestry.

Do We Need a "Third-Generation" Approach for Predicting Long-Term Productivity?

Whether we need a "third-generation" approach to yield and productivity modelling depends largely on whether we accept the assumptions on which the arguments presented above are founded.

The major criticism of the HB approach is based on the assumption that future growing conditions will differ from the past conditions. Estimates of population growth, deforestation, and future timber

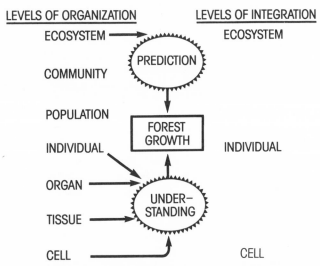

FIG. 11.3. Levels of biological organization and integration: relationships to understanding and predicting forest growth (based on Rowe 1961). *Understanding* stand growth (a population- or individual-level phenomenon) requires knowledge of photosynthesis and resource allocation at the cellular, tissue, organ, and whole-individual levels. *Predicting* stand growth requires an ecosystem approach because only at that level are all the major antecedent determinants of forest growth over a rotation accounted for. Certainly, knowledge gained at the population and community levels does contribute to an understanding of forest growth, but for simplicity these arrows are omitted. Prediction, on the other hand, must necessarily be made at the ecosystem level (from Kimmins 1986).

supply:demand ratio, though tentative and uncertain, lead almost inevitably to the conclusion that forest management will become more intensive. As the demand for traditional and nontraditional forest products increases, as the remaining old-growth commercial forests are harvested and replaced by managed stands, and as the commercial forest land base declines, there will be an intensification of site preparation, weed and insect pest control, stand density control, intermediate harvests, fertilization, and use of nitrogen-fixing "nurse" crops. Rotations will be shorter. Forest-floor biomass, the nutrient content of the soil, the efficiency with which nutrients are recirculated, and the characteristics of noncrop vegetation will change. These interrelated changes are complicated by the anticipated regional and global shifts in climate that are expected to result from the "greenhouse effect" (continuing enrichment of the earth's atmosphere with carbon dioxide and other gases), and by alterations in the forest environment associated with "acid rain" and other air pollutants (see chapter 6, this volume). All these changes will alter the conditions under which future tree crops will grow, thus invalidating the unmodified HB as the basis for yield prediction.

Modifying the historical bioassay with the results of short-term (up to 10 years) research has been suggested as a way of overcoming the inflexibility of that approach. Where the effects of various management practices (e.g., site preparation, spacing, fertilization, whole-tree harvesting) have been or can be monitored for many decades, this would seem a satisfactory solution. Generally, such long-term monitoring has not been, and will not be, conducted. Most research is short term because of the policies of agencies which fund such research, and because of changes in research personnel and research interests. Yet recent evidence from Sweden on the longer term (40-year) effects of scarification and slash burning provides a warning about extrapolating short-term results to the longer term. On some sites, tree height growth was increased by the treatment for the first 15–20 years but was reduced over the subsequent 20–25 years, with little or no net positive effect by midrotation (Lundmark 1977). It is common to observe temporarily accelerated growth in the decade after clearcutting as a result of the "assart effect"[1] (Martin 1985), followed by a period of significantly slower growth. However, such treatment-response growth patterns have rarely been monitored over an entire rotation, and we generally lack the empirical evidence by which to relate short- and long-term treatment responses.

Short-term research in vegetation management may also give an inaccurate picture of the effects of weed control over an entire rotation. Improving crop-tree growth at stand establishment by preventing growth of red alder (*Alnus rubra* Bong.), a nitrogen-fixing hardwood, may lead to the need for nitrogen fertilization later in the rotation. Conversely, nitrogen losses due to slash burning to eliminate salal (*Gaultheria shallon* Pursh) may be

---

[1]The flush of nutrients accompanying the period of accelerated forest-floor decomposition that characteristically occurs for several years after a forest is clearcut.

offset by improved stocking and early growth of crop trees and reduced competition for moisture. Although fertilization may be required later in the rotation to replace the nitrogen losses, the net present value of the crop may nevertheless be maximized by a site treatment which short-term research would suggest is edaphically and nutritionally undesirable. Obviously, treatment effects must be evaluated over the whole rotation as well as over shorter periods before we can judge their desirability. Similarly, shortening the rotation and thinning the stand commercially may increase first-rotation productivity, but may sometimes lead to reduced productivity in subsequent rotations and an overall loss of productivity in the long term. If we are truly concerned about long-term productivity, we must consider multirotational effects of our management decisions.

We conclude, then, that the basic assumption behind the criticism of the historical bioassay is sound, and that making the HB approach more flexible by incorporating results of short-term field research may be difficult. Thus, there *is* a need for a "third-generation" modelling approach which is flexible enough to project growth in altered future environments, but which avoids the problem of excessive model complexity inherent in the mechanistic, process-simulation approach to predicting the long-term productivity of forest ecosystems.

THIRD-GENERATION, STAND-LEVEL MODELS OF LONG-TERM PRODUCTIVITY

Design Criteria and Desired Simulation Capabilities

A stand-level productivity simulation model must be able to represent individual silvicultural activities (from site preparation and crop establishment through final harvest) within a stand, represent the total crop-tree production system (the sum of all individual activities) at the stand level, and produce predictions that become the input to higher level productivity models. The stand-level model must be flexible so it can examine and compare the economic and productivity implications of numerous alternative stand-management systems for various crop species and sites. In other words, it must be an ecosystem-level model. However, the model should be simple enough and have modest enough input (calibration) data requirements that it can be a practical predictor for forest management.

Although these design specifications might seem mutually exclusive, they are not. There is a solution. HB models, which have relatively modest input-data requirements, are implicitly ecosystem-level models because all growth determinants are integrated in the historical pattern. If we combine the HB approach with a simulation of those growth-determining processes likely to be most changed in the future, we can create a hybrid, third-generation productivity model that uses the strengths of each of the component approaches to compensate for the shortcomings of the other. Such a model satisfies most of the previously specified design criteria.

The growth-determining processes that must be simulated explicitly depend on the model's intended purposes. However, a basic set of parameters needed to address management questions includes nutrient cycling and nutritional regulation of growth, and canopy light conditions and their implications for photosynthesis. Competition for water and the effects of management thereon should be included if the model is to be used in areas in which significant soil moisture deficits occur during the growing season; and soil compaction or erosion should be represented for simulating the impacts of management on susceptible soils. "Acid rain" and associated air pollution, important generally in Europe and eastern North America and locally in other parts of the world, should be accounted for in any yield models to be used in affected areas, although inclusion has been hampered to date by persistent uncertainties about how "acid rain" affects soil and plant processes. A more widespread problem causing increasing concern is changes in climate resulting from the "greenhouse effect" (Solomon et al. 1984). As evidence continues to grow that these atmospheric phenomena are real and that their effects on forest ecosystems must be accounted for, it becomes increasingly important that stand productivity models be able to examine the consequences, over rotation-length time scales, of human-induced changes in atmospheric chemistry and climate.

Because forestry is first and foremost an economic activity, yield models should be able to predict future production of economic value as well as tree biomass or volume. Although economic analyses can be done separately, it is convenient if they are conducted automatically by a yield model. One difficulty with economic analyses—the sensitivity of management scenarios to future changes in oil prices, which are uncertain—can be mitigated by conducting an energy benefit:cost analysis (cf. Steinhart and Steinhart 1974 Pimental et al. 1975, 1976). Such an energy analysis is particularly desirable for forests which may be grown as a renewable source of energy.

Currently Available Third-Generation Models

Several third-generation models with which to examine future forest productivity and management effects thereon are available. Most of these models—e.g., FORTNITE (Aber and Mellilo 1982), LINKAGES (Pastor and Post 1985), and FORET[2] (Shugart and West 1977)—had their origin in the JABOWA[3] model (Botkin et al. 1972), which simulates canopy light conditions and the effects of light and elevationally induced temperature change on tree growth. Both JABOWA and FORET were originally designed as models of community development and ecological succession rather than of the productivity of managed stands, and therefore will not be discussed further here even though they are excellent models for their intended purpose and can be used to simulate some aspects of forest management. FORTNITE is essentially JABOWA with nitrogen cycling and limitation added. LINKAGES builds on the modification of JABOWA by Shugart and West (1977), incorporating ideas developed by Weinstein et al. (1982; the FORNUT model, which added nutrient limitation to FORET), Aber et al. (1982), and Solomon et al. (1981).

LINKAGES[4] represents the most recent, sophisticated level of the JABOWA class of model, incorporating temperature, moisture, light, and nitrogen limitation (Fig. 11.4). However, as with FORTNITE and FORNUT, there is no detailed mechanistic accounting of the three pathways—that is, geochemical, biogeochemical, and biochemical (internal)—of nutrient cycling. Although litter decomposition in the forest floor is simulated in detail, the biogeochemical role of noncrop vegetation, and the change in plant-growth allocation strategies and internal cycling as nutrient availability varies, are not represented. These omissions are significant for certain types of forests. For example, it may be difficult to simulate the growth of boreal (northern) forests without simulating overstory foliar leaching and the biogeochemical role of mosses. Growth of fertilized *Eucalyptus* plantations on phosphorus-deficient soils in Brazil depends heavily on internal cycling. Harvest index may be more sensitive to nutrient availability than is total production. Lack of representation of these ecosystem components and processes may limit the application of this otherwise admirable model in situations where these processes are important. A hybrid ecosystem model that does provide a detailed accounting of biomass and of nutrient pools and cycling pathways is FORCYTE-11. It lacks the treatment of moisture and temperature that is present in LINKAGES and FORET, and therefore is currently less suitable than these models for, among other things, predicting the long-term effects of climatic change. However, because FORCYTE-11 has certain advantages as a

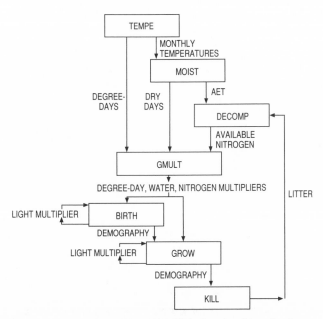

FIG. 11.4. Flow chart of the overall structure of LINKAGES showing how the factors of temperature, moisture, available nitrogen, and light are used as multipliers to modify the historical bioassay growth functions. AET = actual evapotranspiration (Pastor and Post 1985; used with permission).

[2]See also other models by Shugart (1984).

[3]JABOWA (and the models derived therefrom) is a "gap model" that simulates the secondary succession occurring in a relatively small gap created in a forest by some disturbance.

[4]For a recent discussion of a variety of models of forest ecosystems, see the papers in Ågren (1986).

forest-management gaming tool over the other models previously mentioned, it is described as an example of a hybrid, third-generation yield prediction model. Readers are encouraged to consult descriptions of alternative models in Ågren (1986), of the models of Mohren (1987), Solomon (1986), and Barclay and Hall (1986), and of the models mentioned above. According to the objectives of the user, these models may be more or less appropriate than FORCYTE.

FORCYTE-11[5]

Introduction

Like other third-generation models, FORCYTE-11 predicts future forest productivity by combining a historical bioassay with process simulation. In contrast to these other models it simulates forest growth at both the individual-tree and stand levels for either managed or unmanaged forests. At an ecosystem level, it examines change over time in community composition (secondary succession over the stand cycle); production and biomass of mosses, herbs, shrubs, and trees; nutrient budgets and circulation for up to five nutrients; inventory and dynamics of soil organic matter; and economics and energy benefit:cost ratio of crop management (Fig. 11.5).

File and Program Structure

FORCYTE-11 provides a modelling framework rather than a single model in order to combat the "dinosaurism" syndrome of simulation models: as models are improved they tend to get larger, until they may become so large as to be useless. Models may be "too large" in a variety of ways: too large to compile or run on the available computer; too complex to understand; too demanding of input data; too expensive to use; or too difficult to modify for alternative uses. FORCYTE-11 is manageable, and therefore useful, because simulation is divided into three major activities, some of which are subdivided. With this modular approach, FORCYTE-11 can be "customized" for a wide range of crop production situations, including even-aged plantations, agroforestry, agriculture, and mined land that is being revegetated.

All of the plant and soil input data described in the next section are required for the first of the three activities, *Setup*, which establishes the basis for simulating the plant and soil components and processes of the simulated ecosystem (Fig. 11.6). It is the HB component of the hybrid simulation. Data that define the management scenario are required for the second activity, *Management Forecast*, which accepts summaries of information about plant growth and soil processes on different site types (prepared by the *Setup* programs), and uses these summaries (and relationships calculated therefrom) to simulate how growth will change as the growth environment is altered by the defined management regime. The third and final activity is *Output*, in which the results of the *Management Forecast* are analyzed and presented.

Model Input

Two main types of empirical data are required as input to the *Setup* programs: data that define plant growth, and data that define soil processes. If possible, these data should be obtained from unmanaged stands, or at least from stands that have not been disturbed recently, so that the natural processes of self-thinning and stand development are active again. The data for each plant species to be simulated should come from pure stands (monocultures) of that species. These requirements reflect the use of the data as a bioassay of the growth potential of each species on that site in the unmanaged condition. This bioassay is then used as the basis for simulating the growth of managed monoculture or mixed-species communities.

Data that define the management scenario to be simulated in the Management Forecast activity must also be provided in the appropriate input file.

---

[5]FORCYTE-11 is the latest of a series of ecosystem management models. FORCYTE-1 to FORCYTE-8 were development stages in the production of the first publicly available version, FORCYTE-9, which was subsequently upgraded to FORCYTE-10. All these versions focused on the biogeochemical aspects of forest growth and management. FORCYTE-11 constitutes a major redirection in model development, adding a simulation of canopy light conditions, competition for light, and several additional processes and management options.

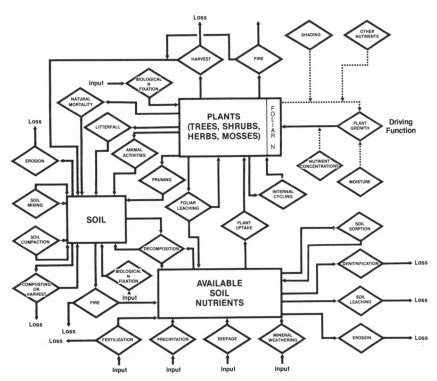

FIG. 11.5. Major compartments (boxes)—plant biomass and nutrient content, soil (including organic matter and its nutrient content, and mineral soil), and "available soil nutrients"—and transfer processes that are represented in FORCYTE-11. Solid arrows represent transfers of biomass and/or nutrients. Dashed arrows represent a modifying influence. The model is driven by an empirically derived index of foliage production efficiency [kilogram of biomass produced per kilogram of foliar nitrogen (N), corrected for shading] and the availability of up to four other nutrients. In this version of the model, moisture is represented only in terms of the maximum foliage biomass that a site can carry. In a future version (FORCYTE-12), moisture will be modelled in greater detail. (Although shown in this flow chart, the soil compaction, soil erosion, and denitrification pathways were not yet operational when this chapter went to press).

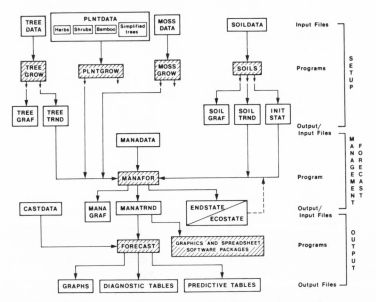

FIG. 11.6. Flow chart of FORCYTE-11 organization, showing the separate programs (shaded) and the three major activities involved in using the model. The *Setup* activity typically involves a forest scientist or research forester. The *Management Forecast* and *Output* activities are conducted by whoever is using the model. The output from the microcomputer-based MANAFOR program can be analyzed and presented by a special output analysis program or by using one of several commercially available spreadsheet programs.

Plant data. The model requires data that define biomass accumulation over time, height/age curves, natural mortality curves (stand density over time), age-class structures of live biomass components [e.g., number of years foliage is retained, number of annual sapwood rings (for trees)], and concentrations of the nutrient elements being simulated in each biomass component of each plant species. For trees, stand-table data (distribution of the tree stems over a range of stem biomass classes for a range of stand ages) must be provided. For all plant species, data that describe the response of plants to shade (photosynthetic light-saturation curves) and the degree of shade they produce (percent light reduction beneath canopies of known foliage biomass) should be given. Data that define foliar leaching may be included but are not essential. Where the model is to simulate vegetative reproduction and growth as opposed to growth from seed, data must be given on many of the above parameters from a coppice as well as from a seedling crop. Plant data are required from sites of at least two different qualities so that the response of plants to management-induced changes in site quality can be simulated. The greater the number of different site types for which data are provided, the more accurate the definition of changes in plant strategy (e.g., allocation of net growth, tissue chemistry, internal cycling) in response to changes in site quality.

One of the design criteria of the FORCYTE series of models is that the requirements for model input should be as simple as possible. Much of the above plant data can be obtained from existing yield tables, from the output of traditional HB yield models, from the scientific literature, or from relatively simple field inventories. Whenever possible, the more complex information requirements of the model are satisfied by calculation and/or simulation within the model from the relatively simple input data [see, for example, Kimmins et al. (1986) for the simulation of foliage production efficiency].

Soil data. FORCYTE-11 simulates several soil processes, the rates of which must be defined by input data. These include litter decomposition (weight-loss rates, changes in the chemistry of decomposing materials) and soil leaching, mixing, and phosphorus sorption-desorption processes (if phosphorus cycling is to be simulated). These and other soil data, required for each site from which plant data are collected, can be measured directly, inferred from a knowledge of soil processes, or estimated from the literature. If possible, the data should be for unmanaged, or at least not recently disturbed, forests.

With the FORSOILS program, users have the option to simulate a variety of soil processes and explore their consequences. However, if users are not satisfied with the representation of a particular process, have insufficient calibration data, or are unwilling to make certain assumptions about the process, they can eliminate the simulation of that process from the model by appropriate entries in the input file. This permits the user to reduce FORCYTE-11 to a much simpler model that demands less input data. However, in doing this the user must accept that omitting the simulation of a process may result in a greater error in the model's predictions than including a "best estimate" simulation of that process.

Management scenario. Data defining rotations, crop sequences, site-preparation techniques, regeneration methods, weeding strategies, regimes for thinning, pruning, and fertilization, and utilization standards must be provided. Episodic events such as fire and defoliation by herbivores can also be simulated if desired. Economic and energy costs of management and benefits of harvested products should be defined. Users may choose to completely eliminate the simulation of nutrient control of growth, thereby reducing the process-simulation component of the model to canopy light conditions and the response of plant growth to these conditions (cf. TASS, Mitchell and Cameron 1985). However, this is not the intended use of the model.

Modelling Strategy

Simulation of changes in plant growth and ecosystem processes in response to management activities is based on empirical data that define growth and ecosystem processes under a variety of site conditions. Unless data that describe these parameters for several different site conditions are provided, FORCYTE's ability to simulate the consequence of management is reduced. In the case of nutrients, data should be gathered from at least two sites that differ in fertility. These data are used to define how parameters such as shoot:root ratio, allocation of net growth to fine roots, internal cycling, plant nutrient concentrations, decomposition rates, soil animal activity, and nutrient chemical forms (e.g., nitrate vs. ammonium nitrogen) change as soil nutrient availability changes. As noted above, the data should be collected from closed stands that have not been disturbed recently. In the case of light, data should be gathered from a series of stands that vary in crown biomass (i.e., canopy closure). These data are used to simulate the shade-related processes of stand self-thinning and branch mortality.

Any branches receiving less than the simulated light levels at the bottom of the live canopy will die. Similarly, any tree receiving less light at its apex than the simulated light intensity of the top of the smallest live-canopy tree will die. Both of these shade-related simulations are based upon the empirical input data in the *Setup* activity.

Plant growth in FORCYTE-11 is based on stand-level data on biomass accumulation, from which a measure of total stand increment is derived. However, the model also simulates growth at the individual-tree level by allocating the total stand increment for each simulation time interval to each of the trees in the simulated stand. This individual tree growth is "distance independent"—that is, the spatial arrangement of the trees is not represented in the model. The allocation of increment to the individual trees is simulated on the basis of stand-table information. This is assumed to be the best, easily available measure of the tendency of the species being simulated to become differentiated into various size classes over time on a particular site. Figure 11.7 compares the results of simulating the frequency of stem sizes at various stand ages with the stand-table data from which the simulation was derived.

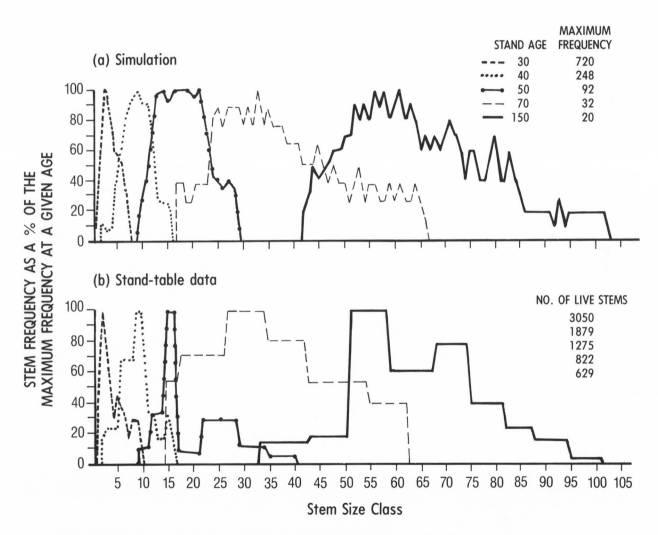

FIG. 11.7. (a) Simulated frequency distribution of stem size classes at five different stand ages, from FORCYTE-11's TREGROW program, compared with (b) the original stand-table data on which the simulation in (a) was based. The stand age (in years) for each distribution curve is shown. For each curve, the highest frequency is given a value of 100. Actual numbers of trees represented by the curves decline as the stand gets older. For each age, the number of stems in the class with the maximum frequency, and the total number of stems alive at that age, are shown.

One of the major functions of the plant *Setup* programs is to prepare an ecologically sound driving function[6] for plant growth in the *Management Forecast* program MANAFOR. The driving function must be site specific, and must be responsive to simulated changes in nutrient availability and light. The approach is similar to Ågren's (1983) *nitrogen productivity* concept (kilogram of foliage produced per kilogram of foliar nitrogen), but is based on the concept of *foliage nitrogen efficiency* (FNE; kilogram of total plant increment produced per kilogram of foliar nitrogen), corrected for shading (Comeau and Kimmins 1986, Kimmins et al. 1986). Foliar nitrogen is assumed to be a good index of the magnitude of the photosynthetic capacity of a plant (Ågren 1983; Brix 1983), and the correction for shading accounts for the reduction in photosynthetic activity as a function of light intensity. This relationship was derived from output of FORCYTE-10 (Kimmins et al. 1982), but was reported earlier by Ingestad et al. (1981). Further details are given in Kimmins et al. (1986) and Kimmins and Scoullar (1989).

Output

The model output summarizes economic production (biomass yield), total biomass production (i.e., NPP), and loss of NPP to litterfall, by species and plant biomass component; reports the simulated inputs, the standing crops, and the outputs of nutrients in various geochemical and biogeochemical cycle pathways, and the magnitude of internal cycling of nutrients; and presents ecosystem nutrient budgets for each rotation, recording the timing and source of all simulated inputs and outputs. Furthermore, the model provides an economic analysis of individual management activities and of crop production as a whole. It also examines energy efficiency in terms of the fossil fuel costs of management and the energy content of harvested materials. This permits an evaluation of the sensitivity of economic predictions to future changes in the price of oil.

ARE THIRD-GENERATION MODELS IMPROVED PREDICTORS OF LONG-TERM PRODUCTIVITY?

There is still debate about whether adding process simulation to a traditional HB model improves the predictive ability of the resulting hybrid, third-generation model. Decisions concerning whether or not it is advantageous to add a simulation of a particular process can be based on the following criteria (Fig. 11.8). If a factor or process (e.g., temperature, or nutrient release by litter decomposition) is known to determine tree growth and is thought to be subject to change in the future, simulation of its action should be added to a traditional HB yield model *if* both the direction of action (a positive or negative effect) and the magnitude of action are known and can be adequately represented. However, such an addition can increase error if the direction of action is not known or the magnitude is incorrectly represented. In such cases, little may be gained by adding process simulation, and error may even be increased. On the other hand, if the direction of action is known but not the magnitude, predictive ability may be improved with process simulation if the magnitude of action can be conservatively estimated.

We do know that management intensification affects site nutrient status, and can affect soil aeration and moisture. We also know that canopy light conditions change as stand density regimes and nutrient availability change. And we know that both production and harvest index are altered by changes in site fertility, soil aeration and moisture, and canopy light conditions. The direction of action of all these processes is understood and can be represented. The magnitude of their action can be simulated, but care must be taken that it is not overestimated. However, considering our current state of knowledge, the risk of increasing error by adding a simulation of these processes is almost certainly less than that of simply omitting these processes from models that are to be used to predict yield under changing future growth conditions. In fact, leaving an important growth-determining process out of a yield model generally involves making just as large an assumption, or an even larger assumption, as including it. On the basis of this argument, we feel that both nutrient- and light-related processes should be included in all hybrid models, and that moisture and temperature-related processes will be needed if we wish to consider the effects of global climatic change on forest structure, species composition, and productivity.

---

[6]The term "driving function" (or "forcing function") refers to the algorithm(s) [i.e., the mathematical equation(s)] which is (are) the basis for a computer model's calculations and simulations. In the case of FORCYTE, the algorithms which "cause" plants to grow in turn "drive" the simulation of biomass dynamics, nutrient cycling, and canopy light conditions.

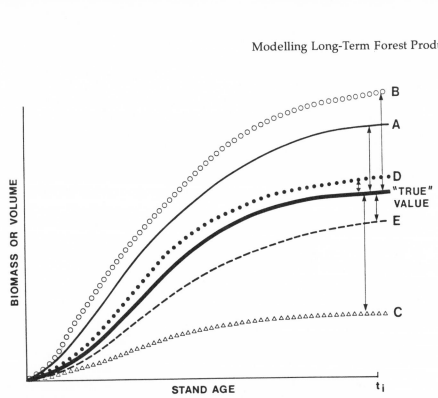

FIG. 11.8. Possible prediction errors arising from hybrid, third-generation models of long-term forest productivity (Kimmins and Scoullar 1989):

"True" value: This curve represents how the forest will actually grow.

A: Prediction from a traditional historical bioassay (HB) yield model.

B: Prediction after adding process simulation to HB model when the *direction* of action is incorrect (increased error).

C: Prediction after adding process simulation to HB model when the *magnitude* of action is incorrect (increased error).

D, E: Predictions after adding process simulation to HB model when both the direction and magnitude of action are correct (reduced error). Vertical arrows show relative magnitudes of error at time t_i.

RESOURCE RENEWABILITY AND ECOLOGICAL ROTATIONS

Accurate assessment of the impacts of management on long-term productivity cannot be made by short-term studies of environmental impacts alone. The sustainability and renewability of forest resources (Kimmins 1973) depend on the combination of degree of ecosystem disturbance accompanying management, frequency of disturbance, and rate at which the ecosystem recovers towards its predisturbance condition. Severe soil erosion, compaction, and/or loss of site nutrient capital may not be very significant for long-term productivity if trees are growing over a very long rotation in a climate and on a soil parent material which promote rapid recovery of soil resources and high levels of net primary production. For short rotations, or in ecosystems with slow recovery from such management impacts, these disturbances may be completely unacceptable and may result in significant loss of productivity.

For each ecosystem-management system combination, there will be a unique period of time for recovery from disturbance: the "ecological rotation" (Kimmins 1974). Ecosystem-level management models offer the possibility of estimating the ecological rotation for a particular ecosystem under a variety of different management regimes. Where economic and management constraints impose a certain level of disturbance on a site, such models can predict how frequently disturbance can occur without degrading productivity over the long term. On the other hand, if the rotation length has been fixed, such models can estimate how much disturbance can be tolerated without loss of productivity, or how much site amelioration will be required to prevent such loss. The economic impacts of having to invest in such site amelioration can also be estimated.

CONCLUSIONS

All yield and productivity predictions involve making and using models—whether an internal conceptual model based on experience, an empirically based (i.e., HB), mensurational computer model, or a hybrid simulation model that includes some process-based simulation. All these models are inevitably less than 100% accurate because they are all merely abstract representations of real forest growth. Thus, evaluation of models should be based less on whether they are right or wrong, than on whether they are accurate enough for their intended purpose. We should use the model that gives predictions of the desired level of accuracy and reliability at the lowest cost and greatest ease of use.

Traditional HB yield models have sufficed in the past because the rate of change in management practices and growing conditions was slow enough that the record of past growth was both a satisfactory predictor, and the best available predictor, of future growth. However, increasing demands on the forest and increasing alteration of the atmosphere and climate have resulted in the need for yield models that are flexible enough to account for changing future conditions. Although the mechanistic approach of process-based simulation is not, of itself, a satisfactory alternative, a hybrid model combining the HB approach with the process simulation-based approach appears to offer some useful improvements. The hybrid model does not seek to replace the traditional approach but rather to complement it by building on its strengths and improving its capabilities.

QUESTIONS FROM THE SYMPOSIUM FLOOR

Q: How can a potential user obtain a copy of FORCYTE?

A: FORCYTE is public-domain software in Canada, but the funding agency, Canadian Forestry Service (CFS), has in the past required that all users agree to certain terms of usage. Permission to obtain a copy involves writing to J. P. (Hamish) Kimmins, Department of Forest Sciences, University of British Columbia, Vancouver, B.C., Canada V6T 1W5. The CFS intends to license future usage of the model, and is currently arranging for the model to be copyright protected and licensed prior to further distribution. This is not to impose any impediments on its use, but only to protect the model and its creators from unauthorized modifications and usages, and from the difficulties which could arise from failure to arrange such protection.

Q: Given your emphasis on differences between productivity and yield, and given that the Pacific Northwest contains about 400–500 species, what potential increase in yield could be projected if we utilized more species as crops?

A: Relatively few plant species in Northwest forests have current or probable future economic value. We are not, however, taking full advantage of all those that do. The long history of treating alder (*Alnus*), cottonwood (*Populus*), birch (*Betula*), cherry (*Prunus*), and other native deciduous hardwoods as "weed" species appears to be changing. Cottonwood, red alder, and aspen (*Populus*) are all being utilized in British Columbia now, and I see an increasing trend in this direction. I believe that on many brush-prone sites, present net value could probably be maximized by using fast-growing pioneer hardwoods instead of, in mixture with, or as alternating crops with conventional coniferous species. Because of our lack of experience with these silvicultural strategies, models like FORCYTE will probably see increasing use, at least until we have data from long-term growth and yield plots.

Q: For which parts of the Northwest is FORCYTE calibrated?

A: FORCYTE-10 has been calibrated for coastal western hemlock [*Tsuga heterophylla* (Raf.) Sarg.] (by Don Sachs). It has also been used in northern California (Alan Strangenberger, USDA Forest Service). Don Sachs is now involved in calibrating FORCYTE-11 in western Oregon, on behalf of the Bureau of Land Management (BLM). The BLM is testing the model as a management decision support tool with which to assess the long-term sustainability of planned management strategies. This is in response to U.S. Environmental Protection Agency requirements that adequate evidence of the sustainability of forest productivity be presented by public land managers.

Q: What efforts have been made in Region 5 (California) to use models like FORCYTE (author's interpretation of question) in relation to land management planning on National Forests, and what are the findings? What work has been done to use FORCYTE to analyze the long-term implications of site-preparation methods?

A: To my knowledge, the only applications of FORCYTE in Oregon have been those by Don Sachs (M.S. thesis, Oregon State University) and the BLM. Weyerhaeuser Company reviewed FORCYTE-10, but concluded correctly that they really needed FORCYTE-11 or some other more advanced model. There are no current applications of the model as a management decision support tool by the USDA Forest Service, but FORCYTE-10 has been tested as a research tool by the Forest Service in California (Alan Strangenberger), and Dick Miller (chapter 7 author) is interested in developing a co-operative project in the fairly near future.

Q: Where does a forest manager get a "tame" forest scientist to help him/her calibrate and use FORCYTE?

A: Department of Forest Science, Oregon State University (Corvallis), Forest Service research stations,

University of Washington (Seattle), or other forestry-oriented research institutions.

Q: Your understanding and ability to communicate the difference between modelling and reality were out-standing. Could you put this difference in perspective by addressing two possible conclusions:

(1)   Foresters should not meddle with forests because we know so little about possible long-term effects ("no risk" position).

(2)   Foresters can move ahead with management because the risks, although unknown, are tolerable ("can do" position).

A: A very good question. Although it is certainly true that science still has a great deal to learn about ecosystems, I feel that the publicly funded forest science of the past 30 years or more has provided a basis on which we can undertake a worthwhile "trend analysis" of the long-term impacts of forest manage-ment. I believe that we do know enough about the basics of production ecology to answer some, though certainly not all, questions with respect to long-term impacts. The difficulty has been in harnessing the diversity of available knowledge, and focusing it in a way that can give us a believable trend analysis. The advent of computer models like JABOWA, LINKAGES, and FORCYTE has provided the tools needed to allow a practically useful synthesis of existing information so that such trends can be predicted.

Q: In view of what we are getting to know of "chaos," in the scientific sense, and the uncertainties it intro-duces, how do you justify mechanistic, deterministic models of forest productivity?

A: The modelling strategy in FORYCTE is to take the historical pattern of forest growth (which integrates all of the stochastic events of the past rotation), and to see, by deterministic simulation, if that historic pattern can be reproduced in the future under a particular, defined set of future growing conditions. These future conditions include both natural events (e.g., wildfire, defoliation, windthrow) and human-induced events (a wide variety of stand-level management activities). Deterministic simulation is used because the major objective of the model is to compare the probable long-term consequences of various management strategies, with or without natural disturbances. Such comparisons could not be made if natural disturbances were simulated stochastically because the outcome of a given simulation would be deter-mined as much by the random occurrence of disturbance effects and the random variations in process rates as by management interventions. The stochastic approach normally involves making many hundreds of runs for each set of management activities, taking the average of the predictions, and com-paring the averages. The result gives you only a comparison of averages, however, which may not be the particular future conditions that you wish to explore. The stochastic approach is ideal for making quantita-tive predictions about a particular future and estimating the confidence one should have in those predic-tions. But for the purposes for which FORCYTE was designed (multiple comparisons of different manage-ment strategies under a variety of possible future conditions), the deterministic, mechanistic approach is best.

Q: You stated that soil texture and depth are unaffected by forest management. Does not the acceleration of erosional processes by harvesting, thinning, site preparation, and other practices reduce depth and alter texture? Does FORCYTE address these effects as related to shorter rotations?

A: I have classified the major determinants of forest productivity into three major categories: those largely unaffected by stand-level management, those which may or may not be affected depending on circum-stances, and those almost inevitably affected. The third category includes canopy architecture and light conditions and competition, soil nutrient availability, and competition for soil moisture. The second category includes the intensity and frequency of disturbance due to insects, diseases, wind, and fire, and alterations in soil architecture, aeration, and moisture. The first category includes climatic parameters, position in the landscape, slope, geology, and soil depth, texture, and coarse-fragment content.

In the hybrid simulation approach, it is necessary to simulate growth-determining processes that are likely to be changed in the type of future for which you wish to make predictions. This will normally require that most of the factors in the third category *must* be simulated, that factors in the second category *should* be simulated, and in many cases, that none of the factors in the first category need be simulated. If, on the other hand, you wish to make predictions of productivity, yield, economics, etc. under changed conditions *not* related to changes in stand management (e.g., global climatic change), then you may indeed have to simulate factors in the first category (e.g., temperature, precipitation).

For some types of stand-level management, it is necessary to be able to simulate soil erosion and soil compaction (alteration of soil structure and bulk density), and FORCYTE-11 will be able to do this. I am not sure that management significantly alters soil texture, except possibly in the case of catastrophic erosion.

Q: Can we get copies of FORCYTE to run on IBM PCs or other personal computers? Can FORCYTE be used to model different yarding impacts (e.g., skidder vs. cable yarding)?

A: The availability of FORCYTE is noted in the answer to a previous question. FORCYTE-10 can be run on an IBM-AT, -XT, or compatible. It can be run with 512K RAM and two floppy disk drives, but is much faster and more convenient with a hard drive, a math coprocessor (80287 or 8087), and 640K RAM. It runs much faster again if you have a 386-CPU or a 32-bit coprocessor (e.g., a DSI board). The current formulation of FORCYTE-11 *requires* the 386-CPU or 32-bit coprocessor. For further details, please contact J. P. Kimmins.

      FORCYTE-11 can simulate some aspects of the difference between skidder and cable yarding *if* you have data on the degree of site disturbance (percentage of area disturbed, degree of soil compaction or stirring), and an estimate of how long it takes for the soil to recover its structure after various intensities of disturbance.

Q: Historically, have models predicting productivity (forestry, agriculture) tended to *overestimate* productivity when compared to reality? What can be done to avoid this?

A: In many cases, management of previously unmanaged ecosystems has increased their productivity. Where prediction of system productivity has been based on premanagement levels, these predictions have been conservative. For example, many managed forests are much more productive than the previous unmanaged forests or other types of vegetation on the site. Unfortunately, there are also widespread examples where the opposite is true, and many examples where the increased productivity of the first managed rotation is not maintained into subsequent rotations. In such cases, the traditional, historical-bioassay type of yield predictor has proven to be overly optimistic, and site productivity has been overestimated. We can avoid both over- and under-estimation by utilizing hybrid-simulation yield predictors such as FORCYTE, or by obtaining data from long-term empirical field trials that lead to managed stand yield tables. However, the latter only gives the yield for the first rotation, whereas a model can predict the probable trend of yield over several future rotations.

Q: How does FORCYTE account for past disturbances and their effects on current productivity? If it cannot account for these disturbances, can it be modified to do so?

A: An excellent and perceptive question. *All* models suffer from the fact that the data on which future predictions are based reflect the historical pattern of disturbance. Where the frequency, intensity, and timing of such disturbance are not changed in the future, this does not invalidate the predictions; if these parameters do change, however, the prediction will be wrong. For example, if a forest has been periodically defoliated in the past, the historical bioassay of forest growth will reflect the growth and stand development which was achieved *with* that particular historical pattern, frequency, and intensity of defoliation. If one wishes to simulate the growth of the forest *without* any defoliation, it is necessary to obtain calibration data from stands that did not suffer significant defoliation, or to correct the calibration data for the effects of the defoliation. This can be done by obtaining empirical data on the impacts of defoliation on growth, or, in the absence of such data, by simulating the effects of defoliation using the model, and using the simulated effects to correct the input data. If the historical pattern of defoliation is unknown, there is little that you can do. All yield prediction methods are susceptible to this latter deficiency, but process-based simulation offers some advantages in this situation.

Q: If using herbicides to prevent alder competition may reduce optimum rotation-length growth of Douglas-fir [*Pseudotsuga menziesii* (Mirb.) Franco] on some sites, are you suggesting that alder should be controlled by manual release?

A: Alder may benefit Douglas-fir growth by symbiotic nitrogen (N) fixation, or may be detrimental by competing for light. Herbicides may completely kill alder, eliminating any further N fixation, whereas manual control *may* permit resprouting and continued N fixation while reducing light competition. It would thus appear that manual control is superior. However, against this, manual control may be ineffective because of the rapid coppice regrowth, it may be much more expensive, and if the Douglas-fir have been suppressed for several years, it could be ecophysiologically less desirable than chemical control. Herbicides generally result in a relatively slow increase in light intensity and leave significant amount of shade cast by the standing dead trees. This can give the Douglas-fir the sometimes critically important opportunity to adjust their shade-adapted foliage for life in full sunlight. Manual removal of alder in midsummer can cause severe physiological trauma to suppressed Douglas-fir, negating many of the benefits of release. Thus, a decision as to which is the more desirable—manual or chemical release—must depend on a site-specific evaluation of the precontrol condition and a consideration of the ecophysiological consequences of the alternative strategies. Process-based or hybrid simulation models can be used to explore and predict these ecophysiological consequences where empirical experience is lacking.

Q: Can you elaborate (perhaps by example) on the conflicts between stand- and forest-level productivity; i.e., where could something that is beneficial at the forest level not be beneficial at the stand level, or vice versa?

A: Forest-level productivity is related to annual allowable cut and regional timber supply. In the short term, it is determined more by the inventory (volume by piece size, and the age-class and area-class structure of the inventory) than by the productivity of individual stands or by the intensity, quality, and success of stand-level management. Sustained timber supply in the short to medium term will be increased more by activities which "normalize" the area and age-class structure of mature and intermediate-aged stands and which reduce the time taken by trees in the stands to reach harvestable size, than by activities which promote the overall rotation-length productivity of individual stands, especially young stands. However, too great a focus on maximizing short- and medium-term regional timber supply could result in important management impacts on individual stands (soil compaction, nutrient depletion, and regeneration delay) being overlooked because they do not have much effect on timber supply in the nearer future. These impacts could lead to later abnormalities in the age-class structure, volume by age, and tree size structure of the regional forest, which will adversely affect the long-term timber supply. Thus, maintenance of stand-level productivity has its greatest importance for long-term sustained yield, while maximization of short- to medium-term regional timber supply can, if care is not taken, lead to or permit reductions in stand-level productivity.

ACKNOWLEDGMENTS

The development of the FORCYTE series of models was funded by the ENFOR program of the Canadian Forestry Service. The contributions of K. A. Scoullar, P. G. Comeau, W. A. Kurz, K. M. Tsze, M. Apps, L. Chatarpaul, and many other individuals to the development of the model, and the numerous contributions of P. Quay, are gratefully acknowledged.

REFERENCES

Aber, J. D., and J. M. Melillo. 1982. *FORTNITE: A computer model of organic matter and nitrogen dynamics in forest ecosystems.* Research Bulletin R3130. Madison, Wis.: College of Agriculture and Life Sciences, University of Wisconsin.

Aber, J. D., J. M. Melillo, and C. A. Federer. 1982. Predicting the effects of rotation length, harvest intensity and fertilization on fibre yield from northern hardwood forests in New England. *Forest Science* 28:31–45.

Ågren, G. I. 1983. Nitrogen productivity of some conifers. *Canadian Journal of Forest* Research 13:494–500.

Ågren, G. I. (editon). 1986. *Predicting consequences of intensive forest harvesting on long-term productivity.* Report 26. Sweden: Department of Ecology and Environmental Research. Swedish University of Agricultural Sciences.

Barclay, H. J., and T. H. Hall. 1986. *SHAWN: a model of Douglas-fir ecosystem response to nitrogen fertilization and thinning: a preliminary approach.* Information Report BC-X-280. Victoria, B.C.: Pacific Forest Centre, Canadian Forestry Service.

Baskerville, G. L. 1986. "The state of forest research in Canada." In *The E. B. Eddy distinguished lecture series,* 27–47. Toronto, Ont.: Faculty of Forestry, University of Toronto.

Botkin, D. B., J. F. Janak, and J. R. Wallis. 1972. Some ecological consequences of a computer model of forest growth. *Journal of Ecology* 60:849–872.

Brix, H. 1983. Effect of thinning and nitrogen fertilization on growth of Douglas-fir: relative contribution of foliage quantity and efficiency. *Canadian Journal of Forest Research* 13:167–175.

Comeau, P. G., and J. P. Kimmins. 1986. "The relationship between net primary production and foliage nitrogen content, and its application in the modelling of forest ecosystems: a study of lodgepole pine (*Pinus contorta*)." In *Crown and canopy structure in relation to productivity,* edited by T. Fujimori and D. Whitehead, 202–223. Proceedings of a IUFO Symposium Workshop. Ibaraki, Japan: Forestry and Forest Products Research Institute.

Ingestad, T., A. Aronsson, and G. I. Ågren. 1981. "Nutrient flux density model of mineral nutrition in conifer ecosystems." In *Understanding and Predicting tree growth,* edited by S. Linder, 61–71. Studia Forestalia Suecica No. 160.

Kimmins, J. P. 1973. The renewability of natural resources: implications for forest management. *Journal of Forestry* 71:290–292.

———. 1974. Sustained yield, ecological rotation, and timber mining: a British Columbia view. *Forestry Chronicle* 50(1):27–31.

———. 1985. Future shock in forest yield forecasting: the need for a new approach. *Forestry Chronicle* 61(6):503–513.

———. 1986. "FORCYTE in forestry: the need for a systems approach in forestry education, yield prediction and management." In *The E. B. Eddy distinguished lecture series,* 1–25. Toronto, Ont.: Faculty of Forestry, University of Toronto.

Kimmins, J. P., and K. A. Scoullar. 1984. "The role of modelling in tree nutrition research and site nutrient management." In *Nutrition of plantation forests,* edited by G. D. Bowen and E. K. S. Nambiar, 463–387. London: Academic Press.

Kimmins, J. P., and K. A. Scoullar. 1989. *FORCYTE-11.4 user's manual.* Contract Report. Ottawa, Ont.: Canadian Forestry Service.

Kimmins, J. P., K. A. Scoullar, R. E. Bigley, W. A. Kurz, P. G. Comeau, and L. Chatarpaul. 1986. "Yield prediction models: the need for a hybrid ecosystem-level approach incorporating canopy function and architecture." In *Crown and canopy structure in relation to productivity,* edited by T. Fujimori and D. Whitehead, 26–48. Proceedings of a IUFRO Symposium Workshop. Ibaraki, Japan: Forestry and Forest Products Research Institute.

Kimmins, J. P., K. A. Scoullar, and M. C. Feller. 1982. "FORCYTE-10." In *Proceedings of the 3rd bioenergy research and development seminar.* Ottawa, Ont.: Energy Project Office, National Research Council, Canada.

Lundmark, J. E. 1977. ["The soil as part of the forest ecosystem."] "Markem som del av det skogliga ekosystemet." [*The Care of the soil. Properties and utilization of forest soils.*] *Markuård. Skogsmarkens egensleaper och utnyttjande.* Sveriges Skogsvårdsforbunds Tidskrift 75:109–122.

Martin, W. L. 1985. *Post-clearcutting forest floor nitrogen dynamics and regeneration response in the Coastal Western Hemlock wet subzone.* Ph.D. Thesis. Vancouver, B.C.: University of British Columbia.

Mitchell, K. J., and I. R. Cameron. 1985. *Managed stand yield tables for coastal Douglas-fir: initial density and precommercial thinning.* Land Management Report No. 31. Victoria, B.C.: British Columbia Ministry of Forests.

Mohren, G. M. J. 1987. *Simulation of forest growth, applied to Douglas-fir stands in the Netherlands.* Ph.D. Thesis. Netherlands: Landbouwuniversiteit, Wageningen.

Pastor, J., and W. M. Post. 1985. *Development of a linked forest productivity soil process model.* Environmental Science Division Publication No. 2455. DSORNL/TM-9519. Oak Ridge, Tenn.: Oak Ridge National Laboratory.

Pimentel, D., W. Dritschilo, J. Krummel, and J. Kutzman. 1975. Energy and land constraints in food protein production. *Science* 190:754–761.

Pimentel, D., E. C. Terhune, R. Dyson-Hudson, S. Rochereau, R. Samis, E. A. Smith, D. Denman, D. Reifschneider, and M. Shepard. 1976. Land degradation: effects on food and energy resources. *Science* 194:149–155.

Rowe, J. S. 1961. The level-of-integration concept and ecology. *Ecology* 42:420–427.

Shugart, H. H. 1984. *A Theory of Forest Dynamics. The Ecological Implications of Forest Succession Models.* New York: Springer-Verlag.

Shugart, H. H., and D. C. West. 1977. Development of an Appalachian deciduous forest succession model and its application to assesssment of the impact of chestnut blight. *Journal of Environmental Management* 5:161–179.

Solomon, A. M. 1986. Transient response of forests to CO_2-induced climatic change: simulation modelling experiments in eastern North American. *Oecologia* 68:567–579.

Solomon, S. M., M. L. Thorp, D. C. West, G. E. Taylor, J. W. Webb, and J. L. Trimble. 1984. *Response of unmanaged forests to CO_2.* DOE/NBB-0053-TR009. Washington, D.C.: Research Division, Department of Energy.

Solomon, S. M., D. C. West, and J. A. Solomon. 1981. "Simulating the role of climate change and species immigration in forest succession." In *Forest succession,* edited by D. C. West, H. H. Shugart, and D. B. Botkin. New York: Springer-Verlag.

Steinhart, J. S., and C. E. Steinhart. 1974. Energy use in the US food system. Science 184:307–316.

Weinstein, D. A., H. H. Shugart, and D. C. West. 1982. *The long-term nutrient retention properties of forest ecosystems: a simulation investigation.* ORNL/TM-8472. Oak Ridge, Tenn.: Oak Ridge National Laboratory.

Chapter 12

Economic Perspectives on Maintaining the Long-Term Productivity of Forest Ecosystems

John H. Beuter and K. Norman Johnson

ABSTRACT

Conventional benefit-cost analysis does not favor constraints on timber management to preserve long-term ecosystem productivity. Even long-term timber productivity fares poorly in such analyses except for the special case in which an allowable cut effect immediately changes harvest level. Policies and regulations aimed at protecting ecosystems infringe on property rights of private landowners and increase the costs of producing marketable forest products and services for both private landowners and public agencies. The challenge is to show that constraints can increase net public benefit. Decision models for considering the costs of long-term ecosystem deterioration have been conceptualized. However, for these models to be useful, long-term effects must be known and understood—a formidable challenge for ecosystem researchers. The key for both economists and biologists is to recognize and establish resource values.

INTRODUCTION

"Resources are not, they become." This anonymous quote cited in Bishop (1978, p. 11) is strong in our consciousness as we economists ponder the long-term productivity of forest ecosystems. What in an ecosystem is of value? To whom? At what price? And where do these values come from?

The term "ecosystem" has attained the standing in modern America of motherhood and apple pie. Our collective wisdom is that one should no more think of harming or doing away with the former than with either of the latter. But realistically, some people are not all that nice to their mothers, some dislike apple pie, and others may never realize how much they can dislike an ecosystem until they have spent a few days beating through the devil's club and vine maple. Not all of our values are self-evident.

As economists, we are comfortable dealing with marketable components of an ecosystem, such as timber. We have no problem focusing on the need to preserve long-term timber productivity. Forecasts in study after study show increasing demand for timber in the face of diminishing supplies. Prices are forecast to rise at or above the rate of inflation, which should attract investment into timber production. Implicitly, investments in timber production are also investments in timber productivity.

But timber is only one aspect of an ecosystem—what about the other aspects, and the ecosystem as a whole? What are they worth? What is a snag or a downed tree worth? A red tree vole or a spotted owl? A brush patch? The soil, or the subsurface water? At what point does the exploitation of one aspect of an ecosystem seriously diminish or destroy the value of the whole? Can we identify a critical zone for ecosystem survival?

Coming from one direction, we have the inexorable evolution of an ecosystem toward its ultimate destiny, be it climax, or wheels of birth, deterioration and rebirth, or extinction. Coming from other directions, we manipulate to meet our needs and wants. Our actions are justified in an economic sense by a distillation to the present of tradition, momentum, and expectations about the future. Most pertinent to this discussion are how assumptions about the future affect decisions being made today—and what the consequences might be if those assumptions are wrong.

CONVENTIONAL BENEFIT-COST ANALYSIS

"In the long run we are all dead," wrote economist John Maynard Keynes in his 1923 *Tract on Monetary Reform* (Heilbroner 1967, p. 238), and sure enough, Keynes is no longer with us. But his quote survives as a clever, concise way for economists to cast aside concerns about long-term consequences of contemporary policies and actions. What difference does it make if we lose 10 or 20% of our forest productivity 100, 300, or 1,000 years from now? The pure economist's answer is: "Not much, if any." To understand this thinking, we need a simple example.

Assume we have a prescription for long-term timber production on a hectare of bare land. The prescription determines the stream of costs and revenues for a timber crop rotation, which in turn can be used to determine the value of the land for timber production. Discounting the value of an infinite series of rotations back to the present, we obtain the "soil expectation value" (SEV)—literally, the present net value of the soil and associated environmental variables as factors of timber production from here to eternity. It is customary to assume that each succeeding rotation will have the same yields as the first, i.e., productivity does not deteriorate over time. But what happens if it does?

For simplicity, let us assume an SEV of $741/ha for the situation of a 100-year rotation, a 5% discount rate, a constant unit price for timber, and no loss of site productivity. If timber productivity were to diminish perpetually by 5% each rotation, SEV would diminish by only 27 cents to $740.73 (Table 12.1). Productivity would have to diminish by over 10% after each rotation before the SEV would drop by $1.00/ha. Even if productivity completely disappeared after the first rotation—the soil slid off the hillside into the ocean—SEV would drop to only $735.36, a loss of less than 1%. Although results vary depending on the discount rate, even at a 1% discount rate, a complete loss of productivity after the first 100-year rotation would drop SEV by only 37%. And, at a 10% discount rate, it would not matter at all!

TABLE 12.1. Soil expectation value (dollars/hectare) under differing assumptions about loss of productivity and discount rate.[1]

Productivity loss, %	Discount rate, %				
	1	3	5	7	10
	100-year rotation				
0	56,722.59	5,307.83	741.00	111.57	7.01
5	55,072.23	5,293.31	740.73	111.57	7.01
10	53,579.73	5,278.86	740.43	111.57	7.01
25	49,495.44	5,235.98	739.59	111.55	7.01
50	43,859.22	5,166.05	738.18	111.50	7.01
100	35,751.60	5,031.66	735.36	111.45	7.01
	50-year rotation				
0	112,507.76	21,432.66	6,928.77	2,548.62	623.13
50	63,361.92	18,673.50	6,618.36	2,504.60	620.46
100	44,098.66	16,543.71	6,324.53	2,388.00	617.82

[1] The calculation of values in this table is explained in the Appendix.

You may think that the economic effects in the example are small because the rotation, at 100 years, is relatively long. To some extent that is true because the farther into the future the loss occurs, the less effect it has on present value. But even if we assume a total loss of productivity after one 50-year rotation (assuming the yield over 50 years is 75% of that over 100 years), the decline in SEV would vary from 61% at a 1% discount rate to only 1% at a 10% discount rate (Table 12.1).

The example may help explain why economists and business people often disagree with biologists and environmentalists about the importance of long-term site deterioration. The former focus on monetary returns from marketable products, using discount rates of 5% and usually higher. Future values discounted at high rates just do not amount to much at present. Besides, economists and business people strongly believe that everything is variable in the long run. As basic resources become scarcer, and thus more expensive, science and technology will find other ways to meet our needs and wants at reasonable prices. It has always happened in the past, so why should things be different in the future? Biologists and environmentalists, on the other hand, focus on endangered plants and animals, advocating constrained exploitation or preservation of forest ecosystems. This can diminish current net revenue from marketable products because of the costs of such constraints—either extra costs for environmental protection or the cost of forgone marketing of products from protected areas.

Both sides argue in terms of opportunity costs, i.e., the values forgone if a course of action eliminates a resource or use, but the measurement of values can differ greatly. When timber production is given up to favor environmental values, the opportunity cost is measured in monetary terms. When environmental values are given up to favor timber production, the opportunity cost is measured by less tangible criteria such as heritage, diversity, ethics, aesthetics, responsibility to future generations—and the ultimate criterion, survival.

Metaphysically, we are faced with differing perspectives on opportunity cost across a spectrum that has, at one end, hope for the immortality of individuals, species, societies, the planet, and the universe, and at the other end, resignation to the inevitability of extinction and death. It should not be surprising that conventional benefit-cost analysis does not lead to results acceptable to everyone.

THE ALLOWABLE CUT EFFECT

An allowable cut effect (ACE) on SEV may occur when there is a constraint on current harvest related to long-term productivity, e.g., nondeclining even flow on National Forest lands. If future productivity for a forest property can be increased by growth-enhancing management, the productivity constraint will be relieved, allowing an immediate increase in the harvest of mature timber that had previously been held in reserve to meet the constraint (Schweitzer et al. 1972).

ACE benefits may be significant. In evaluating the growth benefits of reforesting an area not previously in the timber base, Beuter and Handy (1974) calculated a bare land SEV of $5,590/ha, compared to an SEV of only $894/ha for a property not subject to ACE.

The negative economic effect of future declines in timber productivity may be similarly magnified on properties subject to ACE. For example, a discovery that future productivity will be lower than assumed for the initial harvest calculation might require an immediate decrease in harvest. The change in SEV might be the reverse of that shown above. This is one instance where the immediate economic impact of a future decrease in productivity might be significant enough to be of concern to economists and business people, as well as biologists.

The applicability of ACE varies from forest to forest, depending on the distribution of inventory by age class, the management regime, and the constraints affecting current harvest. Generally speaking, ACE is applicable to few situations at present (mainly on some national forests), and will be even less so as those forests evolve toward a fully managed, regulated condition.

PRODUCTIVITY OF WHAT?

It is easy to focus on timber productivity because it is so important economically, socially, and politically. The perspective of professional foresters rests on an underlying assumption about the inherent capability of our forests to produce timber from here to eternity. Recall that the SEV calculation usually presumes endless cycles of the same silvicultural prescription with the same yields, a prophecy reflecting the commitment of foresters to sustained yield.

The challenge of timber management is to accelerate or otherwise enhance what could occur naturally, i.e., to undertake activities to achieve full stocking of desirable species, increase timber growth, and, in a business sense, turn over the inventory as rapidly as possible. The site is prepared by eliminating undesirable vegetation and debris so that seedlings, once planted, can flourish. Basic yields are enhanced by investing in genetically improved stock, spacing and fertilization, and protecting seedlings from predators, pests, and competing vegetation. The substantial costs of burning, spraying, animal-damage control, and other activities aimed at improving tree survival and growth are readily accepted as costs of doing business—investments in timber productivity.

But how does *ecosystem* productivity relate to *timber* productivity? The distinction can be confusing. Many people equate the two, which makes sense as long as one assumes a direct relationship between what is proposed for maintaining ecosystem health and what is needed to produce merchantable timber. But what happens when the focus shifts from board feet per acre (cubic meters per hectare) per year to nonmarketable concepts such as nutrient cycling rates, diversity and quantity of soil organisms, and diversity of flora and fauna?

This shift is troubling for timber managers. The relationship between ecosystem and timber productivity blurs with proposals to set aside 2,000 acres (about 810 ha) for spotted owls, with restrictions on herbicides and burning, or with other regulations that raise the costs of timber management and thus decrease, rather than increase, timber productivity.

Long-term productivity depends on maintaining and controlling basic ecosystem processes and characteristics-nutrient cycling, soil biology and properties, erosion, and ecological diversity. There are all sorts of implications for how we might define ecosystem productivity and the measures needed to protect it in the long run.

Timber management practices can be adapted to maintain long-term ecosystem productivity, presumably at an acceptable cost to society, but it is obvious we still have a lot to learn. Every new idea for preserving ecosystem productivity that is not linked to maintaining or increasing SEVs is in for a battle in the real world of economics and politics.

MANAGEMENT AND POLICY ISSUES

Property Rights

The major underlying social issue for ecosystem productivity involves property rights—what will land-owners do if left to their own devices? Economic theory suggests that unregulated forest landowners will use their land to maximize their return on investment, even though criteria will differ among them—some measuring returns in dollars, others in status or psychic rewards. Many of us recoil in horror at the thought of a rare and fragile ecosystem being converted to a parking lot or tennis courts. But it happens all the time, although probably less frequently since the dawning of environmental awareness in the 1960s.

To varying degrees, depending upon where you live, society has decided that private interests in forest land ownership do not coincide with the public interest. This has lead to zoning to limit land use and regulations to limit forest practices. In the case of public lands, concerns that the interests of managing agencies such as the USDA Forest Service do not coincide with the public interest have prompted legislation requiring comprehensive land-use planning and restricting management activities, e.g., the Forest and Rangeland Renewable Resources and Planning Act (Act of August 17, 1974; P. L. 93–878, 88 Stat. 476) and the National Forest Management Act of 1976 (Act of October 22, 1976; P. L. 94–588, 90 Stat. 2949).

Managers of private and public forests are protective of their traditional "rights." Neither likes to have "outsiders" tell them how to manage their land. And, like all the rest of us, they want to see results fast and take credit for their accomplishments. Add to that, faith in the resilience of the ecosystem to produce perpetual timber crops, and you have a context in which it is hard to sell forest managers new concepts of ecosystem protection. Within their perception of objectives and constraints, and the limits of their knowledge, most forest managers believe they follow best management practices—it would be rare to find one who admitted to willingly doing less than best, given the circumstances. Yet new requirements aimed at protecting ecosystems, such as restricted harvesting in streamside zones, are often perceived as losses of personal property rights and value for the benefit of special or public interests.

Increased Costs of Timber Production

It is easy to understand why landowners become upset when land is taken out of timber production, but what about reforestation requirements or logging restrictions to avoid soil compaction and erosion—measures aimed directly at fostering timber productivity? Why would landowners resist such measures when they are clearly aimed at preserving timber growing capability?

Attitudes here are tempered by knowledge and perceptions. It is hard for some people to imagine that a little compaction will make a big difference in timber growth rates over the next rotation, or that some microscopic soil organism is important to long-term productivity. What they are conscious of is the extra costs associated with the constraints imposed upon them. For example, even though an herbicide ban does not necessarily diminish the capability to grow timber, it might significantly increase the costs for site preparation and control of vegetation that competes with growing trees. It helps if the benefits of constraints can be documented by good research. Research may not reduce the extra costs, but it might increase willingness to accept constraints as a moral obligation.

Net Public Benefit

The impact of constraints that increase costs of timber management often go beyond the landowner. To the extent that timber supplies might diminish because of costly constraints, there would likely be less economic activity associated with timber production—road building, logging, hauling, manufacturing, reforestation, and related services. That private landowners might be forced out of the timber business by increased costs is obvious to most people. Less obvious is the possibility that public agencies also might be forced out.

Prodded by both economists and environmentalists, the U.S. Congress has taken an increased interest in the costs of timber management on the National Forests. They question whether the Forest Service should make below-cost timber sales, i.e., sales for which costs exceed revenues (U.S. General Accounting Office 1984,

Le Master et al. 1987). Economists question these sales from a business perspective—it does not make sense to continue doing something that loses money. Environmentalists question below-cost sales because many occur in undeveloped, environmentally sensitive areas. In its defense, the Forest Service argues that below-cost sales increase net public benefit by contributing to the economic and social well-being of timber-dependent communities.

Ironically, costs associated with environmental protection and preservation of long-term productivity contribute to the negative cash flow of some below-cost timber sales. The Forest Service builds these costs into timber-sale contracts to protect the site, insure reforestation, and in some cases enhance nontimber values. Thus, even though timber sales may cause environmental problems, they are also a means of mitigating them, and perhaps, in some cases, even increasing environmental values on balance. Whether the nontimber benefits of timber sales offset the negative cash flow for timber-related activities, and thus increase public net benefit, should be evident in National Forest plans. Whether the public believes or accepts what is in the plans is another matter.

BEYOND TIMBER PRODUCTION

The management and policy issues described above are largely oriented toward timber production, and with good reason. The weight of public opinion rests with what people are accustomed to in terms of economic activity, community services, and amenities. Residents in timber-dependent communities are apt to associate their personal welfare with timber management activity rather than with nutrient cycling, soil biology, and other measures of ecosystem health.

But "Resources are not, they become." Nothing is valuable until people decide that it is. Compare, for example, the value of western hemlock [*Tsuga heterophylla* (Raf.) Sarg.] and alder (*Alnus* spp.) 20 years ago with their values today. Changing technology, expanding markets, and new consumer acceptance created value where little existed previously. Values are determined by society's ever-changing tastes and preferences, which in turn are related to how well the basic needs for survival have been met. Goods that remain in favor over time will become more valuable as their supply diminishes, e.g., 1965 Ford Mustang convertibles. Things not previously in favor may gain favor, and thus become valuable as their supply diminishes, e.g., wilderness. Certain goods become resources as a society becomes more confident about its basic survival and can afford to be more concerned about natural and cultural heritage and aesthetics.

Our willingness to pay for the preservation of ecosystem health will be determined by our perceptions of its worth. With a focus on economic activity, however, components of the ecosystem that do not directly affect timber production may be treated as "externalities," as would the responsibilities and costs of maintaining them. Analogously, unregulated pollution of water and air is an externality to the activities that generate the pollutants. With regard to pollution, Pearce (1976, p. 99) states: ". . . if people do not care about biological changes in species (or, indeed in themselves) no 'economic effect' can be said to exist." He goes on to point out this is also the case if people are ignorant of how biological changes caused by pollution may affect them. Pollution—a dynamic externality that is difficult to bring into conventional benefit-cost analysis—is much like long-term declines in ecosystem productivity for which no "economic effect" can be identified. As already noted, such declines are not usually included when timber-management alternatives are evaluated.

So, how can we account for undesirable externalities?

This is a tough question because the answer depends on the extent of the externalities and how much they threaten our well-being. If they are perceived as a threat to our health, safety, and welfare, little analysis is needed to justify changes to eliminate or mitigate them. Witness the recent outpouring of resources to combat AIDS. Paraphrasing Pearce (1976, p. 110): ". . . at some point [economic analysis] should give way to [setting standards] based on a cautious attitude to [biological] and other physical information."

At what point should probable losses in long-term productivity lead us to change the way we do business? Recently, Sachs and Sollins (1986) reported on how management practices in western hemlock stands might affect the availability of nitrogen and soil organic matter (SOM), and, in turn, long-term productivity of timber. They found that shorter rotations used in intensive timber management would likely lead to significant losses of soil and forest-floor nitrogen, compared to longer rotations with less intensive management. However, the decline in yields from one rotation to the next over their 540-year simulation period was relatively small; in fact, at times yields increased (Fig. 12.1). Over 540 years, the projected declines in timber yield for all management regimes were less than 10%. So where is the economic effect?

After noting that their results are tenuous because of uncertainty and poor information about ecosystem processes, Sachs and Sollins (1986, p. 35) conclude: "Whether to believe or act upon these predictions is problematic . . . Nevertheless, given the inevitable uncertainty in long-term predictions, it may be more pru-

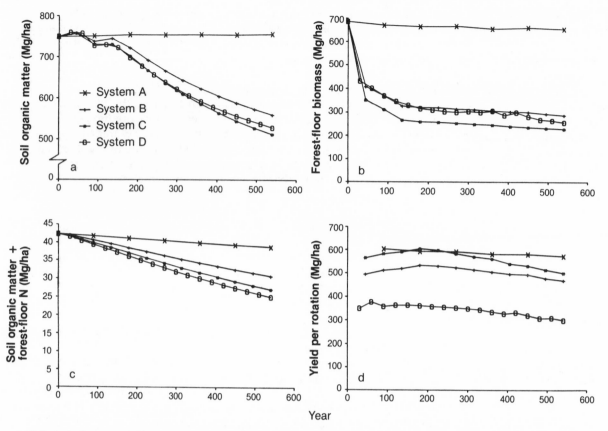

FIG. 12.1. Projected effect of four management systems on forest health over a 540-year simulation (from Sachs and Sollins 1986, p. 33; used with permission):
System A: Low-intensity management; 90-year rotations; no thinning; clearcut harvest, only stems removed.
System B: Management for maximum biomass; 45-year rotations; precommercial thinning at age 30; clearcut harvest, only stems removed.
System C: Same as B but whole trees removed at harvest; N = nitrogen.
System D: 30-year rotations; clearcut harvest, whole trees removed.

dent to protect SOM levels by using longer rotations and less intensive harvest methods until further research and improved models can . . . sharpen our predictions. Certainly it appears much easier to lose SOM than to replace it." What Sachs and Sollins recommend is not necessarily wrong just because they cannot support it with economic evidence. They simply urge "setting standards," as suggested by Pearce (1976) above.

Longer rotations and less intensive harvest methods may be worthy of consideration, but, for reasons noted earlier, timber managers and business people can be expected to do battle with biologists if anyone seriously tries to impose standards by law or regulation. Sachs and Sollins' (1986) recommendation is not on solid ground economically or politically because no crisis exists or is likely to exist in the foreseeable future.

Economist S. V. Ciriacy-Wantrup (1968, p. 253) developed the concept of a "safe minimum standard of conservation" for resources with a critical zone, i.e., a point beyond which it would be uneconomical to halt and reverse depletion. He goes beyond economics in stating (1968, p. 252):

"From a certain degree onward—for example, if more and more acres of land or species of plants and animals are affected—irreversibility in the depletion of critical zone resources limits opportunities of adaptation and narrows the potential development of society. Both the biological and social sciences have come to the conclusion that such a limiting and narrowing force directs development toward specialization rather than diversification. Such a direction has been held responsible for retarded and abortive growth—in the sense of growth toward a dead end—stagnation, and death of species and civilizations."

Specifically referring to forest ecosystems, Ciriacy-Wantrup continues (1968, pp. 257–258):

"Forests . . . are plant (species) associations of often great complexity and sensitivity with respect to influences which upset the ecological balance ... [with regard to a safe minimum standard] ... modern ecology has made it practical to define a plant association and to check its maintenance periodically."

He subsequently proposes (1968, p. 268):

"The objectives and criteria of conservation decisions are best formulated in a way that takes uncertainty explicitly into account ... by subjecting the economic optimum to the restriction of avoiding immoderate losses, or by formulating it as 'minimizing maximum possible losses.' "

Bishop (1978, pp. 12–13) later proposed a "mini-max" approach for assessing the benefits and costs of species extinction. To illustrate the concept he developed a hypothetical trade-off between a hydroelectric dam and the extinction of an endangered species, constructing a hypothetical matrix of probable losses for two strategies and two states of nature:

Strategies	States of nature		Maximum losses
	1	2	
E	0	y	y
SMS	x	x − y	x

where
E = Build dam and make species extinct.
SMS = Safe minimum standard (no dam, protect species).
1 = Nothing unanticipated in future to create large social losses because the species became extinct.
2 = The species unexpectedly turns out to have great value, e.g., the key to curing cancer.
0 = Base point for payoffs.
y = Expected present net value of the possible large future value of the endangered species.
x = Expected present net value of the dam project.
x, y > 0 and y > x.

For convenience, if the dam gets built, and the species does not turn out to be valuable, the loss is zero (base point). If the dam gets built, the species becomes extinct (E). If the species proves to be valuable, the loss is the value of the species (y). If SMS is adopted, the dam does not get built and the species does not prove to be valuable, the loss is the value of the dam (x). If SMS is adopted, and the species turns out to be valuable, the value of the dam is lost, but that of the species is gained (x − y).

Bishop's (1978) endangered-species example represents an extreme situation, but the mini-max approach may still be helpful for analyzing the costs of declines in long-term ecosystem productivity. Is there a critical zone for ecosystem productivity? What is the probability of a substantial loss of public net benefit? When will the critical zone be reached?

The critical zone is defined by economic irreversibility. If declines in ecosystem productivity can be offset by investments such as introducing nitrogen-fixing vegetation or artificial fertilization, and such investments have a positive present net worth, there really is no problem, at least not an economic one. This presumes that all externalities are accounted for, and that the resources brought to bear on solving the problem are priced to reflect their long-term effect on society. However, this may not always be the case. For example, fertilizers made from petroleum-based resources may be underpriced because their supply may eventually be exhausted (Beuter 1979). If the market does not recognize this eventuality, then the market price will not reflect it. Likewise, if the market does not recognize the possibility of long-term productivity loss, market prices will not reflect it. With this observation we have come full circle. It may not be wise to trust the market to set values for resources having a critical zone. We should heed Ciriacy-Wantrup's (1968) admonition that we go beyond the market and take uncertainty into account to minimize our maximum possible losses.

SUMMARY

We started with the problem of evaluating in economic terms the long-term changes in ecosystem productivity. Conventional benefit-cost analysis was found unlikely to favor constraints on timber management for the purpose of preserving long-term ecosystem productivity. Even long-term timber productivity does not fare well in these analyses, except for the special case of the allowable cut effect. Conventional economists and business people are likely to have faith that science, technology, and the marketplace will work everything out. If we cannot afford to "fix" deteriorating ecosystem productivity, the marketplace will surely recognize this and value ecosystems more highly than the activities that cause them to deteriorate.

Not all economists agree with this assessment. Some concede that there is a place where economic analysis breaks down—perhaps because there is no way to correctly price some things that we intuitively feel have great value, or because lack of knowledge prevents us from even being aware of the true value of something or, alternatively, the cost of not having it.

We can conceptualize models to incorporate the likelihood of future losses due to the policies and actions of today. However, a conceptually good model is useless for solving problems if we do not know with some degree of certainty the consequences of our actions. If critical zones for ecosystem survival exist, every effort must be made to identify them. For without such information, it may be impossible to make a strong case for the protecting ecosystem productivity, except when obvious economic values, such as timber productivity, are at risk.

All this suggests there will be plenty of work for researchers of ecosystem processes and modellers of long-term effects of management practices. Answers will not be easy to find and may be long in coming. In the meantime, it is important for us to recognize that we do not have all the answers, neither economists, nor biologists. It is no more prudent to seriously disrupt the established economic and social structure of a community that depends on timber than it is to seriously disrupt an ecosystem structure needed for the long-term survival of valuable organisms. The key is to recognize and establish values. Resources are not valuable unless we make them so.

Nobody said it was going to be easy.

ACKNOWLEDGMENTS

We thank Bill Atkinson, professor and head, Department of Forest Engineering, Oregon State University, for helpful comments.

REFERENCES

Beuter, John H. 1979. "Forest fertilization and the economics of perpetual motion machines." In *Symbiotic nitrogen fixation in the management of temperate forests, proceedings of a workshop,* edited by J. C. Gordon, C. T. Wheeler, and D. A. Perry, 4–13. Corvallis, Ore.: Forest Research Laboratory, Oregon State University.

Beuter, John H., and J. K. Handy. 1974. *Economic guidelines to reforestation for different ownerships: a case study for the Coast Range of western Oregon.* Research Paper 23. Corvallis, Ore.: Forest Research Laboratory, Oregon State University.

Bishop, Richard C. 1978. Endangered species and uncertainty: the economics of a safe minimum standard. *American Journal of Agricultural Economics* 60:10–18.

Ciriacy-Wantrup, S. V. 1968. *Resource conservation economics and policies.* 3rd ed. Berkeley, Calif.: Agricultural Experiment Station, University of California.

Davis, Lawrence S., and K. Norman Johnson. 1987. *Forest Management.* 3rd ed. New York: McGraw-Hill.

Heilbroner, Robert L. 1967. *The Worldly Philosophers.* New York: Simon and Schuster.

Le Master, Dennis C., Barry R. Flamm, and John C. Hendee (editors). 1987. *Below-cost timber sales.* Washington, D.C.: The Wilderness Society.

Pearce, David. 1976. The limits of cost-benefit analysis as a guide to environmental policy. *Kyklos* 29 (1976):97–112.

Sachs, D., and P. Sollins. 1986. Potential effects of management practices on nitrogen nutrition and long-term productivity of western hemlock stands. *Forest Ecology and Management* 17:25–36.

Schweitzer, D. L., R. W. Sassaman, and C. H. Schallau. 1972. Allowable cut effect: some physical and economic implications. *Journal of Forestry* 70(7):415–418.

U.S. General Accounting Office. 1984. *Congress needs better information on below-cost timber sales.* GAO/RCED-84-96, report to the President of the Senate and Speaker of the House. Washington, D.C.: U.S. Government Printing Office.

APPENDIX: Explanation of the calculations in Table 12.1

Soil expectation value (SEV), defined as the present net value of an infinite series of rotations, is calculated as follows (Davis and Johnson 1987):

$$SEV = a/[(1 + i)^w - 1] \tag{A1}$$

where a = future net value of a silvicultural prescription at the end of one rotation (w).
i = discount rate (guiding rate of interest).

Table 12.1 is based on a silvicultural prescription for a 100-year rotation that yields an SEV of $300/acre at a 5% discount rate:

$$SEV = a/(1.05^{100} - 1)$$
$$= 300.$$

It follows that

$$a = 300(1.05^{100} - 1)$$
$$= 39{,}150.38.$$

For simplicity, it was assumed that a = $39,150.38 regardless of the discount rate. This could be the case if there was only a final harvest at age 100. Thus, at a 7% discount rate:

$$SEV = 39{,}150.38/(1.07^{100} - 1)$$
$$= 45.17/\text{acre } (111.57/\text{ha}).$$

If productivity after each rotation is reduced by p percent, SEV must, in turn, account for the reduction for n rotations. Thus, the values in Table 12.1 for a 100-year rotation were calculated as follows:

$$SEV_{ip} = \sum_{n=1}^{\infty} [a(1 - p/100)^{n-1}]/[(1 + i)^{100n}]$$

where SEV_{ip} = soil expectation at discount rate i and a p-percent reduction in productivity after each rotation. When $p = 0$, this equation reduces to Equation (A1) above.

For any combination of discount rate ($0.01 \leq i \leq 1$) and productivity decrease, SEV stabilizes in cents in 20 or fewer rotations, i.e., $n \leq 20$. There is no need to go to infinity.

The values in Table 12.1 for a 50-year rotation were calculated as follows:

$$SEV_{ip} = \sum_{n=1}^{\infty} [0.75a(1 - p/100)^{n-1}]/[(1 + i)^{50n}].$$

230

Chapter 13

Applied Concepts of Ecosystem Management: Developing Guidelines for Coarse, Woody Debris

Steve Eubanks

ABSTRACT

Coarse, woody debris (harvest residues and standing dead or unmerchantable trees) is an important component of forest ecosystems. The Blue River Ranger District seeks to perpetuate this component over time in harvest areas by reducing cleanup of residues to ensure adequate supplies of soil organic matter and leaving more standing trees to ensure wildlife habitat. The District has developed guidelines that not only deal with the technical aspects (what kind, how much) to manage for, but also address how to deal with key people to ensure that the guidelines are met.

INTRODUCTION

Recently, there has been increased interest in ecosystem management—the concept of managing forests with consideration for all parts of the ecosystem. In order to address the concepts of ecosystem management, the Blue River Ranger District, Willamette National Forest, has, in concert with researchers on the H. J. Andrews Experimental Forest (located on the Blue River District), developed several management techniques that are implemented when timber is logged for sale on the District. This chapter describes how the Blue River Ranger District manages the coarse, woody debris—both downed harvest residues (slash) and standing dead or unmerchantable trees—after harvest.

MANAGING FOR RESIDUES

The work with ecosystem management/long-term site productivity on the Blue River Ranger District began several years ago when our staff realized that harvest units were ending up too "clean" after YUM (yarding of unmerchantable material) yarding. Our concern was heightened when we realized that much of the harvest residue being yarded to the landing was not utilizable in any way—it was just too rotten. To address the situation, we convened a task force composed of researchers, resource specialists, and technical experts from Oregon State University, the Pacific Northwest Research Station, the Willamette National Forest Supervisor's Office, and the Blue River Ranger District. The objective of the task force was to determine the level (by amount and size class) of slash that *should be left* on site following harvest to ensure adequate supplies of soil organic matter in future. We felt it was important to look at slash from this perspective rather than from the traditional perspective of how much to remove.

The result of the task force's effort is the Blue River Residue Guideline (Fig. 13.1), which has several important features. First, the Guideline uses common terminology and graphics to enhance understanding. Second, the Guideline calls for a "target" weight per hectare rather than a maximum weight per hectare because we consider the weight per hectare to be just that—a target, as much a minimum as a maximum. Third, for residue larger than 20.1 in. (51.1 cm), the Guideline deals in number of logs rather than weight per hectare because weight per hectare is not a good measure of impacts to the two common areas of concern in Douglas-fir [*Pseudotsuga menziesii* (Mirb.) Franco] forests—fire intensity and planting barriers—for larger residue. As an example, 15 logs 24 in. × 20 ft. (61 cm × 6.1 m) weigh 14 tons (31 Mg) whereas 15 logs 48 in. × 20 ft. (1.2 × 6.1 m) weigh 54 tons (119 Mg) (Table 13.1). While this is a dramatic difference in weight per hectare, there would be little difference in the effect on fire intensity and reforestation because the total area actually covered is virtually the same in both cases. One caveat concerning the Blue River Residue Guideline: it is not the actual numbers in the Guideline that are important, but rather the process used in developing the Guideline. The numbers themselves were developed for the Blue River District and may not apply to other areas.

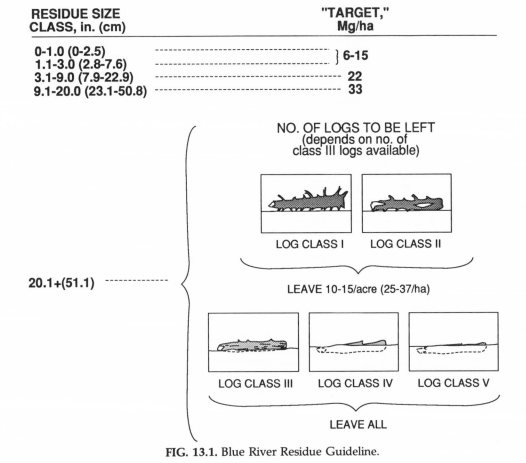

RESIDUE SIZE CLASS, in. (cm)	"TARGET," Mg/ha
0-1.0 (0-2.5)	} 6-15
1.1-3.0 (2.8-7.6)	
3.1-9.0 (7.9-22.9)	22
9.1-20.0 (23.1-50.8)	33

NO. OF LOGS TO BE LEFT
(depends on no. of
class III logs available)

LOG CLASS I   LOG CLASS II

20.1+(51.1)

LEAVE 10-15/acre (25-37/ha)

LOG CLASS III   LOG CLASS IV   LOG CLASS V

LEAVE ALL

FIG. 13.1. Blue River Residue Guideline.

TABLE 13.1. Weight of 15 Douglas-fir logs [12% moisture content, 30 lb/ft.^{3} (480 kg/m^3) density].

Small-end log diameter, in. (cm)	Log length, ft. (m)		
	20 (6.1)	32 (9.8)	48 (14.6)
	tons (Mg)		
12 (30.5)	3 (7)	5 (11)	6 (13)
24 (60.9)	14 (31)	21 (46)	27 (60)
36 (91.4)	30 (66)	46 (101)	64 (141)
48 (121.9)	54 (119)	84 (185)	120 (265)
60 (152.4)	87 (192)	132 (291)	192 (423)

Implementation of Guidelines

Our work really had just begun when the Residue Guideline was completed—because the key step is getting results on the ground. To do that effectively, our fire management and sale administration sections developed a process to address the various situations that would be encountered (Fig. 13.2). Implementation is very simple for new timber sales—just build the Guideline into the sale prescription and reflect the Guideline in the contract and appraisal. But new sales were not our biggest concern because they are so easy to handle. We have about 3 years of existing sales under contract at any given time, and it was these existing sales for which the implementation strategy was primarily developed.

To start with, existing sales were each assessed on the ground in terms of volume per hectare, defect levels, and other variables that affect residue amounts following logging. After each sale was assessed, the decision was

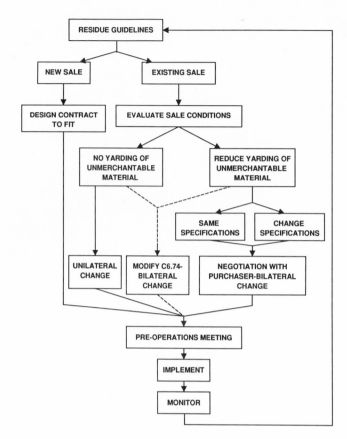

FIG. 13.2. Process for implementing the Blue River Residue Guideline.

made to either eliminate YUM yarding or just reduce it in some way. If YUM yarding was to be eliminated, we simply notified the purchaser and completed a unilateral (the purchaser did not have to agree) contract change. If YUM yarding was to be reduced, we either changed the YUM size specifications (size of the material to be yarded) or retained the same specifications and reduced the amount to be yarded. Both of these strategies required working with the purchasers to complete a bilateral (both parties agreeing) contract change. Concurrently, we worked with purchasers to modify contract clause C6.74 to require logs to be left in the harvest units because a good wood chip market can encourage purchasers to yard residues (unless there is a contractual constraint against doing so).

Once contracts are settled for both new and existing sales, we focus on a key step—the sale pre-operations meeting. Having well-thought-out guidelines or implementation processes, or even good contracts, does not ensure success: you must also spend time explaining your objectives to the people out on the ground doing the work. In most cases, this means not only the timber sale operator but also some of the operator's employees. This explanation is especially important because we have for years been exhorting these people to "be sure not to miss any of those YUM logs."

Our intent now is to monitor the results of implementing our Residue Guideline to see if any changes are warranted and, if so, what those changes should be. We intend the Guideline to be a dynamic product that is fine tuned as needed.

MANAGING FOR WILDLIFE TREES

Completion of the Residue Guideline left us feeling good about the log component of coarse, woody debris but we realized that we needed to improve our management of the other key component of coarse, woody debris—wildlife trees. We were particularly interested in perpetuating the availability of wildlife trees into future rotations. We began by using chapter 7 of *Management of Wildlife and Fish Habitats in Forests of Western Oregon and Washington* (Neitro et al. 1985) as a reference for doing some basic modelling of wildlife-tree management alternatives.

Some basic assumptions guided our modelling. The first was an assumption about the "residence time" (expected life) of the various stages of wildlife trees (Fig.13.3). The second was an assumption about the minimum habitat requirements of the five primary cavity nesters of the Douglas-fir Region at the 40% biological potential level—that is, the habitat needed to support at least 40% of the maximum potential populations of these cavity-nesting species (Fig. 13.4). The minimum needs, when all tree size classes are added together, total about 250 trees/100 ha, or about 2.5 trees/ha. (Remember, this is the *minimum* that must be present at any given time to meet the 40% biological potential level.)

Using the preceding assumptions, we started our modelling with the composite of the minimum needs at year 100—about the end of the next rotation (Fig. 13.5a). We estimated what the wildlife tree mix would have to be at year 80 of the next rotation to ensure that the minimum needs would be met at year 100, and what mix would be needed at year 60 for year 80, and so on back to year 0 (Fig. 13.5b). The year 0 figure, therefore, represents what wildlife tree mix would have to be left in a harvest unit today to ensure that minimum needs are met 100 years from now—approximately 1,000 trees/100 ha or about 10 trees/ha. Since some wildlife trees are lost during burning or logging even in a careful operation, the actual number needed to ensure the proper succession to year 100 would probably be closer to an average of 15 trees/ha. Note that most of the wildlife trees called for are live culls (green trees with defect) and not snags (standing dead trees).

We also wanted to ensure that the wildlife tree mix could be met in future rotations as well as in the current one. To do that, we assumed that we would want to start each successive rotation with the same "year 0" mix deemed necessary in a harvest unit today. Therefore, for the sake of modelling, we needed to determine if we could replace (regrow) that "year 0" mix during successive rotations (Fig. 13.5c). Using "snag replacement"

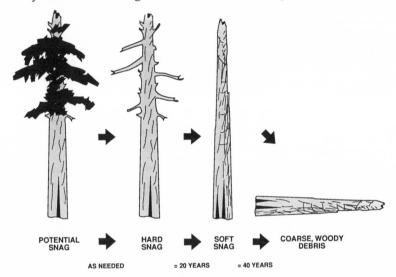

FIG. 13.3. Evolution of a wildlife tree.

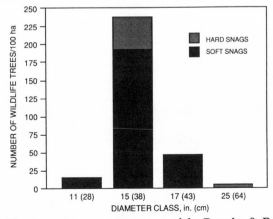

FIG. 13.4. Minimum needs of the five primary cavity nesters of the Douglas-fir Region at the 40% biological potential level (adapted from Neitro et al. 1985).

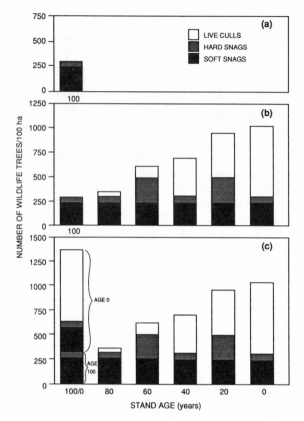

FIG. 13.5. Managing wildlife trees over time to meet the minimum needs of the five primary cavity nesters of the Douglas-fir Region (all size classes combined).

tables in chapter 7 of Neitro et al, 1985 and our own knowledge of timber stands on the Blue River District, we concluded that we could, in fact, regrow the "year 0" mix. There is, however, a "catch"—there must be a commitment to consciously manage for that wildlife tree mix. It will mean less salvage and less volume removed at intermediate harvests so that cull trees will be present at the end of the rotation.

To better assess some of the issues associated with such a management scheme, the Blue River District is completing a pilot project that implements our findings and examines the various trade-offs involved (for example, extra yarding costs and loss of yields). We feel that another issue, that of safety of workers near wildlife trees, has been addressed since we developed a marking guide for wildlife trees in conjunction with representatives of Associated Oregon Loggers, Willamette Timbermen Association, and the Oregon State Accident Prevention Division. In addition, because most of our wildlife trees will be live culls, there should be no more concern about safety in the case of wildlife trees than there is with most normal shelterwood cuts.

FUTURE CONSIDERATIONS

Where do we go next? I think we need to find better ways of perpetuating harvest residues—the log component of coarse, woody debris—into future rotations. At present, it is easy to get support for reducing or eliminating YUM yarding because, with the large amount of defect generally found in old-growth stands, there is an ample supply of logs to leave with no product value. But what happens in future rotations when there is little defect and little likelihood of large cull logs? This is especially of concern when you consider that the large, fast-grown logs of the future will decompose much faster than the tight-grained, old-growth logs of today.

QUESTIONS FROM THE SYMPOSIUM FLOOR

Q: How do you designate the trees to be left in a harvest unit—Forest Service mark or "faller select"?
A: We have used both methods and feel the "faller select" method is best for our conditions. With the larger number of trees being designated, it would take much more time for us to do the marking, and we are

unable to take into account the variables faced by fallers.

Q: How much logging cost increase is associated with extra wildlife trees?

A: The amount of increase hasn't been determined yet—that information will be in our pilot project final report. I don't think it will be that significant. After all, the number of trees being left represents about the same density as that of a light shelterwood.

Q: Do your calculations for coarse, woody debris consider the logs provided by the wildlife trees you are leaving?

A: The wildlife trees will provide logs over time, but not in the numbers that we are leaving to start with. For example, a typical old-growth clearcut may have 30+ Class III, IV, and V logs/acre (74+ logs/ha), and we are leaving 10–15 Class I and II logs/acre (25–37 logs/ha) in addition to that. Even the number of wildlife trees left in the pilot project will not provide that number of logs over time. I think perpetuation of the log component of coarse, woody debris is probably the next issue we will tackle—probably with modelling similar to that used for wildlife trees but more complex.

Q: How do your silviculturists feel about leaving 4–6 cull trees/acre (10–15 culls/ha)—seed sources, disease, etc.?

A: There shouldn't be a problem with the cull trees as seed or disease sources. First of all, we need the genetic diversity over time, and it can be argued that you need some unhealthy individuals to provide the diversity needed to ensure a healthy stand—certainly, we need a future source of wildlife trees, and these culls may provide some of that source. Second, many of the cull trees may actually be superior trees that have been dominants throughout most of their lifetime and are just getting old.

Q: Have you considered clumping the wildlife trees?

A: Some of the wildlife trees, mainly the few soft snags that will be left, may be clumped to minimize safety problems. We want other wildlife trees to be fairly evenly scattered around the stands so that we receive greater benefit from them as coarse, woody debris when they eventually fall to the ground.

Q: Have you considered how your wildlife trees will affect aerial silvicultural treatments such as halitorch burning, fertilization, and herbicide application?

A: Yes. Our fire managers feel that helitorch burning should still be possible—it's a matter of adjusting the viscosity of the mix. Fertilizer and herbicide can be applied from a higher altitude but may require better conditions (less wind for example).

Q: How will you keep the wildlife trees standing (avoid blowdown)?

A: I think the problem with wind is often overstated. I have seen little real problem with blowdown in wildlife trees in most areas I have visited around the West. Many of the trees we are leaving are old former dominants that established windfirmness early in their lifetimes, and even if some of the trees blow down, they can function as coarse, woody debris a little ahead of schedule. However, the process of topping trees is pretty well established and the cost is reasonable, so topping can be used if blowdown is a real concern.

Q: In reference to rewording C6.74 to require that logs be left (part of the Blue River Residue Guideline), the standard B provisions are set up to include removal or substandard removal. If the purchaser chooses to remove the cull logs because of market conditions, how can you stop it?

A: Our interpretation is that the most constraining clause controls, particularly when we have established through the Environmental Assessment Report and prospectus (notice to prospective timber-sale purchasers) the intent to leave logs on site. Ultimately, I think a new clause should be developed to reflect our intent.

Q: What management changes have you made to protect understory duff?

A: We now broadcast burn only when we have "spring burn" conditions, i.e., high duff and soil moisture content.

Q: Why did you use old-growth ecosystems as the base for your guideline for harvest residues and wildlife trees? Historically, extensive disturbance has been the rule.

A: Actually, there has been much more small-scale disturbance in the Douglas-fir Region than was once believed. However, I think the key in looking at old-growth systems is that old growth is nature's way of restoring the "bank account" of productivity. If that is the case, we need to look at that model as a way of at least maintaining the "bank account" as long as possible.

Q: Are you planning to assess differences in seedling survival, plantability, stocking levels, cost of reforestation, etc. If so, how?

A: We are already monitoring those variables on a routine basis. It should be fairly simple to compare the results of our old and new residue treatments.

Q: Having the H. J. Andrews Experimental Forest on your district must make it easier for you to transfer research into application. How can other locations facilitate this transfer of information?

A: I have been involved in ecosystem management for about 10 years and have seen many of the concepts I discussed implemented on other units. Having a close working relationship with the research community has allowed us to progress faster at Blue River than would have been possible in other places, but the real key in getting things started is to have a few people who are interested and committed. I have found the researchers involved in long-term site productivity/ecosystem management to be more than willing to help—all you have to do is ask. A set of videotapes addressing the kinds of issues covered in this symposium, and much more about ecosystem management—both theory and practice, is now available from the College of Forestry's Media Center at Oregon State University.

Q: The options you discussed for land management are often frustrated by political forces or people in higher positions. How can we overcome that?

A: I believe that real improvements tend to begin at the field level (Ranger District or equivalent)—generally, mandating them from above doesn't work as well in the long run. I also believe we can influence the political process and people in higher authority and get them in tune with needed improvements. To do so, we need to communicate the facts. In this case, we must show what we are dealing with and risking if we ignore the needs of the ecosystem over time and develop practical solutions that can be implemented effectively. We must ensure that politicians and those with authority at least are making informed decisions. That can help change policies over time.

REFERENCES

Neitro, W. A., V. W. Binkely, S. P. Cline, R. W. Mannan, B. G. Marcot, D. Taylor, and F. F. Wagner. 1985. "Snags (wildlife trees)." In *Management of wildlife and fish habitats in forests of Oregon and Washington.* Publication no. R6-F&WL-192-1985. Washington, D.C.:U.S. Government Printing Office.

Chapter 14
Symposium Summary: A Manager's Perspective

Bob Metzger

The papers presented in this symposium were of high quality, never boring, and well prepared. Information on short-term productivity was excellent; that on long-term—that is, multirotational—productivity was as good as possible, given the paucity of data available. Symposium attendees' questions were of consistently high caliber and right on target; moreover, questioners allowed very little "artful dodging" on the part of questionees. All in all, the presentations and related question and answer sessions reminded us forestry professionals that we just do not know what we should at this stage about long-term forest productivity, and made clear that we need to get serious about long-term research **now**.

What follows in this chapter is an annotated recap of some of the highlights from my 47 pages of notes, extracted roughly in chronological order, by presenter (chapter author). To the extent possible, a limited synthesis and cross-referencing have been undertaken.

DAY 1

Bob Powers (chapter 1 author) observed: "Most of our work in the Northwest tends to be retrospective. Because our rotations are longer, we tend to go to sites years after harvest and reforestation to see what happened, and then use that information to forecast the performance of current treatments." (Summarizer: Economists and fly-fishermen call that "backcasting.")

Powers mentioned modelling as another approach to determining long-term productivity naming FORCYTE as perhaps the best current modelling tool. He warned, however, that computer models tend to contain "the biases of their builders." This morning, Hamish Kimmins (chapter 11 author and FORCYTE's creator) confirmed that observation for us.

Bob Edmonds (chapter 2 author) remarked that the Europeans may have something to teach us. "The Germans have known about the effects of forest nutrition on productivity for centuries." He briefly explained the Swedes' "optimum nutrition" theory: "Trees can't utilize nitrogen at a uniform rate over their lifetimes, so nitrogen should be metered out when trees can use it best." Edmonds later indicated that one key point for fertilizing Douglas-fir might be at about age 40–50. Apparently, it doesn't pay to add too much too early.

He also reported that "poor" (that is, infertile, or unproductive) sites respond better to fertilization than "rich" (fertile, or productive) sites, and that effects of harvesting on organic matter content and subsequent conifer growth are much more marked on poor than on rich sites. This thesis was endorsed for coastal Douglas-fir/western hemlock forests the next day by Dick Miller (chapter 7 author): on a test area fertilized with nitrogen, the poor site (site index 85) gained 600 ft.^{3}/acre (42 m^3/ha), the rich site (site index 145) only 150 ft.^{3}/acre (10 m^3/ha).

From Edmonds' ensuing question and answer session:

Q: "Is timber productivity an adequate expression of ecosystem health?"

A (actually answered by Bob Powers): "No, but it's the best yardstick we have, with the longest set of measurements. Leaf area is a good yardstick too, but hard to quantify on an operational land unit."

Q: "Is weed competition really a serious problem?"

A: "Not so much in British Columbia and northwest Oregon, where there's plenty of water. But in southwest Oregon it is a serious problem."

(Summarizer: Tell that to a forester in northwest Oregon fighting salmonberry or one who still feels that red alder and bigleaf maple are aggressive weeds!)

Another question with a pithy answer:

Q: "What is the importance of large woody debris?"

A: "It's great for wildlife; but for forest nutrition, it's the small woody debris that contributes most to tree growth."

There was not unanimous regional support on this one. The next day, Al Harvey (chapter 9 author), reporting on interior mixed-conifer and pine forests, stated: "One of the best asymbiotic nitrogen sources is old rotting logs."

From Mike Amaranthus (chapter 3 author), we learned that cool, dry sites hold the toughest regeneration problems. They stay cold and frozen into spring, then thaw, only to dry out quickly, producing in effect a short growing season. So harsh, hot, dry sites are not the only regeneration challenge in southwest Oregon.

Amaranthus put in a kind word for manzanita as a mycorrhizal nurse crop! He also reported that mycorrhizal inoculations from mature forests had much less effect on seedling growth than those from vigorously growing plantations. His observation that nutrition in young forests should be geared to life-cycle stage reinforced earlier remarks on the changing nutritional needs of trees over their lifetimes. Amaranthus' credo—"We human beings are the most important soil organisms!—" brought an important perspective of natural resource management into clear focus.

A good question and answer session followed:

Q: "What are your views regarding the timing of planting?"

A: "The more rapidly you can plant seedlings, the more residual mycorrhizae there are available, and the better the chance of reforestation success." (Summarizer: Not to mention the better the head start on brush competition.)

Q: "Can mycorrhizal inoculation in the nursery overcome other nursery problems?"

A: "There is no one 'silver bullet', but mycorrhizal inoculates can help alleviate drought stress later encountered on the planting site."

(Summarizer: Finally, I wondered to myself whether mycorrhizal inoculation is really necessary in the nursery, or whether seedlings wouldn't obtain mycorrhizae in short order on the planting site anyway . . . this might be a good question to address with research.)

We now know for sure that light soil is good soil. Stuart Childs (chapter 4 author) told us that "Forest soils west of the Cascades have low bulk densities—0.6–1.0." The rule of thumb is that $0.5 \text{ m}^3/\text{m}^3$ soil porosity is ideal. As compaction increases, available water supply decreases, and so does aeration. Childs explained that the first pass by a tractor is the worst pass for compaction. Each successive pass adds only a little more. He also confirmed that high-intensity burns hurt!

Later we heard regional practitioners advise us to try to keep the heat of prescribed burns under 400°F (204°C); burns at 200°F (93°C) with 2–4 ft. (0.6–1.2+m) flame height would be best.

The following question and answer session ensued:

Q: "Which causes the least disturbance to soil: scarification, herbicides, or fire?"

A (by Steve Shade, Bureau of Land Management): "Herbicides cause the least soil impact."

Someone then remarked that herbicides in soil do not biodegrade.

(Summarizer: This remark probably should have been prefaced by "Not according to our evidence," with the appropriate research findings then cited.)

Q: "If you could bar one practice, what would it be?"

A: "Machine piling!"

Q: "On multiple re-entries, should the same roads or new road locations be used?"

A (by Steve Shade): "Stick to the original skid trails as much as possible."

Q: "Are scheduled harvest rotations too short in the Pacific Northwest?"

A (by Bob Meurisse, USDA Forest Service): "It's more a biological than physical problem."

(Summarizer: This seemed an escape. More follow-up is deserved.)

Fred Swanson (chapter 5 author) told us: "We don't know yet if headwall 'leave areas' work. In the Mapleton area they average about 2 acres (0.8 ha), about twice the area of the potential slides, but it is an effort to buffer and prevent windthrow of the key trees."

Swanson continued: "Long rotations in our region don't beat up the soil as much as short ones. But we do a lot of manipulation that affects biological stability and magnifies the results of the way we treat our soils." He urged foresters to "look back historically under forest disturbances and understand the 'pulse beats' of impacts to forest soils."

A couple of the questions and answers that followed:

Q: "What is the best, approved way to stabilize soils on headwalls?"

A: "The jury is still out. You might even try a 'brush leave'—take the conifer, leave the brush, but don't burn on the headwalls."

Q: "Have European forests, which have histories of multiple rotations, shown more erosion and landslides and also reduced organic matter content?"

A: "I don't know."

(Summarizer: Let's visit European Forest Records and Archives and find out.)

Jerry Franklin (chapter 6 author) stressed that "The key to long-term productivity is to maintain resilience through ecological diversity." Waxing philosophical, he observed that we demand endless evidence to prove our theories while accepting without question the most shabbily wrought conventional wisdom.

Franklin warned of three kinds of simplification: genetic, spatial (stand and landscape), and successional. He also cautioned against living constantly at the limit with no reserves: "We wouldn't do it with our health or finances, but it is standard operating procedure for forest management." As an improvement, he suggested that foresters accept earlier natural successional stages and lower regeneration densities after harvest. He also proposed that we let the deadwood rest in peace, in its place.

Franklin's other prescriptions included using a greater diversity of "minor" tree species—for instance, western redcedar, which produces a very base-rich litter—and developing mixed stand structures by leaving a number of older trees at final harvest for the next rotation. He seriously questioned the neat patch-quilt pattern of small, staggered harvests, urging foresters to develop a philosophy favoring "disorder in the forest."

This set the stage for the following question and answer session:

Q: "How would you break the pattern of small, staggered-setting harvests?"

A: "I'm not ready to advocate continuous clearcutting, but maybe through small drainage cuts and limited progressive clearcuts with up to 200–300 acre (80–200 ha) leave settings.

(Summarizer: This is tough to achieve in the O&C land ownership checkerboard of alternating 640-acre and smaller tracts.)

Q: "How do you reconcile your position with the exhortations given public land managers to 'get out the allowable cut'?"

A: "I don't have that responsibility, but you can practice while you cut, and probably, eventually, policies will have to be changed."

(Summarizer: Another escape.)

Q: "What do you think about the practice of leaving two wildlife trees per acre in clearcuts?"

A: "Foresters need to move from small, tidy clearcuts to big, sloppy, even slovenly ones."

Q: "I can't see any proof that diversity equals stability. Can't you also have stable *simple* systems?"

A: "Yes, you can."

Q: "What do you think of using highly productive sites for intensive short rotations, and using steeper, less productive sites for less intensive, longer rotations?"

A: "That's an excellent idea."

DAY 2

The second day, the symposium addressed maintaining site productivity in specific Northwest subregions. Dick Miller offered a simple key for identifying the major players in long-term forest productivity as an introduction to his observations on coastal Douglas-fir/hemlock forests. In his view, there are the optimists, who believe that intensive management increases productivity, and there are the pessimists, who feel that productivity will be lost with repeated harvests and that management may or may not be able to offset some of this loss. Miller's major concerns are nutrient removal and physical soil loss, especially in the face of whole-tree harvesting of younger stands, which leaves "much less biomass on the ground after harvesting" than standard logging practices.

There was conflict about the foregoing point, however. At the poster session that evening (see poster summaries, this volume), one exhibit on whole-tree harvesting proclaimed no significant loss of site productivity from complete crown removal. Yet Hamish Kimmins reported the next morning that the Swedes, who have recently shifted to whole-tree harvest and thinning, project a loss of 10–15%.

Speaking on prescribed fires, Miller summarized the recent work of Sue Little (USDA Forest Service, Pacific Northwest Research Station) in reviewing the 62 pairs of burned and unburned plots from the 40-year-old "Morris study" in western Oregon. On the 32 plots revisited, overall growth declined 8% on the burned relative to the unburned subplots. However, some burned subplots had greater relative growth, some less. Results were not significant.

Turning to mixed stands, Miller touted the Wind River "Isaacs test area," where the Douglas-fir interplanted with nitrogen-fixing red alder stand head and shoulders above the adjoining pure Douglas-fir and are a markedly darker green. Not only do the interplanted Douglas-fir grow better, but they are great bear food, as evidenced by the occasional mortality of trees stripped of bark by bears. In conclusion, warning that even our knowledge of short-term productivity is limited and weak, Miller prescribed that we take a cautious, conservative stance and monitor the impacts of our intensive practices.

The following exchange ensued during the question and answer session:

Q: "Could you please discuss the obvious benefits of herbicides in site preparation and minimization of disturbance?"

A (by Bill Stein, Oregon State University): "Let's not say 'obvious', but remember that using herbicides with fire is almost always better than using herbicides alone."

Kristiina Vogt (chapter 8 author) suggested that we manage upper slope (high-elevation) forests for much more than wood fiber. Water, wildlife, and recreation are of major concern.

[Summarizer: Cross-country skiers in the Northwest know that forest roads above 3,000 ft. (914 m) in elevation were built for ski trails and clearcuts spaced to provide panoramic viewpoints.]

Foresters seldom talk much about starch as a forest food, but Vogt introduced us to the value of starch applications on upper slope stands. She also reminded us that root growth can be more important than top growth and advised a "go-slow" approach to managing upper slope forests, perhaps 120–140 year rotations. As to harvest regime, she noted that there is little research to support either even-aged or uneven-aged management as the better approach.

From Vogt's question and answer session:

Q: "It's been said that we could do some heavy cutting of upper slope forests during the next 2 decades to bridge the timber supply gap at lower elevations. What do you think of that?"

A: "That would be potentially disastrous!"

Al Harvey, discussing the mixed-conifer and pine forests of the interior West, cited mycorrhiza activity and nitrogen dynamics as bellwethers for productivity. He stated: "When you harvest a forest and then go back to try to establish the same stand, you could find yourself in real trouble. You might well be dealing with an entirely changed site." Harvey went on to prescribe: "Don't fix what ain't broke. . . . Scalping can have serious impacts on nutrient and moisture loss; but mounding of humus material around seedlings can be helpful."

Harvey concluded with the following recommendations:

—Prevention is the best prescription.
—Manage with a light hand.
—Try to keep equipment off the soil.
—Limit scarification (this could even save foresters 40% in regeneration costs).
—Keep burns cool [ideally, 200–400°F (93–204°C) with 2–4 ft. (0.6–1.2 m) flames].
—Treat competing vegetation only when necessary.
—Be careful with harsh sites.
—Be aware of site-soil interrelationships.

The allowable cut issue during follow-up question and answers drew another "escape response," however:

Q: "What do you consider viable arguments for non-entry, given allowable cut targets?"

A: "Fortunately, I'm not on the firing line, but we must do what is responsible."

Tom Atzet (chapter 10 author), examining long-term forest productivity in southwest Oregon and northern California, noted that inland fire cycles run 60–70 years, coastal cycles about 100 years. However, in the Ashland watershed, major fires have been returning at about 25-year intervals and people are getting nervous.

Atzet observed that "scalping helps seedlings survive, but not necessarily with much productivity," perhaps because mineralizable nitrogen can be reduced 40% by scalping. Also, Atzet cited a case in which Jeffrey pine grew very well on an "off-site," harsh area, but at age 20, the stand "stalled" and stopped growing!

In summary, Atzet warned foresters not to do "risky things" without good site data. "It's the application of practices that really counts—practices like Jerry Franklin's 'big, slovenly clearcuts', designated skid trails, and fertilization. Soil tillage as a practice for promoting productivity is rather doubtful."

Atzet further commented that "Organic matter is the 'spotted owl' of long-term productivity."

The question and answer session followed:

Q: "Couldn't we get better site productivity with prescribed burns rather than risk wildfire?"

A: "I agree."

Q: "Wouldn't it be better to manage so as not to use fertilizer for a 'quick fix'?"

A (by Bob Powers): "Preventive management definitely is good, but let's use fertilizers to boost productivity."

DAY 3

Opening the final session, on economics and modelling, Hamish Kimmins underscored that forest-management practices are changing. For example, the Swedes, who have recently shifted to whole-tree final harvests and thinnings, are now projecting a resultant decline in site productivity of 10–15%.
(Summarizer: As noted earlier, there is some debate about this.)

Kimmins observed that present yield tables cannot account for future changes in management. As to the establishment of long-term experimental research plots, he noted the obstacle of "future shock": "We have to wait so long to get answers that by the time we do, the results are no longer interesting."

Kimmins proposed combining historical projection with experimental evidence to obtain a hybrid "bioassay" such as his FORCYTE model, a hybrid stand-analysis and individual-tree model that incorporates aspects of forest economics, even to the point of cost shifts in fossil fuels.
(Summarizer: In perhaps the understatement of the week, Kimmins dubbed FORCYTE "rather complicated.")

Describing FORCYTE as "a pretty realistic bird that can fly," he observed that "it cannot, however, 'lay an egg'." Summing up, Kimmins stated: "We should predict long-term productivity as well as yield; we need to marry economics into our decision modelling."

John Beuter (chapter 12 author), directly addressing the economics of long-term productivity, classified himself as a "reformed economist." He noted that under the "soil expectation value" (SEV) technique of classical forest economics, site productivity was assumed constant over time.

By applying assumptions about site-productivity decline to classical discounting of a hypothetical $300/acre ($750/ha) net SEV, Beuter generated provocative results:
—Assuming a 5% productivity loss per rotation, SEV is reduced by just $0.11/acre ($0.27/ha).
—Assuming a 25% productivity loss per rotation, SEV is reduced by $0.57/acre ($1.43/ha).
—Assuming 100% productivity loss per rotation, SEV is reduced by $2.27/acre ($5.68/ha)!!
. . . . So much for the perspective of classical economics.

Beuter then observed that the "allowable cut effect" (ACE) tends to eliminate the anomalies of classical discounting as it applies projected growth and productivity to determining current harvest levels in available mature timber. The "downside" (or "upside," depending on perspective) is that if future productivity is predicted to decline, then current harvest levels must be reduced in anticipation of the future productivity shortfall. Beuter observed that although ACE tends to let us harvest old growth faster now, its effects will diminish as excess stocks of mature timber are diminished.

He also noted the difficulty of trying to require landowners to protect long-term nontimber or nonmarket resource productivity, perhaps largely because such rules impose extra costs today on landowners who may not be around when the future benefits accrue.

Asking why the USDA Forest Service defends below-cost timber sales based on other public nontimber benefits, Beuter suggested that Ciriacy-Wantrup's "safe minimum standard of conservation" for critical zones could provide a valid approach.

Beuter concluded by telling us of a graffiti inscription he'd seen in Washington, D.C., that read: "Be a good American. . . . Don't think!" He advised the audience to "Be good foresters. . . . Think, think, and think!"

Steve Eubanks (chapter 13 author) demonstrated how research can translate into management prescriptions by focusing on snag and wildlife-tree management on the Blue River Ranger District of the Willamette National Forest. He indicated that to meet the target of 40% of cavity dwellers' current needs (about 2 snags/acre, or about 5 snags/ha), 4–6 wildlife trees and snags/acre (about 10–15/ha) must be left after harvest. Eubank's sustained-yield snag model called for leaving a mixture of old "soft" snags, new "hard" snags, and mature dead, green, unmerchantable, or, in some cases, live merchantable trees.

Eubanks summed up the manager's predicament relative to long-term productivity: "We don't know it all, but we must use enough of what we do know to maintain options."

SOME ADDITIONAL RECOMMENDATIONS

First, I want to share with you Bill Stein's concern that we do not have a baseline from which to measure and manage for productivity. Even though that baseline will continuously shift, we need to set one to work from.

Next, I believe we need to establish really long-term research **now.** People like Munger and Isaacs set up some important long-term forest research 50–70 years ago. Now it is time for us to contribute—to leave something of value to future generations of foresters.

We need to reread the published literature and perhaps take trips to the forests of Germany, Sweden, and Japan to learn from histories of numerous rotations of intensive forest management.

We should go into our own stands like ecological detectives and find out where our forests have been and how they got to where they are today. We need to backcast this line of information, and then forecast with it through model building.

Finally, as my high school English teacher, Miss Hyrkin, advised us as seniors: "Drink life to the lees, but always go around with a big question mark furrowed into your forehead!"

Poster Summaries

LONG-TERM PRODUCTIVITY, A CONSERVATIVE APPROACH

Jack Hulsey

The Department of Natural Resources (DNR), the land-management agency for the state of Washington, oversees 2.1 million acres (840,000 ha) of forest land, half of which is in western Washington. The management of the productive potential of these assets is critical both biologically and economically.

Since 1987, a new conservative strategy has redefined the role of burning in forest management in western Washington. The use of burning is now strongly circumscribed to minimize the intensity of site modification and the acceptance of increased risk. The costs of burning, coupled with the recent legislative redistribution of fire-suppression charges, have led DNR to restrict application of broadcast burning to one silvicultural purpose: artificial regeneration of a site.

Burning may be acceptable when required to satisfy hazard abatement (removal of harvest residues to avoid fuel buildup). However, the law is being modified such that the landowner can either remove the residues or assume financial liability for costs incurred by the state, should a wildfire break out and require suppression. There will be circumstances under which DNR, as a landowner, will risk wildfire in lieu of removing slash.

This conservative strategy removes arguments for burning predicated on other rationales (e.g., vegetation management). As such, it clearly states silvicultural objectives.

TIMBER HARVESTING DISTURBANCE ON STEEP SLOPES: EFFECT ON SOIL PHYSICAL PROPERTIES

Bill Carr and Bob Mitchell

We have begun a research project to quantify changes in soil properties—especially soil degradation associated with skid-trail construction—brought about by ground-based logging on steep slopes in the Kamloops Forest Region, British Columbia. The type, degree, and aerial extent of site disturbance were assessed with a line intercept method. Soil bulk density was determined in the field with a nuclear densitometer, and soil cores were taken for laboratory analysis. To date, soil physical properties have been determined, and plantations in which long-term growth will be monitored have been established. Soil chemical analysis should be completed in 1988.

Two study installations were established during 1986 within the Vernon Forest District: in the Winnifred Creek area (rolling topography; 30–70% slopes; winter logged with rubber-tired skidders), and the Railroad Creek area (60–90% slopes; summer logged with rubber-tired skidders). About 25% of the area at Winnifred and 39% at Railroad were deeply disturbed (25+ cm). In both areas, soil density within the skid-trail running surface exceeded 1,600 kg/m^3; density within sidecast material was similar to that of undisturbed sites. Total porosity and aeration porosity were also substantially reduced.

SOIL RECONSTRUCTION OPTIONS FOR SEVERELY DEGRADED FOREST SITES IN THE PRINCE GEORGE FOREST REGION, BRITISH COLUMBIA

Bill Carr and Angus McLeod

In September 1986, a 6-year research project was initiated in the Mossvale area, Prince George Region, in conjunction with Lakeland Mills, Ltd., to evaluate options for improving the nutrition of forest soils degraded by construction of landings and skid trails. The treatments (eight replications) consist of soil tillage, followed by either topsoil replacement or establishment of a legume cover crop, or a combination of the two.

First-year data showed that tillage with a winged subsoiler significantly reduced soil density to levels in undisturbed areas; replacing topsoil improved soil pH and percent carbon and allowed nitrogen, mineralizable nitrogen, phosphorus, and potassium to approach levels in undisturbed areas. Legume establishment, further soil enhancement, and assessment of plantation performance are planned for years 3 and 6 of the project.

ECOLOGICAL APPROACH TO MODELLING DOUGLAS-FIR SITE INDEX

K. Klinka, R. E. Carter, and D. S. McLennan

Climate, soil moisture, and soil nutrients have been used to characterize vegetation environment relationships and ecosystem units in British Columbia. These factors were employed as class variables for predicting Douglas-fir site index (height at specified base age). The LOGIT regression model, based on measured site-index data, explained over 72% of the variation in site index, and had a standard error of the estimate of less than 1.1 m.

MAINTAINING PRODUCTIVITY OF WESTERN LARCH THROUGH BIOLOGICAL CONTROL OF AN IMMIGRANT INSECT

Roger B. Ryan, Robert E. Denton, Scott Tunnock, and Frederick W. Ebel

Populations of pests that affect tree growth must be kept below critical densities if site productivity is to be maintained. One such pest is the larch casebearer, *Coleophora laricella* (Hbn.) (Lepidoptera: Coleophoridae), an immigrant defoliator that has significantly retarded growth of western larch, *Larix occidentalis* Nutt. Parasitic insects from Europe and Japan were imported to help control high population levels of larch casebearer. Parasites were reared both in the laboratory and in field cages, then released at strategic locations within the infestation. *Agathis pumila* (Ratz.) (Hymenoptera: Braconidae) and *Chrysocharis laricinellae* (Ratz.) (Hymenoptera: Eulophidae) have become permanently established and have contributed to drastically reduced casebearer densities. On the basis of samples, radial growth of western larch has returned to previous rates (Fig. 1).

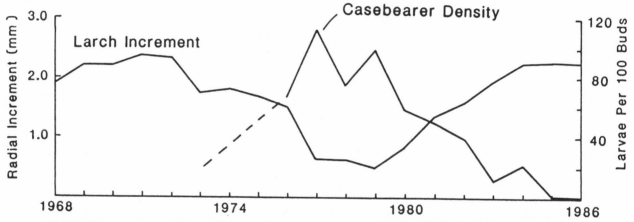

FIG. 1. Larch increment was severely reduced during years when larch casebearer density was high, but returned to normal as introduced parasites reduced casebearer densities, as typified by data for this one site in the Blue Mountains, Boise Cascade Corporation Plot 10 near Elgin, Oregon, between 1968 and 1986.

EFFECTS OF SLASH BURNING ON STAND DEVELOPMENT AND SITE PRODUCTIVITY

Richard E. Miller and Richard E. Bigley

Data from a widely distributed set of 40-year-old pairs of burned and unburned plots—describing physical plot characteristics, interactions among competing vegetation, and conifer establishment and growth—will be analyzed to assess the effects of slash burning on forest development, yield, and productivity in western Washington and Oregon. Preliminary analysis of 30 plot pairs measured in 1986 shows considerable variation in site index and cumulative volume for Douglas-fir [*Pseudotsuga menziesii* (Mirb.) Franco]. However, when all plots were considered together, burning did not significantly affect either site index or cumulative volume. Future analysis of stand development will use plot pairs stratified into ecological groups and will consider conditions created by burning and plant succession.

BIOMASS AND ENERGY RESEARCH

James O. Howard, Michael B. Lambert, Susan N. Little, Dale R. Waddell, Frank R. Ward, and Elsie H. Himes

The Biomass and Energy Project, Pacific Northwest Research Station, is charged with providing land managers with effective tools for determining economically and environmentally acceptable strategies for harvesting and utilizing forest biomass. The multidisciplinary approach includes engineering, biometrics, economics, and ecology research. For each timber resource studied, we:

(1)   develop tools which allow the user to determine total resource availability and to evaluate product potential (quantity and quality) for traditional and nontraditional markets;

(2)   assess the amount and distribution of nutrients on site in a way that allows for analysis of trade-offs between harvest strategy and site productivity. How will harvesting affect nutrient reserves? Site-preparation needs? Subsequent site nutrient capital? and;

(3)   evaluate innovative biomass harvest systems for technical feasibility and economic efficiency, with a focus on emerging technologies for multiproduct marketing and whole-tree harvesting.

We have completed a series of studies on old-growth logging residues and on stagnant, overstocked conifer stands on the Olympic Peninsula, Washington, and are currently studying lodgepole pine (*Pinus contorta* Dougl. ex Loud.) on pumice soils in south-central Oregon. Future research will focus on the issues of harvesting second-growth Douglas-fir [*Pseudotsuga menzies* (Mirb.) Franco] west of the Cascade crest.

PODZOLIZATION AND WINDTHROW: NATURAL FLUCTUATIONS IN LONG-TERM PRODUCTIVITY AND IMPLICATIONS FOR MANAGEMENT

Bernard T. Bormann

Site productivity may be far less constant than previously thought. Evidence from studies in southeast Alaska suggests that natural podzolization greatly reduces soil fertility in as little as 300 years. Windthrow appears to be the principal natural mechanism that reverses the process of podzolization. A single instance of windthrow can disturb from 5 to 77% of the soil surface. The disturbance mixes large accumulations of organic matter with mineral soil, greatly increasing decomposition rate. Soil fertility and tree growth are postulated to decline without mixing through windthrow or through alternative management activities that reverse the effects of podzolization.

ORGANIC MATTER CONTENT AND AGGREGATION OF FOREST SOILS WITH DIFFERENT TEXTURES IN SOUTHWEST OREGON CLEARCUTS

J. G. Borchers and D. A. Perry

The presence of structure in soil has long been recognized as beneficial to plants. Soil aggregate structure is maintained by plant and microbial organic matter. In turn, soil organics are protected from microbial decomposition by physical and chemical processes within aggregates. Organic matter forms stable complexes with clay particles, which can greatly reduce decomposition rates. Thus, both soil structure and texture may exert considerable control over the decomposition phase of nutrient cycles.

Our preliminary work in two pairs of forested/clearcut sites in southwest Oregon (Cedar Camp and Holcomb peak) is directed toward understanding these processes. We have measured significant decreases in soil aggregation that are associated with clearcutting and broadcast burning at both sites. However, differences in organic matter content were significant only in the finer textured Holcomb Peak soil, where predisturbance levels of organic matter greatly exceeded those in the coarser textured Cedar Camp soil.

YELLOWJACKET REHABILITATION PROJECT, MALHEUR NATIONAL FOREST

Tim Sullivan

Twenty-one acres (8.4 ha) of moist and dry meadow in poor condition were rehabilitated in summer 1984. Sixty-one acres (24.4 ha) around the project area were fenced to provide long-term livestock control and protection. Treatment included gopher control, disking, and seeding. Production in the moist meadow is expected to increase 600%, that in the dry meadow 350%.

USE OF A WINGED SUBSOILER IN AMELIORATING COMPACTED CLAYEY FOREST SOILS

Scott Davis

The ineffectiveness of conventional rock rippers and brush rakes to loosen compacted soils and create suitable soil conditions for tree growth has led to less tractor logging and machine piling of slash since the mid-1970s. High-lead logging, coupled with broadcast burning, has taken precedence on most sites. However, several factors of concern are forcing managers to seek alternative methods to prepare harvested sites for reforestation: (1) growing air-quality restrictions on available days for broadcast burning of slash; (2) high costs and liabilities of conducting broadcast burns; and (3) increasing research evidence displaying the persistence of soil compaction from tractor harvest and piling and high-lead logging on moist, clayey soils.

Use of a winged subsoiler may be one cost-effective method for ameliorating soil compaction due to harvesting and piling. First developed in the 1980s through the cooperation of the Department of Forest Engineering, Oregon State University, winged subsoilers were capable of shattering 80% of compacted soil layers, compared to only 20–40% with conventional rock rippers. Recently, Ed Fields (of Monroe, Oregon) has constructed winged subsoilers that can be mounted on suitable tractors; the subsoilers produce a shearing and lifting action while fracturing compacted soils. These machines have separate tripping mechanisms for individual shanks, which automatically reset after encountering stumps or large roots. Use of these subsoilers throughout Oregon and in British Columbia has successfully loosened compacted skid trails and landings, improved soil tilth and drainage, and made sites easier and cheaper to plant.

In October 1986, Yoncalla Timber Products had Ed Fields use a winged subsoiler on machine-piled portions of a 50-acre (20-ha) harvest unit northwest of Cottage Grove, Oregon (Eugene District, Bureau of Land Management), where air-quality restrictions had limited broadcast burning. Soils were brown silty clay loams overlying dark reddish-brown clays; soil moisture was 30–40%. Soil bulk densities were monitored in 1987 to detect changes where soils were both undisturbed and piled, with and without tillage with the winged subsoiler.

THE REGIONAL FOREST NUTRITION RESEARCH PROJECT

H. N. Chappell, L. S. Heath, and D. Opalach

The Regional Forest Nutrition Research Project (RFNRP) was initiated in 1969 with the primary objective of providing forest managers with information on response to fertilization of second-growth stands of Douglas fir [*Pseudotsuga menziesii* (Mirb.) Franco] and western hemlock [*Tsuga heterophylla* (Raf.) Sarg.]. This research cooperative comprises organizations representing forest industry, state and federal agencies, and fertilizer manufacturers. Administration and direction for the project come from the University of Washington's College of Forest Resources.

During the past 17 years, the RFNRP has established almost 3,000 permanent growth plots in western Washington and western Oregon across a wide range of stand ages, stocking levels, and site productivity classes in Douglas-fir and western hemlock stands. Commonly, plots have been fertilized with 200 or 400 lb./acre (80 or 160 kg/ha) of nitrogen applied as urea; unfertilized plots serve as controls. Additional treatments include nitrogen in slow-release forms and as ammonium nitrate, as well as application of other nutrient elements. Growth trends both after a single fertilization and after multiple fertilizations (to determine cumulative effects) are evaluated. Further, data are collected on site and soil characteristics and on soil and foliage nutrient levels.

The RFNRP database is the largest in the world on growth response of Douglas-fir and western hemlock to nitrogen fertilization, providing opportunities for monitoring and modelling long-term productivity in managed forests and forming much of the basis for operational forest-fertilization programs in the Pacific Northwest. Future work will improve fertilization prescriptions; a major priority is developing techniques for identifying stands with potentially high response to fertilization.

A PROTOTYPE TIMBER PRODUCTIVITY SPATIAL DATABASE

G. O. Klock and P. Gum

A prototype spatial database of the estimated current and future timber productivity of the Okanagan National Forest was developed from data [drawn from 207.5-ft. (63-m) quadrangles of forest land] produced by classification of 1981 MSS LANDSAT imagery and further stratified by topography and other site attributes.

Cell data were calibrated by field measurements. Current estimates are based on annual increases in stem volume calculated by equations for estimating biomass of plants in the Pacific Northwest. Future estimates for key tree species and SDICU index classes (annual cubic feet per acre, or cubic meters per hectare, adjusted by the stand density index) are based on forest plant associations.

In addition, individual timber stands have been identified and mapped by computer software through classification and stratification of LANDSAT imagery. Each stand represents a continuous area 10 acres (4 ha) or larger with similar tree species, crown closure, and current productivity class. Site attributes, including current and future productivity estimates for each stand, are stored in the Forest's computer relational database.

The calibration of spatial databases by traditional field measurements is a challenge because of the significant timber-stand diversity often created by forest management. Questions remain regarding the most accurate method of predicting both current and future timber productivity. The higher resolution Thematic Mapper imagery now available should significantly improve mapping accuracy formerly limited by basic vegetation classification data from MSS imagery.

NUTROSS: A SIMPLE MODEL TO PREDICT NUTRIENT LOSS FROM TIMBER HARVEST IN THE NORTHERN ROCKIES

N. Stark and H. Zuuring

A new model, NUTROSS, has been developed to evaluate nutrient losses from harvest of aboveground tree biomass and slash burning in the northern Rocky Mountains. The model is based on the assumption that debris not removed during harvest will be available to supply nutrients through mineralization to grow the same ecosystem components in the next rotation. The debris that is removed should not contain more than 25–30% of any one biologically essential nutrient; these values are guidelines based on estimated weathering rates. At the time of logging, the soil must be able to supply from the *available* nutrient pool enough nutrients to replenish those removed in fiber for the next three to four rotations to prevent deterioration of the site.

The NUTROSS model is useful for:
(1) Moderately permeable soils with low rainfall (less than 76 cm/year);
(2) Forested land that does not export appreciable amounts of nutrients to streams either before or after logging;
(3) Soils with greater than 28% clay content and less than 40% gravel and sand content;
(4) Forests with less than 6 cm of litter and duff;
(5) Forests that have good understory coverage and vigorous resprouting capabilities;
(6) Soils without sand lenses that "pipe" water;
(7) Areas in which major nitrogen-fixing organisms reside in rotten wood or lichens; and
(8) Sites on which radial growth is most likely limited by nutrient availability early in the growing season.

To use NUTROSS, the above conditions must be known and the following data taken:
(1) Diameter at breast height and height of trees or volume by species before and after harvest to convert data to kilograms per square meter using tables;
(2) Available nutrients (up to 14) in the feeder root zone, as milliequivalents per square meter, to the depth of the feeder root zone;
(3) Total nutrient concentrations (up to 14 nutrients) in needles, to judge possible deficiencies;
(4) Depth of the feeder root zone (90% of feeder roots) and soil bulk density; and
(5) Percentage of coarse fragments greater than 2 mm in diameter.
Other useful but not essential data are total nutrient content of the soil and fuel analysis by size classes.

The model was applied to seven stands thinned to spacings of 3 × 3, 4 × 4, and 6 × 6 m and to unthinned controls. Two sites were found to be chemically fragile (unable to withstand the level of harvest projected). None of the stands were able to withstand whole-tree (aboveground) harvest without losing 30% of one or more of eight essential nutrients. Copper and zinc were most often insufficient in available form to support harvest of trees over three or four rotations.

PESTS LINK SITE PRODUCTIVITY TO THE LANDSCAPE

T. D. Schowalter and J. E. Means

The importance of changes in landscape pattern to the potential productivity of a site is rarely recognized. One way in which landscape pattern influences site productivity is through its effects on pest epidemiology. Little concern has been shown for these consequences of change in forest landscapes.

Landscape pattern can be characterized by at least three components: intersection by roads or other corridors (Fig. 1), patch size, and diversity of stand age classes (Fig. 2). Changes in these components affect the ability of potential pests to find and exploit suitable resources.

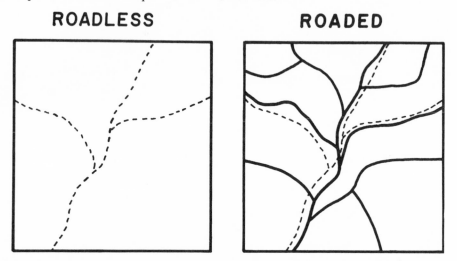

FIG. 1. Forest landscape before (riparian corridors only) and after road construction. Road construction stresses edge trees and increases forest access for dispersing pests. Black-stain root disease. Port-Orford-cedar root rot, and gypsy moth are examples of pests associated with roads. Several are known to be spread along roads via harvest, replanting, and recreational activities.

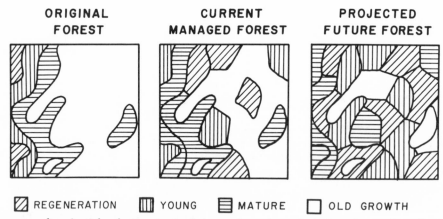

FIG. 2. Current and projected reduction in stand size and stand age-class diversity resulting from harvest and replanting schedules. Such landscape simplification removes physical and biological barriers to pest dispersal and allows pest populations to grow. Despite inherent resistance to pest activity, the shrinking old growth will lose its influence as a barrier to pests and as a source of predators and will become increasingly vulnerable to continuous pest pressure from surrounding managed stands.

Populations of potential pests are controlled naturally by availability of suitable host trees interacting with abundances of predators and by weather. Typically, insects and pathogens can survive on a relatively small number of host tree species, usually at particular stages of tree development or during periods of tree stress (Schowalter 1986). For insects, finding a suitable host often involves orientation to attractive odors. Nonhost plants or stands can hide suitable hosts or stands visually (Courtney 1986) or chemically, by producing odors which interfere with insect orientation (Visser 1986).

Pest success increases when intersection by roads, planting of monocultures (single-species stands) and decreased average size and age-class diversity of stands reduce the time necessary to find or reach suitable hosts (Fig. 3; also Hansen et al. 1986, Schowalter 1986). Forest simplification also reduces the diversity of habitats and prey species necessary to maintain populations of generalist predators, such as spiders and birds. These predators are more important in preventing pest outbreaks than are host-specific predators, such as parasitic wasps, which must be able to find and exploit a particular prey species. Thus, old-growth forests, with their complex array of tree and predator species, large stand size, and high age-class diversity, should be less vulnerable to pest outbreaks than are the simplified forests created through current harvest and regeneration practices (Table 1, Fig. 3).

TABLE 1. Mean arthropod densities in Douglas-fir [*Pseudotsuga menziesii* (Mirb.) Franco] canopies in old-growth (greater than 400-year-old) and young (10-year-old) intermixed stands in western Oregon.

	Old-growth stands		Young stands	
	Individuals/kg of green branch	Number of species	Individuals/kg of green branch	Number of species
Predators				
Ants	0.8	2	2.4	1
Host-specific predators	4.5	12	17	7
Generalist predators	21	31	22	8
Potential pests				
Sap suckers	97	5	29,000	3
Defoliators	3.4	4	0	0
Predator:potential pest	0.26		0.0014	

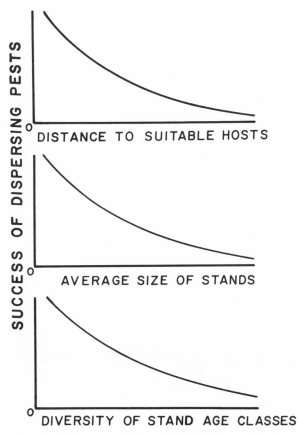

FIG. 3. Pest success depends largely on the pest's ability to find or reach a suitable host. This ability is determined by the distance to suitable hosts (top), as influenced by the average size of stands (middle), which determines that distance, and by the diversity of stand age classes (bottom), which determines the proportion of the landscape occupied by suitable host stands. The right side of each curve characterizes old-growth forest conditions, the left side managed-forest conditions.

Current forest-management concerns in the Pacific Northwest include root beetles, woolly aphids, gypsy moth, black-stain root disease, and Port-Orford-cedar root rot, all promoted by road construction and/or young monocultures. These concerns indicate the severity of future problems if we continue to convert landscapes dominated by old-growth forests with their physical and biological barriers to pest activity to landscapes dominated by extensively roaded young monocultures with no impediment to pest activity (Figs. 1-3; Hansen et al. 1986, Schowalter 1986). Remnant old-growth forests also may become more vulnerable because pest pressure from surrounding young stands will increase as old growth is cut. Meanwhile, old-growth forests will be increasingly valued for genetic diversity and as sources of biological control agents and of biomedical compounds such as the taxol derivatives, unique anticancer drugs derived from the bark of Pacific yew, *Taxus brevifolia* Nutt. (Kingston et al. 1982).

In conclusion, forest penetration by roads increases site access and tree susceptibility to a number of potential pests. Simplifying forest landscapes from large, multispecies, multilayered stands that include trees up to 1,000 years old to small monocultures of trees less than 150 years old removes predators and physical barriers to dispersing pests, thereby increasing the likelihood of regionwide pest outbreaks. Current management practices also are restricting the options available to forest managers for crop tree or stand selection in the event of insect and disease activity or of changes in markets for different tree species over the next rotation. Future site productivity depends in part on how landscape pattern affects pest epidemiology.

REFERENCES
Courtney, S. P. 1986. The ecology of pierid butterflies: dynamics and interactions. *Advances in Ecological Research* 15:51–131.
Hansen, E. M., D. J. Goheen, P. F. Hessburg, J. J. Witcosky, and T. D. Schowalter. 1986. "Biology and management of black-stain root disease in Douglas-fir." In *Forest pest management in southwest Oregon,* edited by O. T. Helgerson, 13–19. Corvallis, Ore.: Forest Research Laboratory. Oregon State University.
Kingston, D. G. I., D. R. Hawkins, and L. Ovington. 1982. New taxanes from *Taxus brevifolia. Journal of Natural Products* 45:466–470.
Schowalter, T. D. 1986. Ecological strategies of forest insects: the need for a community-level approach to reforestation. *New Forests* 1:57–66.
Visser, J. H. 1986. Host odor perception in phytophagous insects. *Annual Review of Entomology* 31:121–144.

EFFECT OF TIMBER HARVESTING ON CELLULOSE AND LIGNIN DEGRADATION IN A NORTHERN ROCKY MOUNTAIN FOREST SOIL

James A. Entry, Nellie M. Stark, and Howard Loewenstein

INTRODUCTION
Timber harvesting alters the activity and distribution of soil microorganisms by changing the amount and type of organic matter and the pH, temperature, and moisture of the soil (Harvey et al. 1980). This study was designed to determine the influence of harvesting treatments on the rate of cellulose and lignin degradation in the organic layer of a Rocky Mountain forest soil. Such information enhances our ability to maximize nutrient availability and site productivity after harvest, especially on nutrient-deficient soil.

MATERIALS AND METHODS
The study site is located in the Graves Creek drainage near Lolo Pass, Montana (Entry et al. 1986). Four harvesting treatments, each applied to one 40- by 40-m plot, were a clearcut on which stems were removed by hand and organic residue was left (RL); a clearcut on which whole trees (needles, branches, stems) were harvested and removed by hand (RR); a clearcut on which stems were removed by hand and organic residue was broadcast burned (RB); and an uncut control (C).

The ^{14}C-labeled cellulose and lignin were prepared with methods described in Crawford (1981). To determine degradation rates for lignin and cellulose, we mixed 100 mg of either ^{14}C-lignin lignocellulose (17,500 dpm/mg) or ^{14}C-labeled cellose (13,500 dpm/mg) with approximately 10 g (dry weight) of soil sample. The preparation was placed in a 1.9-L jar containing a vial of distilled water to maintain the moisture level and a vial of $2M$ NaOH to trap CO_2. The jar was sealed and incubated for 10 days at 22°C. All samples were indexed at 22°C, regardless of field temperature at the time of sampling. Trapped ^{14}C was quantified by liquid scintillation.

Data were subjected to analysis of variance for a completely randomized design; means were compared by Fisher's Protected LSD (p < 0.05).

RESULTS AND DISCUSSION

Cellulose degradation increased in the fall in all treatments (Fig. 1) and was significantly higher in the RL treatment than in the others regardless of season. Lignin degradation was significantly higher in the summer in all treatments but did not differ significantly among treatments during any one season (Fig. 1).

The higher levels of cellulose degradation suggest that nutrients are readily released from the more easily degradable components of forest residues, such as hemicellulose and cellulose. Increased lignin degradation during summer could have been a result of higher temperature, which would increase the activity of lignin-degrading enzymes. Brenner et al. (1986) also reported that temperature was the main factor influencing lignin degradation in the salt marshes and in the Okefenokee Swamp of Georgia. The rate of lignin degradation exerts major control over the rate of woody decomposition in forest ecosystems.

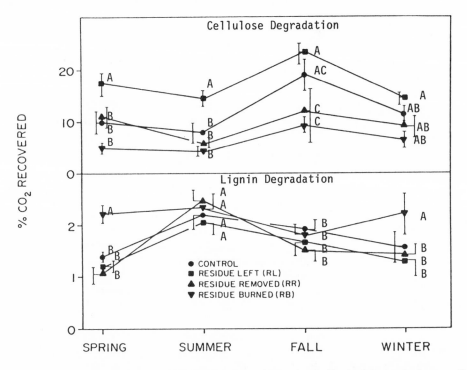

FIG. 1. Cellulose and lignin degradation in the organic horizon of a Rocky Mountain forest soil after four different harvesting treatments (adapted from Entry et al. 1987). Means identified by the same upper case letters are not significantly different (p < 0.05) from one another (Fisher's Protected LSD).

REFERENCES

Brenner, R., A. E. Maccubbin, and R. E. Hodson. 1986. Temporal variation between the deposition and microbial degradation of lignocellulosic detritus in a Georgia salt marsh and the Okefenokee Swamp. *Microbial Ecology* 12:291–298.

Crawford, R. L. 1981. *Lignin Biodegradation and Transformation.* New York: John Wiley and Sons.

Entry, J. A., N. M. Stark, and H. Loewenstein. 1986. The effects of timber harvesting on soil microbial biomass fluxes in a northern Rocky Mountain forest soil. *Canadian Journal of Forest Research* 16:1076–1081.

Entry, J. A., N. M. Stark, and H. Loewenstein. 1987. Timber harvesting: effects on degradation of cellulose and lignin. *Forest Ecology and Management* 22:79–88.

Harvey, A. E., M. F. Jurgensen, and M. H. Larsen. 1980. "Ecology of ectomycorrhizae in northern Rocky Mountain forests." In *The environmental consequences of timber harvesting in Rocky Mountain coniferous forests,* 189–208. General Technical Report INT-90. Ogden, Utah: Intermountain Forest and Range Experiment Station, USDA Forest Service.

EVIDENCE FOR FERTILITY DECLINE ASSOCIATED WITH SALAL INVASION IN OLD-GROWTH CEDAR/HEMLOCK STANDS IN THE NORTHERN COASTAL ZONE OF BRITISH COLUMBIA

G. F. Weetman

Sitka spruce [*Picea sitchensis* (Bong.) Carr.] planted on old-growth cedar/hemlock cutover sites on northern Vancouver Island exhibit severe chlorosis and growth decline 7–8 years following planting. This decline in fertility is coincident with salal (*Gaultheria shallon* Pursh) reinvasion of planted cutovers (Germain 1985, Spencer 1986), although it is not clear whether the apparent productivity declines and chlorosis are due to the direct influence of salal or to the development of mor humus conditions which constrain productivity (Read 1984).

Two ecosystem phases of the old-growth cedar/hemlock on the same mineral soil have been identified on northern Vancouver Island:

(1) The cedar-hemlock (CH) phase—undisturbed for many centuries and characterized by a thick, compact humus layer and a dense salal cover; and

(2) The hemlock-amabilis (HA) phase—produced by periodic windthrow and characterized by a thin, friable humus layer and a sporadic salal cover (Lewis 1982, Tamas 1985).

Single-tree and conventional-plot fertilization experiments have shown that nitrogen (N) and phosphorus (P) are deficient on CH sites for spruce, hemlock, and cedar plantations. A single N and P fertilizer application has temporarily restored height growth rate to the same as that of spruce growing on salal-free HA sites (Schnorbus 1985, MacGregor 1987). There appears to be a very close ecological parallel here with the nutritional problems of Sitka spruce plantations growing on Calluna-dominated oligotrophic peats and moorlands in the United Kingdom (Zehetmayr 1960. Malcolm 1975, Taylor 1987). Handley (1963) suspected that ericaceous plants such as salal, Calluna, Ledum, and Kalmia have mycorrhizal associations which can outcompete those of the trees for N and P. In the wet north coast climate, salal invasion on cutovers and old-growth stands may lead to the phenomenon of "heathland degeneration" seen in eastern Canada and Europe (Meades 1986).

A 28-year-old test of Douglas-fir [*Pseudotsuga menziesii* (Mirb.) Franco], western hemlock [*Tsuga heterophylla* (Raf.) Sarg.], western redcedar (*Thuja plicata* Donn ex D. Don), and Sitka spruce planted in replicated blocks on salal-dominated CH cutovers at two wet Vancouver Island locations indicates that Douglas-fir is not constrained by salal (Exp. Project 571). Yet in drier locations, removing salal from Douglas-fir stands enhances tree growth because of higher soil-water potential (Price et al. 1986). The following hypotheses for the fertility decline associated with salal invasion of these CH cutovers are being investigated:

(1) Ericaceous salal, like Calluna, checks growth in Sitka spruce, hemlock, and cedar by reducing N and P availability to trees.

(2) Growth check can be relieved by a single N and P fertilizer addition and crown closure attained by repeated fertilization.

(3) Douglas-fir nutrition is not affected by salal.

(4) Mycorrhizal associations on salal either inhibit or outcompete those on conifers for P.

(5) Salal litter and roots reduce the rate of N mineralization.

(6) Long-term (200-year) occupancy of old-growth cedar/hemlock sites by salal leads to declines in site fertility.

(7) Salal can be removed from cutovers by herbicide application (Garlon®), physical means, or rapid crown closure of plantations.

From a forest-management view, the extensive areas of extremely valuable old-growth cedar forests on CH sites should be converted into vigorous HA sites. Currently, most CH cutovers are not growing vigorous conifers. The historical precedence of windthrow on HA sites may indicate that radical soil disturbance is necessary to "revitalize" CH forests; this hypothesis is being tested by eradicating salal with backhoes before planting.

Because of the economic importance of the problem, and the obvious need for coordinated research, the Salal/Cedar/Hemlock Integrated Research Project, or SCHIRP (SCHIRP 1986), was established. The cooperators are MacMillan Bloedel Company, Western Forest Products Company, B.C. Ministry of Forests and Lands, the Pacific Forestry Centre, and the University of British Columbia. Most of the current studies are being conducted at Port McNeill, B.C. A bibliography on salal has been published (Vales 1986).

REFERENCES

Germain, A. 1985. *Fertilization of stagnated Sitka spruce plantations on northern Vancouver Island.* M.S. Thesis. Vancouver, B.C.: Faculty of Forestry, University of British Columbia.

Handley, W. R. C. 1963. *Mycorrhizal associations and Calluna heathland afforestation.* Bulletin 36. London: Forestry Commission.

Lewis, T. 1982. *Ecosystems of the Port McNeill (Block 4) of tree-farm licence 25.* Contract Report. Vancouver, B.C.: Western Forest Products.

MacGregor, D. M. 1987. *Fertilization of western red cedar with nitrogen. phosphorus and potassium: a screening trial.* B. S. F. Thesis. Vancouver, B.C.: Faculty of Forestry, University of British Columbia.

Malcolm. D.C. 1975. The influence of heather on silvicultural practice: an appraisal. *Scottish Forestry* 29:14–24.

Meades, W. J. 1986. *Successional status of ericaceous dwarf-shrub heath in eastern Newfoundland.* Ph. D. Dissertation. Storrs, Conn.: University of Connecticut.

Price, D. T., T. A. Black, and F. M. Kelliher. 1986. Effects of salal understory removal on photosynthetic rate and stomatal conductance of young Douglas-fir trees. *Canadian Journal of Forest Research* 16:90–97.

Read, D. J. 1984. Interactions between ericaceous plants and their competitors with special reference to soil toxicity. *Aspects of Applied Biology* 5:195–209.

SCHIRP. 1986. Salal/Cedar/Hemlock Integrated Research Project outline. Vancouver, B.C.: University of British Columbia.

Schnorbus, E. 1985. *Successful release of "checked" Sitka spruce plantations on northern Vancouver Island by fertilization: second year response.* B. S. F. Thesis. Vancouver, B.C.: Faculty of Forestry, University of British Columbia.

Spencer, D. 1986. *The effects of nitrogen and phosphorus fertilization and salal eradication on checked Sitka spruce plantations in northern Vancouver Island.* B. S. F. Thesis. Vancouver, B.C.: Faculty of Forestry, University of British Columbia.

Tamas, M. A. 1985. *A comparison of foliar nutrient status between disturbed and undisturbed western hemlock-western red cedar-salal-moss ecosystems in northern Vancouver Island.* B. S. F. Thesis. Vancouver, B.C.: Faculty of Forestry, University of British Columbia.

Taylor, C. M. 1987. The effects of nitrogen fertilizer at different rates and times of application on the growth of Sitka spruce in upland Britain. *Forestry* 60:87–99.

Vales, D. J. 1986. *A bibliography on salal.* Vegetation Management Research Report VMR 1. Victoria, B.C.: British Columbia Ministry of Forests.

Zehetmayr, J. W. L. 1960. *Afforestation of upland heaths.* Bulletin 32. London: Forestry Commission.

ASSOCIATION OF NITROGEN-FIXING BACTERIA WITH ECTOMYCORRHIZAE IN DOUGLAS-FIR

Chih-Hao Niu, Kermit Cromack, Jr., and C. Y. Li

INTRODUCTION

Many higher plants have mycorrhizae associated with their roots. These mycorrhizae are often essential for plant survival and growth (Harley and Smith 1983). Mycorrhizae are known for their ability to enhance nutrient absorption, although mycorrhizal fungi are not known to fix nitrogen (Trappe and Fogel 1977).

In this study, we exploited the role of mycorrhizal fungi in rhizosphere nitrogen (N) fixation (1) to determine if N fixation is occurring in the rhizosphere of the Douglas-fir [*Pseudotsuga menziesii* (Mirb.) Franco] ectomycorrhizae formed with *Hysterangium setchelli* Fischer and *Gautieria monticola* Harkness in the Woods Creek area of Marys Peak; (2) to evaluate seasonal changes in N-fixation activity and N fixing bacteria populations; and (3) to isolate and identify N-fixing bacteria associated with ectomycorrhizae.

METHODS AND FINDINGS

Soil samples with and without (control) mats of fungal hyphae were collected monthly from October 1985 to September 1986.

N-fixation activity, as indicated by acetylene reduction, was significantly higher in the Douglas-fir mycorrhizosphere than in the control soils. Change in acetylene reduction rate with log-transformed incubation time can be adequately expressed as a linear relationship (Fig. 1). Average nitrogenase activity associated with *H. setchelli* and *G. monticola* was 1.36 and 1.44 nmoles g^{-1} (dry wt.) day^{-1}, whereas that for controls was 0.38 nmoles g^{-1} day^{-1} (Fig. 2). Nitrogenase activity in spring, fall, and winter was not significantly different but was significantly greater than that in summer (Fig. 2).

Number of N-fixing bacteria associated with mycorrhizae was estimated by the most probable number method. Population size was found to vary considerably over the year; the trends in some months (March, August, September; Table 1) paralleled those of nitrogenase activity.

Three different N-fixing bacteria were isolated from the fungal sheaths of *H. setchelli* and *G. monticola* and within the sporocarps of *H. setchelli*. According to Tarrant et al. (1978), these were identified as probable strains of *Azospirillum brasilense*.

The potential of N-fixing bacteria associated with coniferous ectomycorrhizal roots and their associated fungal sporocarps is of considerable importance. Such bacteria could be inoculated into the soil to utilize the protective and nutritional advantage of the mycorrhizae. These discoveries increase our understanding of the role of mycorrhizae in N cycling and help us develop information on how management practices might be modified to optimize biological N fixation in the rhizosphere of young Douglas-fir.

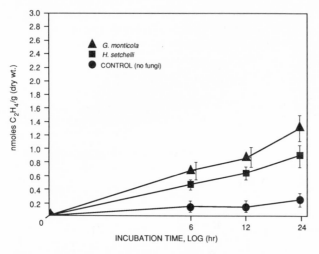

FIG. 1. Nitrogenase activity, as indicated by acetylene reduction, in soils with and without ectomycorrhizal fungi over a 24-hour incubation period. April 1986. These same trends were found year-round.

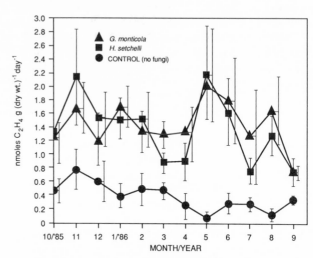

FIG. 2. Nitrogenase activity, as indicated by acetylene reduction, in soils with and without ectomycorrhizal fungi over 1 year.

TABLE 1. Number of nitrogen-fixing bacteria per gram fresh weight of mycorrhizal fungi, 1986.

	No. of bacteria (1 × 10s)	
Month	H. setchelli	G. monticola
March	30 ± 11.5	80 ± 21.1
May	130 ± 38.7	75 ± 30.2
June	268 ± 81.2	60 ± 11.1
July	9 ± 0.9	14 ± 6.2
August	80 ± 3.5	150 ± 34.7
September	36 ± 9.1	24 ± 13.9

REFERENCES

Harley, J. L., and S. E. Smith. 1983. *Mycorrhizal Symbiosis*. New York: Academic Press.

Tarrant, J. J., N. R. Krieg, and J. Dobereiner. 1978. A taxonomic study of the *Spirillum lipoferum* group, with descriptions of a new genus Azospirillum ger. nov. and two species, *Azospirillum lipoferum* (Beijerinck) comb. nov. and *Azosnirillum brasilense* sp. nov. *Canadian Journal of Microbiology* 24:967–998.

Trappe, J. M., and R. D. Fogel. 1977. "The belowground ecosystem: a synthesis of plant-associated processes." In *Range Science Series No. 26*. 205–214. Fort Collins, Colo.: Colorado State University.

EFFECTS OF HAND PULLING SNOWBRUSH CEANOTHUS 8 YEARS AFTER TREATMENT ON A 10-YEAR-OLD DOUGLAS-FIR PLANTATION, MCKENZIE RANGER DISTRICT

Bruce E. Wilson

INTRODUCTION

Manual release of Douglas-fir [*Pseudotsuga menziesii* (Mirb.) Franco] from snowbrush ceanothus (*Ceanothus velutinus* var. *velutinus*) on the Willamette National Forest and elsewhere in the Pacific Northwest has yielded mixed results (Bernstein 1977, Roberts 1980, USDA Forest Service 1980). Hand pulling of snowbrush ceanothus as a release method was first introduced on the Willamette National Forest in 1978 (Farr 1979), and an administrative study was established that same year on the McKenzie Ranger District to monitor its effectiveness. This account is a 5-year follow-up report to the initial third-year report (Wilson 1982) of the administrative study.

STUDY AREA

The study area lies 7 miles (11 km) southeast of the McKenzie Ranger Station at 3,600 feet (1,100 m) elevation. Slopes range from 0 to 35%; annual average precipitation at the McKenzie Ranger Station is 75 in. (185 cm), with most of the rain falling in the winter months. Area soils, belonging to the SRI 66 (Legard and Meyer 1973) mapping unit, are derived from volcanic ejecta and glacial till. The deep, nonplastic landtype is well drained; permeability is rapid in the surface soils and slow in the subsoils. This landtype supports Site III and IV Douglas-fir.

The study site, typified by the western hemlock/silver fir/rhododendron ecoclass classification (Hall 1979) and further refined to western hemlock/rhododendron/twinflower association (Hemstrom et al. 1985), was clearcut and broadcast burned in 1975. During cool, damp weather in spring 1976, 605 2-0 Douglas-fir trees/acre (1,500 trees/ha) were hoe planted. First-year stocking averaged 474 trees/acre (1,185/ha), or approximately 78% survival. Three growing seasons after planting, stocking was 456 trees/acre (1,140/ha). The stand was certified as stocked at that time.

When the study was established, vegetation was primarily resprouting western rhododendron (*Rhododendron macrophyllum*) and snowbrush ceanothus 1 ft. (0.3 m) high.

METHODS

Twelve individual plots, each measuring 124 × 124 ft. (38 × 38 m), were installed in the stand; within each plot, a 0.25-acre (0.1-ha) internal subplot was established to minimize edge influences. Each plot was surrounded by a 30-ft. (9-m) buffer.

In 1978, four treatments were randomly assigned to the 12 plots: 100% removal of snowbrush ceanothus in the plot, 100% removal of snowbrush taller than 8 in. (20 cm), 100% removal of snowbrush within 3 ft. (1 m) of the planted Douglas-fir on the plot, and no removal of snowbrush (control). Each of the three "pull" treatments was replicated 3 times, the control twice.

In 1981, height of all Douglas-fir trees in each internal subplot (986 trees: 264 control, 248 8-in. pull, 283 3-ft. pull, 191 100% pull) was measured. The sampling scheme was modified for the 1985 measurements: a line transect was established in each subplot, along which roughly 33 trees were subsampled for combined 1982–85 height growth and diameter at 6 in. (15 cm) above the ground and at DBH, or 4.5 ft. (1.4 m) above ground. In total, 354 trees (69 control, 92 8-in. pull, 93 3-ft. pull, 100 100% pull) were measured in this subsampling.

Data were subjected to analysis of variance to ascertain treatment effects and t-tests to assess differences in treatment means.

RESULTS AND DISCUSSION

Height growth was not significantly affected (analysis of variance and t-test, $p \leq 0.05, 0.01$) by treatment as the stand approached age 10 (Table 1), when snowbrush was expected to exert competitive influence. In fact, height growth achieved was outstanding, compared to that on other similar sites on the McKenzie District; some Douglas-fir less than 10 years old were approaching 20 ft. (6 m) tall. Trees in control plots averaged the greatest diameter growth, though differences were not statistically significant (Table 2).

Patterns of vegetational succession were different on the plots where snowbrush had been hand pulled, compared to the control. The 100% pull plots were dominated by the established conifers, with minor amounts of willow (*Salix* spp.), rhododendron, and Oregon boxwood (*Pachistima myrsinites*). Trees were completely open grown. The 8-in. and 3-ft. pull treatments contained relatively more snowbrush ceanothus, and relatively less

TABLE 1. Mean Douglas-fir height growth after release from hand-pulled snowbrush ceanothus.

Treatment	Height growth				Total tree height, 1985
	1979	1980	1981	1982–85	
	------ in. ------				
Control (no pull)	9.96	12.24	13.70	67.20	116.06
8-in. pull	11.72	11.65	11.96	66.12	113.35
3-ft. pull	10.04	12.63	13.09	68.76	120.47
100% pull	9.93	13.50	14.50	70.68	123.80

TABLE 2. Mean Douglas-fir diameter growth 8 years after release from hand-pulled snowbrush ceanothus.

Treatment	Diameter (in.) at	
	6 in.	DBH (4.5 ft.)
Control	1.83	3.68
8-in. pull	1.36	2.65
3-ft. pull	1.38	2.57
100% pull	1.53	3.17

rhododendron and Oregon boxwood. The controls, in contrast, were dominated by snowbrush; densities were 2–3 times those on the hand-pulled plots. Trees on all plots now overtop the snowbrush and are essentially free to grow.

Although successful, early establishment of the Douglas-fir plantation seems to have negated any competitive influence from snowbrush, the conclusions that may be drawn are limited by the small scope of the study. However, it appears that (1) Douglas-fir release from snowbrush ceanothus may be unnecessary if the conifer stand is quickly established and juvenile height growth rapid, (2) 100% pull is not required to achieve release objectives, and (3) the McKenzie District should explore the possibilities of precommercial thinning at stand age 8 because stands approach 15 ft. (4.5 m) at age 10.

REFERENCES

Bernstein, Art. 1977. *Seven immediate-impact consequences resulting from the use of a chainsaw to control brush.* Grants Pass, Ore.: Josephine County Forestry Department.

Farr, Leonard. 1979. *New approach to accomplish roadside brushing.* Employee Suggestion W 430. Eugene, Ore.: Willamette National Forest, USDA Forest Service.

Hall, F. 1979. *Codes for Pacific Northwest ecoclass vegetation classification.* R6-ECOL 79-002. Portland, Ore.: Pacific Northwest Region, USDA Forest Service.

Hemstrom, M. A., S. A. Logan, and W. Pavlat. 1985. *Preliminary plant association and management guide.* Eugene, Ore.: Willamette National Forest, USDA Forest Service.

Legard. H. A., and C. Meyer. 1973. *Willamette National Forest soil resource inventory.* Eugene, Ore.: Willamette National Forest, USDA Forest Service.

Roberts, Catherine. 1980. *Cooperative brush control study: second year report.* Corvallis, Ore.

USDA Forest Service. 1980. *Willamette National Forest 1978 hand brushing second year interim report.* Eugene, Ore.

Wilson, B. 1982. *Effects of hand pulling snowbrush ceanothus on the height growth of a six-year-old Douglas-fir plantation on the McKenzie Ranger District.* Eugene, Ore.: Willamette National Forest, USDA Forest Service.